The Cambridge Handbook of Community Psychology

This comprehensive handbook provides community psychology approaches to addressing the key issues that impact individuals and their communities worldwide. Featuring international, interdisciplinary perspectives from leading experts, the handbook tackles critical contemporary challenges. These include climate change, immigration, educational access, health care, social media, wellness, community empowerment, discrimination, mental health, and many more. The chapters offer case study examples to present practical applications and to review relevant implications within diverse contexts. Throughout, the handbook considers how community psychology plays out around the world: What approaches are being used in different countries? How does political context influence the development and extension of community psychology? And what can nations learn from each other as they examine successful community psychology-based interventions? This is essential reading for researchers, students, practitioners, and policymakers involved with community well-being.

CAROLINE S. CLAUSS-EHLERS is Professor of Psychology in the Department of Psychology at the School of Health Professions, Long Island University, Brooklyn, USA. Her research focuses on child and adolescent development with an emphasis on understanding cultural resilience and trauma within diverse community contexts.

The Cambridge Handbook of Community Psychology

Interdisciplinary and Contextual Perspectives

Edited by

Caroline S. Clauss-Ehlers
Long Island University, Brooklyn

CAMBRIDGE
UNIVERSITY PRESS

University Printing House, Cambridge CB2 8BS, United Kingdom

One Liberty Plaza, 20th Floor, New York, NY 10006, USA

477 Williamstown Road, Port Melbourne, VIC 3207, Australia

314–321, 3rd Floor, Plot 3, Splendor Forum, Jasola District Centre,
New Delhi – 110025, India

103 Penang Road, #05–06/07, Visioncrest Commercial, Singapore 238467

Cambridge University Press is part of the University of Cambridge.

It furthers the University's mission by disseminating knowledge in the pursuit of
education, learning, and research at the highest international levels of excellence.

www.cambridge.org
Information on this title: www.cambridge.org/9781108492188
DOI: 10.1017/9781108678971

© Cambridge University Press 2022

First published 2022

A catalogue record for this publication is available from the British Library.

Library of Congress Cataloging-in-Publication Data
Names: Clauss-Ehlers, Caroline S., editor.
Title: The Cambridge handbook of community psychology : interdisciplinary and
    contextual perspectives / Caroline S. Clauss-Ehlers.
Description: 1 [edition]. | New York : Cambridge University Press, 2022. | Series:
    Cambridge handbooks in psychology | Includes bibliographical references and index.
Identifiers: LCCN 2020051630 (print) | LCCN 2020051631 (ebook) | ISBN
    9781108492188 (hardback) | ISBN 9781108729093 (paperback) | ISBN 9781108678971
    (epub)
Subjects: LCSH: Community psychology—Handbooks, manuals, etc.
Classification: LCC RA790.55 .C36 2022 (print) | LCC RA790.55 (ebook) |
    DDC 616.89—dc23
LC record available at https://lccn.loc.gov/2020051630
LC ebook record available at https://lccn.loc.gov/2020051631

ISBN 978-1-108-49218-8 Hardback
ISBN 978-1-108-72909-3 Paperback

To my dear mom, Carole P. Clauss, – a pioneer in support of community well-being, a fierce advocate for children, a committed educator, and a wife, parent, aunt, and grandma who loved her family.

Contents

Figures

Tables

Contributors

RENATO D. ALARCÓN
Mayo Clinic School of Medicine, USA; Peruvian University Cayetano
Heredia, Peru

SETH ASAFO
University of Ghana Medical School, Ghana

JOHN BAKALY
California School of Professional Psychology at Alliant International
University, USA

DONNA BAPTISTE
The Family Institute at Northwestern University, USA

DAVID BELSHAM
University of the Sunshine Coast, Australia

ALEXIS M. BENJAMIN
Wellnest, Los Angeles, USA

BETH BINGHAM
The Graduate Center, City University of New York, USA

ELIZABETH H. BRADLEY
Vassar College, USA

W. JOSHUA BRADLEY
University of South Carolina, USA

PATRICK M. BRESNAN
Pee Dee Mental Health Center, USA

KESHA BURCH
The Family Institute at Northwestern University, USA

TAYMY CASO
New York University, USA

NAOMI CHEE
Rutgers University, USA

CAROLINE S. CLAUSS-EHLERS
Long Island University, Brooklyn, USA

COURTNIE COLLINS
University of South Carolina, USA

DARIEN M. COLLINS
University of South Carolina, USA

CORINNE C. DATCHI
William Paterson University, USA

RONDA DOONAN
Community Memorial Health System, USA

JOSEPH DREW
University of Technology, Australia; Tokyo Metropolitan
University, Japan

LAKEESHA EURE
City of Newark Office of Violence Prevention, USA

KIMBERLY FAZIO-RUGGIERO
Independent Researcher, USA

ZACHARY FOLEY
Rutgers University, USA

ERICA R. GARAGIOLA
Rutgers University, USA

TAMEKA L. GILLUM
Russell Sage College, USA

LAURA D. GONZALEZ
Boston College, USA

TANYA GRAHAM
University of the Witwatersrand, South Africa

MARIA GUEVARA CARPIO
Rutgers University, USA

HELEN P. HAILES
Boston College, USA

SAMANTHA N. HARTLEY
University of South Carolina, USA

MARTHA HERNÁNDEZ
Ronald McDonald House Charities Bay Area, USA

SCOTT J. HUNTER
The University of Chicago, USA

MARGO A. JACKSON
Fordham University, USA

ELIZABETH JENSEN
JSF Professional Counseling Services, USA

GRACE KOGUC
Rutgers University, USA

CARA LOMARO
Rutgers University, USA

ARIANA MANGUAL FIGUEROA
The Graduate Center, City University of New York, USA

MEREDITH MCCONNOCHIE
University of Saint Joseph, USA

DAVID W. MCMILLAN
Fisk University, USA

ELIZABETH W. MILLER
Mott Hall Charter School, USA

GAYLE SKAWENNIO MORSE
Russell Sage College, USA

KWADWO OBENG
Ankaful Hospital, Ghana

PATRICIA O'CONNOR
Russell Sage College, USA

ANGELA OFORI-ATTA
University of Ghana Medical School, Ghana

SUSAN OPOTOW
John Jay College of Criminal Justice, USA and The Graduate Center,
City University of New York, USA

MEGHAN F. OPPENHEIMER
Mott Hall Charter School, USA

TRACEY O'SULLIVAN
University of Ottowa, Canada

LYNN PASQUERELLA
Association of American Colleges and Universities, USA

MARIA PRENDES-LINTEL
Private practice, retired

SUSAN REGAS
California School of Professional Psychology at Alliant International
University, USA

RICHARD L. RENFRO
Loyola University Chicago, USA

ROBERT ROSENHECK
Yale University, USA

MEGAN N. SCOTT
The University of Chicago, USA

RENNIE SLOAN
The Carter Center, USA

ALEXA STERN
Loyola University Chicago, USA

CARLOS STORCK-MARTINEZ
Rutgers University, USA

MELISSA STROMPOLIS
Children's Trust of South Carolina, USA

LISA SUZUKI
New York University, USA

MANJARI SWARNA
Rutgers University, USA

TSE YEN TAN
Vassar College, USA

CHRISTOPHER M. THOMPSON
Seton Hall University, USA

KIP THOMPSON
Fordham University, USA

ELYSE JOAN THULIN
University of Michigan, USA

MICHELE M. TUGADE
Vassar College, USA

PRATYUSHA TUMMALA-NARRA
Boston College, USA

MARY ANN VILLARREAL
University of Utah, USA

LOUISE S. WACHSMUTH
Vassar College, USA

SHANNON R. WAITE
Fordham University, USA

ELICIA C. WARTMAN
Loyola University Chicago, USA

MARK D. WEIST
University of South Carolina, USA

CIRECIE WEST-OLATUNJI
Xavier University, USA

MARC A. ZIMMERMAN
University of Michigan, USA

Foreword

Rennie Sloan
Assistant Communications Director, The Carter Center

As I write this in Spring 2020, I'm missing terribly my weekly visits with a two-year-old toddler who lives eleven miles away. Games of hide and seek with my niece and her shrieks of delight have been replaced with video chats, for which I'm grateful. But my attempts at funny faces through FaceTime are no match for tangible toys in front of her.

Through the self-quarantine of the coronavirus, I'm staying connected with friends and family and coworkers through my phone and laptop, but the isolation has made me more aware than ever of the importance of relationships to my well-being, and even my identity.

Long before the coronavirus outbreak, US Surgeon General, Dr. Vivek Murthy, noted that we were in the midst of another pandemic: loneliness. "During my years caring for patients, the most common pathology I saw was not heart disease or diabetes; it was loneliness. Loneliness is also associated with a greater risk of cardiovascular disease, dementia, depression, and anxiety."[1]

Loneliness, or social alienation, can occur even when surrounded by people. More than half a century ago, psychologists began examining the relationship between individuals, their communities, and the surrounding social environment. At the landmark Swampscott Conference in 1965, and in the context of the deinstitutionalization of mental health care and the civil rights movement, psychologists discussed the concept of "community psychology" as a way to address broader social issues that influenced mental health and community well-being. Recognizing that a multidisciplinary approach was needed, many psychologists proposed gathering and synthesizing data that looked at the cultural, economic, social, political, and environmental aspects that shape and influence lives and communities. Community psychology seeks to address social issues within communities that can contribute to individual and societal problems. Doctoral training programs in community psychology were established and community-based research projects were implemented.

This volume builds on this early work with contributions that consider the question: How can overall health and wellness truly be evaluated without a

---

[1] Murthy, V. (2017, September). Work and the loneliness epidemic: Reducing isolation at work is good for business. *Harvard Business Review*: The Big Idea Series, Connecting at Work. https://hbr.org/2017/09/work-and-the-loneliness-epidemic

close look at how the community supports a sense of belonging within greater society?

In this book, community psychology is viewed through the lens of a modern and globally connected society. Religion, gender, race, ethnicity, sexual orientation, socioeconomic status, ability status, and more are examined in addition to rapidly changing technology and social media. Authors reveal how structural inequalities – such as a lack of educational access, health and mental health disparities, geographic location, and dynamics of power and engagement – all contribute to a person's experience in the world.

When individual connections to others are compromised through inadequate social structures, research points us to the negative impact these structural inequalities have on mental and physical health.

The global pandemic shines a light on hidden societal problems that need to be unearthed or reexamined. Health experts, policymakers, academic and religious institutions, advocacy groups, nonprofits, and the public are urged to see how the fabric of connectedness determines our path, health, and productivity during this time.

Since prehistoric times, humans have depended on each other for sustenance and safety. And while there is evidence of an increasingly disconnected society, there is reason to be optimistic.

During the pandemic, cravings for social connection surfaced in unprecedented ways. Mandatory "social distancing" brought about balcony concerts, drive-by birthday parties, and the introduction of Zoom chats into our daily lexicon.

And while technology and social media may push some to feel inadequate or isolated, they bring new tendrils of connectedness for others. While I desperately shout "Don't forget Auntie Rennie who loves you!" through a phone screen to my niece, her Ukrainian grandparents can marvel at her daily developments through video chats while five thousand miles away.

Our dependence on each other for survival and well-being has never been more clear or more necessary. The contributors to this book have shared a solid framework that can help ignite a cohesive movement to reclaim our roots of interdependence.

This is the world I hope to see for my niece.

PART I

Foundational Concepts

Interdisciplinary, Culturally Responsive, and
Contextual Approaches

1 Promoting Change amid Systemic Oppression

A Twenty-First-Century Call to Action for Communities and Community Psychologists

Caroline S. Clauss-Ehlers

The events of 2020 remind us that community is absolutely critical to who we are and our connections with one another (Clauss-Ehlers et al., 2019). Experiences such as the global COVID-19 pandemic tell us that we are inextricably linked across the globe. They underscore the reality that the experiences of a community in one nation can mirror and connect with those of others. At the same time, the differential impact of COVID-19 on communities of color, those who are incarcerated, people with disabilities, and the elderly tell us that there are systemic challenges to reducing medical and mental health disparities. The deaths of Ahmaud Marquez Arbery, Breonna Taylor, and George Floyd in February 2020, March 2020, and May 2020, respectively, highlight national and transnational concerns with police brutality and racial violence. Questions emerging from these events include: What does it mean to belong to a community? How do systemic racism and discrimination interfere with belongingness, access to freedom, and life and survival? How can communities push macro-level change in the face of systemic oppression?

The events of 2020 appear to demonstrate varying community dynamics. On the one hand, dynamics related to COVID-19 show how communities can learn and quickly adapt new behaviors in response to a deadly virus and global pandemic. When COVID-19 made its appearance, communities around the world responded to sheltering-in-place and quarantine orders. Children stayed home from school, adults in nonessential roles and those who lost their jobs stayed home from work, and essential workers faced the pandemic in health, nursing, retail, food-related, supermarket, and community facilities. Communities adapted to protect themselves in response to recommendations from the medical community (Centers for Disease Control [CDC], n.d.). Wearing masks, maintaining a six-foot distance from one another, using gloves, and being even more mindful about washing hands were precautions communities around the globe adapted in a short period of time.

These rapid-response behaviors demonstrate community change. Communities can adapt to crises presented before them and work together to promote health, safety, and save lives. Communities can support their members through community rituals, for example the 7 p.m. clapping for essential workers every evening in New York City (Gleason, 2020). They can give voice to not being able to honor all rituals, for example the devastating

3

impact of being separated from loved ones who were hospitalized. For those who died, this meant that family members could not be together to say goodbye. Funerals were no longer gathering places for larger communities, leaving many devoid of closure and with no formal process to deal with grief and collectively mourn (Weir, 2020).

Communities can learn from each other. Countries made decisions about transnational travel. Social media platforms allowed for communication with people across countries and globally. Families connected across generations in new ways, sharing technology that promoted regular family discussions (Cohen, 2020).

The way teachers teach and students learn abruptly changed. For instance, in the United States many schools were closed the first week of quarantine while school personnel worked to roll out an online curriculum for students that sought to engage them despite a remote learning environment. For many students and families, the online platform presented equity issues related to not having internet access and/or access to a device (Seale, 2020). Students had mixed responses to online learning. Some appreciated the work-at-your-own-pace schedule, the lack of peer pressure and distraction from classmates, and benefited from being able to focus on course material with the added support of parents at home. For other students, the online format was overwhelming. They feared they would miss class sessions and realized how much they missed the routine of school and being with their friends (The Learning Network, 2020).

The quarantine introduced sudden shifts in the implementation of mental health treatment. While recent barriers to teletherapy usage included concerns regarding a lack of Health Insurance Portability and Accountability Act (HIPAA)-compliant online platforms, such platforms emerged, with teletherapy being implemented as a common quarantine practice. This shift indicates further how policies can promote rapid change through concerted efforts and a coordinated crisis response (Goode & Shinkle, 2020).

However, while in many ways COVID-19 was greeted with rapid policy and personal changes to promote safety, thus showing how communities can shift and change in response to efforts to protect themselves, the virus was also met with great inequities. Magnification is a term that refers to health and economic disparities, and has been applied to the disparity resulting from COVID-19. Pappas (2020) states: "The virus and the resulting economic shutdown are exacerbating long-standing inequities in American society, widening economic gaps and health disparities. And the impacts – both physical and psychological – are likely to be long-lasting." Such disparities include, but are not limited to, those suffering from unemployment and unable to access food, those with disabilities who have higher rates of unemployment and underemployment, the elderly who may have fewer resources and less protection if they are in residential care, data that indicate African Americans and Latinx communities are disproportionately affected by the virus with regard to being infected and dying, anti-Asian xenophobia and violence in response to comments such as those by the US President describing

COVID-19 as the "Chinese virus," and outbreaks of the virus in prisons and jails, among which those who are incarcerated disproportionately represent people of color (Pappas, 2020). Despite the changes that were instituted to protect communities against COVID-19, these realities underscore the great inequities that emerged and exist amid such efforts.

On May 25, 2020, George Floyd was killed in police custody after police officer Derek Chauvin arrested him. The arrest was made in response to a 911 call that accused Floyd of trying to purchase cigarettes with a counterfeit $20 bill. A timeline of events published by the *StarTribune* (Xiong, 2020) based on charging documents, indicates that George Floyd was calm when arrested and told officers he was claustrophobic and couldn't get into the back seat of the police car, all the while sharing that he was not resisting arrest. In response, Derek Chauvin pulled George Floyd out of the car and put him on the ground at 8.19 p.m. Officer Kueng held onto George Floyd's back while Officer Chauvin had his knee on George Floyd's neck. George Floyd told the officer that he was about to die. Another policeman, Officer Thao, continued to stand watch and ignored the pleas of witnesses to stop the police brutality. None of the officers moved from their positions during the incident. According to the *StarTribune* timeline, by 8.25 p.m. the officers were unable to find a pulse. George Floyd was pronounced dead at the Hennepin County Medical Center at 9.25 p.m. (Xiong, 2020).

The murder of George Floyd follows the loss of many African Americans due to police brutality. In response to George Floyd's death, on May 31, 2020, National Public Radio (NPR)'s program *Code Switch* published a "non-comprehensive list of deaths at the hands of police in the U.S. since Eric Garner's death in July 2014" and on June 5, 2020, SCAPE (2020) presented names of African Americans who have been murdered by police on their website (Demby & Miraji, 2020; SCAPE, 2020): Eric Garner, John Crawford III, Michael Brown, Ezell Ford, Dante Parker, Michelle Cusseaux, Laquan McDonald, George Mann, Tanisha Anderson, Akai Gurley, Tamir Rice, Rumain Brisbon, Jerame Reid, Matthew Ajibade, Frank Smart, Natasha McKenna, Tony Robinson, Anthony Hill, Mya Hall, Phillip White, Eric Harris, Walter Scott, Freddie Gray, William Chapman II, Alexia Christian, Brendon Glenn, Victo Emmanuel LaRosa III, Jonathan Sanders, Joseph Mann, Salvado Ellswood, Sandra Bland, Albert Joseph Davis, Darrius Stewart, Billy Ray Davis, Samuel DuBose, Michael Sabbie, Bryan Keith Day, Christian Taylor, Troy Robinson, Asshams Pharoah Manley, Felix Kumi, Keith Harrison McLeod, Junior Prosper, Lamontez Jones, Paterson Brown, Dominic Hutchinson, Anthony Ashford, Alonzo Smith, Tyree Crawford, India Kager, La'Vante Trevon Biggs, Michael Lee Marshall, Jamar Clark, Richard Perkins, Nathaniel Harris Pickett, Jr., Bennie Lee Tignor, Miguel Espinal, Michael Noel, Kevin Matthews, Bettie Jones, Quintonio LeGrier, Keith Childress, Jr., Janet Wilson, Randy Joe Nelson, Antronie Scott, Wendell Celestine, David Joseph, Calin Roquemore, Dyzhawn L. Perkins, Christopher Davis, Marco Antonio Loud, Peter Gaines, Torrey Lamar Robinson, Darius Robinson,

Kevin Hicks, Mary Tuxillo, Demarcus Semer, Willie Tillman, Terrill Thomas, Sylville Smith, Alton Sterling, Philando Castile, Paul O'Neal, Terence Crutcher, Freddie Blue, Alteria Woods, Jordan Edwards, Aaron Bailey, Ronell Foster, Stephon Clark, Antwon Rose II, Botham Jean, Pamela Turner, Dominique Clayton, Atatiana Jefferson, Christopher Whitfield, Christopher McCorvey, Eric Reason, Michael Lorenzo Dean, Breonna Taylor, George Floyd, and Tony McDade (Demby & Meraji, 2020; SCAPE, 2020).

When we see this list, and how police brutality has led to the deaths of African Americans consistently since Eric Garner, other questions emerge: How is it that this keeps happening? Why can't police brutality against African Americans be stopped? What is preventing us as a society from learning how to protect all of our citizens? Such questions show how we keep getting it wrong – resulting in a consistent pattern of murder, loss of life, trauma, and systemic oppression.

In response to systemic police brutality and racism, communities around the world protested to communicate the injustice of George Floyd's murder. Like the response to COVID-19, communities joined globally – and this time for protection from another disease: injustice and racism. Communities organized to collectively promote systemic change. NBC News published a map of global protests (ones that included a hundred people or more) that extended from the United States to Argentina, Australia, Austria, Belgium, Brazil, Bulgaria, Canada, China, Denmark, England, Finland, France, Germany, Greece, Hungary, the Republic of Ireland, Israel, Italy, Jamaica, Japan, Kenya, Liberia, Mexico, Netherlands, New Zealand, Northern Ireland, Norway, Poland, Portugal, Scotland, Senegal, South Africa, South Korea, Spain, Sweden, Switzerland, Thailand, Tunisia, Turkey, and Wales (Smith, Wu, & Murphy, 2020). Such global protests demonstrate the important impact that communities can have when joining together to voice oppression in search of justice and systemic change. The protests in the face of George Floyd's murder demonstrate key aspects of community that are at the heart of this book: empowerment, social power, citizen participation, and community organizing (see Chapter 3, this volume).

1.1 The Founding of Community Psychology

Community psychology in the United States developed in response to the limitations of psychology in addressing social issues (Tebes, 2016). As a result, community psychology emerged amid a backdrop of mental health policies that promoted deinstitutionalization of people with mental illnesses, a focus on community-based mental health, the civil rights movement, the publication of *Action for Mental Health: Final Report, 1961* (Joint Commission on Mental Illness and Health, 1961), and the passage of the Community Mental Health Act in 1963 (see Chapter 13, this volume).

Community psychology as a formal discipline within psychology in the USA was founded at the Swampscott Conference in 1965. Here, community psychology was defined as an action-oriented approach to psychology that sought to address social issues through prevention, intervention, and community-based research (Society for Community Research and Action [SCRA], n.d.a; Tebes, 2016). SCRA presented organizing community psychology principles for research and practice that included:

> 1. Considering individual vs. systems change, including first order vs. second order change; 2. Understanding social ecological levels of analysis and intervention; 3. Focusing on wellness, strengths, and competence (vs. deficits and disorder), including an emphasis on prevention, resilience, and health promotion; 4. Valuing and promoting empowerment and social justice, including liberation from oppression; 5. Understanding human diversity and cultural contexts; 6. Advancing stakeholder participation, multi-level collaboration, and sense of community; 7. Developing empirically-based models for action; [and] 8. Promoting theoretical and methodological pluralism.   (SCRA, n.d.a)

These community psychology principles introduced critical competencies for community psychology practice. Hence, a Task Group designated by the Community Psychology Practice Council and the Council of Education Programs developed key competencies in the community psychology field (SCRA, n.d.b). The community psychology competencies are not standards. Rather,

> SCRA proposes the Competencies for Practice to promote dialogue and innovation in community psychology training and practice. These competencies are not intended as standards for accrediting programs or licensing individuals. Instead, they provide a common framework for discussion of the skills involved in community psychology practice, and how those skills can be learned. Skills for practice and the processes of learning them are contextual, and methods and opportunities for learning are always evolving. However, a common framework for discussion of these skills can promote a more articulate, productive dialogue about the nature of community psychology practice and how students can learn the skills for that practice. This common framework also can promote constructive dialogue with potential employers about practice competencies that community psychologists may have, in general.   (Dalton & Wolfe, 2012, p. 9)

The eighteen competencies are divided under key community psychology areas that include Foundational Principles, Community Program Development and management, Community and Organizational Capacity-Building, Community and Social Change, and Community Research. Table 1.1 presents an overview of these key areas and relevant competencies based on information presented in Dalton and Wolfe (2012; see www.scra27.org/files/8713/8557/6003/TCP_Fall_2012.pdf for more detail). Table 1.1 presents *The Cambridge Handbook of Community Psychology* chapters that are largely representative of each competency area, while also acknowledging that each chapter overlaps with other areas of competence.

Table 1.1 *Community psychology competencies*

Competency Area	Specific Competencies	Overall Competency Area Theme(s)	Relevant *Handbook* Chapters*
Foundational Principles	1. Ecological Perspectives The ability to articulate and apply multiple ecological perspectives and levels of analysis in community practice 2. Empowerment 3. Sociocultural and Cross-Cultural Competence The ability to value, integrate, and bridge multiple worldviews, cultures, and identities 4. Community Inclusion and Partnership 5. Ethical, Reflective Practice	This group of competencies focuses on engagement of a contextual, ecological perspective in community psychology research and practice; systemic, ecological community empowerment; incorporation of diverse perspectives and an ability to incorporate cultural humility; active engagement in efforts that support full community representation and let diverse voices be heard; and involvement in ethical practice and intervention.	Chapters 1, 2, 3, 4, 5
Community Program Development and Management	6. Program Development, Implementation, and Management 7. Prevention and Health Promotion	This group of competencies focuses on collaboration with community partners to forge community programs within diverse community contexts and incorporation of prevention- and health-promoting efforts in community-based initiatives.	Chapters 15, 17, 18, 26, 27
Community and Organizational Capacity-Building	8. Community Leadership and Mentoring 9. Small and Large Group Processes 10. Resource Development 11. Consultation and Organizational Development	This group of competencies focuses on the promotion of community leadership by encouraging diverse constituencies to be involved in community efforts as defined by them; the mentoring and support community leaders and future community leaders	Chapters 10, 19, 20, 25, 27, 28

Table 1.1 (*cont.*)

Competency Area	Specific Competencies	Overall Competency Area Theme(s)	Relevant *Handbook* Chapters*
		can provide in efforts designed to promote leadership capacity and engagement; an awareness of dynamics in small and large group processes in efforts such as working across diverse constituencies; conducting culturally responsive community-based needs assessments; and to consult with organizations to promote their development and attainment of goals.	
Community and Social Change	12. Collaboration and Coalition Development 13. Community Development 14. Community Organizing and Community Advocacy 15. Public Policy Analysis, Development, and Advocacy 16. Community Education, Information Dissemination, and Building Public Awareness	This group of competencies focuses on efforts to promote systemic change at the community level. Such efforts include work to build coalitions; communicate lived experiences; actively engage in community development within one's community; engage in active community organization and advocacy; engagement with the community to promote policy change and implementation; and the promotion of awareness of key issues through dissemination of knowledge and information.	Chapters 3, 11, 12, 13, 14, 16, 21, 22, 23, 24, 30
Community Research	17. Participatory Community Research 18. Program Evaluation	This group of competencies focuses on research and evaluation within an ecological, community-based	Chapters 6, 7, 8, 9, 29, 30

Table 1.1 (*cont.*)

Competency Area	Specific Competencies	Overall Competency Area Theme(s)	Relevant *Handbook* Chapters*
		perspective. Such competencies address the importance of developing true collaborations with community partners where the research process is shared and gives back to the communities where data are collected and where collaboration with community partners engages in comprehensive evaluation processes designed to promote program efficacy and accountability.	

Note: * Themes overlap across chapters, however, cross-reference with the main theme is presented here.
Source: This is an original table based on the competencies presented in Dalton and Wolfe (2012).

1.2 Rationale: A Grounded Ecological Approach

The Cambridge Handbook of Community Psychology: Interdisciplinary and Contextual Perspectives is timely given the global events we are experiencing. A review of current books on community psychology suggests that many of these existing works discuss various aspects of community psychology (e.g., social change, prevention) without taking an interdisciplinary, grounded ecological approach to what it means to be a community. The contributions in this volume address this gap given that they will (1) take a grounded ecological approach to specific aspects of the community psychology field; (2) consider global components of key community psychology concepts; (3) adopt a multicultural, transnational approach to understanding community psychology; (4) present practical applications and relevant implications within diverse contexts; (5) present critical case analyses that illustrate local/bottom-up programs that meet community needs; and (6) incorporate contributing authors from diverse disciplines and nationalities. The grounded ecological approach that is a central focus of this volume is a valuable framework for community psychology given that the "essence of the ecological perspective is to construct an understanding of the interrelationships of social structures and social processes of the groups, organizations, and communities in which we live and work. The concept of interdependence is the basic axiom of the ecological perspective" (Kelly et al., 2000, p. 133).

The rationale for taking an ecological approach is further understood when we consider that the science and practice of community psychology is advanced when one understands how to create "new interdependencies" (Kelly et al., 2000, p. 133). The assertion by Kelly and colleagues (2000) supports this perspective: *"To create a resourceful social system requires that the initiator have a view of how people and social systems affect each other*. The ecological perspective is proposed as a point of view that can elaborate structures and processes for both people and social systems" (p. 134). The grounded aspect of the ecological approach taken is to provide a practical ecological aspect to our understanding of community psychology. The rationale here is to not lose sight of the practical application of community psychology theory. Taking a grounded ecological approach means that contributors are encouraged to apply theoretical constructs within the community ecologies presented.

In sum, *The Cambridge Handbook of Community Psychology* integrates (1) ecological factors that influence community psychology practice, (2) global considerations that examine how community psychology is experienced in different nations, (3) transnational considerations that demonstrate how community psychology concepts can be adapted for diverse country and community contexts, (4) interdisciplinary perspectives from colleagues who represent a range of professional disciplines, (5) a practical aspect that examines how community psychology frameworks play out in the local context with bottom-up solutions, and (6) current research and methodological approaches.

1.3 Community Psychology for the Twenty-First Century: Doesn't All Psychology Incorporate Community Psychology?

Community psychology began during a time of social change. The mental health system was moving from institutionalization to deinstitutionalization, the civil rights movement began, and psychologists were committed to making sure the discipline was responsive to social action change. Just as community psychology has its roots in these historical movements, so too can it reintroduce itself today as an aspect of psychology that focuses on community efforts to promote social action. The killings of Breonna Taylor and George Floyd, among many other African Americans, and the disparity in medical and mental health care demonstrated by COVID-19, are social issues that underscore the need for a reintroduction to community-focused psychology.

Community psychology has an important role to play in response to the tension between our ability to change and our ability to maintain the status quo. Perhaps at no other more recent time in history has a commitment to and an understanding of community been so important. In effect, community is everywhere – and yet many would propose that we lack community in the twenty-first century. This is ironic given that technology and social media have made community more possible in some ways. This duality of experience suggests the notion of community as one that is elusive. It raises the questions: What causes isolation for a community? What makes community members feel marginalized from their community? What encourages a sense of community membership? At the same time, psychology as a science is very much moving into an understanding of how behavioral science can be implemented in a community context.

While some might say that community psychology is a relatively young field – with roots in experiences such as the Swampscott Conference in 1965 – if we consider the fact that communities across the globe have been organizing for justice and well-being for centuries, we can consider community psychology as a discipline with a long history. Community psychology is growing in response to science and practice that takes us into real-world/real-life settings that represent lived experiences. The chapters that follow present examples of community psychology in action transnationally. *Handbook* chapters describe community-organizing efforts that include Black Lives Matter; #MeToo; March for Our Lives; #AbolishICE; the experience of Flint, Michigan; the Public Health Action Plan implemented in 2013 after the train derailment and explosion in Lac-Mégantic, Québec; the Newark Anti-Violence Coalition in Newark, New Jersey; The Carter Center Mental Health Program; the Gowanus Canal Community Advisory Group in Brooklyn, New York; Family Support Services (FSS) at Ronald McDonald House; mental health services in prayer camps in Ghana; crowdfunding via social media; the Strengthening Guided Pathways and Career Success by Ensuring Students Are Learning program; global community responses to climate change; a toolkit to develop school–family–community partnerships; interventions with young adults who have neurodevelopmental disabilities; school-based mental health programs in rural settings; mental health programs on college/university campuses; supporting LGBTQ+ communities, and many more. These advancements are fueled in part by access to emerging evidence-based interventions that can be adapted to diverse community settings.

These examples also illustrate that ours is an increasingly global society. What we experience as a community is influenced by access to global outreach through the Internet, social media, and transportation technologies. Relevant to globalization is consideration as to how community psychology plays out on the world stage. What community psychology approaches are being used in different countries? How does political context influence the development and extension of community psychology? What can nations learn from one another as they examine successful community psychology-based interventions?

1.4 Orientation to *The Cambridge Handbook of Community Psychology: Interdisciplinary and Contextual Perspectives*

The *Cambridge Handbook of Community Psychology* is divided into four parts. *Part I – Foundational Concepts: Interdisciplinary, Culturally Responsive, and Contextual Approaches* includes five chapters focused on foundational aspects of community psychology. Key themes presented in Part I include defining what is meant by having sense of community, stages of community development, and theories that apply to the work of community psychologists (Chapter 2); definitions of empowerment with a focus on how communities can promote local, national, and global change (Chapter 3); ethical guidelines in community-based research and how to assess ethical concerns within a community psychology context (Chapter 4); and defining wellness across diverse world regions including Africa, Asia, Europe, the Americas, and Australia/ New Zealand (Chapter 5).

Part II – Research, Assessment, and Program Evaluation: Ecological Considerations includes four chapters that focus on research methodologies, program evaluation, and assessment. Chapters presented in Part II consider culturally responsive community assessment processes and community action plans (Chapter 6), promotion of youth resilience in rural communities through a school–community–university partnership alongside program evaluation strategies (Chapter 7), implementation of the Constructive Diversity Pedagogy Participatory Action Research project to promote social justice and dialogues focused on diversity in higher education and beyond (Chapter 8), and the application of a critical ethnography approach to community-based research (Chapter 9).

Part III – Community Psychology in Action: Critical Themes and Areas of Application focuses on specific domains where community psychology can play a role and have significant impact. The 19 chapters in Part III discuss concepts from an applied perspective and incorporate case studies to highlight key concepts in action. While it was beyond the scope of this book to include all potential areas, chapters seek to cover a broad range of important systemic themes. They complement one another by focusing on the role of community psychology in diverse, but related, ecological contexts. Topics presented in this part of the *Handbook* include discussion of feminist community leaders with a focus on strategies to promote leadership among women who face barriers to leadership (Chapter 10); components of resiliency theory with an application to the experience of the Flint, Michigan community (Chapter 11); building community resilience through disaster reduction efforts (Chapter 12); discussion of the consumer recovery movement (Chapter 13); examining the concept of neighborhood with a focus on neighborhood empowerment in the South Ward of Newark, New Jersey (Chapter 14); the application of a transculturally informed approach to developmental neuropsychology (Chapter 15); the relationship between community well-being and environmental policies via a case study of the Gowanus community in Brooklyn, New York (Chapter 16);

discussion of FSS offered at Ronald McDonald House in response to families with children facing severe medical illnesses (Chapter 17); consideration of the implementation of mental health services within prayer camps in Ghana (Chapter 18); the impact of social media on our sense of community (Chapter 19); promoting educational access via the case study presentation of the Association of American Colleges and Universities' Guided Pathways Project (Chapter 20); the psychological impact of climate change with consideration of experiences in Syria, Tuvalo, Haiti, and Central America (Chapter 21); understanding the connection between government size and the implementation of public services (Chapter 22); a public health approach to delinquency and incarceration with a focus on the USA and Australia (Chapter 23); presentation of a toolkit to develop school–family–community connections at urban middle schools (Chapter 24); experiences of immigration among women (Chapter 25); a transcultural approach to working with youth with neurodevelopmental disabilities (Chapter 26); provision of mental health services on college campuses (Chapter 27); and supporting LGBTQ+ communities (Chapter 28).

Part IV – Where Do We Go from Here? Gaps and Opportunities for Community Psychology focuses on next steps and future directions for community psychology. The two chapters that make up this section focus on significant gaps in research and practice in community psychology (Chapter 29). The *Handbook*'s concluding chapter presents a call for action for community psychology with a focus on ways to address gaps in research and practice moving forward within an interdisciplinary, transnational, ecological approach (Chapter 30).

References

Centers for Disease Control. (n.d.). *What you can do.* www.cdc.gov/coronavirus/2019-ncov/need-extra-precautions/what-you-can-do.html

Clauss-Ehlers, C. S., Chiriboga, D., Hunter, S. J., Roysircar, G., & Tummala-Narra, P. (2019). APA Multicultural Guidelines executive summary: Ecological approach to context, identity, and intersectionality. *American Psychologist, 74*(2), 232–244. doi.org/10.1037/amp0000382

Cohen, R. B. (2020, March 24). *Intergenerational programs & physical distancing: What to do when we can't be together.* Generations United. www.gu.org/app/uploads/2020/03/Generations-United-Zoom-Meeting-Slides-3.24.20.pdf

Dalton, J., & Wolfe, S. (2012). Joint column: Education connection and the community practitioner. *The Community Psychologist, 45*(4), 7–13.

Demby, G., & Miraji, S. M. (2020, May 31). *A decade of watching Black people die.* Code Switch, National Public Radio. www.npr.org/2020/05/29/865261916/a-decade-of-watching-black-people-die

Gleason, W. (2020, April 3). *Watch videos of tonight's massive citywide clap for essential workers.* TimeOut. www.timeout.com/newyork/news/watch-videos-of-tonights-massive-citywide-clap-for-essential-workers-040320

Goode, H., & Shinkle, E. (2020, April 15). *COVID-19 has fueled the rapid rise of teletherapy*. Global Teletherapy. https://globalteletherapy.com/covid-19-has-fueled-the-rise-of-teletherapy/

Joint Commission on Mental Illness and Health. (1961). *Action for mental health: Final report, 1961*. New York: Basic Books.

Kelly, J. G., Ryan, A. M., Altman, B. E., & Stelzner, S. T. (2000). Understanding and changing social systems: An ecological view. In J. Rappaport and E. Seidman (Eds.), *Handbook of community psychology* (pp. 133–160). New York: Kluwer Academic/Plenum Publishers.

The Learning Network. (2020, April 9). What students are saying about remote learning. *The New York Times*. www.nytimes.com/2020/04/09/learning/what-students-are-saying-about-remote-learning.html

Pappas, S. (2020, June 1). Fighting inequity in the face of COVID-19. *American Psychological Association, COVID-19 Special Report*. www.apa.org/monitor/2020/06/covid-fighting-inequity

SCAPE (2020, June 5). Black Lives Matter. https://www.scapestudio.com/news/2020/06/black-lives-matter/

Seale, C. (2020, March 17). *Distance learning during the Coronavirus pandemic: Equity and access issues for school leaders*. Forbes. www.forbes.com/sites/colinseale/2020/03/17/distance-learning-during-the-coronavirus-pandemic-equity-and-access-questions-for-school-leaders/#3605145b1d4d

Smith, S., Wu, J., & Murphy, J. (2020, June 9). *Map: George Floyd protests around the world*. NBC News. www.nbcnews.com/news/world/map-george-floyd-protests-countries-worldwide-n1228391

Society for Community Research and Action. (n.d.a). *History of community psychology*. www.communitypsychology.com/what-is-swampscott-and-why-is-it-important/

Society for Community Research and Action. (n.d.b). *Competencies for community psychology practice*. www.scra27.org/what-we-do/practice/18-competencies-community-psychology-practice/

Tebes, J. K. (2016). Reflections on the future of community psychology from the generations after Swampscott: A commentary and introduction to the Special Issue. *American Journal of Community Psychology, 58*(3–4), 229–238. doi.org/10.1002/ajcp.12110

Weir, K. (2020, April 6). *Grief and COVID-19: Saying good-bye in the age of physical distancing*. American Psychological Association. www.apa.org/topics/covid-19/grief-distance

Xiong, C. (2020, June 4). A timeline of events leading to George Floyd's death as outlined in charging documents. *StarTribune*. www.startribune.com/a-timeline-of-events-leading-to-george-floyd-s-death-as-outlined-in-charging-documents/570999132/

2 Community Psychology

Getting to Work

David W. McMillan

2.1 Introduction

In the late 1960s, J. R. Newbrough received a grant from the National Institute of Mental Health (NIMH) to develop a nationwide social indicators movement. His ideas were rooted in optimistic wishes of social scientists dating back at least to C. P. Snow's (1959) vision of a third culture that would use the scientific method to address humanitarian problems. E. O. Wilson echoed these ideas in his book *Consilience* (1998). The hope was to treat decisions made by governments as naturally occurring experiments, turning political discussion into rational discourse rather than a blood sport (Pinker, 2018). Newbrough's project fit the mission of most community psychologists – to use social science to develop better communities through influencing public policy.

In the mid-1970s the project died. Newbrough understood that it was terminated by Lyndon Johnson who did not want "egg-headed" intellectuals constraining politicians. In today's world, when public sentiment is even more extreme in its anti-science and anti-intellectual bias (see Donald Trump and global warming), it is easier to understand why Newbrough's vision overshot the possible. His student, David McMillan (i.e., the author of this chapter), had a much less ambitious goal for his contribution to community psychology. McMillan was inspired by Theodore Sarason's (1974) challenge for the field to focus on sense of community as its core mission. He wrote that "the lack of a sense of community was extraordinarily frequent ... and [was] a destructive force in living and ... dealing with its consequence and prevention should be the overarching concern of community psychology" (Sarason, 1986, p. 406). Sarason's challenge was limited by the difficulty in defining sense of community. Like the term "love" (with which it had a great deal in common) its definition seemed illusive to Sarason (1974).

McMillan accepted the challenge and he offered a definition in his 1976 major area paper required for his Ph.D. from Peabody College (McMillan, 1976), and later published in the McMillan and Chavis (1986) version. McMillan's vision for a focus of community psychology was less on public policy and more on communities, from two-person relationships to clubs, companies, teams, towns, cities, states, or nations. Each of the communities in this range would, he believed, have its own level of sense of community that could be measured and evaluated.

From his theory, he and others developed measures that have been validated (Chavis et al., 1986; Peterson, Speer, & McMillan, 2008) and extensively used (Fisher, Sonn, & Bishop, 2002). Hundreds of studies have used some version of this theory and its measures confirming the theory validity. More than five thousand articles reference the McMillan theory. It has been used successfully in communities all over the world from South America to Australia, New Zealand, Thailand, Europe, and China, among other countries.

Although there is criticism from postmodern social scientists who consider the theory and its measures to be positivistic and modern and too absolutist for postmodern social science, the theory and its measures continue to be the primary paradigm for psychological sense of community (PSOC) in community psychology. Debates around the question of what is an appropriate definition of PSOC center around McMillan's theory (Chipuer & Pretty, 1999; Hill, 1996; Puddifoot, 1996; Rapley & Pretty, 1999; Sonn, Bishop, & Drew, 1999; Wiesenfeld, 1996). While the large-scale systemic focus of community psychologists on public policy and government is laudable, perhaps a more effective intervention strategy would focus on smaller communities. Instead of trying to hit a "home run," perhaps community psychologists might work for "base hits" and hope for a "few yards and a cloud of dust."

This is the focus of this chapter: *How can community psychologists use their tools to help all communities, especially smaller dysfunctional communities and developing ones?* This chapter illustrates the practical usefulness of McMillan's PSOC theory along with four other theories that may have practical usefulness in treating community dysfunction and promoting community well-being. The four other theories are (1) a community typology, (2) community emotional contagion, (3) the ten stages of community development, and (4) the third position (Newbrough, 1995).

2.2 Psychological Sense of Community

Many articles on PSOC consider McMillan's theory to be simple-minded common sense (Nowell & Boyd, 2010). They do not recognize that McMillan's four elements each have about six sub-elements, with a total of thirty-three sub-elements or sub-sub-elements. Following McMillan's PSOC paradigm, one can construct a decision-tree intervention model that can be used on communities at any level. Below are the four elements and thirty-three sub-elements or sub-sub-elements.

1. Membership (McMillan & Chavis, 1986)/Spirit (McMillan, 1996)
   a. Boundaries
      i. Barriers marking who belongs and who does not
      ii. Symbols denoting membership

      b. Emotional safety
         i. Able to speak honestly
         ii. Safe to be vulnerable
      c. Sense of belonging
         i. Expectation of belonging
         ii. A feeling of acceptance
         iii. Awareness of being welcome
      d. Personal investment/dues-paying to belong[1]
2. Influence (McMillan & Chavis, 1986)/Trust (McMillan, 1996)
      a. Personal investment
         i. Sacrificing to be a member gives one a sense that membership is earned
         ii. Personal investment makes a community more attracted to the investing member
      b. Community norms influence members to conform
         i. Norms
         ii. Conforming behavior
      c. Members need to conform for consensual validation just as a community needs its members to conform to maintain cohesiveness
      d. Members are attracted to groups that allow members influence over or in the group
      e. Influence between community and members and members and community operates concurrently
3. Reinforcement/Integration of Needs (McMillan & Chavis, 1986)/Trade (McMillan, 1996)
      a. Communities meet members' needs
      b. Strong reinforcements to belong include status, success, competencies of other members
      c. Shared values – or consensual trading
      d. Integrating needs and resources or complementary trading
      e. Transformative trading[2] – teaching skills
      f. Generative trading – handing off responsibilities and roles from one generation to the next
4. Shared Emotional Connection (McMillan & Chavis, 1986)/Art (McMillan, 1996)
      a. Members must share time
      b. There must be a certain quality to time shared
         i. Events must have valence (McMillan & Chavis, 1986) or drama (McMillan, 1996)

---

[1] Note that personal investment has two parts. One belongs in Membership/Spirit. The second belongs in Influence/Trust. McMillan reconsidered this sub-element for this chapter.

[2] Transformative trading and generative trading are new ideas added to the theory and first presented here.

ii. Events must have closure
ii. Events must honor members
c. Events become symbolized in rituals, common symbols, and traditions. Shared stories emerge.
d. A spiritual bond emerges from shared history.

The elements and sub-elements act like subatomic particles, swirling about, overlapping, and compounding the effects of one another. PSOC is a "sense of" spirit more than it is a thing. It is part of the constellation of ideas that are commonly called "love." Terms included in this sphere of human influence are attachment, group cohesiveness, intimacy, empathy, relationships, mirroring, compassion, caring, social glue, and affection. The point is that PSOC is a spirit. Understanding it and reducing it to numbers required precise wording and luck (Bess et al., 2002). Figures 2.1–2.5 together show an example of a decision-tree map that community consultants might apply in evaluating relationships and communities that wish to strengthen their PSOC.

This decision tree can be used when consulting a community when the goal of the consultation is to build stronger PSOC.

An appendix was prepared for this chapter, but space constraints did not allow for its publication here. Instead, it is published on the website www.drdavidmcmillan.com under the heading of "Sense of Community" articles.

2.3 A Community Typology

Every science has a taxonomy of types of species that scientists in the field use to divide the specimens or the live creatures that they study. The most often used community typology was developed by Ferdinand Tönnies (1855–1936) in the 1880s (Tönnies, 1957). Many social thinkers of his time protested the alienation that was a product of industrialization, Max Weber and Karl Marx prominent among them (Worsley, 1987). But Tönnies was the one who created a paradigm contrasting rural and industrial communities. He is the person referenced as the first to develop a community typology. He termed the rural community the *Gemeinschaft* community and the urban community the *Gesellschaft* community. Weber later used a similar comparison using the terms *Vergemeinschaft* and *Vergesselschaft*. Community scholars also acknowledge a variety of types of community (Bess et al., 2002; Heller, 1989). Many contemporary social thinkers often use Tönnies' two types of community to describe how communities may differ (Dokecki, 1996; Newbrough, 1992, 1995). Tönnies proposed two contrasting types. McMillan's community typology adds two more types to Tönnies' two. His four types are *Gemeinschaft* (organic communities), *Gesellschaft* (market communities), *Gefolgschaft* (faith communities), and *Notschaft* (emergency communities).

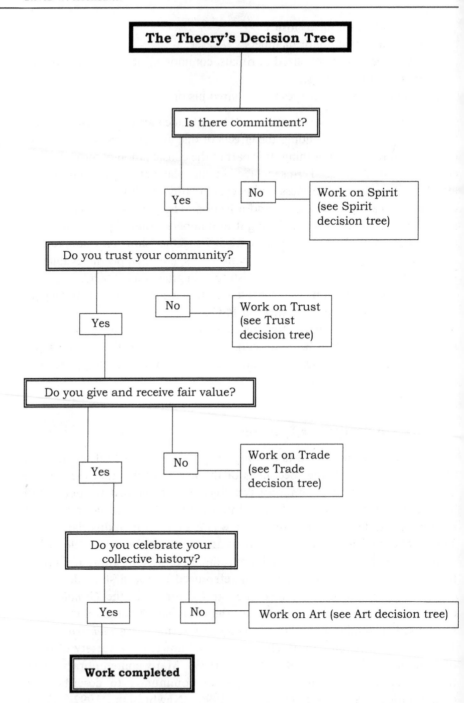

Figure 2.1 *The theory's decision tree*

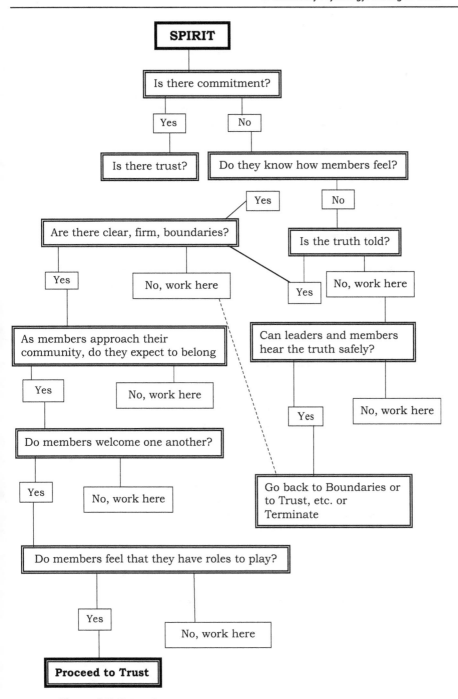

Figure 2.2 *Spirit decision tree*

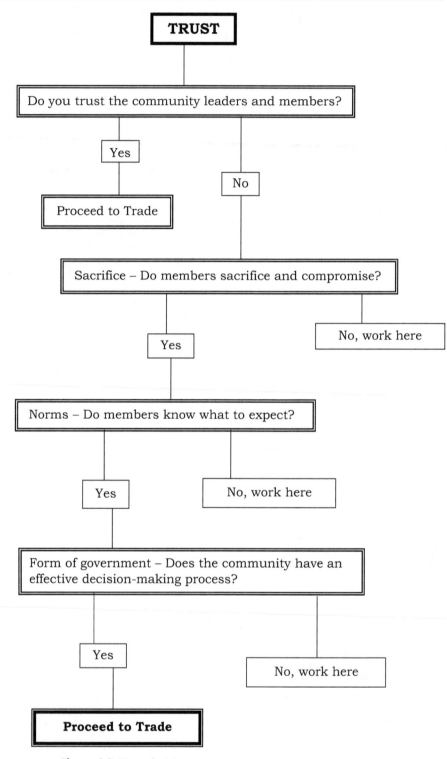

Figure 2.3 *Trust decision tree*

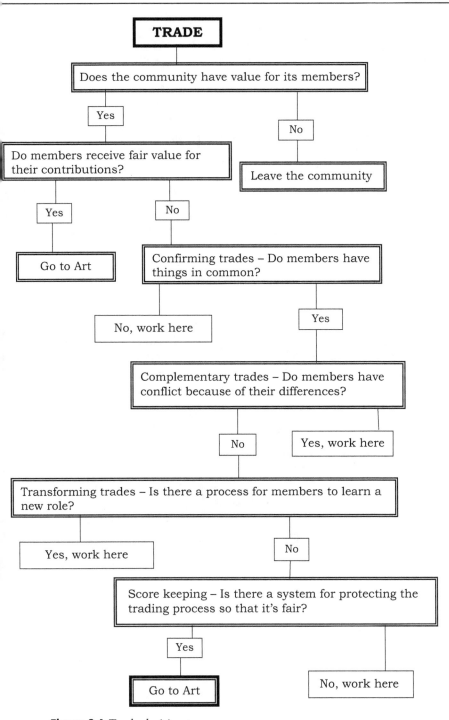

Figure 2.4 *Trade decision tree*

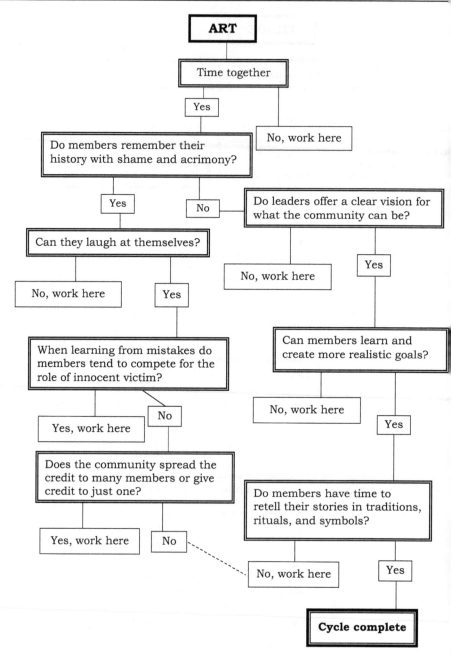

Figure 2.5 *Art decision tree*

2.3.1 *Gemeinschaft*/Organic Communities

2.3.1.1 Glass Half-Full

Tönnies in his time and Putnam (2000) in our time idealized the organic community because of its strong PSOC. Authors George Steinbeck, George Orwell, Elizabeth Gilbert, and Barbara Kingsolver praise the tribal warmth and loyalty that is endemic to an organic community. An organic community takes care of its own. In an organic community, when there is a fire, people respond. They come to put out the fire, to help rebuild, to bring food, and to find beds and shelter if needed. Members of an organic community are committed to the care and nurture of one another and their community. In Biblical terms, they fill the widow's cruse and expand a few loaves and fish to feed multitudes. Less fortunate members are taken in and cared for. There is a place at the community's mythical table for all members. The key values in an organic community are loyalty and commitment. In an organic community, a promise has no time limit. The above describes the organic community's glass as half-full.

2.3.1.2 Glass Half-Empty

The glass half-empty involves roles being clearly and rigidly defined. Social class lines are starkly drawn and movement beyond one's station is rare. There is little upward mobility in an organic world (Bess et al., 2002). Power comes from the question: Who do you know? Success is a product of patronage. Merit and ability count for little. The most qualified person is of little relevance. Corruption is rampant; "the good ole boy network" prevails. Intolerance, stereotyping, racism, and misogyny are markers in the glass half-empty.

2.3.2 *Gesellschaft*/Market Communities

2.3.2.1 Glass Half-Full

David Brooks (2015) calls the market community a "meritocracy." In this community, who you know does not matter. Talent, qualifications, and competence open the doors to membership and belonging. Potential members are encouraged to develop their abilities and compete for a place. If one is to have a place at the community's mythical table, it must be earned. Skills must be mastered. One must do well in school, sports, and politics. To reach a safe place in a market community, one builds résumés, masters intimacy skills, changes careers at the right time, and builds a retirement. In a market community, self-fulfillment is encouraged (Gerwirth, 1998). Life is about what one does to contribute (Taylor, 1994). The goal of a market community is to eliminate corruption and create a fully functioning society where the best qualified are given power and authority and the marketplace will operate efficiently building wealth. While success in an organic community depends on who you know, success in a market community depends on what you can do. That is the market community's glass half-full.

2.3.2.2 Glass Half-Empty

The glass half-empty is that a market community has no compassion, no commitment, no loyalty. It is about "what you can do for me today." What one did yesterday does not matter. This is a world of elites, not a world for the average. Donald Trump, if he is to be believed, is the epitome of where power should reside in a market community. It should not take a village to know what's best. It should be the best judgment of the most qualified person, an *ubermensch*. This is a throwaway society epitomized by the National Football League. Once a member loses a step, she is put out to pasture, disposed of. She receives a "your services are no longer needed" notice. PSOC is irrelevant in a glass half-empty market community.

2.3.3 *Gefolgschaft*/Faith Communities

In the *Gefolgschaft*/faith community, it is not about who you know. It is not about what you can do. It is about what you believe. Churches, political parties or movements, the Boy and Girl Scouts, cults like the Branch Davidians, Jim Jones' the People's Temple, Hitler's Brown Shirts, are examples of this type of community. These communities come together around a charismatic leader. They usually form in a time of rapid change, societal chaos, and confusion, when people feel overwhelmed and are looking for simple solutions. People drawn to these communities are having trouble coping. They do not have faith in themselves or in their traditional institutions. They are relieved when charismatic, confident leaders present themselves as "the one who knows the way." Members eagerly delegate authority to this hero/*ubermensch*. They are expecting their leader to rescue them from their ethical morass.

These communities are characterized by "holy" books that contain "the answer to everything." The contents of these texts often offer contradicting solutions to life's problems. Only the hero/*ubermensch* or their disciples can correctly interpret "the word." Dogma emerges from these leaders. The community develops a special language. Members of many southern faith communities can be recognized by the words they use, such as "Have a blessed day," "You are anointed for this work," "This is a God thing," "God will give us a miracle," etc.

Members tend to think in rigid good/bad, black/white, dichotomous thinking. "You either believe or you don't." Charismatic leaders often exploit their position, for example, priest sex abuse in the Catholic Church, or charity leaders embezzling money or using the charity's resources as if these resources were their personal property.

There are healthy faith communities. They understand the importance of doubt in development of faith. Just as courage recognizes the reasonableness of fear and then provides the strength to act in spite of it, so too do healthy faith and the wisdom that comes from it understand that there are mysteries or unknowables and that beliefs are simply pretense that one "knows" when knowing is impossible. Doubt balanced with faith helps one adapt and revise beliefs in the face of contradictory reality. Festinger's (1957) famous study of cognitive dissonance illustrates one faith community's rigid belief system that thought the world was ending at a certain moment. When it didn't, and the members had to face a new reality, their cognitive dissonance would not allow them room for doubt that they may have been wrong to sell all of their possessions.

A healthy faith community allows for dissent for the many ways to define the unknowable. Such communities respect that other faith communities may have a different understanding of metaphysical questions and answers. They appreciate other faith communities for being fellow communities, building a belief system and a disciplined path to make sense of life.

For some, political parties have replaced churches as faith communities in Europe. The same is happening in the USA. David Brooks on the *PBS Newshour* on October 26, 2018 warned that people in the USA were putting too much emotional investment into their political leaders and political beliefs and that this devotion to party was dangerously dividing the country. Implicit in this criticism is the notion that worship should not become political; that one's investment in the spiritual and political should be divided.

2.3.4 *Notschaft*/Crisis Communities

The fourth type of community is a *Notschaft* or crisis community. It is organized around potential emergent, perhaps dangerous events, in which time is of the essence. Such communities are fire departments, police forces, military units, hospitals, sports teams, and theater troops. What characterizes these types of communities is practice, repetition, protocols, drills, memorized procedures, order, and a chain of command authority structure. People's lives may be at stake. The performance may be jeopardized. It's not who you know that matters. It's not what you can do that matters. It's not what you believe. It is: Can you play your part?

Hospital teams must be fluid. Pharmacists, physicians, nurses, and surgical assistants must synchronize their efforts to respond to health emergencies.[3]

---

[3] Academics have a habit of rediscovering an idea, giving it a new name, and passing if off as a new theory. McMillan might be accused of doing this in his initial formulation of PSOC (McMillan, 1976). In that paper he used studies on group cohesiveness to build his theory.

These communities are funded externally, by taxes, insurance, or ticket sales. Fear or the promise of excitement is used to justify the funding. Money for fire departments, the military, or for hospitals arrives because people outside crisis communities are afraid some tragedy might happen and they will need a response from a competent prepared emergency team. Such communities thrive on the misery of others.

Crisis communities are prepared to respond quickly with well-rehearsed teams. Synchronous movement is required by members. They must work together as if they were a machine. Roles are strictly defined. Members are responsible for a specialized task. Each member is required to master their role and be able to proficiently perform the task allocated to it.

A crisis community contains a rigid hierarchy of authority. The lines of authority are carefully drawn and well-known. Members do not step outside of their designated authority. Members know to whom they report and are willing to follow instructions from their superior. This rigid hierarchy is important in emergencies because responses must be quick. There is no time to debate or experiment. There is a victim to be tended to, a danger to be averted, an audience to be entertained, and a game to be played. "The show must go on."

Crisis communities are supported by their larger societies in many ways. Funding has already been mentioned. The larger community must certify crisis community members as persons proficient to fill their roles. Trainings are offered. Tests are administered. Licenses are given. Auditions are organized.

The larger community advertises or allows advertisements for crisis communities. Signage is placed directing people where to find the crisis community. Performances are advertised. Tickets are sold. Or secrecy is maintained to protect the planning and the development of interventions. Uniforms are given to crisis community members, designating their role and perhaps their rank.

Such communities can develop a number of problems. For example, instead of existing to serve the broader community, a crisis community can use fear to manipulate the larger community to serve the purposes and agendas of people inside the crisis community. (See the movie *The Tail Wags the Dog* or President Eisenhower's speech on the military industrial complex.) Crisis communities can develop in such a way that they strangle the larger community that they are meant to serve. (See healthcare costs rising faster than personal income in the USA.)

Medical care has evolved into healthcare silos that don't connect. Reactive treatment with overlapping specialists and professionals is the norm. In our current medical system, it is expensive and difficult to develop collaborative treatment teams. Yet, interdisciplinary treatment teams of geneticists, psychologists, social workers, nurses, and physicians are needed to address issues

McMillan has noticed other community psychology authors proposing a "new idea" or aspect of PSOC and simply stating one of the thirty-three sub-elements or sub-sub-elements and calling it by another name. This is academic inside of baseball and occurs frequently.

like tobacco use, addiction, and diabetes. Medical billing practices and payment for medical care need to be changed so that medical professionals are rewarded for teamwork and collaboration rather than punished. Developing such an intervention for building and supporting interdisciplinary medical teams would be helpful to medical communities.

People given visibility by their roles in crisis communities (e.g., famous generals, sports and movie stars) can exploit their position and pose as the charismatic leader/savior transferring their authority in their crisis community to authority in the larger community, pretending that their competence in an operating room, a war room, or on a television show qualifies them for the role of leader of government (Donald Trump and *The Apprentice*).

2.4 Community Moods

It is commonly acknowledged that emotions are contagious. Neuroscientists discovered what they called mirror neurons in the human brain (Duncan & Small, 2017; Rizzolatti & Craighero, 2004; Rizzolatti, Fogassi, & Gallese, 2001). These neurons perceive emotions expressed by others. They fire, triggering the brain neurons of the emotion circuit perceived by the mirror neurons. The hormones associated with the emotion are released. This happens in a nanosecond before our neocortex, the human brain, is aware of these feelings. Most of the time emotions are reactive responses to the social environment rather than chosen expressions of feelings. This is visible in communities. Consider the recent Florida Parkland School shooting. This event emotionally bonded the students, staff, and community in shared grief. Unconsciously, they followed a grief recovery script that community psychologists should know. The sadness that is the heart of grief comes from how much it hurts to want. Since they cannot possibly have what they wanted, thinking about their most important desire, for their friends to survive, hurts too much. Their wants only caused them pain.

Yet, of the eight other emotions besides sadness (fear, shame, anger, surprise/startle, disgust, joy, desire, sleep/trance; McMillan, 2005) only two emotions can create energy that will resolve sadness. One is anger and the other is desire (and desire hurts too much). After a time, the Parkland students had the courage to want again. They wanted a safe world without guns. They merged their desire and rage into determination and they marched out of their sadness into a campaign for gun control.

The Starbucks Coffee Company was startled and shamed by the arrest of two men of color for simply sitting in a booth for five minutes waiting for a friend. Surprise/startle/wonder paralyzes us. It is the emotions' version of a clutch in a stick-shift car on neutral. The Starbucks community found its energy and sense of direction from feeling shame. Shame gave the community direction. And from this confession of a mistake, Starbucks closed all of its

Table 2.1 *Emotional resolves*

Emotion	Resolve
Anger	Sadness
Fear	Relaxation/Trance
Sadness	Desire and Anger
Surprise/Startle/Wonder	Desire, Disgust, i.e., likes and dislikes
Desire/Excitement	Sadness and Shame
Shame/Guilt	Joy
Disgust	Shame and Sadness
Joy	Shame and Sadness
Relaxation/Trance/Sleep	Feel the emotion that you used the trance to avoid

stores all over the world for a day to try to learn from what happened. It hoped to create a more respectful company culture.

Each emotion that a community shares has an appropriate constructive emotional resolve. Too often people are told "don't feel that way" or to "stop feeling and think." We cannot stop feeling. We are always feeling something. Emotions are fluid. They move from one emotion to the other, sometimes in seconds. Telling someone to not feel a certain emotion only traps them in that emotion. Knowing how to guide people to the next constructive emotion can be an effective community tool for community interventions. These are McMillan's (2005) nine basic emotions and their emotional resolves (Table 2.1):

Space does not permit a full description of how each community emotional knot is healthily resolved. Community anger will be used as an example of how this is done. The process is based on Steven Stosny's (1995) HEALS ritual that he developed for programs treating perpetrators of domestic violence. This treatment approach has been shown to be arguably the most and only effective treatment for domestic rage that becomes violence in homes (1995). Stosny's HEALS ritual involves five steps:

H – Halt. Do not act impulsively. Give time for feelings below anger to emerge.

E – Examine the feelings below anger. For 99% of the time, Stosny believes feelings of hurt and threat will be discovered. He nominates the following terms to help bring to emotional awareness these painful feelings. It takes courage to feel these unpleasant emotions. Feeling and expressing anger is so much easier. The terms that Stosny nominates are:

1. Unimportant	2. Disregarded	3. Devalued
4. Rejected	5. Powerless	6. Unlovable
7. Accused	8. Disgusting or unfit for human contact	

Once the term (or terms) that best represents the painful, sad feelings beneath the anger is chosen, Stosny suggests engaging the imagination and memory to conjure another event in which these feelings were prominent and feel those sad, painful feelings that came from that event.

A – Once these feeling are felt and the brain circuits and the neurohormones associated with this sadness are released in the brain and body diluting the anger neurohormones and focusing our brain away from anger, the angry tension that had possessed the body is released.

The problem is the sadness and shame that replace anger can also become a problem. So, in this step, self-compassion is Applied. The question is asked: Are we really, for example, powerless or unimportant or disgusting? Whatever the chosen word was the answer is always "No" and the community reaffirms its basic goodness.

L – The next step is to Look inside the community, person, or threat that was once considered the enemy and imagine how they feel. Use the same terms used in Step 2, the "E" step: unimportant, disregarded, devalued, rejected, powerless, unlovable, accused, and disgusting or unfit for human contact.

Once this is done, the community discovers that its enemy's feelings mirrored the community's. They expressed the same emotions below their warring rage. In realizing this, the community discovers its compassion.

S – Work together to move forward and Solve the problem.

2.4.1 The Marshall Plan: An Example of a Healthy Anger Resolve

After World War I the angry victors extracted reparation from the defeated countries, causing even more suffering in those countries after the war, while the victorious countries enjoyed a great surge of wealth and prosperity (the USA and Britain in the 1920s). Many historians believe that the rise of Hitler, Nazism, and consequently World War II were caused by the revenge reparations imposed on Germany and her allies after World War I. After World War II, the victorious allies could have followed a similar path but instead they chose to fund the Marshall Plan in Germany and a similar plan for the rebuilding of Japan.

The Marshall Plan basically used Stosny's five-step process. Before impulsively seeking revenge for the damage and hurt the enemy had inflicted, the Allies considered their own pain and sadness they felt below their anger during the war (Step 1). Their sadness replaced their anger (Step 2). They were aware of their power and in the rightness of their cause (Step 3). The Allies saw the tremendous suffering and sadness of the defeated countries and had compassion for their people (Step 4). And together the Allies helped Germany and Japan rebuild their countries (Step 5).

2.5 Stages of Community Development

Many community theorists have imagined that communities have developed stages. The Chicago School of Sociology in the 1920s and 1930s (Park, Burgess, & McKenzie, 1925) focused on urban development and decay. It developed a theory of stages of urban growth and urban decline. Its theory predicted land values, population density, and personal income of areas in a city as it changes over time.

The various accounts of the declines and falls (Gibbon, 2013) of various empires draw conclusions and offer theories about how communities develop. There are other theories of community development based on technological change (Diamond, 1997; Eisler, 1987). Perhaps the earliest theoretical thinkers who focused on theories of community development were Social Darwinist (Fisher, 1877; Galton, 1894; Haeckel, 1899; Malthus, 1960; Nietzsche, 1996; Spencer, 1860; von Hellwald, 1874). These theorists applied Darwin's principle of natural selection to human society. The term "Social Darwinism" was mostly used in a pejorative sense to discredit those extrapolating Darwin's ideas to human development. The construct of Social Darwinism has been highly divisive and those pejoratively accused by this phrase have used Darwin's ideas in contradictory ways, from Francis Galton, the founder of Eugenics, to Ernst Haeckel, who used Darwin's notion of evolution to propose that Socialism was the goal of human evolution.

It would be easy to fall into the debates around Social Darwinism and stray from the mission of developing a psychological theory of the stages of community development. Suffice it to say that as an aside or a basic assumption, all Social Darwinists contended that human communities evolve through predictable stages of development. Rather than develop theories to define these stages, Social Darwinists focused on race, arguing over which racial group deserved to be called the fittest in the race to survive. Hopefully, for most serious thinkers, this issue is moot.

This chapter will borrow its community developmental template from Eric Erikson and his wife Joan's eight stages of individual development (Erikson, 1968; Erikson and Erikson, 1998). The systems theory idea of isomorphy, which, for the purposes of this chapter, is defined as the principle that "what is lawful at one level of a system is also lawful at the other levels of that system," justifies applying the Eriksons' template to communities.

If one assumes that the developmental stages of an individual are replicated in human communities, then the Eriksons' stages are applicable. Hopefully, it is generally accepted that communities have two stages in common with humans: beginning and endings. If there are community beginnings and endings, there is at least a third stage: the middle. In this chapter, the Eriksons' eight stages are the middle. The resulting ten stages are (1) conception, (2) contracting, (3) authority-testing, (4) evaluation or resignation, (5) accountability, (6) communion, (7) mission, (8) generativity,

(9) authenticity, and (10) termination. Each stage has its particular form of expression. There are eight aspects that differ at each stage. They are (1) thought patterns, (2) emotional climate, (3) metaphysical foundation, (4) form of government, (5) stage two member expectations of the community, (6) type of economy, (7) value dilemmas, and (8) developmental defenses to overcome, ordeals to be passed. Space in this chapter does not permit a complete description of these stages. A brief description follows, then a more expansive example of a single stage, Stage 2, and its eight aspects or qualities.

Stage 1: *Conception* includes exuberant excitement in this initial stage. An exciting idea is presented. It strikes a passionate chord in others. People gather with a hopeful vision. In American history this was the American Revolution of 1776.

Stage 2: *Contracting*: The baby is born. The idea takes shape. Oh my God, what is the community to do next? It has to figure out how this is going to work. Rules, norms, and laws are created. Structures for decision-making are put in place. In American history this was the Constitutional Convention held in Philadelphia in 1787.

Stage 3: The structure formed in Stage 2 is tested in Stage 3, the *authority-testing* stage. The questions here involve who is in charge of what. This is a community's adolescent stage. Conflict and projection of blame are rampant in this stage. In American history this was the Civil War, 1861–1865.

Stage 4: This is the *evaluation* stage. Here members discover that their community has become something different than they had hoped. They are disillusioned and disappointed. They must decide whether or not to disband or to make the best out of what they have. In American history this was the Reconstruction period after the Civil War. It was a time of genocide for Native Americans and exploiting migrant, African American, female, and child labor.

Stage 5: This is the *accountability* stage. This is the time when we clearly see how we have failed our community. We begin to change and do better. We make reforms and we stop expecting heroes to save us or that we will strike gold. In American history this was the Reform movement of the early twentieth century that included the labor movement, anti-trust legislation, and women's suffrage. The Great Depression and the country's recovery from that Depression in the 1940s were part of this stage.

Stage 6: The *communion* stage in US history began with the postwar optimism: the GI Bill and what it did to transform America's working class, and the vision of the United States as the champion of democracy around the world. The community consolidates its gains from what it learned in the accountability stage. However, this stage does not last long (e.g., in American history it was from 1946 to 1957).

Stage 7: The *mission* stage lasts much longer. This is the stage in which the community gets to work accomplishing its mission, the mission discovered in the communal stage. In American history our mission has been to be that "City on the Hill," a "Beacon for Democracy." Another way to say this is to build the American Empire and to "Keep America Great."

Stage 8: The next stage is the *generativity* stage. The mission is over. It was accomplished or not and there is no more to accomplish. In this stage, the community searches for a new *raison d'être*. Members attempt to serve transcendent values rather than to keep consuming, gathering, and acquiring. This can be a depressing and difficult time, especially if a new purpose is not found. In English history this is England today after it has divested itself of its empire.

Stage 9: The penultimate stage is *authenticity*. In this stage members can sense that the end is near. As they anticipate the end, they let go of their community ties. They begin their community bucket list. They have last suppers. They gather their members and write down their stories.

Stage 10: *Termination* is the last community stage. It represents the end of the community. These stages form a circle and next to termination is rebirth or conception. In termination the remaining members hold dear the memories of their former community. They preserve the community's values and try to use them as they begin their search for a new community.

2.5.1 Stage 2: Contracting Defined

This is the, "Oh my God, what have we done?" stage: "Wait a minute. We want to run away, but not just yet. We want to stay around and see what we've gotten ourselves into and if we don't like it, then we will jump overboard." "We want to read the fine print before we sign on." "We have risked more than we meant to." In Stage 2 members begin to realize the big risk they took in joining. Expectations of a future of some sort have been created and the members are not sure that they can live up to these expectations.

In this stage members smile and appear pleased, but behind their smile they try to figure out how this is going to work. Talk is surface conversation with little depth and little risk. Members feel out one another to see if they can develop some working assumptions in their relationships. They look for information about other members and how the community might function. They worry about losing their individual autonomy. Members have the urge to flee. They feel a version of buyer's remorse.

In this stage, members begin to realize that much of what they felt and believed in Stage 1 came from their longing and wishing. In Stage 1, they had created an image of a perfect community. They projected onto this community all the qualities they yearned for. Now, they are beginning to realize the community is not what they imagined. Yet, members feel proud to belong. It's not perfect, but it's not bad. They begin to wonder, how will this community work? What are the rules? What matters most here?

In this community members wonder what it will cost to play the role they are given. They may pretend to want their role or that they can master it, but they fear that they will become stuck playing a role they cannot master or that they hate. They watch carefully to see what is unfolding, not knowing what to do next. In this stage members watch and wonder. They want to discover what kind of contract they have made by joining. What will be expected of them? Can they play their part? What can they avoid? What do they realistically expect from the community? Suddenly, in this stage, fear hits. They may feel trapped by the obligations that come with their commitment. They have uncomfortable ties that bind them.

And then there is the question about members' other obligations and/or other entanglements. What about the family? Can they balance membership with life's other demands? In this stage it is the member's job to learn the new rules of the new relationships that will define their future and to adjust their lives accordingly. In this phase members figure out how decisions will be made in the community. Rules of relating are developed. Members spend enough time together to figure out whether and how they become a working community, and how do activities begin and end. Members wonder how and if their promises and promises made to them will be binding and enforced. And, if they are, what will that mean? If these questions are answered satisfactorily and if the members get past the urge to flee, the community moves to the next stage.

The following ideas reflect the author's work titled *Defining A Community's Developmental Paths* (McMillan, n.d.) that presents stages of community development and is quoted and paraphrased below (see https://www.drda vidmcmillan.com/sense-of-community/defining-a-communitys-developmental-paths):

2.5.2 Stage 2: Thought Patterns

"The magical thinking of Stage 1 has become fragile. It is now giving way to doubt and second thoughts. The passion is wearing off, but it is certainly not gone, and [members don't want to lose this exciting potential] by voicing [their] doubts. Yet, [they] can't seem to push the doubts out of [their minds]" (McMillan, n.d.). They wonder: Are things in their community as they appear? Will the community always serve the members' interests? "In Stage 3, [members] will find out. In Stage 2, it is difficult enough to think these heretical thoughts, yet alone express them" (McMillan, n.d.).

2.5.3 Stage 2: Emotional Climate

"Fear is the major emotion. Anytime [members] are thinking a thought that is not politically correct" or that they know will threaten their standing in the community, "[they] are afraid" (McMillan, n.d.). "They jumped in the water at Stage 1. In Stage 2 [they] wonder if [they] shouldn't have stepped in carefully, one foot at a time. [They] are afraid [they] might drown. [They] try to cover [their] fear with a smile. [They] don't want to lose a good thing, if that is what [they] have, but [they] don't want to be consumed by a [community in which they have no] control" (McMillan, n.d.). "Fear and doubt are [a member's] constant companions in Stage 2."

"Balance is Stage 2's most important [goal]" (McMillan, n.d.) The probing of their membership choice begins to be answered with the question of whether or not there is fairness and reciprocity among members. This back-and-forth transfer of power among members can create a harmony. The establishment of reciprocal power is important for the conflict at Stage 3.

2.5.4 Stage 2: Metaphysical Foundations

"The question here is to figure out what pieces of the magic of Stage 1 [are] real... Hopefully, in Stage 2, [members] discover... symbols that... nurture [their] relationships [and] represent values of respect, compassion, and forgiveness. This is the time to identify [the community's] false magic and to hold on to [values that are] true and eternal" (McMillan, n.d.).

2.5.5 Stage 2: Form of Government

"Members begin to understand that dominance or the will of the stronger party as the governing force can destroy [relationships]. There is a wish for law to rule, rather than [a] person. It was at this stage that civilization invented primogeniture so that power transitions did not destroy the clan. There is still not enough structure at this stage for a democracy or ... a government that allows power to be invested in principles, values, and norms rather than persons, but the [community] is taking steps in that direction. Perhaps the dominant position has shifted once or twice [during the forming of the community] and the community has learned something from the pain of these power shifts when power [belongs] to persons rather than principles" (McMillan, n.d.).

2.5.6 Stage 2: Members' Expectations

"The clear expectations of Stage 1 are breaking down, as are the clear lines of dichotomous thoughts of "in" or "out." Now [the community members] are not sure what to expect. Questions emerge here and that is as it should be. They will be answered in the contests that come. [Members] see that [they] can't have [their] cake and eat it too, as they thought in Stage 1. [They] are beginning to understand that [the community] will require sacrifice, but [they] have no idea how much. What in Stage 1 seemed so certain, no longer does" (McMillan, n.d.).

2.5.7 Stage 2: Type of Economy

"Here there [are] the beginnings of a medium of exchange. The issue in Stage 2 is trust ... As the community demonstrates the strength to entertain doubt and contain ambiguity, trust emerges. The more trust the easier it is to invest value in a symbol, like the coin of the realm" or like the promise that I will be here when you come back, or the promise that I will come back, or the wearing of a uniform that symbolizes commitment (McMillan, n.d.).

2.5.8 Stage 2: Value Dilemma

"The philosophical tension at this stage is even more basic than in Stage 1 where the question was [: Are you "in" or "out"?] That question remains but it is based on the answer to another question: Do [members] have enough reason to trust or do [they] have sufficient reason not to trust? In Stage 2, the doubting stage, the pendulum swings between trust and mistrust. If there is enough reason to trust, [members] move on to Stage 3 where [they] test [their] decision once again. In the next stage, the test will be in [member] behavior not in [their] internal conversations" (McMillan, n.d.).

2.5.9 Defenses to Be Overcome at Stage 2

Defenses protect members like clothes protect them from the elements. Clothes can become worn, out of date. Members can grow so that the clothes no longer fit and they need new clothes. It is the same for personality defenses. It is the collective members' job to outgrow their psychological defenses against connection at each stage and to take on the new defenses of the next stage until they, too, are no longer necessary.

2.5.10 Defenses at Stage 2 to Be Shed

2.5.10.1 Repression

When members use repression as a defense, they hold back their true feelings. They imagine themselves to be on shaky ground in the eyes of other members. They do not say what is on their minds. They try to forget what they feel and think. A great deal remains unsaid. They hold back because they fear the loss of control that comes from telling the truth and being exposed. This constrains the flow of communication. They hold back on expressing what they think of other members and matters in the world around them. More importantly, they try to convince themselves that they accept what once was unacceptable to them; statements members have made or procedures that they find disagreeable for one reason or another. This defense eventually chokes the life from a community, life that comes from the truth about how members feel about one another and what they believe is right.

2.5.10.2 Sublimation

This is the defense of expecting the community to make the member happy. Because the community has conferred membership to the member, the member may expect the community to give them whatever they want, whenever they want it. When they give the community the job of taking complete care of them, they are arresting their own personal development, becoming dependent and addicted to their community. This forfeits a member's opportunity for growth and learning. This will exhaust other community members, expecting them to sublimate their needs in the service of the dependent member.

2.5.10.3 Dissociation

Members do not speak their true feelings and thoughts. They put on an act to please others. They disguise their true thoughts and feelings and pretend to be what they believe the community expects them to be. If any rejection is going to occur, members want it to be their rejection of the community. Therefore, members disassociate from their real selves, leaving the community with a false image of the member.

2.6 The Third Position

Perhaps the most practical of the five ideas presented here is J. R. Newbrough's notion of the third position (Newbrough, 1980, 1995). He had always been bothered by the irreconcilable polarity of the individual versus the collective posed in a Hegelian dialectic. This Hegelian dichotomy seemed to Newbrough to create an insoluble conundrum requiring compromise pitting the community's interests for members to conform to community laws and rules versus liberty and individual freedom of choice. He saw compromise as incomplete negotiation and a rush to resolution. He believed there had to be a way to marry community and individual values.

As Newbrough thought about the opposition of community and individual values, he remembered this drama and he knew there had to be a third position in addition to the values of individual freedom and community conformity. Then he remembered the values chant from the French Revolution "Liberty [individual values], Equality [fairness and justice for all], Fraternity [community values, law and order, conformity to community norms]." He discovered his third position. For him this was the end of the necessity of dichotomous thought. Of course, there was always a third position. Never are humans constricted to only two values. The mammalian brain can only manage two options, but the human brain (the neocortex) can manage many more (Batson et al., 1991; Buck et al., 1992; LeDoux, 1996; Roth, 1994). A third position literally opens the mind, and human creativity is released when three options are considered at once and the mind swirls and juggles three ideas. This opens the door to human imagination. What

Newbrough discovered was a naturally occurring avenue to resolving impasses. The third position gave people a way to negotiate beyond compromise into creative problem-solving (Bess et al., 2002). Newbrough discovered this third position around the same time mediation was emerging as a popular way of resolving disputes.

Newbrough's disciple, David McMillan, was, at the time (and is) a practicing clinical psychologist, mediator, and couples and family therapist. He joined Newbrough and the two of them developed a mediation process based on Newbrough's idea. McMillan brought with him three principles needed to help couples move from acrimony to constructive problem-solving. They are:

1. Shift focus from the personal to the system.
   a. Stop blaming a person.
   b. Begin describing the systems.
2. Identify important roles played in the system by opposing parties.
3. Frame these roles so that they are valued and honored.

Once McMillan understood Newbrough's idea of a third position he proposed a way of categorizing conflicts into three levels. A level-one conflict, the most primitive form of social conflict, is a battle of "I wants." It puts what one person wants against what the other person wants. This is a crass power struggle. The most powerful wins. In a level-two conflict, there is potential to take the conflict out of the personal and to frame it as a system's struggle, natural to all systems. Here the parties are playing their roles assigned to them consciously or unconsciously by the system. Each party serves the relationship by advocating for an important value. In a level-two contest both parties are worthy opponents who deserve respect. What is absent in a level-two conflict is creativity to help open what appears to be a deadlock. It is easy to imagine a level-two conflict falling back into a level-one crass power struggle and another win/lose moment. If these moments continue to pile one on top of the other, one partner will tend to be the winner. This creates a dangerous imbalance and sets up the framework for passive-aggressive guerrilla warfare in relationships.

A level-three conflict includes the system focus rather than the person focus of level one and adds a third-value position. The third value forces both parties to reevaluate their positions in light of an additional third-value position. This consideration of three valid value postures creates a third vote. It adds creativity and imagination to problem-solving. It validates the other two value positions and, at the same time, challenges the parties to think beyond their entrenched postures. Professional mediators often say that the key to a win/win solution is to enlarge the pie (Rose, 1996). When the issue is clear and the contest is joined, it seems counterintuitive to add complexity to the debate. That is exactly what the third position proposes. It is a paradoxical truth that adding an agreed-upon third value will reduce chaos and bring order to the discussion (Kuhn, 1991; Smith & Berg, 1997). The third position breaks up the entrenched postures. It civilizes the debate and creates options neither party ever imagined.

Imagine a line connecting the two opposing points of view. In a level-two conflict whatever decision that is reached represents a point on that line somewhere between the two opposing points. Now imagine a third point above that line. Three points, of course, make a triangle and also a geometric plane. An exponentially greater number of points exist inside the plane than exist on the line between the two opposing points of view. Any point that two opposing sides can agree on inside the plane can become a potential plan of action. The third position forces contending parties to expand their options (Newbrough, 1995; Newbrough, McMillan, & Lorion, 2008). Their creativity can be engaged. They are no longer frozen in place between two opposite points on a line. Every time contending parties develop a third position, it forces them to move out of their one-dimensional or two-dimensional value system. The conversation is no longer pro versus con. It becomes a conversation that explores options to find an answer that serves all three values.

2.6.1 A Third Position Is Not a Compromise or a Synthesis

Some might suggest that the third position is the synthesis or the compromise between two polar opposites. This is not how the originators of the third position think about it. A compromise or a synthesis is a mixture of the two polar positions. The third position allows contending ideas or parties to rise above the two positions and find a creative solution that is not a compromise and not a synthesis of two positions but a point above the line, a mixture of three value positions that becomes something much different than a compromise or a synthesis of two values. It is the third note in music that creates a chord. The chord is a completely different sound than a merger of two dissonant notes. A line between two points becomes a tightrope. A third position creates a three-legged stool. With a third position, the deadlocked parties can serve a higher value as opposed to personal interest. Both parties are able to do the right thing. Nobody has to lose or compromise. Everybody, however, must be creative and respectful to get to a third-position solution (Mellers, Hertwig, & Kahneman, 2001).

2.6.2 Qualifying Participants for Third-Position Negotiations

Not everyone can use the third-position process successfully. Participants must agree to some qualifying process ground rules (Mercier & Sperber, 2011, 2017). There are five of them:

1. There is no one right answer. The only right answer is the one both parties accept.
2. Human memory is fluid. Memories distort past events. What happened in the past is distorted by all of us. Everyone has selective memories. People

conveniently forget facts that do not fit their story. They selectively attend to only facts that help their story and then interpret all information to fit their biases (Hastorf & Cantril, 1954; Mercier & Sperber, 2011). Therefore, participants must agree to be open to ways of looking at a reality other than their own (Sloman & Fernbach, 2017).

3. Everyone needs to be opposed. Often when a person proposes a solution, their partner naturally opposes them. When one says, "I want to buy a new car," their partner naturally says, "Can we afford one?" Or when they say, "I am planning to spend Saturday with a friend," their partner naturally responds, "Who will take care of the children?" Questioning partners serve the system's role of being a worthy opponent. Their opposition helps make better plans and devise better solutions to problems. In third-position negotiations both parties must acknowledge that their adversary is doing them a favor. Who enjoys conflict? The purpose of their opposition is to make the other person and the relationship better. Though parties are not always grateful, they must acknowledge that opposition does not equal malice or stupidity. It may mean compassion and concern. This is the notion of the "worthy opponent" in politics and is the basis of the USA's constitutional checks and balances.

4. Though no one knows The Truth, each person is the ultimate authority on what they think and believe and their worthy opponent deserves the same respect from them.

5. There should be no character attacks. Both parties agree to refrain from "You are a ..." statements. Instead, the parties pledge to speak of their experience using "I feel ..." or "I think ..." or "I believe ..." statements.

If the parties begin their conversation with these five agreements in place, the third position is very likely to lead to a constructive agreement that builds future trust between the parties.

2.6.3 Seven Steps to a Third-Position Civil Conversation

Step 1: Parties agree they have an impasse (Smith & Berg, 1997).
Step 2: Once the community concludes that the debate has become entrenched, it identifies the two values represented by the polarities in the debate. For example, a mother might say to the opposing father, "You are not going to have my child go on a roller coaster." The father might say, "I will not let you take all of the excitement out of my child's life. I will see that she faces fear and builds her courage." The two positions represent important value positions in any system. The mother's value position might be labeled as "security and safety." And the father's position as "building courage and risk-taking." When seen in this way, both parties serve the family system by representing an important value. Labeling the value positions takes the debate out of the personal and the dramatic and

places it into a system. The parties take on important and necessary family roles that someone needs to play for the family system. This step creates the concept of the respected worthy opponent and it ennobles the conversation. It elevates the problem from a personal problem to a system problem. For many practitioners, the most difficult step is naming the two noble values that the parties represent. Remember, as Newbrough suggested, a community always has at least three working values: liberty, equality, and fraternity. The parties' positions usually are somewhere inside one of these values. The practitioner can always fall back on them.

Step 3: Nominate other values that might become a third-position value. This begins the process of collaboration and takes the conversation further away from the entrenched, angry, threatened, frightened positions. This process moves the emotional tone into imaginative, creative, cooperative problem-solving. This should be a playful, fun, not too serious, imaginative process.

Step 4: Encourage the parties to choose a value together to represent their third position. It can be any value that the two currently opposing parties agree to serve. The choice of a value stops the momentum of disagreement and begins the process of seeing areas of agreement. It creates the possibility in the minds of the opposing parties that more can be added to the discussion. It begins the commitment to opening the process to new ideas.

Step 5: Once a third position is agreed upon, retreat. Each party withdraws from the conversation and reconsiders their position in light of the new third-value position. Their goal is to reconstruct their argument so that they serve their original value as well as the new third-value position – and perhaps even their opponent's value. This new position creates opportunities for consensus-building.

Step 6: Present the new ideas and options. Look for areas of agreement. Be willing to discover new ways of solving problems. Begin building an agreement by finding areas where ideas overlap. Use your imagination. Make bold, new, sometimes silly proposals. Be creative. Laugh and enjoy putting the puzzle together.

Step 7: Build a consensus solution. This is done by taking the idea overlaps from Step 6 and looking toward a particular solution. One should not expect a solution beyond the issue at hand. There is no answer for all problems. But there usually is an answer for the next problem. Keep adding newly discovered areas of agreement until the parties find a direction for the next step. The reason the focus should not be beyond the next step is because once the next step is taken previously unimagined ideas and circumstances are discovered. These new circumstances may open doors that make further agreements easy or they may present more difficult challenges. If there are more difficult challenges, simply repeat the third position's seven-step process for each of those.

2.7 Conclusion

Robert Putnam's book *Bowling Alone* (Putnam, 2000) was not the first to decry the loss of sense of community and the rise of alienation. Marx, Weber, Rousseau, Sarason and so many others have preached the same sermon so often that it has become a cliché. With this as a given, it would appear that sense of community is a good thing and that time alone is not. Just as love can be misplaced, just as a baby duck can imprint on a coyote, sense of community can hold violent, criminal gangs together. Even in the best of communities, the glue of sense of community can promote corruption, nepotism, and social calcification.

In romantic relationships, love is not enough. For couples to maintain a lasting love they must have an economic base, shared social norms, an effective decision-making process, and the couple must avoid negativity and cynicism. In communities, sense of community is a positive force only in the right type of community. Just as love is defined as the willingness to absorb and feel the emotions of another, sense of community opens the door for emotions to move and flow through a community. For communities to be successful and healthy, it is important for leaders to know how emotions move from one to the other and how to direct community emotions.

Just as love has many faces (e.g., unconditional accepting love, challenging-show-me-what-you're-made-of love, or romantic love, and so on), so too does sense of community take various forms depending on the community's developmental stage. In Stage 1, sense of community is an exuberant know-no-boundaries spirit. In Stage 2, it is careful and protective. In Stage 3, it must be challenging and creative. In Stage 4, it must be forgiving and compassionate.

Community thinkers are encouraged to use the third position to manage the polar juxtaposition between the love/corruption, messy *Gemeinschaft*/organic community and the egalitarian, heartless, pristine, *Gesellschaft*/market community. *Gefolgschaft*/faith communities could be the third position. The ideal "City on the Hill" might be a combination of tribal, urban, and holy communities, taking the best of each and avoiding their worst qualities. With only two typologies, Dokecki (1996) tried to use third-position thinking to bridge the gap between the organic community and the market community.

The third position eliminates dichotomous impasses and opens doors to limitless human creativity. Many might criticize these ideas as too sappy for academic community psychologists, and perhaps they are. But if the reader wants a path into the real painful messy world of human connection and attachment, these ideas provide one. The author of this chapter knows that these ideas are ineptly constructed and inadequately formulated. He would welcome collaborators who can expand these ideas into an intellectual/practical marketplace of useful potential interventions that nurture and challenge communities to discover their best versions.

Among life's paradoxes is that life stages and community stages are cycles with beginnings and endings, births and deaths. And these cycles exist in another universe that is ever-expanding and never-ending. In this universe death opens the door for birth and the next cycle begins. May Eisler (1987) and Pinker (2018) be right in their hypothesis about the moral improvement of the human community. And may community psychologists and our ideas about communities play a role in that improvement.

References

Batson, D., Batson, J., Slingsby, J., et al. (1991). Empathetic joy and the empathy-altruism hypothesis. *Journal of Personality and Social Psychology*, *61*(3), 413–423. doi.org/10.1037//0022-3514.61.3.413

Bess, K. D., Fisher, A., Sonn, C. C., & Bishop, B. J. (2002). Psychological sense of community: Theory, research and application. In A. Fisher, C. C. Sonn, & B. J. Bishop (Eds.), *Psychological sense of community: Research, applications and implications* (pp. 3–22). New York: Plenum Publishers.

Brooks, D. (2015). *The road to character*. New York: Random House.

Buck, R., Lasaw, J., Murphy, M., & Costanzo, P. (1992). Social facilitation and inhibition of emotional expression and communication. *Journal of Personality and Social Psychology*, *63*(6), 962–968. doi.org/10.1037//0022-3514.63.6.962

Chavis, D. M. M., Hogge, J. H., McMillan, D. W., & Wandersman, A. (1986). Sense of community through Brunswick's lens: A first look. *Journal of Community Psychology*, *14*(1), 24–40. doi.org/10.1002/1520-6629(198601)14:1<24::AID-JCOP2290140104>3.0.CO;2-P

Chipuer, H. M., & Pretty, G. M. (1999). A review of the sense of community index: Current uses, factor structure, reliability and further development. *Journal of Community Psychology*, *27*(6), 643–658. doi.org/10.1002/(SICI)1520-6629(199911)27:6<643::AID-JCOP2>3.0.CO;2-B

Diamond, J. (1997). *Guns, germs, and steel: The fate of human societies*. New York: W. W. Norton & Company.

Dokecki, P. R. (1996). The place of values in the world of psychology and public policy. *Peabody Journal of Education*, *60*, 108–125. doi.org/10.1080/01619568309538411

Duncan, E. S., & Small, S. L. (2017). Imitation-based aphasia therapy increases narrative content: A case series. *Clinical Rehabilitation*, *31*(11), 1500–1507. doi.org/10.1177/0269215517703765

Eisler, R. (1987). *The chalice and the blade: Our history, our future*. New York: Harper Collins.

Erikson, E. (1968). *Identity: Youth and crisis*. New York: W. W. Norton & Company.

Erikson, E., & Erikson, J. (1998). *The life cycle complete* (extended version). New York: W. W. Norton & Company.

Festinger, L. (1957). *A theory of cognitive dissonance*. Stanford, CA: Stanford University Press.

Fisher, A., Sonn, C. C., & Bishop, B. J. (2002). *Psychological sense of community: Research, applications and implications*. New York: Plenum Publishers.

Fisher, J. (1877). The history of landholding in Ireland. In *Transactions of the Royal Historical Society* (Vol. V, pp. 228–326). London. doi.org/10.2307/3677953. JSTOR 3677953, as quoted in the *Oxford English Dictionary*.

Galton, F. (1894). *Natural inheritance*. London and New York: Macmillan & Co.

Gerwirth, A. (1998). *Self-fulfillment*. Princeton, NJ: Princeton University Press.

Gibbon, E. (2013). *History of the decline and fall of the Roman Empire*. Harrington, DE: Delmarva Publications.

Haeckel, E. (1899). *Kunstformen der Natur*. Germany: Marix Verlag (Reprinted 2004).

Hastorf, A. H., & Cantril, H. (1954). They saw a game: A case study. *Journal of Abnormal and Social Psychology*, *49*(1), 129–134. doi.org/10.1037/h0057880

Heller, K. (1989). Return to the community. *American Journal of Community Psychology*, *17*(1), 1–15. doi.org/10.1007/BF00931199

Hill, J. L. (1996). Psychological sense of community: Suggestions for future research. *Journal of Community Psychology*, *24*(4), 431–438. doi.org/10.1002/(SICI)1520-6629(199610)24:4<431::AID-JCOP10>3.0.CO;2-T

Kuhn, D. (1991). *The skills of argument*. New York: Cambridge University Press.

LeDoux, J. E. (1996). *The emotional brain*. New York: Simon & Schuster.

Malthus, T. R. (1960). A summary view of the principle of population. In *Three essays on population* (pp. 1–59). New York: Mentor Books.

McMillan, D. W. (n.d.). *Defining a community's developmental paths*. https://www.drdavidmcmillan.com/sense-of-community/defining-a-communitys-developmental-paths

McMillan, D. W. (2005). *Emotion rituals*. New York: Brunner-Routledge.

McMillan, D. W. (1976). *Sense of community: An attempt at definition*. [Unpublished manuscript]. Nashville, TN: George Peabody College for Teachers.

McMillan, D. W. (1996). Sense of community. *Journal of Community Psychology*, *24*(4), 315–325. doi.org/10.1002/(SICI)1520-6629(199610)24:4<315::AID-JCOP2>3.0.CO;2-T

McMillan, D. W., & Chavis, D. M. (1986). Sense of community: A definition and theory. *Journal of Community Psychology*, *14*(1), 6–23. doi.org/10.1002/1520-6629(198601)14:13.0.CO;2-I

Mellers, B. A, Hertwig, R., & Kahneman, D. (2001). Do frequency representations eliminate conjunction effects? An exercise in adversarial collaboration. *Psychological Science*, *12*(4), 269–275. doi.org/10.1111/1467-9280.00350

Mercier, H., & Sperber, D. (2011). Why do humans reason? Argument for an argumentative theory. *Behavioral and Brain Sciences*, *34*(2), 57–111. doi.org/10.1017/S0140525X10000968

Mercier, H., & Sperber, D. (2017). *The enigma of reason*. Cambridge, MA: Harvard University Press.

Newbrough, J. R. (1980). Community psychology and the public interest. *American Journal of Community Psychology*, *8*(1), 1–17. doi.org/10.1007/BF00892277

Newbrough, J. R. (1992). Community psychology in the postmodern world. *Journal of Community Psychology*, *20*(1), 10–25. doi.org/10.1002/1520-6629(199201)20:1<10::AID-JCOP2290200104>3.0.CO;2-O

Newbrough, J. R. (1995). Toward community: A third position. *American Journal of Community Psychology, 23,* 9–37. doi.org/10.1007/BF02506921

Newbrough, J. R., McMillan, D. W., & Lorion, R. (2008). A commentary on Newbrough's third position. *Journal of Community Psychology, 36*(4), 515–533. doi.org/10.1002/jcop.20248

Nietzsche, F. (1996). *Human, all too human: A book for free spirits.* New York: Cambridge University Press.

Nowell, B., & Boyd, N. (2010). Viewing community as responsibility as well as resource: Deconstructing the theoretical roots of psychological sense of community. *Journal of Community Psychology, 38*(7), 828–841. doi.org/10.1002/jcop.20398

Park, R. E., Burgess, E. W., & McKenzie, R. D. (1925). *The city.* Chicago: University of Chicago Press.

Peterson, A., Speer, P., & McMillan, D. W. (2008). Validation of a brief sense of community scale: Confirmation of the principal theory of sense of community. *Journal of Community Psychology, 36*(1), 61–73. doi.org/10.1002/jcop.20217

Pinker, S. (2018). *Enlightenment now: The case for reason, science, humanism and progress.* New York: Viking (imprint of Penguin Random House).

Puddifoot, J. E. (1996). Some initial considerations in the measurement of community identity. *Journal of Community Psychology, 24*(4), 327–336. doi.org/10.1002/(SICI)1520-6629(199610)24:4<327::AID-JCOP3>3.0.CO;2-R

Putnam, R. D. (2000). *Bowling alone: The collapse and revival of American community.* New York: Simon & Schuster.

Rapley, M., & Pretty, G. M. H. (1999). Playing procrustes: The interactional production of a "psychological sense of community." *Journal of Community Psychology, 27*(6), 695–713. doi.org/10.1002/(SICI)1520-6629(199911)2

Rizzolatti, G., & Craighero, L. (2004). The mirror-neuron system. *Annual Review of Neuroscience, 27,* 169–192. doi.org/10.1146/annurev.neuro.27.070203.144230

Rizzolatti, G., Fogassi, L., & Gallese, V. (2001). Neurophysiological mechanisms underlying the understanding and imitation of action. *Nature Reviews Neuroscience, 2,* 661–670. doi.org/10.1038/35090060

Rose, C. (1996). *Collaborative family law practice.* Santa Cruz, CA: Mediation Center, Inc.

Roth, B. L. (1994). Multiple serotonin receptors: Clinical and experimental aspects. *Annals of Clinical Psychiatry, 6*(2), 67–78. doi.org/10.3109/10401239409148985

Sarason, S. B. (1974). *The psychological sense of community: Perspectives for community psychology.* San Francisco: Jossey-Bass.

Sarason, S. B. (1986). The emergence of a conceptual center. *Journal of Community Psychology, 14*(4), 405–407. doi.org/10.1002/1520-6629(198610)14:4<405::AID-JCOP2290140409>3.0.CO;2-8

Sloman, S. & Fernbach, P. (2017). *The knowledge illusion: Why we never think alone.* New York: Penguin.

Smith, K. K. & Berg, D. N. (1997). *Paradoxes of group life: Understanding conflict, paralysis, and movement in dynamics.* San Francisco: Jossey-Bass.

Snow, C. P. (1959). *The two cultures and the scientific revolution: The Rede Lecture.* New York: Cambridge University Press.

Sonn, C. S., Bishop, B. J., & Drew, N. M. (1999). Sense of community: Issues and considerations from a cross-cultural perspective. *Community, Work & Family, 2*(2), 205–218. doi.org/10.1080/13668809908413941

Spencer, H. (1860). The social organism. *The Westminster Review, 73*, 51–68. Reprinted in Spencer's (1892) *Essays: Scientific, political and speculative.* London and New York: D. Appleton.

Stosny, S. (1995). *Treating attachment abuse: A compassionate approach.* New York: Springer.

Taylor, C. (1994). *Multiculturalism: Examining the politics of recognition.* Princeton, NJ: Princeton University Press.

Tönnies, F. (1957). *Community and society: Gemeinschaft and gesellschaft* (C. P. Loomis, Trans.). Michigan: Michigan State University Press.

Von Hellwald, F. (1874). *The Russians in Central Asia: A critical examination down to the present time of the geography and history of Central Asia.* London: Henry S. King.

Wiesenfeld, E. (1996). The concept of "we": A community social psychology myth? *Journal of Community Psychology, 24*(4), 337–363. doi.org/10.1002/(SICI) 1520-6629(199610)24:4<337::AID-JCOP4>3.0.CO;2-R

Wilson, E. O. (1998). *Consilience: The unity of knowledge.* New York: Random House.

Worsley, P. (1987). *New introductory sociology.* London: Penguin.

3   Now Would Be a Great Time to Raise Your Voice

Empowerment as a Critical Community Psychology Concept

Kip Thompson and Alexis M. Benjamin

At the stroke of midnight on December 22, 2018, the longest government shutdown in US history began, lasting thirty-five days. During this time, approximately eight hundred thousand federal employees were furloughed or required to work without pay; countless US government subcontractors and businesses that depended upon government patronage also experienced a negative impact based on this turn of events. The economic ripple effect of the shutdown was experienced financially and in terms of role conflicts as well. Mortgages and car payments were late, college tuitions were put on hold, and daycare costs became an even greater challenge ("The Government Shutdown Will Hit Home," 2018). A *New York Times* report estimated that each of those furloughed federal employees lost more than $5,000 over the first four weeks of the shutdown (Patel, 2019). Living day to day for many became a Herculean effort of survival. It would be difficult to overestimate the emotional toll these hardships had on communities across the USA.

It could be easy to say that the average citizen lacks the ability to change their circumstances when policies have been set by those in the highest levels of government and the individual has no recourse to change them. However, we argue that it is these challenging experiences that can create opportunities for citizens to equip themselves to take steps to regain their equilibrium and reciprocate some of those ripple effects. Empowerment, a core value in the field of community psychology, is just one vehicle for these changes. It is the focus of the current chapter.

First, we will present a contextual definition of empowerment and discuss what we believe distinguishes it from other similar constructs. We will then discuss different forms of power with a keen eye to the reality that no two community problems can be solved the exact same way. As a result, an understanding of the different paths one can take to resolve conflict will also be provided. Altman and Rogoff's (1987) transactional theory will guide this chapter and help explain how empowerment is enacted in neighborhoods both within the United States and across the globe. Finally, we will provide recommendations for what readers and would-be activists can do to ignite a sense of empowerment in their neighborhoods and communities to effect positive change.

3.1 What Is Empowerment?

Even though empowerment has become a bit of a buzzword in our present culture, we do not necessarily share a common definition of what this construct means. Empowerment is often conflated with resilience, and while these two constructs have a lot in common, the latter can be more concerned with internal assets and is derived from the developmental psychology literature (Brodsky & Cattaneo, 2013; Luthar & Cicchetti, 2000). Here, resilience is defined as the ability to mobilize one's internal assets (e.g., optimism, the strengthening effect of stress, viewing change as an opportunity) to mitigate the impact of adversity on one's personal trajectory. A person can demonstrate resilient qualities and still lack the power to change their challenging circumstances.

More recent resilience researchers describe it as a reflection of the interactions an individual has with the systems within which they are embedded (Clauss-Ehlers et al., 2019; Ungar, Ghazinour, & Richter, 2013). The focus on psychopathology has been replaced with the pursuit of understanding the unique factors that contribute to the individual's capacity to overcome adversity (Betancourt et al., 2015; Clauss-Ehlers, 2008). For example, in a study on resilience among Syrian refugee and Jordanian host-community adolescents, Panter-Brick and colleagues (2018) conceptualized support from one's friends as an individual factor, ethnic pride as a context factor, and perceptions of safety when among one's family as a relational factor. The American Psychological Association's *Multicultural Guidelines* (2017) implore psychologists to consider strengths-based approaches that include the aforementioned factors while also acknowledging the individual's multiple lived identities when building resilience. Such a contextually based approach pulls in families, schools, and communities toward the pursuit of building capacity for overcoming adversity.

Empowerment is also sometimes confused with citizen participation, a value that focuses on assuming one's responsibility in community decision-making via democratic processes like voting or signing a petition for an important cause (Lee & Schachter, 2019). Again, there is some overlap between this construct and empowerment, and while they have both been identified by leaders in community psychology as having a significant role in defining their field (Kloos et al., 2021), they are distinct constructs. The idea here is that merely showing up to the voting booth every two to four years and pulling a lever alone does not make one empowered.

Douglas and colleagues (2016) proposed that the core of empowerment lies in individuals, communities, and organizations participating in decision-making that ultimately have an impact on macro systems (e.g., the legal system, media). This is similar to Urie Bronfenbrenner's social-ecological theory, which suggests there are five environmental systems – microsystem, mesosystem, exosystem, macrosystem, and chronosystem – with which individuals interact, and that these interactions factor heavily in those persons' development (Bronfenbrenner, 1979; Leonard, 2011). Empowerment also adopts certain tenets from liberation psychology, that seeks to instill critical consciousness within individuals so they can identify for themselves where their needs are not being met by the systems responsible for meeting those needs (Chavez et al., 2016). By focusing on how power structures provide and deny important resources, liberation psychologists empower clients and communities to break the cycle of oppression.

We conceptualize empowerment as an ecological, contextual variable that prompts and nurtures social movements. In their seminal work in organizational psychology, Altman and Rogoff (1987) proposed a transactional perspective that suggests that all psychological phenomena occur within the context of changing relationships between individuals and their environments. This perspective places the historical event within its surrounding context, and which unfolds as time progresses. This is like Bronfenbrenner's *chronosystem* that proposes that all of the nested relationships occurring within individual development are situated in time and change based on this context (Bronfenbrenner, 1979; Leonard, 2011).

The 2018 US government shutdown became a historical event, not just because it was the longest of its kind yet, but also because the event will have an economic, legislative, and cultural impact on US society for years to come. More recently, the COVID-19 US pandemic of 2020 has caused more than twenty million layoffs leading to a 14.7% US unemployment rate in May 2020, the highest since the Great Depression of the 1930s (US Bureau of Labor Statistics, 2020). *The Washington Post* reported that these job losses have hit Latinx and Black/African American communities, women, teenage workers, and those without high school diplomas the hardest (Jan, 2020). Whether these historical events lead US citizens to become empowered to prevent such episodes in the future remains to be seen, but we know that historical events in this society have set the stage for other powerful social movements. Next, we will examine four such movements that were established in the United States, but in many cases have developed global influence.

3.2 Examples of Empowerment in Context

3.2.1 Black Lives Matter

The deeply unjust murders of Trayvon Martin in Sanford, Florida in 2012 and Michael Brown in Ferguson, Missouri in 2014 became historical events that laid the groundwork for the Black Lives Matter (BLM) social movement (Botelho, 2012; McLaughlin, 2014) (see https://blacklivesmatter.com/). More recent Black American murders with similar circumstances – Breonna Taylor, Ahmaud Arbery, and George Floyd, all in early 2020 – have kept this movement in the media (Bogel-Burroughs, 2020; Rojas, Mervosh, & Fausset, 2020). Our contention is that these murders became historical events because their deaths were so reminiscent of historical lynchings that Black Americans experienced throughout Reconstruction and Jim Crow, despite the passage of legislation designed to steepen the consequences for committing such crimes. As a result, loved ones and friends of these victims, along with social justice activists from around the country, have engaged with their local police departments and the US Justice Department to improve the relationship between these two systems and the US Black American community.

For example, in 2016, BLM activists took a leadership role in the removal of prosecutors responsible for two high-profile BLM cases (Lussenhop, 2016). These protesters helped to lead canvassing activities that removed Cook County State Attorney Anita Alvarez from office who allegedly concealed footage of the 2014 shooting death of Laquan McDonald to protect Chicago police who murdered him. Chicago BLM activists chartered a plane with a banner that discouraged voters from choosing Alvarez that flew over the city on election day. BLM activists in Cleveland, Ohio derailed the reelection of Cuyahoga Prosecuting Attorney Timothy McGinty, who influenced a grand jury not to charge the two police officers responsible for shooting Tamir Rice, a twelve-year-old Black American with a toy gun at a recreational center. BLM activists reportedly picketed McGinty's home all throughout his campaign and drummed up public outrage for him helping to avert the responsible police officers' indictment for Rice's murder. BLM activists have also met with and influenced the presidential campaigns for Joaquin Castro and Bernie Sanders on the issues of criminal justice, police brutality, and economic justice (City News Service, 2019; Graham, 2015). In the wave of George Floyd's death in May 2020, BLM protests have sprung up in small towns and big cities across the country and the world, and have influenced local government leaders to reallocate funds away from policing toward equitable mental health services, education, housing, and other community-based services (Perano, 2020).

3.2.2 #MeToo

The #MeToo campaign is another example of how context and timing can influence the historical events that give rise to powerful social movements. Around 2006, activist and nonprofit organization founder Tarana Burke was leading a youth camp for girls of color when one privately confided in her about her experiences with sexual abuse, assault, or exploitation (SAAE). Inspired by this confession, Burke started the me too Movement™ to remove cultural barriers between advocacy groups and young women of color who have survived SAAE. Indeed, part of the vision for this movement is "empowerment through empathy," which encourages SAAE survivors to reach out to other women to collaborate on how to advocate for themselves and others to prevent this social problem from continuing (see https://justbeinc .wixsite.com/justbeinc/the-me-too-movement-c7cf).

It took a short series of events to occur before women (and men) across the USA became more publicly empowered to share stories of sexual harassment and abuse at the hands of male authority figures. One obstacle that made sharing these narratives difficult was likely rape culture, the social and cultural context where aggressive male sexuality is normalized and sexual assault is considered excusable since the targets of these assaults are assumed to enjoy being overpowered (Herman, 1978, as cited by Keller, Mendes, & Ringrose, 2018).

The first of these events occurred in 2016. Donald J. Trump, the Republican nominee for US President, was elected to office after admitting to sexually assaulting women on an audio recording. The day after his eventual inauguration an estimated two million people from across the USA coalesced to form the Women's March on Washington, an event designed to push back against those actions and statements perceived as anti-woman made by Trump during and before his campaign (Fisher, Dow, & Ray, 2017). Many political scientists agree that this march was the largest single-day protest in US history (Broomfield, 2017).

Second, in 2017, Harvey Weinstein, a powerful Hollywood movie producer, was publicly exposed for engaging in similar actions against actresses across decades. In the third event, activist and actress Alyssa Milano used the social media platform Twitter to invite women who had been sexually harassed or assaulted to reply with the phrase "Me Too" to expose the problem within society (Parker, 2017).

In the weeks following this third event, more than two hundred powerful men in journalism, commerce, labor, entertainment, the US Senate and Congress, and countless other industries were similarly exposed and roundly dismissed for inappropriate sexual behavior (Carlsen et al., 2018). This national reckoning largely fueled the creation of Time's Up (https:// timesupnow.org/), a social welfare organization by women activists to increase gender parity and protect the safety of women across cultural, industry, and regional boundaries in the USA. Time's Up has also founded its Legal Defense Fund (https://nwlc.org/times-up-legal-defense-fund/) to help provide for the legal costs of women who want to seek legal counsel when holding their assailants accountable in court. Together, the #MeToo campaign and the Time's Up organization have empowered women to resist systemic inequality and dismantle rape culture in ways never before possible. With renewed focus on the campaign she began, Burke has established the official Me Too[TM] website (see https://metoomvmt.org/), created public service announcements, and begun making relationships with Hollywood writers on how to appropriately discuss sexual abuse in television and movies (Harris, 2018).

3.2.3 March For Our Lives

On February 14, 2018, a young man named Nicholas Cruz opened fire at Marjory Stoneman Douglas (MSD) High School in Parkland, Florida, killing seventeen students in the process (Chuck, Johnson, & Siemaszko, 2018). This is not the first school shooting in the USA – there have been many. Part of what made this specific school shooting a historical event is that the MSD shootings eclipsed the 1999 Columbine, Colorado high school shooting in total number of deaths. Another unique circumstance of this historical event is that the national Federal Bureau of Investigation (FBI) was previously tipped off regarding Cruz's death threats directed toward MSD. Yet, the local FBI office denied ever receiving this tip that compounded the preventable nature of this incident.

Several of the survivors were galvanized by their experience and empowered to demand legislative action on gun violence, establish a nationwide campaign to promote gun violence prevention measures, and initiate sponsor boycotts for those media figures interested in undermining their student-led movement. The name of this movement is March For Our Lives (see www.marchforourlives.com). The young leaders of this movement have been featured on international magazine covers and talk shows and testified before the US Congress (Canfield, 2018; Cummings, 2018; "Gun Violence Is an Epidemic," 2019). On March 24, 2018, these survivors led a march on Washington, DC where they sought to have a direct impact on the upcoming midterm election by amplifying the push for gun control legislation and imploring other young adults to vote for elected officials who share their passion ("March For Our Lives Highlights," 2018). More than 830 demonstrations occurred across the USA and the globe to persuade local lawmakers to include gun control in their policy agendas (Langone, 2018).

3.2.4 #AbolishICE

In the wake of the September 11, 2001 attacks, many Americans were united in the mandate that terrorism attacks should never be allowed to occur on US soil again. Congress heard the people and pressed the George W. Bush administration to create an agency designed specifically to enhance domestic security (Levinson-Waldman & Hinkle, 2018). What was formerly called the Immigration and Naturalization Service was dismantled and, in its place, three new agencies emerged within the Department of Homeland Security (DHS): US Citizenship and Immigration Services (USCIS), Customs and Border Protection (CBP), and the Immigration and Customs Enforcement (ICE). According to the DHS website (DHS, n.d.), the mission of ICE is "to protect America from the cross-border crime and illegal immigration that threaten national security and public safety."

The Center for Migration Studies estimates that in 2003, the average number of immigrants detained on a daily basis was about twenty-one thousand – that number increased to more than thirty-eight thousand in 2017 (Reyes, 2018). Former US President Barack Obama's administration reportedly used this agency to deport more immigrants than any of his predecessors; however, in the last two years of his second term he pulled back on these activities (Lind, 2018). In the article "Donald Trump Is Deporting Fewer People Than Barack Obama Did" (2017), it was indicated that although the number of undocumented immigrants removed directly from the border has decreased, President Trump's expansion of the eligibility criteria for removal caused a significant uptick in deportations since his term began (paragraph 5). *The Economist* further reported that while Obama's administration directed ICE officials to focus on immigrants who posed immediate public safety concerns only, Trump's administration moved beyond that criteria to include even those with minor traffic violations and family disputes, causing much disruption in the justice system across the USA (A. Johnson, 2018). In short, ICE has become a nightmare for many families in search of the American Dream.

The term "#AbolishICE" was coined on Twitter by Sean McElwee shortly after President Trump's inauguration (Breland, 2018). However, one could argue that the historical moment that put the movement to eradicate ICE on the map was the family separation catastrophe that unfolded in ICE detention facilities along the US/Mexico border in the summer of 2018 (Levinson-Waldman & Hinkle, 2018). Then the US media caught wind of detained children as young as a year old (O'Leary, 2019), and it became nightly news. During their successful campaigns for the House of Representatives, Alexandria Ocasio-Cortez, Ayanna Pressley, and Ilhan Omar all made abolishing ICE a major component of their respective policy agendas. In Ocasio-Cortez's case, she unseated an incumbent who helped to establish ICE back in 2002 (McElwee, 2018). Other lawmakers have joined in the push to reorganize ICE's priorities, if not eliminate the agency altogether, including former US presidential candidates Cory Booker, Bernie Sanders, Amy Klobuchar, Kirsten Gillibrand, Elizabeth Warren, Bill de Blasio, and Kamala Harris (Godfrey, 2018). Representative Mark Pocan (D-Wisconsin) has introduced legislation to abolish ICE, which is designed to reverse the "blanket directive" that the Trump administration has enforced with arresting and detaining undocumented immigrants and to create a commission that would distinguish which ICE functions are appropriate and should continue from those that have been abused and should be halted (Sarlin, 2018).

One significant difference between the first three movements described here and #AbolishICE is that most of the heavy lifting has so far been done by elected officials. Another is that there is no one central website that speaks for he entire movement – a Google search yields multiple results (see www.afsc org/abolish-ice; https://actionnetwork.org/letters/abolish-ice). However, activists associated with the Occupy ICE movement have led protests in cities across America to generate attention over the issue and demand their law-makers include this issue in their legislative agendas as well (Gabbatt, 2018). These activists have taken up the mantle of improving the US immigration system and they encourage other activists to join them by educating them-selves on these issues, petitioning their local leaders to consider turning their municipalities into sanctuary cities, holding ICE accountable by recording arrests and boycotting private companies that support ICE in its current form, promoting Black immigrants within the ranks of their local activist groups, and using their varied skill sets to organize around changing immigration laws (Uhlmann, 2019).

3.2.5 Empowerment in Context Examples Summary

Each of these four social movements reflects the contextual nature of empower-ment. In each instance, empowered individuals harnessed both internal and external assets to successfully engage their unique positions in time and space to achieve specific goals. Community members chose a social problem to target – White supremacy, rape culture, gun violence, or xenophobia – and took tan-gible actions to reduce these cultural ills. In this way, empowerment can be conceptualized as a construct that shares qualities with resilience and citizen participation, yet the contextual nature of this construct distinguishes it from both. People are embedded within the localities where they live, the social networks they most often interact within, and the institutions that influence their access (or lack of access) to resources. Governmental laws, the culture, and the media all permeate and influence those three levels of analysis (Noffsinger et al., 2012). True empowerment occurs when the individual finds ways to change the dynamics of their relationships at each ecological level, changing themselves and those systems as time progresses.

Thus, thoughts and feelings are considered a type of empowerment at the individual level. Reciprocal helping and mutual influence within role rela-tionships are considered types of empowerment at the setting level. When someone decides to resist forces designed to negate them of their dignity, their resources, or even their sense of comfort, they are demonstrating empowerment. However, an individual feeling empowered does not mean they will act accordingly or empower others. Additionally, a person can be empowered in one setting but not another. Because empowerment is vari-able, contingent on both the individual using it and the context in which they operate, the following paragraphs discuss the root of the word *empowerment* to provide the reader with the underlying components of this construct.

3.3 What Is Power?

There exists a common misconception that the wealthy, the politically connected, and celebrities are the only individuals with power. However, one does not necessarily have to own resources to wield power – sometimes being able to compel those with more power than what the individual has is power unto itself. This illustrates the individual's sphere of influence – their ability to not only wield power but also to become convincing proponents of the sociocultural currents within their community with the ability to determine and direct the development of those currents, as Helen Jennings (1937) wrote in her seminal work on leadership development. For example, the MSD survivors' March For Our Lives event in Washington, DC influenced US Supreme Court Justice John Paul Stevens to pen a *New York Times* editorial calling for the repeal of the Second Amendment (Stevens, 2018). Clearly, a retired Supreme Court justice has more power than a group of high school students. However, we argue that this student-led movement likely had some amount of influence on this highly respected figure, who used his platform to empower others to take up the fight for reasonable gun control. There are multiple forms of power – some are more individual-based, while others are more social-based – that have been identified by Kloos and colleagues (2021). These different forms of power serve as the means of making considerable changes in one's environment and we will detail them in Section 3.3.1.

3.3.1 Four Types of Individual-Based Power

Kloos and colleagues (2021) indicate that the first form of power is the ability to compel others to comply with the individual's will through rewards or punishment. This involves a hierarchy and can lead to just or unjust outcomes depending upon whether large groups share the same vision for change. An unjust example of this is when the US government compelled the removal of Native Americans from their ancestral lands following the 1830 Indian Removal Act (Cave, 2003). Native Americans were threatened with death if they did not comply with the directive to migrate from the Southeastern USA to the western part of the country. A less extreme version of this type of power might be when a parent extinguishes poor academic performance in their child by rewarding them with new game systems for high grades and removes the child's privileges for low grades. This parent would be using their power over their child to place academics as a priority over other pursuits.

The second type of power proposed is when an individual uses their ability to build their own capacities and manifest their dreams. This power helps a person to achieve outcomes that are necessary for individual reinvention (Kloos et al., 2021). Talk show host, author, and CEO Oprah Winfrey exemplifies this type of power. Winfrey experienced innumerable hardships in her early life but focused her talents for communication to establish a successful career in local journalism followed by an iconic daytime talk show with international reach which was on the air for twenty-five years (Garson, 2011). Winfrey empowered herself to change the landscape of media and entertainment, influence gubernatorial and presidential campaigns, and become a voice for women, marginalized groups, and Black people across the globe (T. Johnson, 2018; Zeleny, 2007).

Kloos and colleagues (2021) defined the third type of power as the ability to stand firm against the power wielded by others. If you are in a work setting and your employer tries to compel you to do something you are not comfortable with, you can contact the company's human resources department, your labor union, or an attorney. Doing any of these would demonstrate your power to resist your employer's demands. Another example of this power includes saying "no" and choosing to act in ways that put one in opposition of others who do not have one's best interests at heart. Rosa Parks demonstrated her power from Jim Crow laws when she refused to relinquish her seat per a bus driver's request in Montgomery, Alabama in 1955. In Michael Chabon's 2000 Pulitzer Prize–winning novel *The Amazing Adventures of Kavalier and Klay*, the story protagonists designed a comic book hero whose superpower was his ability to escape the evil clutches of Nazi villains (Chabon, 2000). This novel provided a vivid illustration of the reality that, sometimes, we cannot stop unfortunate things from happening, but we can remove ourselves from these circumstances.

The fourth type of power defined by Kloos and colleagues (2021) is integrative power that refers to the ability to inspire a group of people to achieve collective goals together. Several of the most influential social movements throughout history could not have been successful without this type of power, including the US Postal Strike of 1970 to increase wages and improve working conditions for postal workers (Rubio, 2016). In this example, US President Nixon tried using the National Guard to deliver the mail after US postal workers across the country stopped working before their conditions were improved. This executive tactic proved inefficient and the postal workers successfully negotiated for a higher quality of treatment from the government. This could not have come to pass if there were any chinks in the armor – all postal workers had to agree to sacrifice in the short term to enhance their conditions in the long term. This is integrative power at its finest.

The four terms described above represent sources of power individuals may have at their disposal. Once the individual can identify the source from where their power comes, they can begin using their personal instruments to prompt transactions within their environment. Unlike individual-based sources of power that are yielded solely within systems, the paragraphs that follow describe the category of social-based power that can be used between systems, usually by groups, organizations, and institutions.

3.3.2 Three Instruments of Social Power

The first instrument is controlling resources that are used to bargain, reward, and punish. Kloos and colleagues (2021) defined this as the power to hire professionals to help plead one's case, to use the law and its loopholes, and to drown out "the little guy." This instrument may be used by large corporations, the government, and other entities with immense power. For example, the 2015 Academy Award Best Picture winner *Spotlight* detailed how the Catholic Church used attorneys to protect priests who had been accused of abusing children (McCarthy, 2015). For decades, the parents of most of these children did not have the power to retain attorneys for their families. It was not until *Boston Globe* journalists shared survivor truths that the scales of power tipped in favor of justice (Rezendes, 2002).

The following illustrates a second instrument of social power. An imaginary community member named Jamilah is against the efforts of a large supermarket chain to build its new location in her neighborhood. Jamilah is concerned about regentrification and the quick rise in rent prices that often follows. She organizes her neighbors and they decide to attend the next neighborhood council meeting where the grocery store's bid is put to a vote. However, the grocery store learned of Jamilah's community-organizing efforts so it "negotiated" with the neighborhood council leaders to influence how the meeting would be scheduled. When Jamilah and other community members show up to the meeting expecting to present the case as to why the grocery store should not be allowed to build locally, they find that their time has been cut down from thirty to five minutes.

In this case, the grocery store is implementing the second instrument of social power identified by Kloos and colleagues (2021) described as controlling channels for participation in community decisions. This instrument is concerned with setting the agenda during important interactions between systems to ensure the intentions of the entity (in this case, the grocery store) wielding this instrument come to pass. If Jamilah and her neighbors were not aware of the "hidden rules of the game" or did not have the capital to influence their neighborhood council leaders such as the grocery store, then they would mostly likely end up succumbing to the grocery store's use of this instrument of social power.

When community psychologists are working to change a system, two of the most important things to consider are how to define the problem and selecting the appropriate intervention. Shaping the definition of a public issue, the third instrument of social power defined by Kloos and colleagues (2021), is the ability to make one's argument seem natural and the opposing argument seem unnatural. Illegal immigration has long been an unresolved social issue in the United States; previous policies have served as half measures, but gridlock between the US Senate and the US House of Representatives has curtailed significant progress in this arena (Alvarez, 2019). Using the power of the Oval

Office, the forty-fifth president of the United States, Donald J. Trump, defined the problem of illegal immigration in this country as "a growing humanitarian and security crisis at our Southern border" (Clark, 2019). If American citizens believed that fear was well placed, then the president's proposed solution to the problem of building a new wall along the US/Mexican border might have made sense. In this way, the president was using this particular instrument to take advantage of the historical setting and timing of current events to frame this social issue to reflect his personal feelings.

Whatever type of power an individual has and whatever instrument they choose to use with that power, if they are aligning themselves with the values of community psychology (e.g., psychological sense of community, inclusion, social justice), they have a responsibility to take risks and lead others toward positive change (Brodsky, 2017).

3.4 Avenues toward Empowerment

Suppose there is a community issue that is becoming concerning for you. Hopefully, by now you have begun to consider the instruments of power that may be at your disposal. Below are a few suggestions for how you might activate these tools to shift the dynamics in your favor at a systemic level.

3.4.1 Citizen Participation

As mentioned earlier, block organizations and parent–teacher organizations are excellent avenues toward empowerment as they are local and easily accessible for citizen participation. Voting on important decision points and volunteering to promote the group's mission among your neighborhoods are both meaningful forms of participation. Holding elected officials accountable for protecting the community via their policies through constant correspondence also leads to meaningful change. This type of citizen participation is not only empowerment, it is also a constitutional right secured by the First Amendment. In the era of COVID-19, the Open Government Partnership, a multilateral initiative that promotes the transparency of governments worldwide, encourages citizen-led community responses to inform others of the risks associated with the virus and the necessary steps for tackling misinformation found online (see Open Government Partnership, 2020).

3.4.2 Community Organizing

Decades of research support the idea that community organizing is a powerful empowerment technique for developing and putting plans into action to protect the public health for large groups (Douglas et al., 2016). A four-step framework for community organizing includes (1) growing a community base of affected citizens, (2) building the organization's chosen leaders with training and education, (3) reframing the message such that the prevailing narrative begins to reflect the truths of the residents, and (4) mobilizing the base by encouraging all members of the community to learn about the organization's future directions and giving everyone the opportunity to provide feedback and support.

The Chicago-based Community Organizing and Family Issues, which seeks to train parents to lobby for parent-led policy solutions and included former President Obama in its staff as a community organizer during the 1990s, began promoting tips for community organizing early in the COVID-19 pandemic. Its suggestions included using social media groups to communicate with its community members and sharing information about school meals, unemployment insurance, utility shutoff, eviction freezes, and sick leave (see www .cofionline.org/community-organizing-during-a-pandemic/). This agency's empowered approach to community organizing helped motivate Chicago Mayor Lori Lightfoot to announce a temporary suspension of practices related to debt collection and citations for nonsafety-related incidents (City of Chicago, 2020).

3.4.3 Social Media and Technology

Social media, which has been alluded to several times in this chapter, has emerged as a major resource in empowerment within US culture. This set of technologies and online platforms will almost certainly play some role in all future community-organizing initiatives. Online platforms like TikTok, Instagram, Snapchat, Facebook, YouTube, and Twitter allow users to share their locations, dates, and other information for easy dissemination across the globe at very little cost. For example, each of the movements mentioned in Section 3.2 owe their ubiquity to the social media platform Twitter, which can transform a simple movement name into a rallying cry heard around the world by adding a hashtag. Kia-Keating, Santacrose, and Liu (2017) used social media to empower at-risk, Latinx youth to tell the stories of the community violence they had witnessed in their communities. Participants used their smartphone cameras to take pictures that illustrated community concerns that traditional research and news media may not be equipped to illustrate. This research team used the participatory photography strategy called "Photovoice" to help participants frame their lived experiences and start a dialogue for meaningful, positive change. Some of their photos were curated into videos and published on YouTube, making them instantly available to anyone with an internet connection. The young people's vision of their community "went viral" and empowered them to take control of the narrative as opposed to outsiders who might not understand.

A community-organizing agency, Cincinnati Action for Housing Now, recommends organizers to "warm" text message their friends to promote their agenda instead of messaging strangers, and use OutVote (a platform for emailing contacts and sharing information), Soapboxx (an application that allows users to upload videos created on their mobile devices onto other online platforms like YouTube), and Zoom (an online platform that allows for synchronous conversations between two or more parties) (see Cincinnati Action for Housing Now, n.d.).

The negative impact of technology widens the gap between the informed and the uninformed, creating a digital divide. Indigenous and/or impoverished groups may not have access to phones, though at least someone in their household or village may have access to a radio. Teletherapy is the latest wave in mental health and includes using smartphones and other connected digital devices to provide psychological services like crisis intervention, cognitive behavioral therapy, and exposure-based therapies (Torales, Castaldelli-Maia, & Ventriglio, 2017). One major advantage of this service delivery method is that it can be used to make consulting in rural and more underserved areas much more possible than before (Trombello et al., 2020), in turn increasing the chances that these populations can develop the resources necessary to empower themselves.

3.5 Multicultural Perspectives in Empowerment

Just about every underrepresented identity has its own challenges that can lead to a potentially lessened quality of life. When macro-level systems erode freedoms, faith communities, loci of control, and social tolerance, they ultimately increase the deleterious effects of ableism, racism, sexism, homo/transphobia, classism, and religious persecution. This reinforces why we must discuss power and control when discussing how to promote wellness among marginalized groups.

In underdeveloped countries where women have been historically subjugated through culture, empowerment looks different than it does in more developed countries. In certain parts of Africa, for example, empowerment might mean taking steps to reduce or end child marriages altogether. The practice of marrying girls younger than eighteen years of age makes them vulnerable to health dangers, poverty, and long-term psychological disempowerment (Nour, 2006; Raj, 2010). A Malawian gender rights activist by the name of Memory Banda recently gave a memorable TED Talk (Banda, 2015) where she described the alliance she made with nonprofit organization Girls Empowerment Network to raise awareness and penalize men who initiate young girls into sexual activity. Her advocacy led to policy changes increasing the legal marrying age in Malawi from eighteen to twenty-one years of age.

Another example of communities demonstrating empowerment is the 2019–2020 Hong Kong protests. In 1997, Great Britain handed Hong Kong back to China albeit with a "one country, two systems" agreement, granting this colony considerably more autonomy than mainland Chinese citizens, as reported by BBC News in the article "The Hong Kong Protests Explained in 100 and 500 Words" (2019). However, Hong Kong's constitution includes an article that prohibits any type of secession or sedition that has never been passed; a 2003 attempt to do so resulted in mass demonstrations across the city, considered the largest ever in the city's history at that time (Griffiths & Jiang, 2020). A relative peace lasting seventeen years ended when Hong Kong's government introduced the Fugitive Offenders amendment bill in June 2019 that proposed extraditing suspected criminals in Hong Kong to jurisdictions where that city currently has no extradition agreement. Even though the government rescinded this bill, the mere proposal of it initiated a six-month period of mass protests and demonstrations in the streets of Hong Kong. Protesters clogged busy commercial districts, flew independence flags, and organized flash mob rallies to sing protest anthems, also strictly forbidden by the legal system of Mainland China.

Then, COVID-19 hit, and these protests were temporarily subdued. After weeks of relative quiet due to the social distancing laws caused by the global pandemic, the Chinese government introduced a national security law in late May 2020 that again targeted actions perceived as seditious or subversive to Chinese leadership (Griffiths & Jiang, 2020). These protesters took to the streets again, breaking the social distancing rules in the name of their own empowerment, to protest what they fear may mean increased police brutality and vulnerability for human rights activists, journalists, attorneys, and others who champion democracy. These protests set the stage for a democratic primary, which was held during the summer of 2020. Hundreds of thousands of Hong Kong citizens voted, but the city's leader chose to delay the actual election until late 2021 due to the COVID-19 pandemic to much skepticism and outrage among its citizens. In early January 2021, dozens of politicians and campaigners were arrested for participating in the primary for that election in early morning raids (Davidson, 2021). The Hong Kong fight continues.

In other countries across the globe, the indigenous – cultures whose worldviews often center on an alliance between humans and the natural world (Cunningham & Stanley, 2003) – are often vulnerable to the threat of marginalization. Enn (2012) details how in the 1970s, the Taiwanese government decided to establish a nuclear dumpsite on Orchid Island, a small land mass off the coast where the indigenous Dao people live. From 1982 through 1996, more than a hundred thousand barrels of nuclear waste were brought to Orchid Island. Before this dumping began, the Dao people had little knowledge about toxic waste and radioactivity. Pastors and scholars from the island began collecting information on these problems to fight the government for exploiting their land. These community leaders eventually taught the Dao about the atomic bombs in Hiroshima and Nagasaki and the tremendous negative impacts these events had on their citizens. The Dao had no words for toxic waste, so they adapted the term into their traditional lexicon (Chi, 2001). The Presbyterian Church also sent missionaries to Orchid Island to assist in reading, writing, and translating the Bible into the local tongue while still encouraging the Dao to use their native tongue. The Dao people became educated about their rights under law and successfully petitioned the Taiwanese to halt their dumping practices on Orchid Island. In this instance, empowerment was a result of the people making relationships with the church and, from that collaboration, a unique process was created that included community members who had never been activists before and systems that had never consulted with this particular population before. This specific time window and the space between Orchid Island and Taiwan created a historical event of empowerment that could not have happened any sooner or later.

These examples demonstrate that empowerment in other cultures can take different forms. Sometimes it is a matter of connecting community members to the resources of more developed countries. Other times, empowerment occurs through shared information and greater awareness of human rights. Whether locally or globally, empowerment is about increasing one's capacity to impact the system in which they are embedded.

3.6 Conclusion

This chapter encourages the reader to think of how they might empower themselves through engaging with their communities. Empowerment is a widely discussed concept. Its broad definition can mean different things as applied to the empowerment of an individual, a community, or an organization. Successful empowerment can occur when individuals interact with and within their systems and are open to the dynamics of those relationships shifting. We hope that the examples provided here will generate ideas and templates to follow as the reader charts their own movement for activism and empowerment. Readers are encouraged to take a moment to process the individual power they possess, and with the tools of empowerment discussed here, how they might foster empowerment with one's community on local, national, and/or global levels. Be persistent as such change often takes time. Those in power may be resistant, though with strength and implementation of the concepts mentioned in this chapter, success is possible over the long term. Vote in all elections. Speak with your neighbors, stretch yourself, and speak up about what matters most to you. As a group, identify which lawmakers in your community would be most likely to listen to your calls for action and develop a strategy on how to start that dialogue; better yet, consider running for local positions in government yourself. Your historical event is happening now, so there is no better time to raise your voice than the present.

References

Altman, I., & Rogoff, B. (1987). World views in psychology: Trait, interactional, organismic, and transactional perspectives. In D. Stokols & I. Altman (Eds.), *Handbook of environmental psychology* (Vol. 1, pp. 7–40). New York: Wiley.

Alvarez, P. (2019, December 11). *House votes to provide a pathway to citizenship for thousands of undocumented farmworkers.* CNN. www.cnn.com/2019/12/11/politics/immigration-agriculture-bill/index.html

American Psychological Association. (2017). *Multicultural guidelines: An ecological approach to context, identity, and intersectionality.* www.apa.org/about/policy/multicultural-guidelines.pdf

Banda, M. (2015, July). *A warrior's cry against child marriage.* [Video]. TED Conferences. www.ted.com/talks/memory_banda_a_warrior_s_cry_against_child_marriage?language=en

Betancourt, T. S., Frounfelker, R., Mishra, T., Hussein, A., & Falzarano, R. (2015). Addressing health disparities in the mental health of refugee children and adolescents through community based participatory research: A study in 2 communities. *American Journal of Public Health, 105*(53), S475–S482. doi.org/10.2105/AJPH.2014.302504

Bogel-Burroughs, N. (2020, May 14). Months after Louisville police kill woman in her home, governor calls for review. *The New York Times.* www.nytimes.com/2020/05/14/us/breonna-taylor-louisville-shooting.html

Botelho, G. (2012, May 23). *What happened the night Trayvon Martin died.* CNN. www.cnn.com/2012/05/18/justice/florida-teen-shooting-details/index.html

Breland, A. (2018, July 29). *How Twitter vaulted "Abolish ICE" into the mainstream.* The Hill. https://thehill.com/policy/technology/399303-how-twitter-vaulted-abolish-ice-into-the-mainstream

Brodsky, A. E. (2017). Bridging the dialectic: Diversity, psychological sense of community, and inclusion. *American Journal of Community Psychology, 59*(3–4), 269–271. doi.org/10.1002/ajcp.12135

Brodsky, A. E., & Cattaneo, L. B. (2013). A transconceptual model of empowerment and resilience: Divergence, convergence and interactions in kindred community concepts. *American Journal of Community Psychology, 52*(3–4), 333–346. doi.org/10.1007/s10464-013-9599-x

Bronfenbrenner, U. (1979). *The ecology of human development.* Cambridge, MA: Harvard University Press.

Broomfield, M. (2017, January 23). Women's March against Donald Trump is the largest day of protests in US history, say political scientists. *The Independent.* www.independent.co.uk/news/world/americas/womens-march-anti-donald-trump-womens-rights-largest-protest-demonstration-us-history-political-a7541081.html

Canfield, D. (2018, February 23). Parkland shooting survivors talk gun control and conspiracies on *The Ellen DeGeneres Show. Entertainment Weekly.* https://ew.com/tv/2018/02/23/parkland-survivors-ellen/

Carlsen, A., Salam, M., Miller, C. C., et al. (2018, October 29). #MeToo brought down 201 powerful men. Nearly half of their replacements are women. *The*

New   York   Times. www.nytimes.com/interactive/2018/10/23/us/metoo-replacements.html?searchResultPosition=1

Cave, A. A. (2003). Abuse of power: Andrew Jackson and the Indian removal act of 1830. *The Historian, 65*(6), 1330–1353. doi.org/10.1111/j.0018-2370.2003.00055.x

Chabon, M. (2000). *The amazing adventures of Kavalier and Clay: A novel.* New York: Random House.

Chavez, T. A., Fernandez, I. T., Hipolito-Delgado, C. P., & Rivera, E. T. (2016). Unifying liberation psychology and humanistic values to promote social justice in counseling. *The Journal of Humanistic Counseling, 55*(3), 166–182. doi.org/10.1002/johc.12032

Chi, C.-C. (2001). Capitalist expansion and indigenous land rights: Emerging environmental justice issues in Taiwan. *The Asia Pacific Journal of Anthropology, 2*(2), 135–153. doi.org/10.1080/14442210110001706145

Chuck, E., Johnson, A., & Siemaszko, C. (2018, February 14). *17 killed in mass shooting at high school in Parkland, Florida.* NBC News. www.nbcnews.com/news/us-news/police-respond-shooting-parkland-florida-high-school-n848101

Cincinnati Action for Housing Now. (n.d.). *Organizing in the time of physical distancing.* https://cincihomeless.files.wordpress.com/2020/04/organizing-in-the-time-of-physical-distancing-.pdf

City of Chicago. (2020, March 18). *Mayor Lightfoot announces temporary suspension of debt collection, ticketing and towing practices to provide relief in response to the COVID-19 outbreak* [Press release]. www.chicago.gov/city/en/depts/mayor/press_room/press_releases/2020/march/SuspensionTicketingDebtCollection.html

City News Service. (2019, December 4). *Julian Castro joins Black Lives Matter protest of LAPD shooting.* https://patch.com/california/hollywood/julian-castro-join-black-lives-matter-protest-lapd-shooting

Clark, D. (2019, January 8). *Trump declares a "growing humanitarian and security crisis" on the border in address to the nation.* NBC News. www.nbcnews.com/politics/politics-news/trump-declares-growing-humanitarian-security-crisis-border-address-nation-n956466

Clauss-Ehlers, C. S. (2008). Sociocultural factors, resilience, and coping: Support for a culturally sensitive measure of resilience. *Journal of Applied Developmental Psychology, 29*(3), 197–212. doi.org/10.1016/j.appdev.2008.02.004

Clauss-Ehlers, C. S., Chiriboga, D. A., Hunter, S. J., Roysircar, G., & Tummala-Narra, P. (2019). APA Multicultural Guidelines executive summary: Ecological approach to context, identity, and intersectionality. *American Psychologist, 74*(2), 232–244. doi.org/10.1037/amp0000382

Cummings, W. (2018, March 23). Stoneman Douglas shooting survivors calling for gun control land 'Time' cover. *USA Today.* www.usatoday.com/story/news/nation/2018/03/22/stoneman-douglas-survivors-time-magazine-cover/451715002/

Cunningham, C., & Stanley, F. (2003). Indigenous by definition, experience, or world view: Links between people, their land, and culture need to be acknowledged. *British Medical Journal, 327*(7412), 403–404. doi.org/10.1136/bmj.327.7412.403

Davidson, H. (2021, January 6). Dozens of Hong Kong pro-democracy figures arrested in sweeping crackdown. *The Guardian*. www.theguardian.com/world/2021/jan/06/dozens-of-hong-kong-pro-democracy-figures-arrested-in-sweeping-crackdown

Department of Homeland Security. (n.d.). *Immigration and customs enforcement*. Retrieved May 25, 2020, from www.dhs.gov/topic/immigration-and-customs-enforcement

Donald Trump is deporting fewer people than Barack Obama did. (2017, December 14). *The Economist*. www.economist.com/united-states/2017/12/14/donald-trump-is-deporting-fewer-people-than-barack-obama-did

Douglas, J. A., Grills, C. T., Villanueva, S., & Subica, A. M. (2016). Empowerment praxis: Community organizing to redress systemic health disparities. *American Journal of Community Psychology*, *58*(3–4), 488–498. doi.org/10.1002/ajcp.12101

Enn, R. (2012). Indigenous empowerment through collective learning. *Multicultural Education & Technology Journal*, *6*(3), 149–161. doi.org/10.1108/17504971211253994

Fisher, D. R., Dow, D. M., & Ray, R. (2017). Intersectionality takes it to the streets: Mobilizing across diverse interests for the Women's March. *Science Advances*, *3*(9), 1–8. doi.org/10.1126/sciadv.aao1390

Gabbatt, A. (2018, July 6). The growing Occupy ICE movement: "We're here for the long haul." *The Guardian*. www.theguardian.com/us-news/2018/jul/06/occupy-ice-movement-new-york-louisville-portland

Garson, H. S. (2011). *Oprah Winfrey: A biography*. Santa Barbara, CA: ABC-CLIO.

Godfrey, E. (2018, July 11). What "Abolish ICE" actually means. *The Atlantic*. www.theatlantic.com/politics/archive/2018/07/what-abolish-ice-actually-means/564752/

The government shutdown will hit home after Christmas with many federal offices shuttered. (2018, December 25). *The Associated Press*. www.latimes.com/nation/la-na-government-shutdown-20181225-story.html

Graham, D. A. (2015, October 16). Black Lives Matter is speaking Bernie Sanders' language. *The Atlantic*. www.theatlantic.com/notes/2015/10/black-lives-matter-and-bernie-sanders-search-for-a-common-language/411001/

Griffiths, J., & Jiang, S. (2020, May 22). *Beijing to propose hugely controversial security law in Hong Kong*. CNN. www.cnn.com/2020/05/21/asia/hong-kong-npc-art icle-23-intl-hnk/index.html

"Gun violence is an epidemic": MSD survivor testifies on Capitol Hill. (2019, February 6). *The Associated Press*. www.nbcmiami.com/news/local/parkland-survivor-testifies-gun-violence-capitol-hill/38/

Harris, A. (2018, October 15). She founded Me Too. Now she wants to move past the trauma. *The New York Times*. www.nytimes.com/2018/10/15/arts/tarana-burke-metoo-anniversary.html?searchResultPosition=1

Herman, D. F. (1978). The rape culture. In J. Freeman (Ed.), *Women: A feminist perspective* (pp. 41–63). Palo Alto, CA: Mayfield.

The Hong Kong protests explained in 100 and 500 words. (2019, November 28). *BBC News*. www.bbc.com/news/world-asia-china-49317695

Jan, T. (2020, May 10). Economic pain falls hardest on minorities, less-educated. *The Washington Post*, G2.

Jennings, H. (1937). Structure of leadership-development and sphere of influence. *Sociometry*, *1*(1/2), 99–143. doi.org/10.2307/2785262

Johnson, A. (2018, February 20). Arrests of undocumented immigrants in Boston are up 50 percent. *Boston Globe*. www.bostonglobe.com/metro/2018/02/20/arrests-undocumented-immigrants-boston-percent/6JXkdwmyXFGRaD4VJe2tEL/story.html

Johnson, T. (2018, November 1). Oprah Winfrey campaigns for gubernatorial candidate Stacey Abrams in Georgia. *Variety*. https://variety.com/2018/politics/news/oprah-campaigns-stacey-abrams-georgia-1203017317/

Keller, J., Mendes, K., & Ringrose, J. (2018). Speaking 'unspeakable things': Documenting digital feminist responses to rape culture. *Journal of Gender Studies*, *27*(1), 22–36. doi.org/10.1080/09589236.2016.1211511

Kia-Keating, M., Santacrose, D., & Liu, S. (2017). Photography and social media use in community based participatory research with youth: Ethical considerations. *American Journal of Community Psychology*, *60*(3–4), 375–384. doi.org/10.1002/ajcp.12189

Kloos, B., Hill, J., Thomas, E., et al. (2021). *Community psychology: Linking individuals and communities* (4th ed.). Washington, DC: American Psychological Association.

Langone, A. (2018, March 25). These photos show how big the March For Our Lives crowds were across the country. *Time Magazine*. https://time.com/5214706/march-for-our-lives-us-photos/

Lee, Y., & Schachter, H. L. (2019). Exploring the relationship between trust in government and citizen participation. *International Journal of Public Administration*, *42*(5), 405–416. doi.org/10.1080/01900692.2018.1465956

Leonard, J. (2011). Using Bronfenbrenner's ecological theory to understand community partnerships: A historical case study of one urban high school. *Urban Education*, *46*(5), 987–1010. doi.org/10.1177/0042085911400337

Levinson-Waldman, R., & Hinkle, H. (2018, July 30). *The Abolish ICE movement explained*. Brennan Center for Justice. www.brennancenter.org/our-work/analysis-opinion/abolish-ice-movement-explained

Lind, D. (2018, June 21). *What Obama did with migrant families vs. what Trump is doing*. Vox. www.vox.com/2018/6/21/17488458/obama-immigration-policy-family-separation-border

Lussenhop, J. (2016, March 16). *Chicago prosecutor loses her fight with Black Lives Matter*. BBC News. www.bbc.com/news/world-us-canada-35817890

Luthar, S. S., & Cicchetti, D. (2000). The construct of resilience: Implications for interventions and social policies. *Development and Psychopathology*, *12*(4), 857–885.

March For Our Lives Highlights: Students protesting guns say 'enough is enough.' (2018, March 24). *The New York Times*. www.nytimes.com/2018/03/24/us/march-for-our-lives.html?searchResultPosition=1

McCarthy, T. (Director). (2015). *Spotlight* [Film]. Participant Media.

McElwee, S. (2018, August 4). The power of 'Abolish ICE'. *The New York Times*. www.nytimes.com/2018/08/04/opinion/sunday/abolish-ice-ocasio-cortez-democrats.html?searchResultPosition=1

McLaughlin, E. C. (2014, August 15). *What we know about Michael Brown's shooting.* CNN. www.cnn.com/2014/08/11/us/missouri-ferguson-michael-brown-what-we-know/index.html

Noffsinger, M. A., Pfefferbaum, B., Pfefferbaum, R. L., Sherrieb, K., & Norris, F. H. (2012). The burden of disaster: Part I. Challenges and opportunities within a child's social ecology. *International Journal of Emergency Mental Health, 14*(1), 3–13.

Nour, N. M. (2006). Health consequences of child marriage in Africa. *Emerging Infectious Diseases, 12*(11), 1644–1649. doi.org/10.3201/eid1211.060510

O'Leary, L. (2019, June 25). 'Children were dirty, they were scared, and they were hungry': An immigration attorney describes what she witnessed at the border. *The Atlantic.* www.theatlantic.com/family/archive/2019/06/child-detention-centers-immigration-attorney-interview/592540/

Open Government Partnership. (2020, May). *Collecting open government approaches to COVID-19.* www.opengovpartnership.org/collecting-open-government-approaches-to-covid-19/

Panter-Brick, C., Hadfield, K., Dajani, R., et al. (2018). Resilience in context: A brief and culturally grounded measure for Syrian refugee and Jordanian host-community adolescents. *Child Development, 89*(5), 1803–1820. doi.org/10.1111/cdev.12868

Parker, N. (2017, December 6). *Who is Tarana Burke? Meet the woman who started the Me Too movement a decade ago.* The Atlanta Journal-Constitution. www.ajc.com/news/world/who-tarana-burke-meet-the-woman-who-started-the-too-movement-decade-ago/i8NEiuFHKaIvBh9ucukidK/

Patel, J. K. (2019, January 16). A typical federal worker has missed $5,000 in pay from the shutdown so far. *The New York Times.* www.nytimes.com/interactive/2019/01/16/us/politics/federal-shutdown-salaries.html

Perano, U. (2020, June 7). *Black Lives Matter co-founder explains "Defund the police" slogan.* Axios. www.axios.com/defund-police-black-lives-matter-7007efac-0b24-44e2-a45c-c7f180c17b2e.html

Raj, A. (2010). When the mother is a child: The impact of child marriage on the health and human rights of girls. *Archives of Disease in Childhood, 95*(11), 931–935. doi.org/10.1136/adc.2009.178707

Reyes, J. R. (2018, March 26). *Immigration detention: Recent trends and scholarship.* Center for Migration Studies. https://cmsny.org/publications/virtualbrief-detention/

Rezendes, M. (2002, January 6). Church allowed abuse by priest for years. *The Boston Globe.* http://archive.boston.com/globe/spotlight/abuse/archive/stories/010602_geoghan.htm

Rojas, R., Mervosh, S., & Fausset, R. (2020, May 11). Investigators call evidence in the Ahmaud Arbery shooting "extremely upsetting." *The New York Times.* www.nytimes.com/2020/05/08/us/ahmaud-arbery-shooting-georgia.html

Rubio, P. F. (2016). Organizing a wildcat: The United States postal strike of 1970. *Labor History, 57*(5), 565–587. doi.org/10.1080/0023656X.2016.1239881

Sarlin, B. (2018, June 30). *This Democrat is writing a bill to 'abolish ICE.' Here's how it would work.* NBC News. www.nbcnews.com/storyline/immigration-border-crisis/congressman-wants-abolish-ice-we-asked-him-how-it-would-n887406

Stevens, J. P. (2018, March 27). John Paul Stevens: Repeal the Second Amendment. *The New York Times*, A23. www.nytimes.com/2018/03/27/opinion/john-paul-stevens-repeal-second-amendment.html

Torales, J., Castaldelli-Maia, J., & Ventriglio, A. (2017). Digital psychiatry and digital psychology: Beyond "traditional" teletherapy. *Medicina Clínica y Social, 1* (3), 190–191.

Trombello, J. M., South, C., Sánchez, A., et al. (2020). Two trajectories of depressive symptom reduction throughout Behavioral Activation teletherapy among underserved, ethnically-diverse, primary care patients: A VitalSign6 report. *Behavior Therapy*, 51(6), 958–971. doi.org/10.1016/j.beth.2020.01.002

Uhlmann, N. (2019, May 13). How activists can fight back against Immigration and Customs Enforcement (ICE). *Teen Vogue*. www.teenvogue.com/story/how-to-fight-back-against-ice

Ungar, M., Ghazinour, M., & Richter, J. (2013). Annual research review: What is resilience within the social ecology of human development? *The Journal of Child Psychology and Psychiatry*, 54(4), 348–366. doi.org/10.1111/jcpp.12025

US Bureau of Labor Statistics. (2020, May 13). *The Economics Daily, Unemployment rate rises to record high 14.7 percent in April 2020*. US Department of Labor. www.bls.gov/opub/ted/2020/unemployment-rate-rises-to-record-high-14-point-7-percent-in-april-2020.htm

Zeleny, J. (2007, December 9). Oprah Winfrey hits campaign trail for Obama. *The New York Times*. www.nytimes.com/2007/12/09/us/politics/09oprah.html?searchResultPosition=1

4 Ethics and Community Psychology

Patricia O'Connor, Tameka L. Gillum, and Gayle Skawennio Morse

4.1 Introduction

The aim of this chapter is to examine the principles and applications of ethics in the community psychology field. The field of community psychology evolved from its beginnings in the 1960s with a general focus on defining community-based theories, such as empowerment and prevention (Rappaport, 1981), sense of community (McMillan & Chavis, 1986), exploring the meaning and importance of working in community settings (Bennett et al., 1966), and improving community well-being (Maton, 2000, 2008) to a more targeted focus on examining ways to address oppression (McDonald, Keys, & Balcazar, 2007; Prilleltensky, 2003), social justice (Prilleltensky, 2001), minority status and concomitant discrimination, and populations and settings in need of assistance (Schwartz et al., 2013; Sonn & Fisher, 2003). Community psychology has evolved into a multifaceted discipline that strives to identify effective place-based strategies to improve the quality of people's lives.

Related to this increasing complexity, Campbell and Morris (2017a, 2017b) argue that the community psychology field needs its own comprehensive ethical framework. To date, we have used our values, such as that of social justice, to serve as our guide in negotiating our ethical positions and actions "on the ground" as we engage in community-based research. We have yet, however, to explicitly establish ethical guidelines to direct us in our efforts, despite the fact that through the very nature of our work we often find ourselves in "conflicted spaces" (Campbell & Morris, 2017b, p. 299). For example, sometimes our goals of fostering systemic change to improve the lives of the oppressed populations with which we partner means forging alliances with those structures that foster the oppression. It can be difficult to navigate those waters, and when conflicts arise, it can be challenging at best to decide the just and right path to take, without clearer guidance.

Through their special issue of the *American Journal of Community Psychology*, Campbell and Morris (2017a, 2017b) effectively highlight ethical dilemmas experienced by twenty-three community psychologists in the field and their challenging processes of negotiating these circumstances without clear and solid ethical guidelines to inform the difficult choices that they were forced to make. Campbell and Morris (2017a, 2017b) argue that while our values can effectively guide us in determining *what ought to be* they are not always sufficient to identify *what is* when we are engaged in ground-level work and facing these ethical dilemmas. In this chapter we aim to link community psychology values with the overarching value of social justice, and more explicitly to intervention contexts, examining the essential role of ethics in the development and implementation of intervention strategies.

4.2 Intervention Strategies: Cultural Components

As intervention becomes a focal point for community psychology, Montero and Winkler (2014) emphasize that such interventions, based on research, must be realistic and meaningful. An intervention approach can be considered within the overall strategy in community psychology that involves identifying people and/or settings in need, for example, people who are homeless or who have functional limitations, or settings that are dysfunctional or chaotic. Carefully structured research assessments can elucidate points for intervention. It is critical that a consensus among all stakeholders, including potential intervention participants, agencies, existing service providers, and other related constituencies, determines that there is a need for change. Therefore, O'Connor (2007) proposes a Systems Guides model in which the norms, standards, and values, termed Systems Guides, of adjacent or overlapping systems can be examined to identify possible points of discord or a lack of consensus. Points of discord or disagreement can become the target of intervention, prior to the design of the program to be implemented. Intertwined with the apparent point of discord requiring attention are the ethical issues underpinning a decision to intervene: Who makes the decision about intervening? Which elements will be essential and which are disposable? Who decides? How are disagreements about the desired outcome resolved, or are they?

4.2.1 Ethical Principles

Many of the recommendations and changes in research practices designed to ensure ethical treatment have emerged from previous ethically questionable research practices. Despite the establishment of the Nuremberg Code in 1947 (primarily developed to guide biomedical research) and the subsequent Declaration of Helsinki in 1964, there is evidence of the continuation of ethically questionable research in the social sciences (i.e., Milgram's Obedience Studies, the Tearoom Trade, the Stanford Prison Study), health (the Barrow Alcohol Study), and medicine (i.e., the Tuskegee Syphilis Study) (Foulks, 1989; Humphreys, 1970; Milgram, 1963; Privitera, 2016; Zimbardo, 2009). These and other concerns prompted the establishment of the National Commission for the Protection of Human Subjects in 1972, which subsequently produced the Belmont Report in 1979.

The Belmont Report would subsequently form the foundation for ethical principles established by various disciplines, including psychology. The report identified three core principles that should guide research including human participants: respect for persons, beneficence, and justice (US Department of Health and Human Services, 1979). Campbell and Morris (2017a) discuss how community psychologists have defined, shaped, and applied these principles to their work in the absence of established ethical guidelines for the field. Particularly relevant here is the emphasis that Campbell and Morris (2017a) place on the risks taken by writers describing ethical dilemmas in their workplace: Others may judge their decisions as improper or even wrong.

As recently as 2012, Padmavati describes that ethical principles such as consent, confidentiality, and competence should underlie community interventions for people with mental illnesses. The complexity of ethical principles is particularly evident in Padmavati's (2012) three-factor description of consent: informed consent or being informed about what is going to happen, consent to have information shared, and consent to participate presuming that the intervention is itself ethical. Confidentiality centers on the participants' understanding of the breadth and limits of disclosing information. Competence refers to the presumed level of expertise in those providing the intervention and in those conducting the research. Padmavati (2012) notes that consistent adherence to those principles and practices is important and evaluations of programs should necessarily be solidly grounded in ethical practices.

The difficulties of involvement in community-based interventions are effectively illustrated by Kesten et al. (2017). Kesten and her academic colleagues became involved in a large urban revitalization project without clearly negotiated roles in it, which itself was fraught with political conflicts. They described their primary challenge as deciding whether and when to remain silent on troublesome issues or to become involved, which might compromise the community's perception of their objectivity. The results were complicated. One member of the research team opted to leave the project; the other members were faced with difficult ethical dilemmas: Would community members understand their research-based roles? Could the researchers collect data for those orchestrating the revitalization without community members knowing their roles? The research team struggled with accountability for their work, ultimately coming to recognize the difficulties associated with their multiple, somewhat overlapping roles in the project. As demonstrated by this example, coming into any project, community psychologists must negotiate clearly articulated roles. Even then they need to be able to exhibit flexibility as new situations emerge.

4.2.2 Meaningful Participant Involvement

Effective systems assessments require that all stakeholders are represented and engaged in the research to ensure that community psychologists can accurately determine the context for intervening. That notion of engagement, however, can have multiple definitions and may require clarification to be meaningful (Pullman et al., 2013). In the past, researchers may have gone into communities and made the decisions about what needed intervention, what the intervention might be, and how the intervention would be delivered, and then delivered the intervention. Contrary to these early practices, Santiago-Rivera et al. (1998) identified the importance of including community members/stakeholders as experts during project development. Both the researcher and community members must be considered experts that bring important information to the development and execution of a project/community intervention. This is highlighted by Ramirez (1998) who compares the views of traditional researchers to the views of the group indigenous to the area with whom they are attempting to work. For example, the researcher or interventionist is viewed as the expert and the participant or patient is viewed as uninformed and in need of education.

Ramirez (1998) considers that community participants view themselves as equal partners or participants. Furthermore, to foster community engagement the project/community intervention should also include community members in the "fruits" of funding streams and publication (García et al., 2017; Santiago-Rivera et al., 1998). For example, a community member may be hired and trained to collect the data rather than hiring from outside the community.

In addition, publications should also include community members in the writing process as their internal view of the project is an important adjunct to the data and the external researcher's interpretations. García and Tehee (2014) point out that there have been serious negative consequences when there is an inappropriate interpretation of study results and outcomes related to a lack of community membership or publications. They recommend that a community member be part of every publication and that publications be presented in clear, concise ways that may be easily understood by community members. Community engagement in all parts of a research project – proposal, intervention, and evaluation – is considered critical to ethical research.

A primary factor in developing effective community interventions through appropriately designed research is ensuring the legitimate, meaningful involvement of participants in intervention-focused research studies. Multiple factors can play a role in achieving such participation, including the perceptions of those who belong in the identified setting compared to those who are outsiders to the setting (Julian, Smith, & Hunt, 2017). Noting that community psychologists are often not indigenous to where they work, Kelly (2002) described such interventionists, these outsiders, as guests who "are required to earn the privilege to become a partner" (p. 47).

Additionally, there are partial insiders who are "at the intersections of insiders and outsiders" (Haarlammert et al., 2017, p. 415) and who may more accurately represent the flexibility of the relationships between the researcher/evaluator and the community. Outsiders clearly understand that they do not know or have access to aspects of the lived experiences of insiders. However, some who are actually outsiders may incorrectly think of themselves as partial insiders. Partial insiders do have that knowledge but are also no longer fully part of the community. This insider–outsider relationship has been discussed in the anthropology literature (Pike, 1967) as emic and etic perspectives and provides an important understanding with regard to the dynamic of researcher/interventionist versus community member/stakeholder worldviews. For instance, community members may have an emic perspective that issues, understandings, or needs for interventions are specific to that community that may not be fully understood by the researcher. Researchers, on the other hand, may have an etic perspective of external issues, understandings, or needs for interventions. If their views clash, there can be difficulty with establishing working relationships, appropriate interventions, completing research, and interpreting outcomes. Therefore, it is incumbent upon the researcher/interventionist who is entering a community to be prepared to work with and value the community's emic view.

Similarly, Nelson, Prilleltensky, and MacGillivary (2001) speak of the importance of building "value-based partnerships" with the communities with whom they work. The authors assert that the forging of such partnerships should be primarily for the benefit of the communities with whom we work. They define the value-based partnership as follows: "[R]elationships between community psychologists, oppressed groups, and other stakeholders that strive to advance the values of caring, compassion, community, health, self-determination, participation, power sharing, human diversity, and social justice for oppressed groups. These values drive both the process and the outcomes of partnerships" (Nelson et al., 2001, p. 651). As such, the authors advise us that partnerships forged in the communities with whom community psychologists work should have the intention of advancing the community rather than the intention of advancing the agenda of the community psychologist. It is this overarching goal that should drive these partnerships. Meaningful involvement of participants from the perspective of Nelson et al. (2001) includes developing a collective vision and shared values from the start of the partnership, building relationships and trust, sharing power, and challenging ourselves to build mutually respectful relationships across differences – all with the aim of fostering solidarity with the communities with whom we work. This echoes Santiago-Rivera and colleagues (1998) who wrote that the foundation of research in community begins with a relationship built upon respect, trust, equity, and empowerment.

In some instances, program participation that is court-mandated may seem to preclude meaningful legitimate involvement. In their attempt to intervene with girls involved in the legal system, Javdani, Singh, and Sichel (2017) described that the constraints of the setting virtually eliminated the possibility of relevant engagement with the girls participating in the program because onsite program staff systematically interrupted potentially productive interactions between the researchers and the girls. The authors realized that they needed to understand the structural issues present in the setting and modify their community-based research plans and expectations accordingly. Thus, they shifted the narrative, paying careful attention to the ethical complexities of the situation and the requisite modifications to ensure the girls' meaningful participation in the design and implementation of the intervention.

Another issue related to meaningful participant involvement is appropriately taking into account potential participants who refuse to be part of the research or even the intervention (Ellison & Langhout, 2017). Although there are strategies to encourage such participation, such implementation cannot become coercive and researchers/interventionists must respect the right of potential participants to refuse. In one study, García and Tehee (2014) describe a situation where a $20 participation stipend led many participants to sign up and subsequently hurry through the study merely to get the stipend. The outcomes under such circumstances might not be useful. Hence, even the definition of what may be coercive should be established with the community. Furthermore, it is beneficial to include community members in all stages of establishing a study as community buy-in may facilitate greater meaningful participation.

Meaningful participant involvement also requires a broadly inclusive approach to the selection of participants, including populations whose limitations might make them seem too vulnerable. For instance, people with intellectual disabilities (ID) value socialization activities and can make substantial contributions (McDonald, 2012). Yet, they may be summarily excluded from relevant research through their automatic designation as a vulnerable population. McDonald and Keys (2008) studied factors related to the inclusion of people with ID in research projects, comparing researchers and Institutional Review Board (IRB) reviewers. They concluded that the researchers familiar with people with ID were less likely to note their ability status as a limiting factor and more likely to have positive attitudes about their potential contributions than IRB members.

4.2.3 The "Fit" of an Intervention

That the intervention fits the setting may seem obvious; that is, that the expectations and desires of those in the setting and the expected objectives and outcomes of the proposed intervention match. Yet, factors such as political forces and ethical constraints may interfere with considerations regarding fit. Developing collaborative relationships among relevant stakeholders can serve as a critical foundation in establishing and maintaining appropriate interventions and offsetting interfering factors. Maton (2000) notes the importance of joint articulations among a wide variety of actual and potential stakeholders to achieve what he describes as social transformation. Overall, extensive collaborations and even conflict resolution processes can assist in moving implementations and evaluations forward (Julian et al., 2017).

The implementation of evidence-based practices/programs relies on the assumption that there will be fidelity to the program design in the application of that practice/program.

4.2.4 Role of the Interventionist

Community psychologists play significant roles in developing and evaluating systemic intervention programs (Kloos et al., 2011) as collaborators, facilitators, organizers, advocates, and evaluators. Endemic to these roles is the need for authentic cultural competence, and specifically, cultural competence with humility (Tervalon & Murray-García, 1998). The role of cultural competence and cultural humility in the community psychologist's toolbox cannot be emphasized enough. Cultural competence has been a focus of the American Psychological Association (APA) for nearly twenty years. The recently published and updated APA guidelines (2017) provide a roadmap for psychologists to better understand how to function appropriately in other cultures. The stated purpose of the guidelines is to "provide psychologists with a framework from which to consider evolving parameters for the provision of multiculturally competent services. Services include practice, research, consultation, and education, all of which benefit from an appreciation for, understanding of, and willingness to learn about the multicultural backgrounds of individuals, families, couples, groups, research participants, organizations, and communities" (APA, 2017, pp. 7–8).

This is an excellent start for community psychologists to learn to be culturally competent, but it is not sufficient in and of itself; rather it must include the notion of cultural humility. Cultural humility is a "process that requires humility as individuals continually engage in self-reflection and self-critique as lifelong learners and reflective practitioners" (Tervalon & Murray-García, 1998, p. 118; also Hook & Watkins, 2015). The necessity of cultural humility as a lifelong process of understanding one's own strengths and limitations within another culture is an important additional step (García et al., 2017; Tervalon & Murray-García, 1998). Those who practice cultural humility apply skills that help them continuously do honest evaluations of their own attitudes of racism and biases. They are consequently more sensitive to people from diverse cultures and their plight and thus treat them with respect, equality, and dignity. As a result of community collaboration, "their organizations [will] build better systems of response and prevention and develop an understanding of the best approaches for sharing information and tools" (Mose & Gillum, 2015, p. 59).

Culturally humble psychologists ask themselves questions such as why clients from underserved communities should accept them and their "expertise." They seek respectful ways to gain entry into these communities, to know how they should best be supportive, and to understand how to incorporate traditional values into intervention development. "They will have a clear understanding of strategies for tapping into the community strengths, such as resiliency… and community interdependence" (Mose & Gillum, 2015, p. 59). In other words, a course or reading in multicultural competence is not sufficient to be competent. Rather, cultural competence with humility requires understanding that one must pay continuous attention to one's biases and prejudices, limits of understanding, and recognition of the expertise of the communities with whom we work.

4.2.5 Sustainability of Interventions

Community-based interventions implemented as research are typically time-limited, continuing only as long as the research is underway. The termination of the intervention, then, is based on the needs of the researcher rather than those in the setting. Thus, community members may participate in an intervention, experience it as valuable, and wish to continue with it, but the researcher has completed the research protocol and ends the intervention. The result may be harmful to the community as a whole, or at least to those who participated in the intervention. To offset this ethical dilemma, researchers should engage community leaders in the development, application, and publications so they can continue working within the context of the intervention beyond the time constraints of the researcher. Many funding sources have addressed this issue by drawing attention to plans for sustainability for grant-funded programs (Substance Abuse and Mental Health Services Administration [SAMHSA], 2019).

4.3 Dissemination: Lessons Learned

An obligation of researchers is to disseminate the results of their successful or unsuccessful efforts to provide useful insights for others who wish to develop similar interventions or to intervene in similar settings. Fairweather (1967) and Fairweather and Tornatzky (1977) emphasize the importance of dissemination, including providing all details of an intervention. Discussing interventions as a process, Sarason (2004) reminds us that there is much to learn from "failed" intervention efforts, hence our obligation to share this process and its challenges. In the spirit of lessons learned, Hutchinson (2019) provides numerous examples of failures in the work of program evaluators. Understanding not only the successes of others but also their challenges should be an underpinning for the ethical conduct of research for community psychology.

4.3.1 Examples of the Application of Ethics in Community-Based Settings

4.3.1.1 Meaningful Participant Involvement

A community action program (CAP) received relatively unrestricted funding to provide services to people who were chronically homeless and had issues with addiction. The program aimed to obtain housing for identified participants and to help them maintain that housing. Program participants could receive a wide variety of supports that would facilitate their becoming housed; for example, the program could pay outstanding utility bills that would enable participants to sign up for utilities in new housing. Three to four representatives of locally involved service programs, including legal services and mental health and addictions programs, plus the program director and staff from the community action program, comprised the program steering committee (SC); one of the authors served as the evaluator.

In the early stages of the program, the SC explored ways to provide additional services. At the end of one intense discussion the SC had created a list of five options. The project director invited two program participants, both of whom had been homeless, to participate as members of the SC, beginning with the next meeting. The SC repeated the discussion regarding additional services. With the two program participants making suggestions, the SC created a list of approximately twenty very viable options, all of which would serve as incentives to seek and maintain housing. The ongoing meaningful engagement of program participants has encouraged and facilitated the implementation of more relevant strategies to support participants in obtaining and maintaining housing.

4.3.1.2 Unethical Directive

A local not-for-profit agency received funding for year one of a two-year planning (year one) and implementation (year two, contingent on the quality of the planning in year one) grant. The aim of year one was to facilitate a collaboration among relevant agencies and service providers with substantial, egalitarian input from stakeholders, including program targets and their family members to plan a systems intervention; approximately thirty individuals participated in the collaborative process. Success in year one, and thereby likely to result in funding for year two, was defined as overall agreement among the variety of service providers and other stakeholders on an implementation plan for year two.

The project evaluator, one of the authors, provided formative feedback during the planning year and then a summative report for the funding source to document the extent to which consensus on the project implementation had been achieved. As the evaluator was completing the final report, the project director left the agency and a new project director, who was unfamiliar with the work of the planning year, was appointed. The summative report included the overall achievement of consensus but also reflected areas of disagreement, identified participants who were less engaged in the planning process, and detailed other factors that might mitigate the success in year two.

The new project director asserted a hierarchal role and strongly requested that any less than positive language in the report be changed or removed. The evaluator refused, noting, first, that the report was an accurate reflection of the status of the project, and second, that the funding source was not likely to find a virtually perfect report credible, decreasing the likelihood that the source would award year two funding. The new program director and the evaluator were not entirely able to resolve their differences. This ethical dilemma (for the evaluator: change the language or leave the project) was reflected in the report submission process. The evaluator responded by providing only a paper copy of the final year one report with the language unchanged.

4.3.1.3 Intervening without Sustaining

Much of the research in community psychology is an effort to introduce change and assess the effectiveness of that change. The nature and extent of the change varies by such factors as the guiding model(s), the target population, and the researchers' resources. Much social action research is a continuing effort to develop effective interventions in particular settings by studying the intervention effort and providing feedback to improve the effort, in an ongoing intervention-feedback loop. However, some research-based interventions are one-trial, single efforts to study a particular setting, or program, or identified group of people. These efforts are time-limited and are completed for the expected knowledge gain, rather than for the enhancement of the participants' quality of life. The ethical concern is whether participants are sufficiently aware that they have only scripted access to the program content, that the programmatic effort is not likely to continue, and that the specific program in which they are participating is not meant to be sustainable even if that were the participants' choice.

4.3.1.4 Challenges in the Use of Social Media

Social media use has become a common form of communication and includes using phones to make digital recordings and to take pictures to document ongoing events. Kia-Keating, Santacrose, and Liu (2017) used Photovoice with twenty-two Latinx youth as part of a high school class, providing each student with a digital camera, though most of the students' photographs were taken with their phones. Their aim was to encourage youth to express their concerns about their lives and their neighborhoods through a collaborative process of taking and discussing their visual representations. The authors document three sets of ethical challenges and describe their efforts to address each set. First was the tension between students' choice of content and the risks associated with inappropriate photos or even photos of illegal behavior. The authors addressed this challenge with training in the ethics of photography, discussions with students about content, and their own recognition of students' ability to make choices. The second challenge was the tension between providing incentives to encourage participation and being coercive, particularly given this project was part of the graded high school photography course.

In addition, encouraging students to post their images on social media as a way to provide external support for their work could engender a competitive environment with comparisons of the number of "likes" or might have led students to engage in inappropriate self-disclosure. To respond, the authors confirmed with students that their grades in the course would not be affected by their choice to participate in the Photovoice project or not, and did not support the posting of images during the course itself.

The third challenge identified by Kia-Keating et al. (2017) related to the typical scientific research expectation for confidentiality, generally recognized by IRBs. For instance, the students in this project wished very much to be identified with their work by having their names posted with any public display of the images they had produced. The authors dealt with this challenge by reviewing their own versus the students' concerns with confidentiality and even their very definition of privacy. Students in the digital age generally do not maintain strict privacy in their use of social media (Madden et al., 2013) and some were more interested in having their personal work recognized. Kia-Keating et al. (2017) addressed this challenge by using a "collective voice" (p. 381), which was a pairing of an image from one student with the voice from another student.

4.4 Summary and Recommendations

Campbell (2016), in an examination of ethics in the current, fifty-year post-Swampscott (the first gathering of researchers who would become community psychologists) field of community psychology, concludes that there is not "a clearly articulated ethical framework" (p. 299). Going forward, Campbell (2016) suggests several steps that would lead to the development of an ethical framework relevant to community psychology. In this chapter focused on ethics in community psychology, we review the origins of the traditional ethical guidelines promoted by the US Department of Health and Human Services in 1979 and the application of those principles in research settings. We describe a number of research studies that illustrate opportunities and challenges in assessing and addressing situations that reflect the need for ethically charged decisions. We also present several examples of the authors' experiences with ethics in community-based research and practice. Overall, we find that three factors emerge, each of which can play a role in how ethical decisions can or will be made. These factors, which are reviewed here, can provide important context for the development of the ethical framework proposed by Campbell (2016).

4.4.1 Variability in Contexts

The ethical principles established in the Belmont Report (US Department of Health and Human Services, 1979) – respect for persons, beneficence, and justice – must be the underpinning for community psychologists as they engage in community-based research and interventions. Yet the complexity and variability in community-based settings, that is, the specific context for the intervention, may require unusual accommodations to ensure appropriate resolution of ethical dilemmas, or ethical concerns. Interventions may take place in widely varying geographic regions, for example, urban versus rural; in significantly different cultural domains, for example, different ethnic or racial groups; and in substantial demographic groupings, for example, developmentally diverse ages. Javdani et al. (2017) offered clear respect for the girls participating in their project by modifying their research design and incorporating the girls/participants into decision-making roles. Similarly, Kia-Keating et al. (2017) faced several unique ethical challenges in their social media project with high school students and identified strategies to address them. Relevant to this notion of variability in intervention contexts is the role of "fit," the need for a match between proposed intervention and the context in which the intervention will occur.

4.4.2 Meaningful Participation

A fundamental community psychology principle is a broad-brush notion of inclusion. In this context inclusion means drawing program participants into the various aspects of designing, developing, implementing, and evaluating potential programs. McDonald and Keys (2008) identify circumstances that yield more inclusion of people with intellectual disabilities in research studies. García and Tehee (2014) emphasize the improved credibility of research results when participants are involved in publications. And Julian et al. (2017) stress the importance of having insiders included in design and implementation stages of community-based interventions.

4.4.3 Issues of Sustainability

In developing community-based interventions, researchers need to examine the potential impact of termination, as they work to take ethical principles, particularly respect for people, into account. Recruiting participants, encouraging meaningful involvement, and providing appropriate incentives for participation all encourage participants to have a sense of commitment to the intervention; researchers have a sense of commitment to the participants but also to the successful implementation of the research design and expected outcome. At the end of the intervention trial, the researcher essentially moves to the process of analysis and report-writing. Of importance in the context of ethics is attention to whether the participants are prepared for, or desire, the termination of the intervention and whether the researcher provides adequate termination support or referrals to a similar or related intervention.

4.5 Conclusion

We have explored the application of traditional ethical principles (e.g., respect for people, beneficence, and justice) and noted the inclusion of cultural competence as an ethical principle in community psychology; we consider social justice embedded in the traditional ethical principle of justice. The aim of this chapter was to examine the application of ethics in community psychology, and, in that context, we have further identified three additional factors that should become central in assessing any ethical concerns within the community psychology arena: taking the variable features of context into account; ensuring meaningful participant involvement; and addressing the sustainability of interventions.

References

American Psychological Association. (2017). *Multicultural guidelines: An ecological approach to context, identity, and intersectionality.* www.apa.org/about/policy/multicultural-guidelines.pdf.

Bennett, C., Anderson, L., Cooper, S., et al. (1966). *Community psychology: A report of the Boston conference on the education of psychologists for community mental health.* Boston: Boston University.

Campbell, R. (2016). "It's the way that you do it": Developing an ethical framework for community psychology research and action. *American Journal of Community Psychology, 58*(3–4), 294–302. doi.org/10.1007/ajcp.12037

Campbell, R., & Morris, M. (2017a). Complicating narratives: Defining and deconstructing ethical challenges in community psychology. *American Journal of Community Psychology, 60*(3–4), 491–501. doi.org/10.1002/ajcp.12177

Campbell, R., & Morris, M. (2017b). The stories we tell: Introduction to the special issue on ethical challenges in community psychology research and practice. *American Journal of Community Psychology, 60*(3–4), 299–301. doi.org/10.1002/ajcp.12178

Ellison, E. R., & Langhout, R. (2017). Sensitive topics, missing data, and refusal in social network studies: An ethical examination. *American Journal of Community Psychology, 60*(3–4), 327–335. doi.org/10.1002/ajcp.12195

Fairweather, G. W. (1967). *Methods for experimental social innovation.* New York: John Wiley & Sons, Inc.

Fairweather, G. W., & Tornatzky, L. G. (1977). *Experimental methods for social policy research.* Oxford, UK: Pergamon Press.

Foulks, E. F. (1989). Misalliances in the Barrow Alcohol Study. *American Indian and Native Alaska Mental Health Research, 2*(3), 7–17. doi.org/10.5820/aian.0203.1989.7

García, M. A., Morse, G. S., Trimble, et al. (2017). Partnership with the people: Skillful navigation of culture and ethics. In S. L. Stewart, R. Moodley, & A. Hyatt (Eds.), *Indigenous cultures and mental health counseling: Four directions for integration with counselling psychology* (pp. 199–218). New York: Routledge.

García, M. A., & Tehee, M. (Eds.). (2014). *Society of Indian Psychologists commentary on the American Psychological Association's Ethical Principles of Psychologists and Code of Conduct*. www.aiansip.org.

Haarlammert, M., Birman, D., Oberoi, A., & Moore, W. J. (2017). Inside-out: Representational ethics and diverse communities. *American Journal of Community Psychology, 60*(3–4), 414–423. doi.org/10.1002/ajcp.12188

Hook, J. N., & Watkins, C.E., Jr. (2015). The cornerstone of positive contact with culturally different individuals and groups? *American Psychologist, 70*(7), 661–662. doi.org/10.1037/a0038965

Humphreys, L. (1970). *Tearoom trade: Impersonal sex in public places*. Chicago: Aldine Publishing Co.

Hutchinson, K. (Ed.). (2019). *Evaluation failures: 22 tales of mistakes made and lessons learned*. Thousand Oaks, CA: SAGE Publications.

Javdani, S., Singh, S., & Sichel, C. E. (2017). Negotiating ethical paradoxes in conducting a randomized controlled trial: Aligning intervention science with participatory values. *American Journal of Community Psychology, 60*(3–4), 439–449. doi.org/10.1002/ajcp.12185

Julian, D. A., Smith II, T., & Hunt, R. A. (2017). Ethical challenges inherent in the evaluation of an American Indian/Alaskan Native Circles of Care project. *American Journal of Community Psychology, 60*(3–4), 336–345. doi.org/10.1002/ajcp.12192

Kia-Keating, M., Santacrose, D., & Liu, S. (2017). Photography and social media use in community-based participatory research with youth: Ethical considerations. *American Journal of Community Psychology, 60*(3–4), 375–384. doi.org/10.1002/ajcp.12189

Kelly, J. (2002). The spirit of community psychology. *American Journal of Community Psychology, 30*(1), 43–63. doi.org/10.1023/A:1014368000641

Kesten, S. M., Perez, D. A., Marques, D. S., Evans, S. D., & Sulma, A. (2017). Fight, flight or remain silent? Juggling multiple accountabilities throughout the formative stage of a neighborhood revitalization initiative. *American Journal of Community Psychology, 60*(3–4), 450–458. doi.org/ 10.1002/ajcp.12191

Kloos, B., Hill, J., Thomas, E., et al. (2011). *Community psychology: Linking individuals and communities*. New York: Cengage Learning.

Madden, M., Lenhart, A., Cortesi, S., et al. (2013, May 21). *Teens, social media, and privacy*. Pew Research Center Internet & Technology Report. www.pewinternet.org/2013/05/21/teens-social-media-and-privacy/

Maton, K. (2000). Making a difference: The social ecology of social transformation. *American Journal of Community Psychology, 28*(1), 27–57. doi.org/10.1023/A:1005190312887

Maton, K. (2008). Empowering community settings: Agents of individual development, community betterment, and positive social change. *American Journal of Community Psychology, 41*(1), 4–21. doi.org/10.1007/s10464-007-9148-6

McDonald, K. E. (2012). "We want respect": Adults with intellectual and developmental disabilities address respect in research. *American Journal on Intellectual and Developmental Disabilities, 117*(4), 263–274. doi.org/10.1352/1944-7558-117.4.263

McDonald, K. E., & Keys, C. (2008). How the powerful decide: Access to research participation by those at the margins. *American Journal of Community Psychology, 42*(1–2), 79–93. doi.org/10.1007/s10464-008-9192-x

McDonald, K. E., Keys, C. B., & Balcazar, F. E. (2007). Disability, race ethnicity and gender: Themes of cultural oppression, acts of individual resistance. *American Journal of Community Psychology, 39*(1–2), 145–161. doi.org/10.1007/s10494-007-9094-3

McMillan, D. W., & Chavis, D. M. (1986). Sense of community: A definition and theory. *Journal of Community Psychology, 14*(1), 6–23. doi.org/10.1002/1520-6629(198601)14:1<6::AID-JCOP2290140103>3.0.CO;2-I

Milgram, S. (1963). Behavioral study of obedience. *Journal of Abnormal and Social Psychology, 67*(4), 371–378. doi.org/10.1037/h0040525

Montero, M., & Winkler, M. I. (2014). Iberian and Latin American ethics in community psychology: The contradiction between facts and academician's perception. *American Journal of Community Psychology, 42*(8), 997–1014. doi.org/10.1002/jcop.21667

Mose, G.B., & Gillum, T.L. (2015). Intimate partner violence in African immigrant communities in the United States: Reflections from the IDVAAC African women's roundtable on domestic violence. *Journal of Aggression, Maltreatment & Trauma, 25*(1), 1–13. DOI:10.1080/10926771.2016.1090517

Nelson, G., Prilleltensky, I., & MacGillivary, H. (2001). Building value-based partnerships: Toward solidarity with oppressed groups. *American Journal of Community Psychology, 29*(5), 649–677. doi.org/10.1023/A:1010406400101

O'Connor, P. A. (2007). Using system differences to orchestrate change: A systems-guides intervention model. *American Journal of Community Psychology, 39* (3–4), 393–403. doi.org/10.1007/s10464-007-9105-4

Padmavati, R. (2012). Community mental health services for the mentally ill: Practices and ethics. *International Review of Psychiatry, 24*(5), 504–510. doi.org/10.3109/09540261.2012.712953

Pike, K. (1967). *Language in relation to a unified theory of the structure of human behavior* (2nd ed.). The Hague, The Netherlands: Mouton.

Prilleltensky, I. (2001). Value-based praxis in community psychology: Moving toward social justice and social action. *American Journal of Community Psychology, 29*(5), 747–778. doi.org/10.1023/A:1010417201918

Prilleltensky, I. (2003). Understanding, resisting, and overcoming oppression: Toward psychopolitical validity. *American Journal of Community Psychology, 31*(1–2), 195–201. doi.org/10.1023/A:1023043108210

Privitera, G. J. (2016). *Research methods for the behavioral sciences* (2nd ed.). Thousand Oaks, CA: SAGE Publications.

Pullman, M. D., Ague, S., Johnson, T., et al. (2013). Defining engagement in adolescent substance abuse treatment. *American Journal of Community Psychology, 52*(3–4), 347–358. doi.org/10.1007/s10464-013-9600-8

Ramirez, M. (1998). *Multicultural/multiracial psychology: Mestizo perspectives in personality and mental health*. Lanham, MD: Rowman & Littlefield Publishers, Inc.

Rappaport, J. (1981). In praise of paradox: A social policy of empowerment over prevention. *American Journal of Community Psychology, 9*(1), 1–25. doi.org/10.1007/BF00896357

Santiago-Rivera, A. I., Morse, G. S., Hunt, A., & Lickers, H. (1998). Building a community-based research partnership: Lessons from the Mohawk Nation of Akwesasne. *Journal of Community Psychology, 26*(2), 163–174. doi.org/10 .1002/(SICI)1520-6629(199803)26:2<163::AID-JCOP5>3.0.CO;2-Y

Sarason, S. (2004). What we need to know about intervention and interventionists. *American Journal of Community Psychology, 33*(3–4), 275–277. doi.org/10 .1023/b:ajcp.0000027012.08088.df

Schwartz, S. E., Rhodes, J. E., Spencer, R., & Grossman, J. B. (2013). Youth initiated mentoring: Investigating a new approach to working with vulnerable adolescents. *American Journal of Community Psychology, 52*(1–2), 155–169. doi .org/10.1007/s10464-013-9585-3

Sonn, A., & Fisher, A. T. (2003). Identity and oppression: Differential responses to an in-between status. *American Journal of Community Psychology, 31*(1–2), 117–128. doi.org/10.1023/A:1023030805485

Substance Abuse and Mental Health Services Administration (SAMHSA). (2019). *Strategic prevention framework: Sustainability.* Retrieved February 27, 2019 from www.samhsa.gov/capt/applying-strategic-prevention-framework/ sustainability

Tervalon, M., & Murray-García, J. (1998). Cultural humility versus cultural competence: A critical distinction in defining physician training outcomes in multicultural education. *Journal of Health Care for the Poor and Underserved, 9*(2), 117–129. doi.org/10.1353/hpu.2010.0233

US Department of Health and Human Services. (1979). *The Belmont report.* Washington, DC: Office for Human Research Protections.

Zimbardo, P. G. (2009). Reflections on the Stanford Prison Experiment: Genesis, transformations, and consequences. In T. Blass (Ed.), *Obedience to authority: Current perspectives on the Milgram Paradigm* (pp. 193–237). Mahwah, NJ: Lawrence Erlbaum Associates.

5 Defining Wellness across World Cultures

Renato D. Alarcón

5.1 Introduction

The term "wellness" has gained prominence, conceptual value, and acceptance in a variety of health- and medical-related areas, only in relatively recent times. For decades before the twentieth century it was mostly used in family-based transactions or as an expression of formal socialization exchanges among community members (Kirkland, 2014). During the nineteenth century, wellness became a sort of symbolic, ultimate purpose of diverse modalities of what was later called alternative medicine, at times difficult to distinguish from what official medicine considered "pseudoscientific" health interventions (Upchurch & Rainisch, 2015; Zimmer, 2010).

As the world and its growing number of health implications rounded up notions of "comprehensiveness" and "thoroughness" as the main objectives of total and integral care, it was gradually considered a broader expression of "well-being," present in the World Health Organization's 1948 historical definition of health. The main emphasis of wellness was, then, provided by notions of full development and accomplishment of an individual's potential physical, mental, emotional, and social capabilities. When considered a nuclear component of specific programs, wellness is said to have nine dimensions: physical, environmental, financial, occupational, social, emotional, spiritual, intellectual, and sexual (Stoewen, 2017). Some authors (and countries like the USA) would add a distinctive legal connotation (Elliott, Bernstein, & Bowman, 2014).

Although not free of critical objections coming from traditional health-related quarters and professions, wellness is now accepted as a sought-for objective and culminating product of efficient care practices dispensed in a fair, adaptable set of procedures entailing "different types of justice" (i.e., distributive, procedural, relational, retributive, informational, and developmental) (Prilleltensky, 2012, p. 6). In fact, wellness entails, for many, an effective overall state of psychological stability surrounded by a variety of biosocial reflections (Beadling et al., 2012). For the purposes of this chapter, the role and relevance of culture and cultural factors will be systematically focused upon, culminating in the presentation of crucial distinctions in the definition, processing, and characteristics of wellness among the main societies and cultures across the world.

5.2 Basic Conceptual Implications

The variety of implications that the concept of wellness contains complicate its definition beyond what an initial approach may suggest. In addition to the concept of well-being and its implied overall description of pleasantness and stability, wellness is also closely associated with the now fashionable label *quality of life* (QoL), research about which is still scarce (Crocker, Smith, & Skevington, 2015). While wellness represents a general, almost overinclusive perspective, QoL strongly suggests a more specific appraisal in need of both subjective estimations and objective, measurable (therefore, also quantitative) data. QoL may have a multitude of smaller components and, in fact, has become a powerful indicator of integral health. It is important to clearly delineate these two fields of knowledge and research to avoid misleading synonymities and, rather, to reinforce useful complementarities.

Furthermore, and in a more traditional way, wellness implies the convergence of both physical and emotional health. Needless to say, the former may be considered by many as an essential component of the definition and content of wellness, perhaps its most obvious, visible, and provable evidence (Boller & Barba, 2006; Lieberman & Ogas, 2015). The numerous features or areas involved in descriptions of good physical health lead to clear, conclusive connections with wellness, but such connections would still be characterized as partial or compartmental.

Emotional health (also commonly called psychological, behavioral, or mental health), on the other hand, emerged later as a component of wellness, coming from a subjective, profoundly personal, unique, and almost unexchangeable perspective. In fact, the definition of emotional health and the assessment of its constituent experiences differ between individuals, communities, societies, and other sociocultural entities. For these reasons, the evaluation of wellness has in its emotional or psychological components the most individualized as well as the most varied and even heterogenous perspective of what it means to have a stable and positive way of life (Freeman, 1999; Golden, Berquist, & Coleman, 1978).

Last but not least, wellness also implies *social harmony* at both micro and macro levels. The former has to do with life in the family circle, the daily or frequent contact and interactions between the members of a family group facing and handling common experiences with either successful or painful outcomes. Such interactions encompass diverse mechanisms (analyses, reflections, explanations, consolations, ethical considerations, etc.) and, ultimately, the sharing of satisfactions, relief, and forward-looking plans and purposes – wellness at its most meaningful dynamics (Gheondea-Eladi, 2017).

The macro-level scenario of wellness refers to the community contacts or factors having to do with the individual's surrounding society (Dahrendorf, 1959). The perception of such factors and of their impact on the everyday life of the population will result – if positive and favorable – in a collective sense of an "accomplished mission" or the most genuine experience of true and productive solidarity. On the contrary, if the results are negative or below expectations, the social harmony component of wellness will serve as a pillar of recovery or a reminding testimony of hope.

Many students of the ontology of wellness would also agree on placing the concept inside the broad field of *public health*, not only as an objective of a variety of principles, practices, and efforts but also as a powerful mechanism in pursuit of a solid, sustainable collective well-being. This would then culminate in the elaboration of norms and laws linking health aspirations and expectations with concrete and evident achievements regarding the patients' whole health (Hinchliffe et al., 2018; Sinkfield-Morey, 2018).

5.3 The Role of Culture and Its Components

All of the above-described conceptual pieces of wellness, health-based and socially related as they are, can be also strongly associated with the various components of what is known as culture (Asad & Kay, 2015; Tseng, 2001). However, there are more, perhaps subtler yet undeniably relevant and equally interactive cultural components: religious/spiritual, teleological, and ethical. The first is a primary element of the feeling of totality and thoroughness that wellness possesses, and the integration between physical and spiritual stability (with tranquility or serenity as synonyms) has been described in multiple ways (Berlinger & Berlinger, 2017). Traditions, beliefs, religious practices, rituals, venerations, and texts (many times called "sacred") shape up notions of health among individuals and groups across the world; nevertheless, these cultural sets differ significantly among societies or cultures established in diverse world regions. The definition and actual experience of wellness respond, sometimes dramatically, to the religious texture of specific individuals and communities.

Closely related to religious and spiritual factors, the teleological component of wellness has to do with the possession and cultivation of values, principles, and norms of significant behavioral impact despite their various levels of strength. Values inspire tolerance or rejection, acceptance or indifference vis-à-vis individual or collective wellness: Breaking or moving away from them destabilizes the nature of wellness as a truly genuine way of living with and among others (Baumeister, 1986). Finally, ethical or moral precepts provide wellness with a unique dimension, a powerful defining summary of the concept and its practice (Bhugra, 2014; Gheondea-Eladi, 2017).

In effect, a healthy interaction of all the above elements leads to integral wellness, the essential objective of social, mental, and public health actions. Regrettably, the opposite can also potentially occur. Deficits or "defects" in family life, deficient conveyance of beliefs, values, or religious notions, inconsistent or misleading educational efforts, and ethically diminished practices are all detrimental factors in the wellness-making processes and the actual wellness experience (Napier et al., 2014). Such conflicting outcomes become eloquent representations of social, cultural, or political failures in the lives of individuals and communities.

The presence of cultural factors in the nature and actual experience of wellness demonstrates the role of culture as an active engine of individual and social behaviors; to use a graphic metaphor, the "anatomy" of wellness is the recognized collection of its bio-psycho-social components, whereas its "physiology" is determined precisely by the active, dynamic nature of culture and cultural factors in the everyday life of individuals and societies. Such influence takes place (and materializes) with specific ingredients in each step of the life cycle, hopefully contributing to a healthy personal development. Family life is the most typical setting of early cultural interactions leading to the delineation of identity through the utilization and enhancement of language resources, the active (and passive) transmission of traditions and beliefs, of history and stories, of social relations and their existential script levels of expressiveness and spontaneity (Bhugra, 2014; Brislin, 2000; Napier et al., 2014).

5.4 Wellness across World Cultures

The following sections of this chapter attempt to review the different versions, components, creations, and outcomes of wellness in the various world regions or continents examined from both geographical and historical perspectives. They will describe the main features of wellness in such regions and examine current experiences of wellness in the field and its impact on people and society. The main obstacles, deficiencies, and needs related to these issues will also be assessed. There is agreement in considering Africa as perhaps the oldest continent, the one where the human race probably emerged from. For its part, Asia was probably the crib of the first organized cultures, from original tribal groups to sophisticated civilizations engendered by and through military and commercial enterprises. Europe then became the "center of civilization" (through explorations, discoveries, conquests, and colonization) with also a variety of subregional compartments. Finally, America, the "New Continent," emerged with its different geographic, ethnic, and language-based segments. Populations or human groups in Australia/New Zealand will also be mentioned.

5.4.1 Africa

The history of Africa makes the continent a vivid example of humanity's stormy journey through the times. Students of this journey have focused mostly on the subjugation of its original inhabitants at the hands of European conquerors that combined adventurous boldness with cruel exploitation and exterminating practices to decimate communities and give birth to the different versions of slavery. Health care of African-born people was not exactly a priority in this process, and their wellness was left up to their centuries-old ideas, and in the hands of their original shamans aided by a few pious Westerners accompanying the invading armies.

There may only be a mild objection to the notion that spirituality is perhaps the strongest component of the notion of wellness in most African countries, even deeper than the formalized religious fervor of the European colonizers. The opening phrase of an article by Mayer and Viviers (2014, p. 265) ("I still believe …") eloquently summarizes this process: Located in South Africa, the narrative reflects "a strong intrapersonal interlinkage of spirituality, culture and mental health" and their impact on personal self-construction and social relationships, a process that repeated itself in subregions and countries that experienced their own versions of apartheid. These notions were certainly born out of mythic legends but could also be practically applied to the everyday life of individuals, families, and communities throughout the continent, whose geography imposed a scenario both majestic and intimidating, mysterious and unpredictable. This context accentuated the coherence of relatively small tribes and groups, but also the separation and differences with many others throughout the jungle, the deserts, and the coastal areas.

An interesting example of these heterogeneous realities is provided by Hill et al.'s (2014) report on the pluralistic maternal and neonatal health care in rural northern Ghana, provided by traditional and "allopathic" (Western-trained) caretakers. From a series of in-depth interviews the researchers extracted three overarching themes: different levels of awareness and information about cultural beliefs and practices; different resulting frameworks for the understanding of health and disease, remedies, and overall management; and, yet, agreement about the need to educate patients and their families to allow a better, more comprehensive care. Thus, wellness in African communities requires an integrated cultural education of the allopathic, non-native providers or healers.

On the basis of such integration, African countries may be the most appropriate settings for the implementation of wellness programs in the health workplace, as experiences in Botswana demonstrate (Ledikwe et al., 2017). According to Ledikwe and colleagues (2017), aspects "such as health screening, therapeutic recreation, and health promotion through observation of various commemorations tended to be implemented more frequently than activities related to occupational health and safety as well as psychosocial services" (p. 872), but "administrative support" and "integration of… activities" into organizational culture effectively contributed to ensure the well-being of many healthcare workers (p. 872).

5.4.2 Asia

By far the largest and probably the most complex continent in the world, Asia has been divided throughout history in a variety of subregions, many times due to the predominance of political actors and diverging ideologies. It includes China and its dominating presence in the Far East, although India on one side and Russia on the other also claim Asian heritage, in addition to Japan and North and South Korea. The Middle East (Israel, Saudi Arabia, Turkey, Syria, Iran, Iraq, Afghanistan and other countries, including Egypt in the northernmost, Asia-bordering area of Africa) is not only a scenario of active political and military turbulence but also a natural bridge toward Europe.

Religion or, better, a variety of religions play a significant role in the everyday life of most of these countries, presiding governmental structures, provoking confrontations, and promoting pervasive, often rigid, beliefs, traditions, habits, and customs. It is also clear that countries like China, North Korea, or Russia do not have an officially sanctioned religion or church practice but either passively accept its presence in large population sectors, or the government's ideology operates within religious-like normative rules.

Thus, the nature and the impact of religion in Africa and Asia present different characteristics when wellness is considered. To be sure, there are countries like Japan, India, Egypt, or Jordan where the religious/spiritual component of wellness is significantly relevant in treatment and recovery processes, sometimes experienced as "faith journeys" (Eltaiba & Harries, 2015) at individual, family, and community levels, independent of governmental participation. There are others, like Saudi Arabia, Iran, or Israel, in which religion and politics are actively mixed in the manifestations of the collective life and, finally, a third group of countries like Turkey, that proclaim a "separation of powers" as an operative independence between religion and politics but may strongly invoke the latter when certain circumstances occur. To be sure, these three perspectives maintain wellness as an emblematic component of their existence.

Assessing health literacy (including nonhealth-related items) is considered critical in Eastern and Middle Eastern populations given the influence of the "social desirability" factor (Nair et al., 2016). Methodologically, most health-related research in Asian countries seems to overlook the heterogeneity within their populations, according to Maty et al. (2011) in a study that describes "associations between general health status and several sociodemographic and health-related factors in pooled and ethnic group-stratified samples" (Maty et al., 2011, p. 555). The psychological and health effects of social class (translated into social stratification) reflect culturally divergent manifestations in Asian cultures where individuals of high social class, unlike their counterparts in Western cultures, tend to show high conformity and other-oriented psychological attributes (Miyamoto, 2017). Furthermore, using a culture-centered approach as a theoretical lens of communication scholarship has enhanced the meanings of health and wellness in many Asian countries: such is the case of biomedical services offered within the larger philosophical understandings of Buddhism in the practices favored by the Tzu Chi Foundation. This perspective cultivates nonbiomedical meanings of health (i.e., wellness) through selfless giving and assistance, simultaneously seeking "purity of the mind, body and soul holistically" (Dillard, Dutta, & Sun, 2014, p. 147) and, thus, broadening the outreach of healthcare delivery "from the narrow focus on curing to the complexly intertwined spaces of health, illness, healing and curing" (Dillard et al., 2014, p. 151). In a more specific context, the same applies to the integrated interventional modality of Kumu Hula-based cardio-vascular disease prevention and management programs in the Hawaiian islands (Look et al., 2014).

According to Bian, Lui, and Li (2015), the essentials of Chinese medicine include promoting "health wellness" instead of disease management, largely preceding modern P4 (personalized, predictive, preventive, and participa-tory/precision) Western medicine. Comparative studies on issues such as geographic features, history, culture of health-seeking behaviors, insurance, and interprofessional relationships assess the overall healthcare environment and its impact on a variety of health professions (Lu, Tung, & Ely, 2016) and healthcare-related outcomes in China and other Asian countries (Jia et al., 2017). In turn, concerns over environmental pollution have enriched the so-called therapeutic landscape theory nourishing notions such as longevity culture and its representation by the town of Bama, the "longevity village," now a preferred target of "wellness tourism" in China (Huang & Xu, 2018): Natural environment, social interaction and symbolic landscape work together in the healing process, longevity symbolizing the alignment of a strong body, a graceful mind, and a pleasant habitat.

In India, traditional medicine branches such as Ayurveda, Siddha, or Unani have, since ancient days, used a large variety of plants with defined pharma-cological effects, adding a natural component to a rich wellness-oriented therapeutic arsenal. Lohiya, Balasubramanian, and Ansari (2016) describe how various tribal populations across the subcontinent apply these plants to treatment of chronic conditions and to a basic component of wellness in men: reproductive health issues such as infertility, contraception, libido, sexually transmitted infections, and even cancerous processes. In a truly eclectic approach, Snodgrass, Lacy, and Upadhyay (2017) present another original Indian contribution to emotional wellness: The development of culturally sensitive scales to local clinical populations neither imposing Western noso-logical categories nor adopting native categories of mental distress. "By sharing traits of both global and locally-derived diagnoses," write the authors, "approaches like ours can help to identify synergies between them" (p. 174); in other words, the assessment of emotional frailties and of potential sources of resilience and balance can "minimize stigma and increase the acceptability and validity of assessment instruments" (p. 175).

In a similar manner, a culture-centered approach finds common ground in surveys conducted in West Bengal's and Bangladesh's rural areas (Dutta & Basu, 2008; Jamil & Dutta, 2012): When resources are limited, the population acknowledges the importance of trust in the relationship with the local provider; health is seen as a collective resource, both an asset and a responsibility of the community. Furthermore, community members negotiate health in terms of poverty, work, and structure, and attempt to solve marginalization through communicative practices and the explorations of "spaces of change." The universal meaning of principles of health and wellness are well reflected here, as they expand to co-constructed experiences of health among Bangladesh immigrants into the USA (Dutta & Jamil, 2013), experiences that constitute a "point of entry" for the potential understanding and integration of migration and healthcare issues.

Saudi Arabia and the Persian Gulf countries present a somewhat unique phenomenon with regards to the provision of health care and its impact on the well-being of the general population. With a majority of their healthcare forces coming from non-Arab countries (e.g., the Philippines), the lack of cultural competence and knowledge about language on the side of non-Muslim health workers constitutes a barrier for the provision of quality care (Almutairi, 2015).

The impact of psychosocial job characteristics, particularly job autonomy, on health and wellness status is definitely important in Western economies. That is not the case among Thailand-born working adults in England, however (Yiengprugsawan et al., 2015), a finding that could reflect the cultural feature of Thais being less troubled by individualistic expressions at work, although job security, job demands, and employer support were shared characteristics, and public health strategies would certainly promote mental health and well-being in both populations. On the other hand, the role of social hierarchy, strongly linked to socioeconomic status (SES), seems to be gaining ground in Asian societies due to their increasing connection with Western countries. Contrary to the latter, however, Asian countries like Japan and other Confucian cultures show higher SES associated with greater other-orientation, whereas in the USA, the same feature is linked to a greater self-orientation (Miyamoto et al., 2018). In another study not focused on religious traits (Balkir, Arens, & Barnow, 2013), healthy Turkish women exhibited relatedness-satisfaction as a better predictor of mental health, whereas autonomy-satisfaction did the same among healthy German women; interestingly, such distinction disappeared among depressed women from both countries.

Culturally appropriate wellness initiatives aimed at improving health behaviors and promoting their sustainability have been effective in programs implemented in a Jewish school system in Chicago. A report by Benjamins and Whitman (2010) makes clear also their effective applicability in Israel (and perhaps in other Middle Eastern countries) through the initial results of a two-year comparative pilot study implemented by a Wellness Council charged with the elaboration and application of policy changes or activities in five target areas: health education, physical education, school environment, family involvement, and staff wellness.

5.4.3 Europe

Mental health and psychiatry, as well as related areas including health culture and wellness, could be assessed in Europe from up to three distinctive perspectives: Continental Europe, subgrouped in turn as Western and Eastern; Anglo-Saxon Europe (mostly England and the British Isles); and Scandinavian or Northern countries. For this chapter's purposes, however, differences will only be pointed out when strictly necessary while similarities and their global message will be emphasized. Europe can certainly be considered the repository of many converging cultures and, on the basis of historical realities, demonstrates the most pluralistic expression of approaches and styles regarding our central topic.

Historically, Continental and Anglo-Saxon (British Isles plus Ireland, Scotland, and Wales) Europe grew up side by side, going overseas and conquering different parts of the world while carefully watching each other, and maintaining an artificial atmosphere of peace until wars became inevitable. In Continental Europe, Germany (with its different names throughout the centuries) and France took the lead (Spain and Italy as well, but the former mostly oriented toward the newly discovered America, and both with the objective of restrengthening Catholicism as the universal religion) and made wellness a seemingly harmonious integration of art, spirituality, wisdom, and an early existentialist component of its powerful Renaissance. For its part, England, the British Isles, or the United Kingdom, combined a nearly invincible military and Navy power full of pragmatic foci with similarly practical, instrumental efforts aimed at research and discoveries in health and related fields. They constituted the essence of wellness, defined then as the full accomplishment of comfortableness, safety, and happiness. Last but not least, the Scandinavian countries ascribed physical health and resilience to their also practical notions of disciplined work, team approaches, and safety as the main ingredients of wellness.

On the basis of the strong role of religion in the construction of wellness in Africa and Asia, it is appropriate to wonder about it in the European continent. Such was the purpose of a study by Nicholson et al. (Nicholson, Rose, & Bobak, 2009) about the association between attendance at religious services and self-reported health in 18,328 men and 21,373 women from twenty-two European countries. The study findings indicated that men who never attended religious services were almost twice as likely to describe their health as poor with a similar but weaker effect seen in women. The relationships were stronger in people with long-standing illness, less than university education, and in more affluent countries with lower levels of corruption and higher levels of religious belief. Two reviews by VanderWeele (2017a, 2017b) commenting mostly on a study by Ahrenfeldt et al. (2017) that correlated "resting" and "crisis" religiousness with good and poor health, respectively, appear to confirm that religious community also constitutes a major pathway to human well-being in Europe.

From another perspective, the role of national European cultures in influencing citizens' attitudes toward their health systems was the subject of a massive survey of more than forty thousand respondents from twenty-one countries (Borisova et al., 2017): "Being female, having low or medium education, experiencing financial strain, and reporting poor health and unmet medical needs were negatively associated with individual satisfaction with national healthcare systems" (Borisova et al., 2017, p. 132); this negative evaluation was more likely to occur in "national cultures associated with autocracy and hierarchy" (i.e., mostly Central and Eastern Europe countries; Borisova et al., 2017, p. 132).

A variety of additional issues emerge from works focused on specific countries. From the use of organizational culture concepts in Cyprus, to understand behaviors of individuals and organizations facing external demands and internal social changes while reformulating its healthcare system (Zachariadou, Zannetos, & Pavlakis, 2013), to the assumptions about culture in documents related to ethnic minority health in Denmark (Jaeger, 2013), wellness becomes a complex, multi-faceted expression of collective efforts. Crucial among them is the training of health professionals and the establishment of professional cultures and subcultures with potential implications for patient safety. The case of Sweden in this regard is eloquently exposed by Danielsson et al. (2018): The "competent physician" is expected to be infallible and responsible, while the "integrated yet independent physician" may face organizational barriers and multiple, sometimes contradictory expectations. Collaborative initiatives in Malta (Bonello, Morris, & Azzopardi Muscat, 2018) and the role of culture in their implementation also confront multiple barriers to principles of interprofessional education and the transfer of didactic and practice innovations.

Another study that explored the understanding of wellness by Black ethnic minority individuals (African and Caribbean) at risk of developing psychosis in the UK (Codjoe et al., 2013) identified six insightful explanations for the concept: a sense of social purpose, a test of a surviving God, internalization of spirituality, attribution of symptoms to witchcraft, avoidance and adversity, and search of help to cope.

5.4.4 America

The "New Continent" formally entered onto the world's scene with Columbus' "discovery" in 1492, but obviously existed for centuries before then, as the testimonies of many cultures demonstrate (De Ventos, 1987). With two great empires (Aztec and Inca) present at the time of the Europeans' (Spaniards') arrival in what are now Mexican and Andean territories, respectively, history registers previous civilizations like the Mayan settled in Central America and the Gulf of Mexico, and several pre-Inca cultures mostly in the currently Peruvian land. This subsection will describe wellness between those periods and contemporary times in North

America (the USA and Canada), Mexico/Central America, South America, and the Caribbean subregion.

It is a well-known fact that the large North American territory was inhabited by numerous native or indigenous tribes whose interactions, when present, were mostly through wars, nomadic mobility, and local conflicts. For about three centuries, these human groups were either tolerated or persecuted by the British forces first, and the new American government and its Army, later. Cornered by the superior military forces, Native Americans, rhetorically named the First Nation, were allowed to live in so-called Indian reservations, mostly located in the North-Midwestern and Central zones of the North American continent, following the "Big March" that killed thousands (American Heritage, 1985).

Relatively little is recorded about the healthcare and wellness practices of these groups except, once again, the dominant religious, ritualistic infra-structure and the rightful use of medicinal plants. A telling example is the Diné (Navajo) *hózhó* wellness philosophy, a belief system that combines "living in health, harmony and beauty" (Kahn-John Diné & Koithan, 2015) and entails an integrative approach. This cultural approach to wellness wisdom offers means to improve whole-person/whole-system well-being, providing an effective, culturally adapted, patient-centered care based on authentic human links. The Diné philosophy is offered as a durable legacy to other American Indian/Alaska native nations, global indigenous cultures, and even nonindigenous peoples across the world. This type of pronounce-ment, emphasizing the benefits of traditional holistic healing, can enhance the sense of community ownership, empowerment, self-determination, acceptance, reciprocal accountability, and participation of today's North American indigenous groups in healthcare decisions (Anderson & Hansson, 2016; Auger, Howell, & Gomes, 2016; Boksa, Joober, & Kirmayer, 2015; Snowshoe et al., 2017).

During colonial times and even through the first periods of the life of the United States as an independent country (Canada became independent from the UK in 1867 but remained as a Commonwealth member, and only "patriated" its Constitution and eliminated the word "Dominion" in 1982), North America followed the models of the European power in terms of philosophy and practice of health care and wellness. A complex immigration process, mostly from English-speaking countries but also, gradually, from many others, contributed significantly to what became "the land of opportun-ity" and "the continent of hope" (American Heritage, 1985; Marías, 1986). In such a context, creativity and tenacity combined with openness, constructive critical assessments, systematic dialogues, and solid thinking consistently paved the way toward North America's advances, not only in the acquisition and dissemination of original knowledge and research, but also in the process of building a genuine culture of health through models, associated metrics, partnerships, and extensive communications to address underlying inequities, affirm life conditions, and improve social cohesion: a modern vision of wellness (Trujillo & Plough, 2016).

Hence, wellness, according to North American parameters, is the result of applying research findings, technological resources, coherent administrative norms, and practical procedures to a receptive, cooperative community of patients, fully aware of their rights, protective of their dignity, and respectful of well-established professional approaches. As said previously, this perspective has been historically nourished by the existential, genuinely humanistic philosophy from Continental Europe, and by the pragmatic, precise, and disciplined Anglo-Saxon legacy. It absorbs three pairs of dialectical tensions (autonomy vs. connection, private vs. public, and control vs. lack of control) (Tang, Bajer, & Meadows, 2016). An equally relevant component is the promotion of health services integration aimed at improving quality and efficiency in a safety net that bridges cultural differences (Ko, Murphy, & Bindman, 2015).

A variety of human actors in this wellness scenario convey different sets of realities and expectations. Beginning with training programs, a beneficial cultural change must include positive educational environments for residents and faculty, raising awareness of, for instance, burnout and its symptoms, decreasing concurrent stigmas, and enabling prevention strategies (Eckleberry-Hunt et al., 2009). A comparison of mental health, quality of life, empathy, and burnout between American and Brazilian medical students revealed that the latter experienced more depression and stress, while US students reported greater wellness and environmental quality of life, and less exhaustion and depression; also US students were older, had smaller class sizes, earlier patient encounters, and more problem-based learning and psychological support (Lucchetti et al., 2018).

A positive, strength-based approach to understanding the toll of an occasionally overwhelming practice by current and future health professionals is justified. Similarly, at the college campus educational stage, a substantial wellness approach must consider the fact that a majority of college students do not seek healthcare help. Perceived campus culture plays an important role in personal mental health treatment beliefs, so campus mental health policies and prevention programming must consider targeting such campus culture to foster positive mental health (Chen, Romero, & Karver, 2016). Even in psychiatric hospitals, experiences with peer-run wellness centers reinforce a more recovery-oriented inpatient culture (Reinhardt-Wood, Kinter, & Burke, 2018).

As host countries for immigrants of many origins, and land of birth for subsequent generations, the topic of wellness in North America shows a unique trait: The mixing of numerous ethnicities throughout centuries. In the United States, the African American community is the oldest and, currently, second-largest minority. A suggestive review by Swierad, Vartanian, and King (2017) concluded that African Americans position both their own ethnic and the mainstream (White majority) culture as important influences on their health behaviors, particularly those pertaining to food intake and physical activity with practical considerations such as affordability and social support. Community-based organizations advance the understanding of a culture of engagement by marginalized populations, according to Bloemraad and Terriquez (2016). Going beyond attention to social networks and identities, these organizations empower civic capacities and personal efficacy of minority group members, foster solidarity, and enhance their voice in health-related policies and programming. Results of clinical effectiveness of culturally tailored wellness programs among African American depressed patients have also been reported (Nicolaidis, McKeever, & Meucci, 2013).

Similar findings have taken place among Asian American, Native American and Canadian, and Latino subpopulations (Barker, Goodman, & DeBeck, 2017; Campos & Kim, 2017; Park et al., 2011). Wellness, culture, and cultural intervention practices, explored from an indigenous perspective with adapted evaluative and therapeutic instruments, demonstrated that culture and culturally focused health promotion interventions had a positive impact on a variety of clinical conditions including alcohol use, abstinence, self-efficacy, depression, and low self-esteem (Fiedeldey-Van Dijk et al., 2017; Gray et al., 2010; Hodge, Limb, & Cross, 2009). By the same token, outreach interventions, contextualized by interpretation and transformation of qualitative data according to characteristics and perspectives of Latino communities (i.e., gender relations and religious affiliations and experiences), show positive outcomes (Erwin et al., 2010). Latinos in the USA (currently the largest minority group) show a significant association between high behavioral *familismo* and increased odds of using informal or religious services but not specialty or medical services; self- and socially perceived (by family members and friends) needs for care were also significant predictors of service use (Stacciarini et al., 2011; Villatoro, Morales, & Mays, 2014). The same feature, the vitality of social and natural connections that emphasize the importance of a traditional lifestyle, plays a critical role in the promotion of optimal health among Alaska Eskimo natives (Wolsko et al., 2006). That is why national dialogues among stakeholders about content and investments to improve population health and wellness are being promoted in different parts of the world, in order to establish a paradigmatic culture of health (Acosta et al., 2017).

Latin America, extended from Mexico to Patagonia and including for practical purposes a number of Caribbean countries, exhibits a rich tradition of wellness evidenced by the history and accomplishments of its main pre-Columbian cultures. Mayan, Aztec, pre-Inca, and Inca cultures embraced wellness through a strong religious approach, a mix of magic, idolatrous, and divine/polytheistic conceptions supported by authoritarian political/military regimes that, nevertheless, paid due attention to spiritual and social harmony, collective progress, and moral principles (Alvear Acevedo, 2000;

Lastres, 1951). The three main moral precepts of the Inca Empire were "Do not lie," "Do not steal" and "Do not be lazy." The shamans or *curanderos* and the wisemen (*Huetlatoani* in Mexico, *Amautas* in Peru) were part of privileged layers in these societies; the use of medicinal plants and persuasive collective ceremonies (including human sacrifices) sustained a healthy population and a productive economy. The arrival of the European *conquistadores* (Spanish and Portuguese, the latter exclusively in the territory that is today's Brazil) did profoundly affect the bases of these political entities, fostering a sense of failure, decadence, and existential confusion. The ulterior exploitation, abuse, and near-slavery conditions of agricultural and mining work in colonial times reduced wellness to a set of nostalgic memories somehow saved in pieces of art, tools, or rustic documents (Vargas Llosa, 2005).

The Independence Wars in Mexico and South America took place during the 1800s, after three centuries of colonial administrations whose religious practices played an important role in health and wellness. Actually, the first schools of medicine in the subcontinent were founded in the sixteenth century in Lima, Santo Domingo, and Mexico. The growing *creole* population (generations of descendants from the Spanish conquerors) occupied the highest portion of the social hierarchy enjoying the wellness of the time, whereas heirs of the subjugated Aztecs or Incas were mostly used as cheap workers. Wellness for the latter became a question of survival from malnourishment, epidemics, poverty, and deprivations. It may not be an exaggeration to say that wellness then turned out to be a political label, a piece of demagoguery, or an anti-cultural assault, particularly for Latin American natives and women (Alarcón, 2003).

The new nations allowed a gradual arrival of new scientific findings and clinical information, mostly from Europe and, with them, a subsequently more consistent conception of wellness. To be sure, traditional values such as religious support and family-based solidarity still occupy preferential levels in the new definitions, but other considerations have been added and gained ground. This is probably due to political uncertainties, for instance, social instability and a massive rejection of realities such as violence, poverty, corruption, and abuse are relevant factors in the process of building a safety culture as part of a new, well-targeted wellness (Lawati et al., 2018; Mitchell, Steeves, & Dillingham, 2015). Challenges for the implementation of this and other measures include leadership education, additional resources, and work on hierarchical relationships; further assessments of clinical outcomes and organizational performance would permit the establishment of this philosophy in a variety of health areas in Latin American and other Low and Middle Income Countries (LMICs) across the world (Castro, Barrera, & Holleran Steiker, 2010; Cunningham & Jacobson, 2018; Rice et al., 2018; World Health Organization, 2017).

In Caribbean countries, a good example of wellness and its tribulations is given by Wagenaar et al. (2013) in a study that examined patterns, determinants, and costs of care-seeking for mild to moderate mental health problems in rural Haiti. One-third of 408 adults surveyed in the country's Central Plateau endorsed God as their first choice for care if suffering from mental distress, and a close 29% endorsed clinics and hospitals; almost half of the respondents chose potential providers on the basis of anticipated efficacy, and for different clinical situations (suicide included) three out of four rural Haitians would prefer community-based providers (herbal healer, church priest or pastor or vodou priest) even though they charged much more than hospitals or clinics. The authors rightly conclude that isolated clinical interventions may have limited impact because of less frequent use, born out of a culturally acquired, and prevalent, notion of wellness and its maintenance.

5.4.5 Australia and New Zealand

The Anglo-Saxon connection of these territories does not discard the strong indigenous heritage from large tribal groups prior to the arrival of the British First Fleet by the end of the eighteenth century. A solid example of this is the concept of health and the practice of health care held by the Maori aboriginal group. Maori methodologies and knowledge are based on principles such as respect for people, cautiousness, and the ability to "look, listen and speak" (Hopkirk & Wilson, 2014, p. 158). In turn, key concepts held by Maori therapists include spirituality, holistic views, client-responsive practice, and favorable environmental contexts emphasizing the importance of the individual within the extended family.

5.5 Discussion: Wellness and the Culture of Health

The semantics of wellness is undoubtedly the first point that needs to be solved when attempting to discuss the meaning of this term across cultures. The risk of such an attempt is a conceptual collision about the priority of its components, so consensus must be sought through careful choices. The first agreement would certainly reside in the acceptance of health as the vertebral column of wellness. Yet, it would not just be health alone, but what has come to be known nowadays as integral health, a total, thorough, complete health. Following the route of the World Health Organization's definition of health initiated near the mid-twentieth century, it is to be reiterated that health is not only "the absence of disease" but a comprehensive sense of well-being that initially was labeled as "bio-psycho-social," with "cultural" being added years later and, finally, "spiritual": Health is a state of bio-psycho-socio-cultural-spiritual well-being, the closest and eventually more acceptable, comprehensive explanation of wellness (Alarcón et al., 1999; Guerrero & León, 2008).

There are more terminological reflections. As the realities of globalization became the challenge they are today, the World Health Organization, again, proclaimed, after decades of hesitating delays, that "There is no health without mental health," thus rescuing the precious combination of psycho-socio-emotional facts and experiences that constitute our mental well-being (it must be noticed that "bio" is not included, because conventionally it belongs to an organ – the brain – and to a system, that of the central nervous system, mostly in charge of physiological, regulatory, and cognitive tasks). And, at a time when biological, neurophysiological research in psychiatry, assisted by unstoppable-looking technological advances, seems to govern all areas of health-related investigations, the world has also seen the solid, persuasive reemergence of cultural and social inquiries, investigations, and, above all, the vindication of human and humanistic considerations in the articulation of a genuine wellness (Montiel, 2000; Swartz et al., 2014). That is why this author would suggest that another phrase must be coined: "There is no mental health without culture and cultural facts."

A crucial point in the assessment of wellness across cultures is that a culture of health (CoH) must be clearly articulated as its main support (Kagawa-Singer, Dressler, & George, 2016; Plough, 2014; Weil, 2016) and as an expression of the human rights movement (Mariner & Annas, 2016) applied to health. Not to be confused with "caring cultures" resulting from compassion- and solidarity-inspired approaches (Gillin, Taylor, & Walker, 2017), the CoH concepts have, in fact, grown exponentially in recent years to the point of being considered an imperative for a multitude of areas having to do with wellness: workforce engagement, patient experience, social interactions, and even financial transactions or value-based purchasing (Gage-Bouchard, 2017; Kagawa-Singer, 2011; Owens et al., 2017); in spite of difficulties in the plausibility of some of its pathways (Hruschka, 2009), CoH can be applied to all areas covered by wellness and, definitely, impacts social processes, teaching/training programs, clinical outcomes, cross-sector collaborations, behavioral economics, and legal initiatives (Daskivich et al., 2015; Flynn et al., 2018; Martsolf et al., 2018; Melnyk et al., 2016; Milner, Bradley, & Lampley, 2018; Volpp & Asch, 2017). Furthermore, it provides wellness with psychometric measurement options at different stages (Lin & Lin, 2014; Melnyk, Szalacha, & Amaya, 2018; Rafferty et al., 2017) through instruments that gauge the attributes of care culture perceived by staff, organizational agencies, patients, and communities.

The field of education for health professions is also essential for a successful development of wellness (McClafferty et al., 2014; Walsh, 2016). It is, indeed, the classical setting in which the contemporary learning health systems require the bridging of two "cultures": health data sciences or bioinformatics and effective healthcare system design and implementation (clinical informatics or digital health) (Scott et al., 2018). In 2017, the Resident Wellness Consensus Summit developed a longitudinal curriculum to address wellness and burnout following an evidence-based research covering self-care, physician suicide and self-help, and clinical-care series (Arnold et al., 2018; Place & Talen, 2013); bullying has fostered a dangerous "culture of silence" in many healthcare workplaces (Fink-Samnick, 2018). Facilitators, barriers, potential best practices, and lessons learned should all lead to wellness-oriented processes based on equity, cultural adaptations, ongoing multi-inputs, adequate incentives, correction of structural inequalities, transformational leadership, and institutionalization of health promotion efforts (Aarons et al., 2017; Beckett et al., 2013; Laurie et al., 2018).

While universal in its presence and value, wellness represents a prominent objective for public policies and even sociopolitical stability in LMICs (Mbau & Gilson, 2018). The challenges of poverty, violence, or corruption have been mentioned. Stigma is one of the biggest obstacles in many clinical/mental health segments of the wellness route (de Figueiredo & Gostoli, 2013; Yang et al., 2013, 2014), but also affects areas in which the use of culturally induced stereotypes accentuate disadvantages, such as aging (Hess et al., 2017; Löckenhoff et al., 2009), discrimination, and racism (Viruell-Fuentes, Miranda, & Abdulrahim, 2012). The latter becomes part of the emotional and behavioral repertoire of immigrants on whom multiple dimensions of inequality intersect in the context of a "dual culture" to have an impact on wellness and health outcomes (Connell, 2014).

A strong research culture in health services can be the optimal resource to a better wellness not only through interventions addressing the needs of the communities and the health workforce that serves them (Harding et al., 2017), but also in areas such as historical context, practice changes (Al-Bannay et al., 2014; Kagawa-Singer, 2012) and health promotion (Lakeman, 2013). A multidisciplinary approach would be a powerful means oriented to respect and preserve the dignity of the populations being served (Vrzina, 2011). At individual and group levels, wellness research also must address features of particular impact in the handling of adversities (e.g., resilience, emotional intelligence, solidarity, or creativity).

5.6 Conclusion

Wellness is, quite probably, the health field with the broadest implications in contemporary times. As it reflects a variety of concurrent factors to reach its place in the life of human beings, its study, research foci, achievements, and challenges occupy the attention of many disciplines. Yet, at the center of such views, a cultural approach operates as the integrating factor of wellness and, as such, its impact is being strongly assessed from many perspectives. Culture penetrates the definitions, concepts, status, quality, operationalization, performance, and results of the many facets of health and health care, pillars of a strong wellness. Cultural variables reinforce comprehensive approaches to wellness and contribute to its commonalities and distinctions in all regions of the world and in all societies and communities along time and history. The main task of those dedicated to this field of health studies and knowledge is to identify theoretical principles and practical applications that will allow and strengthen advances in universal wellness while also adapting it to the respective cultural contexts.

References

Aarons, G. A., Ehrhart, M. G., Farahnak, L. R., Sklar, M., & Horowitz, J. (2017). Discrepancies in Leader and Follower ratings of Transformational Leadership: Relationship with organizational culture in mental health. *Administration and Policy in Mental Health and Mental Health Services Research, 44*(4), 480–491. doi.org/10.1007/s10488-015-0672-7

Acosta, J. D., Whitley, M. D., May, L. W., et al. (2017). Stakeholder perspectives on a culture of health: Key findings. *Rand Health Quarterly, 6*(3), 6–11.

Ahrenfeldt, L. J., Moller, S., Andersen-Ranberg, K., et al. (2017). Religiousness and health in Europe. *European Journal of Epidemiology, 32*(10), 921–929. doi .org/10.1007/s10654-017-0296-1

Alarcón, R. D. (2003). *Los mosaicos de la esperanza. Reflexiones en torno a la Psiquiatría Latinoamericana.* Caracas, Venezuela: APAL.

Alarcón, R. D., Westermeyer, J., Foulks, E. F., & Ruiz, P. (1999). Clinical relevance of contemporary cultural psychiatry. *Journal of Nervous and Mental Diseases, 87*(8), 465–471.

Al-Bannay, H., Jarus, T., Jongbloed, L., Yazigi, M., & Dean, E. (2014). Culture as a variable in health research: Perspectives and caveats. *Health Promotion International, 29*(3), 549–557. doi.org/10.1093/heapro/dat002

Almutairi, K. M. (2015). Culture and language differences as a barrier to provision of quality care by the health workforce in Saudi Arabia. *Saudi Medical Journal, 36*(4), 425–431. doi.org/10.15537/smj.2015.4.10133

Alvear Acevedo, C. (2000). *Historia de México* (3rd ed.). Mexico DF: Editorial Limusa.

American Heritage. (1985). *A sense of history.* New York: American Heritage Press.

Anderson, B., & Hansson, W. K. (2016). Engagement in system redesign: A wellness example to enable a cultural transformation. *Health Management Forum, 29* (5), 205–210. doi.org/10.1177/o840470416649732

Arnold, J., Tango, J., Walker, I., et al. (2018). An evidence-based longitudinal curriculum for resident physician wellness: The 2017 Resident Wellness Consensus. *Western Journal of Emergency Medicine, 19*(2), 337–341. doi.org/10.5811/ westjem.2017.12.36244

Asad, A. L., & Kay, T. (2015). Toward a multidimensional understanding of culture for health interventions. *Social Science and Medicine, 144*(1), 79–87. doi.org/ 10.1016/j.socscimed.2015.09.013

Auger, M., Howell, T., & Gomes, T. (2016). Moving towards holistic wellness, empowerment and self-determination for indigenous peoples in Canada: Can traditional Indigenous health care practices increase ownership over health and health care decisions?. *Canadian Journal of Public Health, 107*(4–5), e393–e398. doi.org/10.17269/cjph.107.5366

Balkir, N., Arens, E. A., & Barnow, S. (2013). Exploring the relevance of autonomy and relatedness for mental health in healthy and depressed women from two different cultures: When does culture matter?. *International Journal of Social Psychiatry, 59*(5), 482–492. doi.org/10.1177/0020764012441428

Barker, B., Goodman, A., & DeBeck, K. (2017). Reclaiming indigenous identities: Culture as strength against suicide among indigenous youth in Canada. *Canadian Journal of Public Health, 108*(2), e208–e210. doi.org/10.17269/cjph.108.5754

Baumeister, R. F. (1986). *Identity: Cultural change and the struggle for self.* New York: Oxford University Press.

Beadling, C., Maza, J., Nakano, G., et al. (2012). Global health language and culture competency. *Journal of Special Operations Medicine, 12*(4), 10–16.

Beckett, P., Field, J., Molloy, L., et al. (2013). Practice what you preach: Developing person-centred culture in inpatient mental health settings through strengths-based, transformational leadership. *Issues on Mental Health Nursing, 34*(8), 595–601. doi.org/10.3109/01612840.2013.790524

Benjamins, M. R., & Whitman, S. (2010). A culturally appropriate school wellness initiative: Results of a 2-year pilot intervention in two Jewish schools. *Journal of School Health, 80*(8), 378–386. doi.org/10.1111/j.1746-1561.2010.00517.x

Berlinger, N., & Berlinger, A. (2017). Culture and moral distress: What's the connection and why does it matter? *AMA Journal of Ethics, 19*(6), 608–616. doi.org/10.1001/journalofethics.2017.19.6.msoc1-1706

Bhugra, D. (2014). Globalization, culture and mental health. *International Review of Psychiatry, 26*(5), 615–616. doi.org/10.3109/09540261.2014.955084

Bian, L. J., Liu, Z. G., & Li, G. X. (2015). Promoting health wellness: The essentials of Chinese medicine. *Chinese Journal of Integrated Medicine, 21*(8), 563–568. doi.org/10.1007/s11655-015-2100-y

Bloemraad, I., & Terriquez, V. (2016). Cultures of engagement: The organizational foundations of advancing health in immigrant and low-income communities of color. *Social Science and Medicine, 165*, 214–222. doi.org/10.1016/j.socscimed.2016.02.003

Boksa, P., Joober, R., & Kirmayer, L. J. (2015). Mental wellness in Canada's Aboriginal communities: Striving toward reconciliation. *Journal of Psychiatry and Neurosciences, 40*(6), 363–365. doi.org/10.1503/jpn.150309

Boller, F., & Barba, G. D. (2006). The evolution of psychiatry and neurology: Two disciplines divided by a common goal? In D. V. Jeste & J. H. Friedman (Eds.), *Current clinical neurology: Psychiatry for neurologists* (pp. 11–15). Totowa, NJ: Humana Press.

Bonello, M., Morris, J., & Azzopardi Muscat, N. (2018). The role of national culture in shaping health workforce collaboration: Lessons learned from a case study on attitudes to interprofessional education in Malta. *Health Policy, 122*(10), 1063–1069. doi.org/10.1016/j.healthpol.2018.06.013

Borisova, L. V., Martinussen, P. E., Rydland, H. T., Stornes, P., & Eikemo, T. A. (2017). Public evaluation of health services across 21 European countries:

The role of culture. *Scandinavian Journal of Public Health*, *45*(2), 132–139. doi.org/10.1177/1403494816685920

Brislin, R. W. (2000). *Understanding culture's influence on behavior* (2nd ed.). Fort Worth, TX: Harcourt.

Campos, B., & Kim, H. S. (2017). Incorporating the cultural diversity of family and close relationships into the study of health. *American Psychologist*, *72*(6), 543–554. doi.org/10.1037/amp0000122

Castro, F. G., Barrera, M., & Holleran Steiker, I. K. (2010). Issues and challenges in the design of culturally adapted evidence-based interventions. *Annual Review of Clinical Psychology*, *6*, 213–239. doi.org/10.1146/annurev-clinpsy-033109-132032

Chen, J. I., Romero, G. D., & Karver, M. S. (2016). The relationship of perceived campus culture to mental health help-seeking intentions. *Journal of Counseling Psychology*, *63*(6), 677–684. doi.org/10.1037/cou0000095

Codjoe, L., Byrne, M., Lister, M., McGuire, P., & Valmaggia, L. (2013). Exploring perceptions of "wellness" in black ethnic minority individuals at risk of developing psychosis. *Behavioral Cognitive Psychotherapy*, *41*(2), 144–161. doi.org/10.1017/S1352465812000707

Connell, J. (2014). The two cultures of health worker migration: A Pacific perspective. *Social Science and Medicine*, *116*, 73–81. doi.org/10.1016/j.socscimed.2014.06.043

Crocker, T. F., Smith, J. K., & Skevington, S. M. (2015). Family and professionals underestimate quality of life across diverse cultures and health conditions: Systematic review. *Journal of Clinical Epidemiology*, *68*(5), 584–595. doi.org/10.1016/j.clinepi.2014.12.007

Cunningham, T. R., & Jacobson, C. J. (2018). Safety talk and safety culture: Discursive repertoires as indicators of workplace safety and health practices and readiness to change. *Annals of Work Exposures and Health*, *62* (Suppl. 1), S55–S64. doi.org/10.1093/annweh/wxy035

Dahrendorf, R. (1959). *Class and class conflict in industrial society*. Stanford, CA: Stanford University Press.

Danielsson, M., Nilsen, P., Rutberg, H., & Carlfjord, S. (2018). The professional culture among physicians in Sweden: Potential implications for patient safety. *BMC Health Services Research*, *18*(1), 543–546. doi.org/10.1186/s12913-018-3328-y

Daskivich, T. J., Jardine, D. A., Tseng, J., et al. (2015). Promotion of wellness and mental health awareness among physicians-in-training: Perspective of National Multispecialty panel of Residents and Fellows. *Journal of Graduate Medical Education*, *7*(1), 143–147. doi.org/10.4300/JGME-07-01-42

de Figueiredo, J. M., & Gostoli, S. (2013). Culture and demoralization in psychotherapy. *Advances in Psychosomatic Medicine*, *33*, 75–87. doi.org/10.1159/000348735

De Ventos, X. R. (1987). *El laberinto de la Hispanidad*. Barcelona, Spain: Editorial Planeta.

Dillard, S. J., Dutta, M., & Sun, W. S. (2014). Culture-centered engagement with delivery of health services: Co-constructing meanings of health in the Tzu Chi

Foundation through Buddhist philosophy. *Health Communication, 29*(2), 147–156. doi.org/10.1080/10410236.2012.729262

Dutta, M. J., & Basu, A. (2008). Meanings of health: Interrogating structure and culture. *Health Communication, 23*(6), 560–572. doi.org/10.1080/10410230802465266

Dutta, M. J., & Jamil, R. (2013). Health at the margins of migration: Culture-centered co-constructions among Bangladeshi immigrants. *Health Communication, 28*(2), 170–182. doi.org/10.1080/10410236.2012.666956

Eckleberry-Hunt, J., Van Dyke, A., Lick, D., & Tucciarone, J. (2009). Changing the conversation from burnout to wellness: Physician well-being in Residency Training Programs. *Journal of Graduate Medical Education, 1*(2), 225–230. doi.org/10.4300/JGME-D-09-00026.1

Elliott, H., Bernstein, J., & Bowman, D. M. (2014). Wellness as a worldwide phenomenon?. *Journal of Health Politics, Policy and Law, 39*(5), 1067–1088. doi.org/10.1215/03616878-2813732

Eltaiba, N., & Harries, M. (2015). Reflections on recovery in mental health: Perspectives from a Muslim culture. *Social Work and Health Care, 54*(8), 725–737. doi.org/10.1080/00981389.2015.1046574

Erwin, D. O., Treviño, M., Saad-Harfouche, F. G., et al. (2010). Contextualizing diversity and culture within cancer control interventions for Latinas: Changing interventions, not cultures. *Social Science and Medicine, 71*(4), 693–701. doi.org/10.1016/j.socscimed.2010.05.005

Fiedeldey-Van Dijk, C., Rowan, M., Dell, C., et al. (2017). Honoring indigenous culture-as-intervention: Development and validity of the Native Wellness Assessment. *Journal of Ethnicity in Substance Abuse, 16*(2), 181–218. doi.org/10.1080/15332640.2015.1119774

Fink-Samnick, E. (2018). The new age of bullying and violence in health care: Part 4: Managing organizational cultures and beyond. *Professional Case Management, 23*(6), 294–306. doi.org/10.1097/NCM.0000000000000281

Flynn, J. P., Gascon, G., Doyle, S., et al. (2018). Supporting a culture of health in the workplace: A review of evidence-based elements. *American Journal of Health Promotion, 32*(8), 1755–1788. doi.org/10.1177/0890117118761887

Freeman, H. (Ed.). (1999). *A century of psychiatry*. London, UK: Harcourt Publishers Ltd.

Gage-Bouchard, E. A. (2017). Culture, styles of institutional interactions, and inequalities in healthcare experiences. *Journal of Health and Social Behavior, 58*(2), 147–165. doi.org/10.1177/0022146517693051

Gheondea-Eladi, A. (2017). Health research ethics: Between ethics codes and culture. *Journal of Empirical Research and Human Research Ethics, 12*(4), 246–260. doi.org/10.1177/1556264617717162

Gillin, N., Taylor, R., & Walker, S. (2017). Exploring the concept of "caring cultures": A critical examination of the conceptual, methodological and validity issues with the "caring cultures" construct. *Journal of Clinical Nursing, 26*(23–24), 5216–5223. doi.org/10.1111/jocn.13858

Golden, J. L., Berquist, G. F., & Coleman, W. E. (1978). *The rhetoric of Western thought* (2nd ed.). Dubuque, IA: Kendall/Hunt Publishing Co.

Gray, N., Mays, M. Z., Wolf, D., & Jirsak, J. (2010). Culturally focused wellness intervention for American Indian women of a small Southwest community: Associations with alcohol use, abstinence self-efficacy, symptoms of depression, and self-esteem. *American Journal of Health Promotion, 25*(2), e1–10.

Guerrero, L., & León, A. (2008). Aproximación al concepto de salud. *Revisión histórica. Fermentum, 18*, 610–633.

Harding, K., Lynch, L., Porter, J., & Taylor, N. F. (2017). Organisational benefits of a strong research culture in a health system: A systematic review. *Australian Health Review, 41*(1), 45–53. doi.org/10.1071/AH15180

Hess, T. M., O'Brien, E. L., Voss, P., et al. (2017). Context influences on the relationship between views of aging and subjective age: The moderating role of culture and domain of functioning. *Psychology and Aging, 32*(5), 419–431. doi.org/10.1037/pag0000181

Hill, E., Hess, R., Aborigo, R., et al. (2014). "I don't know anything about their culture": The disconnect between allopathic and traditional maternity care providers in rural northern Ghana. *African Journal of Reproductive Health, 18*(2), 36–45.

Hinchliffe, S., Jackson, M. A., Wyatt, K., et al. (2018). Healthy publics: Enabling cultures and environments for health. *Palgrave Communications, 4*, 57–62. doi.org/10.1057/s41599-018-0113-9

Hodge, D. R., Limb, G. E., & Cross, T. L. (2009). Moving from colonization toward balance and harmony: A Native American perspective on wellness. *Social Work, 54*(3), 211–219.

Hopkirk, J., & Wilson, L. H. (2014). A call to wellness – Whitiwhitia I te ora: Exploring Māori and occupational therapy perspectives on health. *Occupational Therapy International, 21*(4), 156–165. doi.org/10.1002/oti.1373

Hruschka, D. J. (2009). Culture as an explanation in population health. *Annals of Human Biology, 36*(3), 235–247. doi.org/10.1080/03014460902852593

Huang, L., & Xu, H. (2018). Therapeutic landscapes and longevity: Wellness tourism in Bama. *Social Science and Medicine, 197*, 24–32. doi.org/10.1016/j.socscimed.2017.11.052

Jaeger, K. (2013). Assumptions about culture in discourse on ethnic minority health. *Community Medicine, 10*(2), 141–151. doi.org/10.1558/cam.v10i2.141

Jamil, R., & Dutta, M. J. (2012). A culture-centered exploration of health: Constructions from rural Bangladesh. *Health Communication, 27*(4), 369–379. doi.org/10.1080/10410236.2011.586989

Jia, Y., Gao, J., Dai, J., Zheng, P., & Fu, H. (2017). Associations between health culture, health behaviors and health-related outcome: A cross-sectional study. *PLoS One, 12*(7), Article e0178644. doi.org/10.1371/journal.pone.0178644

Kagawa-Singer, M. (2011). Impact of culture on health outcomes. *Journal of Pediatric Hematology and Oncology, 33* (Suppl. 2), S90–S95. doi.org/10.1097/MPH.0b013e318230dadb

Kagawa-Singer, M. (2012). Applying the concept of culture to reduce health disparities through health behavior research. *Preventive Medicine, 55*(5), 356–361. doi.org/10.1016/j.ypmed.2012.02.011

Kagawa-Singer, M., Dressler, W., & George, S. (2016). NIH Expert Panel. Culture: The missing link in health research. *Social Science and Medicine, 170,* 237–246. doi.org/10.1016/j.socscimed.2016.07.015

Kahn-John Diné, M., & Koithan, M. (2015). Living in health, harmony and beauty: The dine (Navajo) hózhó wellness philosophy. *Global Advances in Health and Medicine, 4*(3), 24–30. doi.org/10.7453/gahmj.2015.044

Kirkland, A. (2014). What is wellness now?. *Journal of Health, Politics, Policy and Law, 39*(5), 957–970. doi.org/10.1215/o3616878-2813647

Ko, M., Murphy, J., & Bindman, A. B. (2015). Integrating health care for the most vulnerable: Bridging the differences in organizational cultures between US hospitals and community health centers. *American Journal of Public Health, 105* (Suppl. 5), S676–S679. doi.org/10.2105/AJPH.2015.302931

Lakeman, R. (2013). Talking science and wishing for miracles: Understanding cultures of mental health practice. *International Journal of Mental Health Nursing, 22* (2), 106–115. doi.org/10.1111/j.1447-0349.2012.00847.x

Lastres, J. B. (1951). *Historia de la medicina peruana* (5 vols.). Lima, Perú: Imprenta Santa María.

Laurie, T. M., Linnea Warren, M., Weilant, S., Acosta, J. D., & Chandra, A. (2018). How cultural alignment and the use of incentives can promote a culture of health: Stakeholder perspectives. *Rand Health Quarterly, 7*(2), 5–9.

Lawati, M. H. A., Dennis, S., Short, S. D., & Abdulhadi, N. N. (2018). Patient safety and safety culture in primary health care: A systematic review. *BMC Family Practice, 19*(1), 104–109. doi.org/10.1186/s12875-018-0793-7

Ledikwe, J. H., Semo, B. W., Sebego, M., et al. (2017). Implementation of a national Workplace Wellness Program for health workers in Botswana. *Journal of Occupational and Environmental Medicine, 59*(9), 867–874. doi.org/10.1097/JOM.0000000000001028

Lieberman, J. A., & Ogas, O. (2015). *Shrinks: The untold story of psychiatry.* London, UK: W&N.

Lin, Y. W., & Lin, Y. Y. (2014). A multilevel model of organizational health culture and the effectiveness of health promotion. *American Journal of Health Promotion, 29*(1), e53–63. doi.org/10.4278/ajhp.121116-QUAN-562

Löckenhoff, C. E., De Fruyt, F., Terracciano, A., et al. (2009). Perceptions of aging across 26 cultures and their culture-level associates. *Psychology and Aging, 24* (4), 941–954. doi.org/10.1037/a0016901

Lohiya, N. K., Balasubramanian, K., & Ansari, A. S. (2016). Indian folklore medicine in managing men's health and wellness. *Andrologia, 48*(8), 894–907. doi.org/10.1111/and.12680

Look, M. A., Maskarinec, G. G., de Silva, M., et al. (2014). *Kumu hula* perspectives on health. *Hawaii Journal of Medicine and Public Health, 73*(12, Suppl. 3), 21–25.

Lu, C. F., Tung, C. C., & Ely, I. (2016). Reflections on the differences and similarities of mental health care in Virginia and Taiwan: Geography, history, culture and nurse practitioners. *Hu Li Za Zhi, 63*(6), 107–113.

Lucchetti, G., Damiano, R. F., DiLalla, L. F., et al. (2018). Cross-cultural differences in mental health, quality of life, empathy, and burnout between US and

Brazilian medical students. *Academic Psychiatry*, *42*(1), 62–67. doi.org/10 .1007/s40596-017-0777-2

Marías, J. (1986). *Hispanoamérica*. Madrid, Spain: Alianza Editorial.

Mariner, W. K., & Annas, G. J. (2016). A culture of health and human rights. *Health Affairs (Millwood)*, *35*(11), 1999–2004. doi.org/10.1377/hlthaff.2016.0700

Martsolf, G. R., Sloan, J., Villarruel, A., Mason, D., & Sullivan, C. (2018). Promoting a culture of health through cross-sector collaborations. *Health Promotion Practice*, *19*(5), 784–791. doi.org/10.1177/1524839918772284

Maty, S. C., Leung, H., Lau, C., & Kim, G. (2011). Factors that influence self-reported general health status among different Asian ethnic groups: Evidence from the Roadmap to the New Horizon: Linking Asians to Improved Health and Wellness study. *Journal of Immigration and Minority Health*, *13*(3), 555–567. doi.org/10.1007/s10903-010-9349-1

Mayer, C. H., & Viviers, R. (2014). "I still believe…" Reconstructing spirituality, culture and mental health across cultural divides. *International Review of Psychiatry*, *26*(3), 265–278. doi.org/10.3109/09540261.2013.866076

Mbau, R., & Gilson, L. (2018). Influence of organizational culture on the implementation of health sector reforms in low- and middle-income countries: A qualitative interpretive review. *Global Health Action*, *11*(1), 1462579. doi .org/10.1080/16549716.2018.1462579

McClafferty, H., Brown, C. W., Vohra, S., et al. (2014). Physician health and wellness. *Pediatrics*, *134*(4), 830–835. doi.org/10.1542/peds.2014-2278

Melnyk, B. M., Amaya, M., Szalacha, L. A., & Hoying, J. (2016). Relationship among perceived wellness culture, healthy lifestyle beliefs, and healthy behaviors in university faculty and staff. Implications for practice and future research. *Western Journal of Nursing Research*, *38*(3), 308–324. doi.org/10.1177/ 0193945915615238

Melnyk, B. M., Szalacha, L. A., & Amaya, M. (2018). Psychometric properties of the perceived wellness culture and Environment Support Scale. *American Journal of Health Promotion*, *32*(4), 1021–1027. doi.org/10.1177/0890117117737676

Milner, K. A., Bradley, H. B., & Lampley, T. (2018). Health professions faculty beliefs, confidence, use, and perception of organizational culture and readiness for EBP: A cross-sectional, descriptive survey. *Nurse Education Today*, *64*, 5–10. doi.org/10.1016/j.nedt.2018.02.003

Mitchell, E. M., Steeves, R., & Dillingham, R. (2015). Cruise ships and bush medicine: Globalization on the Atlantic coast of Nicaragua and effects on the health of Creole women. *Public Health Nursing*, *32*(3), 237–245. doi.org/10.1111/phn .12127

Miyamoto, Y. (2017). Culture and social class. *Current Opinion in Psychology*, *18*, 67–72. doi.org/10.1016/j.copsyc.2017.07.042

Miyamoto, Y., Yoo, J., Levine, C. S., et al. (2018). Culture and social hierarchy: Self- and other-oriented correlates of socioeconomic status across cultures. *Journal of Personality and Social Psychology*, *115*(3), 427–445. doi.org/10.1037/ pspi0000133

Montiel, E. (2000). *El humanismo americano. Filosofía de una comunidad de naciones*. Asunción, Paraguay: Fondo de Cultura Económica.

Nair, S. C., Satish, K. P., Sreedharan, J., & Ibrahim, H. (2016). Assessing health literacy in the Eastern and Middle Eastern cultures. *BMC Public Health, 16*, 831–839. doi.org/10.1186/s12889-016-3488-9

Napier, A. D., Ancarno, C., Butler, B., et al. (2014). Culture and health. *The Lancet, 384*(9954), 1607–1639. doi.org/10.1016/S0140-6736(15)60226-4

Nicholson, A., Rose, R., & Bobak, M. (2009). Association between attendance at religious services and self-reported health in 22 European countries. *Social Science and Medicine, 69*(4), 519–528. doi.org/10.1016/j.socscimed.2009.06 .024

Nicolaidis, C., McKeever, C., & Meucci, S. (2013). A community-based wellness program to reduce depression in African Americans: Results from a pilot intervention. *Progress in Community Health Partnership, 7*(2), 145–152. doi .org/10.1353/cpr.2013.0017

Owens, K., Eggers, J., Keller, S., & McDonald, A. (2017). The imperative of culture: A quantitative analysis of the impact of culture on workforce engagement, patient experience, physician engagement, value-based purchasing, and turn-over. *Journal of Health Leadership, 9*, 25–31. doi.org/10.2147/JHL.S126381

Park, M., Chesla, C. A., Rehm, R. S., & Chun, K. M. (2011). Working with culture: Culturally appropriate mental health care for Asian Americans. *Journal of Advanced Nursing, 67*(11), 2373–2382. doi.org/10.1111/j.1365-2648.2011.05671.x

Place, S., & Talen, M. (2013). Creating a culture of wellness: Conversations, curriculum, concrete resources, and control. *International Journal of Psychiatry and Medicine, 45*(4), 333–344. doi.org/10.2190/PM.45.4.d

Plough, A. L. (2014). Building a culture of health: Challenges for the public health workforce. *American Journal of Preventive Medicine, 47*(5, Suppl. 3), S388–S390. doi.org/10.1016/j.amepre.2014.07.037

Prilleltensky, I. (2012). Wellness as fairness. *American Journal of Community Psychology, 49*(1–2), 1–21. doi.org/10.1007/s10464-011-9448-8

Rafferty, A. M., Philippou, J., Fitzpatrick, J. M., Pike, G., & Ball, J. (2017). Development and testing of the "Culture of Care Barometer" (CoCB) in health care organizations: A mixed methods study. *British Medical Journal Open, 7*(8), Article e016677. doi.org/10.1136/bmjopen-2017-016677

Reinhardt-Wood, D. L., Kinter, K. T., & Burke, K. (2018). Inception of a peer-run wellness center at a state psychiatric hospital. *Journal of Psychosocial Nursing and Mental Health Services, 18*, 1–5. doi.org/10.3928/02793695-2018612-01

Rice, H. E., Lou-Meda, R., Saxton, A. T., et al. (2018). Building a safety culture in global health: Lessons from Guatemala. *BMK Global Health, 3*(2), Article e000630. doi.org/10.1136/bmjgh-2017-000630

Scott, P., Dunscombe, R., Evans, D., Mukherjeee, M., & Wyatt, J. (2018). Learning health systems need to bridge the "two cultures" of clinical informatics and data science. *Journal of Innovation in Health Informatics, 25*(2), 126–131. doi .org/10.14236/jhi.v25i2.1062

Sinkfield-Morey, T. (2018). Diversity, inclusion, and storying: Connecting across cultures to give meaning to patients' whole health. *Creative Nursing, 24*(1), 12–19. doi.org/10.1891/1078-4535.24.1.12

Snodgrass, J. G., Lacy, M. G., & Upadhyay, C. (2017). Developing culturally sensitive affect scales for global mental health research and practice: Emotional balance, not named syndromes in Indian Adivasi subjective well-being. *Social Science and Medicine*, *187*, 174–183. doi.org/10.1016/j.socscimed.2017.06.037

Snowshoe, A., Crooks, C. V., Tremblay, P. F., & Hinson, R. E. (2017) Cultural connectedness and its relation to mental wellness for First Nations youth. *Journal of Primary Prevention*, *38*(1–2), 67–86. doi.org/10.1007/s10935-016-0454-3

Stacciarini, J. M., Wiens, B., Coady, M., et al. (2011). CBPR: Building partnerships with Latinos in a rural area for a wellness approach to mental health. *Issues in Mental Health Nursing*, *32*(8), 486–492. doi.org/10.3109/01612840.2011.576326

Stoewen, D. L. (2017). Dimensions of wellness: Change your habits, change your life. *Canadian Veterans Journal*, *58*(8), 861–862.

Swartz, L., Kilian, S., Twesigye, J., Attah, D., & Chiliza, B. (2014). Language, culture, and task-shifting: An emerging challenge for global mental health. *Global Health Action*, *7*. doi.org/10.3402/gha.v7.23433

Swierad, E. M., Vartanian, L. R., & King, M. (2017). The influence of ethnic and mainstream cultures on African Americans' health behaviors: A qualitative study. *Behavioral Sciences (Basel)*, *7*(3), 49. doi.org/10.3390/bs7030049

Tang, L., Bajer, J. S., & Meadows, C. Z. (2016). Tensions of health narratives of Employee Wellness Program participants. *Workplace Health Safety*, *64*(9), 426–432. doi.org/10.1177/2165079916643966

Trujillo, M. D., & Plough, A. (2016) Building a culture of health: A new framework and measures for health and health care in America. *Social Science and Medicine*, *165*, 206–213. doi.org/10.1016/j.socscimed.2016.06.043

Tseng, W.-S. (2001). *Handbook of cultural psychiatry*. San Diego, CA: Academic Press.

Upchurch, D. M., & Rainisch, B. W. (2015). The importance of wellness among users of complementary and alternative medicine: Findings from the 2007 National Health Interview Survey. *BMC Complementary & Alternative Medicine*, *15*(3), 362–366. doi.org/10.1186/s12906-015-0866-y

VanderWeele, T. J. (2017a). Religion and health in Europe: Cultures, countries, context. *European Journal of Epidemiology*, *32*(10), 857–861. doi.org/10.1007/s10654-017-0310-17

VanderWeele, T. J. (2017b). On the promotion of human flourishing. *Proceedings of the National Academy of Sciences, USA*, *31*, 8148–8156. doi/10.1073/pnas.1702996114

Vargas Llosa, M. (2005). *Diccionario del amante de América Latina*. Barcelona, Spain: Paidós.

Villatoro, A. P., Morales, E. S., & Mays, V. M. (2014). Family culture in mental health help-seeking and utilization in a nationally representative sample of Latinos in the United States: The NLAAS. *American Journal of Orthopsychiatry*, *84*(4), 353–363. doi.org/10.1037/h0099844

Viruell-Fuentes, E. A., Miranda, P. Y., & Abdulrahim, S. (2012). More than culture: Structural racism, intersectionality theory, and immigrant health. *Social Science and Medicine*, *75*(12), 2099–2106. doi.org/10.1016/j.socscimed.2011.12.037

Volpp, K. G., & Asch, D. A. (2017). Make the healthy choice the easy choice: Using behavioral economics to advance a culture of health. *QJM-An International Journal of Medicine*, *110*(5), 271–275. doi.org/10.1093/qjmed/hcw190

Vrzina, S. M. (2011). Talking culture, crying health, hoping for nothing: Surviving the many flyers above the human rights global cuckoo's nests. *College Anthropology*, *35*(4), 969–978.

Wagenaar, B. H., Kohrt, B. A., Hagaman, A. K., McLean, K. E., & Kaiser, B. N. (2013). Determinants of care-seeking for mental health problems in rural Haiti: Culture, cost or competency. *Psychiatric Services*, *64*(4), 366–372. doi .org/10.1176/appi.ps.201200272

Walsh, M. M. (2016). Wellness in graduate medical education: Is it time to pull the Andon Cord?. *Journal of Graduate Medical Education*, *8*(5), 777–779. doi .org/10.4300/JGME-D-16-00547.1

Weil, A. R. (2016). Defining and measuring a culture of health. *Health Affairs (Millwood)*, *35*(11), 1947. doi.org/10.1377/hlthaff.2016.1358

Wolsko, C., Lardon, C., Hopkins, S., & Ruppert, E. (2006). Conceptions of wellness among the Yup'ik of the Yukon-Kuskokwim Delta: The vitality of social and natural connections. *Ethnicity and Health*, *11*(4), 345–363. doi.org/10.1080/13557850600824005

World Health Organization. (1948, April 7). Constitution preamble. *Official Records*, 2, 100–120.

World Health Organization. (2017). *Patient safety: Making health care safer*. Geneva, Switzerland: World Health Organization.

Yang, L. H., Purdie-Vaughns, V., Kotabe, H., et al. (2013). Culture, threat, and mental illness stigma: Identifying culture-specific threat among Chinese-American groups. *Social Science and Medicine*, *88*, 56–67. doi.org/10.1016/j .socscimed.2013.03.036

Yang, L. H., Thornicroft, G., Alvarado, R., Vega, E., & Link, B. G. (2014). Recent advances in cross-cultural measurement in psychiatric epidemiology: Utilizing "what matters most" to identify culture-specific aspects of stigma. *International Journal of Epidemiology*, *43*(2), 494–510. doi.org/10.1093/ije/dyu039

Yiengprugsawan, V., Lazzarino, A. I., Steptoe, A., Seubsman, S. A., & Sleigh, A. C. (2015). Psychosocial job characteristics, wealth and culture: Differential effects on mental health in the UK and Thailand. *Global Health*, *11*, 31–37. doi.org/10.1186/s12992-015-0116-x

Zachariadou, T., Zannetos, S., & Pavlakis, A. (2013). Organizational culture in the primary healthcare setting of Cyprus. *BMC Health Services Research*, *13*, Article 112. doi.org/10.1186/1472-6963-13-112

Zimmer, B. (2010, April 16). *Wellness. The New York Times Magazine*, 8–10.

PART II

Research, Assessment, and Program Evaluation

Ecological Considerations

6 Conducting Culturally Responsive Community Needs Assessments

Lisa Suzuki, Taymy Caso, Cirecie West-Olatunji, and Maria Prendes-Lintel

6.1 Defining Culturally Responsive Community Needs Assessments

"Community-engaged interventions, which are informed by multiple disciplines (e.g., public health education and health promotion, community psychology, and health policy), focus on behavior and social change theories and practice to improve health" (Wallerstein, Yen, & Syme, 2011, p. 822). A major focus in the creation and evaluation of programs and intervention services falls within the domain of community assessment. Community assessment is often equated with a needs assessment:

> A community needs assessment provides community leaders with a snapshot of local policy, systems, and environmental change strategies currently in place and helps identify the areas for improvement. With this data, communities can map out a course for health improvement by creating strategies to make positive and sustainable changes in their communities. (Centers for Disease Control and Prevention [CDC], 2013, p. 6)

Community assessment requires an ecological approach that involves application of both qualitative and quantitative research methods as the gathering of data may take the form of known measures as well as gathering narrative information from multiple stakeholders (Trickett, 2009). The information provided by these sources enables the community assessor to understand the critical role(s) that context may play in the creation and maintenance of the resources, needs, and concerns facing a community.

Community assessments are often conducted by academic faculty and researchers. Given their academic standpoint, it is critical that scholars prioritize the incorporation of multiple perspectives across varying levels of power and privilege. This can be accomplished by ensuring that (1) teams are diversely recruited across disciplines and are offered proper cultural competency training by professionals who are familiar with the community of interest and (2) all team members' perspectives and voices are given adequate consideration and incorporated whenever possible. When recruiting students to join the team, it is important for them to work across all levels of a given project to balance out

115

hierarchical power structures within the team. The interdisciplinary team should reflect individuals who have diverse intersectional identities (age, race, gender, sexual orientation, socioeconomic status, ability, privilege, etc.) related to the community being assessed and amplify those voices as community members with unique perspectives. Prioritizing fostering these team dynamics will facilitate conversations from a range of perspectives that will help identify action steps and solutions to address logistical hurdles that may arise.

We acknowledge that conducting community needs assessments is vital to community-based research. As such, this chapter addresses assessment as a strategy for community psychology research and program development within academic and community contexts. The authors will present key concepts associated with assessment. The application of this approach to questions of community will be discussed. Case examples are provided to illustrate how assessment can prompt community-level change in terms of program creation and evaluation. We cite the *Community Needs Assessment* manual (CDC, 2013) throughout this chapter given its salience to the topic.

Understanding the needs of the larger community is essential to making decisions about intervention planning. As such, conducting a community needs assessment is an essential step to gain perspective from members of the community, as well as practitioners, service providers, and other stakeholders. These individuals can provide invaluable information about the needs of the larger community including barriers to service provision, limitations of the current setting, and successful interventions currently in place. In addition, they can provide information regarding risk factors, community priorities, openness and flexibility with respect to change, and ultimately "how to engage community strengths in effective strategies" (Wallerstein et al., 2011, p. 822).

Additionally, community and government stakeholders can provide historical and contextual insight into the financial cost for staffing and overhead, and ultimately how the community will receive and interact with a new clinic or community resource. These perspectives can inform a community action plan that will guide the decision-making process, implementation of community outreach strategies, and shape the intervention so that it targets improving service provision for a community. Moreover, they can also be instrumental in highlighting the feasibility of certain projects and effectiveness of approaches, as well as areas for future development and growth.

6.1.1 Definitions

There are a number of terms and constructs related to the topic of conducting community assessment in a cultural context. Critical to this work is understanding the construct of community and the role that culture can play in adapting and determining objectives, goals, and questions to be addressed; variables to be explored; as well as applying interventions and prioritizing salient outcomes; as these are all critical to the assessment process.

6.1.1.1 Community

Communities can be defined by geographic area as well as member characteristics (e.g., religion, race, age, occupation). "People within a community come from different backgrounds and have unique cultures, customs, and values." It is critical that assessors have a "clear understanding of the different cultural groups within a community and how to best work with them to solve community issues" (CDC, 2013, p. 6).

6.1.1.2 Community Assessment

This process of evaluation serves to identify the "community's assets, challenges, and specific vulnerabilities and threats related to disasters and other potential adversities" (Pfefferbaum, Pfefferbaum, & Van Horn, 2015, p. 239). Community members are most informed about their own "locality, relationships, and networks, knowledge useful to understand the local context and dynamics ... Risk assessment and other data that detail relevant community characteristics and issues can augment the information provided by community members and organizations" (p. 239).

6.1.1.3 Cultural Adaptation

Adapting measures and assessment procedures involves changes and adjustments to increase cultural and linguistic adequacy (Geisinger, 1994). The process requires linguistic, cultural, and psychometric skills on the part of the team conducting the assessment (Van de Vijver, 2016). Given the variability and complexity of the skills across projects, steps need to be taken to ensure proper cultural sensitivity training is offered to team members.

6.1.1.4 Cultural Competence

This area of competence refers to the "ability to understand, appreciate, and interact with people from cultures and belief systems different from one's own" (DeAngelis, 2015, p. 64). Cultural competence of assessment team members is critical and should include attention to beliefs/attitudes, knowledge, and skills (Sue, 2001) regarding various facets of the community being addressed.

6.1.2 Components

Specific areas of consideration when planning to conduct a community assessment include the following (as noted in CDC, 2013):

- **Policy Change** – laws, regulations, rules, protocols, procedures that are designed to guide or influence behavior (legislative or organizational);

mandate environmental changes and increase the likelihood that they will become institutionalized or sustainable.

- **System Change** – change that affects all community components including the social norms of an organization, institution, or system; this may include a policy or environmental change strategy. Here it is important to note that policies are often the driving force behind system change.
- **Environmental Change** – physical, social, or economic factors designed to influence people's practices and behaviors: physical (e.g., structural changes or the presence of programs or services); social (e.g., positive change in attitudes or behavior about policies that promote health or an increase in supportive attitudes regarding a health practice, including an increase in favorable attitudes of community decision makers); and/or economic (e.g., presence of financial disincentives or incentives to encourage a desired behavior).

6.2 The Process

Planning a community assessment is a challenging and complex process given the need to understand numerous data sources alongside the importance of defining the scope of the assessment and data collection strategies (e.g., quantitative measure to be used, qualitative questions to be asked). The planning process requires balancing multiple objectives, availability of resources, collaboration of community partners, and integrating perspectives of stakeholders. The overall steps to be addressed in a community needs assessment include beginning with the planning phase and moving toward an action plan based upon the data obtained (CDC, 2013):

- planning the assessment
- conducting the assessment
- reviewing the data
- recording and consolidating the data
- developing a community action plan

While this may appear to be a linear process, in application there may be re-directions, modifications to data collection, and mid-course corrections as salient information is obtained from stakeholders. Additional steps and questions may be added to the process to improve the quality of the assessment.

There are many useful strategies for conceptualizing the initial planning stages, including concept mapping: "a structured method for translating complex qualitative data into a pictorial form [that] displays the interrelationships among ideas" (Shorkey, Windsor, & Spence, 2009, p. 63). As explained by Shorkey et al. (2009), concept mapping consists of several stages including:

- **Preparation** – Identifying participants or respondents for focus groups and establishing focal themes (e.g., research aims or questions) and objectives for consideration

- **Generation of Statements** – Brainstorming and generating ideas during focus groups
- **Structuring of Statements** – Visually displaying statements from the focus group and conducting an exercise wherein participants determine the importance of the statements and organize them accordingly
- **Representation of Statement** – Analyzing the "sortings and ratings" using computer software
- **Interpretation of Maps** – Using analytic software to create potential names for each "dimension" in the concept map
- **Utilization of Maps** – During this final stage, the focus group will decide on final names for each "dimension" and engage in thoughtful discussions about the utility of the instrument

Overall, the general goals of many community assessments are to decrease the mental health and educational burden experienced by underserved community members and provide effective and culturally relevant services aimed at establishing and building community partnerships. Engaging in the assessment process serves to increase the visibility and access of services, decrease stigma, reduce barriers, and create professional training experiences. As with many projects, establishing a tentative timeline with built-in flexibility, targets, goals, objectives, and deliverables is essential. This can help the team determine the pace at which the project can be conducted, and when deliverables can be produced. Moreover, it is important to note that moving too quickly between project stages (i.e., determining goals and objectives) may leave out critical voices that can potentially have an impact on the success of the assessment and action plan moving forward.

6.2.1 Recruiting a Team

The assessment should incorporate stakeholder perspectives across various levels of power and privilege. Establishing collaborative relationships with various stakeholder groups is critical to the process of community assessment. Spending time to learn about the community and communicating with professionals and community members who can serve as informants and cultural brokers contributes to the richness and relevant discourse to follow in the assessment process. The team should include individuals who have diverse intersectional identities related to the communities being served (e.g., age, race, gender, sexual orientation, socioeconomic status, ability, privilege, among others). In this way, the team can help facilitate conversations aimed at identifying potential logistical challenges and implementing effective solutions.

6.2.2 Recruiting a Community Advisory Board

Once selected, the team is encouraged to assemble a community advisory board. This board consists of service providers, community advocates, and members across levels of access that serve as an important sounding board through the assessment, action planning, and implementation stages (Newman et al., 2011). Although in rural areas and/or places that lack racial and ethnic diversity recruiting a diverse team might be difficult to accomplish, the community advisory board can supplement this deficit by prioritizing the needs of the larger community and challenging the team to think through their structural power, institutional privilege, and potential blind spots resulting from being disconnected to sources of adversity that have an impact on community members.

6.2.3 Identifying Location and Informants

With this information, the team can select and prioritize a geographic region for the project and begin to construct a comprehensive needs assessment that gathers data about policies (i.e., limitations associated with service provision; local and institutional regulations that might have an impact on service delivery), systems (i.e., organizations, institutions, and resources that already provide services), community needs (i.e., needing more psychological assessment, intakes, and referrals vs. individual or group psychotherapy; bilingual or multilingual services for monolingual or non-English-speaking clients; psychoeducation that addresses specific concerns such as natural disaster relief; and age-specific services for specific demographics, among other areas).

6.2.4 Finances

It is critical to consider financial resources including potential external sources (e.g., grants) available to the community and the assessment team. Budgetary concerns may include staffing, overhead, recruitment materials, advertising, hardware, software, and other potential costs that may arise. The tentative budget should take into consideration projected goals so that progress can be evaluated through development and implementation. If scarce resources are available, parties are encouraged to determine whether additional funding through external sources is worth pursuing.

6.3 Methods

A comprehensive needs assessment should include both quantitative and qualitative measures that cover potential areas of interest (CDC, 2013). Initially, the team can focus on identifying research questions and constructs of interest, planning logistics, and designing the methods of inquiry, to facilitate the instrument selection process. For projects with a quantitative focus, it is important to consider instruments and measures that have strong validity, reliability, and have been used across cultures to ensure that the needs assessment is culturally responsive and inclusive of ethnic and racially diverse community members.

6.3.1 Quantitative Instruments

Inclusion of instruments and measures that focus on various facets of a community should be prioritized (Kramer et al., 2011). A review of instruments by Kramer et al. (2011) identifies a number of community characteristics including resources, social or group cohesion, social capital, resilience, attitudes, perceptions of neighborhood, and sustainability. They reviewed the utility, reliability, and validity of instruments that are used primarily in South Africa (Kramer et al., 2011). Among the measures reviewed, we provide highlights of the following instruments: (1) the Neighborhood Characteristics Scale (NCS) (Ellaway, Macintyre, & Kearns, 2001); (2) the Sense of Community Index (SCI) (McMillan & Chavis, 1986; Sarason, 1974); and (3) the Community Resilience Measure (Ahmed et al., 2004). These instruments were chosen due to their psychometric properties, cross-cultural adaptations, and popularity in the field.

The NCS measures how community members from different neighborhoods, within the same city, perceive their local communities. This scale is brief, can be completed in a short amount of time, requires minimal effort from respondents, and includes items that cover a wide range of common issues facing local communities. Structurally, the NCS contains several subscales that measure perceptions of neighborhood quality, perceptions of neighborhood cohesion, and perceived standard of living compared with others in the neighborhood (Ellaway et al., 2001). In the NCS, items on the perceptions of neighborhood quality subscale focus on the extent to which social issues (e.g., vandalism, littering, crime) and environmental problems (e.g., burglaries, pollution, access to safe spaces for recreation for children and adults, markers of public substance use) have an adverse impact on a neighborhood (Ellaway et al., 2001). The perceptions of neighborhood cohesion subscale asks respondents to indicate their level of "attraction to neighborhood" – comfort in speaking and connecting with neighbors, as well as willingness to ask for help, and overall sense of community belonging (p. 2304). Lastly, the measure asks respondents to report on a three-point Likert scale whether they feel "better off," "about the same," or "worse off," with regards to their "perception of own standard of living in relation to others living in [their] neighborhood" (p. 2308). Overall, this measure can be used to inform how community members perceive their local environment and their support networks.

The Sense of Community Index (SCI) is the most commonly used scale for measuring sense of community throughout the world and has been translated into ten different languages (Community Science, n.d.) and used in different cultures in North and South America, Asia, and the Middle East, and applied in urban, suburban, rural, tribal, workplace, schools, university, recreational clubs, and internet communities (Community Science, n.d.). The SCI has two versions, the SCI and the SCI-2 (McMillan & Chavis, 1986; Sarason, 1974). The SCI consists of twelve true or false items that make up four subscales: membership, influence, reinforcement of needs, and shared emotional connection (McMillan & Chavis, 1986). The SCI includes items like: "I think my [block] is a good place for me to live," "People on this [block] generally don't get along with each other," and "If there is a problem on this [block] people who live here can get it solved" (McMillan & Chavis, 1986). In addition to being widely used across cultures, this scale is brief, time efficient, and simple to score, making it a valuable tool for measurement.

The Community Resilience Measure (CRM) was developed by Ahmed et al. (2004) in South Africa. This questionnaire is intended to be administered by a trained professional and includes the following subscales: small business and physical security, community cohesion, community structures and leadership, social supports, access to knowledge, and community hope (Ahmed et al., 2004). The CRM has "high" reliability, although more research needs to be conducted to further validate the scale. Other comparable instruments have similar limitations. For instance, the Brief Sense of Community Index (BSCI) (Long & Perkins, 2003) has "confirmed construct validity," but "marginal" scale and subscale reliability (Kramer et al., 2011). In situations where there are limited validated measures available, the research team should consider including exploratory qualitative measures and methods.

6.3.2 Qualitative Measures

Interviews, focus groups, observations, postal survey, telephone survey, face-to-face survey, web-based survey, photo journals, social media applications, and review of documents and examination of demographic, policy, legal, and empirical records and outcomes often take the form of qualitative data in the process of community assessment. There are related strengths and limitations related to each type of qualitative data-gathering method (CDC, 2013). For example, (1) interviews are time-consuming and interviewees may present only a narrow perspective introducing potential biases; (2) focus groups introduce a loss on anonymity for the speakers in the room; (3) observations may provide only a general overview of the community (e.g., examination of physical points of access, pricing in the neighborhood, advertisements of community programs); (4) written surveys may be best suited for short and straightforward questions and require moderate literacy and may result in low response rates; and (5) telephone and face-to-face surveys may increase the potential for socially desirable responses (CDC, 2013).

The preceding listing highlights the numerous and potentially expansive nature of qualitative data-gathering sources. In addition, many community assessments incorporate qualitative participatory, assessment-based, action-oriented processes (e.g., Pfefferbaum, Pfefferbaum, & Van Horn, 2015). For example, in a review of community resilience interventions of participatory, assessment-based, and action-oriented processes, the authors conducted a comparison study of six interventions designed to enhance community disaster resilience utilizing qualitative methods. The authors noted that all interventions incorporated local action planning as identified in program documents (e.g., program manuals, guidebooks, toolkits) as reflecting "strategic planning adapted specifically for community application to build community disaster resilience" (Pfefferbaum et al., 2015, p. 246). In addition, interventions were "sponsored and used by community-based organizations; businesses; service providers; educational institutions; faith-based organizations; local foundations; civic, social, home-owner, or professional associations; government agencies; and affiliated volunteers" (p. 248). The review of interventions concluded that all programs recognized the uniqueness of communities and emphasized the importance of gathering local input into the process.

6.3.3 Mixed-Method Assessment

Community needs assessment studies have also incorporated both qualitative and quantitative data sources. For example, Craig (2011) describes a community assessment designed to develop a system of care for lesbian, gay, bisexual, transgender, and questioning (LGBTQ) youths. Craig describes a research process "flowing from qualitative to quantitative research strategies" incorporating community-based participatory research – "key informant interviews, focus groups, and survey research in a countrywide initiative" (p. 274). Community-based participatory research entails that stakeholders are full and equal partners in all steps of the research process from development to action (Corrigan, 2020). "Professional researchers have the expertise to promote rigorous and valid science within the constraints of the real world. Community stakeholders have the expertise to make sure the science is relevant to their community" (p. 123).

The process of community assessment was designed to be in four phases: (1) Phase 1: environmental scan and key informant interviews; (2) Phase 2: focus groups of LGBTQ youths and straight allies commenting on experiences with close friends and family members; (3) Phase 3: development, implementation, and analysis of a survey of the target population; (4) Phase 4: solicited community feedback regarding results of the community needs assessment. The author notes that the qualitative and quantitative components of the assessment were facilitated by the principal investigator and a research assistant. Inclusion of community members as well as service providers meant that competing agendas and personalities were present in the process, therefore it was critical to have skilled facilitators available. The author states that "partnerships were often tenuous and possessed significant challenges in both implementing the needs assessment and uncovering the needs of youth ... Yet the process is critical to creating systems of care that are relevant for, and sensitive to, marginalized populations" (Craig, 2011, p. 288).

6.4 Case Examples

In this section, we illustrate the dynamic process of community assessment in greater detail in the case examples that follow. Both cases involve developing an assessment that will inform service provision for under-served members of a community. The first case provides an example of an organic process that evolved based upon the growing needs of the local community. The second case provides an evaluative structure based upon predetermined goals and deliverables within a public school context. In reviewing these cases, we ask readers to think critically about the process of community needs assessment and the many voices that are involved in the planning process. The needs assessment includes considerations as founda-tional as which languages are spoken in the community, what the local resources are and barriers to accessing them, socioeconomic status of sur-rounding neighborhood areas, challenges that have an impact on the local community (e.g., lack of insurance, undocumented status), and other relevant factors. Multiple stakeholders may be involved in these discussions as many perspectives were gathered during initial phases of the assessment process. Notably, the critical process of gathering information helped each case define potential resources available and needs within the community.

6.4.1 The For Immigrants and Refugees Surviving Torture Project

The For Immigrants and Refugees Surviving Torture (FIRST) Project was funded by a grant awarded through the Torture Victims Relief Act, adminis-tered through the Office of Refugee Resettlement (www.acf.hhs.go/orr/pro grams/survivors-of-torture/about). The FIRST Project was designed to help "individuals and families overcome adversity and counteract the pain, inhumanity, and degradation of the torture and trauma experienced at the hands of a government" (Prendes-Lintel & Peterson, 2008, p. 220). This mission was integrated into multiple levels of the project and materials. From the beginning of the project to its closing six years later, the following motto appeared on the project website: "FIRST Project clients are incredible people – strong and capable individuals. The staff is honored to serve them." The emphasis embedded in this statement highlights the focus on assets rather than deficits and the importance of incorporating resources to be found within each cultural community relocated to the relocation site.

The grant identified populations to be served, outlined requirements regarding how the funds could be used, and stipulated required collabor-ation between community agencies. At the time of development, approximately forty agencies in Nebraska offered services to the refugee population located in Lincoln.

6.4.1.1 The Call for Assessment

Lincoln, Nebraska was identified as one of the major cities for resettlement in the 1990s as a community for recent arriving refugees due to availability of job opportunities and affordability. Refugees and immigrants from Croatia, Iraq, Vietnam, Mexico, Guatemala, El Salvador, Russia, Serbia, Bosnia, Hungary, Ethiopia, Sudan, Afghanistan, Liberia, Somalia, and Sierra Leone relocated to Lincoln. Due to data archival the statistics for each country are no longer available for the FIRST Project. A general listing of refugee admissions by state to the USA is available from the Office of Refugee Resettlement and inclusive of the community served by the FIRST Project (www.wrapsnet.org/admissions-and-arrivals/). The data on the website indicate that for the State of Nebraska, from 2006 to 2020 456 refugees and Special Immigrant VISAs (SIVs) were issued from Afghanistan; 1,923 refugees and SIVs were issued from Iraq. SIVs were awarded to those who worked with the US Armed Forces or under Chief of Mission authority as a translator or interpreter in Iraq or Afghanistan.

The need for community assessments to determine how to deal with population shifts in the city as well as how to create an agency that could effectively serve the needs of these diverse resettlement communities was of major concern. A partnership among stakeholders was formed through the New Americans Task Force (NATF) and needs were identified by this collaborative group. The NATF is a "network of public and private organizations and community members, dedicated to supporting New Americans in our community ... assisting them to build new lives they seek through the removal of barriers and the provision of culturally competent support services" (https://app.lincoln.ne.gov/city/natf/).

A staff psychologist with expertise in mental health service provision for refugees identified the growing need for mental health services and the utility of implementing a mental health orientation for newly arriving refugees. Under her leadership, the voices of counselors, religious leaders, indigenous healers, physicians, politicians, educators (e.g., K–12 and university level) were included in the process of services development. The disciplinary areas of professional representation grew as the development of the FIRST Project progressed. Cultural brokers and community informants were identified as a critical first step to ensure that the voices of immigrants and refugees were part of the assessment process. The professional staff "mirrored the communities we served, including former refugees and immigrants" (Prendes-Lintel & Peterson, 2008, p. 221).

Community relationships were established with various agencies and programs, such as the Lincoln Family Practice Residency Program, the

University of Nebraska Counseling Psychology Program, Legal Assistance for Southeast Nebraska, and the Center for Legal Immigration Assistance. Simultaneously, collaborations also began at the national level and request for guidance was issued to the Center for Victims of Torture in Minnesota and through the developing consortium of torture treatment programs. Eventually, the FIRST Project was accepted by the National Consortium of Torture Treatment Programs, a "U.S. based network of programs which exists to advance the knowledge, technical capacities and resources devoted to the care of torture survivors living in the United States and acts collectively to prevent torture worldwide" (www.ncttp.org/).

6.4.1.2 Multidimensional Training Program

A major feature of this community assessment was the creation of a training program to equip the staff with skills to best serve the community. As needs arose within the community, the team worked to hire additional staff and provide resources on a continual basis. All staff attended training for the purpose of learning to work cohesively as strength-focused providers including clinicians, case managers, and all personnel regardless of position. Nurses were brought in as a result of participants having difficulty taking medications correctly. As the need for community trainings and consultations increased, services expanded to include working with teachers locally and nationally to address the needs of traumatized refugee children and their families. A local literacy agency also provided volunteers to teach English to participants who often learned better in a one-to-one format.

6.4.1.3 Professional Development Activities

Practicums were developed for doctoral students training to work with refugees and torture survivors. Staff also received access to field-specific training activities to help further their professional development. Psychologists were exposed to lunchtime presentations and a journal club. Similarly, mental health providers (e.g., counselors and social workers), physicians, and volunteers attended community trainings. Overall, these activities were an important element of the FIRST Project services and promoted professional development.

6.4.1.4 Interpreter Training

Early in the assessment process the need for interpreters was identified as stakeholders needed to communicate effectively. Languages spoken within the countries of origin for refugees and immigrants were specifically targeted. The complexities of providing interpreter services based upon the various languages represented was a major challenge. The importance of understanding the lives of community members was paramount. Each individual client brought their own experiences and life journey to this point and issues around language and communication quickly rose to the forefront:

> The unique experiences of individuals, the meaning of their torture, and experiences of multiple losses, acculturation, and adjustment, as well as culture, race, ethnicity, religion, gender, and abilities, all had to be addressed within the context of language … we wanted to understand the meaning and context of the client's pain, needs, and coping.   (Prendes-Lintel & Peterson, 2008, p. 221)

To address this need, interpreters were trained to understand the therapeutic process and encouraged to explore their own personal traumas that they worked through toward their own healing. This was a complex process given the dynamic nature of language and how it is influenced by local cultural, religious, spiritual, sociopolitical, socioeconomic, and environmental contexts. Additionally, the training process for interpreters emphasized the following characteristics: flexibility, trustworthiness, professionalism, full bilingualism, cultural familiarity, and awareness of limitations. Interpreters were also provided with a code of ethics that underscored the importance of confidentiality and prioritized the protection of participants.

6.4.1.5 Community Stakeholders

The need to earn the trust of community members was established in part through "family picnics" where stakeholders and their families openly gathered with immigrant and refugee families to establish cultural bridges. Together, decisions were made regarding the location of the agency away from government buildings near affordable public transportation. Given limited resources transportation passes were provided. Given the history of trauma, the design of FIRST Project offices included subdued lighting, a coffee bar, and a lobby area where staff, service providers, and clients could gather and work on jigsaw puzzles together. A strength-based perspective was discussed among the stakeholders and purposely integrated throughout the treatment program from the training of staff to the selection of assessment measures. The strengths-based model supports a collaborative relationship between the clients and service providers recognizing the innate strength of the whole person moving away from a traditional focus on client deficits. Clients are believed to be capable of making their own decisions and this is critical in the process of recovery as strength can be gained from adversity (Smith, 2006). Rubin et al. (2012) notes the strengths-based approach models of respect, reciprocity, and power sharing as reflected in the core principles of community-engaged pedagogy.

Attorneys volunteered to provide services to those seeking asylum coming to the FIRST Project to meet with clients. Politicians visited the site to learn about the needs of the growing community. Immigrants and refugees who had received services were given opportunities to speak on panels and other professional advocacy venues to share their experiences.

The FIRST Project officially closed its site due to lack of funding after six years. Yet, the services live on through the extensive network of interpreters now available in Lincoln and the passing on of training of mental health, education, and medical personnel. In addition, trainees from a variety of professional disciplines participated in the assessment and resulting services that were provided. As noted earlier, these included physicians, social workers, psychologists, and mental health providers. The team also spread their growing knowledge base as they along with clients were called upon to provide information and consultation services to agencies, hospitals, political venues, and other service providers.

The FIRST Project is a unique example of how community psychology and assessment methods were utilized in a collaborative multidisciplinary effort to provide services to refugee survivors of torture in Lincoln, Nebraska. The strengths-based perspective characteristic of community-based partnerships is evident throughout the formulation of services including the planning of assessment processes, creation of a staff that represented the communities being served, and empowerment of survivors.

6.4.2 A District-Wide Needs Assessment

6.4.2.1 Scope of the Assessment

The impetus for our second case study needs assessment began when a researcher was approached by a representative of their community engagement office within a large school district with more than 250,000 students. This study is still in progress and preliminary data are being analyzed. That office had attempted to gather information from community stakeholders but struggled with making lasting contact. Additionally, since most of the staff were practitioners, they sought assistance with designing an appropriate research study. Their concerns were twofold: First, despite consistent efforts to improve the academic performance of students in two specific school zones (consisting of approximately twenty schools) that served Black and Latinx children from economically challenged families, little headway had been made. Second, although schools within these zones had received trauma-informed interventions aimed at reducing negative outcomes for students, improvements were evident only in some areas and not in others. The administrator recognized that the needs of the community continued to have an impact on the immediate and long-term outcomes for students and their family members. The overarching goal for this project was to engage the community as a full partner in creating and implementing an action plan that would address the needs of the families while supporting academic outcomes among students.

The more specific objective of this needs assessment was to analyze and explore the traumatic events affecting students' developmental, emotional, and psychological well-being. An emancipatory or culturally informed needs assessment was conducted. Culture-centered research and program evaluation methodologies have emerged as alternatives to the cultural hegemony in mainstream research and program evaluation with a focus on empowerment and liberatory practices. Culture-centered research "addresses the inherent ethnocentrism and bias in traditional research methodologies that lead to inaccurate application and interpretation of constructs, faulty generalizations about non-Western client populations, and compromised efficacy among counselors" (West-Olatunji et al., 2014, p. 129). Transcultural theory further enhances this discourse in evaluating cross-national methodological challenges in research design, analysis, and interpretation of findings (West-Olatunji et al., 2017). The plan involved four major stakeholders: students at the elementary, middle, and high school levels; parents/caregivers; educators (including teachers, administrators, school counselors/psychologists/social workers); and community members (e.g., representatives of faith-based institutions, nonprofit organizations, community agencies, businesses, and neighborhood residents).

6.4.2.2 Recruiting a Team

The lead investigator gathered a team of professionals that included three research scholars, two of whom had expertise in curriculum and instruction and experience with emancipatory research methods that incorporated community involvement, while the third was familiar with the Parent Proficiency Questionnaire (PPQ) and had strong quantitative analysis skills. Emancipatory research places culture at the center of inquiry and challenges the way that knowledge and research are constructed. This methodological approach also honors and validates culturally diverse ways of knowing and being in order to empower and liberate participants and improve the lives of culturally diverse people and those who have historically been marginalized by the positivist tradition of social science research and psychology (King, 2005; Tillman, 2006; West-Olatunji et al., 2014, 2017).

Additionally, an external evaluator with a background in culturally responsive program evaluation methods was secured. Other members included two doctoral students in education attending a university close to the school district, a postdoctoral fellow with a background in counseling, and the creator of the Mi Rialiti app. The Mi Rialiti mobile application was proposed to help students to self-assess their community and identify how they perceive trauma in their school setting that ultimately impacts their emotional well-being and cognitive development. Students were provided with an opportunity to participate in an environmental scan to capture and document experiences through pictures, video, interviews, and geolocations (https://mirialiti.com).

Finally, a videographer was enlisted to provide more reflexivity to the overall process and offer a more accessible form of dissemination at the conclusion of the project. Reflexivity is defined as some confirmation of how the researchers' suppositions have been impacted by the logic of the data (Lather, 1986, 2018).

6.4.2.3 Planning the Community Needs Assessment

Study participants included students ($n = 40$), parents/caretakers ($n = 18$), school personnel ($n = 15$), and community members ($n = 15$) who were asked to participate in focus group and/or individual interviews. Additionally, parents/caregivers ($n = 500$) were asked to complete a culturally specific diagnostic instrument, the PPQ. The PPQ for African Americans (PPQ-AA) is a diagnostic tool that was designed to assess parenting practices among low-income African American parents/caregivers from a strength-based, culture-centered approach (Marks, West-Olatunji, & Goodman, 2016). Also, another fifty high school students gathered their own data using the Mi Rialiti app on their smartphones that allowed them to take photos in and around the school campus, write journal notes, and record short videos (thirty seconds maximum).

6.4.2.4 Recruiting Participants

As per the Institutional Review Board (IRB) approval, participants were contacted in a variety of ways. Students were recruited with the assistance of teachers in the identified schools. Parents/caregivers were recruited with assistance from community liaison staff. School personnel were recruited with the assistance of principals in the identified schools. Community members were contacted using a snowball method by attending key meetings where community stakeholders were present and extended an oral invitation as well as distributed written flyers. Once potential participants were identified, they were given an Informed Consent form that outlined the project and what they were being asked to do, including an explanation of the focus on trauma-informed services.

Students, parents/caregivers, school personnel, and community stakeholders engaged in synergistic discussions guided by structured interview questions, facilitated by a member of the research team and a graduate research assistant who served as a process observer. Focus group interviews lasted for ninety minutes and were held at one of the school sites or, in the case of community members, in a local site, such as a public library or church. After the preliminary analysis of the focus groups, some participants were asked to return for a forty-five-minute follow-up individual, structured interview. Some interviews were in person and others were held online using a videoconferencing program such as Zoom or Skype. All interviews were recorded (audio- and videotaped). All of the parents/caregivers of students in the school zones of interest were contacted via email to complete the PPQ. Secondary school students engaged in observations of their campus environments using the Mi Rialiti app over a three-week period.

As the team began planning meetings, they partnered with community members to conduct literature reviews, develop the focus group questions, and finalize interview locations. The research team met weekly via Zoom for roughly sixty minutes to go over the plan and provide updates on various segments of the project. One researcher served as supervisor to the doctoral students and post-doctoral fellow. One researcher focused on the data analysis protocols and the lead researcher coordinated all aspects of the needs assessment project and was responsible for reporting.

6.4.2.5 Conducting the Needs Assessment

After developing the needs assessment plan, implementation began with scheduling the focus group interviews, training the graduate assistants how to serve as process observers, and securing the tools necessary for data collection (e.g., audio and video recording devices). Although the plan was comprehensive, there were times when only one person showed up for the focus group interview and they needed to be rescheduled. Other challenges included receiving calls from the principal of a school of the day of the extended focus group interview and being told that the team could not use the school that day. Rapid reassessment was needed at all times.

It was also important to schedule interviews with educators away from school grounds and without representatives from the school district being present. This enabled educators to feel comfortable in sharing their authentic feelings and opinions with the team during data collection. There were delays from within the school district administration that slowed down the process. For instance, it took two months for the school district to approve the IRB application despite the fact that the host institution had long since approved the project. During these two months there were numerous back-and-forth communications and phone calls made to clarify methodological protocols. Also, there were persistent problems in getting the district to disperse funds to project team members.

6.4.2.6 Reviewing and Rating the Data

At the conclusion of every interview, recordings were sent electronically to a transcription service and promptly returned within twenty-four hours. All materials related to the project were stored on a secure cloud storage system that all members of the research team could access. References were stored and managed in Zotero (i.e., a reference management software designed to manage bibliographic data and research materials; www.zotero.org) and jointly updated by the entire team to facilitate easy access to journal articles for discussion. Once transcriptions were made available, research team members then reached out to participants for member checking.

Data analysis occurred in groups of three in which the transcripts were read and independently coded. Then the group would meet to reach consensus about themes and quotes that reflected those themes. This was followed by the development of definitions of the themes. During the weekly whole team meetings, analysis teams shared their preliminary findings and sought feedback from other members of the team. Once they finalized their analysis, each team included a list of follow-up questions for specific participants of the focus group interviews. These analyses were reviewed by the research scholars who engaged in a comprehensive analysis of the focus group interviews to reach translation of the research.

The individuals selected for individual interviews were contacted to schedule a follow-up interview with a member of the research team and a doctoral student. The transcription, member checking, and analysis procedures followed a similar pattern as with the focus group interviews. The journal notes data from the Mi Rialiti app were collected and pasted into an MS Word document to create a comprehensive transcript. This was analyzed in a similar fashion as other qualitative data. The results of the PPQ analysis were also provided and discussed by the team. Once the analyses from the triadic analysis teams were completed, the research scholars conducted a broad analysis using all of the data.

6.4.2.7 Recording and Reviewing the Consolidated Data

After completing the final analysis, the research team spent most of their weekly sessions engaged in theorizing about the findings. They compared the findings to existing literature on various segments of the student population and invited scholars to sit in on their weekly meetings to share information about their relevant research. Additionally, members of the community were asked to respond to the emerging translation of the findings. In this snowball fashion, the research team continued to develop a final report on the needs assessment that included a conventional dissemination of the qualitative and quantitative data, two conceptual papers that presented a discussion of the key issues, a readers' theater script that will be developed by the lead researcher and performed for the community institute for three hundred community stakeholders, a photo montage designed from the students' photos in the Mi Rialiti app, and the video created by the videographer. The purpose will be to make the findings of the needs assessment to be both translational as well as accessible by members of the community.

Key needs assessment themes were: Trauma and Resilience, Identity and Sense of Belonging, and Teacher Competence/Professionalism. Evidence from all four stakeholder groups suggested that the students were traumatized by their schooling experiences, whether from interactions with teachers, school policies, or lack of necessary resources. Additionally, many of the students were first- or second-generation Afro-Caribbean students who were struggling with their ethnic identity, and shared that they were neither identifying with their home country nor the American experience (Connolly, 1995; Henry, 1998; Jackson & Cothran, 2003).

6.4.2.8 Developing a Community Action Plan

The action plan was designed to be developed at the two-day community institute workshop. The first day consisted of an after-school program on a Friday evening that provided an overview of the project and its findings. The second day was an all-day program for representatives of the school district and community agencies that could make system-wide changes that would impact the students. Based upon the recommendations of the research team, the action planning group developed the community action that would be printed and distributed to all parties. The caveat was that the group would reassemble in six months to review the action plan and deliverables to make modifications, if necessary, and then schedule another meeting in six additional months.

It is too early to determine the success of the action plan. However, the research team successfully gave voice to the four stakeholders groups in this needs assessment. The students articulated ways in which they felt traumatized by their schooling experiences, the educators expressed how they needed guidance on how to make the curriculum relevant to the students, parents/caregivers expressed the need for the schools to link their services to children's needs once they step foot off campus, and community members stated how involved and engaged they are in the success of the students. The research process for this community assessment project is ongoing.

This second case illustrates the complexity of community psychology working to address the needs and academic achievement of Black and Latinx students in the urban school environment. Once again, a collaborative community-based participatory action research process was applied. In this case investigators clearly identified the importance of culture-centered and emancipatory perspectives and collaboration incorporating the strengths of the community. Innovative qualitative mobile apps and culture-based measures were built into the study design. While this study remains in progress the impact of the community assessment will have far-reaching implications and unique dissemination venues.

6.5 Implications of Cases and Future Directions

These two cases illustrate the range of procedures, data sources, and outcomes (i.e., action plans) that can result from a community assessment.

Each case uniquely addresses the complexity of the process of gathering relevant information from stakeholders representing different professional disciplines with their own agendas in relation to the goals of the assessment. In addition, understanding the historical context of what has been tried in the past to meet the needs of respective communities is a critical part of program development and intervention. The importance of cultural competence among members of the assessment team, cultural adaptability in the process, and the diversity of data sources (e.g., qualitative, quantitative, mixed methods) is noted.

Conducting a community assessment is an invaluable skill for educators, researchers, and clinicians. It is only through an inclusive and informed process of data gathering that a relevant and accurate understanding of a community's assets and needs can be obtained. The process of assessment is complex and strategic requiring the assessment team to spend time planning, collecting data from multiple stakeholder groups, analyzing the data, and formulating informed action plans. Given the increasing diversity within our communities, utilizing the information provided in the aforementioned concepts, theoretical frameworks, and case examples to help develop a culturally responsive community needs assessment is a clarion call for our profession.

References

Ahmed, R., Seedat, M., Van Niekerk, A., & Bulbulia, S. (2004). Discerning community resilience in disadvantaged communities in the context of violence and injury prevention. *South African Journal of Psychology, 34*(3), 386–408. doi.org/10.1177/008124630403400304

Centers for Disease Control and Prevention. (2013). *Community needs assessment.* www.cdc.gov/globalhealth/healthprotection/fetp/training_modules/15/community-needs_pw_final_9252013.pdf

Community Science. (n.d.). *Sense of community.* www.senseofcommunity.com/soc-index/

Connolly, P. (1995). Racism, masculine peer-group relations and the schooling of African/Caribbean infant boys. *British Journal of Sociology in Education, 16*(1), 75–92. www.jstor.org/stable/1393127

Corrigan, P. W. (2020). Editorial: Community-based participatory research (CBPR), stigma, and health. *Stigma and Health, 5*(2), 123–124. doi.org/10.1037/sah0000175

Craig, S. L. (2011). Precarious partnerships: Designing a community needs assessment to develop a system of care for gay, lesbian, bisexual, transgender, and questioning (GLBTQ) youths. *Journal of Community Practice, 19*(3), 274–291. doi.org/10.1080/10705422.2011.595301

DeAngelis, T. (2015). In search of cultural competence. *APA Monitor, 46*(3), 64. www.apa.org/monitor/2015/03/cultural-competence

Ellaway, A., Macintyre, S., & Kearns, A. (2001). Perceptions of place and health in socially contrasting neighbourhoods. *Urban Studies, 38*(12), 2299–2316. doi .org/10.1080/00420980120087171

Geisinger, K. F. (1994). Cross-cultural normative assessment: Translation and adaptation issues influencing the normative interpretation of assessment instruments. *Psychological Assessment, 6*(4), 304–312. doi.org/10.1037/1040-3590.6 .4.304

Henry, A. (1998). "Speaking up" and "speaking out": Examining "voice" in a reading/ writing program with adolescent African Caribbean girls. *Journal of Literacy Research, 30*(2), 233–252. doi.org/10.1080/10862969809547997

Jackson, J. V., & Cothran, M. E. (2003). Black versus black: The relationships among African, African American, and African Caribbean persons. *Journal of Black Studies, 33*(5), 576–604. www.jstor.org/stable/3180977

King, J. E. (2005). A transformative vision of Black education for human freedom. In J. E. King (Ed.), *Black education: A transformative research and action agenda for the new century* (pp. 3–17). Mahwah, NJ: Lawrence Erlbaum Associates.

Kramer, S., Seedat, M., Lazarus, S., & Suffla, S. (2011). A critical review of instruments assessing characteristics of community. *South African Journal of Psychology, 41*(4), 503–516. doi.org/10.1177/008124631104100409

Lather, P. (1986). Issues of validity in openly ideological research: Between a rock and a soft place. *Interchange, 17*(4), 63–84. doi.org/10.1007/BF01807017

Lather, P. (2018). Thirty years after: From research to praxis to praxis in the ruins. In H. J. Malone, S. Rincon-Gallardo, & K. Kew (Eds.), *Future directions of educational change: Social justice, professional capital and systems change* (pp. 71–86). New York: Routledge.

Long, D. A., & Perkins, D. D. (2003). Confirmatory factor analysis of the sense of community index and development of a brief SCI. *Journal of Community Psychology, 31*(3), 279–296. doi.org/10.1002/jcop.10046

Marks, L. R., West-Olatunji, C. A., & Goodman, R. D. (2016). A pilot study evaluating the Parent Proficiencies Questionnaire for African American Parents (PPQ-AA). *Urban Education Research and Policy Annals, 4*(1), 99–109.

McMillan, D. W., & Chavis, D. M. (1986). Sense of community: A definition and theory. *Journal of Community Psychology, 14*(1), 6–23. doi.org/10.1002/1520-6629(198601)14:1<6::AID-JCOP2290140103>3.0.CO;2-I

Newman, S. D., Andrews, J. O., Magwood, G. S., et al. (2011). Community advisory boards in community-based participatory research: A synthesis of best processes. *Preventing Chronic Disease, 8*(3). www.cdc.gov/pcd/issues/2011/ may/10_0045.htm

Pfefferbaum, B., Pfefferbaum, R. L., & Van Horn, R. L. (2015). Community resilience interventions: Participatory assessment-based, action-oriented processes. *American Behavioral Scientist, 59*(2), 238–253. doi.org/10.1177/ 0002764214550298

Prendes-Lintel, M., & Peterson, F. (2008). Delivering quality mental health services to immigrants and refugees through an interpreter. In L. A. Suzuki & J. G. Ponterotto (Eds.), *Handbook of multicultural assessment: Clinical, psychological, and educational applications* (3rd ed., pp. 220–243). San Francisco: Jossey Bass.

Rubin, C. L., Martinez, L. S., Chu, J., et al. (2012). Community-engaged pedagogy: A strengths-based approach to involving diverse stakeholders in research partnerships. *Program Community Health Partnerships, 6*(4), 481–490. doi .org/10.1353/cpr.2012.0057

Sarason, S. B. (1974). *The psychological sense of community: Prospects for a community psychology*. San Francisco: Jossey-Bass.

Shorkey, C., Windsor, L. C., & Spence, R. (2009). Assessing culturally competent chemical dependence treatment services for Mexican Americans. *The Journal of Behavioral Health Services & Research, 36*(1), 61–74. doi.org/10.1007/ s11414-008-9110-x

Smith, E. J. (2006). The strength-based counseling model. *The Counseling Psychologist, 34*, 13–79. doi.org/10.1177/0011000005277018

Sue, D. W. (2001). Multicultural facets of cultural competence. *The Counseling Psychologist, 29*(6), 790–821. doi.org/10.1177/0011000001296002

Tillman, L. (2006). Researching and writing from an African American perspective: Reflective notes on three research studies. *International Journal of Qualitative Studies in Education, 19*(3), 265–287. doi.org/10.1080/09518390600696513

Trickett, E. J. (2009). Multilevel community-based culturally situated interventions and community impact: An ecological perspective. *American Journal of Community Psychology, 43*(3–4), 257–266. doi.org/10.1007/s10464-009-9227-y

Van de Vijver, F. J. R. (2016). Test adaptations. In F. T. L. Leong, D. Bartram, F. M. Cheung, K. F. Geisinger, & D. Iliescu (Eds.), *The ITC international handbook of testing and assessment* (pp. 364–376). New York: Oxford University Press.

Wallerstein, N. B., Yen, I. H., & Syme, S. L. (2011). Integration of social epidemiology and community-engaged interventions to improve health equity. *American Journal of Public Health, 101*(5), 822–830. doi.org/10.2105/AJPH.2008.140988

West-Olatunji, C., Shure, L., Jean-Paul, N., Goodman, R. D., & Lewis, D. (2014). Culture-centered research and counselor efficacy. *Turkish Psychological Counseling and Guidance Journal, 5*(42), 129–137. www.turkpdrdergisi.com/ index.php/pdr/article/view/18

West-Olatunji, C., Yang, M. J., Wolfgang, J. D., Henesy, R., & Yoon, E. (2017). Highlighting the challenges when conducting cross-national studies: Use of transcultural theory. *Journal of Counseling and Development, 95*(4), 457–464. doi.org/10.1002/jcad.12160

7 Comprehensive Evaluation of a Rural School Mental Health Program

Samantha N. Hartley, Melissa Strompolis, Courtnie Collins, W. Joshua Bradley, Darien M. Collins, Patrick M. Bresnan, and Mark D. Weist

Evaluating regional programs designed to promote youth resilience and well-being can be challenging, especially when embedded data collection systems are primarily designed to catalogue the number of services rendered rather than the nature of outcomes achieved. This chapter highlights how one school–community–university partnership evaluated efforts to counteract the impacts of adverse childhood experiences (ACEs) in rural South Carolina. First, the chapter describes the wisdom of using an ecological systems approach to promote youth resilience, including a continuum of mental health supports within schools, helping families navigate community resources to address concrete needs, and building community-level ACE awareness and capacity for resiliency promotion. Second, the chapter presents a case study of such an approach in rural South Carolina, called the Pee Dee Resiliency Project. This section includes an overview of the region in which the project took place, components and goals of the initiative, and the evaluation of those efforts. Initial results and helpful strategies for those interested in conducting similar evaluations with school and community partners are provided. The chapter concludes with additional guidance on how communities can take concrete steps to prevent ACEs and build resilience and some final considerations for the field.

7.1 Social, Emotional, and Behavioral Challenges and Adverse Childhood Experiences in Children and Youth

The need to address the social, emotional, and behavioral (SEB) well-being of youth is significant (Merikangas et al., 2010a, 2010b; Patel

The Pee Dee Resilience Project Team would like to thank the BlueCross® and BlueShield® of South Carolina Foundation for their leadership, funding, and support; and the South Carolina Department of Mental Health, Pee Dee Mental Health Center, Darlington County Schools, Florence County Schools, Marion County Schools, and community-based organizations that worked together to build student, school, and community resilience.

et al., 2007). Estimates suggest that approximately 20% of youth in the United States have a diagnosable mental health problem that requires intervention (Merikangas et al., 2010a, 2010b). However, a significant proportion of those in need of mental health supports do not receive them, with 50% of youth with mental health concerns receiving some intervention and only 20%–25% completing treatment (Anderson & Gittler, 2005; Burns et al., 1995; Kataoka, Zhang, & Wells, 2002; Nock & Ferriter, 2005). This gap in the receipt of services is of significant concern, given that untreated mental health concerns tend to result in greater functional impairments that persist over time (Harpin et al., 2016; Lacourse et al., 2002).

There is also growing evidence and increased recognition regarding the negative effects and sequelae of ACEs (Chapman et al., 2004; Dube et al., 2003; Felitti et al., 1998). ACEs include negative childhood experiences related to abuse (e.g., sexual, physical, emotional), neglect (e.g., physical, emotional), and household dysfunction (e.g., domestic violence, mental illness, substance use/misuse, parental separation/divorce, household member in prison; Felitti & Anda, 2010; Felitti et al., 1998). Research has documented an array of negative social and health outcomes associated with ACEs, including increased risk for smoking (Anda et al., 1999), alcohol/substance use/misuse (Anda et al., 2002; Dube et al., 2003), overweight/obesity (Burke et al., 2011), suicide (Dube et al., 2001), heart disease (Felitti et al., 1998), premature mortality (Brown et al., 2009), and mental health problems (Chapman et al., 2004; Edwards et al., 2003). The relation between ACEs and negative outcomes is a dose–response relationship, such that a greater number of ACEs is associated with proportionally greater risk for negative social and health outcomes (Felitti et al., 1998).

Given the myriad of negative outcomes associated with ACEs, the prevalence of ACEs is a significant public health concern. Data from the 2016 National Survey of Children's Health (NSCH) indicate that 45% of children in the United States have experienced at least one ACE (Sack & Murphey, 2018). Approximately 10% of children have experienced three or more ACEs and are at high risk for experiencing negative social and health outcomes (Mersky, Topitzes, & Reynolds, 2013). Data from the NSCH also document racial/ethnic disparities in the probability of experiencing ACEs. A total of 51% of Hispanic youth and 61% of African American youth report experiencing at least one ACE, whereas 40% of White youth and 23% of Asian American youth report the same (Sack & Murphey, 2018). This is particularly concerning given disparity in the experience of ACEs has been shown to contribute to other social and health disparities affecting racial/ethnic minorities (Slopen et al., 2016; Umberson et al., 2014).

7.2 Ecological Systems Approach to Promoting Well-Being

A core principle of a community psychology approach to promoting well-being is to consider the role of contexts and systems (Kloos et al., 2020). An ecological systems approach posits that an individual's development and well-being is influenced by the contexts and systems in which they are embedded, and concurrently, that individuals have agency to influence these contexts and systems (Bronfenbrenner, 1992). Increasingly, an ecological systems approach has informed prevention, promotion, and intervention efforts for youth. One example is the movement to expand the delivery of mental health services to schools.

School mental health (SMH) programs aim to provide mental health supports to youth "where they are" in a universal ecologically relevant context – the school (Weist, 1997). Given SMH services are delivered in a setting that is convenient to youth and families, youth receive care more rapidly and are more likely to be engaged in treatment compared to traditional clinic settings (Atkins et al., 2006; Burns et al., 1995; Green et al., 2013). SMH programs have been demonstrated to improve student academic performance (Suldo et al., 2014), SEB functioning (Kutash, Duchnowski, & Green, 2011; Nabors & Reynolds, 2000), and school attendance (Ballard, Sander, & Klimes-Dougan, 2014). Increasingly, the SMH field has recognized the need for services to extend beyond treatment of mental health problems to address the mental health needs of all youth within a multitiered system of support (MTSS), including prevention and promotion programming (Tier 1), early intervention (Tier 2), and treatment (Tier 3; Barrett, Eber, & Weist, 2013; Sugai & Horner, 2006). Decisions regarding which interventions are selected and implemented in a school are typically made by an MTSS team and informed using data from multiple ecological levels (e.g., school, city/town, county).

For example, a school in a region where many youth experience ACEs and traumatic experiences might consider implementing interventions that provide psychoeducation on the effects of ACEs and trauma at Tier 1, a group-based intervention for youth demonstrating some signs of traumatic stress at Tier 2 (e.g., cognitive behavioral intervention for trauma in schools; Stein et al., 2003), and individual psychotherapy for youth who meet criteria for post-traumatic stress disorder at Tier 3 (e.g., trauma-focused cognitive behavioral therapy [CBT]; Cohen et al., 2000).

There have also been efforts to promote youth resilience and well-being at the community level, including the prevention of ACEs and traumatic experiences. This work has similarly drawn on ecological and public health approaches to conceptualize and address ACEs (Bronfenbrenner, 1992; Verbitsky-Savitz et al., 2016). Community initiatives that aim to promote youth resilience and prevent ACEs have often emphasized (1) a positive youth development perspective that centers on facilitating healthy relationships with others, building competencies (particularly social-emotional), and exposure to positive developmental contexts; (2) coordination of care and interventions across multiple contexts and sectors (e.g., public mental health system coordinating with schools, juvenile justice system); and (3) enhancing community capacity to sustain efforts to promote resilience and prevent ACEs (Blodgett, 2013; Verbitsky-Savitz et al., 2016; Vivolo, Matjasko, & Massetti, 2011). These community-based strategies have been shown to result in community-level reductions of ACEs as well as improved social and health outcomes (Hall et al., 2012; Verbitsky-Savitz et al., 2016).

One approach to build community capacity is through school–community–university (SCU) partnerships (Spoth et al., 2004, 2011). SCU partnerships involve school, community, and university partners coordinating resources and leveraging their relative strengths in order to achieve a desired goal (e.g., reduction of ACEs, promotion of youth SEB functioning). For example, university partners often have expertise and resources to provide technical assistance and capacity-building support, whereas community partners are often positioned to contribute needed services and facilitate linkages to relevant community supports (e.g., community-based parenting programs). Research suggests that SCU partnerships can enhance implementation quality and promote positive youth outcomes (Spoth et al., 2007, 2011).

7.3 Evaluation of Community Programs

Evaluation plays a critical role in monitoring the implementation and effectiveness of community and school programs (Kloos et al., 2020). *Process evaluation* involves assessing the extent to which a program is being implemented as intended and reaching intended consumers. Process evaluation is necessary for identifying implementation problems that need to be addressed in order to maximize the probability that a program achieves desired outcomes. Process evaluation indicators could include intervention fidelity checklists, demographic characteristics of consumers, and key stakeholders' interviews that assess barriers to implementation. *Outcome evaluation* is concerned with determining the extent to which a program reached its overall goals and desired outcomes in the long term. Examples of outcome evaluation indicators include SEB functioning, grades, and school attendance. Evaluation findings can have significant impacts on programs, such as identifying areas where a program should be modified and whether a community decides to fund and sustain a program after grant funding ends.

7.4 The Pee Dee Resilience Project

In this chapter, we provide an example of a community–university partnership aimed at counteracting the impact of ACEs during childhood, the Pee Dee Resiliency Project (PDRP). First, we describe the region in which the project took place, the Pee Dee region of South Carolina (SC). Then, we describe the general structure and goals of PDRP. Finally, we describe the evaluation conducted for PDRP, including helpful strategies and tips for those interested in managing similar evaluations with school and community partners.

7.4.1 Project Setting: The Pee Dee Region of South Carolina

The northeastern corner of SC is referred to as the Pee Dee region. Named for the Great Pee Dee River, several counties encompass this region; for the purpose of this chapter, the focus will be Darlington, Florence, and Marion counties.

The estimated population of these three counties is 237,000 people, with 52.8% of individuals identified as White, 44.4% Black/African American, and 2.5% Hispanic/Latinx. The major industries include health care and social assistance; retail trade; accommodation and food service; manufacturing; education; professional, scientific, and technical services; and finance and insurance. While the region is a proven location for world-class business and industry (e.g., FedEx, General Electric Healthcare, Honda), an average of 33.4% of children are living in households with income below the poverty line, 10.8% are living with an unemployed caregiver, and 15.8% live with a household member who lacks a high school diploma (Children's Trust of South Carolina, 2019).

The largest city within the Pee Dee is the City of Florence, which has an estimated population of thirty-eight thousand residents. Florence's location as the midpoint between New York City and Miami along I-95 and as an intersection of Interstates 20 and 95 has led to the area's growth in many ways, particularly with regard to the hospitality industry.

The three-county Pee Dee region has seven public school districts. Combined, these districts have fourteen high schools as well as multiple middle, elementary, alternative, and magnet schools. The area also boasts three schools of higher education: Francis Marion University, Coker College, and Florence-Darlington Technical College. Challenges related to education in this region include relatively high percentages of students failing grades 1, 2, or 3 (8%); third graders testing below state standards in English/Language Arts (70.3%); and eighth graders testing below state standards in math (78.9%) (Children's Trust of South Carolina, 2019).

The region's largest mental health provider is the Pee Dee Mental Health Center (Pee Dee MHC), a public, outpatient facility of the South Carolina Department of Mental Health. Pee Dee MHC has more than 160 employees, including psychiatrists, nurse practitioners, nurses, licensed professional counselors, master's-level mental health professionals (MHPs), bachelor's-level therapists, and peer support specialists. Twenty-five of Pee Dee MHC's

MHPs provide school mental health services. These clinicians are embedded in schools and provide a range of treatments including individual, group, and family therapy. Pee Dee MHC averages a caseload of 2,500 patients, with more than 4,000 individuals receiving services each year. Because of their established position within the region as a provider of school-based mental health services, the Pee Dee MHC was a natural partner for PDRP.

7.4.2 The Pee Dee Resiliency Project

The Pee Dee Resiliency Project (PDRP) is an innovative partnership between the BlueCross® and BlueShield® of South Carolina Foundation, Children's Trust of South Carolina (Children's Trust), the South Carolina Department of Mental Health, the University of South Carolina School Behavioral Health Team, and the Pee Dee MHC. Through these partnerships, PDRP has been able to address the needs of students and families through a diverse set of lenses, with a focus on building resilience and improving well-being for students, families, and communities within the Pee Dee region.

Overarching aims of the work included increasing student well-being and achievement, increasing family well-being, increasing consistent and quality caregiving, and promoting safe and supportive neighborhoods. In order to achieve these goals PDRP partnered with eight elementary schools across Florence, Darlington, and Marion counties and provided each school with one full-time mental health clinician in the hopes that they became fully integrated in their school culture. This model of one clinician to one school is unlike traditional practice, wherein school mental health clinicians are typically asked to serve multiple schools, not allowing an opportunity for integrating themselves into the daily routines and cultures of the schools that they serve. Additionally, a full-time family engagement specialist (FES) served all PDRP schools to mobilize community and project resources to support the needs of all students and families in the eight target schools (e.g., housing, food, transportation). These eight schools served as a universal entry and delivery point to engage students, families, and communities to address the root causes of ACEs and work toward prevention of such issues.

This work has relied on an MTSS (see Sugai & Horner, 2006) with strategic efforts to engage communities across the continuum of care: prevention, early intervention, and treatment. Prevention and early intervention efforts have primarily included community outreach/trainings, school trainings, family engagement, and safety and support teams (SSTs). A key component to community engagement and outreach has relied on the involvement and guidance of a Community Action Team (CAT). The CAT is a community-based group of stakeholders across the Pee Dee region. CAT members advise PDRP team members on various components of the project such as methods for best engaging families and the community as a whole, as well as continuously drawing in new members who are invested in bettering the Pee Dee ommunity. Children's Trust has engaged members of the Pee Dee and PDRP chools by offering film screenings and trainings on the impact of ACEs, eading to stimulating discussions around ways to build more resilient communities and schools within the Pee Dee.

SSTs at each of the PDRP schools have functioned as a hub for identifying he needs of all students, vulnerable students, and students requiring individual clinical service. The full availability of an FES solely focused on meeting he needs of children and families outside of the school building has filled a ritical role in SSTs. Implementing this MTSS model within the eight elementary schools has provided a space for identifying issues such as schoolwide oncerns with bullying, groups of youth dealing with anger and trauma, and tudents/families who require treatment but would otherwise not have had iccess to a mental health clinician.

7.4.3 Evaluating the Pee Dee Resiliency Project

7.4.3.1 Designing the PDRP Evaluation Strategy

Within our project timeline, the evaluation team was granted the luxury of the entirety of Summer 2017 to thoughtfully design an evaluation plan for PDRP. The original directive of the evaluation was to measure how strategic collaboration and a focus on MTSS, prevention, and empowering community voice can build resiliency and improve well-being for students, families, and communities n the Pee Dee region of South Carolina. PDRP is a fairly expansive project, with intervention components ranging from quality improvement and service expansion in SMH practices to schoolwide trainings and systems interventions e.g., incorporating SMH into positive behavioral interventions and supports PBIS]), assessing and connecting families in need to concrete resources in their community, and impacting the community through a number of resilience/ ACE-focused trainings, community events, and the development of a community action team. The evaluation team worked to develop a mixed methods evaluation strategy that translated broad aims stated within the grant application into eight thematic goals and forty measurable desired outcomes, reduced measurement burden whenever possible, monitored progress on project milestones, and provided actionable progress data that could be used to identify opportunities for improvement during implementation.

7.4.3.2 Determining Goals, Desired Outcomes, and Data Sources

PDRP was designed to have several areas of impact, including the greater Pee Dee community, systems-level improvements within schools, child mental health and functioning, and family well-being. This chapter focuses on evaluating PDRP's impact on child mental health and functioning and family well-being. A key goal for the project was that students enrolled in participating

PDRP schools would demonstrate increased well-being and functioning at the end of the project period. This would be accomplished by implementing a one-to-one clinician model where SMH clinicians provided quality, evidence-based care and were integrated with the school community through an MTSS. Additionally, families in PDRP schools would demonstrate increased well-being by receiving FES services that effectively met their family's concrete resource needs.

Desired outcomes were specified for all students attending PDRP schools and for students who received individualized treatment. Changes in school-wide student outcomes were gathered from school record data (SRD) provided by the school district through PowerSchool, the student information management system used in South Carolina public schools. These targets included data related to discipline (i.e., office discipline referrals, suspensions, expulsions), attendance (i.e., unexcused absences and tardies), and academic achievement (i.e., grade retention, grade point average [GPA]) extracted on the individual-student level. As the evaluation team discovered, creating novel reports was a significant task for districts not previously involved in research studies that required this information. It is recommended that stipulations for gathering SRD be included in project memoranda of understanding (MOUs) and that project staff work collaboratively with PowerSchool coordinators at the district or state level to develop detailed instructional guides for creating desired SRD reports. This may reduce the amount of data cleaning required once SRD reports are received from schools.

Desired outcomes for students receiving individual therapy at school included improvements in symptoms and strengths (i.e., reduction in Pediatric Symptom Checklist [PSC; Jellinek & Murphy, 1988] scores, increase in Child and Youth Resilience Measure-12 [CYRM-12; Ungar & Liebenberg 2009] score, parent report of more positive behaviors at home), achieving a majority of their treatment goals by case closure, and parent satisfaction with SMH services. Several clinician variables were monitored to characterize their work within the schools, including self-reported use of evidence-based interventions with clients, productivity reports for clinical services, and involvement in nonbillable SMH services that promoted their integration within an MTSS at the school (e.g., school engagement, MTSS meetings, Tier 1 and 2 activities). Although the evaluation team wished to reduce measurement burden on the clinicians, it was quickly realized that the electronic medical record system used by their agency was not built to extract easily analyzable subsets of client data. The system functioned exceptionally well at generating detailed productivity and billing reports, which could be quickly generated at specified time points by the Pee Dee MHC. Separate measures were designed to document client and treatment information at intake, ninety-day progress monitoring intervals, and case closure and nonbillable MTSS activities. Efforts were taken to build clinician capacity and motivation for using this separate data collection system (detailed in Section 7.4.3.3 below) and to increase the clinical utility of "extra" forms by programming automated scoring and interpretation into the PSC and CYRM-12 forms.

Finally, desired outcomes for family well-being focused on whether families who received FES services received community-based services and supports that adequately met their needs and reduced their self-reported stress. Outcomes for families receiving FES services were measured using a novel FES database created for PDRP. The database was created collaboratively with the FES as an integrated record and data collection system and included forms documenting referral, needs assessment, service provision, and follow-up. Analysis of FES database data provided valuable information to the community team and school on common needs of Pee Dee families and the availability/accessibility of community resources designed to meet those needs.

7.4.3.3 Managing Data Collection and Anticipating Challenges

As a university partner, the evaluation team decided to collect and manage PDRP data using REDCap electronic data capture tools hosted at the University of South Carolina (Harris et al., 2009, 2019). REDCap (Research Electronic Data Capture) is a secure, web-based software platform designed to support data capture for research studies, providing (1) an intuitive interface for validated data capture, (2) audit trails for tracking data manipulation and export procedures, (3) automated export procedures for seamless data downloads to common statistical packages, and (4) procedures for data integration and interoperability with external sources. REDCap allowed the team the flexibility to develop novel, secure databases for SMH and FES client information with data access rules to prevent evaluation staff from viewing unnecessary protected health information (PHI). This feature was especially useful in the case of the FES database – developed in collaboration with the FES – as REDCap functioned as her primary form of client documentation. For data collection needs that required repeated entries, such as weekly documentation of MTSS activities, REDCap allowed for the development of repeated measure surveys with email invitations that could be sent to clinicians at planned intervals.

REDCap represented a compelling data collection/management option for the evaluation team, but it was a new interface for our community and mental health partners tasked with inputting project data not directly related to billing. Two challenges that the evaluation team encountered with data collection included knowledge/skill-based barriers to engaging with REDCap and minimizing missing data.

To reduce barriers to using REDCap, the evaluation team offered a combination of live trainings with opportunities for clinicians to log in, click through all forms and surveys inputting test data, and real-time assistance with difficulties; drop-in technical assistance sessions at Pee Dee MHC prior to the first data check; as-needed trouble shooting via email and conference calls;

and an illustrated step-by-step user guide for each data collection instrument that included annotated screen captures of important fields and "click" locations. Technology-anxious staff reflected that the illustrated step-by-step instructions gave them confidence to use REDCap on their own after the initial training.

Missing data – particularly data that are collected in a separate location or otherwise in addition to the requirements of daily clinical work – are an ever-present concern in program evaluation work. To minimize the likelihood of missing data, thorough data checks of all clinician-completed database measures and surveys were completed by the evaluation team every two months using project milestones (e.g., an expected number of SST meetings) and active case load reports from Pee Dee MHC. Clinicians were given advance warning of data checks and personalized emails listing all missing data after the initial check and data recheck were performed. User logs on REDCap allowed evaluation team members to look up the most recent site log-ins and activity by clinicians based on their username; periodic outreach to clinicians who were absent from the site allowed for timely technical assistance and more frequent reminders of accountability. An additional strategy for reducing missing data was teaming with clinical supervisors and Pee Dee MHC staff to communicate the importance and priority of inputting PDRP data into REDCap. Clinical supervisors were provided with their own supervision checklist to inquire about data input and clinical events (e.g., new clients, case closures) that would necessitate REDCap tasks. At their request, clinical supervisors and the Department of Mental Health coordinator were also included on the clinicians' data check emails so that they could be aware of their staff's compliance with project expectations.

7.4.3.4 Reporting Back on Progress

Statistically significant change in valued indicators of student well-being and success – such as improvements in schoolwide academic performance and student attendance and reductions in disciplinary incidents and clinically significant behavioral health symptoms – take time to achieve after introducing a suite of interventions like PDRP. The evaluation team provided brief, individualized annual reports to PDRP schools to highlight the impact one-to-one SMH and FES services were having in their school. These one- and two-page update reports emphasized a colorful design that attended to data visualization principles, rather than relied on an abundance of text.

The one-page update flyer for general audiences included a brief description of PDRP and highlights from the mental health (e.g., number of students served, presenting concerns based on PSC scores, and parent feedback on the acceptability and convenience of SMH services as well as the impact on child behavior) and FES services (e.g., number of families referred, most frequent needs, impact of FES services on stress) provided to the school community. It also included information on the school's clinician and FES and how to initiate services for those interested in making a referral. These flyers were distributed to all school staff and provided to SMH clinicians to post outside their office and hand out at school events. Clinicians felt that the flyers helped justify their presence in the school while helping them to connect with administrators and staff on areas of improvement for themselves as well as schoolwide.

The two-page administrator update included data from SMH and FES services as well as information on referral sources, MTSS implementation progress, and goals/expectations for the upcoming school year. This "progress and next steps" section allowed project staff to concisely celebrate accomplishments, specify school-specific improvement goals based on progress data, and orient administrators to upcoming trainings. School administrators valued the succinct nature of the two-sheet reports. They indicated that they could easily digest areas of success and improvement. The sheets were utilized to conveniently share updates with both teachers and parents.

7.4.3.5 Qualitative Evaluation

Although the evaluation team did not initially anticipate having the capacity to complete a thorough qualitative evaluation of PDRP, adding this component in the last year of implementation was determined to be an essential component of understanding the experience and impact of PDRP from various perspectives (e.g., SMH clinicians, FES, school administrators, parents) and informing quality improvement in future iterations of the project model. Projects with greater capacity for qualitative work could benefit from engaging in briefer, more frequent interviews, focus groups, or other forums for qualitative feedback to inform more continuous quality improvement initiatives.

Semi-structured interviews were conducted with the FES, school administrators at each PDRP school, and caregivers of students who had received SMH and FES services. Because of the novelty of the FES position within the project and at the Pee Dee MHC, the semi-structured interview with the FES was designed to enable a more contextual understanding of what allowed the FES to be successful (e.g., her working relationship with SMH clinicians and school staff) and what worked and could be improved procedurally to maximize the position's impact on addressing student/family needs. Interviews with school administrators focused on assessing the current landscape for addressing school community and student mental health needs at their school, reflections on their experience with school-based components of PDRP (e.g., full-time clinician, FES, MTSS, schoolwide trainings and technical assistance), and feedback on barriers to and facilitators for realizing the PDRP model in their school.

Caregivers who completed the phone feedback interview were compensated for their time. They were asked to reflect on their interactions with their child's school, mental health clinician, and the family engagement specialist, including how they would like those interactions to be changed and/or improved. Caregivers expressed that their children greatly benefited from being able to work with the clinicians in the school setting, which removed some of the barriers to receiving treatment. Most recognized that the clinicians were invested in their children's mental health and would request that they attend Individualized Educational Planning (IEP) or other meetings because of their knowledge. Some caregivers reported complications with information sharing over the course of the project. Improved communication between families, clinicians, and school staff could facilitate understanding of the students' needs within the classroom and at home.

SMH clinicians were invited to participate in a ninety-minute focus group that focused on their expanded role delivering services within an MTSS, the value of training/professional development, and reflections on challenges, lessons learned, and ideas for improving impact. To better characterize the impact of well-integrated, well-trained SMH clinicians on individual students, clinicians also completed a semi-structured interview to highlight one or more of their clinical cases within the school. These case highlights were a powerful tool for conveying the impact of context and relationships in improving child well-being that may not have been captured by our quantitative measures. Overall, clinicians reported strong relationships with school staff including principals, counselors, and teachers, who reached out when students were misbehaving even if they were not clients. This reportedly decreased the rate at which students were being suspended for inappropriate behaviors, as the clinicians were able to intervene before disciplinary action was taken. Encouraging the clinicians to leave their offices and become integrated within the schools improved referral rates as principals and teachers became more comfortable with referring students to services.

7.4.3.6 What PDRP Accomplished in Child Mental Health and Family Well-Being

Data collection continues for PDRP schools, but preliminary analyses of PDRP data suggest that the project made a positive impact on children, families, and schools in the Pee Dee region of the state. This section will provide a brief summary of implementation and outcome highlights with respect to providing a continuum of quality, evidence-based services in SMH that benefit child mental health and family well-being.

Interdisciplinary meetings for coordinating MTSS were documented at each of the PDRP schools, although only some schools were able to regularly incorporate these meetings into their school calendar (e.g., one school reported holding twelve meetings per school year). Meetings were most frequently attended by SMH clinicians, principals, teachers, and school counselors. Nearly three-quarters of meetings resulted in specific student referrals to Tier 2 (early intervention), Tier 3 (individual or family therapy), and FES services. This suggests that prioritizing the attendance of SMH clinicians at these meetings could result in a consistent flow of new referrals for students identified as experiencing behavioral and mental health challenges that interfere with their functioning in school. In addition to participating in MTSS meetings, clinicians embraced the opportunity to expand their role in the school community beyond their therapy office. Over two school years, PDRP clinicians reported spending more than 900 hours embedding themselves as a member of the school community by volunteering for school events (e.g., school dances, academic ceremonies, Career Day) and helping with bus and lunch duty; nearly 1,400 hours participating in Tier 1 activities, like consulting with teachers on classroom management strategies and performing classroom observations; and approximately 1,000 hours in Tier 2 activities including Check-In Check-Out (Crone, Hawken, & Horner, 2010) and small groups for anger management, conflict resolution, and self-esteem.

Engaging in a full continuum of services did not prevent clinicians from eventually building school-based caseloads that could sustain a one-to-one model. PDRP clinicians provided individual therapy services to a total of 413 students over the course of the project, resulting in approximately 9,500 billable intervention hours between January 2018 and August 2019. In 96% of cases, clinicians reported using at least one evidence-based practice (EBP) as part of treatment and three-quarters reported using two or more EBPs. The most frequently used EBPs included psychoeducation, CBT, and child-focused interventions from the PracticeWise system (Chorpita & Weisz, 2009). In over 60% of cases, clinicians reported using the family engagement strategies they were trained in as part of their PDRP-provided professional development.

SMH services were effective at improving well-being for students who received individual services. Comparison of PSC scores at intake and case closure indicate statistically significant reductions in parent-reported child symptoms. Increases in child-reported resiliency scores also demonstrated statistically significant improvements from intake to case closure, registering an average improvement of more than three points on the thirty-six-point scale. For cases that included parent feedback at case close (86%), nearly three-quarters of parents reported that they had noticed behavioral improvements in their child since beginning treatment. Parents held positive attitudes of their experience with PDRP SMH clinicians, with 80% of parents saying that they were satisfied with the services their child received, 96% reporting that it was easier for their child to receive services at school than in another setting, and 98% affirming that they would recommend SMH services to another parent. Preliminary analyses indicate that we may not have met our desired outcome of students achieving a majority of their treatment goals by the time they ended treatment. However, this was likely impacted by fewer than one-sixth of students ending treatment in a planned manner due to symptom reduction. Examining reasons given for case closure (e.g., no longer attending school because of Department of Social Services involvement, family moved out of the region, insufficient family engagement) indicates the importance of working with school and community partners to promote positive connections to families, early parenting interventions, and providing support for family needs outside the clinician's control (e.g., lack of transportation, inconsistent cell phone or internet access, moving due to economic hardship).

Schools and SMH clinicians made a total of 363 referrals to the FES. Three-quarters of these families consented to completing a needs assessment, most often identifying needs related to financial support, clothing, housing, and identifying various specific resources within the community (e.g., childcare, furniture, tutors). At follow-up, a majority of families reported that they were successfully able to access at least one of the services recommended to them and 44% reported that those resources partially or adequately met their needs. Even if families' needs were not entirely met, the services provided by the FES appeared to improve their self-assessed well-being: 80% shared that FES services reduced their stress and 97% were satisfied with the help they received. These results indicate that our families generally appreciated and were open to receiving help meeting their concrete resource needs, but that additional work is needed to create communities where all children and families can thrive.

7.5 Next Steps: The Empower Action Model

Research on ACEs helps us understand that adult health and social outcomes are the result of a complex interplay between structurally embedded inequities and early childhood experiences (Bear et al., 2014; Braveman & Barclay, 2009; Larkin, Shields, & Anda, 2012). Considerable evidence demonstrates that toxic stress (i.e., severe, chronic stress resulting from prolonged exposure to adversity) is considered the major mechanism by which ACEs affect health (Garner, 2013; Shonkoff et al., 2012). At the same time, the brain can adapt quickly from adversity when structurally embedded buffers or positive childhood experiences (i.e., protective factors) are put into place (Afifi & Macmillan, 2011; Moore & Ramirez, 2016; Rutter, 1985). Protective factors help children build resilience by providing nurturing environments that can prevent and mitigate the effects of adversity on their life. Through increased resilience, a child's health and well-being is likely to improve physically, emotionally, and psychologically (Ginsburg & Jablow, 2005).

Given the importance of youth mental health, SMH initiatives and approaches are prime opportunities for the integration of ACE and protective factor science and research. The melding of community-based approaches to prevent and address ACEs and build protective factors with SMH initiatives offers an innovative opportunity to not only improve the lives of children and families but also to change organizations, structures, and systems at the community level to prevent adversity and promote resilience. Components of a newly developed model, the Empower Action Model (Srivastav et al., 2019; see Figure 7.1), were piloted with an SMH initiative in a rural, southeastern

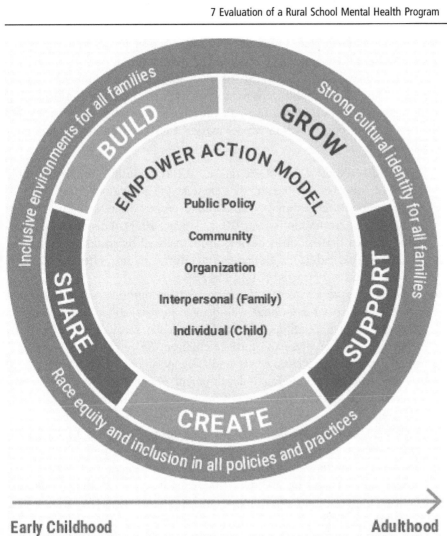

Figure 7.1 *The Empower Action Model developed by Aditi Srivastav and colleagues of the Children's Trust of South Carolina (see www.scchildren .org)*

community. Within PDRP, the CAT was galvanized around promoting mental health awareness and resilience in the Pee Dee. Although initial interest was high among community members, the CAT ultimately struggled to create a cohesive and feasible plan for achieving its goals. The greatest challenge encountered was ensuring consistent member attendance across the three repre- sented counties, likely impacted significantly by a rotating location. Due to inconsistent member attendance, it became difficult for the group to set goals or execute community events. Were we able to gain a consistent community action core team, setting and reaching common goals across the three counties would have been more achievable and the team may have evolved into a sustainable working group as desired. Using the Empower Action Model from the beginning may have helped the CAT achieve its ambitious goals.

The Empower Action Model (Srivastav et al., 2019; see Figure 7.1) aims to provide clear and attainable steps to prevent ACEs and promote resilience and well-being for all individuals through the intentional building of protective factors. The Empower Action Model merges four key frameworks and concepts, including:

1. The *socio-ecological model* recognizes the relationship among multiple levels of influence on health, that include the individual, interpersonal, organizational, community, and public policy (Centers for Disease Control and Prevention [CDC], 2015; Ungar, 2011). This model emphasizes the idea that health behaviors are influenced by social determinants, suggesting that public health prevention efforts are most effective when all of these levels are targeted (CDC, 2015).
2. Building of *protective factors*: *Understand* the importance of positive environments for social-emotional well-being; *Support* children and families through positive relationships; *Build* resilience through learning skills needed to manage stress and nurture children; *Share* resources that allow families to meet their basic needs; and *Grow* positive outcomes by knowing the importance of individual development (Center for the Developing Child, n.d.; Center for the Study of Social Policy, 2018, n.d.; CDC, 2014; Children's Bureau, Administration of Children and Families, 2017).
3. *Race equity and inclusion* tenets of recognizing the need to create an inclusive environment for all families, encouraging a strong cultural identity for all families through the adoption of practices that honor their culture, and recognizing that disparities exist by demonstrating a commitment to equity and inclusion in all policies and practices (Annie E. Casey Foundation, 2015).
4. *Life course perspective* highlights the importance of implementing the factors not only across all levels but across the lifespan to create sustainable improvements in health and well-being. The life course perspective intentionally expands strategies to implement protective factors across all stages of life (Braveman & Barclay, 2009).

"The Empower Action Model can help any individual, organization, or coalition interested in improving equity, health, and well-being in developing a plan for action in each of their respective areas of influence. Traditional players such as parents/caregivers, professionals who serve families, coalitions, and policy advocates or nontraditional players such as local businesses, human resources professionals, or law enforcement could use the model" (Srivastav et al., 2019, p. 529). With an understanding of the significance of structurally embedded inequities, the model recognizes that each of these actions, over time, improves outcomes for all, including students. "The model also promotes cross-disciplinary collaboration by identifying strengths and weaknesses within each system or sector and emphasizing the importance of partnering with existing resources and stakeholders within the community of impact" (Srivastav et al., 2019, p. 529).

7.5.1 School Mental Health

Community advocates, leaders, and professionals in the child health and well-being space have identified a need for concrete steps to prevent and address ACEs and to build strong mental health and general resilience and well-being. "Current frameworks focused on ACEs fall short of including a multilevel approach, considering the role of health equity in well-being, and providing concrete, tangible steps for implementation across the life span. The empower action model is among the first to provide actionable steps to promote well-being by building resilience in all individuals including children and families by bringing together key frameworks and theories in public health that promote upstream approaches to health. This model can be especially useful for states, communities, and organizations seeking to build protective factors and promote resilience among their respective populations as a way to address the root cause of many different poor health outcomes. This can range from employees within an organization to larger systems such as health care or social services. The model can also serve as a foundation for community-based impact, encouraging cross-sector collaboration and a shift in social norms" (Srivastav et al., 2019, p. 532).

This model is especially timely given the momentum around SMH and the growing opportunity for local SMH approaches as pathways to build student, family, and community health and well-being. The relevance and importance of SMH is underscored at the time of this writing in 2020 as the USA is confronting multiple challenges, including the COVID-19 pandemic, associated severe economic challenges for many, and racial injustice and widespread protesting/rioting. Mental health challenges for all people are increasing, including for rural youth and families, and SMH exemplifies the proactive, more accessible, and ecologically valid approach that is critically needed in our country now (Atkins et al., 2006; Weist, 1997). Moreover, these crises create an important opportunity for significant conversations with diverse school and community stakeholders, especially youth and families on tailoring SMH programs to address the stressors families and schools are encountering and to increase the effectiveness of programs to improve student social, emotional, behavioral, and academic functioning (see Clauss-Ehlers, Acosta, & Weist, 2004 and Weist et al., 2002 for two examples).

7.5.2 Summary/Considerations for the Field

In this chapter, we report on an innovative initiative for rural students and families – the Pee Dee Resiliency Project (PDRP), reflecting a school–community–university (SCU) partnership (Spoth et al., 2011) that improved SMH services and addressed ACEs commonly experienced by these families. PDRP developed from a strong foundation of knowledge of evidence-based practices and how to effectively implement them within schools' MTSS in SC, along with excellent collaborative relationships between three state-supported agencies, local school districts, and a highly engaged funder. As the project and its evaluation is moving toward closure, collaborators – reflecting authors of this chapter – are pleased with the many positive impacts shown. This includes proximal outcomes such as SMH clinicians being integrated into MTTS teams, being able to be a part of Tier 1 (prevention/promotion) and Tier 2 (early intervention programs), and increasing delivery of evidence-based modular CBT (Chorpita & Weisz, 2009) to students and families. In addition, the project clearly evinced an ecological systems approach (Bronfenbrenner, 1992; Kloos et al., 2020) in supporting schools and improving prevention and intervention efforts as clinicians and teams interfaced with diverse school and community members in addressing ACEs and other challenges, with programming guided by the voices of school and community members. Importantly, the work of the FES was effectively integrated into these team efforts and was highly appreciated by all stakeholders, including families, school leaders and clinicians, suggesting the importance of this role in future efforts that build effective SMH for rural youth.

Further, evaluation of PDRP was comprehensive, including qualitative and quantitative aspects, and overall, use of the REDCap system (Harris et al., 2019) was highly effective in organizing our evaluation approach and its findings. Notably, evaluation findings documented improvements in students' emotional/behavioral functioning, and consistent ratings of satisfaction with the program by parents and caregivers. The program and its evaluation were guided by the Empower Action Model (Srivastav et al., 2019) considering critical dimensions of functioning for these rural students and families, including socio-ecological considerations, racial/ethnic factors, inequities, and a life course perspective.

Finally, from a systems perspective, the opportunity to develop and evaluate PDRP strengthened collaborative relations among the partnering agencies, school districts, and funder, and contributed to the development of capacity building for effective SMH in SC through other relevant initiatives. These include a certificate training program to recruit recent masters-level graduates into SMH, a statewide Center of Excellence for mental health services for students and families, improved training in child protection and trauma-sensitive programming in schools, and enhanced coordination of programs for students in special education (Shapiro et al., 2020). It is our hope that this chapter, reflecting our comprehensive evaluation of a rural SMH program, exemplifies critical principles of evaluation within community psychology, building research and action toward mental health and education systems working closely together to improve outcomes for children, youth, and families (see special issue of the *American Journal of Community Psychology*; Wandersman et al., 2005).

References

Afifi, T. O., & Macmillan, H. L. (2011). Resilience following child maltreatment: A review of protective factors. *Canadian Journal of Psychiatry/Revue Canadienne de Psychiatrie, 56*(5), 266–272. doi.org/10.1177/070674371105600505

Anda, R. F., Croft, J. B., Felitti, V. J., et al. (1999). Adverse childhood experiences and smoking during adolescence and adulthood. *Journal of the American Medical Association, 282*(17), 1652–1658. doi.org/10.1001/jama.282.17.1652

Anda, R. F., Whitfield, C. L., Felitti, V. J., et al. (2002). Adverse childhood experiences, alcoholic parents, and later risk of alcoholism and depression. *Psychiatric Services, 53*(8), 1001–1009. doi.org/10.1176/appi.ps.53.8.1001

Anderson, R. L., & Gittler, J. J. (2005). Unmet need for community-based mental health and substance use treatment among rural adolescents. *Community Mental Health Journal, 41*(1), 35–49. doi.org/10.1007/s10597-005-2598-0

Annie E. Casey Foundation. (2015, January 8). *Race equity and inclusion action guide.* www.aecf.org/resources/race-equity-and-inclusion-action-guide/

Atkins, M. S., Frazier, S. L., Birman, D., et al. (2006). School-based mental health services for children living in high poverty urban communities. *Administration and Policy in Mental Health and Mental Health Services Research, 33*(2), 146–159. doi.org/10.1007/s10488-006-0031-9

Ballard, K. L., Sander, M. A., & Klimes-Dougan, B. (2014). School-related and social–emotional outcomes of providing mental health services in schools. *Community Mental Health Journal, 50*(2), 145–149. doi.org/10.1007/s10597-013-9670-y

Barrett, S., Eber, L., & Weist, M. D. (2013). *Advancing education effectiveness: An interconnected systems framework for Positive Behavioral Interventions and Supports (PBIS) and school mental health.* Center for Positive Behavioral Interventions and Supports (funded by the Office of Special Education Programs, US Department of Education). Eugene: University of Oregon Press. www.pbis.org/resource/advancing-education-effectiveness-intercon necting-school-mental-health-and-school-wide-positive-behavior-support

Bear, T., Documèt, P., Marshal, M., Voorhees, R., & Ricci, E. (2014, November). *Childhood adversity: A social determinant of health and inequity over the lifespan and across generations.* Paper presented at the 142nd annual meeting and exposition of the American Public Health Association, New Orleans, LA.

Blodgett, C. (2013). *A review of community efforts to mitigate and prevent adverse childhood experiences and trauma.* Spokane: Washington State University Area Health Education Center.

Braveman, P., & Barclay, C. (2009). Health disparities beginning in childhood: A life-course perspective. *Pediatrics, 124*(Suppl. 3), S163–S175. doi.org/10.1542/peds.2009-1100D

Bronfenbrenner, U. (1992). Ecological systems theory. In R. Vasta (Ed.), *Six theories of child development: Revised formulations and current issues* (pp. 187–249). London, UK: Jessica Kingsley Publishers.

Brown, D. W., Anda, R. F., Tiemeier, H., et al. (2009). Adverse childhood experiences and the risk of premature mortality. *American Journal of Preventive Medicine, 37*(5), 389–396. doi.org/10.1016/j.amepre.2009.06.021

Burke, N. J., Hellman, J. L., Scott, B. G., Weems, C. F., & Carrion, V. G. (2011). The impact of adverse childhood experiences on an urban pediatric population. *Child Abuse and Neglect*, *35*(6), 408–413. doi.org/10.1016/j.chiabu.2011.02.006

Burns, B. J., Costello, E. J., Angold, A., et al. (1995). Children's mental health service use across service sectors. *Health Affairs*, *14*(3), 147–159. doi.org/10.1377/hlthaff.14.3.147

Center for the Developing Child. (n.d.). *Three principles to improve outcomes for children and families*. https://developingchild.harvard.edu/resources/three-early-childhood-development-principles-improve-child-family-outcomes/

Center for the Study of Social Policy. (n.d.). *Strengthening Families^{TM}: A protective factors framework*. https://cssp.org/wp-content/uploads/2018/11/About-Strengthening-Families.pdf

Center for the Study of Social Policy. (2018). *Youth Thrive^{TM}*. www.cssp.org/reform/child-welfare/youththrive

Centers for Disease Control and Prevention (2014). *Essentials for Childhood Framework: Steps to create safe, stable, nurturing relationships and environments for all children (Essentials for Childhood)*. Centers for Disease Control and Prevention. www.cdc.gov/violenceprevention/childabuseandneglect/essentials.html

Centers for Disease Control and Prevention. (2015, March 25). *The social-ecological model: A framework for prevention*. www.cdc.gov/violenceprevention/publichealthissue/social-ecologicalmodel.html

Chapman, D. P., Whitfield, C. L., Felitti, V. J., et al. (2004). Adverse childhood experiences and the risk of depressive disorders in adulthood. *Journal of Affective Disorders*, *82*(2), 217–225. doi.org/10.1016/j.jad.2003.12.013

Children's Bureau, Administration of Children and Families. (2017). *Protective factors to promote well-being*. www.childwelfare.gov/topics/preventing/promoting/protectfactors/

Children's Trust of South Carolina. (2019). *Child well-being data county profiles*. https://scchildren.org/resources/kids-count-south-carolina/child-well-being-data-county-profiles/

Chorpita, B. F., & Weisz, J. R. (2009). *Modular approach to therapy for children with anxiety, depression, trauma, or conduct problems (MATCH–ADTC)*. Satellite Beach, FL: PracticeWise.

Clauss-Ehlers, C., Acosta, O., & Weist, M. D. (2004). Responses to terrorism: The voices of two communities speak out. In C. Clauss-Ehlers & M. D. Weist (Eds.), *Community planning to foster resilience in children* (pp. 143–160). New York: Springer.

Cohen, J. A., Mannarino, A. P., Berliner, L., & Deblinger, E. (2000). Trauma-focused cognitive behavioral therapy for children and adolescents: An empirical update. *Journal of Interpersonal Violence*, *15*(11), 1202–1223. doi.org/10.1177/088626000015011007

Crone, D. A., Hawken, L. S., & Horner, R. H. (2010). *Responding to problem behavior in schools: The Behavior Education Program* (2nd ed.). New York: Guilford Press.

Dube, S. R., Anda, R. F., Felitti, V. J., et al. (2001). Childhood abuse, household dysfunction, and the risk of attempted suicide throughout the life span:

Findings from the Adverse Childhood Experiences Study. *Journal of the American Medical Association*, *286*(24), 3089–3096. doi.org/10.1001/jama .286.24.3089

Dube, S. R., Felitti, V. J., Dong, M., et al. (2003). Childhood abuse, neglect, and household dysfunction and the risk of illicit drug use: The adverse childhood experiences study. *Pediatrics*, *111*(3), 564–572. doi.org/10.1542/peds.111.3 .564

Edwards, V. J., Holden, G. W., Felitti, V. J., & Anda, R. F. (2003). Relationship between multiple forms of childhood maltreatment and adult mental health in community respondents: Results from the adverse childhood experiences study. *American Journal of Psychiatry*, *160*(8), 1453–1460. doi.org/10.1176/ appi.ajp.160.8.1453

Felitti, V. J., & Anda, R. F. (2010). The relationship of adverse childhood experiences to adult medical disease, psychiatric disorders and sexual behavior: Implications for healthcare. In R. A. Lanius, E. Vermetten, & C. Pain (Eds.), *The impact of early life trauma on health and disease* (pp. 77–87). Cambridge, UK: Cambridge University Press.

Felitti, V. J., Anda, R. F., Nordenberg, D., et al. (1998). Relationship of childhood abuse and household dysfunction to many of the leading causes of death in adults: The adverse childhood experiences (ACE) study. *American Journal of Preventive Medicine*, *14*(4), 245–258. doi.org/10.1016/s0749-3797(98)00017-8

Garner, A. S. (2013). Home visiting and the biology of toxic stress: Opportunities to address early childhood adversity. *Pediatrics*, *132*(Suppl. 2), S65–S73. doi .org/10.1542/peds.2013-1021D

Ginsburg, K. R., & Jablow, M. M. (2005). *Building resilience in children and teens: Giving kids roots and wings*. Elk Grove Village, IL: American Academy of Pediatrics.

Green, J. G., McLaughlin, K. A., Alegría, M., et al. (2013). School mental health resources and adolescent mental health service use. *Journal of the American Academy of Child & Adolescent Psychiatry*, *52*(5), 501–510. doi.org/10.1016/j .jaac.2013.03.002

Hall, J., Porter, L., Longhi, D., Becker-Green, J., & Dreyfus, S. (2012). Reducing adverse childhood experiences (ACE) by building community capacity: A summary of Washington Family Policy Council research findings. *Journal of Prevention & Intervention in the Community*, *40*(4), 325–334. doi .org/10.1080/10852352.2012.707463

Harpin, V., Mazzone, L., Raynaud, J. P., Kahle, J., & Hodgkins, P. (2016). Long-term outcomes of ADHD: A systematic review of self-esteem and social function. *Journal of Attention Disorders*, *20*(4), 295–305. doi.org/10.1177/ 1087054713486516

Harris, P. A., Taylor, R., Minor, B. L., et al. (2019). The REDCap consortium: Building an international community of software platform partners. *Journal of Biomedical Informatics*, *95*, 103208. doi.org/10.1016/j.jbi.2019.103208

Harris, P. A., Taylor, R., Thielke, R., et al. (2009). Research electronic data capture (REDCap): A metadata-driven methodology and workflow process for providing translational research informatics support. *Journal of Biomedical Informatics*, *42*(2), 377–381. doi.org/10.1016/j.jbi.2008.08.010

Jellinek, M. S., & Murphy, J. M. (1988). *Pediatric symptom checklist.* Massachusetts General Hospital. www.massgeneral.org/assets/MGH/pdf/psychiatry/psc/psc-english.pdf

Kataoka, S. H., Zhang, L., & Wells, K. B. (2002). Unmet need for mental health care among US children: Variation by ethnicity and insurance status. *American Journal of Psychiatry, 159*(9), 1548–1555. doi.org/10.1176/appi.ajp.159.9.1548

Kloos, B., Hill, J., Thomas, E., et al. (2020). *Community psychology: Linking individuals and communities.* (4th ed.). Washington, DC: American Psychological Association.

Kutash, K., Duchnowski, A. J., & Green, A. L. (2011). School-based mental health programs for students who have emotional disturbances: Academic and social-emotional outcomes. *School Mental Health, 3*(4), 191–208. doi.org/10.1007/s12310-011-9062-9

Lacourse, E., Coté, S., Nagin, D. S., et al. (2002). A longitudinal–experimental approach to testing theories of antisocial behavior development. *Development and Psychopathology, 14*(4), 909–924. doi.org/10.1017/s0954579402004121

Larkin, H., Shields, J. J., & Anda, R. F. (2012). The health and social consequences of adverse childhood experiences (ACE) across the lifespan: An introduction to prevention and intervention in the community. *Journal of Prevention & Intervention in the Community, 40*(4), 263–270. doi.org/10.1080/10852352.2012.707439

Merikangas, K. R., He, J. P., Brody, D., et al. (2010a). Prevalence and treatment of mental disorders among US children in the 2001–2004 NHANES. *Pediatrics, 125*(1), 75–81. doi.org/10.1542/peds.2008-2598

Merikangas, K. R., He, J. P., Burstein, M., et al. (2010b). Lifetime prevalence of mental disorders in US adolescents: Results from the National Comorbidity Survey Replication–Adolescent Supplement (NCS-A). *Journal of the American Academy of Child and Adolescent Psychiatry, 49*(10), 980–989. doi.org/10.1016/j.jaac.2010.05.017

Mersky, J. P., Topitzes, J., & Reynolds, A. J. (2013). Impacts of adverse childhood experiences on health, mental health, and substance use in early adulthood: A cohort study of an urban, minority sample in the US. *Child Abuse & Neglect, 37*(11), 917–925. doi.org/10.1016/j.chiabu.2013.07.011

Moore, K. A., & Ramirez, A. N. (2016). Adverse childhood experience and adolescent well-being: Do protective factors matter? *Child Indicators Research, 9*(2), 299–316. doi.org/10.1007/s12187-015-9324-4

Nabors, L. A., & Reynolds, M. W. (2000). Program evaluation activities: Outcomes related to treatment for adolescents receiving school-based mental health services. *Children's Services: Social Policy, Research, and Practice, 3*(3), 175–189. doi.org/10.1207/s15326918cs0303_4

Nock, M. K., & Ferriter, C. (2005). Parent management of attendance and adherence in child and adolescent therapy: A conceptual and empirical review. *Clinical Child and Family Psychology Review, 8*(2), 149–166. doi.org/10.1007/s10567-005-4753-0

Patel, V., Flisher, A. J., Hetrick, S., & McGorry, P. (2007). Mental health of young people: A global public-health challenge. *Lancet, 369*(9569), 1302–1313. doi.org/10.1016/s0140-6736(07)60368-7

Rutter, M. (1985). Resilience in the face of adversity: Protective factors and resistance to psychiatric disorder. *The British Journal of Psychiatry*, *147*(6), 598–611. doi.org/10.1192/bjp.147.6.598

Sack, V., & Murphey, D. (2018). *The prevalence of adverse childhood experiences, nationally, by state, and by race or ethnicity*. Bethesda, MD: Child Trends. www.childtrends.org/publications/prevalence-adverse-childhood-experiences-nationally-state-race-ethnicity

Shapiro, C., Collins, C., Parker, J., et al. (2020). Coalescing investments in school mental health in South Carolina. *Child and Adolescent Mental Health*, *5*(3). doi.org/10.1111/camh.12382

Shonkoff, J. P., Garner, A. S., Siegel, B. S., et al. (2012). The lifelong effects of early childhood adversity and toxic stress. *Pediatrics*, *129*(1), e232–e246. doi.org/10.1542/peds.2011-2663

Slopen, N., Shonkoff, J. P., Albert, M. A., et al. (2016). Racial disparities in child adversity in the US: Interactions with family immigration history and income. *American Journal of Preventive Medicine*, *50*(1), 47–56. doi.org/10.1016/j.amepre.2015.06.013

Spoth, R., Greenberg, M., Bierman, K., & Redmond, C. (2004). PROSPER community–university partnership model for public education systems: Capacity-building for evidence-based, competence-building prevention. *Prevention Science*, *5*(1), 31–39. doi.org/10.1023/b:prev.0000013979.52796.8b

Spoth, R., Guyll, M., Lillehoj, C. J., Redmond, C., & Greenberg, M. (2007). Prosper study of evidence-based intervention implementation quality by community–university partnerships. *Journal of Community Psychology*, *35*(8), 981–999. doi.org/10.1002/jcop.20207

Spoth, R., Redmond, C., Clair, S., et al. (2011). Preventing substance misuse through community–university partnerships: Randomized controlled trial outcomes 4½ years past baseline. *American Journal of Preventive Medicine*, *40*(4), 440–447. doi.org/10.1016/j.amepre.2010.12.012

Srivastav, A., Strompolis, M., Moseley, A., & Daniels, K. (2019). *The Empower Action Model: Mobilizing prevention to promote well-being and resilience*. https://scchildren.org/wp-content/uploads/Empower-Action-Model-research-brief.pdf

Stein, B. D., Jaycox, L. H., Kataoka, S. H., et al. (2003). A mental health intervention for schoolchildren exposed to violence: A randomized controlled trial. *Journal of the American Medical Association*, *290*(5), 603–611. doi.org/10.1001/jama.290.5.603

Sugai, G., & Horner, R. R. (2006). A promising approach for expanding and sustaining school-wide positive behavior support. *School Psychology Review*, *35*(2), 245–259. doi.org/10.1080/02796015.2006.12087989

Suldo, S. M., Gormley, M. J., DuPaul, G. J., & Anderson-Butcher, D. (2014). The impact of school mental health on student and school-level academic outcomes: Current status of the research and future directions. *School Mental Health*, *6*(2), 84–98. doi.org/10.1007/s12310-013-9116-2

Umberson, D., Williams, K., Thomas, P. A., Liu, H., & Thomeer, M. B. (2014). Race, gender, and chains of disadvantage: Childhood adversity, social relationships, and health. *Journal of Health and Social Behavior*, *55*(1), 20–38. doi.org/10.1177/0022146514521426

Ungar, M. (2011). *The social ecology of resilience: A handbook of theory and practice.* New York: Springer Science & Business Media.

Ungar, M., & Liebenberg, L. (2009). *The Child and Youth Resilience Measure (CYRM).* Halifax, Canada: Resilience Research Centre. https://cyrm .resilienceresearch.org/

Verbitsky-Savitz, N., Hargreaves, M. B., Penoyer, S., et al. (2016). *Preventing and mitigating the effects of ACEs by building community capacity and resilience: APPI cross-site evaluation findings.* Washington, DC: Mathematica Policy Research.

Vivolo, A. M., Matjasko, J. L., & Massetti, G. M. (2011). Mobilizing communities and building capacity for youth violence prevention: The National Academic Centers of Excellence for Youth Violence Prevention. *American Journal of Community Psychology, 48*(1–2), 141–145. doi.org/10.1007/s10464-010-9419-5

Wandersman, A., Kloos, B., Linney, J. A., & Shinn, M. (2005). Science and community psychology: Enhancing the vitality of community research and action. *American Journal of Community Psychology, 35*(3–4), 105–106. doi.org/10 .1007/s10464-005-3387-1

Weist, M. D. (1997). Expanded school mental health services: A national movement in progress. *Advances in Clinical Child Psychology, 19*, 319–352. doi.org/10 .1007/978-1-4757-9035-1_9

Weist, M. D., Sander, M. A., Lever, N. A., et al. (2002). School mental health's response to terrorism and disaster. *Journal of School Violence, 1*(4), 5–31. doi.org/10.1300/j202v01n04_02

8 Constructive Diversity Pedagogy for Challenging Classroom Dialogues

Participatory Action Research with Interdisciplinary Faculty

Margo A. Jackson and Shannon R. Waite

Toward promoting health, empowerment, and positive change, the focus of community psychology not only includes understanding of thoughts, feelings, and behavior at the individual level, but also integrates social, cultural, economic, political, environmental, and international influences at systemic levels (www .scra27.org/what-we-do/what-community-psychology/). Community psychology, as an academic discipline and professional specialization, is grounded in values that support community strengths, honor human rights, promote social justice action to reduce oppression, advance scientific inquiry, and foster action-oriented research.

This chapter describes the foundation for a professional development, participatory action research project with an interdisciplinary and diverse group of new faculty that was originated as one response to expand educating for social justice in the context of our university community. (The first author was the principal investigator and facilitator, and the second author was a coresearcher and participant.) Relevant to the focus and values of community psychology, the Constructive Diversity Pedagogy Participatory Action Research (CDP PAR) project was designed to build collaborative relationships with a core group of faculty members new to the university community to help address social injustice issues by engaging in research by and for the participants to develop, implement, and evaluate this initiative. The role of the participant members of the PAR team was to engage in a series of CDP professional development seminars that were foundationally designed by the facilitator, contribute to the evolving content and process, provide formative and summative evaluation data for analysis, and derive recommendations to inform evolving university community efforts to expand educating for social justice.

8.1 Impetus for the CDP PAR Project: Problem, Context, and Focus

In the US national sociopolitical context, there has been a resurgence of attention on racist and other overtly hateful incidents of violence against members of marginalized and oppressed groups. Responses to these issues of racial and social injustice have been broadly publicized, protested, and hotly debated. Furthermore, revealed in this context have been more covert, insidious, and chronic forms of racism, implicit stereotyped biases, and microaggressions. *Microaggressions* are denigrating messages grounded in stereotyped biases that are often communicated automatically, unconsciously, and unintentionally, yet have a cumulative and harmful impact (Sue et al., 2019). As microcosms of the national sociopolitical context, US college and university campuses reflect societal values as well as conflicts about racial and social justice.

Many examples of a nexus of conflicting responses to overt and covert influences of racial injustice occurred on our campus in 2014–2015. Serving as an impetus for the CDP PAR project, in the following we highlight the national sociopolitical context, an unhelpful response of silence on our campus in fall 2014, and a more constructive response in fall 2015. In the national context, there were viral videos, widespread social media, and other publicized accounts of unarmed Black individuals killed by police, prompting conflicting protests such as Black Lives Matter and Blue Lives Matter.

The origin of the movement for Black Lives Matter (n.d.) has been traced to a response by activist Patrisse Cullors following the acquittal in July 2013 of neighborhood watchman George Zimmerman in the fatal shooting of a Black high school student Trayvon Martin (Solomon & Martin, 2019). Cullors created the viral #blacklivesmatter Twitter hashtag in response to a social media post by her friend, Alicia Garza, saying "Black people, I love you. I love us. Our lives matter" (p. 11). These Black community organizers and allies have since worked to advocate for justice, respect, and equity for several other unarmed Black victims of shootings by police and related personnel. They view their activism efforts as needed to counter systemic violence against Black individuals in "a justice system unable or unwilling to hold such shooters accountable or change to prevent future tragedy" (Solomon & Martin, 2019, p. 11).

The movement for Blue Lives Matter (2017) arose to offer support for families of fallen and accused officers, particularly in response to two events: The grand jury investigation of a police officer in the shooting death of Michael Brown in Ferguson, Missouri, and the fatal shootings by ambush of two New York City police officers, reported as motivated to avenge the deaths caused by police officers of Michael Brown and Eric Garner. "Blue Lives Matter continues to provide financial and ideological support to those they believe are targeted by the Black Lives Matter Movement – officers and their families … and shift the national narrative away from the focus on race purveyed by Black Lives Matter. The movement quickly gained an active following on social media, with #bluelivesmatter … designed to counter #blacklivesmatter" (Solomon & Martin, 2019, p. 12).

In the national sociopolitical context of the movements for Black Lives Matter and Blue Lives Matter, two current events in the news were publicized at the end of the fall 2014 semester on our campus during the stressful period of final exams. On November 24, 2014, a grand jury decision in Ferguson, Missouri was announced to not indict the White police officer who fatally shot Michael Brown, an unarmed Black 18-year-old. On December 3, 2014, a grand jury acquitted the White New York City police officer whose chokehold on Eric Garner, an unarmed Black man, led to his death. There was an unhelpful response of silence on these issues by some of our campus leaders and faculty members – an unintentional yet harmful racial microaggression message that was communicated to students. In a discussion at a university-wide faculty senate meeting, some campus leaders and faculty members explained their silence as a conscious decision to avoid distracting students from focusing on their final exams. However, as was noted by others at this meeting, this silence ignored and discounted the real threat, trauma, stress, and emotions elicited by these events that could particularly impair final exam performance for students of color, as well as for all students committed to the university's mission for social justice. Yet, many administrators and faculty members admitted that they did not know how to helpfully discuss these issues and feared they would make matters worse.

In contrast, as one example of a more constructive response, a grassroots coalition of diverse members of the Fordham University community (students, alumni, faculty, administrators, staff, and local community partners from a range of racial/ethnic and other identity groups, both privileged and marginalized) coordinated an intensive Racial Justice Teach-In that was open to the public and well attended. Held in November 2015, this daylong program of workshops was designed as one means to bring together diverse university community members to better understand the realities of racial injustice and take collective action to address personal and structural racism.

In the US national sociopolitical context of conflicting helpful and unhelpful responses to publicized incidents of racial and social injustice, a wide range of members and leaders of our university community engaged in multiple efforts to "recommit ourselves to the work of educating for justice" (Joseph M. McShane, S. J., President, Fordham University, July 12, 2016 message). Promoting social justice in powerfully transformational ways through excellent and caring education of the whole person are core values in the mission of our university. Progress has been made in renewed commitment toward these goals through many initiatives that have been implemented at the university since the relative silence of 2014/2015.

As one such initiative, we describe in this chapter a Constructive Diversity Pedagogy Participatory Action Research (CDP PAR) project with an interdisciplinary group of faculty newly hired in fall 2016. The rationale for including only new faculty for the CDP PAR project was to deepen their orientation to the core educational values of this Jesuit university's mission in promoting social justice via *cura personalis* (a Latin phrase meaning "care for the entire person" and individualized care for the other). Provided with space, time, and support to develop over the course of their first semester, this small voluntary working group connected across disciplines to consider strategies to discern and constructively challenge social injustices in their teaching and learning. New faculty members were expected to bring fresh perspectives to inform subsequent faculty development initiatives. In particular, the CDP PAR collaborative seed project in Fall 2016 was designed by the first author for incoming faculty to help develop together (1) *social justice critical consciousness* and (2) skills to facilitate *challenging diversity dialogues* in our classrooms that promote social justice critical consciousness in ways that include multiple voices, consider alternative perspectives, and expand learning.

8.2 Rationale for the Focus of the CDP PAR Project

8.2.1 Social Justice Critical Consciousness

Social justice has been defined as action that promotes the basic human rights and dignity of all people by fostering equity in access to and distribution of societal resources (Toporek, Sapigao, & Rojas-Arauz, 2017). Nevertheless, social injustices against marginalized group members (for example, overt and covert racism) are pervasive at individual, interpersonal, and systemic levels (Jones, 2000). At all these levels, the exploitative influences of social injustices, of how power and control are manifest, cause significant harm to people's health and well-being (Williams, 2018).

Most people consider themselves as good people who would not condone unfair and harmful social injustices (Chugh, 2018). Paradoxically, social injustices are perpetuated by most people through a common dysconsciousness, or uncritical habits of mind that justify inequality and exploitation by accepting the existing order as a given (King & Akua, 2012). As Paolo Freire (2000) explained in his classic book, *Pedagogy of the Oppressed*, social injustices are perpetuated by the dominant system of social relations that creates a culture of silence by repressing the voices of and instilling negative self-images into the people it oppresses. Freire (2000) advocated that education is needed to engage in a learning process to develop *critical consciousness*, which is defined as not only (1) developing an awareness to perceive, assess, and expose the sociopolitical and economic contradictions inherent in pervasive social injustices, but also (2) taking action against the oppressive elements that are illuminated by that understanding.

One foundational aim of the CDP PAR project was for faculty participants to engage in a learning process to further develop our own social justice critical consciousness relevant to our teaching. Why? Educators are human, too. While we are all vulnerable at times to social justice dysconsciousness, as educators we have the responsibility and power to engage in an ongoing developmental learning process to build social justice critical consciousness.

Thus, we may more critically and helpfully inform our curriculum development, advance our effectiveness in teaching and scholarship, and promote our functioning as role models and mentors with our students and as collaborative partners with our colleagues and communities.

8.2.2 Constructively Facilitating Challenging Diversity Dialogues

The other main focus of the CDP PAR project was to develop, together with faculty participants, skills to constructively facilitate challenging diversity dialogues in our classrooms that promote social justice critical consciousness in ways that include multiple voices, consider alternative perspectives, and expand learning.

Ideally, colleges and universities encourage openness and freedom of inquiry and discourse among multiple perspectives to promote knowledge, understanding, and development of our students as people who make positive contributions in their lives and broader communities. Diversity includes differences within and among individuals' perspectives from their experiences as members of various social identities (for example, race, ethnicity, gender, age, social class, religion, health or ability status, sexual orientation, nationality, geographic location, immigration status, and cultural heritage). Diversity includes multicultural perspectives of individuals from their experiences of their intersecting group memberships with social positions of greater or more limited access to power and resources.

Toward these common goals of higher education, evidence is overwhelming for the value of diversity. Diversity in perspectives may also include differences in expertise from multiple academic disciplines or fields of vocational practice. Evidence for the value of diversity of perspectives has been demonstrated in producing higher quality in scientific research (Phillips, 2014); more accurate financial predictions and probability estimates for policymakers (Levine et al., 2014; Mellers & Tetlock, 2019); workplace health and effectiveness (Haynes et al., 2019); and greater diligence, creativity, and innovation in complex, real-world problem-solving (Phillips, 2014; Proctor & Vu, 2019).

Thus, the benefits to society of promoting diversity in perspectives, by social and other group memberships, include advancing knowledge, understanding, and teamwork. Yet, to realize these benefits, the process of facilitating dialogues that bring the differences in group members' perspectives to the fore is necessary and challenging. Potentially, college faculty members can have a vital role in our classrooms for facilitating these challenging dialogues with students in ways that constructively discern diversity perspectives and expand learning.

Given this focus of the CDP PAR project, following are working assumptions that were articulated to prospective faculty participants:

1. Powerful pedagogy (the art, science, methods, and practice of teaching) includes, first, connecting learning objectives with relevance to students'

personal, social, and broader communities, and second, analysis of complex issues from multiple and alternative perspectives in which all voices are heard and considered.

2. Issues of diversity and social justice are of relevance to examine in all disciplines to teach and learn ethically and powerfully.

3. The process of teaching and learning in higher education that includes developing social justice critical consciousness requires engaging constructively in difficult dialogues of reflection and exchange with diverse others in classroom, mentoring, and collegial relationships.

Yet, challenging diversity dialogues are *difficult dialogues*, defined as exchanges of ideas or perspectives among members of a community that are centered on "an awakening of potentially conflicting views or beliefs or values about social justice issues (such as racism, sexism, ableism, heterosexism/homophobia)" (Watt, 2007, p. 116). While engaging in difficult dialogues is a central component for educating to develop social justice critical consciousness, the process can be challenging, anxiety-provoking, or threatening (Toporek & Worthington, 2014). Even highly knowledgeable and skilled educators are prone to avoid or mismanage difficult dialogues (Placier et al., 2012).

Sue (2013) found that diversity dialogues were difficult for faculty to facilitate in classrooms because of social and academic norms to avoid, ignore, silence, or discourage in-depth exploration of potentially offensive, uncomfortable, and emotionally intense topics such as issues relevant to diversity and social injustices. For example, on issues of race and racism, reasons revealed for why these were difficult classroom dialogues include (1) for educators and students with identities as people of color, they risk being subjected to microaggressions that minimize, discount, invalidate, or assail their own racial/ethnic identities and (2) for White educators and students, they fear "appearing racist, of realizing their racism, of acknowledging White privilege, and of taking responsibility to combat racism" (Sue, 2013, p. 663). When challenging questions, comments, or reactions are raised by students in our classrooms relevant to diversity and social justice, the default response of many faculty members is to avoid discussion. Sometimes, even brave and well-intentioned attempts by faculty members to constructively engage in challenging diversity dialogues in classrooms may have unintentionally adverse consequences on learning: For example, when the exchange of conflicting perspectives elicits entrenched and uninformed biases in ways that become polarizing, adversarial, and vitriolic, thus eroding the potential for constructive dialogue and understanding (Young, 2003). Thus, the concerns of faculty and students as noted by Sue (2013) and Young (2003) are likely reasons why they avoid or fail to engage in constructive diversity dialogues.

Nevertheless, although facilitating difficult dialogues is an understandably challenging classroom dilemma, this is a key opportunity for teachable moments. As faculty members, we can and should develop our pedagogical competencies to more constructively facilitate challenging diversity dialogues in our classrooms. A key focus in the CDP PAR project was to examine how in our classrooms we might facilitate more constructive diversity dialogues that are open, free, inclusive, responsible, respectful exchanges on challenging social justice issues of relevance to our learning objectives. We endorse the following pedagogical goals described by Toporek and Worthington (2014):

> We use difficult dialogues as one of the many ways of grappling with challenging and sensitive issues in our fields of study. The overall goal is to create safer places for the free exchange of ideas and to become more inclusive of voices and ways of knowing that have been absent, unpopular, excluded, or oppressed. The purpose may or may not be to change people's beliefs, values, or perspectives – an issue that depends on the context and nature of the dialogue, as well as the participants – and most often requires participants to deeply listen and work to understand the perspectives, values, and worldviews of people who are sometimes very different from them. Thus, the intention is to create dialogues based on mutual respect, open-mindedness, and an informed exchange of ideas and beliefs, an outcome intended to enhance both the likelihood and the quality of thoughtful discussions, and allow for a respectful and responsible hearing of questions and issues within academic and professional communities dedicated to open inquiry and social justice. (p. 925)

8.2.3 Participatory Action Research

Following is the rationale for using a participatory action research approach to address the focus of this seed project in constructive diversity pedagogy. The initial broad charge of the university president was to develop for all newly hired faculty members, across multiple disciplines, a curriculum to advance the mission of educating for social justice. The president assigned this task to the first author to accomplish in collaboration primarily with the dean of the graduate school of education and the provost. Following consultative meetings with the provost, his associate vice presidents, the vice president for mission integration and planning, and the director of the center on religion and culture, the first author developed and obtained approvals for a proposal and IRB (Institutional Review Board) protocol for a more focused and preliminary CDP PAR project. As faculty members, one place where we have the power to influence developing social justice critical consciousness of relevance to our learning objectives is in the classroom with students through facilitating constructive diversity dialogues. Yet to date, the pedagogical tools to apply toward these goals had been under development, not widely known, and likely to vary in effectiveness for different faculty members and different university contexts. Using research to investigate what pedagogical methods work best with whom and under what conditions, in particular through participatory action research – by and for the faculty participants – seemed like a good starting place. From the perspective that social justice advocacy interventions may be initiated at various entry points, the CDP PAR project focused on the domains of individual empowerment, community collaboration, and "acting with" new faculty members, more than "acting on [their] behalf" (Toporek, Lewis, & Ratts, 2010), to explore, challenge, and support each other's work.

With a focus on empowering their voices and supporting their professional development in this challenging work, the process for building trust and mutual support with a small interdisciplinary CDP PAR team was particularly important with faculty members new to the university. New faculty members are in the process of navigating new roles and responsibilities, developing their professional identities, establishing new relationships, and seeking to understand performance expectations (e.g., to achieve reappointment and tenure). Furthermore, by using this approach to the CDP PAR seed project with a small group of voluntarily committed participants working collaboratively and from multiple diverse perspectives toward problem-solving in this context, we expected the results might lead to constructive ripple effects on the system more broadly at the university.

Since 2016, this model has been extended in part to all faculty and staff of the university community. Various departments, schools, offices, centers, and leaders (including the provost, vice president for mission integration and planning, and a new university diversity officer) now provide support for a range of continuously evolving small group, semester-long, intensive, professional development seminars, led by skilled facilitators and with broad participation, to explore how to constructively address social justice issues from sound grounding in education and *cura personalis*.

8.3 Brief Overview of the CDP PAR Project

8.3.1 Faculty Participants

At the start of the fall semester of 2016, ten faculty members newly hired at Fordham University voluntarily committed to participate in the CDP PAR project with the facilitator-participant/principal investigator (following her summer recruitment efforts via an email video, presentation at the New Faculty Orientation, and reviewing and obtaining informed consent). A summary of the academic disciplines and areas of scholarship focus for each faculty participant on this team is presented in Table 8.1.

Demographic information that participants shared at the start of the CDP PAR project includes the following:

- By gender, six identified as women, four as men, and one as nonbinary.
- Their ages ranged from the twenties (one participant), thirties (six), forties (two), and fifties (one), plus one who did not report age.

Table 8.1 *Summary of academic disciplines and areas of scholarship focus for each faculty participant*

Academic Discipline	Areas of Scholarship Focus
African and African American Studies	African Diaspora; Caribbean immigration; African American history
Communication and Media Studies	Television history; ethnic studies; media studies; gender, race, transnationalism, and fashion
Communication and Media Studies	Cultural studies; critical theory and analysis; theorizing practices of televisual spectatorship in the home entertainment zone; representations of masculinities in film, TV, and videogame genres
Counseling Psychology	Methods to assess and constructively address hidden biases and strengths of counselors, educators, and leaders; career development and social justice advocacy across the lifespan; training and supervision in ethical multicultural counseling and psychology
Educational Leadership and Policy	School improvement; leadership development; teacher support
Educational Leadership and Policy	Educational equity; leadership preparation and development; organizational culture and climate; policy analysis and implementation; principal leadership assessment; program evaluation; research methodology and advanced quantitative techniques; school finance reform; STEM teacher preparation and retention for urban contexts
Educational Leadership and Policy	Teacher diversity; industrial prison complex; economic reality associated with the "pipeline to school" phenomenon
History	Nineteenth-century US history; antislavery and emancipation; American Civil War and Reconstruction era; transatlantic abolitionism; nineteenth-century transnational US and Caribbean histories; Black Atlantic and African Diaspora, Black radicalism, and political thought
Political Science	Gender, sexuality, gender identity, race, and marginalized political identities in politics; social movements and interest groups in US politics
Theology	Intellectual history of late ancient Christianities; Syriac and Coptic literature; religious controversies; psychoanalysis and religion
Theology	Personalism, Christian philosophy in the twentieth century to the present, shaping thinking about "the whole person"; political theology

- By race/ethnicity, responses included Black, Haitian; Black, African American, Caribbean, West Indian; African American; Puerto Rican, Latina; Asian, Chinese American; Middle Eastern, Lebanese American; South Asian, South Indian (Tamil); White, Canadian; White, English, Scottish, Irish; Polish and French; plus one who did not initially share information about identity by race/ethnicity.
- By socioeconomic status of their family of origin, responses ranged from working class/lower middle class (five) to middle class (three), plus three who did not report.
- Regarding relationship status, two reported having a partner, five were married, one was single, and three did not report.
- By sexual orientation, six identified as heterosexual, one as queer, one as questioning queer, and three did not report.
- Regarding religious affiliation, responses included Christian (six; with three specified as Baptist, Roman Catholic, and Presbyterian); agnostic, born Hindu; spiritual; none (two); and one did not report.
- Regarding current health status, two reported living with a chronic illness or disability.
- Regarding immigration status, three identified as first-generation immigrants to the USA; four as second-generation, including one who reported it "sometimes feels like first"; one as third; one as fourth; one as "unknown" yet closest guess was fourth-generation, as a great-grandfather was from the Caribbean; and one identified as a "non-immigrant" who was born in another country and came to the USA as an adult.
- By nationality, most identified as American or US citizens, two had dual citizenship (one with Haiti and one with India), one was a citizen of China, one was a citizen of Canada, and two did not report.
- Responses to the question of what other group identities might also describe them included person of color, Midwesterner, vegetarian, partner and parent of biracial daughters, immigrant, feminist, social justice and environmental care advocate, mom, sorority sister, friend, scholarly community member, public intellectual, educator and life learner.

8.3.2 Pilot Professional Development Program and Data Collection

Throughout the fall semester of 2016, the CDP PAR faculty team met for eight sessions (11:00 am to 2:30 pm on Fridays, for a total of twenty-eight hours) to discuss assigned readings and relevant current events, participate in experiential exercises, share resources, and consult on current challenging cases for facilitating constructive diversity dialogues in our classrooms. The team members completed pre- and post-measures of social justice critical consciousness, a summative evaluation of the fall 2016 professional development program, and formative evaluations following each of the eight sessions. Furthermore, the team generated rich additional data over the course of the program by documenting all our group discussions.

8.3.3 Subsequent Steps Underway in Data Analysis and Sharing Results

In the spring semester of 2017, the team developed a bibliography of key books and other resources relevant to each faculty participant's academic scholarship and pedagogy for facilitating constructive diversity dialogues that promote learning in our classrooms (available on request from the first author). Data analysis is in progress, and the team has discussed potential publication plans for disseminating the evolving results.

To date, preliminary findings and key recommendations from our CDP PAR project for supporting faculty members to develop these challenging and compelling pedagogical competencies include:

- We must foundationally and continuously explore how our diverse perspectives, particularly from our own intersecting identities and experiences with power and oppression, influence both our blind spots in biases and sources of strength for advancing these vital educational efforts.
- We need to cultivate with each other essential networks of trustworthy and informed support for "work-shopping" or helpfully processing our failures and triumphs in this challenging work to promote teaching effectiveness.
- We can share and develop scholarship in all our academic disciplines that serves as resources for promoting social justice by fostering empathic understanding, informed critical analysis, and expanded learning.

8.4 Conclusion

In this chapter, relevant to the values of community psychology, we described the foundation for a professional development, participatory action research project with an interdisciplinary and diverse group of new faculty. The Constructive Diversity Pedagogy Participatory Action Research (CDP PAR) project was originated as one response, in the context of our university community and broader sociopolitical current events, to expand educating for social justice. This collaborative seed project was conducted by and for the CDP PAR faculty team of participants. In an intensive, small-group, semester-long professional development program, the team focused on examining and promoting together our own (1) *social justice critical consciousness* and (2) skills to facilitate *challenging diversity dialogues* in our classrooms that advance social justice critical consciousness, include multiple voices, consider alternative perspectives, and expand learning.

Results are evolving from our analyses of formative and summative sources of data gathered during the course of this pilot professional development program. Potential contributions include considering how these interdisciplinary perspectives might build from other models for facilitating difficult dialogues in teaching and learning (Worthington & Arévalo Avalos, 2017), integrating critical consciousness in the curriculum (Nicotera & Kang, 2009), developing critical consciousness with community partners (Maiter et al., 2012; Toporek & Worthington, 2014), or integrating evidence for intervention effectiveness in community-based participatory research (Clauss-Ehlers, 2017).

Finally, the CDP PAR project sparked a growing interdisciplinary community of scholars and meaningful connections that continue to inform and inspire our evolving personal and professional identities. For example, as noted by the second author (faculty participant; Educational Leadership and Policy, Graduate School of Education):

> As I reviewed the chapter I realize that participating in the CDP PAR significantly contributes to the scholar activist I am becoming. I met Wes [faculty participant; History Department] because of this project and subsequently reached out to him to learn more about the historical readings that shaped his lens as a result of participating in this project. He introduced me to Dr Barbara Fields' "Ideology of Race in American History" and that document shapes and grounds my entire awakening to institutionalized oppression and racism's role in education as a field and, most importantly, how I have been colonized, and it highlighted the assimilationist perspectives I had and have. It influences how I view and think about race and class, influences how I teach, as well as my decision to take a Freirean approach to liberation pedagogy.

References

Black Lives Matter. (n.d.). *Herstory*. http://blacklivesmatter.com/herstory/

Blue Lives Matter. (2017). *Blue Lives Matter: About*. https://bluelivesmatter.blue/organization/#about

Chugh, D. (2018). *The person you mean to be: How good people fight bias*. New York: HarperCollins.

Clauss-Ehlers, C. S. (2017). In search of an evidence-based approach to understand and promote effective parenting practices. *Couple and Family Psychology: Research and Practice*, 6(3), 135–153. doi.org/10.1037/cfp0000082

Freire, P. (2000). *Pedagogy of the oppressed*. New York: Bloomsbury Academic. (Original work published 1970)

Haynes, N. J., Vandenberg, R. J., DeJoy, D. M., et al. (2019). The workplace health group: A case study of 20 years of multidisciplinary research. *American Psychologist*, 74(3), 380–393. doi.org/10.1037amp0000445

Jones, C. P. (2000). Levels of racism: A theoretic framework and a gardener's tale. *American Journal of Public Health*, 90(8), 1212–1215. doi.org/10.2105/AJPH.90.8.1212

King, J. E., & Akua, C. (2012). Dysconscious racism and teacher education. In J. A. Banks (Ed.), *Encyclopedia of diversity in education*. Thousand Oaks, CA: SAGE Publications.

Levine, S. S., Apfelbaum, E. P., Bernard, M., et al. (2014). Ethnic diversity deflates price bubbles. *PNAS Proceedings of the National Academy of Sciences of the United States of America, 111*(52), 18524–18529. doi.org/10.1073/pnas .1407301111

Maiter, S., Joseph, A. J., Shan, N., & Saeid, A. (2012). Doing participatory qualitative research: Development of a shared critical consciousness with racial minority research advisory group members. *Qualitative Research, 13*(2), 198–213. doi .org/10.1177/1468794112455037

Mellers, B. A., & Tetlock, P. E. (2019). From discipline-centered rivalries to solution-centered science: Producing better probability estimates for policy makers. *American Psychologist, 74*(3), 290–300. doi.org/10.1037amp0000429

Nicotera, N., & Kang, H. (2009). Beyond diversity courses: Strategies for integrating critical consciousness across social work curriculum. *Journal of Teaching in Social Work, 29*(2), 188–203. doi.org/10/1080/08841230802240738

Phillips, K. W. (2014, October 1). How diversity makes us smarter. *Scientific American.* www.scientificamerican.com/article/how-diversity-makes-us-smarter/

Placier, P., Kroner, C., Burgoyne, S., & Worthington, R. (2012). Developing difficult dialogues: An evaluation of classroom implementation. *Journal of Faculty Development, 26*(2), 29–36. www.ingentaconnect.com/content/magna/jfd

Proctor, R. W., & Vu, K.-P. L. (2019). How psychologists help solve real-world problems in multidisciplinary research teams: Introduction to the special issue. *American Psychologist, 74*(3), 271–277. doi.org/10.1037amp0000458

Solomon, J., & Martin, A. (2019). Competitive victimhood as a lens to reconciliation: An analysis of the Black Lives Matter and Blue Lives Matter movements. *Conflict Resolution Quarterly, 37*(7), 7–31. doi.org/10.1002/crq.21262

Sue, D. W. (2013). Race talk: The psychology of racial dialogues. *American Psychologist, 68*(8), 663–672. doi.org/10.1037/a0033681

Sue, D. W., Alsaidi, S., Awad, M. N., et al. (2019). Disarming racial microaggressions: Microintervention strategies for targets, white allies, and bystanders. *American Psychologist, 74*(1), 128–142. doi.org/10.1037/amp0000296

Toporek, R. L., Lewis, J. A., & Ratts, M. J. (2010). The ACA advocacy competencies: An overview. In M. J. Ratts, R. L. Toporek, & J. A. Lewis (Eds.), *ACA advocacy competencies: A social justice framework for counselors* (pp. 11–20). Alexandria, VA: American Counseling Association.

Toporek, R. L., Sapigao, W., & Rojas-Arauz (2017). Fostering the development of a social justice perspective and action. In J. M. Casas, L. A. Suzuki, C. M. Alexander, & M. A. Jackson (Eds.), *Handbook of multicultural counseling* (4th ed.; pp. 17–30). Thousand Oaks, CA: SAGE Publications.

Toporek, R. L., & Worthington, R. L. (2014). Integrating service learning and difficult dialogues pedagogy to advance social justice training. *The Counseling Psychologist, 42*(7), 919–945. doi.org/10.1177/0011000014545090

Watt, S. (2007). Difficult dialogues, privilege and social justice: Uses of the Privileged Identity Exploration (PIE) model in student affairs practice. *College Student Affairs Journal, 26*(2), 114–126.

Williams, D. R. (2018). Stress and the mental health of populations of color: Advancing our understanding of race-related stressors. *Journal of Health and Social Behavior, 59*(4), 466–485. doi.org/10.1177/0022146518814251

Worthington, R. L., & Arévalo Avalos, M. R. (2017). Difficult dialogues in counselor training and higher education. In J. M. Casas, L. A. Suzuki, C. M. Alexander, & M. A. Jackson (Eds.), *Handbook of multicultural counseling* (4th ed.; pp. 360–372). Thousand Oaks, CA: SAGE Publications.

Young, G. (2003). Dealing with difficult classroom dialogue. In P. Bronstein & K. Quina (Eds.), *Teaching gender and multicultural awareness: Resources for the psychology classroom* (pp. 347–360). Washington, DC: American Psychological Association.

9 Critical Language Ethnography as a Community-Centered Research Paradigm

Ariana Mangual Figueroa and Meredith McConnochie

9.1 Introduction

In this chapter we outline a critical *language* ethnography approach to community-based research. We propose that this approach can offer rich qualitative insights into those everyday interactions through which children and adults acquire and impart locally accepted norms for language use in their communities while also co-constructing social identities and collective practices that can resist and change oppressive structures. While, arguably, all ethnographic fieldwork is conducted within the context of socially meaningful groupings denoted by the term *community*, this chapter seeks to elaborate on ethnographic projects that work not only to depict the cultural underpinnings of community life but that also seek to disrupt those structural forces that produce inequities across communities. By integrating insights from the fields of language socialization (LS) and critical ethnography (CE), we seek to bring into conversation complementary subfields within anthropology, sociolinguistics, and education that share a commitment to community-centered research.

Our focus on LS as a primary framework for conceptualizing and conducting community-based critical ethnographic research has grown out of our own training in the field. LS was founded in the early 1980s by linguistic anthropologists Elinor Ochs and Bambi Schieffelin, whose own ethnographic research was originally situated in discourse communities in Western Samoa, Papua New Guinea, and the United States (Ochs & Schieffelin, 1984). Integrating theoretical and methodological insights from the ethnography of communication (Hymes, 1964), developmental psychology (Slobin & Welsh, 1973), and linguistic anthropology (Duranti, 1997), Ochs and Schieffelin have shown how people learn to use language in culturally specific ways throughout their lifespan (1984, 2008). Over the last two decades, LS researchers have made critical contributions to our understanding of the ways in which adults and children negotiate macro ideologies regarding communicative competence, developmental appropriateness, and social identities linked to race and class during everyday micro interactions. As third- and fourth-generation LS researchers conducting ethnographic research in schools and homes (first and second author, respectively), we are indebted to foundational research in the field of educational and linguistic anthropology that precedes us (Garrett & Baquedano-López, 2002). The goal of this chapter is to build upon the existing literature as we forge connections between the study of language and the use of critical ethnographic methods while working in and alongside communities.

9.2 Critical Ethnography and Language Socialization

9.2.1 A Conceptual Framework

CE emerged in the 1960s out of a sociological concern with unveiling oppressive societal power structures ignored in traditional ethnographic approaches. Traditional ethnography sought to thickly describe social patterning without accounting for the unequal outcomes that issued from such patterns (Quantz, 1992). Current approaches to CE cohere around several research principles. These principles include (1) integrating critical social theory with empirical approaches that view societal inequities between communities in light of historical and contemporary power structures rather than inherent deficits of the communities themselves; (2) developing ethnographic approaches for centering the voices of nondominant groups and examining the ways in which such communities engage in praxis – a cycle of reflection, action, and transformation; and (3) making reflexivity part of the research process – from data collection through to analysis and presentation – by engaging in dialogue among those occupying participant and researcher roles as they co-construct new knowledge and arrive at shared goals for social change (Madison, 2004; Noblit, Murillo Jr., & Flores, 2004; Palmer & Caldas, 2015; Quantz, 1992). In short, these three principles focus our attention on power, praxis, and positionality as fundamental to the critical ethnographic research tradition.

Language socialization researchers conduct ethnographic research in order to document the ways in which theoretical concepts such as power, praxis, and positionality manifest in everyday life and shape the lives of children and adults in communities around the globe. Early comparative studies rendered the tacit norms underlying kinship interactions visible – for example, Ochs and Schieffelin (1984) worked to unsettle ideologies about universal child-rearing practices by questioning whether White American middle-class discourse practices would be the preferred socializing patterns across speech communities within and beyond the USA. By considering children to be active members of routine interactions – rather than merely passive recipients of adult speech – language socialization researchers recognize the ways in which power is distributed and accorded to experts/novices across the lifespan. It highlights the ways in which the learning process can itself be understood as an ethnographic praxis. By innovating new theories of language learning and childhood, LS has also drawn attention to the ways in which critical reflexivity regarding our own positionality can shape our interactions in the field as well as our analysis and writing processes (Ochs, 1979). Fundamentally, LS views ways of thinking, knowing, feeling, and communicating as ideologically constructed or aligned with beliefs, values, and identities that are indexed through language features and participation structures for interactions. The following three subsections – named for each of the three principles – offer examples of research that attends to power, praxis, and positionality within and across communities.

9.2.1.1 Power

Critical ethnographers, like language socialization researchers, reach for social theory to develop their "critical" stance. Social theory coupled with ethnographic methods makes possible the work of making the everyday strange, thereby allowing us to see more clearly the tacit norms that underlie everyday interactions. By doing so, critical ethnographers render visible the unequal power relations that come to be taken for granted and that constitute cultural practices. While ethnographers may draw on distinct theoretical traditions – for example, the structural economic perspectives that undergird important insights into the role of capital in the development of schooling routines (Bowles & Gintis, 1976; Bourdieu & Passeron, 1977) or Chicana feminist views (in the tradition of Anzaldúa, 1999), for example) that inform important interventions in our understanding of agency and voice in schooling (Cervantes-Soon, 2017; Patel, 2013) – the common goal of CE is to identify the everyday institutional mechanisms that have an impact on students differentially based upon the different social roles that they occupy in society with the hopes of advancing structural change and social justice (Quantz, 1992).

Within the study of language, the question of communicative competence has been a rich site for the study of power in interaction. Hymes (1972) defines communicative competence as the ability to interpret and use social and linguistic cues to communicate in ways considered appropriate by the ideologically constructed expectations of a speech community. In his early treatise titled "On Communicative Competence," Hymes (1972) argued against a Chomskian notion of the ideal hearer-speaker who acquires grammatical knowledge in the early years of life, and instead called for situating language learning within the sociocultural context of what is considered acceptable (Chomsky, 1985). In this formulation, notions of acceptability are never neutral but are instead inextricably linked to power relations that undergird interaction. Early studies of interaction within the developing field of interactional sociology developed this view and included studies of doctor–patient interactions revealing the unequal relations linked to privileged Westernized knowledge that appeared in routine checkups (Cicourel, 1974; e.g., dinnertime conversations that were sites for tracking the role of patriarchy and power among parents and children; Schegloff, 1996) and social experiments that called into question the discursive norms for face-to-face interaction

(Garfinkel, 1964; Goffman, 1974, 1981). This wave of critical interventions in the study of social interaction focused on the study of how communicative behaviors and everyday institutional routines are encoded with power circulating within our broader social and political systems.

Informed by Bourdieu's (1977) theorization of the way in which social class is reproduced through value systems that privilege particular dispositions and behaviors, language socialization research in schools demonstrates how school-based literacy expectations signal what counts as knowledge in schools (Baquedano-López & Kattan, 2008; Garrett & Baquedano-López, 2002). Thus, early studies in LS highlighted discrepancies between knowledge construction in school versus household language and literacy practices.

In her foundational work, Heath (1983) examined early literacy practices in White and Black mill families of low socioeconomic classes in rural Appalachia. Importantly, this work legitimized the language and literacy socialization practices of nondominant groups and highlighted a discontinuity between the household literacy practices of working-class parents and children and middle-class teachers' expectations for student participation in school literacy activities. Heath found that White families living in Roadville frequently asked children "known-answer" questions that prompted children to recount factual narratives using discourse patterns mirrored in the local elementary schools. While this meant that the literacy practices of the White homes and local school were aligned, and that children from these families were generally considered successful, those same Roadville children struggled when asked to apply factual knowledge beyond their frame of reference. In contrast, Black families in Trackton socialized their children to engage in imaginative storytelling employing metaphorical language to capture an audience's attention. These same children had more difficulty answering the factual questions typically asked in the school and were therefore deemed in need of remediation based upon differences in literacy practices judged against a school-based norm. In a similar vein, Phillips (2001) compared first- and sixth-grade classrooms on a Warm Springs Indian Reservation and a primarily Anglo middle-class neighborhood, highlighting differences in verbal and nonverbal communication patterns and raising questions regarding the detrimental impact that assessing cultural practices based upon a mainstream institutional standard can have on young children. Similarly highlighting distinctions between home and school literacy, Vasquez, Pease-Alvarez, and Shannon (1994) draw attention to the ways in which the norms for participating in the classrooms of young Mexican children differed from norms for participation in their homes.

The turn toward situation-centered ethnographies of communication has adhered in critical ethnographies today. Orellana and García Sánchez have studied together and separately the ways in which children take up the important role of language brokers during routine institutional interactions – ranging from parent–teacher conferences (García Sánchez & Orellana, 2006) to doctor's visits (Orellana, 2009). Orellana (2009) defines language brokering as "the meditational work that children do as they advocate for their families and negotiate between monolingual speakers" (p. 25); this can include translation and interpretation work across a range of settings. A close look at these interactions shows that they are laden with power dynamics that uphold the status quo of immigrant families' subservient position in relation to a White monolingual norm. Abu El-Haj's (2015) study of the schooling experiences of transnational Palestinian youth provides us with a new "understanding of the central role that everyday nationalism plays in drawing youth from im/migrant communities into the racialized social fabric of this country" (p. 32). Her work tracks how im/migrant youth are racialized by "the *everyday mechanisms* through which the categories of who can and cannot belong fully to this nation are established in ways that build a complex and uneven map of inequalities" (p. 32). Routine schooling activities communicate beliefs about inclusion and value that reproduce social inequality at the institutional level through embodied schooling practices that position immigrant children as in need of remediation and assimilation (Cekaite, 2012; Mökkönen, 2013). However, children themselves can appropriate everyday schooling practices as sites for resistance, as in the case of Sterponi's (2007) analysis of elementary-aged children who resist mandated silent reading as an individualized academic task devoid of social interaction by surreptitiously engaging in joint meaning-making practices through literacy. By orienting their bodies toward one another, using pointing gestures, and interjecting comments at a whisper, the children in Sterponi's study rejected the privileged school-based norm of demonstrating reading fluency independently and silently; instead, they found creative ways to make meaning and analyze text in peer-led interactions under their teacher's radar.

This emphasis on tracking the reproduction of inequality through institutional interactions has also been coupled with ethnographic work focused on resistance, continuing Hymes' (1972) charge to turn toward performance as a site for studying resistance and social change. Drawing from the fields of sociolinguistics and linguistic anthropology, current approaches to CE focus on engagement in various forms of resistance. As explained by Madison (2004), to engage in CE is to create a performance aimed at deconstructing hegemony and unveil oppression (p. 6 as cited in Palmer & Caldas, 2015).

Mangual Figueroa (2013) demonstrates how undocumented parents give *testimonio* about the difficulties they and their children face living in the USA. She shows how the act of giving *testimonio* functions as a form of civic engagement in a society where a lack of *papeles* (papers) limits their political participation. Within the field of education, ethnographic examinations of resistance have the potential to counter deficit perspectives of nondominant groups by showing the creative ways in which they engage in systems from which they are barred from mainstream participation. In the case of undocumented Latinx communities, for example, educators may believe families are disinterested in their children's education – contributing to deficit perspectives that cast immigrant parents as uncaring. However, critical ethnographic perspectives highlight the ways in which family members are marginalized from traditional forms of parent involvement and instead find other ways to engage fully in their children's learning (Baquedano-López, Alexander, & Hernandez, 2013; Hernandez, 2013; Mangual Figueroa, 2014; McConnochie & Mangual Figueroa, 2017). These ethnographic studies illustrate the ways in which power dynamics become evident in everyday activities inside and outside of schools. These findings have led to changes in the ethnographic process itself, which we turn to now in our discussion of praxis.

9.2.1.2 Praxis

Rooted in a Freirean understanding of knowledge as power, praxis can be thought of as a process through which the construction of knowledge has emancipatory and transformational potential to reorganize power relations (Quantz, 1992). In his posthumously published book, *Pedagogy of Indignation*, Freire (2004) predicates a pedagogy on the felt indignation of the educator at the indignations faced by the educated. In so doing, he acknowledges the falsity of any positivistic detachment of the observer from the observed. The educator, and for our purposes the ethnographer, is implicated – intellectually, bodily, politically – in the processes she aspires to transform. For many critical ethnographers, "indignation" can function as a sign – both a sign of the times and an indicator of what actions they might take (Márquez, 1999; Nash, 1993; Sawyer, 2004). Acknowledging subjectivity in the social processes of co-constructing identity and goals for shared resistance, critical ethnographers call for the use of ethnographic methods aimed at exploring how dominant as well as nondominant groups – and they, alongside them – make sense of and resist systems of oppression (Hamann, 2003; Nader, 1969). As Palmer and Caldas (2015) explain, "what sets critical ethnography apart is its focus on the way individuals within a marginalized community engage in praxis (Freire, 1970) – a cycle of action and reflection – and how members of the community exercise agency for cultural production and transformation" (p. 382). In other words, while engaging in participant observation, the ethnographer works alongside community members to develop ways to use the knowledge articulated in the collaborative research process to make social change.

Language socialization researchers locate the social processes of action – reflection – and change primarily in the notion of indexicality whereby language forms accrue social meaning that points to one's social standing in the society. This may therefore lead to forms of reproduction or resistance of those social roles. For example, the use of certain vernacular registers known as "Spanish" or "Spanglish" derive distinct value based upon differences in the racial and social standing of the speakers (Hill, 1998; Zentella, 2005).

Indexicality has been a rich site for the study of social meaning as it is made evident through language use and interaction, and for the study of contested power relations that emerge during interaction (Ochs, 1996; Rosa, 2018).

Through critical praxis, language socialization researchers and linguistic anthropologists continue to unsettle categories otherwise viewed as stable – the "meaning" of a word or phrase, the "speech community," "culture," and the very notion of "communicative competence," to name a few that have been and continue to be central in language socialization research (Flores & Rosa, 2015; Mangual Figueroa & Baquedano-López, 2011). Using the language of being socialized "to" and "through" language to signal the organizing role of language in being both a mode for socialization and a medium for social transformation, language socialization scholars analyze how reflection and change occurs through socializing interactions. As Baquedano-López and Hernandez (2011) explain, language socialization research examines "trajectories of learning ways of being in social system and the ways of resisting and shaping the system" (p. 199).

Arguably, a prerequisite for the development of praxis is the existence of power imbalances; and ethnographers of language find that unequal social relationships are often rendered visible in moments of cultural contact and conflict (Garrett & Baquedano-López, 2002). Researchers, in turn, develop praxis differently given the varying scales of social interaction to which they attend (for example, in educational studies we might see variety across district-wide, school-based, or classroom-specific modes of engagement) and the role that they believe research itself plays in furthering social change. One area in which critical perspectives on communicative competence meet CE is the study of language shift. Language shift can "occur whenever the members of a local speech community begin pervasively to abandon the use of one linguistic variety in favor of another," even when the language being lost is still used elsewhere (Moore, 2001, p. 60). For example, Wong Fillmore (2000) has shown that language shift among particular racialized communities of Spanish-speaking families in the USA occurs within one generation even when Spanish is widely used by other speech communities both within and beyond the country. Within the field of LS, language shift has been studied in contexts of cultural contact that emerge from colonizing projects across the globe. Och's (1988) work in Samoa longitudinally tracks the ways in which the interventions of British colonial forces in schooling and society show up in the shifting modes of interaction and literacy practices across settings. In the Caribbean context, Garrett's (2003) fieldwork in St. Lucia reveals similar patterns, as does Paugh's (2005) research on children in Dominica, among others.

Ethnographers studying "minoritized" languages in the US context have also merged the study of language shift with efforts at language maintenance in the face of racializing and colonizing forces to implement ethnographic projects in which they become implicated in supporting community's local efforts. We adopt McCarty's term "minoritized" because the shift from a categorical noun (minority) to a verb form captures the dynamic and value-laden nature of assigning labels to social groups and prompts us to examine "the power relations and processes by which certain groups are socially, economically, and politically marginalized within the larger society" (2002, p. xv). Baquedano-López (1997, 2004) demonstrates the integration of scales and ideologies in her study of struggles to resist English-only *doctrina* (catechism) classes in a California parish that reflected community-wide tensions issuing from statewide anti-immigrant legislation. In this instance, conversations between the ethnographer and parish members regarding linguistic and racial oppression led to collaborative efforts to preserve bilingual religious instruction, and resulted in important theoretical insights regarding community members' strategic choices about when to speak up or remain silent as they engage in projects of cultural maintenance.

Ethnographic research enlisting community members in the study of their own educational practices with the goal of changing school practices (González, Moll, & Amanti, 2004) and those in which the ethnographer's research lies in the service of supporting local change (Cervantes-Soon, 2017; Dyrness, 2011) provide additional examples of critical ethnographic praxis. In the area of language loss and language maintenance, Teresa McCarty's (2002) work within and alongside native communities in the Southwestern USA provides a rich model for an ethnographic praxis that involves learning from and working in solidarity with community to develop community-based programs that leverage ethnographic research for social change. Attention to praxis raises the question of the ethnographer's positionality, which is the third guiding principle that we explore here.

9.2.1.3 Positionality

Researcher positionality can be understood as the role that the researcher's values and ideologies play in the production of scholarly knowledge and social transformation (Madison, 2004; Noblit et al., 2004; Palmer & Caldas, 2015). As such, the critical ethnographer recognizes the need for transparency about her beliefs, intentions, and processes by which knowledge is produced and represented (Palmer & Caldas, 2015). The goal of the critical ethnographer is to "use the resources, skills, and privileges available to her to make accessible – to penetrate the borders and to break through the confines in defense of – the voices and experiences of subjects whose stories are otherwise restrained and out of reach" (Madison, 2004, p. 5). Working to achieve this goal requires self-reflection about the possible (intended and unanticipated) consequences of research, about the exchanges that take place between ourselves and those we work alongside, about the relationship between the ethnographic account and the broader social issues it depicts, and about the way in which the ethnography can contribute to equity (Madison, 2004). Madison explains how the researcher's theories are

> hidden forces and ambiguities that operate beneath appearances; to guide judgments and evaluations emanating from our discontent; to direct our attention to the critical expressions within different interpretive communities relative to their unique symbol systems, customs, and codes; to demystify the ubiquity and magnitude of power; to provide insight and inspire acts of justice; and to name and analyze what is intuitively felt. (Madison, 2004, p. 13)

To examine researcher positionality involves analyses of the ways in which the subjective selves of the researcher and others are constructed through dialogue between the researcher, participants, and the historical context (Madison, 2004; Quantz, 1992). Madison (2004) conceptualizes this dialogue as a performance between researcher and "other." She explains that this dialogue moves from ethnographic *present* to ethnographic *presence* by creating opportunities for readers and audiences to experience and grasp the partial presence of a temporal conversation constituted by the Other's voice, body, history, and yearnings (p. 10). Quantz (1992) demonstrates how reflexivity demands not only an examination of knowledge construction between researcher and participants but also an analysis of the way in which the purpose of the research is situated in a historical dialectic of social theory. Likewise, LeCompte and Preissle (1992) call for a continual focus on agency and researcher reflexivity, situating praxis within a disciplinary history that opens on to an ethnographic future.

Language socialization research demonstrates how positionality and subjectivities are developed through moment-by-moment interactions. From its inception, language socialization scholars have understood methods as ideological and have demonstrated the importance of integrating theory and method (Ochs, 1979). Arguing for a view of transcription as theory, Ochs (1979) specifically calls attention to the way in which the structure of the transcription, such as whose language (novice or expert) and what kind of language (verbal or nonverbal) is privileged by being positioned on top or on the left side of the page. In this work, she demonstrates that power is conveyed through transcript structure, and thus sheds light on the importance of reflexivity through stages of research.

Briggs (1984) focuses specifically on data collection and the ways in which researchers' own communicative competence may reproduce what Briggs calls a kind of "communicative hegemony" (p. 22). His focus on the ethnographic interview aligns with Palmer and Caldas' analysis of the interview as a methodological genre and shows how researchers may disrupt conventions for local communication by posing questions that may not be locally appropriate or comprehensible, ultimately revealing the ethnographers' inability to adapt to and respect local norms. Similarly concerned with tensions surrounding interviewing, Fredericks (2019) demonstrates how a structured interview process can intimidate marginalized youth and other vulnerable populations and calls on researchers to learn about participants' experiences through mutual exchanges of stories and dialogue during everyday routines. In these formulations, the onus is on the researcher to develop interview methods (and, more broadly, a communicative repertoire, in Rymes' 2010 formulation) that doesn't impose the researcher's social and linguistic practices but instead acknowledges difference between researcher and researched while acquiring local practices that prompt rather than prevent open exchange.

Like Briggs, Moore (2009) argues that researchers should develop a communicative fluency that doesn't impede their ability to communicate with participants, or at worst, offend and alienate them. She notes that "Most of us report little on our own skills or how we developed them, despite the fact that our field competence has strong bearing on the research questions we ask and how we answer them" (p. 245). Moore calls for ethnographers of language to write about the process of acquiring "field language communicative competence" in the hopes of generating a dialogue about the role of the ethnographer in the field, the relationships between researcher and researched, and those processes that are often idealized and neutralized when left unscrutinized (2009, p. 245). Acknowledging tendencies toward an etic perspective, reflexivity in language socialization research involves analysis of how participants make sense of identities and construct membership boundaries through interaction. Hernandez (2013) argues that by embracing vulnerability and sharing one's own experiences during data collection, researchers can facilitate meaningful conversations with participants. The process of exiting the field can likewise invoke conversations between the researcher and participants about the trajectory of researcher–participant relationships (Mangual Figueroa, 2014). In sum, LS researchers' focus on the micro features of language and the ways in which how power is encoded in interaction leads to new insights into power inequities built into the ethnographic process itself.

9.3 Critical Case Analysis

In this section, we exemplify analytic approaches that are available within a critical language ethnography approach by examining one interaction that took place in the home of a Latinx family residing in a New Latino Diaspora community within the state of New Jersey, referred to by the pseudonym of Smithtown. This interaction took place during an ethnographic study conducted by the second author from 2013 to 2015 in a second-grade bilingual classroom and the homes of seven families of Mexican origin. The second author is an American-born English-dominant White female of European descent who developed Spanish proficiency in formal educational settings and informal contexts living abroad. This study originated from her experience of serving as a volunteer in a Smithtown community organization dedicated to immigrant services and advocacy. While volunteering as an English as a Second Language teacher at the organization, the second author developed relationships with two mothers who would come to participate in the study over time. After obtaining formal permission from the district superintendent to recruit participants and conduct research in the local public elementary school the second author recruited four additional children enrolled in second-grade, along with their teachers, mothers, peers, and siblings. The second author obtained IRB approval for all research protocols and acquired informed consent from all participants in the study. Juan González – whose family is featured in this case analysis – is a pseudonym for one of the students enrolled in this class. We have removed all identifying details from this chapter and use pseudonyms for participants to protect confidentiality. Participant observation was conducted during ten visits to the household of each family including the González family. Data from each visit include field notes, audio-recorded interactions during routines and informal conversations, and written artifacts that were photographed.

The study specifically examined the ways in which elementary-aged emergent bilingual children and their Mexican-born mothers interpreted school-based discourses related to academic competency. When the school issued evaluations of "low academic achievement," the study tracked the ways in which parents and children developed ways of remedying "low" achievement through language and literacy routines. The data presented below draw on informal conversations between one family and the second author on related topics of how to negotiate and repair everyday social interactions characterized as bullying among peers at school. This extended interaction provides insights into the ways in which the family and ethnographer co-constructed their relationship and how they actively negotiated their differing power relations and positionalities throughout the study. Using an adapted Conversation Analytic approach, we examine the ways in which mothers' and children's language use is indexical of their subjective understandings of power structures and researcher positionality (Schegloff, 2007). This approach to the study of interaction attunes us analytically to meaning-making and turn-taking; in other words, the ways in which speakers present and develop ideas over the course of an interaction in order to reach new understandings. The focus on the turn – which readers will see numbered in the following transcript – allows us to focus on the significance of what the adults and children said each time they spoke and responded to one another. This excerpt allows us to explore the three themes of critical language ethnography explored in this chapter: power, praxis, and positionality.

The following exchange was recorded in 2015 during a dinner table conversation that included the second author and members of Juan González's family, a second-grade focal student whose family the second author had known for approximately two months. The González family included Sofia (mother), Antonio (fifth-grade boy), Manuela (fourth-grade girl), Juan (second-grade boy), and an infant. The family had moved to Smithtown during the previous school year. Sofia was born in El Salvador, and all three of her children were born in Mexico. The three oldest children shared a father who remained in Mexico and the youngest sibling's father lived with the family in Smithtown. The three school-aged children spoke Spanish to one another and their mother in the home and were learning English in school. As was typical during visits to the González household, family members communicated with the second author in Spanish. By presenting a transcript that includes Spanish utterances to the left and English translations on the right, we seek to foreground the language of the participants in this exchange and to redistribute the power often granted to English in scholarly publications in the USA. It is common in academic journals to find English translations of Spanish-language interactions without the original text, or to find that the English translations appear above the Spanish. Here, we de-center the dominant academic language of English by providing the reader with the original Spanish words spoken followed by our English translation to the right.

On this afternoon, the dinner table conversation among Sofia, the children, and the second author turned to issues of school bullying and how the siblings could assert their rights in such situations. The example begins as Sofia invited the second author – who we will refer to as Meredith for the purposes of data analysis – to join the family for dinner after she had assisted the children to complete their homework. Sofia begins the sequence by retelling a story to Meredith about a time that Antonio had reported being hit by a peer in school. In turn 1 below, Sofia begins with *y éste* (and this one) – ending one story she had just told about Manuela being bullied by peer and transitioning to the ensuing story about Antonio's experiences of being bullied as well.

1	Sofia:	*Y éste me dijo que un niño le había pegado. ¿Quién te pegó?*	And this one told me that a boy had hit him. Who hit you?
2	Antonio:	*No está en mi salón. No va en quinto grado.*	He isn't in my class. He isn't in fifth grade.
3	Meredith:	*En quinto.*	In fifth.
4	Antonio:	*No. No es en quinto.*	No. No he's not in fifth.
5	Meredith:	*Oh no es en quinto, en otro grado. ¿No sabes el nombre?*	Oh he's not in fifth, in another grade. You don't know his name?
6	Antonio:	*Era americano.*	He was American.
7	Sofia:	*Que hable con la maestra. Porque primero es hablar con la maestra. Si este niño sigue y no le hace caso la maestra, no entendió, allí a hablar con el maestro y el maestro de este niño.*	Talk with the teacher. The first thing is to talk with the teacher. If this boy continues and doesn't pay attention to the teacher, didn't understand, from there talk with the teacher and this boy's teacher.

Part of the way through Sofia's initial retelling (in turn 1), Antonio cut his mother off to provide more information about the boy who had hit him (turn 2). After clarifying that the boy who hit him was not in his class or in the fifth grade, Antonio identified the boy as *Americano* (American) in turn 6, pointing to his perception of the boy's national identity. While Antonio offered this identifier in lieu of the peer's name, which he did not know, Sofia turned her attention to directing Antonio about what steps to take in this kind of situation. Sofia outlined that he should first talk to his own teacher and then the teacher of the offending boy. She offered Antonio a sequence of steps to address this bullying, and suggested an order in which he should communicate his concerns to specific adults in the school setting – first his teacher and, if necessary, the peer's teacher. Shifting from referring specifically to Antonio, Sofia employed the present informal tense (*"primero es* (first is)" instead of first <u>you</u> should) to issue a more general recommendation about what Antonio and his siblings should be prepared to do in similar situations. By making these suggestions, Sofia worked to socialize her children into adopting positive dispositions toward self-advocacy. The exchange continued as Antonio returned to the relevance of the bully's nationality.

8	Antonio:	*Pero Mami, pero este niño es americano, que no habla español.*	But Mommy, but this boy is American, he doesn't speak Spanish.
9	Meredith:	*Y los padres tampoco–*	And the parents neither–
10	Juan:	*Y como lo voy a decir a los maestros de él–*	And how am I going to say to his teachers–
11	Sofia:	*Ah hijo para que tiene la boca uno, para hablar, pedir ayuda. ¿Cómo que va a quedar ahogando sin pedir ayuda? Uno tiene que pedir ayuda.*	Ah son, why does one have a mouth, to speak, to ask for help. How are you going to continue drowning without asking for help? One has to ask for help.
12	Juan:	*Mami, y como le voy a decir algo en inglés que no–*	Mommy, and how am I going to say something to him in English that I don't–
13	Sofia:	*Por eso, pedir ayudar con alguien que sepa inglés y español.*	Because [of that], you ask for help from someone that knows English and Spanish.
14	Juan:	*Uh huh como Meredith.*	Uh huh like Meredith.
15	Sofia:	*O tu maestra.*	Or your teacher.
16	Antonio:	*La maestra de español.*	The Spanish teacher.

In turn 8, Antonio returned to the issue of the peer being American as a metonym for the unequal power relations between the two students and to signal the challenges that Antonio faced in advocating for himself. Antonio repeated that the bullying peer was American, adding this time that the boy did not speak Spanish. Juan, Antonio's younger brother, took up his concern about advocating for oneself in a majority-English schooling context in a new country. Juan questioned *"¿y cómo lo voy a decir a los maestros de él?"* (how am I going to say this to his teachers?) in turn 10. Sofia responded to Antonio's question with a moral lesson about the importance of speaking up to ask for help, stating *"Ah hijo para que tiene la boca uno, para hablar, pedir ayuda. ¿Cómo que va a quedar ahogando sin pedir ayuda? Uno tiene que pedir ayuda"* (Ah son, why does one have a mouth, to speak, to ask for help. How are you going to continue drowning without asking for help? One has to ask for help."). We can see in turn 12 that Juan remained unconvinced in his ability to ask for help and questioned his mother about how to voice his concerns across linguistic difference – a linguistic difference also marked by national identity – thereby reiterating his brother's doubt about being heard in the schooling context. Importantly, Antonio and Juan's questions imply that they both view English as the language of power, a power they do not possess.

Challenging this view, Sofia directed them to ask help from a teacher who spoke English and Spanish (turn 13). Accepting his mother's suggestion, Juan began to identify possible trusted adults *"cómo Meredith"* (like Meredith) in turn 14, suggesting that he could seek the help of the ethnographer to broker his communication. This statement provides insight into the ways in which participants call upon researchers to help resolve dilemmas they experience (see also Mangual Figueroa, 2014). In this case, Meredith was positioned as a trusted advocate for addressing the issue of English dominance and social power as a form of oppression in the everyday life of these elementary school immigrant children. Antonio also suggested his Spanish teacher as a possible broker (turn 16).

17	Sofia:	*Mhmm se puede. Y decirle que está pasando. El hecho de que nosotros no seamos de acá no quiere decirle que los niños van a abusar. ¿Porqué? Todos somos iguales.*	Mhmm you can. And tell them what is happening. The fact that we are not from here does not mean that the kids can be abused. Why? We are all equal.
18	Antonio:	*Yo creo que somos americanos. Canadá, Estados Unidos, México, Guatemala, El Salvador, es América.*	I think that we are all Americans. Canada, the United States, Mexico, Guatemala, El Salvador, it's America.
19	Meredith:	*Claro, el sur de América también.*	Of course, South America too.
20	Antonio:	*Yo soy de norte americano.*	I am from North America.

In the final segment of this exchange, Sofia connected the request for help to a concern about the broader rights of immigrant children in turn 17. Interestingly, Antonio then invoked a pan-North and South American identity in turn 18, juxtaposing his earlier label of the peer bully as American within his own sense of himself as American and rights-bearing by virtue of immigrating from south to north. Ultimately, this excerpt sheds light on the way in which young children can learn to develop a critical consciousness and disposition toward self-advocacy during everyday interactions through narrations of problems in the home.

Across these three segments of the interaction, we can track several developing ideas that link up to this chapter's themes of power, praxis, and positionality. Across several turns of talk, Sofia and her children used the bullying example to raise larger concerns about power and language faced by their immigrant family. They described a sociopolitical context in which "American English" is the expected norm for everyday communication and advocacy, thereby communicating a set of language ideologies equating English with belonging and power in the US nation-state. Accordingly, Sofia called directly upon her children to develop their own critical praxis – socializing them to speak up about injustices they face and to seek help from trusted bilingual individuals. Notably, Juan identified Meredith as one of these trusted adults, implicating the ethnographer in the work of advocating for fairness and respect within the context of the school site where she was conducting research.

9.4 Toward a Critical Language Socialization Ethnography

This chapter has provided a close look at critical ethnographic and language socialization approaches to working within diverse communities, in the hopes of providing a model for rigorous qualitative research that can foster community-led social change. We have traced the ways in which ethnographic modes of inquiry grounded in a theoretical analysis of power can combine with the close study of language and community. Our critical case study analysis draws on insights from LS and CE to examine how adults and children negotiate beliefs about fairness and socialize one another to beliefs and actions that confront power across multiple scales (such as face-to-face and nation-state constructions of who belongs and who is empowered to speak out). By specifically focusing on narratives of advocacy co-constructed by immigrant parents, their children, and the ethnographer, we highlight how beliefs about social problems and their potential solutions are attributed to people, settings, institutions, and nations. As we close this chapter, we return to each of the three principles of power, praxis, and positionality – indicating productive overlaps across all three – to direct our readers to ongoing disciplinary conversations among scholars currently shaping future developments in CE and LS.

Recalling the importance of social theory for developing an understanding of power, we revisit Bourdieu's (1980) theory of habitus. The concept of habitus occupies an important place in critical anthropological approaches to ethnographic research because it provides a working understanding of how individuals come to acquire dispositions and practices that are "socially structured and hence enduring, but also as situated, contextually grounded, and emergent in character" (Garrett & Baquedano-López, 2002, p. 344). The notion of "durable ... dispositions" shaped by histories of structural inequality that become sedimented in our beliefs about language, people, and schooling is simultaneously juxtaposed with the idea that these beliefs are dynamic and subject to renegotiation (Bourdieu, 1980, p. 53). As language socialization scholars Kulick and Schieffelin (2004) have noted, "language socialization studies have enormous potential for enriching social theory. By analyzing ways in which praxis comes to be acquired, and performativity actually operates in situated interactions ..." (p. 352). In other words, critical language socialization ethnographers can document cultural patterns while also paying close attention to how and when long-held beliefs begin to shift in communities and across societies. Here we draw the reader's attention to the conversation regarding the "language gap" taking place in the *Journal of Linguistic Anthropology*, where critical ethnographers of language make clear what is at stake in our continued work to counter deficit models of racially and linguistically diverse communities in the USA. Many of our colleagues are taking on this work through professional organizations such as the Society for Linguistic Anthropology's working group on Language and Social Justice, while others are creating multimedia resources with the goal of shifting the political discourse away from exclusion and toward inclusion (see Otto Santa Ana's site www.thepresidentsintent.org and Mica Pollock's https://USvsHate.org).

Building on the notion of habitus as praxis – as a historically informed, potentially shifting set of practices – we turn to the potential of new studies in LS and CE to focus on reflexivity, or how individuals interpret and adapt social norms across different timescales (Rymes, 2008; Wortham, 2005). We believe that a critical methodological approach can explore how community-based changes emerge, while also continuing to adapt our ethnographic methods based upon community's lived experiences. Take, for example, the articles published in a 2016 issue of *Anthropology & Education Quarterly* in which US-based ethnographers critically examined their own methodological practices in communities living with the everyday effects of state surveillance – ranging from Muslim communities in New York City to high schools serving students of color in Southern California, along with varying field sites that lie in between the two coasts. These scholars account for the ways in which the community members in their studies called upon the ethnographer to rethink her research methods – regarding the norms for audio and video recording, for example – because these methods mirrored the broader experiences of surveillance that these racialized groups experienced in their everyday lives. By offering their accounts of the ethical dilemmas that arise when working in communities living under conditions of state surveillance, these ethnographers reveal their own methodological praxis. The lessons that they share hold promise for enriching all of our research methods, thus extending their insights across projects and timescales.

We end this chapter by considering ethnographer positionality in light of the responsibility that the ethnographer assumes when learning from the communities that welcome her in. As such, we must always attune to the edict in social science research that mandates that we "do no harm" (Erickson, 2016) and the imperative that we have to consider research ethics and dilemmas that arise throughout our research. Rather than assuming that we can anticipate and resolve these dilemmas at the outset of our research, we urge community-based researchers to put in place ethical sounding boards beyond university-based IRBs that can lend support to ethnographers throughout the research process (Mangual Figueroa, 2016). This commitment requires additional planning and relationship building, to be sure, but is essential if we are to be truly accountable to those communities with whom we work (Fox & Fine, 2013).

Having interlocutors within the communities we study, not simply as informants but as coresearchers and trusted advisors, will help us to redistribute power through critical ethnographic praxis. This will also help us continue to shift away from a reliance on home–school conflict models that endure in the field of education (Zentella, 2005) and from overgeneralization that can result when imposing our perspectives on our data (Ochs, 1999; Rymes, 2008). As we heard in our critical case study, seven-year-old Juan urged the second author to reconsider the quintessential ethnographic mode of inquiry found in participant observation. Juan called on her to move out of the observer role and into a more active advocacy role and, in so doing, he leaves us all with the call to remain attuned to our responsibilities to those we work with when engaging in community-based research.

References

Abu El-Haj, T. R. (2015). *Unsettled belonging: Educating Palestinian American youth after 9/11*. Chicago: University of Chicago Press.

Anzaldúa, G. E. (1999). *La frontera/Borderlands: The new mestiza* (2nd ed.). San Francisco: Aunt Lute Books.

Baquedano-López, P. (1997). Creating social identities through *doctrina* narratives. *Issues in Applied Linguistics*, 8(1), 27–45. Reprinted in A. Duranti (Ed.) (2001), *Linguistic anthropology: A reader* (pp. 343–358). Malden, MA: Blackwell.

Baquedano-López, P. (2004). Traversing the center: The politics of language use in a Catholic religious education program for immigrant Mexican children. *Anthropology & Education Quarterly*, 35(2), 212–232. doi.org/10.1525/aeq .2004.35.2.212

Baquedano-López, P., Alexander, R. A., & Hernandez, S. (2013). Equity issues in parental and community involvement in schools: What teacher educators need to know. *Review of Research in Education, 37*(1), 149–182. doi.org/10 .3102/0091732X12459718

Baquedano-López, P., & Hernandez, S. (2011). Language socialization across educational settings. In B. Levinson & M. Pollock (Eds.), *A companion to the anthropology of education* (pp. 197–211). Malden, MA: Blackwell.

Baquedano-López, P., & Kattan, S. (2008). Language socialization in schools. In N. Hornberger & P. Duff (Eds.), *Encyclopedia of language and education, Vol. 8: Language socialization* (pp. 161–173). New York: Springer/Kluwer Academic Publishers.

Bourdieu, P. (1977). *Outline of a theory of practice.* Cambridge, UK: Cambridge University Press.

Bourdieu, P. (1980). *The logic of practice.* Stanford, CA: Stanford University Press.

Bourdieu, P., & Passeron, J. C. (1977). *Reproduction in education, society, and culture.* Beverly Hills, CA: SAGE Publications.

Bowles, S., & Gintis, H. (1976). *Schooling in capitalist America.* New York: Basic Books.

Briggs, C. L. (1984). Learning how to ask: Native metacommunicative competence and the incompetence of fieldworkers. *Language in Society, 13*(1), 1–28. doi .org/10.1017/S0047404500015876

Cekaite, A. (2012). Affective stances in teacher–novice student interactions: Language, embodiment, and willingness to learn in a Swedish primary classroom. *Language in Society, 41*(5), 641–670. doi.org/10.1017/S0047404512000681

Cervantes-Soon, C. (2017). *Juárez girls rising: Transformative education in times of dystopia.* Minneapolis: University of Minnesota Press.

Chomsky, N. (1985). Methodological preliminaries. In J. J. Katz (Ed.), *The philosophy of linguistics* (pp. 80–125). Oxford, UK: Oxford University Press.

Cicourel, A. (1974). Interpretive procedures and normative rules in the negotiation of status and role. In A. Cicourel (Ed.), *Cognitive sociology: Language and meaning in social interaction* (pp. 11–41). New York: The Free Press.

Duranti, A. (1997). *Linguistic anthropology.* New York: Cambridge University Press.

Dyrness, A. (2011). *Mothers united: An immigrant struggle for socially just education.* Minneapolis: University of Minnesota Press.

Erickson, F. (2016). First, do no harm: A comment. *Anthropology & Education Quarterly, 47*(1), 100–103. doi.org/10.1111/aeq.12138

Flores, N., & Rosa, J. (2015). Undoing appropriateness: Raciolinguistic ideologies and language diversity in education. *Harvard Educational Review, 85*(2), 149–171. doi.org/10.17763/0017-8055.85.2.149

Fredericks, D. (2019). Working towards a humanizing research stance. In D. S. Warriner & M. Bigelow (Eds.), *Critical reflections on research methods: Power and equity in complex multilingual contexts* (pp. 110–123). Bristol, UK: Multilingualism Matters.

Freire, P. (1970). *Pedagogy of the oppressed.* New York: Continuum.

Freire, P. (2004). *Pedagogy of indignation.* New York: Paradigm Publishers.

García-Sanchez, I., & Orellana, M. F. (2006). The construction of moral and social identity in immigrant children's narratives-in-translation. *Linguistics and Education, 17*(3), 209–239. doi.org/10.1016/j.linged.2006.07.001

Garfinkel, H. (1964). Studies of the routine grounds of everyday activities. *Social Problems, 11*(3), 225–250. doi.org/10.2307/798722

Garrett, P. B. (2003). An "English Creole" that isn't: On the sociohistorical origins of linguistic classifications of the vernacular English of St. Lucia. In M. Aceto & J. P. Williams (Eds.), *Contact Englishes of the Eastern Caribbean* (pp. 155–210). Philadelphia: John Benjamins.

Garrett, P. B., & Baquedano-López, P. (2002). Language socialization: Reproduction and continuity, transformation and change. *Annual Review of Anthropology, 31*(1), 339–361. doi.org/10.1146/annurev.anthro.31.040402.085352

Goffman, E. (1974). *Frame analysis: An essay on the organization of experience.* Cambridge, MA: Harvard University Press.

Goffman, E. (1981). *Forms of talk.* Philadelphia: University of Pennsylvania Press.

González, N., Moll, L., & Amanti, C. (2005). *Funds of knowledge: Theorizing practices in households, communities, and classrooms.* Mahwah, NJ: Lawrence Erlbaum Associates.

Hamann, E. T. (2003). Reflections on the field: Imagining the future of the anthropology of education if we take Laura Nader seriously. *Anthropology and Education Quarterly, 34*(4), 438–449. doi.org/10.1525/aeq.2003.34.4.438

Heath, S. B. (1983). *Ways with words: Language, life and work in communities and classrooms.* Cambridge, UK: Cambridge University Press.

Hernandez, S. (2013). *When institutionalized discourses become familial: Mexican immigrant families interpreting and enacting high stakes educational reform* [Doctoral Dissertation]. University of California, Berkeley. https://escholarship.org/uc/item/3gh3n8vs

Hill, J. H. (1998). Language, race and white public space. *American Anthropologist, 100*(3), 680–689. doi.org/10.1525/aa.1998.100.3.680

Hymes, D. (1964). Toward ethnographies of communication. *American Anthropologist, 66*(6), 1–34. doi.org/10.1525/aa.1964.66.suppl_3.02a00010

Hymes, D. (1972). On communicative competence. In J. Pride & J. Holmes (Eds.), *Sociolinguistics* (pp. 53–73). Harmondsworth, UK: Penguin Books.

Kulick, D., & Schieffelin, B. B. (2004). Language socialization. In A. Duranti (Ed.), *A companion to linguistic anthropology* (pp. 349–368). Oxford, UK: Blackwell.

LeCompte, M. D., & Preissle, J. (1992). Towards an ethnology of student life in schools and classrooms: Synthesizing the qualitative research tradition. In M. LeCompte, W. Millroy, & J. Preissle (Eds.), *Handbook of qualitative research in education* (pp. 815–859). San Diego, CA: Academic Press.

Madison, D. S. (2004). *Critical ethnography: Method, ethics, and performance.* Los Angeles: SAGE Publications.

Mangual Figueroa, A. (2013). ¡Hay que hablar!: *Testimonio* in the everyday lives of migrant mothers. *Language & Communication, 33*(4), 559–572. doi.org/10.1016/j.langcom.2013.03.011

Mangual Figueroa, A. (2014). *La carta de responsabilidad*: The problem of departure. In D. Paris & M. T. Winn (Eds.), *Humanizing research: Decolonizing qualitative inquiry with youth and communities* (pp. 129–146). Thousand Oaks, CA: SAGE Publications.

Mangual Figueroa, A. (2016). Citizenship, beneficence, and informed consent: The ethics of working in mixed-status families. *International Journal of Qualitative Studies in Education, 29*(10), 66–85. doi.org/10.1080/09518398.2014.974722

Márquez, P. C. (1999). *The street is my home: Youth and violence in Caracas.* Stanford, CA: Stanford University Press.

McCarty, T. L. (2002). *A place to be Navajo: Rough Rock and the struggle for self-determination in indigenous schooling.* Mahwah, NJ: Lawrence Erlbaum Associates.

McConnochie, M., & Mangual Figueroa, A. (2017). *"Dice que es bajo"* ("She says he's low"): Negotiating breaches of learner identity in two Mexican families. *Linguistics and Education, 38*, 68–78. doi.org/10.1016/j.linged.2017.02.005

Mökkönen, C. (2013). Newcomers navigating language choice and seeking voice. *Anthropology & Education Quarterly, 44*(2), 124–141. doi.org/10.1111/aeq.12011

Moore, L. C. (2009). In communicative competency … in the field. *Language and Communication, 29*(3), 244–253. doi.org/10.1016/j.langcom.2009.02.006

Moore, R. E. (2001). Endangered. In A. Duranti (Ed.), *Key terms in language and culture* (pp. 60–63). Malden, MA: Blackwell.

Nader, L. (1969). Up the anthropologist: Perspectives gained from "studying up." In D. Hymes (Ed.), *Reinventing anthropology* (pp. 284–311). New York: Pantheon Books.

Nash, J. (1993). *We eat the mines and the mines eat us: Dependency and exploitation in Bolivian tin mines.* New York: Columbia University Press.

Noblit, G. W., Murillo Jr., E. G.., & Flores, S. Y. (Eds.). (2004). *Postcritical ethnography in education.* Cresskill, NJ: Hampton Press.

Ochs, E. (1979). Transcription as theory. *Developmental Pragmatics, 10*(1), 43–72.

Ochs, E. (1988). *Culture and language development: Language acquisition and language socialization in a Samoan village.* Cambridge, UK: Cambridge University Press.

Ochs, E. (1996). Linguistic resources for socializing humanity. In J. J. Gumperz & S. C. Levinson (Eds.), *Rethinking linguistic relativity* (pp. 407–437). Cambridge, UK: Cambridge University Press.

Ochs, E. (1999). Socialization. *Journal of Linguistic Anthropology, 9*(1–2), 230–233.

Ochs, E., & Schieffelin, B. (1984). Language acquisition and socialization: Three developmental stories and their implications. In R. A. Shweder & R. A. LeVine (Eds.), *Culture theory: Essays on mind, self, and emotion* (pp. 276–320). New York: Cambridge University Press.

Ochs, E., & Schieffelin, B. (2008). Language socialization: An historical overview. In P. Duff & N. H. Hornberger (Eds.), *Encyclopedia of language and education* (2nd ed.; pp. 2580–2594). New York: Springer.

Orellana, M. F. (2009). *Translating childhoods: Immigrant youth, language, and culture.* New Brunswick, NJ: Rutgers University Press.

Palmer, D., & Caldas, B. (2015). Critical ethnography. In K. King, Y. Lai, & S. May (Eds.), *Research methods in language and education: Encyclopedia of language and education* (pp. 381–392). Cham, Switzerland: Springer International Publishing.

Patel, L. (2013). *Youth held at the border: Immigration, education and the politics of inclusion*. New York: Teachers College Press.

Paugh, A. (2005). Multilingual play: Children's code-switching, role-play and agency in Dominica, West Indies. *Language in Society*, *34*(1), 63–86. doi.org/10.1017/0S0047404505050037

Phillips, S. (2001). Participant structures and communicative competence: Warm Springs children in community and classroom. In A. Duranti (Ed.), *Linguistic anthropology: A reader* (pp. 302–317). Malden, MA: Blackwell.

Quantz, R. A. (1992). On critical ethnography (with some postmodern considerations). In M. D. LeCompte, W. L. Millroy, & J. Preissle (Eds.), *The handbook of qualitative research in education* (pp. 447–505). New York: Academic Press, Inc.

Rosa, J. (2018). *Looking like a language, sounding like a race: Raciolinguistic ideologies and the learning of Latinidad*. Oxford, UK: Oxford University Press.

Rymes, B. (2008). Language socialization and the linguistic anthropology of education. In P. Duff & N. Hornberger (Eds.), *Encyclopedia of language and education, Vol. 8: Language socialization* (2nd ed.; pp. 1–14). New York: Springer/Kluwer Academic Publishers.

Rymes, B. (2010). Classroom discourse analysis: A focus on communicative repertoires. In N. H. Hornberger & S. L. McKay (Eds.), *Sociolinguistics and language education* (pp. 528–546). New York: Multilingual Matters.

Schegloff, E. A. (1996). Turn organization: One intersection of grammar and interaction. In E. Ochs, E. A. Schegloff, & S. A. Thompson (Eds.), *Grammar and interaction* (pp. 52–133). Cambridge, UK: Cambridge University Press.

Schegloff, E. A. (2007). *Sequence organization in interaction: A primer in conversation analysis* (Vol. 1). Cambridge, UK: Cambridge University Press.

Slobin, D. I., & Welsh, C. A. (1973). Elicited imitation as a research tool in developmental psycholinguistics. In C. Ferguson & D. Slobin (Eds.), *Studies of child language development* (pp. 485–497). New York: Holt, Rinehart & Winston.

Sterponi, L. (2007). Clandestine interactional reading: Intertextuality and the double-voicing under the desk. *Linguistics and Education*, *18*(1), 1–23. doi.org/10.1016/j.linged.2007.04.001

Vasquez, O. A., Pease-Alvarez, L., & Shannon, S. M. (1994). *Pushing boundaries: Language and culture in a Mexicano community*. Cambridge, UK: Cambridge University Press.

Wong Fillmore, L. (2000). Loss of family languages: Should educators be concerned? *Theory into Practice*, *39*(4), 203–210. doi.org/10.1207/s15430421tip3904_3

Wortham, S. (2005). Socialization beyond the speech event. *Journal of Linguistic Anthropology*, *15*(1), 95–112. doi.org/10.1525/jlin.2005.15.1.95

Zentella, A. C. (2005). Premises, promises, and pitfalls of language socialization research in Latino families and communities. In A. C. Zentella (Ed.), *Building on strength: Language and literacy in Latino families and communities* (pp. 13–30). New York: Teachers College Press.

PART III

Community Psychology in Action

Critical Themes and Areas of Application

10 Women and Leadership

Building Community

Donna Baptiste and Kesha Burch

10.1 Introduction

Women's leadership has been pivotal in movements for social change in the United States over the past century, including the women's suffrage movement (Mazur, McBride, & Hoard, 2016), the civil rights movement, the women's rights movement, and more recently, in Black Lives Matter (Matthews & Noor, 2013). While women have made tremendous strides in their leadership standing, they have not achieved practical or symbolic parity with men. Women are underrepresented in executive leadership positions, comprising just 5% of chief executive officers (CEOs) in the USA (Catalyst, 2020b). Women are also underrepresented in nonprofit leadership. Typically, around 75% of nonprofit employees are women, but they make up only 47% of CEOs (Catalyst, 2020b). Women make up around 24% of the US Congress and hold nine of fifty state governorships (Center for American Women and Politics, 2020). Similarly, women are underrepresented in leadership roles in unions, faith organizations, as heads of legal practices, in law enforcement, and in higher education (American Association of University Women [AAUW], 2016).

For racial/ethnic and sexual minority women, the leadership gap with White women and men is severe. At every level of leadership in Fortune 500 companies, women of color are significantly underrepresented (Catalyst, 2020a). They make up about 12% of the managerial and professional workforce but hold less than 1% of executive leadership positions and are less than 5% of board members of Fortune 500 companies (Catalyst, 2020a). The same is true in academic leadership, medicine, and other sectors, where there is a scant representation of minority women as leaders (AAUW, 2016). Women who hold different marginalized identities, such as trans women, face just as much or even more discrimination in leadership (Mishel, 2016). It is with this background that we consider the importance of women's leadership, and the unique strengths and opportunities women bring as community change agents.

Although women are underrepresented in leadership roles across civil society, they are a force in community settings, exerting powerful influence in response to complex problems. By community, we mean *collective entities* united around integrated purposes or shared values and missions (Delanty,

2018). Communities coalesce around locations (e.g., urban communities), identities (i.e., lesbian, gay, bisexual, transgender, and queer/questioning or LGBTQ communities), or organizations (e.g., a community mental health center) (Delanty, 2018). Across definitions of community, women are leading others to challenge the status quo, redistribute influence, and rally for inclusion in policymaking. Women are influential in community-building on small and large scales, bringing uplifts and improvements in local and social settings (Hinton, 2013; Reisen, 2015). There are many examples of women who begin locally, moved by an important need, who go on to build large-scale and international operations. The following is one example of a woman nominated for the Cable News Network (CNN) Hero's Initiative for her service.

> In the mid-90s, Najah Bazzy was working as a nurse when she visited an Iraqi refugee family to help care for their dying infant. She knew the situation would be difficult, but she wasn't prepared for what she encountered. There, at the house, she got her first glimpse of poverty. ... "They absolutely had nothing," she said. "There was no refrigerator, there was no stove, there was no crib. ... The baby was in a laundry basket, laying on clean white towels. ... I was so devastated by that. ... I decided that this wasn't going to happen on my watch." That day Najah and her family gathered all the furniture and household items that they could – including a crib – and delivered everything to the family. She hasn't stopped since. For years, Najah ran her goodwill effort from her home [in Detroit], transporting donated goods in her family's minivan. Eventually, her efforts grew into Zaman International, a nonprofit that now supports impoverished women and children of all backgrounds in the Detroit area. The group has helped more than 250,000 people. Today, Zaman operates from a 40,000-square-foot facility in the suburb of Inkster. The group's warehouse offers aisles of food, rows of clothes and vast arrays of furniture free to those in need. The group's case managers help clients access housing and other services. The group's donated clothing and furniture are also available to the public through its Good Deeds Resale Shop. The nonprofit also offers clients free education and job placement, as well as vocational training through its sewing and culinary arts programs. The goal is to help women become self-sufficient.   (Toner, 2019)

Though women have been catalysts in community-building, their leadership in this area is also underappreciated (Hinton, 2013). Often, women's savvy as heads of community entities, especially grassroots organizations, is intermingled with the work and progress of their teams. Women themselves rarely tout their leadership accomplishments (Goryunova, Scribner, & Madsen, 2017). The lack of recognition of women's leadership capacities in community-building and women's reluctance to promote their expertise emanate from the same sex and gender biases that pervade other sectors. However, rather than viewing women's penchant to emphasize the *collective* versus *individual* leadership accomplishments as a vulnerability, we will explore why it is a considerable strength that predicts leadership success. We view women's philosophy of leadership as desperately needed and well-matched to the moral, social, and ethical leadership zeitgeist of modern times (Chin et al., 2007).

Below, we explore leadership frameworks that are complementary for community-building and discuss how women leaders can draw on these frameworks to maximize their effectiveness. We will also discuss strategies for developing women as leaders with consideration of the unique circumstances and needs of women who represent underprivileged backgrounds. Our discussion emphasizes aspects of leadership that reflect complementary, interactional processes among persons in leadership roles and their members or followers in social and organizational environments. We place less emphasis on leader behaviors or the individual-level capacities that leaders display.

10.2 Women and Leadership

A universal definition of leadership is elusive, but most accept that leadership unfolds in multiple contexts, formally and informally, and in various ways. Leadership is linked to positions people hold, to personality traits, to a display of authority, to moral influence, to power and status, or to capacities that emerge in the face of need (Northouse, 2015). Being moved to action based on the challenges of geographical or social communities is characteristic of women's leadership, and there is a long history of women rising to prominence under such conditions. Sojourner Truth and Harriet Tubman fought for the liberation of African Americans at a time when women and racial/ethnic minority leadership roles were constrained (Sharp, 2013). Teen activist Greta Thunberg has earned *Time* magazine's "Person of the Year" for her leadership on climate change impacts. She is inspiring many of her peers to embrace environmental advocacy (Knowles, 2019).

Other women have led movements to improve public education, reform welfare, promote health initiatives, press for better work conditions, and stave off poverty (Keohane, 2012; Tetzloff, 2007). In such efforts, women are not handpicked to lead. They see a need, feel driven to act, and grow in leadership as their organizations grow. This sequence is a typical story of women's community-building efforts, and the work of Dr. Jean Kalilani in Malawi is one example. Dr. Kalilani started HIV/AIDS education in Malawi at a time when many people did not know about the virus (Chin et al., 2007). Moved to action as described below, her radio program to improve HIV/AIDS literacy was so successful that the World Health Organization replicated it in other African countries (Chin et al., 2007). In 2014, Dr. Kalilani was appointed Malawi's minister of health.

> Back in 1985, when I went to do my master's in public health at Emory University in Atlanta, Georgia, United States, I learned about AIDS at the Centers for Disease Control which was adjacent to our school. I thought of how I could help people back home. So, when I returned home, I talked to the authorities and I mobilized resources and initiated an outreach where we were teaching people how to prevent AIDS. I was the first person to go on the national radio to teach people about AIDS.   (Chin et al., 2007, p. 45)

10.2.1 Gender and Leadership

Leadership may seem to be androgynous; however, masculinized leadership has long been the dominant paradigm. Koenig et al. (2011) conducted a meta-analysis of more than sixty-five studies on the extent to which stereotypes of leaders are culturally masculine. They confirm that stereotypical masculine qualities such as aggression, dominance, rationality, and objectivity seem to be "leadership" views held across genders. Other studies have found no reliable gender differences in leadership effectiveness, suggesting that men and women leaders can equally display useful traits (Hyde, 2014). Eagly (2007) identifies nuances and contradictions when comparing women's leadership experiences to men's. Women's leadership has proven to be as effective as men's, while women are simultaneously inhibited by sexist attitudes and constrained by lack of leadership resources (Eagly & Carli, 2003). This duality in women's leadership experience is impressive because, in many settings, women fight potent forces that can mitigate their success. Recent studies suggest that women's leadership styles might be exemplars of the qualities needed for contemporary leadership (Crites, Dickson, & Lorenz, 2015). This sentiment is also ours, and in Section 10.2.2, we discuss how feminist leadership approaches embody our ideals.

10.2.2 Feminist Notions of Leadership

We view women's leadership contributions through the lens of *feminist leadership*, which is leadership capacities that emerge out of women's gender socialization, gendered scripts, and worldviews (Chin et al., 2007). Feminism rests on the belief that women make contributions to society that are worthwhile and distinct from the contributions of men (Chin et al., 2007). At the heart of feminism is the idea that women can and should achieve equality with men in all areas of civil society (Chin, 2007). Women's leadership often unfolds through collaboration and concern for the well-being of others. Many women leaders also tackle the unequal status of women and minorities, brought on by bias and oppression in work, family, and social life (Suyemoto & Ballou, 2007).

Differences in women's worldview, socialization, and life experiences nudge them toward feminist leadership styles. They may often value shared versus hierarchical leadership to avoid replication of the "take-charge" styles that maintain male-dominated status quos. Democratic and collaborative relationships may seem more attractive than autocratic, hierarchical ones (Chin, 2007). Historical feminism has not been always attuned to the unique needs of underrepresented minority women. There has also been a muted response to the hurdles women of marginalized social identities face in pursuing leadership (Bass & Avolio, 1994). However, we believe that contemporary feminism can elevate the needs and priorities of women and articulate the daunting standards to which minority women are held. This is articulated well by one leader:

> These rules ["rules of the game"] are different depending on who you are – Black, female, male, lesbian, heavy, disabled, young, old, a northerner, etc. We must be aware of the fact that the rules are not the same for all of us and don't apply equally to us. We are accorded varied amount of privilege by others based on our age, race, ability, class, sexual orientation, education, gender and other areas of classification. Some of us are allowed to learn from our mistakes while in other cases, we must perform under high and unforgiving standards. (Penny Sanchez)   (Suyemoto & Ballou, 2007, p. 39)

Feminist leadership endorses these leadership ideals: (1) a collective versus heroine vision; (2) use of self, nurturance, empathy, and interpersonal connectedness; (3) intuition and emotions in assessing motives; (4) a democratic and participatory management style and appreciation for consensus-building; (5) positive reinforcement as rewards; and (6) commitment to gender-equitable environments and diversity and inclusion (Chin, 2007; Madden, 2007).

Raelin (2003) described the modern leader as concurrent, collective, collaborative, and compassionate, traits that are quintessentially feminist.

In our opinion, feminist leadership is not about the sex or gender identities of leaders but qualities that instill respect and cultivate an engaged followership to meet unique demands. A man can be a feminist leader. One male leader comments on this:

> Most models of leadership are deeply patriarchal, so feminist leadership has to be ... transformational leadership, leadership with, rather than leadership over. Leadership that fights to create space for others to lead, especially those denied that space by patriarchy ... The number one challenge in being a guy who aspires to achieving feminist goals, is to get other guys to think. (John Coonrod)   (The Feminist Leader Project, 2019)

Feminist leadership still invites stereotypes and bias in that collaborative and nurturing styles may seem weak, ineffective, or too nice, nurturing, and empathic. Women leaders may be liked for these qualities but not respected and they may have to choose between competence or likeability, when they should not have to choose at all (Chin, 2007). The literature on qualities of effective leadership for community-building also shows a striking alignment with feminist thought. In Section 10.2.3, we summarize preferred traits in community leadership that are synergistic with feminism.

10.2.3 Leadership of Community Initiatives

Studies have highlighted the leadership qualities associated with effective community-building, and these qualities are empirically associated with women's leadership. Goodman et al. (1998) identify a range of leadership capacities for community-building that align with a collaborative style.

Capabilities include a responsive and accessible style, skills to engage well in group processes, cultivating an environment where all can participate, and respect, generosity, and service to others, in addition to other strengths. Similarly, other studies in community leadership (Crosby & Bryson, 2005) emphasize collaboration in developing an organizational vision, personal influence, gutsiness in decision making, selflessness, and an ability to command respect. Team-mindedness and participatory styles are also more successful than authoritarian approaches (Bryson, Crosby, & Stone, 2015). In addition, active community leaders often have a good understanding of social, political, and economic contexts and are devoted to equality and social change (Bryson et al., 2015).

Taken together, the styles and qualities associated with community-building make a robust case for promoting a feminist leadership framework for community-building anchored by distinctive traits. We believe that women are well-placed for community leadership in local, domestic, and international communities. They have the will and energy to address old problems that persist (e.g., poverty, the unequal status of women, human rights violations) and new issues that are increasing (e.g., climate change, civil conflicts, and cybercrimes). Feminist leadership approaches will be core to success in many matters. Kniffin and Patterson (2019) note that the "challenges of the 21st century, post-industrial society are increasingly complex. They will not be solved by the actions of individual, 'heroic' leaders; instead, they require the participation of diverse stakeholders in order to make progress" (p. 188). Increasingly, women leaders in various types of communities are embracing this charge.

10.3 Women's Community-Building: A Feminist Framework

Women are leading coalitions and movements of all types in various communities. This speaks to the premise of this chapter (Folta et al., 2012; Stefanco, 2017). We believe that gendered worldviews place women on center stage to care about the well-being of others, sometimes beyond themselves, and many are rebuilding and improving conditions for their families and their neighbors (Folta et al., 2012).

Expanding women's capacities as leaders benefits civil society. This is the view of the CEO/president of the National Association of Software and Services Company (NASCOMM), a nonprofit industry association in India with links to the technology industry worldwide.

> We are having real conversations now about getting more women into every level of our organizations and onto boards, and that's a good thing. But we need to get beyond conversations. We need to get to the point where every CEO believes that if we don't do this, we will lose relevance and customers,

and realize that competitors who are embracing diversity will win. (Debjani Ghosh, president, NASSCOM)   (Ready & Cohen, 2019)

For women involved in community-building, we endorse six leadership frameworks that align well with feminized thought. Rather than recommending one approach, we suggest that women incorporate components of all, in a manner that fits their personalities, the dynamics of their organizations, their people, and relevant contexts. The approaches described in the sections below overlap, and some may fit some settings more than others. We illustrate how the core qualities of a feminist leader might powerfully impact community development initiatives, using the example of Ana L. Oliveira:

Ana L. Oliveira became the President & CEO of The New York Women's Foundation in 2006 and still retains this position. Under her leadership, The Foundation has grown in several dimensions, establishing a new strategic plan, sponsoring landmark research reports, increasing visibility and public awareness of The Foundation's presence in NYC; and dramatically increasing the impact of The Foundation with the distribution of a record $5 million in grants in its 25th year, in 2012. The Foundation has distributed over $58 million to 371 organizations. The Foundation has also cultivated critical partnerships influencing policy changes in equal pay and financial investments, focusing on areas of social and economic inequity for women and families.

Ana has worked in the health and human services field for over 22 years, developing programs for vulnerable populations throughout NYC. She has served as the Executive Director of Gay Men's Health Crisis for more than seven years, overseeing a complete turn-around of the agency. Ana has also directed innovative community-based programs at Samaritan Village, the Osborne Association, Kings County, and Lincoln Hospitals.

Ana has served as a member of the New York City HIV Planning Council, in the New York City Commission on AIDS, chaired the NYC Commission for LGBTQ Runaway and Homeless Youth, and Co-Chaired Mayor Bloomberg's Young Men's Initiative. Ana has served as a Co-Chair of the Board of the Women's Funding Network, has led critical cross-sectoral partnerships to advance women's rights as a proud co-chair of The New York City Council Speaker's Young Women's Initiative and a Commissioner of Human Rights for NYC. She sits on the Independent Commission to Study Criminal Justice Reform in NYC and is on the board of Philanthropy New York.

In 2005, Newsweek profiled Ana as "America's Best," a series highlighting ordinary individuals using their extraordinary vision on behalf of others. Her awards include the Liberty Award (Lambda Legal & Education Defense Fund), Community Service Award (Empire State Pride Agenda), the Rosie Perez Fuerza Award, (Latino Commission on AIDS), and the New York City Civil Liberties Union Liberty Award, among others.

Ana was born and raised in Sao Paulo, Brazil, and resides in Manhattan. She has an M.A. in Medical Anthropology from the New School for Social Research.   (Women's Media Center, n.d.)

10.3.1 Transformational Leadership

As a transformational leader Ana may prioritize individual professional development as well as team identity development (Porter & Daniel, 2007). Transformational leaders are role models, challenging followers to push well beyond perceived capacities to own their ideas and work. Ana may be adaptive, self-aware, and self-disciplined and may drive positive change around core values. She may use a variety of strategies, including *inspirational motivation*, inviting her team to engage in reasonable and relevant goal-setting, and articulating a shared vision that integrates the team's expectations. She also uses *moral influence* by serving as a stable and ethical role model, leading by example in good times and in challenging times.

Such qualities model principled and composed leadership in conflicts and crises and recovery from organizational missteps. Her *intellectual stimulation* encourages followers to think for themselves, to innovate, to use creativity, and generate new solutions to problematic processes. A leader like Ana will not be afraid to tackle obsolescence through new approaches. Through *individualized consideration*, she establishes relationships with individuals, workgroups, and teams, helping them to appreciate how they contribute to the mission and achievements of the organization (Bass & Avolio, 1994; Rumsey, 2013). As a transformational leader, Ana must be patient and tolerant about team members and herself and works hard to motivate by communicating well around the tangible markers of growth and positive change (Bass & Avolio, 1994; Rumsey, 2013).

10.3.2 Servant Leadership

Ana can serve her organization versus the other way around. As a servant leader, she turns away from a rigid hierarchical model of leadership where power and authority reside at the top. Ana leads an organization staffed by women and works for and on behalf of women. She should create an inverted leadership hierarchy that attends to the needs and advancement of the lowest in the organization. Servant leaders operationalize these values by seeking to understand and sponsor enhancements to productivity and morale, that excite all levels of the organization, by sharing ownership of initiatives and helping individuals to advance toward their stated potential (Liden et al., 2014).

Research has shown the growth of service leadership infrastructure and values embodied in this approach such as promoting greater leadership success, increasing revenue and profits, organizational achievement goals, and expanding institutional footprint, more so than traditional systems (Qiu & Dooley, 2019). Research on servant leadership notes its impact on markers of success, including revenue, morale and productivity, and the success of organizations. Servant leadership serves as a counterforce to decades of leadership trends in which leaders are the greatest benefactors of organizational success and yet rupture trust through self-focused values and actions (Qiu & Dooley, 2019). In the last three decades, there has been a proliferation of servant leaders in the USA.

10.3.3 Collaborative Leadership

Ana will showcase collaborative leadership in designing and managing strategic partnerships that link stakeholders, allies, cheerleaders, and even competitors, in advancing a vision and mission with broad and deep impact (Kramer & Crespy, 2011). Such influence was mainly seen through her role in her previous organization as the executive director of the Gay Men's Health Crisis as she engaged in networking with several partners with urgency to ramp up a response to the virus and to end discrimination against gay men. A collaborative approach requires a leader with robust interpersonal and social skills, a capacity to manage high-level frustrations and tensions, and one that can stay the course during crises and pressures.

Typically, collaborative leadership has been deemed necessary in traditional sectors such as businesses, governments, social, and technological organizations. But increasingly, the collaborative leader is needed where there are entities of different climates and cultures, seeking the strategic advantages of alignment and integration, to promote collective social goals and outcomes (Echavarria, 2015). The complex problems of our times will require collaborative leadership that can integrate a variety of organizational climates and cultures.

Ana should showcase qualities that Lovegrove and Thomas (2013) identify as collaborative leadership traits. These qualities include influencing sectors to work together, working strategically with data-driven management analytics, tolerance for intersectoral cultural differences modeled by acceptance of each partner, innovation, willingness to work with novel ideas, and an appreciation for the value of connectedness among sectors. Ana is strategic in risk-taking and passionate, attuned, optimistic, and generous in sharing credit. As a leader, she manages conflict well, is empathic, action-oriented, and future-thinking; she is a good listener, able to hold difficult conversations, and skilled in coalition-building (Kramer & Crespy, 2011).

10.3.4 Innovation Leadership

As an innovation leader, Ana will facilitate the creativity of ideas and outcomes in pursuit of strategic goals. This approach emphasizes novel methods, research-based enhancements, and consumer or end-user feedback from both inside and outside an organization to remain competitive. In managing community enterprises for the twenty-first century, an innovative leader pays attention to both organizational climate and culture (Sarros, Cooper, & Santora, 2008). The emphasis is on inviting individuals and workgroups to generate creative solutions, with recognition rewards for good ideas. The innovation leader encourages all levels of the organization – C-suite, managerial, supervisory staff, and well as entry-level employees – to collaborate in planning (Mumford & Licuanan, 2004). The innovation leader has extensive social and interpersonal skills and can manage transitions and successions to keep vision and outcomes alive. Innovation leaders pay attention to organizational development and change and understand that some degree of pressure can have a positive effect that emanates from intellectual challenges associated with innovating (Mumford & Licuanan, 2004).

10.3.5 Diversity and Inclusion Leadership

As a diversity and inclusion leader, Ana must send powerful signals internally and externally related to creating an organizational climate and culture that includes people of diverse social identities, showing value for equity and equality in process and practices (Chin, 2007; Hinton, 2013). Ana will weed out stereotypes, prejudice, and discrimination through education and training as well as advocacy and zero-tolerance policies. This advocacy starts with multiculturally informed hiring practices, cultural proficiency training, and sanctions to dismantle inequitable structures. Diversity and inclusion leaders are not shy in targeting gender-based equity. Apart from the underrepresentation of women in the organization, gender diversity and inclusion also means tackling traditional masculine climates to create an appreciation of women's leadership prowess and styles. Related to the idea of demasculinized work contexts is the sponsorship of family-friendly policies that support women's reproductive functions and parenting demands (Chin et al., 2007). Ana will also tackle obstacles and barriers to the advancement of those pregnant and parenting women, promoting a culture of success for each gender that embraces the reality of women's roles in the care of children and households. Appreciation for this work–family interface will also support men to increase their responsibilities in family life (Chin, 2007).

10.3.6 Emotionally Intelligent Leadership

A vital responsibility of any leader is to manage change. Change processes in organizations and teams can invoke a range of positive, combative, and even hostile emotions. Such emotions can have an impact on trust, optimism, and morale, leading to resistance to new ideas or opportunities (Barbuto & Burbach, 2006; Issah, 2018). As an emotional leader, Ana must embrace the range of emotions in herself, in individual members, and in the team as a whole. Through her leadership she strives to help both herself and her team to channel those emotions into positive and constructive energy.

Any experience or conflict can produce growth and organizational intimacy in the hands of an emotionally skilled leader (Barbuto & Burbach, 2006; Issah,

2018). The emotionally intelligent leader can understand, read, and label emotions. She integrates emotional valence and language in presenting ideas and requests; manages her own emotions through a high level of self-awareness and self-soothing; and encourages and challenges others to understand and manage their feelings through awareness, empathy, and conflict management skills. Thus, emotional intelligence in leaders and followers can enrich intellectual stimulation and personal growth (Barbuto & Burbach, 2006; Issah, 2018).

Emotional intelligence in leadership can explain organizational and leadership success. Watkins et al. (2017) state that "reflecting on experiences, interpreting environmental cues, relating to followers and developing relationships, intelligent, emotional competencies are a necessity of modern leadership" (p. 150). Radical empathy for followers, and a capacity to gain their trust, are signs of emotional intelligence and these qualities are especially needed in twenty-first-century leaders.

10.4 Developing Women as Community Leaders

We have argued for a feminist approach to community leadership and suggested several leadership qualities and traits that feminist community leaders embrace to become influential in shaping the tone and pace of change (Chin, 2007). In community-building, many women begin this journey tackling cultural, social, and economic barriers to their leadership success (Chin, 2014). For women, their prowess as leaders may become visible when their initiatives show tangible markers of success. This dynamic means that women's pioneering efforts in the trenches of leadership, driving change in their communities, may not be appropriately credited or acknowledged (Hinton, 2013). This reality is especially the case in grassroots initiatives that begin locally with few resources. Women themselves may be reluctant to promote their own stories of success, and this may be related to internalized bias that affects how they see themselves (Hoyt, 2005).

Schuh et al. (2014) suggest that gender bias partially explains the confidence gap between men and women. Where men are self-promoting and confident, women may feel imposter anxiety and a sense of reluctance to take on leadership roles. Eagly and Carli (2007), in discussing this self-defeating capacity in women, suggest that the concept of a "labyrinth" may be more appropriate than a glass ceiling in explaining women's pathways. One aspect of the labyrinth versus glass-ceiling metaphor is that women might be their own worst enemies in leadership advancement, needing solid developmental supports and opportunities to build confidence and skills. One can argue that women's hesitations to take on leadership roles as well as their lack of confidence (internalized dynamics) are also connected to gendered social norms that privilege men's leadership and that drive gender discriminations against women leaders. If women show drive and ambition to advance, they are often viewed as pushy or demanding and so women may elect to mute their ambitious rather than battling misperceptions.

In the following sections, we recommend five strategies that have proven successful in women's advancement as leaders in many industries and can be applied to women leading community-building efforts. Each approach highlights the value of resources women lack when the status quo prevails, and we encourage women to be proactive and assertive in connecting to such opportunities. Each strategy is useful for women's leadership overall, but we are especially mindful of their application for women who are underrepresented in leadership roles such as women of color. Strategies include (1) self-awareness programs to build self-confidence, (2) participation in Women's Leadership Programs, (3) expanding informal networks, (4) support to balance work and family life, and (5) attending to career development needs.

10.4.1 Self-Awareness to Build Leadership Confidence

Self-awareness is one of the essential qualities in leadership that women leaders are encouraged to seek. Bradberry, Greaves, and Lencioni (2009) refer to self-awareness as an aspect of emotional intelligence and a capacity to understand, recognize, and manage aspects of self and others, especially in interpersonal relationships. High self-awareness is empirically related to more robust performance and greater productivity. Self-awareness is a crucial skill for feminist community leaders. A worldwide study of almost twenty thousand leaders (Business Wire, 2012) found that 19% of women as compared to 4% of men demonstrated self-awareness.

The focus of self-awareness is on the "self" and several strategies are essential to increasing awareness. One such strategy includes soliciting feedback from trusted sources. Such information helps a leader to understand her impact on others and address blind spots. Leaders can identify factors and triggers that have an impact on how people respond to leaders and how leaders respond to them. Feedback can also reveal how cultural dynamics shape the leadership context, what personality traits and styles increase optimism and trust and convey empathy. Leaders should understand how personal features strengthen leadership and stay curious about the self and open to personal evolution and the management of pressures (Gonzalez, 2012). Self-awareness can improve through recognized tools (e.g., 360-degree assessment), informal feedback, and via coaching or mentoring. Self-awareness is critical to a collaborative style of leadership and contributes to the creation of a dynamic work team.

For grassroots women leaders with limited resources for leadership training, straightforward methods of seeking and using feedback can help. Individually or in a group, women may identify people whom they trust to provide specific feedback on leadership climate, leader skills, strengths, and weaknesses. Such information can then be related and processed personally or with the help of an informal coach. Women leaders can also forge linkages with a senior community leader of any gender for tips on eliciting and using follower feedback for growth (Lester & Kezar, 2012). A tried and true method to gain awareness is "debriefing" of key moments and events, positive or negative, in the organization or movement. The leader's questions should relate to what she may have done that helped or hindered the event. The main point here is that a radical openness to feedback from others enhances self-awareness skills and women, as well as men, are encouraged to be open to integrating and using such feedback (Lester & Kezar, 2012).

10.4.2 Participation in Women's Leadership Programs

A confident leadership identity is a significant asset. Our view is that women have far less support than men for leadership identity consolidation. Identity development requires the availability of role models leaders can imitate, a supportive arena in which fledging leaders can try out different managerial features, and internal and external feedback loops to assess the impact of self- improvements (Ely, Ibarra, & Kolb, 2011). Disparities in leadership opportunities for women create a shortage of role models that women leaders can model. For women of color, there are even fewer exemplars of leadership, and this can represent an impediment to accessing resources that promote leadership as well as their leadership development (Schmitz, 2011). Relatedly, women may be afraid to experiment and try new skills because the margin for error is low, and women may become risk-averse (Debebe et al., 2016).

Women's Leadership Programs (WLPs) create a formalized structure for women to work together to advance their leadership potential. There has been a proliferation of such programs recently, and women are taking advantage of them (Ely et al., 2011; Schmitz, 2011). WLPs can include a formal curriculum, assessment, and other tools. Informal WLPs are less structured and can still be useful in linking senior women leaders to women aspiring toward leadership. For WLPs within organizations, a cadre of diverse female leaders from inside or outside an organization, including male feminist leaders, can coach women on navigating male-dominated settings (Ely et al., 2011). In general, WLPs can provide women with groups related to their organizations and missions. Women mentors are encouraged to energize WLPs. Training opportunities should be available (e.g., assessments, resource guides) where participants can center themselves in activities that match their organizations.

In WLPs, the needs of underrepresented women of color are encouraged to have priority (Hall, Garrett-Akinsanya, & Hucles, 2007). At the very least, WLPs can strive to ensure diverse representation within the mentoring team with regular in-person or virtual meetings for women of color and opportunities for segmented coaching for women interested in this support.

10.4.3 Expanding Informal Networks

Informal networks play an essential role in leadership development. The right networks influence trajectories, create access to resources, provide emotional support, facilitate high-level linkages, and offer career protection (O'Neil, Hopkins, & Sullivan, 2011). A leader's informal networks can also drive referrals, channel information, boost reputations and credibility, and influence promotions (O'Neil et al., 2011). In this arena, men are far more privileged than women. Where men are a majority, they can generate a substantive pool of same- gender leadership contacts to whom they can turn for advice, support, and resources. Men's informal contacts can seal promotions, increase salaries, and reroute high-profile tasks and projects (Chin, 2014). Men of high status are more likely to offer opportunities for advancement to male mentees. Women, by their lower share in leadership hierarchy as thus potentially having fewer and less efficient networks, can remain outside of these influential spheres (O'Neil et al., 2011).

Women of all backgrounds have noted a lack of networks as a constraint and may need to join or create networking groups to develop their own cheerleaders (Chin, 2014). Women can initiate meetups on issues of equality, gender parity, sex, and gender discrimination. Sharing such narratives can increase awareness and build women's confidence in their organizations. Building self-confidence is especially important for women of color. Mentoring to develop networks can become a part of a WLP assessment to help women leaders understand where they need concentrated activity. Women might also seek coaching on self-assessment, exploring how gender or marginalized identities may have an impact on their network success, and identify ways to expand their reach (Dworkin, Ramaswami, & Schipani, 2013). For community women connecting with one influential leader of any gender may open pathways to communicate with others. With the right coaching, women can then build and nurture their high-profile contacts (Chin, 2014).

Network-building in community-based leadership may happen organically, driven by ad-hoc and emerging encounters that enhance the visibility of the leader, allowing her to voice expectations when opportunities present. In this, local contacts and activities can advance network expansion. For example, personal networks such as family and friends, clergy, and lay membership in religious groups, local businesses, campaigns, and service establishments can also be useful in growing contacts (Dworkin et al., 2013). Connections with local governments, local media, and social media must also be in the mix, especially for grassroots community movements. Women may shy away from the self-promotional activities needed to cultivate such networks, and exposure to success stories and exemplars can provide them with energy and inspiration.

10.4.4 Support to Balance Work and Family Life

In the USA, women make up 47% of the labor force, with a total of 58% of US women working outside the home (US Bureau of Labor Statistics, 2020). In both female-headed and two-parent households, caring for the home, children, and other dependents is a balancing act. Even in homes where there are two full-time working caregivers, women more often take ownership of child-rearing and household responsibilities, and this inevitably has an impact on women's career trajectories and pursuit of leadership opportunities (Eagly & Carli, 2007). Some advocates for women's career advancement and leadership argue that women never achieve real balance, per se. Women who negotiate multiple role demands and obligations might do what one calls juggling of roles and responsibilities (Cheung & Halpern, 2010; Emslie & Hunt, 2009). Most women leaders want to feel satisfied with both their fulfillment of work demands as well as roles and responsibilities in the family.

Ellinas, Fouad, and Byars-Winston (2018) investigated how workplace and family life balance has had an impact on women's advancement and leadership opportunities in academic medicine. When compared to men, women who perceived significant conflicts between work and family responsibilities were less likely to aspire to or seek leadership opportunities in their careers. Fritz and Van Knippenberg (2018) suggest that the availability of workplace solutions for family life demands increases women's aspirations for leadership roles. Both studies demonstrate how work–life balance is a factor in the decision to assume leadership given that conflicts between work and home life have an impact on women's performance in leadership positions. When women leaders simultaneously carry a larger share of family and home life responsibilities along with the heavy demands of professional leadership, they face challenges that men do not. Such inequities may contribute to opportunity costs for women in the workplace.

Difficulties for women in work–life balance occur across industries and primarily affect women of color in unique ways. One study demonstrated that having marginalized identities such as gender, race, ethnicity, and low socio-economic status disadvantage women's advancement and make work–life balance more complex (Ellinas et al., 2018). Clear work–life balance policies from organizations and employers can help women to identify how professional and personal life trajectories combine in leadership roles. Such conversations are useful for women before experiencing role conflicts between home and work (Hall et al., 2007).

As leaders, women must themselves drive advocacy for family-friendly and gender-friendly policies to support their pregnant and parenting staff and to expand men's roles in family life. Such policies should be endorsed from the top and operationalized through specific benefits. Women leaders might also allow their women team members to self-advocate in their organizations and use mentors and coaches to sort out priorities. Women have been adept at juggling for centuries, and their resilience in this should not be understated. Key factors of support are time management skills, boundary-making, and assertiveness skills. Frequently women in leadership must address their anxieties, guilt, and shame about having to choose between work and family roles, and then they must proactively say "no" to quite a few opportunities, without apologies or defensiveness (Ellinas et al., 2018; Fritz & Van Knippenberg, 2018).

10.4.5 Attending to Career Development Needs

Women in leadership frequently aspire to more challenging positions that might utilize and showcase their skills and talents but may stay put due to comfort in existing roles, or out of fear of change and anxiety that their skills are not transferrable (Vanderbroeck, 2014). In general, women may have a harder time than men making a career transition and need support to embrace opportunities (Kossek & Buzzanell, 2018). Women may worry about their capacity to take on a more significant role, about work–family balance, and may experience stereotype threats based on their anxieties. Stereotype threats, in the above scenarios, are situations in which women worry about becoming the very thing that they fear, in this case embracing leadership opportunities that lead to their neglect of families. Women also have anxiety about professional loneliness as they ascend (Hoyt & Murphy, 2016, Kossek & Buzzanell, 2018). Women who have such anxieties and fears of failure need support to assess and seek promotion opportunities. Such support might also help them to work through ambivalence, step out of their comfort zones, and conduct a realistic appraisal of the transferability of their knowledge and skills (Kossek & Buzzanell, 2018). Career coaching formally or informally can help.

Career consultations can connect women to other women who made leadership transitions and those that switched to different organizations and contexts. Hearing stories of successful women leaders whose ambitions drove them upward can also help (Schmitz, 2011). For underrepresented women, thorough assessments about the diversity and inclusion climates of organizations, through formal or informal career consultations, can help them to decide if a more prominent leadership position is worth it. Even though a woman of color may choose to transition to a less diverse or inclusive setting, with assessments of benefits and risks, she can do so fully informed (Kossek & Buzzanell, 2018).

Career development coaching can help women leaders manage anticipatory anxiety about showcasing their leadership pedigree in a new setting. For example, women working in community contexts often develop an elastic skillset by filling many gaps in their organizations. While their education and training backgrounds may not capture their leadership acumen, career coaching can help grassroots women leaders to appreciate their wealth of experience (Kossek & Buzzanell, 2018; Schmitz, 2011). Women can become loyal to organizations and missions and may not prioritize their career interests. With career development support, women can address a tendency to develop loyalties from which they believe they cannot break free (Schmitz, 2011). Grassroots women leaders in community settings have increased the visibility and pedigree of women's leadership prowess, over decades. It is also true that some women begin leading localized movements, and their prodigious talents outgrow the organizations they manage. As other opportunities that expand their leadership footprint become available, women involved in community-building are encouraged to embrace their potential and consider career choices that expand their leadership influence. Such ambitions do not have to disadvantage their existing organizations. Through mentoring and supporting younger women leaders to replace them, grassroots women leaders can contribute to building up the next generation, while embracing opportunities for their own advancement.

10.5 Implications for Community Psychology

Our discussion thus far has underscored the strengths and contributions of women as feminist leaders, while simultaneously identifying and exploring strategies to bolster both leadership understanding in communities. Leadership, when viewed through a feminist lens, is concerned with empowering groups and individuals, committed to promoting the needs of underserved populations, and concerned with improving critical social problems (Bond & Mulvey, 2000; Chin et al., 2007; Enns & Sinacore, 2005). While the case examples and topics from the literature discussed in this chapter represent a wide variety of leadership contexts – from international activists and health educators, to managers, executives, and politicians – we now pivot to a discussion of the implications of women's leadership specifically for community psychology and in community contexts.

Community psychology is concerned with solutions that empower, heal, and develop communities and improve society. Community psychologists identify inequities and promote social justice (Bond et al., 2017; Dutta, 2018). Individual, family, and community-level health and wellness unfold within an ecological perspective. This perspective involves considering the social, cultural, political, historical, and environmental factors that have an impact on how problems are expressed individually and collectively (Bond et al., 2017; Dutta, 2018). Relatedly, community psychology values research, intervention, and prevention strategies that address individual, family, and community needs.

Community psychologists and feminists have values and approaches that are synergistic. Both value social advocacy and justice, embrace multicultural perspectives, and are committed to improving social conditions, especially for those from underrepresented and underserved populations (Bond & Mulvey,

2000; Enns & Sinacore, 2005). What follows are specific implications and recommendations to leverage women as feminist leaders to address community-based priorities:

1. Encourage, empower, and equip women for leadership. Women's leadership can be pivotal at professional and grassroots levels to solve critical problems in organizations and communities. This requires a commitment to identify, nurture, and elevate women as leaders (Kniffin & Patterson, 2019).
2. Bring awareness to the impact of active women leaders. Women's leadership efforts are often hidden. Showcasing women as leaders gives other women, including young women, models of leadership of community engagement (Crites et al., 2015; Women's Media Center, n.d.).
3. Psychologists, educators, and human service professionals who practice in community settings are encouraged to mainstream gender in their work. This means engaging in efforts to promote women's issues and address problems that are barriers to women's full and equal participation in society.
4. Community psychology can work to address social problems related to women and girls in both domestic and global contexts. Violence against women, reproductive health rights, lack of access to education, and capital are important to women sustaining hard-won successes (Baptiste et al., 2010; Enns & Sinacore, 2005; Hoyt & Kennedy, 2008). Develop workplace, community-level, and public policy interventions that promote equity and support women's leadership development. Women's leadership, feminist leadership, and progressive policies can converge for the benefit of many communities. Investment in family-friendly workplace, educational, and governmental policies will enhance women's leadership access and capacity (Chin et al., 2007; Storberg-Walker & Haber-Curran, 2017).
5. Researchers can investigate women's leadership in various contexts with multicultural and intersectional frameworks in mind. Historically the prototypical leader has been White and male. Women have not been the subject of inquiry for most of the research and scholarship on leadership. Scholars are needed to explore the leadership experiences of women, women of color, and individuals with LGBTQ identities (Chin et al., 2007; Storberg-Walker & Haber-Curran, 2017).

10.6 Conclusion

The strengths and complexities of women's leadership are appropriately documented in historical and contemporary literature. But in this literature, the specific needs and challenges of experiences among grassroots women leaders can be amplified. We contend that women in leadership of local and grassroots initiatives, domestically and internationally, have broken barriers and paved the way for the success and visibility of women leaders in many other sectors, including politics and the corporate world. Grassroots women's leadership, while hidden from mainstream view, carry great promise in confronting contemporary issues of diversity, inclusion, and justice. In closing, we juxtapose two essential ideas. As a social group, we celebrate women's advancement in leadership. This must be juxtaposed against the reality that all women have not equally benefited from leadership progress. Radical improvements in access and opportunity for women of marginalized and underprivileged backgrounds might be the next important frontier of women's leadership scholarship, research, and advancement.

References

American Association of University Women. (2016). *Barriers and bias: The status of women in leadership*. Washington, DC: AAUW. www.aauw.org/research/barriers-and-bias/

Baptiste, D., Kapungu, K., Khare, M., Lewis, Y., & Barlow-Mosha, L. (2010). Integrating women's human rights into global health research: An action framework. *Journal of Women's Health, 19*(11), 2091–2099. doi.org/10.1089/jwh.2010.2119

Barbuto, J. E., & Burbach, M. E. (2006). The emotional intelligence of transformational leaders: A field study of elected officials. *The Journal of Social Psychology, 146*(1), 51–64. doi.org/10.3200/SOCP.146.1.51-64

Bass, B. M., & Avolio, B. J. (1994). *Improving organizational effectiveness through transformational leadership*. Thousand Oaks, CA: SAGE Publications.

Bond, M., García de Serrano, I., Keys, C., & Shinn, M. (Eds.). (2017). *APA handbook of community psychology*. Washington, DC: American Psychological Association.

Bond, M., & Mulvey, A. (2000). A history of women and feminist perspectives in community psychology. *American Journal of Community Psychology, 28*(5), 599–630. doi.org/10.1023/A:1005141619462

Bradberry, T., Greaves, J., & Lencioni, P. (2009). *Emotional intelligence 2.0*. San Diego, CA: TalentSmart.

Bryson, J., Crosby, B., & Stone, M. (2015). Designing and implementing cross-sector collaborations: Needed and challenging. *Public Administration Review, 75*(5), 647–663. doi.org/10.1111/puar.12432

Business Wire. (2012, March 12). *Overall competencies required to successfully lead matrix teams are in short supply*. www.businesswire.com/news/home/20120327005180/en

Catalyst. (2020a). *Too few women of color on boards: Statistics and solutions*. www.catalyst.org/research/women-minorities-corporate-boards/

Catalyst. (2020b). *Women CEOs of the S&P 500*. www.catalyst.org/research/women-ceos-of-the-sp-500/

Center for American Women and Politics (2020). *Women in elective office*. www.cawp.rutgers.edu/current-numbers

Cheung, F. M., & Halpern, D. F. (2010). Women at the top: Powerful leaders define success as work + family in a culture of gender. *American Psychologist, 65*(3), 182–193. doi.org/10.1037/a0017309

Chin, J. L. (2007). Overview: Women and leadership: Transforming visions and diverse voices. In J. L. Chin, B. Lott, J. K. Rice, & J. Sanchez-Hucles (Eds.), *Women and leadership: Transforming visions and diverse voices* (pp. 1–18). Malden, MA: Blackwell.

Chin, J. L. (2014). Women and leadership. In D. V. Day (Ed.), *The Oxford handbook of leadership and organizations* (pp. 733–753). Oxford, UK: Oxford University Press.

Chin, J. L., Lott, B., Rice, J. K., & Sanchez-Hucles, J. (2007). *Women and leadership: Transforming visions and diverse voices*. Malden, MA: Blackwell.

Crites, S. N., Dickson, K. E., & Lorenz, A. (2015). Nurturing gender stereotypes in the face of experience: A study of leader gender, leadership style, and satisfaction. *Communications, and Conflict, 19*(1), 1–23.

Crosby, B. C., & Bryson, J. M. (2005). *Leadership for the common good: Tackling public problems in a shared-power world* (2nd ed.). San Francisco: Jossey-Bass.

Debebe, G., Anderson, D., Bilimoria, D., & Vinnicombe, S. (2016). Women's leadership development programs: Lessons learned and new frontiers. *Journal of Management Education, 40*(3), 231–252. doi.org/10.1177/1052562916639079

Delanty, G. (2018). *Community: Key ideas* (3rd ed.). New York: Routledge.

Dutta, U. (2018). Decolonizing "community" in community psychology. *American Journal of Community Psychology, 62*(3–4), 272–282. doi.org/10.1002/ajcp.12281

Dworkin, T., Ramaswami, A., & Schipani, C. (2013). The role of networks, mentors, and the law in overcoming barriers to organizational leadership for women with children. *Michigan Journal of Gender & Law, 20*(1), 83–128.

Eagly, A. H. (2007). Female leadership advantage and disadvantage: Resolving the contradictions. *Psychology of Women Quarterly, 31*(1), 1–12. doi.org/10.1111/j.1471-6402.2007.00326.x

Eagly, A. H., & Carli, L. L. (2003). The female leadership advantage: An evaluation of the evidence. *Leadership Quarterly, 14*(6), 807–834. doi.org/10.1016/j.leaqua.2003.09.004

Eagly, A. H., & Carli, L. L. (2007). *Through the labyrinth: The truth about how women become leaders*. Boston, MA: Harvard Business School Press.

Echavarria, M. (2015). *Enabling collaboration: Achieving success through strategic alliances and partnerships*. New York: LID Publishing Inc.

Ellinas, E. H., Fouad, N., & Byars-Winston, A. (2018). Women and the decision to leave, linger, or lean in: Predictors of intent to leave and aspirations to leadership and advancement in academic medicine. *Journal of Women's Health, 27*(3), 324–332. doi.org/10.1089/jwh.2017.6457

Ely, R. J., Ibarra, H., & Kolb, D. M. (2011). Taking gender into account: Theory and design for women's leadership development programs. *Academy of Management Learning & Education, 10*(3), 474–493. doi.org/10.5465/amle.2010.0046

Emslie, C., & Hunt, K. (2009). "Live to work" or "work to live"? A qualitative study of gender and work–life balance among men and women in mid-life. *Gender,*

Work and Organization, 16(1), 151–172. doi.org/turing.library.northwestern
.edu/10.1111/j.1468-0432.2008.00434.x

Enns, C. Z., & Sinacore, A. L. (2005). Second-wave feminism and their relationships to pedagogy. In C. Z. Enns & A. L. Sinacore (Eds.), *Teaching and social justice: Integrating multicultural and feminist theories in the classroom* (pp. 25–39). Washington, DC: American Psychological Association.

The Feminist Leader Project. (2019, May 24). *Meet John Coonrod.* https:// feministleadership.org/2019/05/24/meet-john-coonrod/.

Folta, S., Seguin, R. A., Ackerman, J., & Nelson, E. (2012). A qualitative study of leadership characteristics among women who catalyze positive community change. *BMC Public Health, 12*(1), 383. doi.org/10.1186/1471-2458-12-383

Fritz, C., & Van Knippenberg, D. (2018). Gender and leadership aspiration: The impact of work–life initiatives. *Human Resource Management, 57*(4), 855–868. doi.org/10.1002/hrm.21875

Gonzalez, M. (2012). *Mindful leadership: The 9 ways to self-awareness, transforming yourself, and inspiring others.* San Francisco: Jossey-Bass.

Goodman, R., Speers, M., McLeroy, K., et al. (1998). Identifying and defining the dimensions of community capacity to provide a basis for measurement. *Health Education & Behavior, 25*(3), 258–278. doi.org/10.1177/109019819802500303

Goryunova, E., Scribner, R. T., & Madsen, S. R. (2017). The current status of women leaders worldwide. In S. R. Madsen (Ed.), *Handbook of research on gender and leadership* (pp. 3–23). Cheltenham, UK: Edward Elgar Publishing.

Hall, R. L., Garrett-Akinsanya, B., & Hucles, M. (2007). Voices of Black feminist leaders: Making spaces for ourselves. In J. L. Chin, B. Lott, J. K. Rice, & J. Sanchez-Hucles (Eds.), *Women and leadership: Transforming visions and diverse voices* (pp. 281–296). Malden, MA: Blackwell.

Hinton, D. (2013). Unheard voices in the community building process: The role of poor Black women in the U.S. during the mid-20th century. *Journal of International Women's Studies, 14*(1), 40–53. http://vc.bridgew.edu/jiws/vol14/iss1/3

Hoyt, C. (2005). The role of leadership efficacy and stereotype activation in women's identification with leadership. *Journal of Leadership & Organizational Studies, 11*(4), 2–14. doi.org/10.1177/107179190501100401

Hoyt, C., & Murphy, S. (2016). Managing to clear the air: Stereotype threat, women, and leadership. *Leadership Quarterly, 27*(3), 387–387. doi.org/10.1016/j .leaqua.2015.11.002

Hoyt, M. A., & Kennedy, C. L. (2008). Leadership and adolescent girls: A qualitative study of leadership development. *American Journal of Community Psychology, 42*(3–4), 203–219. doi.org/10.1007/s10464-008-9206-8

Hyde, J. S. (2014). Gender similarities and differences. *Annual Review of Psychology, 65*, 373–398. doi.org/10.1146/annurev-psych-010213-115057

Issah, M. (2018). Change leadership: The role of emotional intelligence. *SAGE Open, 8* (3). doi.org/10.1177/2158244018800910

Keohane, N. O. (2012). *Thinking about leadership.* Princeton, NJ: Princeton University Press.

Kniffin, L. E., & Patterson, R. M. (2019). Reimagining community leadership development in the postindustrial era. *Journal of Leadership Education, 18*(4), 188–204. doi.org/10.12806/V18/I4/T1

Knowles, H. (2019, December 11). *Time*'s person of the year is its youngest ever: Greta Thunberg, the teen climate activist. *The Washington Post*. www .washingtonpost.com/nation/2019/12/11/time-person-year/

Koenig, A. M., Eagly, A. H., Mitchell, A. A., & Ristikari, T. (2011). Are leader stereotypes masculine? A meta-analysis of three research paradigms. *Psychological Bulletin*, *137*(4), 616–642. doi.org/10.1037/a0023557

Kossek, E., & Buzzanell, P. (2018). Women's career equality and leadership in organizations: Creating an evidence-based positive change. *Human Resource Management*, *57*(4), 813–822. doi.org/10.1002/hrm.21936

Kramer, M., & Crespy, D. (2011). Communicating collaborative leadership. *The Leadership Quarterly*, *22*(5), 1024–1037. doi.org/10.1016/j.leaqua.2011.07 .021

Lester, J., & Kezar, A. (2012). Understanding the formation, functions, and challenges of grassroots leadership teams. *Innovative Higher Education*, *37*(2), 105–124. doi.org/10.1007/s10755-011-9191-y

Liden, R., Panaccio, A., Meuser, J., Hu, J., & Wayne, S. (2014). Servant leadership: Antecedents, processes, and outcomes. In D. V. Day (Ed.), *The Oxford handbook of leadership and organizations* (pp. 357–379). Oxford, UK: Oxford University Press.

Lovegrove, N., & Thomas, M. (2013, February 13). Why the world needs tri-sector leaders. *Harvard Business Review*. https://hbr.org/2013/02/why-the-world-needs-tri-sector.html

Madden, M. (2007). Strategic planning: Gender, collaborative leadership, and organizational change. In J. L. Chin, B. Lott, J. K. Rice, & J. Sanchez-Hucles (Eds.), *Women and leadership: Transforming visions and diverse voices* (pp. 192–308). Malden, MA: Blackwell.

Matthews, S., & Noor, M. (2013). *Black Lives Matter: Celebrating 4 years of organizing to protect Black lives*. https://drive.google.com/file/d/ 0B0pJEXffvS0uOHdJREJnZ2JJYTA/view

Mazur, A., McBride, D., & Hoard, S. (2016). Comparative strength of women's movements over time: Conceptual, empirical, and theoretical innovations. *Politics, Groups, and Identities*, *4*(4), 652–676. doi.org/10.1080/21565503.2015 .1102153

Mishel, E. (2016). Discrimination against queer women in the U.S. workforce: A résumé audit study. *Socius: Sociological Research for a Dynamic World*, *2*. doi.org/10.1177/2378023115621316

Mumford, M., & Licuanan, B. (2004). Leading for innovation: Conclusions, issues, and directions. *The Leadership Quarterly*, *15*(1), 163–171. doi.org/10.1016/j .leaqua.2003.12.010

Northouse, P. G. (2015). *Leadership: Theory and practice* (7th ed.). Los Angeles: SAGE Publications.

O'Neil, D., Hopkins, M., & Sullivan, S. (2011). Do women's networks help advance women's careers? Differences in perceptions of female workers and top leadership. *Career Development International*, *16*(7), 733–754. doi.org/10 .1108/13620431111187317

Porter, N., & Daniel, J. H. (2007). Developing transformational leaders: Theory to practice. In J. L. Chin, B. Lott, J. K. Rice, & J. Sanchez-Hucles (Eds.),

Women and leadership: Transforming visions and diverse voices (pp. 245–263). Malden, MA: Blackwell.

Qiu, S., & Dooley, L. (2019). Servant leadership. *Leadership & Organization Development Journal, 40*(2), 193–212. doi.org/10.3390/su12166591

Raelin, J. (2003). *Creating leaderful organizations: How to bring out leadership in everyone.* San Francisco: Berrett-Koehler.

Ready, D. A., & Cohen, C. (2019, June 3). Closing the gender gap is good for business. *MIT Sloan Management Review.* https://sloanreview.mit.edu/article/closing-the-gender-gap-is-good-for-business/

Reisen, M. (2015). *Women's leadership in peace building: Conflict, community and care.* Trenton, NJ: Africa World Press.

Rumsey, M. G. (Ed.). (2013). *The Oxford handbook of leadership.* Oxford, UK: Oxford University Press.

Sarros, J. C., Cooper, B. K., & Santora, J. C. (2008). Building a climate for innovation through transformational leadership and organizational culture. *Journal of Leadership & Organizational Studies, 15*(2), 145–158. doi.org/10.1177/1548051808324100

Schmitz, P. (2011). *Everyone leads: Building leadership from the community up.* Hoboken, NJ: Wiley.

Schuh, S., Hernandez Bark, C., Van Quaquebeke, A., et al. (2014). Gender differences in leadership role occupancy: The mediating role of power motivation. *Journal of Business Ethics, 120*(3), 363–379. doi.org/10.1007/s10551-013-1663-9

Sharp, A. W. (2013). *Women civil rights leaders* (Lucent library of Black history). Detroit, MI: Lucent Books.

Stefanco, C. (2017). Beyond boundaries: Millennial women and the opportunities for global leadership. *Journal of Leadership Studies, 10*(4), 57–62. doi.org/10.1002/jls.21505

Storberg-Walker, J., & Haber-Curran, P. (2017). *Theorizing women and leadership: New insights and contributions from multiple perspectives.* Charlotte, NC: Information Age Publishing.

Suyemoto, K. L., & Ballou, M. B. (2007). Conducted monotones to coacted harmonies: A feminist (re)conceptualization of leadership addressing race, class and gender. In J. L. Chin, B. Lott, J. K. Rice, & J. Sanchez-Hucles (Eds.), *Women and leadership: Transforming visions and diverse voices* (pp. 35–54). Malden, MA: Blackwell.

Tetzloff, L. M. (2007). "With our own wings we fly": Native American women clubs, 1899–1955. *American Educational History Journal, 34*(1), 69–84.

Toner, K. (2019, September 12). *She started helping Detroit's impoverished community in her house. Now, her nonprofit has reached 250,000 people.* CNN Heroes. www.cnn.com/2019/09/12/us/cnnheroes-najah-bazzy-zaman-international/index.html

US Bureau of Labor Statistics. (2020, January 22). *Labor force statistics derived from the current population survey: Employment by detailed occupation and sex.* www.bls.gov/cps/cpsaat11.htm

Vanderbroeck, P. (2014). *Leadership strategies for women: Lessons from four queens on leadership and career development* (Management for professionals). Berlin: Springer.

Watkins, D., Earnhardt, M., Pittenger, L., et al. (2017). Thriving in complexity: A framework for leadership education. *Journal of Leadership Education*, *16*(14), 148–163. doi.org/1012806/V16/I4/T4

Women's Media Center. (n.d.). *Bio of Ana. L. Oliveria*. www.womensmediacenter .com/shesource/expert/ana-l.-oliveira

11 Community Resilience

From Broken Windows to Busy Streets

Elyse Joan Thulin and Marc A. Zimmerman

We discuss the concept of community resilience and building community resilience to promote sustainability in neighborhoods. We provide a case presentation as an example of how a community-based, resilience-focused intervention can promote positive community outcomes in the face of adversity. The case example illustrates the importance of tailoring community interventions to specific local communities rather than assuming a one-size-fits-all approach.

11.1 Definition of Resilience

Researchers define resiliency as a process that examines how promotive factors may operate to help individuals overcome the negative effects of a risk factor on a given outcome (Norris et al., 2008). Fergus and Zimmerman (2005) note that resiliency requires both risk and promotive factors to be present. Promotive factors are made up of assets and resources. Assets are factors within or internal to the agent of interest (e.g., individual, organization, community). Resources are external factors outside the agent of interest. Within individuals, assets might be psychological factors such as self-confidence or critical thinking skills. Individual resources might include social support and opportunities to participate in community organizations. Notably, assets and resources are not static qualities. Rather, they are dynamic, may change over time, and can vary depending on the nature of the risk exposure. Although resiliency theory has largely focused on individual resilience (A. S. Masten, 2001), the process and factors of resilience have been examined across various levels of the socioecological system and in the context of different types of risk (Anderson, 2012; Berger, 2017; Bergström & Dekker, 2014; Berkes & Ross, 2013; Sherrieb, Norris, & Galea, 2010).

11.2 Focus on Individual Resilience

Resilience theory was originally applied in the behavioral sciences to individuals with a focus on developmental outcomes among children and adolescents (Betancourt & Khan, 2008; Cicchetti, 2010; Conger & Conger, 2002;

Fergus & Zimmerman, 2005; Fergusson & Lynskey, 1996; Fleming & Ledogar, 2008; Goldstein & Brooks, 2013; Luthar, 1993; Luthar, Cicchetti, & Becker, 2000; A. S. Masten, 2001, 2007; Olsson et al., 2003; Ostaszewski & Zimmerman, 2006; Richardson, 2002; Southwick et al., 2014). A. S. Masten (2001) has noted that resilience is a normal event through the human developmental trajectory. When considering individual resiliency, researchers consider how an individual overcomes risk exposure. Assets or resources the individual has or can access are key factors that may help the person reduce or avoid altogether the negative consequences of the risk factor. Thus, a youth that lives in a neighborhood that has high rates of violence is at risk for adverse mental or physical health outcomes (Assari et al., 2016; Fowler et al., 2009; Gorman-Smith & Tolan, 1998). For youth exposed to neighborhood violence, promotive assets could include coping skills or self-efficacy (Dupéré, Leventhal, & Vitaro, 2012). Promotive resources might be parental support or adult mentorship (Assari et al., 2015). Researchers have found that assets such as racial identity, involvement in organized extracurricular activities, and self-esteem have helped youth overcome risk exposures such as negative peer influences (e.g., alcohol and drug use, violent behavior), experiences of discrimination, and family conflict (Caldwell, Kohn-Wood et al., 2004; Marshal & Chassin, 2000; Reischl et al., 2011; Sellers et al., 2006; Sullivan, Kung, & Farrell, 2004; Zeldin, 2004; Zimmerman et al., 2011). Researchers have also identified several external resources that have helped youth overcome the negative influences of risk exposures including father and mother support (Caldwell, Sellers et al., 2004; Piko & Kovács, 2010; Wills & Cleary, 1996), adult mentors (Beier et al., 2000; Norton & Watt, 2014; L. A. Thompson & Kelly-Vance, 2001), and access to positive community programs for youth (Flay et al., 2004; Reischl et al., 2011; Zimmerman et al., 2011).

11.3 Community Resilience

The basic components of Resiliency Theory – risk exposure, promotive assets and resources – and the dynamic interaction of risk and promotive factors over time can be applied to communities. When the agent of interest is a community, the risks, assets, and resources need to be focused on the community level of analysis. We present a comparison of risk exposure and resiliency factors associated with individual and community levels in Table 11.1. This table provides examples of community-level risk factors related to individual resiliency, and concomitant assets and resources that might help explain a resiliency process at each level. Community resilience has been referred to as a system's ability to adapt and transform in order to sustain a healthy quality of life for residents (Magis, 2010). Community risk exposure might include catastrophic events that are relatively short-term in nature, even if the effects of such events are long-lasting. Short-term exposures

Table 11.1 *Comparison of risk exposure and resiliency factors associated with individual and community levels*

	Individual Level	**Community Level**
Risk Exposure	Interpersonal conflict, low family SES, negative social influences, mental distress, chronic illness	Low home ownership rates, high unemployment, low average household income, high crime rates and violence, high vacancy, high physical deterioration of infrastructure, persistent economic decline
Assets	Beliefs in efficacy and control, tenacity, knowledge and skills, optimism	Residents' attitudes about their community (e.g., pride), social capital (trust, collective efficacy)
Resources	Social support, community (church) engagement, neighborliness	Opportunities for engagement, community programs, institutional support (protective services), physical characteristics

might include a disaster that results from nature (e.g., hurricane, flooding, earthquake) or human-made such as a mass shooting, serial killer, or chemical spill. Risk exposure may also result from long-term or persistent adversity such as community disorganization and poverty, red-lining and other race-based discrimination, and inconsistent protective services (e.g., fire, police, emergency medical).

The Flint, Michigan water crisis (S. J. Masten, Davies, & Mcelmurry, 2016; Pieper, Tang, & Edwards, 2017) is a good example of a persistent risk exposure that did not necessarily start with the discovery of high lead content in the water. The persistent economic decline of the city that began decades ago when General Motors closed all but one manufacturing plant resulted in the appointment of an unelected financial manger to help address the city's budgetary woes (Rushe, 2013). A series of decisions resulted in switching the water from Detroit, Michigan sources to the Flint River and not treating the new source of water to adequately prevent its corrosive nature. The pipes leached lead and the Flint water crisis was born. Understanding community resilience in this context is quite different than understanding how the New Jersey shore communities coped with the aftermath of the disastrous Hurricane Sandy. In the Jersey shore example, communities were resilient in the face of a single transitory catastrophic event that was preceded by a context where economic resources were not already significantly challenged. While Hurricane Sandy had lingering effects and required time and effort to overcome, the Flint example was a slow process of a resource-challenging context that culminated (and in some ways precipitated) the water crisis. Flint had fewer resources to leverage for itself in the aftermath of the water debacle, and as remediation occurs the structural factors that put Flint at risk in the first place remained unchanged.

In settings that are either stable or experiencing economic development, individual, community, and institutional resources may be more readily available for coping with the aftermath of a catastrophic event like a hurricane, wildfires, and mass shootings. In contrast, in settings that are largely challenged by long-term economic and social decline, long-term stress has negative consequences across the entire system, from individual up to policy level. In these communities, endemic deterioration results in a smaller economic base to utilize in institutional, organizational, and system maintenance. Institutional resources may be limited due to a slow decline in investment and community structures to address challenges become depleted, which results in reduced resources to cope with catastrophic events. Thus, the underlying context may define how community resilience is expressed across settings.

Community resilience has most often been studied in the context of a sudden, short-term event or acute disaster that has a discrete start and end point (Norris et al., 2008). In this situation, community resiliency is evaluated relative to the community's ability to respond to and rebuild after that event. These disasters are often sudden and devastating even though they often have long implications for community health and development. These types of events are often natural disasters such as Hurricane Katrina in New Orleans, Louisiana or short-term violent events such as the 9/11 terror attacks on the World Trade Center in New York City (Moore, Chandra, & Feeney, 2013). This type of disaster study focuses on the discrete event, the direct effects of that event, and the negative implications for population health and well-being. Research on a community's resilience in the face of a short-term disaster has helped to further the definition and application of resiliency theory in community settings, and has resulted in work that examines the types of safeguards a community can work to put in place to foster resiliency in case of a disaster (O. Cohen et al., 2013). Yet, definitions and theory regarding short-term disaster do not capture persistent ongoing risk that is not tied to a singular event.

Grassroots and small community-based organizations (CBOs), governmental and regulatory systems, and environmental factors all play roles in a community's ability to respond and adapt to the risk exposure being faced. Although short-term exposures may also result in long-term consequences, the process of resilience may look somewhat different when comparing factors related to short-term and persistent risk and resiliency. Community assets could include community cohesion, presence of well-established CBOs, and attractions such as safe and well-maintained beaches, parks, or sports venues. Community resources might include local government policy regarding economic development, protective services available such as police and fire, and accessible physical and mental health care. Like individual resiliency, the type of risk facing a community will inform the assets and resources that may be most helpful for overcoming the negative consequences of the risk exposure. The experience of a natural disaster in a community may, for example, require a different set of assets and resources for response and adaptation than the experience of persistent poverty in that same community.

Community resilience for short-term disasters may focus on preparation for evacuation, ability to secure infrastructure support, temporary housing, and securing resources for rebuilding (American Red Cross, 2014; O. Cohen et al., 2013; Leykin et al., 2013). Community resiliency for more persistent disasters may focus on addressing institutional racism, allocating protective services, economic development that does not displace residents, and collaboration between CBOs and community institutions (e.g., schools, police, chamber of commerce). Of course, some of these assets and resources may be applicable to all forms of risk exposure, but the form they take and the distribution of them may be quite different for short-term versus more persistent risk exposure because the underlying causes of the risk are also quite different.

11.4 Definition of Community

Communities exist and are defined in many ways. Neighborhoods can be communities, online chat or video gaming groups can be considered communities, formal religious groups can consider their congregation or group a community, even yoga studios can call their practice studio space a place for community. Most communities feature complex social interactions and networks, connecting members to one another, enabling members to achieve a common need (Brennan, 2008). Given certain structural factors we will consider relative to promotive and risk factors that effect and guide community resiliency, the type of community we are focusing on is one that has a geographic spatial component. It may be a neighborhood, a region of a city, or an entire (small) city or town, but we are referring to geographically defined communities with a relatively narrow scope. In addition, we want to focus our attention on the more persistent type of risk exposure or chronic risk because community resilience researchers have typically focused on response to more short-term episodic disaster exposure. Yet, we recognize that the consequences of short-term exposure may be quite long-lasting and differentially affect different kinds of communities. Nevertheless, the underlying causes of chronic stress exposure for communities are quite different than sudden, unexpected, and often nature-based disasters. Similarly, the response of government and public support for assistance for recovery from short-term disasters are typically strong, resource abundant, and benevolent. Public response to chronic risk is often victim-blaming, unsympathetic, and indifferent to racial and economic disparities that often underlie the situation. Yet, chronic risk at the community level is often treated as an individual-level issue with limited attention to the structural inequalities and risks that go far beyond individual factors. This may result in blaming residents for community resource challenges and limiting an understanding of or developing solutions for community-level change that can help prepare a community to face challenges. This notion is similar to blaming an individual who succumbs to the negative effects of a risk factor because they were just not resilient enough to cope with the challenge. The fundamental problem with this perspective at whatever level is that it ignores the historical, structural, and contextual factors that may help or hinder resilience to be expressed.

11.5 Chronic Risks in Communities

Communities exposed to chronic stressors over time face slow disasters (Draus, 2009; Sherval & Askew, 2012; Simms, 2017). In slow-disaster communities, resiliency must be considered across a longer temporal period based on steady and often slowly developing adversity. These communities face both acute risk factors that might inhibit ongoing development (like that of short-term disasters) and chronic risk factors that weaken the potential for future development. Economic decline contributes to neighborhood instability and disadvantage, and elevated rates of violent crime (Krivo & Peterson, 1996; Peterson, Krivo, & Harris, 2000; Spelman, 1993). Abandoned homes and vacant lots perpetuate neighborhood decay and lead to high rates of poverty, drug dealing and use, social isolation, and crime (Accordino & Johnson, 2000; Scafidi et al., 1998; Spelman, 1993). Increases in vacancies and abandoned properties can change perceptions of neighborhoods and choices about future investments in those neighborhoods (Immergluck & Smith, 2006; Leonard & Schilling, 2005). The number of risk and promotive factors and their interactions over time have pervasive effects across the socioecological framework of human development and can lead to negative health and social outcomes across individuals, family, and communities (Wallace & Wallace, 1998).

Few researchers have studied chronic slow-disasters in community resiliency, despite a need to better understand the mechanisms of community survival in the face of chronic stressors. Several researchers have examined natural resource-based communities, which are often characterized as not experiencing similar gains in economic, social, or structural development as urban area counterparts (Brennan, 2008; Brennan & Luloff, 2007; Flint & Luloff, 2005). In these settings, researchers have identified local agency, social networks, social agency, and investment in the locality as important promotive factors for community resiliency. The study of slow-disasters in rural settings, though limited, has helped expand the understanding of resilience associated with persistent risk exposure experiences in urban settings (Brennan & Luloff, 2007; Simms, 2017).

In the United States, urban slow-disasters are exacerbated by "long-term collision between corrosive structural processes, counterproductive social policies, and vulnerable populations" (Draus, 2009, p. 361). This kind of ongoing risk exposure to community well-being may include high levels of vacancy, poverty, crime, and violence. These kind of disasters include longer-term decline in a community that can result in socioeconomic vulnerability, formation of drug cultures, and environmental decline (from global warming or unfettered pollution) (Simms, 2017). These compounding issues influence social relationships within a neighborhood including social capital and cohesion, physical factors including infrastructure, vacancy, and urban decay, and local government operations including protective services, schools, and economic policy.

In these chronic disaster settings, community members are vulnerable due to structural factors such as economies dependent upon few major industries, and are more susceptible to negative outcomes due to inabilities to respond to small or major disasters (Draus, 2009). Vulnerability and susceptibility combine to create risk factors and barriers to community health and well-being, and impediments to a community's ability to adapt and sustain. Our analysis of community resilience focuses on long-term chronic stressors and persistent states of economic decline, urban decay, structural discrimination, and systematic marginalization experienced in many communities across the USA and globally.

11.6 Communities in Abandoned, Postindustrial Cities

In the postindustrial USA, many cities have experienced high rates of exodus because of the economic decline resulting from factories closing and businesses supporting them. This results in significant and negative implications across economic, social, and service sectors that have adverse effects on community development and health. The implications of population and economic decline in these shrinking cities can have negative ramifications for county and state income (Anderson, 2012). This trickles down to local funding for basic services including police, fire, health care, road maintenance, school systems, and just about everything people experience in everyday life. Reduction in the funding and decreasing quality of these services can in turn exacerbate the health and well-being of communities, resulting in a cyclical, slow-disaster decline that persists over time.

Physically, these postindustrial cities have significant unoccupied and often uncared-for infrastructure. Abandoned houses and decaying buildings in a once busy neighborhood transition it into an area with fewer people on the streets, nefarious activity, and social disorganization. Larger prevalence of vacant and derelict buildings has been associated with higher rates of crime, illicit activities, physical breakdown of the infrastructure, and government neglect (Accordino & Johnson, 2000; Furr-Holden et al., 2011; Spelman, 1993). Higher levels of abandonment and decline in a community have also been associated with poorer physical (Chandola, 2001; Ross & Mirowsky, 2001), sexual (D. Cohen et al., 2000; D. Cohen et al., 2003), and mental health outcomes (Latkin & Curry, 2003) across the individual lifespan. Decay and decline of a neighborhood may also increase fear of crime that may result in neighbors being physically absent in their neighborhood because they do not what to expose themselves to risk of victimization (Garvin et al., 2013). This in turn can result in fewer positive social interactions with neighbors that are vital for social support, developing social relationships, and creating a cohesive community character. Increased vacancy and reduced home ownership also results in loss of community, neighbors, and social connections that are associated with poorer social cohesion and negative mental health outcomes (Cagney et al., 2009; Krause, 1993; E. E. Thompson & Krause, 1998). Although residences may become occupied by short-term renters, they often do not replace longer-term residencies that help rebuild social cohesion, relationships, and trust that are vital for a healthy neighborhood.

Economically, rate of foreclosure on houses has been linked with higher rates of crime (Immergluck & Smith, 2006). Properties in neighborhoods with abandoned and declining housing stock lose their value, resulting in the overall decline in a neighborhood (Leonard & Schilling, 2005). Lower housing costs usually result in lower real estate taxes, fewer houses being bought or upgraded, and fewer funds available for various social and civil projects (Anderson, 2012). In neighborhoods where houses are losing value and localities must reduce services (e.g., police, fire, road repair) these costs may be transferred to individual owners who may not be able to afford additional security measures or fixes in their neighborhood. This slippery slope may result in further exodus of citizens from the neighborhood or community that results in a spiraling decline of community well-being (Leonard & Schilling, 2005).

11.7 Broken Windows Theory

The Broken Windows Theory postulates that physical characteristics of neighborhood decay and weakening economic conditions send messages of abandonment that further exacerbate the decline and result in increasing crime and violence (Kelling & Coles, 1997; Kelling & Wilson, 1982). Thus, left unrepaired, one broken window will lead to more broken windows, that eventually leads to increasing illicit activities, and lower mental and physical health (Chandola, 2001; Garvin et al., 2013; Latkin & Curry, 2003; Reisig & Kane, 2014; Ross & Mirowsky, 2001; Sousa & Kelling, 2014). One team of researchers, for example, found that a higher broken windows index was associated with higher rates of gonorrhea, and better explained variation than poverty (D. Cohen et al., 2000). Other researchers found that a rise in vacant land and deteriorating structures in a neighborhood negatively affected social relations and feelings of safety (Garvin et al., 2013). These findings have also been found in the school setting, where physical disorder in the school (e.g. broken windows) predicted social disorder in grade-school-aged children (Plank, Bradshaw, & Young, 2009). A rise in crime paired with shrinking city budgets and reductions in quality and availability of social and protective services often results in increased risk for community safety, social disorganization, and weakening of positive social ties. Researchers have found that crimes are often place-based and cluster around specific areas of a given neighborhood such as a convenience store or a house that is a hot spot for illicit activities (Braga & Schnell, 2013; Eck & Weisburd, 1995; Weisburd, 2018). Such crime hot spots are often associated with the physical characteristics of sites including abandoned buildings and buildings with less secure access points (Braga et al., 1999; Spelman, 1993).

While the Broken Windows Theory has been utilized to expand the understanding of place-based crime it also has informed targeted policing that can create tensions with community residents. This type of policing, which includes stop and frisk, has faced issues with legality of search and seizure activities (Gould & Mastrofski, 2004) and efficacy of these practices (Caudill et al., 2013). Policing activities tied to community disorganization and hotspot approaches have been linked with increased racial disparities (Golub, Johnson, & Dunlap, 2007) that has increased racial discrimination (Sharp-Grier & Martin, 2016) and created tensions and distrust among neighborhood residents and between them and the police. These feelings of distrust and contempt further undermine residents' feelings of local agency, social cohesion, and ownership. Such disparities further divide law enforcement and residents and increase mistrust between them (and by extension the government more generally). The abandonment of protective resources and government attention contributes to feelings of fear, potential victimization, and a lack of control over their community that can increase suspicion and social tension among residents while decreasing social capital and other social resources within their neighborhoods. These conditions exacerbate risk for and reduce a community's ability to be resilient because social institutions are a key resource for helping communities overcome the decline of community infrastructure and social health. Broken Windows Theory, as it has been typically interpreted and applied, however, focuses on risk and community decline. An alternative approach that focuses on community resilience is the Busy Streets Theory.

11.8 Busy Streets Theory

Busy Streets Theory (BST) focuses on the process of building up a challenged community by highlighting promotive factors that bolster community resiliency in the face of adversity resulting from the kind of slow-disaster risk we described above in Section 11.6 (Aiyer et al., 2015). In basic terms, BST postulates that communities with busier streets are healthier, as community members feel free to walk around, shops are open for business, and the community feels safe to be in. It describes how a process of property enhancement, community engagement, and neighborhood improvement can help an economically challenged community overcome the negative effects of deteriorating infrastructure, social disorganization, and government neglect. BST applies empowerment theory at a community level of analysis by describing how internal factors within a community (intracommunity factors), external interactions with outside community organizations and institutions (interactional factors), and community residents' actions (behavioral factors) integrate to help a community overcome the debilitating effects of economic challenges, crumbling infrastructure, and housing vacancy. Intracommunity factors relate to residents' perceptions of neighborhood trust, social cohesion, collective efficacy, and a sense of community. Interactional factors include coalitions across community organizations, collaboration with institutions outside the community (e.g., police), and the development of partnerships with external organizations to help address community decline. One example of the interaction component is the development of a partnership with the police intended to enhance safety and further community development (Reisig & Kane, 2014). Sometimes referred to as community policing, a trusting partnership between police and community can help improve understanding between citizens and officers, enhance protective services, and help police be both more effective and be perceived as an ally for addressing crime and violence within a community. The process of community-building with the police can help citizens and officers get to know one another on a more personal basis that may enable trust-building on both sides and reduce antagonism on both sides so they can work on a common goal of community safety through cooperation.

Finally, the behavioral component of BST emphasizes the actions that neighborhood residents and organizations take to improve the physical and social conditions in their neighborhood, influence policymaking in the city, and organize to have a united voice through neighborhood associations to speak to local power authorities. Communities that create opportunities for resident engagement in community improvement projects is one way that behavioral factors contribute to community resilience. Social engagement with neighbors on a common goal of community improvement can help establish the community cohesion and collective efficacy necessary for communities to address risks they face. Together, the three components of community empowerment integrate to form the ingredients for creating a busy street where residents interact in positive ways, form social capital within and outside their neighborhood, and transform their neighborhoods so that people feel safe to be outside. These three components of community empowerment animate BST for understanding community resiliency. Table 11.2 presents a

Table 11.2 *Comparison of Broken Windows and Busy Street Theory, levels of analysis*

	Broken Windows	Busy Streets
Physical Characteristics	Neighborhood decay, abandoned buildings, crime hot spots	Properties are landscaped, homes and buildings are well-kept and physically sound
Social Factors	Nefarious (or no) street activity, interpersonal violence, disorganized, community fear	Positive street activity, vibrant, collectivism, community identity, community pride
Institutional Response	Heavy-handed policing, fire and ambulance neglect, limited city resources, help in the form of gentrification	Community policing, quick response, economic development, community engaged improvement

comparison of a Broken Windows Theory (as it has been traditionally interpreted) and the more resiliency focused BST.

Several researchers have found that localized community improvement can be an effective strategy to take back the streets and improve neighborhood wellbeing. Heinze et al. (2018) describe how community-engaged greening projects can help reduce assaults and interpersonal injury on the street faces around the enhanced properties. Community greening projects are aimed at improving the physical neighborhood environment, and can include actions such as mowing and cleaning up overgrown lots, planting community gardens, and installing features that demarcate ownership such as signage and fencing. Garvin et al. (2013) have also found that cleaning vacant lots, planting grass and trees, and building fencing to indicate ownership resulted in greater reductions in aggravated assault and improved residents' perceptions of neighborhood safety than control conditions. They conducted a randomized controlled trial with vacant lots randomly assigned to either the greening intervention or no intervention control conditions.

Kondo et al. (2015) found that remediating buildings also improved neighborhood outcomes. They collected pre- and postmeasures of crime incidents around abandoned buildings that were remediated or received permits for remediation, compared to randomly matched abandoned buildings that did not receive remediation or permits for remediation. After controlling for demographic characteristics and other confounders, they found that areas with remediated buildings had greater crime reductions (including firearm-related incidents) compared to the comparison sites. Notably, in this study and the Heinze et al. (2018) study, crime displacement effects were not observed (i.e., crime did not spike in other locations because of the remediation). Researchers have also reported that green spaces (e.g., cleaning up a vacant lot and planting grass or gardens) is associated with improved mental health outcomes (i.e., symptomology) and less stress compared to less greened spaces (Beyer et al., 2014; Krekel, Kolbe, & Wüstemann, 2015; Pun, Manjourides, & Suh, 2018; Sarkar, Webster, & Gallacher, 2018). These effects may be due to empirically supported ideas that cared-for green spaces are visually more pleasing and that community-owned green areas (i.e., parks) promote social interactions (Fan, Das, & Chen, 2011; Souter-Brown, 2014).

11.9 Case Study: Flint, Michigan

Flint, Michigan, USA provides an example of a community that has experienced a slow-disaster of chronic and persistent risk and adversity compounded over a very long period of time. Flint was founded in the 1800s, but became the Vehicle City in the early 1900s when General Motors established factories in Flint. Between the early 1900s and the 1960s, a flood of workers resulted in fast expansion of the city of Flint (Frohlich, 2016). At the height of growth, the population of Flint was close to two hundred thousand individuals. With around eighty thousand individuals in well-paying jobs with General Motors (GM), Flint was one of the wealthiest counties and had one of the highest median income levels in the United States in the 1960s. In the 1970s, the economic benefits to changing manufacturing locations and closing of many GM factories in Flint resulted in a sharp decline in the number of automotive jobs in Flint, a trend that has continued through to the present day (Adams, 2017; Dandaneau, 1996; Lord & Price, 1992). Today only one truck factory is left in Flint with fewer than seven thousand jobs. The closing of factories had catastrophic effects on the local economy including significant out-migration to other areas with greater economic or social opportunities. As of 2017, Flint was declared one of the fastest-shrinking cities in the United States with a total population of 96,448 (US Census Bureau, 2017). This decline in economy and population has created significant disparities and challenges. Table 11.3 compares some demographic characteristics between Flint and the average of similar sized US cities in 2018. The rate of uninsured residents of the Flint metropolitan area in 2018 was 22.8% compared to the average Michigan rate of 12.7% (Klein & McCarthy, 2010). Genesee County (the county where Flint is located) has higher rates of morbidity and mortality, particularly among the top leading causes of death such as heart disease, cancer, stroke, chronic respiratory problems, diabetes mellitus, and kidney disease than state averages, which are already higher than national averages (US Census Bureau, 2017). These morbidity and mortality rates are highly disparate across race, with African Americans experiencing higher rates. As Flint's population is roughly half African American, this disparity exacerbates the negative effects of the economic decline the city and county have experienced over the last forty years. Over the last decade Flint has also consistently

Table 11.3 *Demographic characteristics of Flint, MI and the USA (US Census Bureau, 2017)*

Demographic Characteristics	Flint, MI	United States
Race/Ethnicity		
White	40%	74%
Black/African American	55%	13%
Hispanic	4%	17%
Income		
Median income	$26,330	$57,652
All families below poverty	35.5%	11%
Families with children <18 below poverty	54%	18%
Highest Level of Education Attained		
Less than high school	18%	8%
High school diploma	36%	28%
Bachelor's degree	7%	18%
Housing		
Owner occupied	57%	88%
Median home value (owner occupied)	$41,700	$176,700

had one of the highest crime rates per capita in the United States (US Census Bureau, 2015; FBI, 2016).

Fast expansion during the growth years followed by mass exodus resulted in a large proportion of vacated properties in the city of Flint. Private and public infrastructure built to accommodate the budding population of the mid-twentieth century is now largely empty, with thousands of vacant buildings (City of Flint, 2014). In some cases, vacant properties are retained by their owners and in others they are abandoned. For those retained, some owners have the resources and motivation to attend to their properties in terms of maintenance and structural integrity. Most, however, do not have adequate resources to maintain their structures or do not feel motivated to spend the resources they do have given the widespread prevalence of disrepair of structures throughout Flint.

Abandoned and neglected houses also pose various risks including fire hazards, crime and violence, and psychological distress as feelings of trust and safety and security among residents are challenged (Accordino & Johnson, 2000; D. Cohen et al., 2003; Garvin et al., 2013; Immergluck & Smith, 2006; Leonard & Schilling, 2005; Scafidi et al., 1998; Spelman, 1993). One community resource that addresses vacancy is the Genesee County Land Bank, which with support from the US Department of the Treasury's Hardest Hit Fund, has demolished more than five thousand abandoned properties since 2014 (Genesee County Land Bank, 2018). The aim of this demolition is to transform these properties to make them productive once again or to at least improve them so they are viable green spaces versus rundown and vacant overgrown and uncared-for lots.

The slow developing disaster in Flint was intensified by the 2014 Flint water crisis. In April 2014, Flint changed its water source to the Flint River that was not treated with anticorrosives resulting in leaching of lead from old pipes into the water supply and causing elevated levels of lead exposure (Butler, Scammell, & Benson, 2016; Gostin, 2016; Hanna-Attisha et al., 2015; Sadler, LaChance, & Hanna-Attisha, 2017). Flint changed the water source to reduce cost, but the ramification of unpotable water and inadequate resources to address the failing pipes are lingering. An estimated 140,000 individuals were exposed to heightened lead levels, and as of January 2016 a federal emergency was declared over the water crisis (Ruckart et al., 2019). Although substantial work has been done to replace pipes and treatment of water sources, the effects of the water crisis persist because of the damage done to trust in government and lingering feelings of abandonment (Clark, 2016; Cuthbertson et al., 2016; Krings, Kornberg, & Lane, 2018). As of 2019, prosecutors dropped criminal charges against local government officials, calling for a reinvestigation due to concerns over evidence collection (CNN Editorial Research, 2019; Hsin Hsuan Sun & Walker, 2019).

Despite all the adversity, however, Flint has proved to be a resilient city with committed and proud residents. The senior author of this chapter (Zimmerman) has been working in Flint since 1994 and has seen their resilience firsthand (https://prc.sph.umich.edu/). In partnership with local and state community organizations, health departments, and other universities, our research has focused on the promotion of safe and healthy futures through prevention research in Flint, Michigan. Our research covers a range of topics, including violence prevention, sexual health, drug and alcohol use, physical activity, healthy eating, and maternal and child health. Building on theories of positive youth development, youth and community empowerment, and resiliency, we have conducted several research projects including prospective longitudinal studies to inform intervention development, and evaluation studies of the interventions using comparison group and randomized control designs. Results of a 2013 community survey we did with community partners indicated that a third of Flint residents participated in neighborhood cleanups, were involved in crime watches, and/or acted with neighbors to solve neighborhood problems (Prevention Research Center – UM SPH, 2019). Flint also has many nonprofit organizations that promote positive environmental and social change, as well as several universities (University of Michigan-Flint, University of Michigan-Ann Arbor, Kettering University) that are vested in sustainable development and growth of a safe community. Despite the interest of individual community members, nonprofit community organizations, and local institutions to work on community development, having the skills to come together to collaborate on goals, plans, and community development activities requires skills such as organization, vested interest, resources (time, leadership), and consistency of interest. When communities can come together through collaboration of the public and private sectors, and across organizational levels from grassroots to state institutions, they might be able to pair assets to produce resources and enhance community resilience.

Such a collaboration began in 2012, when organizations from various sectors in Flint, representing public and private interests, including community-based organizations, hospitals, public and private universities, and civic agencies including law enforcement, came together to form the University Avenue Coalition (UACC) (Wyatt, 2017). The UACC has the organizational skills, leadership, and structural empowerment necessary to plan, implement, and evaluate projects to foster community revitalization and development. One key component of the Coalition's work is its investment in engaging and collaborating with citizens. Another key component is the dedication of the multiple organizations and interests to work together and pool limited resources to better serve sustainable community development and not devote scarce resources to replicate existing projects.

Through its engagement, the UACC has devised, planned, and implemented a variety of community greening projects to clean up empty lots, mow them, beautify them, and engage residents in the revitalization process in Flint. The UACC focus area represents a downtown zone, that if revitalized could draw interest and resources into Flint and begin a boomerang effect to other parts of the city. The goal was to increase neighborhood safety, improve community health, and expand economic opportunities in the targeted four downtown Flint communities, and to create a busy street with positive social interaction.

Our team evaluated community development activities led by the UACC from 2014 to 2017, finding increases in community engagement and participation in activities and a reduction in crime. Utilizing qualitative and quantitative research designs, we have found increased community cohesion, decreased crime in greened areas, and increased interest of community members in community development projects (Heinze et al., 2018; Rupp et al., 2019). Since 2012, Coalition membership has grown to more than a hundred organizations, and resident involvement has continually increased with more than two thousand residents participating in UACC activities over the last year of evaluation activities (2017). Over the course of the evaluation period, more than 375 unique community development and greening activities were implemented across the UACC corridor, including transformations of parcels of land (such as infrastructure changes, major remodeling, new construction and landscaping), organization events (meetings, workshops), and safety and crime prevention activities (including the formation of citizen and police patrols). The UACC was also able to plan and help support more than sixty social events that allowed community members to socialize and participate in recreation, including Friday Nights at the University Square, where community members enjoyed events such as lawn games and food trucks. In terms of vacancy and crime, community-engaged greening of vacant lots reduced violent crimes including assaults by nearly 40% (Heinze et al., 2018; Zimmerman, 2019).

Involving community members in the planning and execution of community greening is beneficial to improve neighborhood satisfaction. Community involvement appears to have had an effect on some communities' perception of neighborhood disorder (Rupp et al., 2019). For instance, residents reported feeling more pride over the areas where they lived and having less fear of crime after the greening activities. In some cases residents reported more ownership over their community and communal spaces (Japowicz, 2017; Rupp & Alberts, 2017). Quotes from residents collected during the project indicate that residents support the underlying ideas of BST. One resident noted that the reduction in crime increased street activity and feelings of safety:

> There's definitely more street activity. People walking … we didn't have that before. You know … what you saw before was a lot of open alcohol, people with beer cans in paper bags, and cars slowing, stopping, talking to people … indicative of an open air drug market. With gun violence in the area there was just a fear of even being out in the community, of being outside the home … So this guy has a wife and a newborn baby and now all of a sudden he is out in front of his home, barbecuing and spending time with his family, whereas before he wouldn't have done that. I see it happening more and more.

Another resident noted the effects of greening on the community:

> It's not just about crime prevention, it's also about creating a sense of brightness and hope because you are clean and constantly getting better. It gives that appearance of something happening, something good coming … the perception that maybe encouraged people to be part of the community … helped our state of community, saying "You know, I can handle this."

Engagement grew over time, with initial community member participation inspiring other members to get involved. As one resident explained:

> We have seen a couple people that came out while we were cleaning on projects that were … where they had kind of let their places go, and they came out and said, "Yunno, we need to step up our game, we are looking a little sloppy" and they actually asked, can we borrow some tools from you, and of course we said sure go ahead. And it's definitely a keeping up with the Jones's effect, if someone isn't trying hard next to you, you might not either, you might just give up out of frustration, but if you've got someone who is keeping up, I'm not going to say that it works with everybody but they are gonna say "Well, they are keeping up, I should probably make an effort myself."

Psychological well-being of residents improved, with fear of crime or victimization decreasing. Mental health outcomes improved across time, with residents reporting fewer mental health symptoms across time. The Rupp et al. (2019)

findings are consistent with other researchers that have found engagement of communities, decreases in crime (Branas et al., 2018; Kondo et al., 2016), and improved mental health outcomes (Kuo & Sullivan, 2001; South et al., 2018).

11.10 Conclusion

Community-engaged efforts to revitalize a community can benefit the community infrastructure while also having positive effects on residents' mental health, including decreased depressive symptoms. Investing in revitalization and community engagement can give agency and feelings of ownership to community members, and the number of community members who engage with a given project may grow. The greening process and the engagement by a variety of organizations from grassroots to state institutions allow for a combination of assets across groups to create resources for the community. Engaging community members is also applying an asset of the community, and may allow this asset to grow in the sense that resident interest and investment in their community and how it looks may grow. While greening is not a panacea for community resiliency, the process fosters resiliency. This process fosters busy streets and at minimum can slow or stop the slide of broken windows, and can potentially create momentum for continued community social and economic growth and revitalization.

References

Accordino, J., & Johnson, G. T. (2000). Addressing the vacant and abandoned property problem. *Journal of Urban Affairs, 22*(3), 301–315. doi.org/10.1111/0735-2166.00058

Adams, D. (2017, September 21). *Here's how Flint went from boom town to nation's highest poverty rate.* MLive. www.mlive.com/news/flint/2017/09/heres_how_flint_went_from_boom.html

Aiyer, S. M., Zimmerman, M. A., Morrel-Samuels, S., & Reischl, T. M. (2015). From broken windows to busy streets: A community empowerment perspective. *Health Education & Behavior, 42*(2), 137–147. doi.org/10.1177/1090198114558590

American Red Cross. (2014). *Community resilience assessment tool: Household and committee surveys for measuring overall community resilience and for tracking changes following Red Cross integrated interventions ("Ritaline").* www.preparecenter.org/sites/default/files/rita_baseline_methodology_for_community_resilience-_guide.pdf

Anderson, M. W. (2012). Dissolving cities. *The Yale Law Journal, 121*(6), 1364–1446.

Assari, S., Moghani Lankarani, M., Caldwell, C. H., & Zimmerman, M. A. (2016). Fear of neighborhood violence during adolescence predicts development of obesity a decade later: Gender differences among African Americans. *Archives of Trauma Research, 5*(2). doi.org/10.5812/atr.31475

Assari, S., Smith, J. R., Caldwell, C. H., & Zimmerman, M. A. (2015). Gender differences in longitudinal links between neighborhood fear, parental support, and depression among African American emerging adults. *Societies*, *5*(1), 151–170. doi.org/10.3390/soc5010151

Beier, S. R., Rosenfeld, W. D., Spitalny, K. C., Zansky, S. M., & Bontempo, A. N. (2000). The potential role of an adult mentor in influencing high-risk behaviors in adolescents. *Archives of Pediatrics & Adolescent Medicine*, *154*(4), 327–331. doi.org/10.1001/archpedi.154.4.327

Berger, R. (2017). An ecological-systemic approach to resilience: A view from the trenches. *Traumatology*, *23*(1), 35–42. doi.org/10.1037/trm0000074

Bergström, J., & Dekker, S. W. A. (2014). Bridging the macro and the micro by considering the meso: Reflections on the fractal nature of resilience. *Ecology and Society*, *19*(4). doi.org/10.5751/ES-06956-190422

Berkes, F., & Ross, H. (2013). Community resilience: Toward an integrated approach. *Society & Natural Resources*, *26*(1), 5–20. doi.org/10.1080/08941920.2012.736605

Betancourt, T. S., & Khan, K. T. (2008). The mental health of children affected by armed conflict: Protective processes and pathways to resilience. *International Review of Psychiatry*, *20*(3), 317–328. doi.org/10.1080/09540260802090363

Beyer, K. M. M., Kaltenbach, A., Szabo, A., et al. (2014). Exposure to neighborhood green space and mental health: Evidence from the survey of the health of Wisconsin. *International Journal of Environmental Research and Public Health*, *11*(3), 3453–3472. doi.org/10.3390/ijerph110303453

Braga, A. A., & Schnell, C. (2013). Evaluating place-based policing strategies: Lessons learned from the Smart Policing Initiative in Boston. *Police Quarterly*, *16*(3), 339–357. doi.org/10.1177/1098611113497046

Braga, A. A., Weisburd, D. L., Waring, E. J., et al. (1999). Problem-oriented policing in violent crime places: A randomized controlled experiment. *Criminology*, *37*(3), 541–580. doi.org/10.1111/j.1745-9125.1999.tb00496.x

Branas, C. C., South, E., Kondo, M. C., et al. (2018). Citywide cluster randomized trial to restore blighted vacant land and its effects on violence, crime, and fear. *Proceedings of the National Academy of Sciences*, *115*(12), 2946–2951. doi.org/10.1073/pnas.1718503115

Brennan, M. A. (2008). Conceptualizing resiliency: An interactional perspective for community and youth development. *Child Care in Practice*, *14*(1), 55–64. doi.org/10.1080/13575270701733732

Brennan, M. A., & Luloff, A. E. (2007). Exploring rural community agency differences in Ireland and Pennsylvania. *Journal of Rural Studies*, *23*(1), 52–61. doi.org/10.1016/j.jrurstud.2006.04.003

Butler, L. J., Scammell, M. K., & Benson, E. B. (2016). The Flint, Michigan, water crisis: A case study in regulatory failure and environmental injustice. *Environmental Justice*, *9*(4), 93–97. doi.org/10.1089/env.2016.0014

Cagney, K. A., Glass, T. A., Skarupski, K. A., et al. (2009). Neighborhood-level cohesion and disorder: Measurement and validation in two older adult urban populations. *The Journals of Gerontology: Series B*, *64B*(3), 415–424. doi.org/10.1093/geronb/gbn041

Caldwell, C. H., Kohn-Wood, L. P., Schmeelk-Cone, K. H., Chavous, T. M., & Zimmerman, M. A. (2004). Racial discrimination and racial identity as risk or protective factors for violent behaviors in African American young adults. *American Journal of Community Psychology, 33*(1), 91–105. doi.org/10.1023/B:AJCP.0000014321.02367.dd

Caldwell, C. H., Sellers, R. M., Bernat, D. H., & Zimmerman, M. A. (2004). Racial identity, parental support, and alcohol use in a sample of academically at-risk African American high school students. *American Journal of Community Psychology, 34*(1), 71–82. doi.org/10.1023/B:AJCP.0000040147.69287.f7

Caudill, J. W., Getty, R., Smith, R., Patten, R., & Trulson, C. R. (2013). Discouraging window breakers: The lagged effects of police activity on crime. *Journal of Criminal Justice, 41*(1), 18–23. doi.org/10.1016/j.jcrimjus.2012.09.005

Chandola, T. (2001). The fear of crime and area differences in health. *Health & Place, 7*(2), 105–116. doi.org/10.1016/s1353-8292(01)00002-8

Cicchetti, D. (2010). Resilience under conditions of extreme stress: A multilevel perspective. *World Psychiatry, 9*(3), 145–154. doi.org/10.1002/j.2051-5545.2010.tb00297.x

City of Flint. (2014). *Imagine Flint: Master plan for a sustainable Flint: Summary of goals & objectives.*www.cityofflint.com/wp-content/uploads/Flint%20Master%20Plan%20Summary.pdf

Clark, K. (2016). The value of water: The Flint water crisis as a devaluation of natural resources, not a matter of racial justice. *Environmental Justice, 9*(4), 99–102. doi.org/10.1089/env.2016.0007

CNN Editorial Research. (2019, July 2). *Flint water crisis fast facts.* Retrieved July 22, 2019, from www.cnn.com/2016/03/04/us/flint-water-crisis-fast-facts/index.html

Cohen, D., Mason, K., Bedimo, A., et al. (2003). Neighborhood physical conditions and health. *American Journal of Public Health, 93*(3), 467–471. doi.org/10.2105/ajph.93.3.467

Cohen, D., Spear, S., Scribner, R., et al. (2000). "Broken windows" and the risk of gonorrhea. *American Journal of Public Health, 90*(2), 230–236. doi.org/10.2105/ajph.90.2.230

Cohen, O., Leykin, D., Lahad, M., Goldberg, A., & Aharonson-Daniel, L. (2013). The conjoint community resiliency assessment measure as a baseline for profiling and predicting community resilience for emergencies. *Technological Forecasting and Social Change, 80*(9), 1732–1741. doi.org/10.1016/j.techfore.2012.12.009

Conger, R. D., & Conger, K. J. (2002). Resilience in Midwestern families: Selected findings from the first decade of a prospective, longitudinal study. *Journal of Marriage and Family, 64*(2), 361–373. doi.org/10.1111/j.1741-3737.2002.00361.x

Cuthbertson, C. A., Newkirk, C., Ilardo, J., Loveridge, S., & Skidmore, M. (2016). Angry, scared, and unsure: Mental health consequences of contaminated water in Flint, Michigan. *Journal of Urban Health, 93*(6), 899–908. doi.org/10.1007/s11524-016-0089-y

Dandaneau, S. P. (1996). *A town abandoned: Flint, Michigan, confronts deindustrialization.* New York: State University of New York Press.

Draus, P. J. (2009). Substance abuse and slow-motion disasters: The case of Detroit. *The Sociological Quarterly, 50*(2), 360–382. doi.org/10.1111/j.1533-8525.2009.01144.x

Dupéré, V., Leventhal, T., & Vitaro, F. (2012). Neighborhood processes, self-efficacy, and adolescent mental health. *Journal of Health and Social Behavior, 53*(2), 183–198. doi.org/10.1177/0022146512442676

Eck, J. E., & Weisburd, D. (1995). Crime places in crime theory. In J. E. Eck & D. Weisburd (Eds.), *Crime and place* (pp. 1–33). Monsey, NY: Criminal Justice Press.

Fan, Y., Das, K. V., & Chen, Q. (2011). Neighborhood green, social support, physical activity, and stress: Assessing the cumulative impact. *Health & Place, 17*(6), 1202–1211. doi.org/10.1016/j.healthplace.2011.08.008

FBI. (2016). *Crime in the United States, 2012: Michigan, Table 8, state listing.* Retrieved February 11, 2019 from https://ucr.fbi.gov/crime-in-the-u.s/2012/crime-in-the-u.s.-2012/tables/8tabledatadecpdf/table-8-state-cuts/table_8_offenses_known_to_law_enforcement_by_michigan_by_city_2012.xls

Fergus, S., & Zimmerman, M. A. (2005). Adolescent resilience: A framework for understanding healthy development in the face of risk. *Annual Review of Public Health, 26*(1), 399–419. doi.org/10.1146/annurev.publhealth.26.021304.144357

Fergusson, D. M., & Lynskey, M. T. (1996). Adolescent resiliency to family adversity. *Journal of Child Psychology and Psychiatry, 37*(3), 281–292. doi.org/10.1111/j.1469-7610.1996.tb01405.x

Flay, B. R., Graumlich, S., Segawa, E., Burns, J. L., & Holliday, M. Y. (2004). Effects of 2 prevention programs on high-risk behaviors among African American youth: A randomized trial. *Archives of Pediatrics & Adolescent Medicine, 158*(4), 377–384. doi.org/10.1001/archpedi.158.4.377

Fleming, J., & Ledogar, R. J. (2008). Resilience, an evolving concept: A review of literature relevant to Aboriginal research. *Pimatisiwin, 6*(2), 7–23.

Flint, C., & Luloff, A. (2005). Natural resource-based communities, risk, and disaster: An intersection of theories. *Society & Natural Resources, 18*(5), 399–412. doi.org/10.1080/08941920590924747

Fowler, P. J., Tompsett, C. J., Braciszewski, J. M., Jacques-Tiura, A. J., & Baltes, B. B. (2009). Community violence: A meta-analysis on the effect of exposure and mental health outcomes of children and adolescents. *Development and Psychopathology, 21*(1), 227–259. doi.org/10.1017/S0954579409000145

Frohlich, T. C. (2016). *America's fastest shrinking cities.* 24/7 Wall St. https://247wallst.com/special-report/2016/04/04/americas-fastest-shrinking-cities-3/

Furr-Holden, C. D. M., Lee, M. H., Milam, A. J., et al. (2011). The growth of neighborhood disorder and marijuana use among urban adolescents: A case for policy and environmental interventions. *Journal of Studies on Alcohol and Drugs, 72*(3), 371–379. doi.org/10.15288/jsad.2011.72.371

Garvin, E., Branas, C., Keddem, S., Sellman, J., & Cannuscio, C. (2013). More than just an eyesore: Local insights and solutions on vacant land and urban health. *Journal of Urban Health: Bulletin of the New York Academy of Medicine, 90*(3), 412–426. doi.org/10.1007/s11524-012-9782-7

Genesee County Land Bank. (2018). *Funded demolitions.* Retrieved March 12, 2019, from www.thelandbank.org/blightfree.asp

Goldstein, S., & Brooks, R. B. (Eds.). (2013). *Handbook of resilience in children* (2nd ed.). New York: Springer.

Golub, A., Johnson, B. D., & Dunlap, E. (2007). The race/ethnicity disparity in misdemeanor marijuana arrests in New York City. *Criminology & Public Policy*, *6*(1), 131–164. doi.org/10.1111/j.1745-9133.2007.00426.x

Gorman-Smith, D., & Tolan, P. (1998). The role of exposure to community violence and developmental problems among inner-city youth. *Development and Psychopathology*, *10*(1), 101–116. doi.org/10.1017/s0954579498001539

Gostin, L. O. (2016). Politics and public health: The Flint drinking water crisis. *Hastings Center Report*, *46*(4), 5–6. doi.org/10.1002/hast.598

Gould, J. B., & Mastrofski, S. D. (2004). Suspect searches: Assessing police behavior under the U.S. Constitution. *Criminology & Public Policy*, *3*(3), 315–362. doi .org/10.1111/j.1745-9133.2004.tb00046.x

Hanna-Attisha, M., LaChance, J., Sadler, R. C., & Champney Schnepp, A. (2015). Elevated blood lead levels in children associated with the Flint drinking water crisis: A spatial analysis of risk and public health response. *American Journal of Public Health*, *106*(2), 283–290. doi.org/10.2105/AJPH.2015 .303003

Heinze, J. E., Krusky-Morey, A., Vagi, K. J., et al. (2018). Busy streets theory: The effects of community-engaged greening on violence. *American Journal of Community Psychology*, *62*(1–2), 101–109. doi.org/10.1002/ ajcp.12270

Hsin Hsuan Sun, M., & Walker, T. (2019, June 14). *Prosecutors drop criminal charges in Flint water scandal*. CNN. www.cnn.com/2019/06/13/us/flint-prosecutors-drop-charges/index.html

Immergluck, D., & Smith, G. (2006). The impact of single-family mortgage foreclosures on neighborhood crime. *Housing Studies*, *21*(6), 851–866. doi.org/10 .1080/02673030600917743

Japowicz, M. (2017, March 26). *Flint Blight Squad works to make neighborhood "something to be proud of."* NBC. http://nbc25news.com/news/local/flint-blight-squad-works-to-make-neighborhood-something-to-be-proud-of

Kelling, G. L., & Coles, C. M. (1997). *Fixing broken windows: Restoring order and reducing crime in our communities*. New York: Simon & Schuster.

Kelling, G. L., & Wilson, J. Q. (1982, March). Broken windows: The police and neighborhood safety. *The Atlantic*. www.theatlantic.com/magazine/archive/ 1982/03/broken-windows/304465/

Klein, S., & McCarthy, D. (2010). Genesee health plan: Improving access to care and the health of uninsured residents through a county health plan. *Commonwealth Fund Publication*, *52*(14), 1–12.

Kondo, M., Hohl, B., Han, S., & Branas, C. (2016). Effects of greening and community reuse of vacant lots on crime. *Urban Studies (Edinburgh, Scotland)*, *53* (15), 3279–3295. doi.org/10.1177/0042098015608058

Kondo, M. C., Keene, D., Hohl, B. C., MacDonald, J. M., & Branas, C. C. (2015). A difference-in-differences study of the effects of a new abandoned building remediation strategy on safety. *PLoS ONE*, *10*(7), Article e0129582. doi.org/ 10.1371/journal.pone.0129582

Krause, N. (1993). Neighborhood deterioration and social isolation in later life. *International Journal of Aging & Human Development*, *36*(1), 9–38. doi.org/ 10.2190/UBR2-JW3W-LJEL-J1Y5

Krekel, C., Kolbe, J., & Wüstemann, H. (2015). *The greener, the happier? The effects of urban green and abandoned areas on residential well-being* (SSRN Scholarly Paper No. ID 2554477). https://papers.ssrn.com/abstract=2554477

Krings, A., Kornberg, D., & Lane, E. (2018). Organizing under austerity: How residents' concerns became the Flint water crisis. *Critical Sociology*. doi .org/10.1177/0896920518757053

Krivo, L. J., & Peterson, R. D. (1996). Extremely disadvantaged neighborhoods and urban crime. *Social Forces, 75*(2), 619–648. doi.org/10.2307/2580416

Kuo, F. E., & Sullivan, W. C. (2001). Aggression and violence in the inner city: Effects of environment via mental fatigue. *Environment and Behavior, 33*(4), 543–571. doi.org/10.1177/00139160121973124

Latkin, C. A., & Curry, A. D. (2003). Stressful neighborhoods and depression: A prospective study of the impact of neighborhood disorder. *Journal of Health and Social Behavior, 44*(1), 34–44. doi.org/10.2307/1519814

Leonard, J., & Schilling, J. (2005). *Vacant properties: The true costs to communities*. National Vacant Properties Campaign. www.communityprogress.net/filebin/ pdf/toolkit/NVPC_VacantPropertiesTrueCosts.pdf

Leykin, D., Lahad, M., Cohen, O., Goldberg, A., & Aharonson-Daniel, L. (2013). Conjoint Community Resiliency Assessment Measure-28/10 items (CCRAM28 and CCRAM10): A self-report tool for assessing community resilience. *American Journal of Community Psychology, 52*(3), 313–323. doi .org/10.1007/s10464-013-9596-0

Lord, G. F., & Price, A. C. (1992). Growth ideology in a period of decline: Deindustrialization and restructuring, Flint style. *Social Problems, 39*(2), 155–169. doi.org/10.2307/3097035

Luthar, S. S. (1993). Methodological and conceptual issues in research on childhood resilience. *Journal of Child Psychology and Psychiatry, 34*(4), 441–453. doi .org/10.1111/j.1469-7610.1993.tb01030.x

Luthar, S. S., Cicchetti, D., & Becker, B. (2000). The construct of resilience: A critical evaluation and guidelines for future work. *Child Development, 71*(3), 543–562. doi.org/10.1111/1467-8624.00164

Magis, K. (2010). Community resilience: An indicator of social sustainability. *Society & Natural Resources, 23*(5), 401–416. doi.org/10.1080/ 08941920903305674

Marshal, M. P., & Chassin, L. (2000). Peer influence on adolescent alcohol use: The moderating role of parental support and discipline. *Applied Developmental Science, 4*(2), 80–88. doi.org/10.1207/S1532480XADS0402_3

Masten, A. S. (2001). Ordinary magic: Resilience processes in development. *The American Psychologist, 56*(3), 227–238. doi.org/10.1037//0003-066x.56.3.227

Masten, A. S. (2007). Resilience in developing systems: Progress and promise as the fourth wave rises. *Development and Psychopathology, 19*(3), 921–930. doi.org/ 10.1017/S0954579407000442

Masten, S. J., Davies, S. H., & Mcelmurry, S. P. (2016). Flint water crisis: What happened and why? *Journal of the American Water Works Association, 108* (12), 22–34. doi.org/10.5942/jawwa.2016.108.0195

Moore, M., Chandra, A., & Feeney, K. C. (2013). Building community resilience: What can the United States learn from experiences in other countries?

Disaster Medicine and Public Health Preparedness, 7(3), 292–301. doi.org/10 .1001/dmp.2012.15

Norris, F. H., Stevens, S. P., Pfefferbaum, B., Wyche, K. F., & Pfefferbaum, R. L. (2008). Community resilience as a metaphor, theory, set of capacities, and strategy for disaster readiness. *American Journal of Community Psychology, 41*(1–2), 127–150. doi.org/10.1007/s10464-007-9156-6

Norton, C. L., & Watt, T. T. (2014). Exploring the impact of a wilderness-based positive youth development program for urban youth. *Journal of Experiential Education, 37*(4), 335–350. doi.org/10.1177/1053825913503113

Olsson, C. A., Bond, L., Burns, J. M., Vella-Brodrick, D. A., & Sawyer, S. M. (2003). Adolescent resilience: A concept analysis. *Journal of Adolescence, 26*(1), 1–11. doi.org/10.1016/S0140-1971(02)00118-5

Ostaszewski, K., & Zimmerman, M. A. (2006). The effects of cumulative risks and promotive factors on urban adolescent alcohol and other drug use: A longitudinal study of resiliency. *American Journal of Community Psychology, 38*(3), 237–249. doi.org/10.1007/s10464-006-9076-x

Peterson, R., Krivo, L., & Harris, M. (2000). Disadvantage and neighborhood violent crime: Do local institutions matter? *Journal of Research in Crime and Delinquency, 37*(1), 31–63. doi.org/10.1177/0022427800037001002

Pieper, K. J., Tang, M., & Edwards, M. A. (2017). Flint water crisis caused by interrupted corrosion control: Investigating "ground zero" home. *Environmental Science & Technology, 51*(4), 2007–2014. doi.org/10.1021/acs .est.6b04034

Piko, B. F., & Kovács, E. (2010). Do parents and school matter? Protective factors for adolescent substance use. *Addictive Behaviors, 35*(1), 53–56. doi.org/10.1016/j .addbeh.2009.08.004

Plank, S. B., Bradshaw, C. P., & Young, H. (2009). An application of "broken-windows" and related theories to the study of disorder, fear, and collective efficacy in schools. *American Journal of Education, 115*(2), 227–247. doi.org/ 10.1086/595669

Prevention Research Center – UM SPH. (2019). *Speak To Your Health! community survey.* http://prc.sph.umich.edu/projects/speak-to-your-health-community-survey/

Pun, V. C., Manjourides, J., & Suh, H. H. (2018). Association of neighborhood greenness with self-perceived stress, depression and anxiety symptoms in older U.S adults. *Environmental Health: A Global Access Science Source, 17* (1), Article 39. doi.org/10.1186/s12940-018-0381-2

Reischl, T. M., Zimmerman, M. A., Morrel-Samuels, S., et al. (2011). Youth empowerment solutions for violence prevention. *Adolescent Medicine: State of the Art Reviews, 22*(3), 581–600, xiii.

Reisig, M. D., & Kane, R. J. (2014). *The Oxford handbook of police and policing.* Oxford, UK: Oxford University Press.

Richardson, G. E. (2002). The metatheory of resilience and resiliency. *Journal of Clinical Psychology, 58*(3), 307–321. doi.org/10.1002/jclp.10020

Ross, C. E., & Mirowsky, J. (2001). Neighborhood disadvantage, disorder, and health. *Journal of Health and Social Behavior, 42*(3), 258–276. doi.org/10.2307/ 3090214

Ruckart, P. Z., Ettinger, A. S., Hanna-Attisha, M., et al. (2019). The Flint water crisis: A coordinated public health emergency response and recovery initiative. *Journal of Public Health Management and Practice*, 25(Suppl. 1: Lead Poisoning Prevention), S84–S90. doi.org/10.1097/PHH.0000000000000871

Rupp, L., & Alberts, J. (2017, November). *Revitalizing community spaces through environmental design: Telling the story of revitalization in Flint, Michigan.* Presented at the GIS Day Conference, Dearborn, MI.

Rupp, L., Zimmerman, M., Sly, K., et al. (2019). Community engaged neighborhood revitalization and empowerment: Busy streets theory in action. *American Journal of Community Psychology*, 65(1–2), 169–178. doi.org/10.1002/ajcp .12358

Rushe, D. (2013, July 19). "Detroit is basically broke": Cuts, cuts and cuts to follow bankruptcy filing. *The Guardian*. www.theguardian.com/world/2013/jul/19/detroit-broke-bankruptcy

Sadler, R. C., LaChance, J., & Hanna-Attisha, M. (2017). Social and built environmental correlates of predicted blood lead levels in the Flint water crisis. *American Journal of Public Health*, 107(5), 763–769. doi.org/10.2105/AJPH .2017.303692

Sarkar, C., Webster, C., & Gallacher, J. (2018). Residential greenness and prevalence of major depressive disorders: A cross-sectional, observational, associational study of 94 879 adult UK Biobank participants. *The Lancet Planetary Health*, 2(4), e162–e173. doi.org/10.1016/S2542-5196(18)30051-2

Scafidi, B. P., Schill, M. H., Wachter, S. M., & Culhane, D. P. (1998). An economic analysis of housing abandonment. *Journal of Housing Economics*, 7(4), 287–303. doi.org/10.1006/jhec.1998.0235

Sellers, R. M., Copeland-Linder, N., Martin, P. P., & Lewis, R. L. (2006). Racial identity matters: The relationship between racial discrimination and psychological functioning in African American adolescents. *Journal of Research on Adolescence*, 16(2), 187–216. doi.org/10.1111/j.1532-7795.2006.00128.x

Sharp-Grier, M. L., & Martin, J. L. (2016). Broken windows, broken promises: Grief, privilege, and hope in the mythical post racial, a call and response. *Qualitative Inquiry*, 22(7), 561–567. doi.org/10.1177/1077800415624716

Sherrieb, K., Norris, F. H., & Galea, S. (2010). Measuring capacities for community resilience. *Social Indicators Research*, 99(2), 227–247. doi.org/10.1007/s11205-010-9576-9

Sherval, M., & Askew, L. E. (2012). Experiencing "drought and more": Local responses from rural Victoria, Australia. *Population and Environment*, 33 (4), 347–364. doi.org/10.1007/s11111-011-0149-x

Simms, J. R. Z. (2017). "Why would I live anyplace else?": Resilience, sense of place, and possibilities of migration in coastal Louisiana. *Journal of Coastal Research*, 33(2), 408–420. doi.org/10.2112/JCOASTRES-D-15-00193.1

Sousa, W., & Kelling, G. (2014). Order maintenance policing. In G. Bruinsma & D. Weisburd (Eds.), *Encyclopedia of criminology and criminal justice* (pp. 3349–3358). New York: Springer. doi.org/10.1007/978-1-4614-5690-2_267

Souter-Brown, G. (2014). *Landscape and urban design for health and well-being: Using healing, sensory and therapeutic gardens.* London, UK: Routledge. doi.org/10 .4324/9781315762944

South, E. C., Hohl, B. C., Kondo, M. C., MacDonald, J. M., & Branas, C. C. (2018). Effect of greening vacant land on mental health of community-dwelling adults: A cluster randomized trial. *JAMA Network Open*, *1*(3), e180298–e180298. doi.org/10.1001/jamanetworkopen.2018.0298

Southwick, S. M., Bonanno, G. A., Masten, A. S., Panter-Brick, C., & Yehuda, R. (2014). Resilience definitions, theory, and challenges: Interdisciplinary perspectives. *European Journal of Psychotraumatology*, *5*(1). doi.org/10.3402/ejpt.v5.25338

Spelman, W. (1993). Abandoned buildings: Magnets for crime? *Journal of Criminal Justice*, *21*(5), 481–495. doi.org/10.1016/0047-2352(93)90033-J

Sullivan, T. N., Kung, E. M., & Farrell, A. D. (2004). Relation between witnessing violence and drug use initiation among rural adolescents: Parental monitoring and family support as protective factors. *Journal of Clinical Child & Adolescent Psychology*, *33*(3), 488–498. doi.org/10.1207/s15374424jccp3303_6

Thompson, E. E., & Krause, N. (1998). Living alone and neighborhood characteristics as predictors of social support in late life. *The Journals of Gerontology: Series B, Psychological Sciences and Social Sciences*, *53*(6), S354–S364. doi.org/10.1093/geronb/53B.6.S354

Thompson, L. A., & Kelly-Vance, L. (2001). The impact of mentoring on academic achievement of at-risk youth. *Children and Youth Services Review*, *23*(3), 227–242. doi.org/10.1016/S0190-7409(01)00134-7

US Census Bureau. (2015). *American community survey 5-year estimates*. Retrieved February 11, 2019, from www.census.gov/programs-surveys/acs

US Census Bureau. (2017). *QuickFacts: United States*. Retrieved January 28, 2019, from www.census.gov/quickfacts/fact/table/US/PST045218

Wallace, D., & Wallace, R. (1998). *A plague on your houses: How New York was burned down and national public health crumbled*. London, UK: Verso.

Weisburd, D. (2018). Hot spots of crime and place-based prevention. *Criminology & Public Policy*, *17*(1), 5–25. doi.org/10.1111/1745-9133.12350

Wills, T. A., & Cleary, S. D. (1996). How are social support effects mediated? A test with parental support and adolescent substance use. *Journal of Personality and Social Psychology*, *71*(5), 937–952. doi.org/10.1037/0022-3514.71.5.937

Wyatt, T. (2017). *The University Avenue Corridor Coalition: A collaborative effort of over 80 stakeholders along University Avenue, Flint, Michigan*. Flint, MI: Kettering University.

Zeldin, S. (2004). Preventing youth violence through the promotion of community engagement and membership. *Journal of Community Psychology*, *32*(5), 623–641. doi.org/10.1002/jcop.20023

Zimmerman, M. (2019, February). *Busy streets theory and research: Transforming neighborhoods for safe and healthy futures*. Oral presented at the Keep America Beautiful conference, Stamford, CT. www.kab.org/news-info/press-releases/national-nonprofit-keep-america-beautiful%C2%A0hosts-2019-national-conference

Zimmerman, M. A., Stewart, S. E., Morrel-Samuels, S., Franzen, S., & Reischl, T. M. (2011). Youth empowerment solutions for peaceful communities: Combining theory and practice in a community-level violence prevention curriculum. *Health Promotion Practice*, *12*(3), 425–439. doi.org/10.1177/1524839909357316

12 Building Community Resilience and Supporting Disaster Risk Reduction through Social Action Efforts

Tracey O'Sullivan

12.1 What Is Community Resilience?

Community resilience has been studied extensively and the literature surrounding it has expanded considerably in the past fifteen years (Castleden et al., 2011; McCleary & Figley, 2017). Resilience is a common term, yet definitions vary depending on the field of study, unit of analysis (e.g., individual vs. community), and context (Davidson et al., 2016). Holling (1973) introduced ecological resilience as the capacity of a complex adaptive system to resist and absorb disturbances, while maintaining structural integrity and functioning. Applied to human systems and across different levels, the term has evolved with a variety of interpretations (Southwick et al., 2014).

The American Psychological Association (APA) defines resilience as "the process of adapting well in the face of adversity, trauma, tragedy, threats or significant sources of stress – such as family and relationship problems, serious health problems, or workplace and financial stressors" (APA, 2020). While this definition focuses more on the individual, the concept of resilience has also been applied to families, organizations, and communities, as adaptive human systems. A common discussion point related to resilience across different levels and contexts is an emphasis on bouncing back after a stressor is experienced, but also the potential for growth from that adaptation by bouncing forward to an improved state of functioning (Cox & Perry, 2011; Southwick et al., 2014).

In social sciences, the psychosocial perspective presents resilience as a set of adaptive capacities within individuals and communities and the process of returning to positive functioning after a disruption (Norris et al., 2008). Viewed through an ecological lens, resilience is a complex, integrated process where systems resist or absorb the impacts of a disruption and adapt (Berkes & Ross, 2013; Folke, 2016; Tyler & Moench, 2012).

The lack of agreement on a definition for community resilience is one of the perplexing issues in this multidisciplinary field (Davidson et al., 2016). Some authors define resilience in terms of a process or set of processes linked to adaptive capacity (Norris et al., 2008; Walker et al., 2004), whereas other authors regard community resilience as an outcome of adaptation to a disruption (United Nations Office for Disaster Risk Reduction [UNDRR], 2009). Regardless of which perspective, adaptation in the face of environmental change is a common element. Table 12.1 provides some sample definitions for each to show the distinctions.

12.2 Bouncing Back ... or Forward

An important concept within the resilience discussion is whether it is optimal for a community to bounce back after a disturbance – or to bounce forward – as Cox and Perry (2011) suggest. Following a crisis or disaster, it is

Table 12.1 *Example definitions for resilience*

Term	Definition	Reference
Community Resilience	"A process linking a set of networked adaptive capacities to a positive trajectory of functioning and adaptation in constituent populations after a disturbance"	Norris et al., 2008 (p. 131)
Community Resilience	"The processes that community members collectively use to develop and engage collective capacities (adaptation and self-organization) and resources (physical, economic, and social) in order to thrive in communities subject to change, uncertainty, unpredictability, and surprise"	Davidson et al., 2016 (p. 32)
Disaster Resilience	"A measure of how well people and societies deal with disruptive change through capacities for anticipation, adaptation, and improvization, and their ability to capitalize on the new opportunities offered or to innovate"	Davidson et al., 2016 (p.32)
Resilience	"The ability of a system, community or society exposed to hazards to resist, absorb, accommodate to and recover from the effects of a hazard in a timely and efficient manner, including through the preservation and restoration of its essential basic structures and functions"	UNDRR, 2009 (p. 24)
Socioecological Resilience	"... the capacity of a system to absorb disturbance and reorganize while undergoing change so as to still retain essentially the same function, structure, identity, and feedbacks"	Walker et al., 2004 (p. 6)

not always optimal for people to return to circumstances that were detrimental to their well-being in the first place. Vulnerable settings are often clustered around the social determinants of health (e.g., income insecurity combined with transitional or inadequate housing; Baum & Friel, 2017). Settings and inequities are essential considerations when looking at recovery following an adverse event. An example related to the COVID-19 pandemic is households where there is domestic violence. The physical distancing measures required people to stay home as much as possible and resulted in many people – disproportionately women and children – being confined at home with family members who abuse them (United Nations, 2020). Bouncing back to "normal" following the pandemic is not ideal for persons in relationships where there is abuse. Instead, recovery for these individuals and families must include improvements to living arrangements and access to mental health and social services supports, to reduce vulnerability going forward.

Southwick et al. (2014) present an anthropologist perspective emphasizing the process of resilience leading to sustained well-being. Following a disaster, such as pandemic, a health-promoting recovery plan that addresses vulnerabilities within settings and persistent inequities is warranted to ensure recovery trajectories are equitable for the whole community. Health-promoting plans must address social determinants of health, such as housing, income, or food security, to ensure equity in recovery. Equitable access to mental health services is another example that supports people in their recovery trajectory.

Rebuilding is an opportunity to strengthen the assets within a community (Moser & Satterthwaite, 2008) – a process that may be commonly referred to as "build back better" (UNDRR, 2015, p. 36). This may include adaptive structural improvements to reduce risk (e.g., construction improvements to withstand flooding), environmental mediators to reduce adverse impacts of future events, or changes in social service delivery. Beyond adaption, however, there are increasing global recommendations to build back better by aligning disaster risk reduction strategies with transformative development (Gall, Cutter, & Nguyen, 2014). An example could include financial mechanisms for reducing risk during a rebuild, instead of limiting insurance funding to building back to the original state (UNDRR, 2018). This type of policy supports economic development, which is one of the adaptive capacities Norris et al. (2008) deemed essential for supporting community resilience and disaster resilience.

Walker and colleagues (Walker et al., 2004) discuss resilience, adaptability, and transformability as attributes that contribute to stability in dynamic social-ecological systems. Transformability refers to "the capacity to create a fundamentally new system when ecological, economic, or social (including political) conditions make the existing system untenable" (Walker et al., 2004, p. 7). Transformative development is an approach to community development that prioritizes social justice and changing or creating systems that address root causes of inequities; these inequities exacerbate disaster risk and vulnerability (Thomalla et al., 2018).

From a social-ecological lens, *adaptation and transformation* are essential elements of resilience thinking (Folke, 2016). When disruptions occur, it is important to think about solutions to stay on a current trajectory – and to recognize when it is better to switch to a new path. People and systems will tend to adapt to changes in the environment to maintain a given trajectory; that adaptability "helps turn changes and surprises into opportunities" (Folke, 2016, p. 4). However, transformative development requires thinking innovatively and switching pathways, if necessary, to improve environmental surroundings and maintain functioning (Walker et al., 2004).

Transformations tend to occur around tipping points or thresholds when an opportunity to switch gears becomes apparent (Folke, 2016). These points provide action levers for social action initiatives to propel change within a community. Eliminating or reducing silos in collaborative practice are examples of transformative development that supports disaster risk reduction. Alignment of action strategies in response to different global agreements and planning frameworks, which has been a priority in recent years, is one way to reduce silos and combine investment. For example, the Sendai Framework for Disaster Risk Reduction (UNDRR, 2015), the Paris Agreement on Climate Change (United Nations Framework Convention on Climate [UNFCCC], 2015), and the Sustainable Development Goals (United Nations Development Programme [UNDP], 2015) are three global agreements (all published the same year), that support community resilience as described below:

- The Sendai Framework for DRR provides global recommendations to reduce disaster risk, with particular emphasis on supporting resilience among populations at disproportionate risk due to the intersection of functional capacity, existing inequities, and vulnerable settings (UNDRR, 2015).
- The Paris Agreement is a global agreement to reduce carbon emissions and slow the adverse impacts of climate change, which includes more frequent and severe disasters. This agreement supports community resilience by providing parameters for countries around the globe to address the drivers of climate change (UNFCCC, 2015).
- The Sustainable Development Goals are a set of 17 goals and 169 targets that are part of an action plan outlined by the United Nations to promote peace, human rights, gender equity and health, end poverty, and protect the planet. The SDGs focus on sustainability and resilience across the world (UNDP, 2015).

In the wake of the COVID-19 crisis, the need for sound investment and prioritization of the recommendations in these global frameworks and agreements could not be more pertinent. As observed in other pandemics, COVID-19 magnified the social gradient of risk (O'Sullivan & Phillips, 2019) and inequities around the globe. It has underscored the urgent need for social justice, investment in strategies to reduce disaster risk, and resources to support adaptive capacity among people at heightened risk due to the vulnerable settings and circumstances in which they live. For example, care facilities for older adults have been impacted disproportionately by the COVID-19 pandemic and the impacts have exposed serious weaknesses in these systems. Going forward, there will be a need for rights-based policy development to address the factors that exacerbate these risks (UN, 2020).

Many strategies that support climate change adaptation align with the SDGs and address the drivers of risk that make communities more vulnerable to disasters (UNDRR, 2018). For example, investment in green affordable housing projects demonstrates sustainable building practices, while addressing barriers to affordable housing options for people with limited income. Quality housing can contribute to reducing risk of adverse impacts for different types of disasters, such as pandemics. As seen during the COVID-19 response, physical distancing can be challenging in contexts where there is crowded housing. Investment and coordination to support transformative action is an example of how silos can be dismantled to address the complexity of upstream health promotion and disaster risk reduction – both of which support community resilience (O'Sullivan et al., 2013).

12.3 Elements That Support Community Resilience

There are many factors known to influence resilience within a community. This is one of the reasons community resilience is a complex issue. In general, factors that promote healthy vibrant cities support community resilience; these factors include but are not limited to social cohesion, social justice, intersectoral collaboration to improve the quality of life of citizens, and prioritized investment in public health (Kickbusch & Sakellarides, 2006). Southwick et al. (2014) suggest that resilience can be enhanced by creating environments to support development of natural protective mechanisms to support health and people's abilities to cope with adverse events. These could include social opportunities to reduce social isolation and loneliness, affordable housing and neighborhood kitchens, or skill development programs to assist people with finding stable employment.

Norris et al. (2008) outline four adaptive capacities that are integrated, foundational elements of community resilience: (1) *economic development*, (2) *social capital*, (3) *community competence*, and (4) *information and communication*. Investment of time, money, and energy to build each of these adaptive capacities upstream (before an adverse event occurs) can support resilience downstream after an event, enabling communities to mobilize resources and manage the impacts when an adverse event occurs (O'Sullivan et al., 2014). Each of these four adaptive capacities is described in the sections that follow.

12.3.1 Economic Development

Economic development, as an adaptive capacity, includes ensuring there is diversity in economic drivers in the community, opportunities for employment, social safety net programs, and macro political-economic factors, such as strategies to stabilize the economy when there is a disturbance and equitable distribution of resources. Fairness and equity are essential elements of sustainable economic development (Norris et al., 2008). The global SDGs focus on eradicating poverty because of its link with adverse health outcomes (UNDP, 2015). When people are struggling to make ends meet on a daily basis, they do not have the capacity to bounce back or forward when there is a crisis or disaster.

Distress about finances can put people at heightened risk as they look for strategies to make ends meet. For example, despite recommendations to engage in physical distancing during a pandemic, some people may feel they have no choice but to go to work when ill, because they need the money to feed their family. During the COVID-19 pandemic, many people were laid off or had reduced hours because there were so many closures in an effort to control the spread of the virus. Markets were volatile due to uncertainty about how the pandemic would unfold. To alleviate stress and ensure the public followed distancing guidelines, within the first month of the pandemic the Canadian federal government implemented an economic stimulus package equivalent to C\$82 billion, and restructured employment insurance programs. These adaptive capacities were mobilized to ensure people did not experience undue financial stress and the economy could withstand the market fluctuations and reduced consumer spending during the pandemic (Harris, 2020). It was also a support mechanism to help individuals and families follow distancing guidelines, knowing there was financial help to offset the costs of staying home.

12.3.2 Social Capital

A community can be thought of as a social system, made up of individuals, groups, organizations, and interdependent relationships. Social capital and social trust are fundamental assets that help people navigate and improve their quality of life, manage in adverse circumstances, and thrive (Lechner et al., 2016). Resilient communities have strong social networks (Norris et al., 2008; Pfefferbaum, Van-Horn, & Pfefferbaum, 2017) and partnerships within these social networks benefit from synergy, which is a similar construct to trust (Jones & Barry, 2011).

Social capital stems from social networks and represents an essential adaptive capacity to support people in their daily activities and to recover after an adverse event (Chandra et al., 2011; Pfefferbaum et al., 2017). As social beings, people are influenced by their social networks and culture in terms of prioritizing different values, views on health, how they interpret guidelines from authorities, and what activities they choose to engage in (Yong & Lemyre, 2019). Poortinga (2012) describes three different types of social capital: bonding, bridging, and linking; each can contribute to community resilience in different ways.

- *Bonding social capital* describes connections within groups that share common identities (e.g., LGBTQ2+, ethnic origin, living in the same neighborhood). Bonding social capital can support resilience by reinforcing a sense of belonging, providing companionship, and providing sources of information and practical support, when needed.
- *Bridging social capital* refers to the connections people have between social groups, such as people who hold different beliefs, affiliations, and cultural identities. Bridging social capital supports resilience by expanding the pool of resources and connections people can turn to for information, ideas, practical support, or opportunities to participate in their community.
- *Linking social capital* refers to connections people have with people and institutions involved in decision-making, who can be turned to for support in advocacy. The benefits of linking social capital is that people can access opportunities to participate in and influence discussions of issues that affect them, which in turn can support the process of resilience, when faced with adverse events or circumstances.

An important concern with physical distancing measures during the COVID-19 pandemic was the detrimental impact of social isolation. While public health risk messaging emphasized the need to self-isolate, there was complementary risk messaging emphasizing the need to stay in contact with other people, to promote mental health at a time when people needed social contact to help cope with the stress of the pandemic. Three months into the pandemic, Statistics Canada (2020) reported mental health among people living in Canada had decreased. Of the forty-six thousand respondents to a crowdsourced survey administered between April 24 and May 11, 2020, approximately half reported their mental health had worsened during the pandemic, and 88% indicated they had experienced at least one symptom of anxiety within the previous two weeks. With a prolonged response period and uncertainty regarding subsequent waves and vaccine availability, the implications for overall well-being of the population and long-term demands on mental health and social services have been profound.

12.3.3 Community Competence

Norris et al. (2008) describe community competence in terms of community action, critical reflection and problem-solving skills, flexibility and creativity, collective efficacy and empowerment, and political partnerships. Many of these elements require engagement and an approach to community life where participation, innovation, and collaboration are valued. Social action depends on people working together – collaborating – through formal or informal partnerships. Where there is social action, there is often innovation, provided people have opportunities to engage in discussions that are important to them and express their ideas. Social action initiatives provide space for participation in community discussions and initiatives, and when there is recognition of the need for inclusion of different community groups and organizations, people can be empowered to contribute (O'Sullivan et al., 2014).

Leadership is emphasized in the literature as a critical factor influencing community resilience (Leykin et al., 2016). Developing and refining governance structures is part of transformative leadership that includes collaborative decision-making, accountability, meaningful participatory consultation, and transparency (UNDRR, 2018). The importance of strong, trusted leadership was evident in the response to the COVID-19 pandemic, in terms of communication, implementation of precautionary measures, transparency in decision-making, and reassuring the public in the face of uncertainty.

As described by Caldwell et al. (2012), transformative leadership is "an ethically based leadership model that integrates a commitment to values and outcomes by optimizing the long-term interests of stakeholders and society and honoring the moral duties owed by organizations to their stakeholders" (p. 176). Upstream-oriented leadership embodies a transformative approach and understanding of the underlying causes of risk and how social inequities exacerbate risk; it is based on a recognition of the need to invest proactively in people and critical social infrastructure to support adaptive capacity and community resilience (O'Sullivan et al., 2014).

To promote social action, leadership does not have to follow traditional structures. In fact, empowerment of citizens to take on leadership roles is one way to recognize different types of expertise and embrace new ways of doing things. Transformative development can include leadership structures where power is shared, and citizens have opportunities to contribute through leadership roles they find meaningful. As suggested by plenary panelist at a 2013 conference of the International Society for Traumatic Stress Studies, Dr. Catherine Panter-Brick, an expert in the area of resilience, "interventions targeted at readiness for jobs and education, targeted at alleviating violence and human insecurity, or targeted at social justice to enhance fairness in access to resources are among the most effective ways to enhance resilience" (Southwick et al., 2014, p. 10). This is the essence of community competence, where individuals have adaptive capacities that can contribute to the resilience of communities.

12.3.4 Information and Communication

Communication is central to building community resilience because people need information. However, communication needs to be multidirectional, emphasizing that citizens have information to share. Communication channels need to be open both ways. The emergent ways in which social media is being used is a good example of this. Public health and emergency management organizations now realize the importance of drawing on citizens for information to enhance situational awareness around a disaster. Social media is used as a virtual gathering space by many people, and has changed the way politicians, government, and other organizations interact with the public (Wang et al., 2019).

Social media use by governmental departments, humanitarian organizations, politicians, and public health units exemplifies how tipping points can trigger transformation. While social media has proliferated information exchange, misinformation spreads rapidly and can undermine recommendations around preventive health behaviours (e.g., vaccination), disaster preparedness, and response actions (e.g., when to evacuate; Wang et al., 2019; Yong & Lemyre, 2019). Maintaining credibility among public health and emergency management organizations, as a legitimate source of accurate information, is dependent upon keeping up with the public conversation and communicating quickly (Khan et al., 2019). Many organizations have had to change practice guidelines and structural aspects of how they operate to adapt to public reliance on social media. For example, in focus groups we conducted about social media use in the context of public health emergency preparedness, many public health professionals reported a change in how they work, to ensure messaging about important topics is distributed as quickly as possible (Khan et al., 2019). Organizational learning was apparent in how approval protocols for risk communication were adjusted to ensure Twitter feeds kept pace with public discussions (Khan et al., 2019). Hence transformation in this example represents the change in path toward new channels of communication and organizational protocols – driven by changes in how the public accesses health information.

The use of social media as a tool in pandemic response was evident during COVID-19; information flow – particularly spread of misinformation – has been referred to as an "infodemic" (Zarocostas, 2020). Case numbers, changing response strategies, public health guidelines, and business closures are among the myriad of issues making up the vast information flow associated with COVID-19; misinformation is of particular concern given its influence on population health and behavioral compliance with public health response measures, such as physical distancing and unproven pharmaceutical interventions (Krause et al., 2020).

12.4 The EnRiCH Project: Social Action to Promote Community Resilience in Canada

Disasters are by nature complex and characterized by the disproportionate impact on marginalized and otherwise high-risk groups (UNDRR, 2015). Pandemics and other large-scale outbreaks present unique challenges that disproportionately have an impact on people who, due to the intersection of preexisting inequities, personal circumstances, and vulnerable settings, are more susceptible when exposed (O'Sullivan & Phillips, 2019).

Because disasters cause disruptions in social and physical environments, it is important to consider multilevel factors that influence resilience among people at greater risk.

The EnRiCH (Enhancing Resilience and Capacity for Health) Project was a community-based participatory research initiative developed in 2009 through partnerships with five Canadian geographic communities (Gatineau, Truro, Québec City, Region of Waterloo, and Calgary). Institutional partners spanned jurisdictional levels and sectors, including various governmental organizations, nongovernmental organizations (The Canadian Red Cross), and academic institutions. The initial project was funded by Defense Research and Development Canada.

Between 2009 and 2013, our team collaborated with the EnRiCH pilot communities to explore strategies to enhance community resilience by focusing on inclusion and engagement of populations at heightened risk (e.g., persons with disabilities that require supports for daily living, persons with visual or hearing limitations, persons with limited access to transportation – due to geography, limited finances, medical condition, or suspension of a driver's license – and persons living with food or housing insecurity). The premise behind our approach was to build adaptive capacity among populations at heightened risk, which would contribute to the resilience of the whole community through enhanced adaptive capacity.

As part of the EnRiCH community resilience intervention, the pilot communities engaged in an asset-mapping exercise. The purpose of this activity was multifold: to foster social connectedness across different sectors involved in the asset-mapping exercise, increase awareness of the assets and needs in each community, and to create a database that could contribute to adaptive capacity for disaster response. Respecting the needs and preferences – and unique context within each community – the asset-mapping exercise was implemented in different ways. Each community determined the approach they would use, in accordance with the skills, resources, and preferences of the people and organizations involved in the exercise.

One of the outputs from the EnRiCH Project was a framework combining empirical evidence from working with five communities in Canada and the available literature on community resilience. The EnRiCH Community Resilience Framework for High-Risk Populations (O'Sullivan et al., 2014) is summarized in Figure 12.1 as an example of social action to support community resilience.

As can be seen by the emphasis on adaptive capacity as the focal point, surrounded by empowerment, collaboration, and innovation in Figure 12.1, the EnRiCH framework built on the work of Norris et al. (2008) incorporating different adaptive capacities to support community resilience. In this model we referred to them as action levers that include awareness/communication, connectedness/engagement, upstream leadership, and asset/resource management (O'Sullivan et al., 2014). The complexity of community resilience

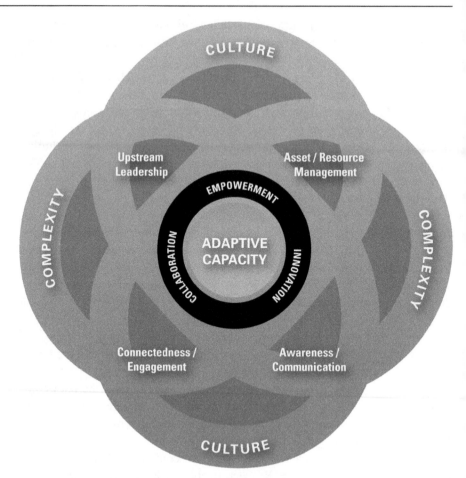

Figure 12.1 *The EnRiCH Community Resilience Framework for High-Risk Populations.*
Source: Reprinted with permission from O'Sullivan et al., 2014

is also emphasized as encompassing all the components that support adaptive capacity. This feature recognizes the social-ecological lens, which embeds resilience within interconnected components of all the systems within a community (Berkes & Ross, 2013; Tyler & Moench, 2012).

Adaptive capacity can be at the individual, organizational, or community level. It is supported through connectedness and strong relationships between different sectors and organizations in a community (Norris et al., 2008), and can be mapped according to assets that can be used to support resilience (Kretzmann & McKnight, 1996). Through our experiences working with the pilot communities, we identified the drivers of adaptive capacity to be collaboration, innovation, and empowerment (O'Sullivan et al., 2014). Social action levers are depicted in the surrounding circles in Figure 12.1. These four areas emphasize where action can support community resilience, specifically focused on high-risk populations: upstream leadership, connectedness/engagement, awareness/communication, and asset/resource management.

In the EnRiCH framework the action lever "connectedness/engagement" emphasizes social connections and opportunities to build social capital and opportunities for social participation in the community. Given that poverty and exclusion are drivers of social and economic vulnerability (Moser & Satterthwaite, 2008), inclusive engagement and empowerment of typically marginalized or high-risk groups in the community is central to many of the key concepts around resilience (O'Sullivan et al., 2014). Inequity contributes to vulnerability and undermines adaptive capacity (Southwick et al., 2014). This critical point underscores how strategies to support community resilience can be addressed through investment in the social determinants of health (UNDRR, 2018). Systems must consider how services are delivered, not simply whether they are available. To support community resilience, services need to be provided in nonjudgmental spaces, demonstrate respect, and support dignity (Bartley, 2006). Listening to and responding to the voiced needs – and preferences – of citizens is an essential part of empowerment.

UNDRR (2018) emphasizes the dynamic nature of risk profiles and the need to focus on the local level to pinpoint risk and potential strategies to reduce exposure. However, it is also important to acknowledge the dynamic nature of asset-profiles, and recognize that risk and assets work as two sides of the coin. Asset-mapping, therefore, is as important as mapping vulnerability. Asset-mapping was introduced by Kretzmann and McKnight (1996) as a proactive strategy to support asset-based community development (ABCD).

Within the literature and fields of health promotion, community development, and disaster risk reduction, there is considerable discussion about assets that support resilience and the need to map them to ensure communities know which resources are available when they need them. In addition to the direct and indirect benefits of mapping assets, one concept that emerged from the EnRiCH Project was the importance of asset literacy, as a fundamental element of resiliency.

Asset literacy is an individual's capacity to understand what an asset is, why it is important, and how to activate it to enhance or maintain functional independence (O'Sullivan et al., 2014). Awareness is part of asset literacy, and it evolves from the process of identifying different assets and how they might contribute to enhance well-being. From there, an individual can develop confidence and motivation to act on knowledge of assets and it can inspire creativity when people understand the value of different assets. An important part of asset literacy is to develop motivation and self-efficacy to take adaptive action. It is a cyclic process that moves from awareness to empowerment to participation – and finally to innovation and engagement; at which point the cycle starts again as people recognize new assets they have developed or become aware of through their social connections.

Asset literacy is not just about receiving information about assets, but extends to the processing of the information to conceptualize one's personal asset profile and activate the assets in adaptive response. Three critical components of any strategy to enhance asset literacy are empowerment, inclusive engagement, and fostering a community culture where innovation is embraced. Programs that train leaders to foster inclusive communities and value different types of expertise across the population can contribute to collective asset literacy in a community and promote resilience (O'Sullivan et al., 2014). Asset literacy and inclusive citizen engagement are important across all phases of a disaster from prevention/mitigation to preparedness, response, and recovery. As seen in the next example, they can contribute to adaptation and transformation in long-term postdisaster recovery.

12.5 Social Action in Rural Québec

An inspiring example of how adaptation and transformation can support community resilience is the Public Health Action Plan following the 2013 train derailment and explosion in the small rural town of Lac-Mégantic, Québec. Forty-seven people lost their lives in this tragedy, and the city's downtown was decimated from the explosion and environmental contamination. In 2016, the public health department partnered with the municipality to host a Day of Reflection and develop an action plan to support the community recovery process (Généreux et al., 2018).

The plan was developed in consultation with the citizens and local organizations to empower the community and ensure their priorities and preferences informed the recovery efforts over the long term. Details of this action plan are provided by Généreux et al. (2018). The four axes of the public health action plan included:

1. "Establishment of a gathering place for the community to support connection and communication;
2. Promotion of a positive campaign to share citizen visions for the community, including a Photovoice Initiative where citizens would share their ideas and experiences through photography;
3. Development of a child/youth psychological profile and expansion of the EPHS [Estrie Public Health Survey] to monitor the health of children and youth; and
4. Recurrent investment through the creation of a permanent community outreach team." (pp. 158–159)

The creation of a permanent outreach team (consisting of a team of social workers and community organizers) to support the community in recovery represents a transformation within the community and public health department. It is an example of upstream leadership where a need was recognized, and the initiative was championed to obtain stable, recurrent investment in this new structure within the community.

The community outreach team did not exist before the tragedy and was put in place by the local government as a structural system-level change resulting from social action in the community. This outreach team has been instrumental in implementing activities to address the other axes of the plan. This team has become a hub for connecting with citizens and facilitating engagement, as well as collaborating with the reconstruction team for the community. The public health outreach team published a detailed explanation of all the activities they have been involved with during the recovery process (www.santeestrie.qc.ca/clients/SanteEstrie/Publications/Sante-publique/Promising_Initiatives_DSPublique2019-11-01.pdf). These activities included, but not are limited to, the creation of a community garden, youth council, and Photovoice initiative to engage citizens in developing a vision for the community through 2025. In addition, the Greeters program was established to manage the influx of disaster tourists in the years following the explosion. Citizens in Lac-Mégantic found themselves confronted with questions about the disaster from interested tourists, which contributed to recurrent reminders of the event and made it difficult to cope and progress in their recovery. To alleviate the burden on community citizens, the Greeters program provides a space for tourists to ask questions, and for the community to provide information about their experience in a way that they can manage misinformation and insensitivity from visitors. Many of the initiatives within the community of Lac-Mégantic have been highly innovative and provide examples of how citizen empowerment and social action can contribute to substantial gains in community resilience.

12.6 Conclusion: A Call to Action

Engagement is possible when citizens, and local groups/organizations are given a voice (Quaranta et al., 2019). Resilience thinking can contribute to the development of adaptive capacity, building on local knowledge and networks, and fostering buy-in to disaster risk reduction strategies. The success of social action initiatives is also dependent on whether people are willing to participate. Citizen participation and grassroots community initiatives must be supported by local governments to leverage power to change policy, programs, and system structures (UNDRR, 2018). What is needed is the creation of opportunities to build awareness and relationships – these are key factors to engage communities to become more resilient. These types of opportunities can include – but are not limited to – public consultations, invitations for citizens to be part of planning exercises, intergenerational councils, and artistic and cultural hubs to build social capital.

Leaders from all levels need to reach out to community stakeholders to engage them – and empower everyone to participate. This is the essence of a "whole of society" approach to promote resilience, where individuals, households, organizations, and groups are invited and encouraged to contribute to the adaptive capacity of the community (Federal Emergency Management Agency [FEMA], 2009; World Health Organization [WHO], 2009). The messaging needs to be consistent, however, to be authentic. When people are invited to the table to express their views, it is important to take action on the issues that are raised and to create an atmosphere of respect for the different types of knowledge citizens bring to the discussion.

Finally, and perhaps most importantly, there is a need to change the lens to look for assets within individuals, organizations, and communities. Upstream transformative leadership is needed to champion this type of paradigm shift to promote community resilience through social action. In community psychology, this shift requires a balanced approach to research and practice, recognizing how individual and collective asset literacy can support community capacity and, hence, resilience.

References

American Psychological Association. (2020). *Building your resilience.* www.apa.org/topics/resilience.

Bartley, M. (Ed.). (2006). *Capability and resilience: Beating the odds.* UCL Department of Epidemiology and Public Health on behalf of the ESRC Priority Network on Capability and Resilience. www.ucl.ac.uk/capabilityandresilience/beatingtheoddsbook.pdf

Baum, F., & Friel, S. (2017). Politics, policies and processes: A multidisciplinary and multimethods research programme on policies on the social determinants of health inequity in Australia. *British Medical Journal Open, 7*(12), e017772. doi.org/10.1136/bmjopen-2017-017772

Berkes, F., & Ross, H. (2013). Community resilience: Toward an integrated approach. *Society and Natural Resources, 26*(1), 5–20. doi.org/ 10.1080/08941920.2012.736605

Caldwell, C., Dixon, R. D., Floyd, L. A., et al. (2012). Transformative leadership: Achieving unparalleled excellence. *Journal of Business Ethics, 109*(2), 175–187. doi.org/10.1007/s10551-011-1116-2

Castleden, M., McKee, M., Murray, V., & Leonardi, G. (2011). Resilience thinking in health protection. *Journal of Public Health, 33*(3), 369–377. doi.org/10.1093/pubmed/fdr027

Chandra, S., Acosta, J., Stern, S., et al. (2011). *Building community resilience to disasters.* Santa Monica, CA: RAND Corporation. www.rand.org/pubs/technical_reports/TR915.html

Cox, R. S., & Perry, K. E. (2011). Like a fish out of water: Reconsidering disaster recovery and the role of place and social capital in community disaster resilience. *American Journal of Community Psychology, 48*(3–4), 395–411. doi.org/10.1007/s10464-011-9427-0

Davidson, J. L., Jacobson, C., Lyth, A., et al. (2016). Interrogating resilience: Toward a typology to improve its operationalization. *Ecology and Society*, *21*(2), Article 27. doi.org/10.5751/ES-08450-210227

Federal Emergency Management Agency (FEMA). (2011). *A whole community approach to emergency management: Principles, themes, and pathways for action* (FDOC Publication 104-008-1). Washington, DC: US Department of Homeland Security. www.fema.gov/media-library/assets/documents/23781

Folke, C. (2016). Resilience (republished). *Ecology and Society*, *21*(4), Article 44. doi.org/10.5751/ES-09088-210444

Gall, M., Cutter, S. L., & Nguyen, K. (2014). *Transformative development and disaster risk management* (IRDR AIRDR Publication No. 4). Beijing: Integrated Research on Disaster Risk.

Généreux, M., Petit, G., Lac-Mégantic Community Outreach Team, & O'Sullivan, T. (2018). Public health approach to supporting resilience in Lac-Mégantic: The EnRiCH Framework. In E. Ziglio (Ed.), *Health 2020 priority area four: Creating supportive environments and resilient communities – A compendium of inspirational examples* (pp. 156–162). Geneva, Switzerland: World Health Organization. www.euro.who.int/en/publications/abstracts/health-2020-prior ity-area-four-creating-supportive-environments-and-resilient-communities.-a-compendium-of-inspirational-examples-2018

Harris, K. (2020, March 18). *Trudeau unveils $82B COVID-19 emergency response package for Canadians, businesses*. CBC News. www.cbc.ca/news/politics/economic-aid-package-coronavirus-1.5501037

Holling, C. S. (1973). Resilience and stability of ecological systems. *Annual Review of Ecology and Systematics*, *4*, 1–23. www.jstor.org/stable/2096802

Jones, J., & Barry, M. M. (2011). Developing a scale to measure synergy in health promotion partnerships. *Global Health Promotion*, *18*(2), 36–44. doi.org/10.1177/1757975911404762

Khan, Y., Tracey, S., O'Sullivan, T., Gournis, E., & Johnson, I. (2019). Retiring the flip phones: Exploring social media use for managing public health incidents. *Disaster Medicine and Public Health Preparedness*, *13*(5–6), 859–867. doi.org/10.1017/dmp.2018.147

Kickbusch, I., & Sakellarides, C. (2006). Flu city – smart city: Applying health promotion principles to a pandemic threat. *Health Promotion International*, *21*(2), 85–87. doi.org/10.1093/heapro/dal014

Krause, N. M., Freiling, I., Beets, B., & Brossard, D. (2020). Fact-checking as risk communication: The multi-layered risk of misinformation in times of COVID-19. *Journal of Risk Research*, 23(7–8), 1052–1059. doi.org/10.1080/13669877.2020.1756385

Kretzmann, J. P., & McKnight, J. (1996). *Voluntary organizations in low-income neighbourhoods: An unexplored community resource*. Evanston, IL: ABCD Institute. https://resources.depaul.edu/abcd-institute/publications/publica tions-by-topic/Documents/VoluntaryAssociations.pdf

Lechner, S., Jacometti, J., McBean, G., & Mitchison, N. (2016). Resilience in a complex world: Avoiding cross-sector collapse. *International Journal of Disaster Risk Reduction*, *19*, 84–91. doi.org/10.1016/j.ijdrr.2016.08.006

Leykin, D., Lahad, M., Cohen, R., Goldberg, A., & Aharonson-Daniel, L. (2016). The dynamics of community resilience between routine and emergency situations. *International Journal of Disaster Risk Reduction*, *15*, 125–131. doi.org/10.1016/j.ijdrr.2016.01.008

McCleary, J., & Figley, C. (2017). Resilience and trauma: Expanding definitions, uses, and contexts. *Traumatology*, *23*(1), 1–3. doi.org/10.1037/trm0000103

Moser, C., & Satterthwaite, D. (2008). *Towards pro-poor adaptation to climate change in the urban centres of low- and middle- income countries* (Human Settlement Development series: Climate Change and Cities Discussion Paper 3). London: International Institute for Environment and Development (IIED). www.iied.org/pubs/display.php?o=10564IIED

Norris, F. H., Stevens, S. P., Pfefferbaum, B., Wyche, K. F., & Pfefferbaum, R. L. (2008). Community resilience as a metaphor, theory, set of capacities and strategy for disaster readiness. *American Journal of Community Psychology*, *41*(1–2), 127–150. doi.org/10.1007/s10464-007-9156-6

O'Sullivan, T. L., Kuziemsky, C. E., Corneil, W., Lemyre, L., & Franco, Z. (2014). The EnRiCH Community Resilience Framework for High-Risk Populations. *PLoS Currents Disasters*. doi.org/10.1371/currents.dis.11381147bd5e89e38e78434a732f17db http://currents.plos.org/disasters/article/the-enrich-community-resilience-framework-for-high-risk-populations/.

O'Sullivan, T. L., Kuziemsky, C. E., Toal-Sullivan, D., & Corneil, W. (2013). Unraveling the complexities of disaster management: A framework for critical social infrastructure to promote population health and resilience, *Social Science & Medicine*, *93*, 238–246. doi.org/10.1016/j.socscimed.2012.07.040

O'Sullivan, T. L., & Phillips, K. (2019). From SARS to pandemic influenza: The framing of high-risk populations. *Natural Hazards*, *98*(1), 103–117. doi.org/10.1007/s11069-019-03584-6

Pfefferbaum, B., Van-Horn, R. L., & Pfefferbaum, R. L. (2017). A conceptual framework to enhance community resilience using social capital. *Clinical Social Work Journal*, *45*, 102–110. doi.org/10.1007/s10615-015-0556-z

Poortinga, W. (2012). Community resilience and health: The role of bonding, bridging, and linking aspects of social capital. *Health & Place*, *18*(2), 286–295. www.sciencedirect.com/science/article/abs/pii/S1353829211001912?via%3Dihub

Quaranta, G., Dalia, C., Salvati, L., & Salvia, R. (2019). Building resilience: An art–food hub to connect local communities. *Sustainability*, *11*(24), 7169–7183. doi.org/10.3390/su11247169

Southwick, S. M., Bonanno, G. A., Masten, A. S., Panter-Brick, C., & Yehuda, R. (2014). Resilience definitions, theory, and challenges: Interdisciplinary perspectives. *European Journal of Psychotraumatology*, *5*(1), Article 25338. doi.org/10.3402/ejpt.v5.25338

Statistics Canada. (2020, May 27). *Canadians' mental health during the COVID-19 pandemic*. www150.statcan.gc.ca/n1/en/daily-quotidien/200527/dq200527b-eng.pdf?st=AuLLfteM

Thomalla, F., Boyland, M., Johnson, K., et al. (2018). Transforming development and disaster risk. *Sustainability*, *10*(5), Article 1458. doi.org/10.3390/su10051458

Tyler, S., & Moench, M. (2012). A framework for urban climate resilience. *Climate and Development, 4*(4), 311–326. doi.org/10.1080/17565529.2012.745389

United Nations. (2020). *COVID-19 and human rights: We are all in this together.* Geneva, Switzerland: United Nations. www.un.org/sites/un2.un.org/files/un_policy_brief_on_human_rights_and_covid_23_april_2020.pdf

United Nations Development Programme (UNDP). (2015). *Transforming our world: The 2030 agenda for sustainable development.* Geneva, Switzerland: United Nations. https://sustainabledevelopment.un.org/content/documents/21252030%20Agenda%20for%20Sustainable%20Development%20web.pdf

United Nations Framework Convention on Climate (UNFCCC). (2015). *Paris agreement.* Geneva, Switzerland: United Nations. https://unfccc.int/sites/default/files/english_paris_agreement.pdf

United Nations Office for Disaster Risk Reduction (UNDRR). (2009). *2009 UNISDR terminology on disaster risk reduction (non-UN language translations).* Geneva, Switzerland: United Nations. www.undrr.org/publication/2009-unisdr-terminology-disaster-risk-reduction-non-un-language-translations

United Nations Office for Disaster Risk Reduction (UNDRR). (2015). *Sendai framework for disaster risk reduction 2015–2030.* Geneva, Switzerland: United Nations. www.unisdr.org/we/inform/publications/43291

United Nations Office for Disaster Risk Reduction (UNDRR). (2018). *Implementation guide for local disaster risk reduction and resilience strategies: A companion for implementing the Sendai Framework target E.* Geneva, Switzerland: United Nations. www.uncclearn.org/sites/default/files/inventory/unisdr_-_57399_drresiliencepublicreview.pdf

Walker, B., Holling, C., Carpenter, S., & Kinzig, A. (2004). Resilience, adaptability and transformability in social-ecological systems. *Ecology and Society, 9*(2), Article 5. www.ecologyandsociety.org/vol9/iss2/art5/

Wang, Y., McKee, M., Torbica, A., & Stuckler, D. (2019). Systematic literature review on the spread of health-related misinformation on social media. *Social Science & Medicine, 240*, Article 112552. doi.org/10.1016/j.socscimed.2019.112552

World Health Organization. (2009). *Whole-of-society pandemic readiness: WHO guidelines for pandemic preparedness and response in the non- health sector.* Geneva, Switzerland: World Health Organization. www.who.int/influenza/preparedness/pandemic/2009-0808_wos_pandemic_readiness_final.pdf

Yong, A. G., & Lemyre, L. (2019). Getting Canadians prepared for natural disasters: A multi-method analysis of risk perception, behaviors, and the social environment. *Natural Hazards, 98*(1), 319–341. https://link.springer.com/article/10.1007/s11069-019-03669-2

Zarocostas, J. (2020). How to fight an infodemic. *The Lancet, 395*(10225). www.thelancet.com/action/showPdf?pii=S0140-6736%2820%2930461-X

13 The Consumer Recovery Movement in the United States

Historical Considerations, Key Concepts, and Next Steps for Action

Maria Guevara Carpio, Naomi Chee, Manjari Swarna, and Caroline S. Clauss-Ehlers

13.1 Introduction: The Consumer Recovery Movement and Early Policies

Throughout history various underrepresented groups have catalyzed social movements to advocate for federal recognition and support (Clauss-Ehlers et al., 2019; Parham & Clauss-Ehlers, 2016). The United States has progressed as a nation due to the efforts of various movements that fought for civil rights, women's rights, human rights, the rights of people of color, the rights of children, and the rights of LGBTQ+ communities, among others. In addition, another movement began in the 1930s. This movement focused on gaining rights and federal support for those with mental health issues, and became known as the *consumer recovery movement* (Gehart, 2011). This movement, like others in our history, advocated for change and a better quality of life. More specifically, the consumer recovery model emphasized autonomy, advocacy, and community engagement. Present-day consumer recovery movement goals focus on people with mental illness leading their lives and contributing to society while engaging in treatment, through principles of recovery (Davidson, 2016; Substance Abuse and Mental Health Services Administration [SAMHSA], 2012).

The consumer recovery movement continued to develop in response to feelings of helplessness engendered by a mental health system focused on pathology and stigma. As research increasingly demonstrated hopeful outcomes for serious mental illnesses such as schizophrenia (Bellack & Drapalski, 2012), consumers, family members, communities, and healthcare professionals increasingly supported a consumer-driven recovery movement focused on hope and empowerment. Bellack and Drapalski (2012) state:

> [T]here is growing recognition that traditional paternalistic mental health services have generated feelings of hopelessness and helplessness among many consumers, promoting dependence, and fostering stigma. In response to the failure of traditional services, consumers and many professionals have promoted a recovery movement, based on a model of recovery and health care that emphasizes hope, respect, and consumer control of their lives and mental health services. (p. 156)

The word "consumer" in the consumer recovery movement emerged from a consumer movement in the 1970s that addressed a range of health considerations (ourconsumerplace.com, n.d.). The impetus for this movement came from people who used health care wanting to have more say about healthcare decisions. This led to the idea of consumers influencing healthcare policy (ourconsumerplace.com.au, n.d.).

In this spirit, SAMHSA convened a working group in 2010 to address recovery as "a primary goal for behavioral health care" (SAMHSA, 2012, p. 2). This working group consisted of a range of constituencies including consumers of mental health and substance abuse services. The group was pioneering in efforts to develop one overall definition for recovery. Having one unified term for recovery was a historical shift in the recovery movement as previous models presented different definitions of recovery for mental health and substance use disorders (SAMHSA, 2012). The group derived an overall "working definition of recovery from mental health disorders and/or substance use disorders [as]: A process of change through which individuals improve their health and wellness, live a self-directed life, and strive to reach their full potential" (p. 3). The Recovery Support Strategic Initiative, SAMHSA identified four areas that support recovery – health, home, purpose, and community. The ten guiding principles of recovery that emerged from these areas were: "Recovery emerges from hope"; "Recovery is person-driven"; "Recovery occurs via many pathways"; "Recovery is holistic"; "Recovery is supported by peers and allies"; "Recovery is supported through relationship and social networks"; "Recovery is culturally-based and influenced"; "Recovery is supported by addressing trauma"; "Recovery involves individual, family, and community strengths and responsibility"; and "Recovery is based on respect" (SAMHSA, 2012, see www.samhsa.gov/recovery for more information).

These ten principles underscore key themes in the consumer recovery movement. The importance of hope is a critical factor in recovery and can be considered the "catalyst of the recovery process" (SAMHSA, 2012, p. 4). The recovery process is person-driven and reflects many different pathways. This means that there is no one way to move forward in recovery efforts. Pathways are not necessarily linear, leading directly from point A to point B. Rather, it is important for all of us to acknowledge that pathways, as implied by the term, are characterized by different routes, some leading back to point A and others winding their way forward to point B. These efforts seek to increase resilience and decrease trauma in holistic and culturally responsive ways (Clauss-Ehlers et al., 2019).

This chapter describes the history of the consumer mental health movement with a focus on legislation and the shift from institutionalization to community-based mental health centers (see Table 13.1 for a timeline of events that influenced the consumer recovery movement). Obstacles to the consumer movement are presented such as the role of ambiguity, challenges faced by consumer-operated services organizations, and mental health-related

Table 13.1 *A timeline of key events that supported the consumer recovery movement*

Timeframe/Dates	Events/Policies
1900s–1950s	Number of people with mental illnesses admitted to state hospitals exponentially increases
1930s	Early stages of the consumer recovery movement in the USA
July 3, 1946	National Mental Health Act of 1946 becomes law; this calls for the National Institute of Mental Health to be developed
July 1, 1947	US Public Health Service Division of Mental Hygiene awards first research grant
1948	The Fountain House building is purchased and Fountain House emerges as the first clubhouse in the clubhouse model
April 15, 1949	The National Institute of Mental Health (NIMH) is launched
1955	Mental Health Study Act of 1955
1961	*Action for Mental Health* is published
1963	Community Mental Health Act is passed
1965	Authorized by Title XIX of the Social Security Act, Medicaid was signed into law in 1965 alongside Medicare
February 17, 1977	President Jimmy Carter establishes the President's Commission on Mental Health
1978	*Report to the President's Commission on Mental Health* is published
February 7, 1979	First Lady Rosalynn Carter testifies before the Senate Human Resources Committee's Subcommittee on Health and Scientific Research, stressing the importance of supporting mental health programs and the 117 recommendations made by the Commission
1980	Mental Health Systems Act of 1980 legislation signed by President Jimmy Carter
August 13, 1981	President Ronald Reagan signs the Omnibus Budget Reconciliation Act of 1981, thus repealing much of the 1980 Mental Health Systems Act
July 26, 1990	American with Disabilities Act (ADA) signed into law by President George H. W. Bush
1990s	Paid positions emerge to hire peers to support people with mental illnesses
June 22, 1999	The United States Supreme Court ruled in *Olmstead* v. *L. C.* that segregation of people with mental health issues and development disabilities in institutions when community-based treatment is appropriate is in violation of the ADA's title II
March 23, 2010	President Barack Obama signs the Patient Protection and Affordable Care Act into law
May 2010 (originally September 23, 2010)	The Patient Protection and Affordable Care Act extends coverage on a family health insurance plan until twenty-six years of age
August 2010	Meeting of diverse constituencies, including consumers and SAMHSA to provide one overall working definition of recovery that includes recovery from mental health disorders and/or substance use disorders; the Recovery Support Strategic Initiative presents 4 areas that support recovery (e.g., health, home, purpose, and community)
2014	The Patient Protection and Affordable Care Act requires small group and individual health insurance plans to include ten essential health categories, including mental health and substance use services

stigma (van Zelst, 2020). An interview conducted with Dr. Eve Byrd, director of The Carter Center's Mental Health Program, demonstrates principles of recovery in action. It describes programmatic efforts committed to the recovery model and person-directed care. The chapter concludes with considerations of next steps to further the consumer recovery movement.

13.2 State Hospitals

Community-based mental health programs became a point of emphasis for the consumer recovery movement in response to the rampant use of state institutions for the treatment of mental illnesses. From the beginning of the 1900s to the mid-1950s, the number of patients admitted to state hospitals increased threefold (Gronfein, 1985). The immense increase in state hospital admissions was in part due to the social stigma that surrounded mental illness. Due to a lack of education and public understanding, people with mental illnesses were feared by the larger society and ultimately sent to hospitals, often involuntarily (Gronfein, 1985). As a result, there was a lack of emphasis on helping those with mental illnesses learn skills that would help them reintegrate into society, as they were treated as a subgroup to be kept separate from society. The deinstitutionalization of state hospitals was promoted through the creation of advocacy efforts and policies that led to a focus on community-based mental health care and supported the consumer recovery movement.

13.3 Critical Mental Health Policies: 1946–1990

13.3.1 National Mental Health Act of 1946

Goals of the consumer recovery movement were slowly achieved over time through the enactment of policies, beginning with the National Mental Health Act of 1946 (Grob, 2005). The National Mental Health Act of 1946 came as a byproduct of the practices and observations gleaned from working with soldiers with mental illnesses during World War II (Grob, 2005). Preceding World War II, the common belief surrounding mental health treatment was based on the view that state mental hospitals were the most efficient mode of treatment. However, once the military began "treating soldiers with psychiatric symptoms and returning them to their units" it became evident that outpatient treatment was more effective than the previous methods of isolation (Grob, 2005, p. 426).

Following this shift in ideology, the National Mental Health Act of 1946 was passed and in 1949 the National Institute of Mental Health (NIMH) was created, serving as the foundation for mental health policy reforms. NIMH was a turning point in mental health treatment because it focused more on community-based programs as opposed to state hospitals for those with mental illnesses. By creating community-based programs, the aim of NIMH was to decrease the amount of patients being sent to hospitals (Grob, 2005). On July 1, 1947, the first mental health research grant was awarded (titled *Basic Nature of the Learning Process*, given to Dr. Winthrop N. Kellogg at Indiana University) by the US Public Health Service Division of Mental Hygiene (National Institutes of Health [NIH], n. d.). This initial grant award had significant implications for the consumer recovery movement as it indicated a shift toward supporting research to understand mental health issues.

13.3.2 Mental Health Study Act of 1955

One key policy passed shortly after the creation of the NIMH was the Mental Health Study Act of 1955. This occurred during President Dwight Eisenhower's administration. The Mental Health Study Act called for "an objective, thorough, nationwide analysis and reevaluation of the human and economic problems of mental health" (NIH, n.d.). It led to the creation of a commission that published an extensive report known as the *Action for Mental Health* in 1961 (Mechanic & Rochefort, 1992). This publication was yet another vital turning point for the consumer recovery movement, as it again emphasized the importance of community with regard to mental health outreach programs and assessed the status of the mental health system in the United States.

13.3.3 Community Mental Health Centers Act of 1963

President John F. Kennedy developed a committee in response to the *Action for Mental Health* (1961) publication that considered the federal response to this contribution. In 1963, President Kennedy passed the Community Mental Health Centers Act, which was significant in providing support for mental health programs at a federal level (Mechanic & Rochefort, 1992). Further, at this time, the NIMH was charged with overseeing community mental health centers (CMHCs) throughout the USA.

Despite providing federal recognition of the need for community-based outreach programs, however, the CMHCs "at best, [had] a minor impact on reducing hospital populations after 1965" (Grob, 2005, p. 427). Although having the intentions to reduce mental hospital populations, the CMHC Act was not very successful in accommodating those with severe mental illnesses. It lacked the ability to provide those with mental illnesses proper access to clinics and psychiatrists (Grob, 2005).

This was due in large part to insufficient funding and a lack of trained professional staff who could support the transitions of those moving from institutions to community care as well as supporting those in the community who were vulnerable to being institutionalized (Young Minds Advocacy, n.d.). Young Minds Advocacy (n.d.) states:

> Despite this progress, however, public mental health systems largely failed to develop sufficient resources and staffing adequate to treat and support individuals in home and community-based settings. The service array in many communities was, and often continues to be, insufficiently comprehensive and intensive to meet the needs of young people and adults returning from or at risk of institutional care. Many public mental health systems were, and remain, critically underfunded and understaffed.

As a result, despite making strides for the mental health community, the consumer recovery movement had still much to accomplish in terms of establishing reforms with long-lasting impact.

13.3.4 The Carter Administration's Efforts to Support the Consumer Recovery Movement

It was not until the 1970s that reforms, especially under the Carter administration, would provide greater focus on community programs and support for those with mental health illnesses. The creation of various federally funded programs such as Medicaid and Medicare in 1965 allowed for the transition of patients from hospitals to nursing homes and other subsidized forms of living and was an attempt at integration into the community (Grob, 2005; Mechanic & Rochefort, 1992). However, due to individualized efforts made state by state, the deinstitutionalization from mental health hospitals to communities was not uniform around the country (Mechanic & Rochefort, 1992).

Such an attempt at uniform policy and reform for mental health issues came with the election of Jimmy Carter as president in 1977. One of President Carter's first steps toward addressing mental health nationally was through the creation of the President's Commission on Mental Health (PCMH; Parham & Clauss-Ehlers, 2016). An important aspect of the title of the Commission was a shift from using the term mental illness to using the term mental health. The change in terms suggests a paradigm shift "based on the application of a public health model that emphasized the role of the environment, social services, and prevention rather than the traditional psychiatric focus on the diagnosis and treatment of severe and persistent mental disorders" (Grob, 2005, pp. 429–430).

A direct statement made by the Commission was to give the mental health community recognition on a federal level with the rationale that "groups composed of individuals with mental or emotional problems are in existence or are being formed all over the United States" (PCMH, 1978, p. 14–15). First Lady Rosalynn Carter served as honorary chair of the PCMH. Her advocacy and contributions in this role set the stage for the passage of the Mental Health Systems Act in 1980. Commission members were selected to represent a very diverse group of leaders who could take a broad view of the issues and actions necessary to protect and promote the mental health of all Americans. A consumer with a history of serious mental illness also served as a member of the Commission. The PCMH members were appointed by President Carter as follows: Thomas E. Bryant, Chairperson; First Lady Rosalynn Carter, Honorary Chair; Ruth B. Love; Priscilla Allen; Allen Beigel; José A. Cabranes; John J. Conger; Thomas Conlan; Virginia Dayton; LaDonna Harris; Beverly Long; Florence Mahoney; Martha Mitchell; Mildred Mitchell-Bateman; Harold Richman; Julius B. Richmond; Reymundo Rodriquez; George Tarjan; Franklin E. Vilas, Jr.; Glenn E. Watts; and Charles V. Willie (see Grob, 2005 for additional details regarding members).

The PCMH sought the expertise of more than four hundred volunteers who served on task panels and subpanels focused on specific mental health topics and legislation to support the community. After six months and four public hearings, the PCMH issued a preliminary *Report to the President*. This report addressed four main areas of concern, one of which focused on community-based mental health services. Here the report advocated for the delivery of community-based mental health services. Current definitions of community mental health care incorporate a recovery perspective that focuses on

> the principles and practices needed to promote mental health for a local population by: a) addressing population needs in ways that are accessible and acceptable; b) building on the goals and strengths of people who experience mental illnesses; c) promoting a wide network of supports, services and resources of adequate capacity; and d) emphasizing services that are both evidence-based and recovery-oriented. (Thornicroft, Deb, & Henderson, 2016, p. 276)

Other recommendations included the creation of group care housing at state and local levels, increased funding for CMHCs, and increased training for those interested in working in community-based programs (Grob, 2005). Additional areas of concern conveyed in the report included the financing needed for health services, supporting research, developing intervention and prevention efforts, and supporting public education to further an overall understanding of mental health issues (Grob, 2005; Parham & Clauss-Ehlers, 2016).

Through subsequent research and additional efforts made by PCMH panels, the final report, *Report to the President's Commission on Mental Health*, was issued in April 1978, just a little more than a year since the Commission had been appointed (Grob, 2005). The report acknowledged that there were still many groups who were not receiving proper support and resources, such as those with "chronic illnesses, children, adolescents and older Americans" (Grob, 2005, p. 441). Many of the points previously discussed in the preliminary report were emphasized, including fortifying community mental health services, providing benefits for emergency, outpatient, and inpatient care with regard to public and private mental health services, and increasing funds for training. However, there was also the inclusion of reforms that dealt with protecting patients' rights and creating an advocacy system for those with mental illnesses, including accessibility to mental health services by those in prison and fighting against discrimination (PCMH, 1978, 1: pp. 42–45).

As honorary chairperson, Mrs. Carter played a critical role in promoting awareness of mental health issues and leading efforts that led to the 1980 Mental Health Systems Act being signed into law. For instance, on February 8, 1979, Mrs. Carter testified before the Senate Labor and Human Resources Committee's Subcommittee on Health and Scientific Research about the importance of supporting mental health programs (Hunter, 1979). Senator Kennedy had great praise for Mrs. Carter's testimony, stating that it was important to "take the issue of mental illness out of the closet and into the sunlight" (as cited in Hunter, 1979). Mrs. Carter was the second First Lady in history to testify before a Congressional Committee. A First Lady had not testified before Congress since the 1940s when First Lady Eleanor Roosevelt testified, followed by a second time while serving as the Office of Civilian Defense's assistant director (Chicago Tribune, 1993; Hunter, 1979).

After reviewing the report, President Carter directed the Secretary of Health, Education, and Welfare to prepare legislation that would implement many of its recommendations. President Carter announced the legislation at a White House briefing in May 1980. The Mental Health Systems Act was enacted in October of 1980 (Grob, 2005). This was a milestone in mental health efforts that supported community-based mental health and the consumer recovery movement. At the forefront of the policy was the intent to develop and implement programs, especially those with an emphasis on community support and involvement (Grob, 2005). The law also focused on increasing funding for mental health services, such as the subsidization of grants from the government to CMHCs (Grob, 2005). Yet, despite addressing many of the concerns made by the panels and commissions from the Carter administration, the Mental Health Systems Act faced difficulties under the Reagan administration. Much of the law was repealed by President Reagan and the US Congress when President Reagan signed the Omnibus Budget Reconciliation Act of 1981.

13.3.5 The Americans with Disabilities Act

A next major policy reform that supported principles of the consumer recovery movement came with the passing of the Americans with Disabilities Act (ADA) in 1990. The ADA was signed into law by President George H. W. Bush on July 26, 1990. The ADA acknowledged the struggles faced by those with mental illnesses, stating how "historically, society has tended to isolate and segregate individuals with disabilities" (ADA, 1990). The purpose of this

Act was to convey a "clear and comprehensive national mandate for the elimination of discrimination" and "clear, strong, consistent, enforceable standards addressing discrimination" (ADA, 1990).

The ADA redefined mental illness as a mental disability, being that it restricts an individual's ability to partake in "major life activities" (ADA, 1990). By changing the classification of mental illness from a sickness to a disability, the ADA allowed those with mental health illnesses to gain greater support from the government and access various accommodations. A major point of emphasis was the facilitation of recovery through inclusion in the community (Davidson, 2016). Efforts sought to provide the most integrated setting for recovery and aid (ADA, 1990).

While focusing heavily on preventing discrimination against those with mental illnesses, the ADA can also be applied to instances that promote community-based outreach programs. The 1999 decision made by the United States Supreme Court in the case of *Olmstead* v. *L. C.* is one such example. *Olmstead* v. *L. C.* came about when two women with mental illnesses and developmental disabilities, Lois Curtis and Elaine Wilson, were treated at Georgia Regional Hospital-Atlanta. Although the women were not admitted against their will, they were kept in the confines of the psychiatric unit for years after the clinical recommendation that they should be integrated into community-based programs (Olmstead v. L. C., 1999).

In the face of such confinement, Lois Curtis and Elaine Wilson sued under the ADA. Following deliberation, the United States Supreme Court ruled on June 22, 1999 that the detainment of those with mental illnesses in isolated institutions was a form of discrimination and that states must comply with professional orders of admittance to community-oriented programs (Burnim, 2015). The ruling of this case showed how the government was beginning to prioritize community-based methods of recovery as opposed to individual recovery in institutions.

13.4 Current Consumer Recovery Movement Programs

Self-advocacy programs are one result of the consumer recovery movement. Self-advocacy refers to a person with a mental illness knowing one's rights to engage in important decision-making. Self-advocacy has been defined as "the ability to speak up for yourself about things that are important for you" (Equip for Equality, n.d., p. 2). Equip for Equality describes key components of self-advocacy, including "understanding your needs and strengths, learning how to get information, knowing your rights, making your own decisions about important issues affecting you, and reaching out to others for support and help when you need it" (n.d., p. 2). Some people with serious mental illnesses may be in a position where there are substantial impediments associated with their ability to make decisions for themselves. A more recent term, supported decision-making (SDM), addresses such concerns. SDM refers to "recruitment of trusted supports to enhance an individual's capacity in the decision making process, enabling them to retain autonomy in life decisions" (Jeste et al., 2018, p. 28). Here we see the role of advocacy emerge via SDM when an individual needs support with decision-making.

13.4.1 Consumer Operated Services Organizations

Peer-support programs were started by consumer volunteers who mentored individuals struggling with mental illnesses. Peer supporters are defined as people "who have experienced a mental illness and are either in or have achieved some degree of recovery" (Davidson, 2015). "Peer supporters use personal experiences of illness and recovery – along with relevant training and supervision – to facilitate, guide, and mentor another person's recovery journey by instilling hope, role modeling recovery, and supporting people in their own efforts to reclaim meaningful and self-determined lives in the communities of their choice" (Davidson, 2015).

Peer support developed in the 1980s out of the consumer recovery movement. However, Professor Larry Davidson, who serves as the director of the Yale Program for Recovery and Community Health at Yale University's School of Medicine, shares that the idea of peer support programs actually started in France in the 1790s when Jean Baptiste Pussin, the superintendent of Bicêtre Hospital's mental health ward, had patients take on the role of supporting other patients (Davidson, 2015). By the 1990s, paid positions emerged to hire peers to engage in roles that ranged from "those of case manager aide or housing support staff to the new roles of recovery educator" (Davidson, 2016, p. 1094). Consumer-operated services organizations (COSOs) are one type of advocacy program that developed in response to the importance of peer support.

Consumer-operated services organizations, also known as consumer-operated service programs, consumer-run organizations, peer support programs, peer services, and peer agencies, provide peer support to support those with mental illnesses (US Department of Health and Human Services [USDHHS], n.d.). COSOs have the purpose of empowering consumers and promote self-governing, with at least 51% of governing boards consisting of mental health consumers (USDHHS, n.d.). The underlying philosophy of COSOs is that "people with psychiatric difficulties can and do recover, living meaningful lives" and that "peers can help one another with the recovery process in ways that professionals cannot" (USDHHS, n.d.).

COSOs include services such as peer counseling, drop-in centers, educational groups, support groups, and crisis response initiatives (USDHHS, n.d.). Services provided through these venues include advocacy, support with basic needs, and support with concerns linked to housing, employment, and education (USDHHS, n.d.). COSO participation seeks to further the ten principles of recovery discussed at the outset of this chapter. Through peer support, for instance, COSOs seek to promote a sense of hope by helping people with mental illnesses see that recovery is possible. This is done by allowing those who are suffering to have a safe space to share their experiences, develop coping skills, build a support network by engaging with others, address trauma, and build resilience (Clauss-Ehlers, 2008).

Empirical research on COSOs has consistently demonstrated that peer support programs promote positive outcomes among those with mental illnesses (Campbell, 2005; Goldstrom et al., 2006; Rogers et al., 2007). Jean Campbell's seminal research on peer programs identified

> 46 common ingredients (CIs) of consumer-operated service programs and identified key peer practices that effectively promote psychological well-being, empowerment and hope of recovery among participating adults diagnosed with severe mental illness or impairment. The multi-site findings suggest that when consumer operated services programs are integrated within the continuum of community care they enhance opportunities for mental health consumers to live, work, learn, and participate fully in the community.   (Campbell, 2008, p. 1)

The forty-six common ingredients (CIs) are listed under six categories: operating structure (e.g., COSOs are operated by consumers); environment (e.g., COSO environments are accessible, safe, and informal); belief system (e.g., peer principle, helper's principle, recovery, empowerment, respect for diversity, spirituality); peer support (e.g., supporting peers, storytelling, arts and creativity, consciousness raising, crisis prevention, peer mentoring); education (e.g., problem-solving strategies, receiving and providing informal problem-solving support, skills practice, job readiness); and advocacy (e.g., self-advocacy, peer advocacy, participant outreach) (see Campbell, 2008 for a detailed description of CIs).

Two specific examples of advocacy programs are Project GREAT (Georgia Recovery-Based Educational Approach to Treatment) and the Fountain House Movement. Each program takes a different approach, with the former supporting the consumer movement through academia, and the latter exploring unique settings for recovery that incorporates the clubhouse model (Mabe et al., 2014; Norman, 2006).

13.4.2 Project GREAT

Project GREAT (Georgia Recovery-Based Educational Approach to Treatment) developed as an effort to "transform the education and practice of an academic department of psychiatry into a recovery-oriented one with the focus on shaping the recovery knowledge, attitudes, and practices of psychiatry and psychology faculty and trainees" (Mabe et al., 2014, p. 347). The context for the development of this partnership was the Department of Psychiatry and Health Behavior's observed need for a transformation of the "mental health care system" amid increasing criticism of traditional mental healthcare practices alongside increasing increased advocacy and recovery-oriented practices (Mabe et al., 2014, p. 348).

In response to this context, the partnership developed a curriculum to educate physicians, and train psychologists and other professionals within their department on recovery-related approaches. Project GREAT's goal was to achieve cultural changes in trainees and the overall department. Before developing the curriculum, the researchers analyzed the environment and the learners' characteristics, established partnerships, identified core principles as the framework for the project, and combined two method approaches (Mabe et al., 2014). Given the curriculum was focused on educating about recovery-oriented practices, dismantling stigmatization against people with mental illnesses, and integrating the consumer input, the researchers hired two certified peer specialists (CPSs). Their participation was critical as it offered a consumer's perspective on mental health services.

The researchers acknowledged that "both psychiatrists and psychologists were well indoctrinated in traditional 'illness views' of mental health care" (Mabe et al., 2014, p. 349). This meant that traditional views of treatment in this hospital context defined the relationship between the clinician and the patient as one where the professional is viewed as the "expert" with the responsibility to "cure." In contrast, a recovery approach highlights patients' strengths and resources in addition to the clinician's expertise (Mabe et al., 2014). Such an approach is reflected in the American Psychological Association's (APA) revised multicultural guidelines that emphasize a bidirectional relationship that involves a give and take between the person offering services and the person receiving them (Clauss-Ehlers et al., 2019). Project GREAT researchers found their work was challenging but rewarding. They emphasized the lack of empirical data regarding recovery model training. Overall, they concluded that the participation of CPSs was crucial to transforming clinicians' attitudes (Mabe et al., 2014).

13.4.3 Fountain House Movement

A second example of consumer recovery programs is the Fountain House Movement (see www.fountainhouse.org). This is a method of consumer support based on the clubhouse model (Norman, 2006). Similar to COSOs, in the clubhouse model, people with mental health illnesses advocate for themselves and form an organization. Clubhouses provide memberships, relationships, employment, and more. Members have communal responsibility and daily tasks to complete. There are morning meetings and board meetings as well. Clubhouses often have an advisory board that consists of people from the local community, administrators, staff, and people with lived experience (Norman, 2006). The clubhouse focus on community reflects the view that "the process of rehabilitation includes not only the service given by the professional but also the effort made by the social network and by the individual" (Norman, 2006, p. 185).

There are hundreds of clubhouses throughout the world. The first club-house, Fountain House, was founded in New York City in 1948 by six patients who wanted to recreate the respect and support they shared with one another when they met as a group in a hospital clubroom (see www .fountainhouse.org/about/history for more information about the history of Fountain House). Fountain House aimed to promote a nonpsychiatric environment for people with mental illnesses that offered support and encouraged autonomy. Employment training sought to facilitate better employment outcomes (Norman, 2006).

Empirical research has explored members' opinions of the clubhouse model (Norman, 2006). Christina Norman was one such researcher whose work specifically focused on a clubhouse in Gothenburg, Sweden (Norman, 2006). Interviewees' responses indicated that clubhouse members connected daily tasks to personal growth and that the clubhouse experience was meaningful once they viewed themselves as members (Norman, 2006). Many of the research participants highlighted the support of the staff and their own willpower as key factors in their recovery and moving forward (Norman, 2006). Overall, programs such as those that follow the clubhouse model seek to advocate for consumers and the consumer movement either through peer support, nonprofit efforts, training professionals in the mental health field, and creating supportive communities. Notwithstanding these heroic efforts, for the consumer recovery movement to continue forward and for funding to be allocated to this area, it is necessary to address obstacles and have policies in place.

13.5 Obstacles to the Consumer Recovery Movement

13.5.1 Ambiguity

The consumer movement is a relatively new construct, making it difficult to assess its current effectiveness with regard to treatment programs due in part to a lack of solid parameters that define the treatment. The ambiguity surrounding treatment models and methods is reflected in the dearth of research and assessments about the effectiveness of the consumer movement (Bellack & Drapalski, 2012). This introduces a need for new research methodologies that account for potential challenges associated with evaluating changes in the status of a person's mental health when following the recovery model.

Though there is little empirical evidence surrounding the recovery model, there is a body of research that demonstrates the efficacy of COSOs (Segal, 2011). Based on the peer support model, social integration, personal empower-ment, and self-efficacy all increased in conjunction with the treatment of mental illness within the recovery model. New assessment methods are also being developed to better assess the effectiveness of the model, such as the creation of the Maryland Assessment of Recovery in People with Serious Mental Illness (MARS; Drapalski et al., 2012). For the consumer recovery movement to continue to grow, decreasing ambiguity is important with measures such as MARS (Drapalski et al., 2012) that seek to operationalize and document recovery processes.

13.5.2 Challenges Faced by COSOs

Nevertheless, the consumer movement still faces challenges and is not completely accepted by some communities. For instance, research by Tanenbaum (2011) indicated that COSOs' directors described their relationships with providers as "difficult." Tanenbaum (2011) reports: "[the providers] may ignore the presence of COSOs in their communities or even advise patients against joining them" (p. 197). Here study findings are thought to reflect providers' beliefs that peer-provided services have no capacity to be beneficial for people with mental illnesses.

13.5.3 Mental Health-Related Stigma

"The US National Institute of Mental Health considers stigma to be the most debilitating aspect of a mental illness. It is easy to see why. Stigma increases mental distress and leads to shame, avoidance of treatment, social isolation, and, consequently, a deterioration in health" (Seeman, 2015, p. 309). One of the major goals of the consumer movement is to transform current treatment so that it resonates with the recovery model. A central goal of this transformation is to destigmatize mental illness and to decrease the levels of discrimination faced by people with mental health disorders (Ahmed, Buckley, & Mabe, 2012). Part of what promotes stigma is the ongoing distinction that is made between physical and mental health and related practices. It might be said that differentiating physical versus mental health concerns perpetuates the idea that mental illness is less important than physical illness (Hunt & Resnick, 2015). Mental health recovery and physical health recovery have very similar goals and yet are treated very distinctly amongst the public. More work is needed to incorporate responsiveness to mental health practices within the primary care setting.

A central part of the recovery model is good social relationships during and following integration into the community. This can be severely hindered due to the way people with mental disorders are treated in society because of the stigma associated with mental illness. Seeman and colleagues (Seeman et al., 2016) conducted a global study about mental health-related stigma. Study findings indicated that while 45%–51% of participants from developed countries believed that "mental illness [was] similar to physical illness, only 7% of the same people believe that mental illness could be overcome" (Seeman, 2015, p. 309). Further, 7%–8% of participants from developed countries, and 15%–16% of participants from developing countries, supported the view that people with mental illness were more violent than people who did not have a mental illness. These results speak to the very real impact that mental health-related stigma has on people with mental illness, and has implications for family members in caretaking roles, as well as discrimination experienced by people with mental illnesses on a community level.

Another stigma-related issue that people with mental illnesses face is discrimination from medical professionals (Silversides, 2009). Research has indicated that "people with mental illness experience high levels of discrimination from family doctors, psychiatrists and emergency staff, and that mental health professionals are more likely than the general populace to support restrictions on people with mental illness" (Silversides, 2009, p. E317). These findings are in direct contrast with the goals and principles of the consumer recovery movement. A potentially negative outcome of mental health-related stigma is that people decide not to seek treatment due to the understandable fear of being stigmatized, labeled, and discriminated against (Henderson, Evans-Lacko, & Thornicroft, 2013). There is movement from the mental health community to develop programs that reduce stigma against mental health and promote mental health literacy (Clauss-Ehlers et al., 2020; Henderson et al., 2013; Silversides, 2009). Examples of some of these initiatives are illustrated in the interview that follows in Section 13.6.

13.6 Consumer Recovery in Action: An Interview with Dr. Eve Byrd, Director of The Carter Center Mental Health Program

The interview that follows highlights contemporary themes and efforts that characterize the consumer recovery movement. Dr. Eve Byrd, the director of The Carter Center (TCC) Mental Health Program is interviewed by the *Handbook* editor (who was a Rosalynn Carter Fellow for Mental Health Journalism in 2004–2005 and currently serves as an advisory board member for this program). The two main goals of TCC's Mental Health Program are "To reduce stigma and discrimination against people with mental illnesses" and "To achieve equity for mental healthcare comparable to other health care." The program aims to advance promotion, prevention, and early intervention services and focuses on improving access to care for the most vulnerable populations including children and older adults (TCC, n.d.). The interview seeks to capture these goals in action.

Caroline Clauss-Ehlers: How would you describe consumer recovery?

Dr. Eve Byrd: Consumer recovery from the Georgia perspective is person-centered, strengths-based, and individually goal directed. It's also participatory, with the person in recovery making choices. As stated by Mark Baker (Director of the Office of Recovery Transformation at the Georgia Department of Behavioral Health and Developmental Disabilities), the main question to be asked is: "What is working for you?" The focus is then building on those strengths.

And it's important to acknowledge that personal strengths don't need to be defined by one's mental illness or symptoms. I have found the participatory aspect of the consumer recovery movement to be very effective in my work. If we go in with our own preconceived notions as professionals, it doesn't work. We need to learn from the people we are working with about what's working for them.

Caroline Clauss-Ehlers: What gets in the way of supporting the consumer recovery movement?

Dr. Eve Byrd: We need to move away from thinking we know what's best for people. A central question for patient-centered care and person-centered care is: *How do you empower the person in their need for self-sufficiency?* Stigma also still exists. We see stigma playing out in the faulty belief that when someone has a mental illness, that person is unable to make decisions. We also don't necessarily take the time needed to build trust between consumers and their interactions with mental healthcare professionals and the healthcare system. If someone doesn't trust you, they don't share all the factors that influence their experiences – so we can be somewhat limited in helping someone and supporting their process.

Caroline Clauss-Ehlers: What are some program examples the Mental Health Program is engaged in that support the consumer recovery movement?

Dr. Eve Byrd: Mrs. Carter has always been sensitive to and concerned about the individual's lived experience. She has instilled in the Mental Health Program that what we do needs to be informed by that lived experience. We've incorporated work with the RESPECT Institute of Georgia that advocates for people with lived experience and facilitates people sharing their stories with the larger community (see www .gmhcn.org/respect-institute-of-georgia).

The Rosalynn Carter Fellowship Program for Mental Health Journalism is another program. The Journalism Fellowship program is meant to improve the way people write about mental illness – and, in so doing, provides a hope perspective. For instance, the Fellowship program considers how a solutions journalism perspective relates to mental health. This approach is opposite to a "If it bleeds it leads" perspective where media portray stories that use fear as a central mechanism to increase their readership/viewership. In the "If it bleeds it leads" approach, there can be a story of a situation based on fear – and people are left to take the story from where it ends, and do what they want with it. The Journalism Fellowship program takes a very different perspective. Our focus is to take the lead from the story the person with lived experience is sharing. If we read one story after another that portrays mental illness in a negative way (e.g., the "If it bleeds it leads" approach), that can be retraumatizing. It is the journalist's responsibility to obtain information from accurate sources in telling the whole story, including the "solutions" which are a part of the story that encourages hope, resilience, and that "recovery" is real, and so that journalists aren't reinforcing stigma.

Caroline Clauss-Ehlers: Moving forward, how can we engage in advocacy efforts to support the consumer recovery movement?

Dr. Eve Byrd: I think we have to remember the science and point to the science of the consumer recovery movement. For instance, working with peer specialists in mental health has been shown to be both effective clinically as well as cost effective. What peer specialists bring to the treatment team is effectiveness in engaging the person with lived experience and building trust. Private insurance companies are engaging peer specialists because they know it works. In light of COVID-19 and the current situation we are facing with regard to racism and discrimination, peer specialists are more important than ever. All people want to be understood. Peer specialists bring the trust factor which comes in working with someone with a lived experience to the strengths-based recovery movement.

13.7 Conclusion: Policy Developments and Implications for the Consumer Recovery Movement

Many policy developments have bolstered the ability of the government to provide support for the consumer movement and a recovery model. As mentioned, the Americans with Disabilities Act of 1990 helped redefine mental illness as a form of disability, allowing for accommodations to help those struggling with a mental health issue to have greater support for their recovery (Davidson, 2016). One of the most current policies affecting the consumer movement is the Patient Protection and Affordable Care Act (ACA) signed into law by President Barack Obama on March 23, 2010. Further, in May 2010 (a date that was going to initially be September 23, 2010) the ACA extended dependent care coverage to all individuals younger than age twenty-six (Centers for Medicare and Medicaid Services, n.d.). This was a critical shift as it meant that families worried about their children losing healthcare insurance coverage after milestones like graduating college and becoming young adults now had extended healthcare coverage for their dependents. Further, a high percentage of the age of onset (AOO) for psychotic disorders occurs during the teenage years and through emerging and early adulthood.

Research indicates, for instance, that psychotic disorders increase in prevalence between fifteen and seventeen years of age (Kessler et al., 2007). The AOO for schizophrenia is often between fifteen and thirty-five years of age (Kessler et al., 2007). As a result, the ACA extending dependent coverage to age twenty-six is particularly important for young adults (and their families) in need of mental health care during a first onset of psychosis.

Starting in 2014, the ACA provided a landmark expansion of healthcare coverage for mental health and substance use services, expanding such protections for more than sixty-two million Americans (Beronio et al., 2013).

> Beginning in 2014 under the law, all new small group and individual market plans will be required to cover ten Essential Health Benefit categories, including mental health and substance use disorder services, and will be required to cover them at parity with medical and surgical benefits. The Affordable Care Act builds on the Paul Wellstone and Pete Domenici Mental Health Parity and Addiction Equity Act of 2008 (MHPAEA, or the federal parity law), which requires group health plans and insurers that offer mental health and substance use disorder benefits to provide coverage that is comparable to coverage for general medical and surgical care.   (Beronio et al., 2013, p. 1)

This legislation promoted access and utilization of mental health services as evidenced by the increased number of people seeking treatment for various mental illnesses (Golberstein et al., 2015). However, the federal legislation is not necessarily being enforced at the state level. Compared to insurance coverage for physical health treatments, individuals needing behavioral health treatment (mental health and addiction treatment services) continue to have to pay more out of pocket because the majority of the states' statutes poorly define mental illness and do not enforce equitable coverage of mental health and addiction treatment by public and private insurers (Douglas et al., 2018; Melek, Davenport, & Gray, 2019).

Since 2011, there have been multiple ongoing attempts to repeal or modify the ACA (Riotta, 2017), rolling back the advances that have been made. As reported by *Newsweek*, at least seventy Republican-led attempts have sought to repeal or change the ACA (Riotta, 2017). The Economic Policy Institute (EPI) estimates that repealing the ACA would lead to a loss of health insurance coverage for 29.8 million people throughout the USA and a loss of 1.2 million jobs in healthcare and in other sectors (EPI, n.d.). EPI (n.d.) data indicate that increases in those who would lose their health insurance if ACA was repealed range from 53% (Alaska) to 273% (Massachusetts).

Sustained advocacy efforts are critical to supporting access to mental health and substance use services as provided for by the ACA. The ACA reflects critical recovery principles by bringing the healthcare system closer to being more holistic and recovery-oriented. Moving forward, initiatives are underway that seek to contribute to the consumer recovery movement.

For example, consumers are advocating for "several levers for person-centered clinical care" (Davidson, 2016, p. 1094). These would require trained professionals, called "health navigators," who assist patients with complex medical needs (Davidson, 2016).

Another initiative is to establish partnerships with mental health services (Happell & Scholz, 2017). Though consumers are involved in the recovery movement, it may be the case that they do not hold as much power as medical professionals and policymakers, who are in a position to intervene, design, and fund recovery supports. This power differential speaks to the importance of partners of the consumer recovery movement being invested in consumer goals. A related future goal of the consumer recovery movement is to increase organizational support and involvement and to find ways for partners to improve the recovery model through ongoing collaboration.

Community psychologists (e.g., psychologists who examine larger systemic and contextual factors that have an impact on people and organizations in efforts to promote empowerment, equity, and wellness) are instrumental partners to the consumer recovery movement and in a position to make a significant impact on the direction of mental health practices. Future directions for community psychology contributions to the consumer recovery movement include the development and implementation of empirical research that further explores principles and processes connected to the recovery model. Community psychologists can incorporate training and supervision that encourages trainees to be aware of the consumer-oriented recovery approach. Community psychologists can incorporate key values of empowerment and belonging through interventions and programmatic efforts that integrate peer support throughout a person's experience with services. Overall, collaboration between and among professional groups, building ongoing supports and partnerships for consumers, research designs that further the science of the consumer recovery movement, and funding for peer specialist recovery programs are key to continued advancement for the consumer recovery movement.

The histories of community psychology and the consumer recovery movement in the United States have some shared, overlapping themes. Just as community psychology developed out of the psychology field's limitations in addressing social issues, so too the consumer recovery movement developed out of mental health system limitations. Just as community psychology developed "amid a backdrop of mental health policies that promoted deinstitutionalization of people with mental illnesses" (Clauss-Ehlers, Chapter 1, this volume), so too the consumer recovery movement developed in response to consumers, family members, friends, mental health professionals, advocates, policymakers, educators, and many others who pushed away from a paternalistic system of care toward a holistic path of recovery.

References

Ahmed, A. O., Buckley, P. F., & Mabe, P. A. (2012). Recovery: International efforts at implementing and advancing the recovery model. *International Psychiatry: Bulletin of the Board of International Affairs of the Royal College of Psychiatrists, 9*(1), 4–6.

Americans with Disabilities Act. (1990). 42 U.S.C. §§ 12101–12141.

Bellack, A. S., & Drapalski, A. (2012). Issues and developments on the consumer recovery construct. *World Psychiatry: Official Journal of the World Psychiatric Association (WPA), 11*(3), 156–160. doi.org/10.1002/j.2051-5545.2012.tb00117.x

Beronio, K., Po, R., Skopec, L., & Glied, S. (2013). *ASPE Research Brief: Affordable Care Act will expand mental health and substance use disorder benefits and parity protections for 62 million Americans.* US Department of Health and Human Services.

Burnim, I. (2015). The promise of the Americans with Disabilities Act for people with mental illness. *Journal of the American Medical Association, 313*(22), 2223–2224. doi.org/10.1001/jama.2015.4015

Campbell, J. (2005). The historical and philosophical development of peer-run support programs. In S. Clay, B. Schell, P. W. Corrigan, & R. O. Ralph (Eds.), *On our own together: Peer programs for people with mental illness* (pp. 17–64). Nashville, TN: Vanderbilt Press.

Campbell, J. (2008). *Key ingredients of peer programs identified.* Missouri Institute of Mental Health. www.researchgate.net/publication/242273575_KEY_INGR EDIENTS_OF_PEER_PROGRAMS_IDENTIFIED

The Carter Center. (n.d.). *Mental health program.* www.cartercenter.org/resources/ pdfs/factsheets/mental-health-facts.pdf

Centers for Medicare and Medicaid Services. (n.d.). *Young adults and the Affordable Care Act: Protecting young adults and eliminating burdens on families and businesses.* www.cms.gov/CCIIO/Resources/Files/adult_child_fact_sheet

Chicago Tribune. (1993, September 27). *Hillary Clinton one of three first ladies to testify.* www.chicagotribune.com/news/ct-xpm-1993-09-27-9309280024-story.html

Clauss-Ehlers, C. S. (2008). Sociocultural factors, resilience, and coping: Support for a culturally sensitive measure of resilience. *Journal of Applied Developmental Psychology, 29*(3), 197–212. doi.org/10.1016/j.appdev.2008.02.004

Clauss-Ehlers, C. S., Chiriboga, D., Hunter, S. J., Roysircar, G., & Tummala-Narra, P. (2019). APA Multicultural Guidelines executive summary: Ecological approach to context, identity, and intersectionality. *American Psychologist, 74*(2), 232–244. doi.org/10.1037/amp0000382

Clauss-Ehlers, C. S., Guevara Carpio, M., & Weist, M. D. (2020). Mental health literacy: A strategy for global adolescent mental health promotion. *Adolescent Psychiatry, 10*(2), 73–83. doi.org/10.2174/2210676610666200204104429

Davidson, L. (2015, March 20). *History of the peer support movement.* International Association of Peer Supporters (iNAPS). https://na4ps.files.wordpress.com/ 2015/03/history-of-peer-support-davidson-webinar-19.pdf

Davidson, L. (2016). The recovery movement: Implications for mental health care and enabling people to participate fully in life. *Health Affairs, 35*(6), 1091–1097. doi.org/10.1377/hlthaff.2016.0153

Douglas, M., Wrenn, G., Bent-Weber, S., et al. (2018). *Evaluating state mental health and addiction parity laws: A technical report*. The Kennedy Forum. https://wellbeingtrust.org/areas-of-focus/policy-and-advocacy/reports/evaluating-state-mental-health-and-addiction-parity-statutes/

Drapalski, A. L., Medoff, D., Unick, G. J., et al. (2012). Assessing recovery of people with serious mental illness: Development of a new scale. *Psychiatry Services, 63*(1), 48–53. doi.org/10.1176/appi.ps.201100109

Economic Policy Institute. (n.d.). *How would repealing the Affordable Care Act affect health care and jobs in your state?* www.epi.org/aca-obamacare-repeal-impact/

Equip for Equality. (n.d.). *Personal decision-making: Self-advocacy for people with mental illness.* www.equipforequality.org/wp-content/uploads/2015/12/35_Self_Advocate_Mental_Illness_03.pdf

Gehart, D. R. (2011). The mental health recovery movement and family therapy, Part I: Consumer-led reform of services to persons diagnosed with severe mental illness. *Journal of Marital and Family Therapy, 38*(3), 429–442. doi.org/10.1111/j.1752-0606.2011.00230.x

Golberstein, E., Busch, S. H., Zaha, R., et al. (2015). Effect of the Affordable Care Act's young adult insurance expansions on hospital-based mental health care. *American Journal of Psychiatry, 172*(2), 182–189. doi.org/10.1176/appi.ajp.2014.14030375

Goldstrom, I., Campbell, J., Rogers, J., et al. (2006). Mental health consumer organizations: A national picture. In R. W. Manderscheid and J. T. Berry (Eds.), *Center for Mental Health Services: Mental health, United States, 2004* (DHHS Pub No. [SMA]-06-4195, pp. 247–255). Rockville, MD: Substance Abuse and Mental Health Services Administration.

Grob, G. N. (2005). Public policy and mental illnesses: Jimmy Carter's Presidential Commission on Mental Health. *The Milbank Quarterly, 83*(3), 425–456. doi.org/10.1111/j.1468-0009.2005.00408.x

Gronfein, W. (1985). Incentives and intentions in mental health policy: A comparison of the Medicaid and community mental health programs. *Journal of Health and Social Behavior, 26*(3), 192–206. doi.org/10.2307/2136752

Happell, B., & Scholz, B. (2017). Doing what we can, but knowing our place: Being an ally to promote consumer leadership in mental health. *International Journal of Mental Health Nursing, 27*(1), 440–447. doi.org/ 10.1111/inm.12404

Henderson, C., Evans-Lacko, S., & Thornicroft, G. (2013). Mental illness stigma, help seeking, and public health programs. *American Journal of Public Health, 103*(5), 777–780. doi.org/10.2105/AJPH.2012.301056

Hunt, M. G., & Resnick, S. G. (2015). Two birds, one stone: Unintended consequences and a potential solution for problems with recovery in mental health. *Psychiatric Services, 66*(11), 1235–1237. doi.org/ 10.1176/appi.ps.201400518

Hunter, M. (1979, February 8). Mrs. Carter, in Capitol debut, praised by Kennedy. *The New York Times.* www.nytimes.com/1979/02/08/archives/mrs-carter-in-capitol-debut-praised-by-kennedy-you-can-depend-on-it.html

Jeste, D. V., Eglit, G., Palmer, B. W., et al. (2018). Supported decision making in serious mental illness. *Psychiatry, 81*(1), 28–40. doi.org/10.1080/00332747.2017.1324697

Kessler, R. C., Amminger, G. P., Aguilar-Gaxiola, S., et al. (2007). Age of onset of mental disorders: A review of recent literature. *Current Opinion in Psychiatry*, *20*(4), 359–364. doi.org/10.1097/YCO.0b013e32816ebc8c

Mabe, P., Ahmed, A., Duncan, G., Fenley, G., & Buckley, P. (2014). Project GREAT: Immersing physicians and doctorally-trained psychologists in recovery-oriented care. *Professional Psychology: Research and Practice*, *45*(5), 347–356. doi.org/10.1037/a0037705

Mechanic, D., & Rochefort, D. A. (1992). A policy of inclusion for the mentally ill. *Health Affairs*, *11*(1), 128–150. doi.org/10.1377/hlthaff.11.1.128

Melek, S., Davenport, S., & Gray, T. J. (2019, November 19). *Addiction and mental health vs. physical health: Widening disparities in network use and provider reimbursement: A deeper analytical dive and updated results through 2017 for 37 million employees and dependents*. Milliman Research Report. http://assets.milliman.com/ektron/Addiction_and_mental_health_vs_physical_health_Wi dening_disparities_in_network_use_and_provider_reimbursement.pdf

National Institutes of Health. (n.d.). National Institute of Mental Health (NIMH). *The NIH almanac*.www.nih.gov/about-nih/what-we-do/nih-almanac/national-institute-mental-health

Norman, C. (2006). The Fountain House Movement, an alternative rehabilitation model for people with mental health problems, members' descriptions of what works. *Scandinavian Journal of Caring Sciences*, *20*(2), 184–192. doi.org/10.1111/j.1471-6712.2006.00398.x

Olmstead v. L. C. (1999). (98–536) 527 U.S. 581.

ourconsumerplace.com.au. (n.d.). *Help sheet: Our consumerism*. www.ourconsumerplace.com.au/consumer/helpsheet?id=3563

Parham, W. D., & Clauss-Ehlers, C. S. (2016). Following inspiration: A conversation with Former First Lady Rosalynn Carter. *Journal of Multicultural Counseling and Development*, *44*(3), 156–175 (Archived at the Drs. Nicholas and Dorothy Cummings Center for the History of Psychology, The University of Akron). doi.org/10.1002/jmcd.12044

President's Commission on Mental Health. (1978). *Report to the President from the President's Commission on Mental Health*, 4 vols. Washington, DC: US Government Printing Office.

Riotta, C. (2017, July 29). GOP aims to kill Obamacare yet again after failing 70 times. *Newsweek*. www.newsweek.com/gop-health-care-bill-repeal-and-replace-70-failed-attempts-643832

Rogers, E. S., Teague, G., Lichtenstein, C., et al. (2007). The effects of participation in adjunctive consumer-operated programs on both personal and organizationally mediated empowerment: Results of a multi-site study. *A Special Issue of the Journal of Rehabilitation Research and Development*, *44*(6), 785–800. doi.org/10.1682/JRRD.2006.10.0125

Seeman, N. (2015). Use data to challenge mental-health stigma. *Nature*, *528*(7582), Article 309. doi.org/10.1038/528309a

Seeman, N., Tang, S., Brown, A. D., & Ing, A. (2016). World survey of mental illness stigma. *Journal of Affective Disorders*, *190*, 115–121. doi.org/10.1016/j.jad.2015.10.011

Segal, S. P. (2011). Outcomes from consumer-operated and community mental health services: A randomized controlled trial. *Yearbook of Psychiatry and Applied Mental Health*, *62*(8), 915–921. doi.org/10.1016/j.ypsy.2011.11.003

Silversides, A. (2009). Medical profession urged to end mental health discrimination. *Canadian Medical Association Journal*, *181*(12), E317–E318. doi.org/10.1503/cmaj.081304

Substance Abuse and Mental Health Services Administration. (2012). *SAMHSA's working definition of recovery: 10 guiding principles of recovery* [Brochure]. https://store.samhsa.gov/sites/default/files/d7/priv/pep12-recdef.pdf

Tanenbaum, S. J. (2011). Mental health consumer-operated services organizations in the US: Citizenship as a core function and strategy for growth. *Health Care Analysis*, *19*(2), 192–205. doi:10.1007/s10728-010-0151-y

Thornicroft, G., Deb, T., & Henderson, C. (2016). Community mental health care worldwide: Current status and further developments. *World Psychiatry: Official Journal of the World Psychiatric Association (WPA)*, *15*(3), 276–286. doi.org/10.1002/wps.20349

US Department of Health and Human Services. (n.d.). *Consumer-operated services*. Substance Abuse and Mental Health Services Administration, Center for Mental Health Services. https://mnprc.org/wp-content/uploads/2019/01/COSP_PowerPoint8.25.pdf

Young Minds Advocacy (n.d.). *The Community Mental Health Act of 1963*. www.ymadvocacy.org/the-community-mental-health-act-of-1963/

14 Taking Back the Streets

Violence Prevention and Neighborhood Empowerment in the South Ward of Newark

Christopher M. Thompson, Corinne C. Datchi, and Lakeesha Eure

14.1 Introduction

In the field of community psychology, the concept of neighborhood has been defined using a variety of theoretical frameworks. Theories that are used to understand the characteristics that have an impact on neighborhoods fall into two distinct categories: social disorganization and pluralistic neighborhood theories. Social disorganization theory is a deficit-based approach that identifies structural factors (i.e., poverty, residential instability, racial and ethnic heterogeneity) that weaken social ties and lead to maladaptive behaviors among youth (Shaw & McKay, 1942). Alternatively, pluralistic neighborhood theory is rooted in the constructivist tradition and attempts to identify sources of neighborhood resiliency through the lived experiences of residents (Aber & Nieto, 2000). Researchers have used both social disorganization and pluralistic neighborhood theories to offer a contextual understanding of neighborhoods (Witherspoon & Ennett, 2011).

This chapter provides an overview of neighborhood theories and research with a focus on the social disorganization and pluralistic neighborhood frameworks and their limitations in understanding the complexity of neighborhood life and interactions. To fill perceived gaps in these theoretical models, we draw on the systemic epistemology of couple and family psychology to contextualize neighborhood violence and highlight the reciprocal and interdependent relations between individual behaviors and neighborhood characteristics, including social cohesion and trust. The South Ward of Newark, New Jersey, is used to illustrate the application of key family systems concepts to describe a neighborhood and its efforts to reduce crime and violence at the local level. Specifically, we use these concepts to understand how the interventions of the Newark Anti-Violence Coalition in the South Ward activate processes that increase neighborhood engagement and collective efficacy. Implications for community psychology are discussed.

14.2 Social Disorganization Theory

Social disorganization is considered the most prominent neighborhood theory in the field of community psychology. It is rooted in the structural characteristics model that focuses on the physical and social conditions of neighborhoods as they relate to resident well-being (Wandersman & Nation, 1998). Earlier structural frameworks include the neighborhood disorder model that examines the physical (e.g., abandoned buildings, litter, vandalism) and social (e.g., public drunkenness, street harassment) characteristics of neighborhoods, and their effects on crime, juvenile delinquency, fear of crime, and mental health (White et al., 1987), and the environmental stress model that links environmental stressors (e.g., noise, crowding, pollution) and built environment (e.g., high-rise housing) with mental health outcomes (Baum, Singer, & Baum, 1981; Wandersman et al., 1983).

The core assumptions of social disorganization theory are that communities in distress lack a shared set of values and beliefs, and structural factors such as residential instability, poverty, single-parent households, and racial and ethnic heterogeneity undermine the likelihood of developing strong social ties and community norms (Osgood & Chambers, 2000; Sampson, 2001; Shaw & McKay, 1942). These factors are characteristics of neighborhood disadvantage that have been found to be associated with delinquency and crime (Anderson, 2002; Boggess, 2017; Fajnzylber et al., 2000; Lee, Lee, & Hoover, 2016).

Socioeconomic conditions such as poverty are believed to influence the experiences of community members in ways that erode social cohesion and trust in neighborhoods. Theorists of social disorganization assert that this occurs because no consensus can be made about community norms and values. Although social disorganization theory attempts to explain individuals' perceptions of their neighborhood, the core focus is on the structural patterns of poverty, residential instability, and racial heterogeneity, and how they relate to crime, delinquency, and other maladaptive behaviors (Shaw & McKay, 1942; Witherspoon & Ennett, 2011).

The effects of macro-level processes in relation to crime and victimization have been well documented (Jencks & Mayer, 1990; Leventhal & Brooks-Gunn, 2000; Sampson, 2001; Wilson, 2012). In particular, the seminal work of Shaw and McKay (1942) highlighted the geographical concentration of crimes: The authors used spatial maps to plot the residential locations of juveniles who were referred to court and found that when juveniles moved to low-crime areas, their antisocial activities decreased. They also noted that crime rates were not associated with changes in racial demographics and concluded that neighborhood factors may be more influential than resident characteristics (Shaw & McKay, 1942). Later research confirmed this finding and provided support for the relationship between juvenile delinquency, poverty, and neighborhood instability (Figueira-McDonough, 1993).

Shaw and McKay's (1942) research examined socioeconomically deprived neighborhoods that experienced high crime rates and rapid social and economic changes, also called "zones of transition." Their work tested the theory that poverty made neighborhoods undesirable and therefore influenced residents to leave when they had the means to do so. Shaw and McKay also argued that racial heterogeneity and high resident mobility were characteristics of socioeconomically deprived neighborhoods that contributed to their social disorganization. They posited that traditional institutions of social control such as family, schools, churches, and other systems were key contextual factors in preventing youth delinquency (Shaw & McKay, 1942). By the 1980s, neighborhood research also established the role of factors such as proximity among poor and middle-class residents, number of families in poverty, divorce rates, and number of female-headed households as predictors of crime and violence (Block, 1979; Shihadeh & Steffensmeier, 1994).

Social disorganization research has many limitations. In particular, it has relied on census and crime data that focus on what is *not* working in communities; these data do not capture neighborhood-level resiliency processes that explain how communities thrive despite structural disadvantages. Aber and Nieto (2000) described neighborhoods where high poverty rates, residential mobility, and racial and ethnic heterogeneity coexisted with relatively low crime rates and high social organization, which suggests the negative and positive characteristics of neighborhoods may be unrelated, mutually exclusive constructs. Studies have found that residents vary in how they perceive the living conditions of their neighborhood and their perceptions mediate the effect of environmental characteristics on individual adjustment (Korbin et al., 1998; Seidman et al., 1998). In addition, Seidman and colleagues (1998) found that urban adolescents' perception of neighborhood risk factors such as poverty-related adversities were not associated with neighborhood cohesion and other neighborhood strengths.

Social disorganization theory emphasizes physical infrastructure and demographic characteristics when defining neighborhoods. As previously described, studies that operate from this structural framework rely on census data, block groups, and zip codes rather than residents' perceptions of their neighborhood. However, residents' subjective experiences are equally important to consider when studying the ecology of neighborhoods and are a central focus of pluralistic neighborhood theory.

14.3 Pluralistic Neighborhood Theory

While social disorganization theory emphasizes the negative effects of poor neighborhood conditions and identifies neighborhood factors that influence crime, pluralistic neighborhood theory offers a constructivist approach to the concept. This approach shines light on the processes that promote human development in communities that are deemed structurally disadvantaged (Aber & Nieto, 2000). Moreover, pluralistic neighborhood theory aims to describe the neighborhood-level resiliency factors that support at-risk youth's ability to adapt to their circumstances and overcome adversity (Cowen, 1994).

Pluralistic neighborhood studies use research methods such as photovoice, interviews (Fernández & Langhout, 2014), focus groups (Geller et al., 2014), and surveys (Lewicka, 2005) that facilitate engagement with community members and make it possible to understand the subjective experiences of residents and how these experiences lead to neighborhood well-being. Social cohesion, trust, and informal social control (e.g., monitoring of youth by the community) have been a focus of investigation among social disorganization researchers to identify what factors contribute to reductions in violence and increased social organization (Sampson, Raudenbush, & Earls, 1997). However, pluralistic neighborhood theory posits that structural disadvantage and social resiliency factors are distinct constructs from one another. Thus, communities can have the structural indicators of social disorganization (i.e., family instability, poverty, racial heterogeneity), while also demonstrating that social resources and resiliencies concurrently exist. These studies have highlighted the existence of neighborhoods where crime is low and social ties are strong despite family instability, poverty, and racial heterogeneity (Aber & Nieto, 2000). They have also investigated the social resources – cohesion, trust, informal social control – that create opportunities for community members to thrive (Witherspoon & Ennett, 2011).

Collective efficacy is one of the main constructs that explain neighborhood resiliency. Collective efficacy is defined as social cohesion among residents along with a willingness to intervene for the common good of the neighborhood (Sampson, Raudenbush, & Earls, 1997). The capacity for residents to intervene, also referred to as informal social control, is an important aspect of neighborhoods' collective efficacy. Informal social control does not refer to forced conformity by the state such as zero-tolerance policing or punitive measures by schools. Rather, it is characterized by community members regulating other residents based on common principles and values for the greater good of the community (Janowitz, 1975).

Informal social control can promote safety and order within neighborhoods. Research examining the relationship between informal social control and crime shows that collective efficacy is negatively associated with violence. Furthermore, collective efficacy was shown to mediate the relationship between residential stability, disadvantage, and violence (Sampson et al., 1997). These informal mechanisms of support can take the form of monitoring children's play, engaging positively with youth to prevent loitering or truancy, confronting other residents who are causing a disturbance in the community (Hackler, Ho, & Urquhart-Ross, 1974; Maccoby, Johnson, & Church, 1958; Sampson & Groves, 1989; Taylor, Gottfredson, & Brower, 1984; Thrasher, 1963), and intervening to prevent violence, victimization, and other illegal activity among adults (Reiss & Roth, 1994).

Social capital is a construct related to collective efficacy that describes those aspects of neighborhoods' social life that facilitate willing engagement among residents. There have been many conflicting definitions of social capital (Lin, Cook, & Burt, 2001; Putnam, Leonardi, & Nanetti, 1993); the most common one refers to mutual help among citizens, trust, and strength of organizational life such as the ability to bridge social divisions and manage conflict (Kawachi & Berkman, 2000; Moore et al., 2005).

Onyx and Bullen's (2000) research identified the key components of social capital as participation in networks, reciprocity among community members, trust, social norms, and communal agency. Participation in networks is the process by which people and groups engage with one another on a voluntary basis and in a mutually beneficial way. This process is important to the development of social capital. Reciprocity refers to community members' acts of altruism and their willingness to help each other. In communities where reciprocity is strong, residents care about each other's interests and expect their acts of kindness will be returned. Trust represents the degree to which community members perceive other residents to be supportive of their needs and feel confident to take risks in social contexts.

Research has also found that trust among neighborhood residents occurred as a result of social capital. There are two types of neighborhood-level trust: "Thick trust" is established within close, personal relationships and "thin trust" develops among individuals who do not personally know each other (Putnam, 2000; Putnam et al., 1993). Social norms are unwritten rules that define which behaviors are socially sanctioned by the community; they are also mechanisms of informal social control that promote prosocial behaviors (Onyx & Bullen, 2000). When informal social control is high, there is less of a need for formal control (e.g., law enforcement). Another aspect of social capital is known as the commons, which refers to a community resource shared by all, where individuals are concerned about the greater good of the neighborhood rather than their own personal interests (Putnam et al., 1993). Lastly, social agency corresponds to community members' willingness and capacity to actively engage other residents in the broader community. In this sense, community members on an individual level take ownership of their circumstances by collectively working together (Onyx & Bullen, 2000).

Like social capital, place attachment and place identity are key concepts that explain community engagement (Brown, Perkins, & Brown, 2003; Hay, 1998; Lenzi et al., 2013; Lewicka, 2005). Place attachment is defined in terms of the positive emotions that individuals develop toward a specific neighborhood (Hernández et al., 2007; Lewicka 2005). The interaction between individuals and their social contexts can facilitate place identity or sense of belonging to a specific place. Karacor and Parlar (2017) argue that place attachment plays a significant role in reducing residents' fear of crime.

14.4 Systems Theory

In couple and family psychology (CFP), neighborhoods are naturally occurring contexts of family life and relationships. They constitute broader systems that interact with families and family members in ways that influence individual and relational functioning (Smalls Glover et al., 2019). Many contemporary, evidence-based CFP interventions emphasize the role of families' ecology and integrate considerations of neighborhood-level risk and protective factors into the conceptualization and treatment of clinical problems (e.g., multidimensional family therapy [Liddle, 2016]; functional family therapy [Sexton, 2011]; multisystemic therapy [Shoenwald, Henggeler, & Rowland, 2016]). Neighborhoods are viewed as informal social networks and sources of support that can be engaged in the life of families to promote and maintain positive outcomes over time (Sexton, 2011).

14.4.1 The Neighborhood System

The systemic epistemology of CFP offers a complex mode of thinking about neighborhoods with a focus on the interactions between each constituent part. Complexity, reciprocity, adaptability, and self-organization are key systemic concepts used to describe family structure and dynamics (Fiese, Jones, & Saltzman, 2019; Stanton & Welsh, 2011). In this section, we consider how these concepts help us understand neighborhoods as social systems where individuals, families, and neighbors have mutual, interactive effects on each other.

Systems theory emphasizes holism or the view that systems are complex and greater than the sum of their parts (Stanton, 2009). Complexity and non-summativity contrast with reductionism or the assumption that it is possible to understand how systems work by analyzing their discrete elements, such as the physical infrastructure of neighborhoods in structural disorganization theory or residents' individual experiences in pluralistic neighborhood theory. To think systemically is to examine how residents' interactions with each other and with aspects of their environment influence their experiences of their neighborhood as well as the development of social cohesion, community engagement, place attachment, and place identity.

Reciprocity is a concept that highlights circular causality in living, social systems, and the mutual effects of person–context interactions (Stanton, 2009; Stanton & Welsh, 2011). It represents a shift in perspective from a focus on linear relationships where more of A (e.g., poverty, family instability) is associated with less of B (e.g., strong social ties) to the recognition that individuals, families, and neighbors are influencing each other and aspects of their environments, simultaneously rather than sequentially, as they interact with one another. Reciprocal influence between persons and contexts may explain empirical findings that invalidate the hypothesis that neighborhood poverty undermines social cohesion from the perspective of vulnerable youth (Aber & Nieto, 2000). It raises questions about possible relational processes that operate at the neighborhood level to promote cohesion and protect individuals and families from the effects of poverty. Reciprocity also calls attention to mutual person–context influences in the development of place attachment and place identity.

Adaptation and self-organization are properties of social systems that refer to their capacity to adjust and develop new structures in response to internal and external changes (Stanton, 2009). They are mechanisms that support the flexibility as well as the integrity and continuity of living systems. The concepts of adaptation and self-organization may help to expand our understanding of neighborhood resiliency, in particular, collective efficacy or residents' decision to intervene for the common good of their neighborhood community. They may clarify how disadvantaged neighborhoods persist rather than disintegrate, and how individuals, families, and neighbors' inter-actions around internal and external stressors such as neighborhood violence and neighborhood policing contribute to both continuity and change in their community.

The next sections offer a portrait of the South Ward of Newark, New Jersey, a neighborhood characterized by high levels of unemployment, pov-erty, residential mobility, and fear of crime (Sanzone, Weidman, & Doykos, 2016). The theoretical lens of family systems theory is used to discuss the characteristics of the neighborhood and the development of the Newark Anti-Violence Coalition (NAVC) in response to crime against women and children in the South Ward. The principles that guide NAVC's activities are also examined in relation to the concept of community ownership and collective efficacy.

14.5 The South Ward of Newark, New Jersey

Newark is the largest and second most diverse city in the state of New Jersey. Approximately 50% of the city's population is African American, 36.4% Hispanic or Latino, and 10% White (US Census Bureau, 2019). Newark is also a multicultural city composed of many ethnic communities including Brazilians, Dominicans, Italians, Irish, Haitians, Jamaicans, Latin Americans, Portuguese, Puerto Ricans, and Spaniards. Newark counts approximately 285,000 residents with a median age of 34.4 years and a household median income of $35,167 (US Census Bureau, 2017).

Newark is divided into five distinct wards. The North, Central, and West Wards are primarily residential neighborhoods, while the East and South Wards are places with a large concentration of commerce and industry (Newark Community Economic Development Corporation [Newark CEDC], 2016). The South Ward is the site of many small businesses, storefront churches, and single-family homes, and has two major neighborhoods: Clinton Hill, with its residential community, and Weequahic, with its lake and parks. Newark Beth Israel Medical, the second-largest hospital in the city, and Newark Liberty International Airport are also located in the South Ward (Newark CEDC, 2016).

The South Ward has been the birthplace and residence of famous artists, activists, and politicians such as Kenneth Gibson, the first Black mayor of Newark, and Ras Baraka, the current mayor of the city. Mayor Baraka's father, author and activist Amiri Baraka, lived in Weequahic from the late 1960s until he died in 2014. Amiri was very influential in the Black political power movement in Newark; he is known as a visionary of Black art and culture. Pulitzer prize-winning author Philip Roth also lived in the South Ward and wrote about Jewish life in Weequahic in the 1940s and 1950s.

Neighborhood statistics suggest the residents of the South Ward may experience low levels of place attachment (Sanzone et al., 2016): Between 2000 and 2014, the population decreased from 47,057 to 46,171; 46% said they would leave their neighborhood if they had the chance; 38% would stay if conditions improved; and 17% would stay no matter what. Parents were more likely to express dissatisfaction with the South Ward compared to nonparents (Sanzone et al., 2016): 48% of parents and 35% of nonparents stated that they would leave the South Ward if they were able to; 12% of those who would stay no matter what were parents and 35% nonparents. These numbers point to the residents' dissatisfaction with everyday life conditions for children and families in the South Ward. Among those, economic difficulties and safety are primary concerns.

The South Ward has experienced many social and economic challenges including high crime rates, high unemployment, low-wage jobs, high levels of social service participation, and high rates of poverty, particularly among children (Sanzone et al., 2016; US Census Bureau, n.d.). In 2014, approximately one-third of South Ward households earned less than $20,000 and 60% earned less than $40,000. Approximately 32.4% of all residents fell below the poverty line (Sanzone et al., 2016; US Census Bureau, n.d.). The unemployment and poverty rates in the South Ward are 31% and 41% respectively, higher than the city of Newark and the state of New Jersey. Approximately 95% of individuals who worked in the South Ward did not live there. The ratio of highest-paying jobs among nonresidents versus residents was greater than three to one (Sanzone et al., 2016; US Census Bureau, 2016).

Crime and violence in the South Ward of Newark are an endemic issue that affects the everyday life and well-being of individuals and families in the community. In 2015, 30% of all city homicides occurred in the South Ward. This corresponds to thirty out of ninety-nine murders citywide and shows that killings are more than twice as likely to occur in the South Ward compared to other neighborhoods of Newark (Sanzone et al., 2016). Crime data from the Newark Police Department indicate that in 2015 there were 356 burglaries,

216 aggravated assaults, 185 disorderly offenses, 382 drug arrests, 243 thefts, 239 robberies, 275 theft from auto, and 347 auto thefts in the South Ward (Sanzone et al., 2016). These numbers illustrate both the significance of the problem and its geographical concentration.

Crime and violence produce fear and mistrust (Kruger et al., 2007; Perkins & Taylor, 1996). Exposure to community violence increases the likelihood of trauma-related symptoms and other forms of psychological distress (Affuso et al., 2014; Bacchini & Esposito, 2020; Margolin et al., 2010; Pierre, Burnside, & Gaylord-Harden, 2020; Zinzow et al., 2009). It also increases children's risk of associating with delinquent peers as well as their risk of offending in young adulthood (Eitle & Turner, 2002). Community violence restricts physical movement and thus limits residents' capacity to address individual and family needs (Loukaitou-Sideris & Eck, 2007). Businesses are often discouraged from moving in, which reduces property values in the neighborhood (Hipp, 2011; Oh, 2005) and contributes to low levels of place attachment (Sanzone et al., 2016).

High crime rates are linked to a low sense of safety in the community. In 2015, the South Ward Children's Alliance surveyed South Ward residents and found that 38% lived in fear and 65% were afraid of crime; 71% reported that a murder had occurred in the past twelve months (Sanzone et al., 2016). When asked about their perceptions of their neighborhood, three-quarters of the respondents described incidents of public drinking, drug use, public drug sales, loitering, neglected or abandoned buildings, panhandling, trash, and empty lots. They also expressed dissatisfaction with and lack of safety in public transportation. About 75% reported vandalism and overgrown vegetation in the neighborhood, and 50% reported incidents of prostitution (Sanzone et al., 2016).

Newark's past and present response to crime and violence in the South Ward has contributed to the community's increased sense of insecurity and distrust toward law enforcement and the local government. This distrust can be traced back to the history of race and police–community relations in the city, in particular the 1967 Newark uprising. The uprising lasted five days (Rojas & Atkinson, 2017) and was the culmination of more than a hundred years of poor city planning and policymaking that had a disproportionate impact on Black residents (for more information about the 1967 Newark uprising, see Mazzola & Yi, 2017 and Parks, 2007a, 2007b).

In 2006, the Newark police department adopted a zero-tolerance approach to the problem of community violence that resulted in historically low homicide rates but questionable policing practices, including racial profiling and excessive use of force (Corasaniti & Saul, 2019). A three-year federal investigation revealed that approximately 75% of pedestrian stops by the Newark police were unconstitutional: Individual behaviors that were perceived as insubordinate or disrespectful were often charged as obstruction of justice, disorderly conduct, or resisting arrest. A disproportionate number of stops and arrests were carried out in Black communities: While Black residents represented 53.9% of the city population, they accounted for 85% of pedestrian stops and 79.3% of arrests (US Department of Justice [DOJ], 2014). In addition, evidence emerged that the police had engaged in criminal acts against citizens such as money and property theft and failed to provide adequate supervision and training to their officers, to properly investigate complaints, and to hold officers accountable for their actions (DOJ, 2014).

Taken together, the geographical concentration of crime and the history of policing in the South Ward show the local government's failed attempts at resolving the problem of violence. Section 14.6 describes how South Ward residents took matters into their own hands and formed the NAVC in partnership with various city organizations. NAVC illustrates the resilience of disadvantaged neighborhoods and their capacity to identify and implement effective solutions to crime.

14.6 The Newark Anti-Violence Coalition

On July 20, 2009, Nakisha Allen, the thirty-five-year-old mother of two children, was killed in a drive-by shooting outside her apartment near Weequahic Park. In a period of eight months, she was the eleventh person shot and the second killed within a half block radius of her residence (Peet, 2009). Her death was a major event that shook the community of the South Ward. Two days later, dozens of protesters gathered at the scene of her shooting and blocked traffic to demand resources to fight crime in the neighborhood and the city. They viewed her killing as a violation of the "street code of conduct" that says women and children are off limits when it comes to gang-related and other forms of community violence.

This neighborhood gathering was the first step toward the formation of NAVC (www.navcoalition.org), a community-based organization that Newark historian Clement Price described as a "seismic shift" in the culture of grassroots activism (Queally, 2010, p. 1). NAVC was developed to hold residents responsible for creating solutions to community violence and to address broader societal issues such as racism and police misconduct. Its founding members, including Newark Mayor Ras Baraka, were Newark residents who had experienced crime directly and indirectly through family relationships and friends. Because they were Newark residents, they already had the trust of the South Ward; and they used that trust to engage the neighborhood in the activities of NAVC. The identity of NAVC as a volunteer coalition and a partnership between community-based organizations was also important in building and maintaining trust with the neighborhood. NAVC is *not* a for-profit or nonprofit association. It is a coalition that pulls together the resources of the neighborhood, the residents, and anti-violence organizations for the purpose of helping victims of crime. These resources include referrals to trauma-informed care specialists, grief and support groups, domestic violence counseling, youth educational and employment services, and programs that provide compensation and support for survivors of violent crime. NAVC is the glue that brings together community-based organizations and other groups that share the common goal of stopping violence. It organizes and leads the community meetings where these organizations and groups discuss and exchange information and resources. The sharing of resources and the development of partnerships with community-based organizations contribute to strengthen collective efficacy and social cohesion in the neighborhood of the South Ward.

NAVC operates on democratic norms: Power is distributed equally among its members, elections are held to fill positions, decisions are based on a majority of votes, and individuals have the option of participating or not in the activities of the coalition. Everyone has a specific role (e.g., ensuring security, public speaking, interaction with law enforcement) and is equally responsible. In the neighborhood, during street rallies in particular, NAVC serves as a model of being and relating that emphasizes consensus, accountability, transparency, and unity as well as empowerment in the face of violence and fear. These values constitute the foundations of community healing and speak to the importance of interdependence in promoting resilience.

The activities of NAVC are carried out by outreach workers who are from the community and who live in neighborhoods with a high level of violence. These workers have first-hand knowledge of street and gang life; they derive credibility and influence from their affiliation with the neighborhood and from the relationships they have developed with other residents. These relationships form a social network that can be activated to detect conflict and to prevent violence.

14.7 Systemic Solutions to Neighborhood Violence

When we examine the goals of NAVC closely, we see the principles that guide the Coalition's approach to the reduction and prevention of crime in the South Ward: increasing the residents' awareness and shared responsibility for the problem of violence; taking back the streets and fostering a sense of collective ownership to encourage the residents to police their own neighborhood; promoting a both/and rather than either/or approach to violence (i.e., individuals who commit crimes are also residents of the South Ward); and building bridges between the neighborhood and other systems (e.g., law enforcement, schools).

These goals are based on the view that neighborhoods are systems where cohesion results from individuals' awareness of their interdependence as well as their perception of crime as a collective loss that affects the unity of the community not only the integrity of the person and the person's family. Dualities are eschewed – us versus them, residents versus criminals, police versus community – and linkages emphasized to promote a sense of inclusivity or we-ness in the community. We-ness is a necessary condition for shared responsibility and collaborative action against violence, not only in the neighborhood but also in those places where the community comes into contact with other systems such as police and schools.

To achieve the goals above, NAVC uses a variety of interventions that fall under four broad categories: outreach, education, advocacy, and mediation. Outreach is the primary mechanism for delivering material and emotional support to residents and families who have been affected by acts of violence in the neighborhood. It is a home-based, proactive intervention that involves taking resources to the people rather than waiting for them to come to the office and ask for help. Material and emotional support takes many forms, such as giving furniture; assisting with employment, food, transportation; relocating the family to another residence; calling the family to check in; finding a summer camp for the children; supervising the children to give their mother a break; sitting in court with the family; attending funerals and weddings; and encouraging the family to use counseling services. In fact, NAVC's outreach activities are not only a source of support; they also are the means by which the Coalition strengthens as well as makes visible the relationships of the South Ward's extended family system. "If you say you're from the South Ward, you'll get this overwhelming love from people who are from the South Ward even if they don't know you." This quote by the third author highlights the sense of filiation that develops from living in the neighborhood. It is this sense of filiation that NAVC outreach activities maximize to encourage the residents of the South Ward to protect each other from violence.

NAVC views neighborhood crime and violence as a form of self-loathing that stems, in part, from the internalization of negative images about the South Ward. Education is therefore an intervention that aims to reveal the greatness of South Ward residents, instill pride in their community, and challenge biases about the neighborhood. It involves expanding the high schools' curriculum and building upon students' knowledge of Black and Latinx history by telling them about South Ward residents and the broader historical figures who have influenced the social and political landscape of their city and country. When youth learn about Black and Latinx South Ward leaders, they are able to form personal connections with their local history and take position in the multigenerational map of their neighborhood's extended family system. They can also visualize the place that their community occupies in a broader, historical context. In sum, cultural education or consciousness-raising is a strategy to counter the negative effects of oppressive systems, promote self-worth, increase self-confidence, and thereby encourage the community to take care of the neighborhood and its residents (Freire, 2006).

Community advocacy corresponds to the act of supporting the neighborhood's right to weigh in on decisions that influence the residents' everyday life. NAVC provides the channel through which the South Ward influences local policymaking. It facilitates bidirectional communication and exchanges between the neighborhood and other systems like the police, the city government, and the schools. For example, when a resident of the South Ward is afraid to report a crime, NAVC serves as an intermediary, relaying the information from the neighborhood to local law enforcement. NAVC also seeks to increase the police's understanding of the impact of violence on community dynamics, to support a trauma-informed approach to law enforcement, avoid revictimization, and promote positive interactions between police officers and South Ward residents. In addition, NAVC works to create a space in city government where residents' stories about the South Ward (e.g., their experience of violence and crime in the neighborhood) are heard and considered a credible source of information. It does so by polling the community to identify what residents perceive as critical issues and by reporting their findings to the mayor or/and the councilmen.

Rallies are the epitome of NAVC's efforts to encourage South Ward residents to take ownership of their neighborhood and address the problem of violence. They symbolize the impact of crime on the community: A person was killed, a life was interrupted, and so is life in the community when NAVC stops traffic, takes back the streets, and gives residents the opportunity to express their loss and pain in public. Neighbors stand together in solidarity. Loudspeakers carry the voices and stories of family members who have lost a loved one to violence. NAVC rallies are interventions that highlight the residents' interrelatedness as well as their capacity to come together, speak up about their needs, take a stand against violence, and police their community. They encourage the community to use their own experience and understanding of violence to intervene and prevent crime in the neighborhood.

NAVC rallies are a collective demonstration of the community's power to heal itself. They take place in the streets of the neighborhood; the perimeter is secured by the Coalition and the police; and the participants form a circle that symbolizes the cohesiveness and inviolability of their relationships. The circle is sacred, and no one walks through it; it is the space where neighbors and relatives communicate their message of hope to the community and where they engage in a dialogue with representatives of other systems like the mayor. In other words, the rallies represent the need for a multisystemic approach to violence prevention where residents, families, community and religious organizations, and city government talk and work together to develop and implement solutions.

Shutting down traffic with no permits during busy traffic hours was a form of direct action that was initially perceived as aggressive and disruptive by law enforcement and elected officials. Residents also became frustrated, as they were often late to work, or could not get to their homes because NAVC was rallying on their block. Over time, NAVC successfully gained the trust and respect of the police, the community, and the city. Their success rests on its presence, visibility, and involvement in the neighborhood, showing up at crime scenes, at the hospital, and at the funeral home; educating gang-affiliated youth and empowering them to redefine their filial relationships in and with gangs to foster positive community dynamics; providing information and support to residents and families; and facilitating the resolution of violence through mediation. Mediation is an activity that brings together the parties involved in a crime to reduce the likelihood that violence will escalate. It involves the creation of a safe space to promote dialogue and understanding and to explore how residents and families can protect the safety of their neighborhood.

14.8 Conclusion

The ecology of neighborhoods has been described in terms of structural conditions (e.g., poverty, heterogeneity) and residents' subjective experience (e,g,, place attachment and place identity). Neighborhood research has highlighted the social processes that contribute to neighborhood resilience in the face of adversity, including collective efficacy, trust, informal social control, and social agency. This chapter emphasized the systemic character of neighborhoods where individuals influence and are influenced by their immediate environment in the context of their interactions with other systems like the school and law enforcement. We described the activities of the Newark Anti-Violence Coalition (NAVC) in the South Ward to illustrate the reciprocal and interdependent relationships between persons and contexts: The characteristics of the South Ward (e.g., poverty, violence) are not structural factors that limit the behaviors of residents or conditions that the residents experience negatively or positively; they are the sites of action and collective empowerment. The residents that participate in NAVC rallies and outreach act upon the neighborhood; they take back the streets not only to stop violence but also to redefine the South Ward as a space of healing and a system of cross-generational relationships where neighbors learn to appreciate and validate their worth.

The purpose of community psychology is to empower and alleviate the suffering of marginalized communities through theory, action-oriented research, and practice (Iscoe, 1974; Revenson & Seidman, 2002). In the past twenty years, the field has witnessed a growing interest in the study of community organizing (Hartmann et al., 2014; Orsi, 2014; Peterson et al., 2008; Serrano-García, 2020; Suyemoto & Tree, 2006; Zanbar & Itzhaky, 2013). However, few studies have investigated the role of neighborhood initiatives in the prevention of violence and their effects on community cohesion, trust, and the building of social capital (Bhatt & Tweed, 2018; Housman, Siddons, & Becker, 2000). Future research in community psychology should look at successful community projects like those led by NAVC, to identify principles for effective community-based anti-violence organizing.

Community psychology emphasizes a contextual understanding of neighborhoods and communities (Goodstein & Sandler, 1978). This chapter has demonstrated how the core principles of couple and family psychology can enhance the conceptual approach of community psychology by highlighting the systemic processes that operate within the neighborhood (e.g., between the residents; between the residents and community organizations) and between the neighborhood and other contexts (e.g., the neighborhood and local law enforcement). Future studies of community organizing and anti-violence interventions should examine which of those processes are most relevant to the resilience of disadvantaged communities.

References

Aber, M. S., & Nieto, M. (2000). Suggestions for the investigation of psychological wellness in the neighborhood context: Toward a pluralistic neighborhood theory. In D. Cicchetti, J. Rappaport, I. Sandler, & R. P. Weissberg (Eds.), *The promotion of wellness in children and adolescents* (pp. 185–219). Washington, DC: CWLA Press.

Affuso, G., Bacchini, D., Aquilar, S., De Angelis, G., & Miranda, M. C. (2014). Esposizione alla violenza in contesti multipli e sintomi post-traumatici da stress: uno studio con adolescent (Exposure to violence in multiple contexts and post-traumatic stress symptoms: A study with adolescents). *Maltrattamento e Abuso all'Infanzia, 2*(16), 13–33. doi.org/10.3280/mal2014-002002

Anderson, A. L. (2002). Individual and contextual influences on delinquency: The role of the single-parent family. *Journal of Criminal Justice, 30*(6), 575–587. doi.org/10.1016/s0047-2352(02)00191-5

Bacchini, D., & Esposito, C. (2020). Growing up in violent contexts: Differential effects of community, family, and school violence on child adjustment. In N. Balvin & D. J. Christie (Eds.), *Children and peace: From research to action* (pp. 157–171). Cham, Switzerland: Springer.

Baum, A., Singer, J. E., & Baum, C. S. (1981). Stress and the environment. *Journal of Social Issues, 37*(1), 4–35. doi.org/10.1111/j.1540-4560.1981.tb01056.x

Bhatt, G., & Tweed, R. (2018). University and community acting together to address youth violence and gang involvement. *Canadian Psychology/Psychologie canadienne, 59*(2), 151–162. doi.org/10.1037/cap0000149

Block, R. (1979). Community, environment, and violent crime. *Criminology, 17*(1), 46–57. doi.org/10.1111/j.1745-9125.1979.tb01275.x

Boggess, L. N. (2017). Disentangling the reciprocal relationship between change in crime and racial/ethnic change. *Social Science Research, 68*, 30–42. doi.org/10.1016/j.ssresearch.2017.08.011

Brown, B., Perkins, D. D., & Brown, G. (2003). Place attachment in a revitalizing neighborhood: Individual and block levels of analysis. *Journal of*

Environmental Psychology, 23(3), 259–271. doi.org/10.1016/s0272-4944(02)00117-2

Bursik, R. J., & Grasmick, H. G. (1992). Longitudinal neighborhood profiles in delinquency: The decomposition of change. *Journal of Quantitative Criminology, 8*(3), 247–263. doi.org/10.1007/bf01064548

Corasaniti, N. & Saul, S. (2019, March 27). "Newark's original sin" and the criminal justice education of Cory Booker: Mr. Booker's road from enforcer to reformer began with rocky oversight of the Newark Police Department. *The New York Times.* www.nytimes.com/2019/03/27/us/politics/cory-booker-2020-criminal-justice.html

Cowen, E. L. (1994). The enhancement of psychological wellness: Challenges and opportunities. *American Journal of Community Psychology, 22*(2), 149–179. doi.org/10.1007/bf02506861

Eitle, D., & Turner, R. J. (2002). Exposure to community violence and young adult crime: The effects of witnessing violence, traumatic victimization, and other stressful life events. *Journal of Research in Crime and Delinquency, 39*(2), 214–237. doi.org/10.1177/002242780203900204

Fajnzylber, P., Lederman, D., Loayza, N., et al. (2000). Crime and victimization: An economic perspective [with comments]. *Economia, 1*(1), 219–302. doi.org/10.1353/eco.2000.0004

Fernández, J. S., & Langhout, R. D. (2014). "A community with diversity of culture, wealth, resources, and living experiences": Defining neighborhood in an unincorporated community. *American Journal of Community Psychology, 53*(1–2), 122–133. doi.org/10.1007/s10464-014-9631-9

Fiese, B. H., Jones, B. L., & Saltzman, J. A. (2019). Systems unify family psychology. In B. H. Fiese, M. Celano, K. Deater-Deckard, E. N. Jouriles, & M. A. Whisman (Eds.), *APA handbook of contemporary family psychology: Foundations, methods, and contemporary issues across the lifespan*, Vol. 1 (pp. 3–19). Washington, DC: American Psychological Association.

Figueira-McDonough, J. (1993). Residence, dropping out, and delinquency rates. *Deviant Behavior, 14*(2), 109–132. doi.org/10.1080/01639625.1993.9967933

Freire, P. (2006). *Pedagogy of the oppressed* (30th anniversary ed.). New York: Continuum.

Geller, J. D., Doykos, B., Craven, K., Bess, K. D., & Nation, M. (2014). Engaging residents in community change: The critical role of trust in the development of a promise neighborhood. *Teachers College Record, 116*(4), 1–42.

Goodstein, L. D., & Sandler, I. (1978). Using psychology to promote human welfare: A conceptual analysis of the role of community psychology. *American Psychologist, 33*(10), 882–892. doi.org/10.1037/0003-066x.33.10.882

Hackler, J., Ho, K. Y., & Urquhart-Ross, C. (1974). The willingness to intervene: Differing community characteristics. *Social Problems, 21*(3), 328–344. doi.org/10.2307/799902

Hartmann, W. E., Wendt, D. C., Saftner, M. A., Marcus, J., & Momper, S. L. (2014). Advancing community-based research with urban American Indian populations: Multidisciplinary perspectives. *American Journal of Community Psychology, 54*(1–2), 72–80. doi.org/10.1007/s10464-014-9643-5

Hausman, A. J., Siddons, K., & Becker, J. (2000). Using community perspectives on youth firearm violence for prevention program planning. *Journal of Community Psychology*, *28*(6), 643–654. doi.org/10.1002/1520-6629(200011) 28:6%3C643::aid-jcop7%3E3.0.co;2-k

Hay, R. (1998). Sense of place in developmental context. *Journal of Environmental Psychology*, *18*(1), 5–29. doi.org/10.1006/jevp.1997.0060

Hernández, B., Hidalgo, M. C., Salazar-Laplace, M. E., & Hess, S. (2007). Place attachment and place identity in natives and non-natives. *Journal of Environmental Psychology*, *27*(4), 310–319. doi.org/10.1016/j.jenvp.2007.06.003

Hipp, J. R. (2011). Spreading the wealth: The effect of the distribution of income and race/ethnicity across households and neighborhoods on city crime trajectories. *Criminology: An Interdisciplinary Journal*, *49*(3), 631–665. doi.org/10 .1111/j.1745-9125.2011.00238.x

Iscoe, I. (1974). Community psychology and the competent community. *American Psychologist*, *29*(8), 607–613. doi.org/10.1037/h0036925

Janowitz, M. (1975). Sociological theory and social control. *American Journal of Sociology*, *81*(1), 82–108. doi.org/10.1086/226035

Jencks, C., & Mayer, S. E. (1990). The social consequences of growing up in a poor neighborhood. In National Research Council, *Inner-city poverty in the United States* (pp. 111–186). Washington, DC: The National Academies Press.

Karacor, E., & Parlar, G. (2017). Conceptual model of the relationship between neighbourhood attachment, collective efficacy and open space quality. *Open House International*, *42*(2), 68–74. doi.org/10.1108/ohi-02-2017-b0010

Kawachi, I., & Berkman, L. (2000). Social cohesion, social capital, and health. In I. Kawachi & L. Berkman (Eds.), *Social epidemiology* (pp. 174–190). New York: Oxford University Press.

Korbin, J. E., Coulton, C. J., Chard, S., Platt–Houston, C., & Su, M. (1998). Impoverishment and child maltreatment in African American and European American neighborhoods. *Development and Psychopathology*, *10*(2), 215–233. doi.org/10.1017/s095457949800158

Kruger, D. J., Hutchison, P., Monroe, M. G., Reischl, T., & Morrel-Samuels, S. (2007). Assault injury rates, social capital, and fear of neighborhood crime. *Journal of Community Psychology*, *35*(4), 483–498. doi.org/10.1002/jcop .20160

Lee, B., Lee, J., & Hoover, L. (2016). Neighborhood characteristics and auto theft: An empirical research from the social disorganization perspective. *Security Journal*, *29*(3), 400–408. doi.org/10.1057/sj.2013.35

Lenzi, M., Vieno, A., Pastore, M., & Santinello, M. (2013). Neighborhood social connectedness and adolescent civic engagement: An integrative model. *Journal of Environmental Psychology*, *34*, 45–54. doi.org/10.1016/j .jenvp.2012.12.003

Leventhal, T., & Brooks-Gunn, J. (2000). The neighborhoods they live in: The effects of neighborhood residence on child and adolescent outcomes. *Psychological Bulletin*, *126*(2), 309–337. doi.org/10.1037/0033-2909.126.2.309

Lewicka, M. (2005). Ways to make people active: The role of place attachment, cultural capital, and neighborhood ties. *Journal of Environmental Psychology*, *25*(4), 381–395. doi.org/10.1016/j.jenvp.2005.10.004

Liddle, H. A. (2016). Multidimensional family therapy. In T. L. Sexton & J. Lebow (Eds.), *Handbook of family therapy* (pp. 231–249). New York: Routledge/ Taylor & Francis Group.

Lin, N., Cook, K. S., & Burt, R. S. (Eds.). (2001). *Social capital: Theory and research.* New Brunswick, NJ: Transaction Publishers.

Loukaitou-Sideris, A., & Eck, J. E. (2007). Crime prevention and active living. *American Journal of Health Promotion, 21*(4), 380–389. doi.org/10.4278/ 0890-1171-21.4s.380

Maccoby, E. E., Johnson, J. P., & Church, R. M. (1958). Community integration and the social control of juvenile delinquency. *Journal of Social Issues, 14*(3), 38–51. doi.org/10.1111/j.1540-4560.1958.tb01415.x

Margolin, G., Vickerman, K. A., Oliver, P. H., & Gordis, E. B. (2010). Violence exposure in multiple interpersonal domains: Cumulative and differential effects. *Journal of Adolescent Health, 47*(2), 198–205. doi.org/10.1016/j .jadohealth.2010.01.020

Mazzola, J., & Yi, K. (2017, July). 50 years ago, Newark burned. www.nj.com/essex/ 2017/07/what_you_need_to_know_about_the_1967_newark_riots.html

Moore, S., Shiell, A., Hawe, P., & Haines, V. A. (2005). The privileging of communi-tarian ideas: Citation practices and the translation of social capital into public health research. *American Journal of Public Health, 95*(8), 1330–1337. doi .org/10.2105/ajph.2004.046094

Newark Community Economic Development Corporation (Newark CEDC). (2016). *Neighborhoods and wards.* www.newarkcedc.org/neighborhoods_and_wards

Oh, J. (2005). Social disorganizations and crime rates in U.S. central cities: Toward an explanation of urban economic change. *The Social Science Journal, 42*(4), 569–582. doi.org/10.1016/j.soscij.2005.09.008.

Onyx, J., & Bullen, P. (2000). Measuring social capital in five communities. *The Journal of Applied Behavioral Science, 36*(1), 23–42. doi.org/10.1177/ 0021886300361002

Orsi, R. (2014). A method for articulating grassroots community organizing outcomes. *Journal of Community Psychology, 42*(4), 398–413. doi.org/10 .1002/jcop.21617

Osgood, D. W., & Chambers, J. M. (2000). Social disorganization outside the metro-polis: An analysis of rural youth violence. *Criminology, 38*(1), 81–116. doi .org/10.1111/j.1745-9125.2000.tb00884.x

Parks, B. (2007a, July). *Crossroads pt. 1: Before 1967, a gathering storm.* http://blog.nj .com/ledgernewark/2007/07/crossroads_part_1.html

Parks, B. (2007b, July). *Crossroads pt. 2: 5 days that changed a city.* http://blog.nj.com/ ledgernewark/2007/07/crossroads_pt_2.html

Peet, J. (2009, August). *A block in Newark known for drugs and gangs is safe, for NOW.* www.nj.com/news/2009/08/a_block_in_newark_known_for_dr.html

Peterson, N. A., Speer, P. W., Hughey, J., et al. (2008). Community organizations and sense of community: Further development in theory and measurement. *Journal of Community Psychology, 36*(6), 798–813. doi.org/10 .1002/jcop.20260

Perkins, D. D., & Taylor, R. B. (1996). Ecological assessments of community disorder: Their relationship to fear of crime and theoretical implications. *American*

Journal of Community Psychology, 24(1), 63–107. doi.org/10.1007/BF02511883

Pierre, C. L., Burnside, A., & Gaylord-Harden, N. K. (2020). A longitudinal examination of community violence exposure, school belongingness, and mental health among African-American adolescent males. *School Mental Health, 12*, 388–399. doi.org/10.1007/s12310-020-09359-w

Putnam, R. D. (2000). *Bowling alone: The collapse and revival of American community.* New York: Simon & Schuster.

Putnam, R. D., Leonardi, R., & Nanetti, R. Y. (1993). *Making democracy work: Civic traditions in modern Italy.* Princeton, NJ: Princeton University Press.

Queally, J. (2010, August). *Newark anti-violence group holds 1-year anniversary march.* www.nj.com/news/2010/08/newark_anti-violence_group_hol.html

Reiss Jr., A. J., & Roth, J. A. (1994). *Understanding and preventing violence, Vol. 4: Consequences and control.* Washington, DC: The National Academies Press.

Revenson, T. A., & Seidman, E. (2002). Looking backward and moving forward: Reflections on a quarter century of community psychology. In T. A. Revenson et al. (Eds.), *A quarter century of community psychology: Readings from the* American Journal of Community Psychology (pp. 3–31). New York: Kluwer Academic/Plenum Publishers.

Rojas, R., & Atkinson, K. (2017, July). 50 years after the uprising: Five days of unrest that shaped, and haunted, Newark. *The New York Times.* www.nytimes.com/2017/07/11/nyregion/newark-riots-50-years.html

Sampson, R. J. (2001). How do communities undergird or undermine human development? Relevant contexts and social mechanisms. In A. Booth & A. Crouter (Eds.), *Does it take a village? Community effects on children, adolescents, and family* (pp. 3–30). Mahwah, NJ: Lawrence Erlbaum.

Sampson, R. J., & Groves, W. B. (1989). Community structure and crime: Testing social-disorganization theory. *American Journal of Sociology, 94*(4), 774–802. doi.org/10.1086/229068

Sampson, R. J., Raudenbush, S. W., & Earls, F. (1997). Neighborhoods and violent crime: A multilevel study of collective efficacy. *Science, 277*(5328), 918–924. doi.org/10.1126/science.277.5328.918

Sanzone, J., Weidman, M., & Doykos, B. (2016). *Needs and segmentation analysis of the South Ward of Newark, New Jersey.* https://steinhardt.nyu.edu/scmsAdmin/media/users/atn293/reval/needs_segmentation_alalysis_south_ward.pdf

Seidman, E., Yoshikawa, H., Roberts, A., et al. (1998). Structural and experiential neighborhood contexts, developmental stage, and antisocial behavior among urban adolescents in poverty. *Development and Psychopathology, 10*(2), 259–281. doi.org/10.1017/s0954579498001606

Serrano-García, I. (2020). Resilience, coloniality, and sovereign acts: The role of community activism. *American Journal of Community Psychology, 65*(1–10). doi.org/10.1002/ajcp.12415

Sexton, T. L. (2011). *Functional family therapy in clinical practice: An evidence-based treatment model for working with troubled adolescents.* New York: Routledge/Taylor & Francis Group.

Shaw, C. R., & McKay, H. D. (1942). *Juvenile delinquency and urban areas*. Chicago: University of Chicago Press.

Shihadeh, E. S., & Steffensmeier, D. J. (1994). Economic inequality, family disruption, and urban black violence: Cities as units of stratification and social control. *Social Forces, 73*(2), 729–751. doi.org/10.2307/2579828

Shoenwald, S. K., Henggeler, S. W., & Rowland, M. D. (2016). Multisystemic therapy. In T. L. Sexton & J. Lebow (Eds.), *Handbook of family therapy* (pp. 271–285). New York: Routledge/Taylor & Francis Group.

Smalls Glover, C., Smith, E., Yu, D., & Lewis, C. (2019). Families and community-based programs: Characteristics, engagement, and dissemination. In B. H. Fiese, M. Celano, K. Deater-Deckard, E. N. Jouriles, & M. A. Whisman (Eds.), *APA handbook of contemporary family psychology: Foundations, methods, and contemporary issues across the lifespan*, Vol. 2. (pp. 351–364). Washington, DC: American Psychological Association.

Stanton, M. (2009). The systemic epistemology of the specialty of family psychology. In J. H. Bray & M. Stanton (Eds.), *The Wiley-Blackwell handbook of family psychology* (pp. 5–20). Oxford, UK: Wiley-Blackwell.

Stanton, M., & Welsh, R. (2011). *Specialty competencies in couple and family psychology*. New York: Oxford University Press.

Suyemoto, K. L., & Tree, C. A. F. (2006). Building bridges across differences to meet social action goals: Being and creating allies among people of color. *American Journal of Community Psychology, 37*(3–4), 237–246. doi.org/10.1007/s10464-006-9048-1

Taylor, R., Gottfredson, S., & Brower, S. (1984). Block crime and fear: Defensible space, local social ties and territorial functioning. *Journal of Research in Crime and Delinquency, 21*(4), 303–331. doi.org/10.1177/0022427884021004003

Thrasher, F. M. (1963). *The gang: A study of 1313 gangs in Chicago* (Rev. ed.). Chicago: University of Chicago. (Original work published 1927)

US Census Bureau. (n.d.). *American community survey (ACS)*. www.census.gov/acs/www/data/data-tables-and-tools/data-profiles/2014/

US Census Bureau. (2016). *LEHD origin-destination employment statistics (2002–2015)*. Washington, DC: US Census Bureau, Longitudinal-Employer Household Dynamics Program. https://onthemap.ces.census.gov

US Census Bureau. (2017). *American community survey (ACS)*. https://datausa.io/profile/geo/newark-nj/#about

US Census Bureau. (2019). *Quick facts. Newark City, New Jersey*. www.census.gov/quickfacts/fact/table/newarkcitynewjersey/RHI525217#qf-headnote-a

US Department of Justice. (2014). Investigation of the Newark Police Department. United States Attorney's Office, District of New Jersey. www.justice.gov/sites/default/files/crt/legacy/2014/07/22/newark_findings_7-22-14.pdf

US Department of Justice. (2016). *United States v. City of Newark. Consent decree*. www.justice.gov/opa/file/836901/download

Wandersman, A., Andrews, A., Riddle, D., & Fancett, C. (1983). Environmental psychology and prevention. In R. Felner et al. (Eds.), *Preventive psychology: Theory, research and practice* (pp. 104–127). New York: Pergamon Press.

Wandersman, A., & Nation, M. (1998). Urban neighborhoods and mental health: Psychological contributions to understanding toxicity, resilience, and interventions. *American Psychologist, 53*(6), 647–656. doi.org/10.1037/0003-066x.53.6.647

White, M., Kasl, S. V., Zahner, G. E., & Will, J. C. (1987). Perceived crime in the neighborhood and mental health of women and children. *Environment and Behavior, 19*(5), 588–613. doi.org/10.1177/0013916587195003

Wilson, W. J. (2012). *The truly disadvantaged: The inner city, the underclass, and public policy.* Chicago: University of Chicago Press.

Witherspoon, D., & Ennett, S. (2011). An examination of social disorganization and pluralistic neighborhood theories with rural mothers and their adolescents. *Journal of Youth and Adolescence, 40*(9), 1243–1253. doi.org/10.1007/s10964-009-9499-4

Zanbar, L., & Itzhaky, H. (2013). Community activists' competence: The contributing factors. *Journal of Community Psychology, 41*(2), 249–263. doi.org/10.1002/jcop.21527

Zinzow, H. M., Ruggiero, K. J., Resnick, H., et al. (2009). Prevalence and mental health correlates of witnessed parental and community violence in a national sample of adolescents. *Journal of Child Psychology and Psychiatry, 50*(4), 441–450. doi.org/10.1111/j.1469-7610.2008.02004.x

15 Promoting Adolescent Mental Health

A Transculturally Informed Approach to Engaging Developmental Neuropsychology in the Support of Prevention and Intervention

Scott J. Hunter

15.1 Introduction

Adolescence is a period of significant change, one where expectations increase with regard to both independence and how demands will be managed (Galvan, 2017; Steinberg, 2011). Adolescence is defined as a period between the ages of ten and nineteen (World Health Organization [WHO], 2014). This period is consistent with an array of biological and psychological changes that unfold starting with puberty, and which end when emerging adulthood begins to, as defined by each society, allow individuals to function independently (Spear, 2000; Steinberg, 2011).

Mental health is a particularly important component of adolescent development. The risk for challenges behaviorally and emotionally and the capacity to understand and address one's health and mental health care needs emerge during adolescence (Steinberg & Morris, 2001). As such, it has become increasingly important that this period and its demands, given the changes that take place in cognitive and behavioral regulatory skill, be best appreciated and addressed scientifically (Steinberg & Morris, 2001; Suleiman & Dahl, 2017). Neuroscience in particular has been informative across the latter twentieth century and now into the twenty-first, regarding how to best appreciate what is unfolding neurodevelopmentally, and how we can translate that into a more robust understanding of what is both possible and challenging across adolescence into emerging adulthood.

For the purposes of this chapter, neuroscience refers to the examination of "the structure and function of the human brain and nervous system. Neuroscientists use cellular and molecular biology, anatomy and physiology, human behavior and cognition, and other disciplines, to map the brain at a mechanistic level" (*Psychology Today*, April 17, 2020, retrieved from www .psychologytoday.com/us/basics/neuroscience). However, much of this neuroscientific research has taken place in Western cultures (Galvan, 2017; Pedraza & Mungas, 2008). While there is increasing data to indicate that the biological processes that unfold during adolescence are relatively universal across world cultures (Galvan, 2017; Steinberg, 2011), how these processes vary in response to differences in contextual and social demands deserves greater attention (Galvan, 2014, 2017; Steinberg, 2011).

In 2016 and 2017, the current author had the opportunity to participate in a series of cross-national symposia and consultations in Cuba and China, addressing how, within varied medical and rehabilitation settings, clinical neuropsychologists, psychiatrists, neurologists, and other allied medical and mental health clinicians can utilize current neuroscientific research to inform best practices that address a range of psychological and psychiatric sequelae of neurodevelopmental and neurological concerns in pediatric and adolescent populations. With each of these engagements came the opportunity to share relevant models of clinical neuroscience practice, and to learn about differing approaches to scientific investigation and clinical practice in pediatric specialties, where collaboration with the West has been often constrained by geopolitical considerations.

These international opportunities importantly occurred simultaneous to the author's participation on the task force to revise the American Psychological Association's (APA) multicultural guidelines for the practice of professional psychology (see Clauss-Ehlers et al., 2019). The emphasis of the work undertaken by the task force was to address intersectionality and international considerations across all aspects of professional psychological efforts (e.g., science, clinical practice, teaching, and consultation). This confluence of collaborations addressed the multicultural practice of mental and behavioral health, both within the broadening diversity of the United States and in conjunction with international colleagues, and was pivotal in terms of how the author has come to think about multicultural considerations within clinical work, as well as research in neuropsychological development. The range of issues raised during these efforts served to have a significant impact with regard to considerations about how pediatric neuropsychology is currently practiced within the USA. Central to these considerations is an acknowledgement about how we as a profession are remiss in our efforts to effectively address the demands of working with diverse patients and their families that have arisen over time. This need has played out both locally and as pediatric neuropsychology has expanded, internationally as well; it has required that the profession more effectively address the needs of a global population of practitioners and consumers.

These opportunities led the author of this chapter to attempt to confront a challenge that exists for clinical neuropsychology as it is conceptualized through a primarily Western lens. This challenge was to attend to the impact of broader clinical neuroscience itself and its implications for understanding adolescent development in particular. This involves addressing how models presently being utilized in assessment and diagnosis within mental health and neuropsychological care are able to meet the needs (or not) of a growing diversity of individuals requiring intervention and diagnostic services within the United States, as well as internationally (Byrd et al., 2008; Rivera Mindt et al., 2010).

If our goal is to seek to minimize the negative impact of trauma and adversity that emerges during childhood and adolescence, within societies where low resource availability is increasingly commonplace, and to increase cognitive and behavioral capabilities and growth developmentally, then it is imperative that we work to improve our capacity to address these needs as they exist within an international populace. This involves gauging whether the translation of what we have come to know neuroscientifically is appropriate within a broader cultural lens.

In developing this chapter, it has been necessary to engage a wider literature than might typically be done when thinking about neuropsychological practice. To understand the current necessity for those of us practicing in clinical neuroscience, it is important to move beyond traditional literatures of neuroscience and neuropsychology. Here it is critical to engage in work being conducted by globally based researchers and clinicians who consider how to best address what the WHO (2005) has characterized as a crisis in our investment in pediatric health worldwide: The assessment and intervention of mental health disorders in children and adolescents across cultures and environments (see also Moleiro, 2018). Underlying this review is a question readily seen as most relevant to adolescent practice at this time in the twenty-first century: How to attempt to find a more common language to consider opportunity, challenge, and resilience as it unfolds for adolescents and their families. What this chapter hopes to discuss and guide is a broader set of developmental considerations with regard to the practice of pediatric mental health care, and pediatric neuropsychology in particular; a shared commitment to interdisciplinary care that is culturally considered, and yet utilizes and applies scientifically supported approaches and models in a thoughtful and collaborative, integrated manner.

The chapter begins with a review of what is known neuroscientifically regarding puberty, adolescence, and emerging adulthood, and how this is conceptualized within a cross-cultural framework. It then considers pediatric neuropsychological assessment specifically, as a principal method to address questions of risk and resilience in adolescence, and how that can be accomplished through a multicultural and intersectional lens. Following a brief example regarding pediatric neuropsychology as it is practiced in China in comparison with the United States, a culturally responsive model of assessment to support prevention and intervention for mental health needs in adolescents is presented.

15.2 A Brief Review of the Neuroscience of Adolescence

A detailed understanding of the importance and significance of brain development and resulting maturity that unfolds during adolescence has emerged in the last decades of the twentieth century and the beginning of the twenty-first (Galvan, 2017). Neuroscientific explorations of cognitive and behavioral development, focusing specifically on the organization and refinement of neural networks that occur in response to the substantial brain reorganization that takes place during adolescence, have informed us of the significance this period holds developmentally (Galvan, 2014, 2017; Steinberg, 2011; Suleiman & Dahl, 2017). More directly, the results from these studies have had an impact on and altered how, particularly in the northern and western hemispheres, teenagers and emerging adults are considered with regard to autonomy and agency (Steinberg, 2011).

Among the clearest representations of this change in our understanding of adolescent neural development are the dramatic improvements that have emerged in legal and ethical considerations about how and when an individual can be seen as competent in the USA, in other words, showing adult-level reasoning, judgment, and the capacity for independent decision-making (see recent decisions by the US Supreme Court abolishing the death penalty for individuals under the age of eighteen – *Roper* v. *Simmons* [2005] – and banning sentences of life without parole for individuals under eighteen convicted of crimes other than homicide – *Graham* v. *Florida* [2010] – and then with *Miller* v. *Alabama* / Jackson v. Hobbs [2012], the determination that life without parole for any juvenile offense is unconstitutional; see Galvan, 2017). We have come to better understand that adolescence is a period that encompasses significant alterations and improvements in how the brain both processes and then utilizes information to support increasingly more effective choices and decisions. This understanding has come to strongly influence how we regard capacity as well as how youth are capable of managing their experiences and controlling their behaviors (Grootens-Wiegers et al., 2017).

One of the ideas most associated with adolescence in the USA is that it is a time of exploration of self, ideas, and identification (Steinberg, 2011). Cultural norms about adolescence in the USA consider how youth move from a childhood period of attachment and socialization more directly tied to the home and family to, following the changes that occur with puberty that engage greater social interest, a more peer-centered period, where friends and acquaintances hold greater sway and influence (Albert, Chein, & Steinberg, 2013; Steinberg, 2011). Concurrent with this greater engagement with peers is also a strong motivation to seek out and explore what a range of new experiences can offer (Crone & Dahl, 2012; Galvan, 2014). This highlights an understanding of adolescence as a period of time where self-efficacy, self-identity, and self-actualization are directed toward meeting the goals of both biological and psychological needs to come: specifically, reproductive maturity, the ability to use knowledge to guide independence, and the initiation of an adult life (Galvan, 2017; Steinberg, 2011).

As a result, adolescence can be a period where significant risks unfold, both in terms of mental health status and being capable of meeting enhanced demands (Steinberg, 2011). Notably, adolescence is known as a period when many mental health challenges that can impede adult development begin to emerge; depressive and anxiety disorders, and more significantly, the psychotic disorders, most typically start to impede development during adolescence (Allott et al., 2013; Steinberg, 2011). For example, while symptoms of major depressive disorder do occur in childhood, at a prevalence rate of around 1%–3% of the population, recurrent depression occurs at a prevalence rate consistent with adults by age fifteen (i.e., 5%–7%; Wilson et al., 2015). Similarly, the increased vulnerability to the onset of symptoms of a psychotic disorder typically occurs between the ages of fifteen and seventeen, with a median age at which a psychotic disorder diagnosis is made in community tracked samples of twenty-two years (Kessler et al., 2007). For both young men and women, changes that begin with puberty can often serve to contribute to greater variabilities in mood and behavioral regulation (Hamlat et al., 2019). For example, youth with comorbid Attention-Deficit/Hyperactivity Disorder (ADHD; a disorder of attention, impulse regulation, and behavioral and cognitive motivation – APA, 2013; Fine et al., 2018) and Oppositional Defiant Disorder (ODD; a disruptive behavior disorder impacting social compliance and motivation – APA, 2013) may show an increase in impulsive and poorly regulated behaviors, including onset of disruptive conduct during adolescence that impedes both learning and peer relationships, and may contribute to challenges with opportunity when entering adulthood (Burke, Row, & Boylan, 2014; Pardini & Fite, 2010). Youth with neurodevelopmental disorders, like Autism Spectrum Disorder (ASD; a neurogenetic syndrome that affects social communication, language, and executive functioning – APA, 2013) or intellectual disability syndromes, are also vulnerable to showing a more challenging presentation between puberty and adolescence (Klein-Tasman & Janke, 2010; Janke & Jacola, 2018; Janke & Klein-Tasman, 2012). This includes both physical change with regard to such challenges as increased seizure activity that disrupts cognitive and behavioral functioning (Felix & Hunter, 2010; Janke & Jacola, 2018), and the emergence of increased impulse and regulation disorders (Einfeld et al., 2006).

Cross-cultural studies have contributed to our understanding that these enhanced risks for the onset of mental health challenges are international in their presentation. Although there are epidemiological differences tied to cultural factors (i.e., how mood disorders may be experienced in Chinese mainland communities versus in Toronto Canada, for example; see Liu, Tein, & Zhao, 2004), age of onset of mood and behavioral disorder profiles are relatively stable across most communities globally (Achenbach & Rescorla, 2006; Kessler & Bromet, 2013; Laceulle, Vollebergh, & Ormel, 2015). Kessler and colleagues (2007), examining WHO Mental Health surveys, have shown that nearly one-half of all mental disorders emerge across the world by the mid-teens to early twenties, highlighting the vulnerability of the adolescent period to the expression of underlying genetic and environmental risks for disorder onset.

To support how we think about adolescence more directly, it is important to review what we have come to understand takes place neurodevelopmentally, to make sense of risk, and to consider how to best address both risk and resilience to mental health concerns during adolescence. With the onset of puberty, occurring typically between nine and twelve years of age (and generally one to two years earlier for girls versus boys; Galvan, 2017), a torrent of hormonally influenced changes occur that begin to reorganize physical and psychological functioning (Galvan, 2017).

Children undergoing puberty experience an increase in adrenal androgens, gonadal steroids, and growth hormones that signal to the body that it is time to undergo significant physical growth and maturation, metabolic changes, neural reorganization, and accompanying cognitive, behavioral, and emotional alterations. Appetite, motivation, physical activity, circadian rhythms, and sleep are all disrupted as a result of these hormonal signals that support growth in size and shape, and the maturation of the capacity to meet reproductive drives. As adolescence settles in, myelination of brain white matter, thinning of grey matter, and dendritic growth and refinement of neural networks occurs, setting in place the foundation for the individual to engage greater cognitive control skills (Galvan, 2014, 2017; Hunter et al., 2012b). Particularly important is the elaboration of subcortical, frontal, and broader networks across the brain, and their interaction, supporting enhanced and more automatic information processing that allows for increases in memory, attention, visuoperceptual and spatial analysis, language, and executive functioning (Galvan, 2017; Hunter et al., 2012a, 2012b; Steinberg, 2011).

The use of neuroimaging technologies has allowed the move from animal models (e.g., mouse models of the expression underlying risk to OCD, that examine disruptions in neural patterning; see Zike et al., 2017) to more directly being able to demonstrate how, in the human brain, puberty and adolescence come to sculpt neural networks for increasing adult-level functioning (Galvan, 2017). Work beginning with Casey and her team (Casey & Caudle, 2013; Casey et al., 1997; see also Steinberg, 2011) has shown how the immature brain, particularly the subcortical areas related to attentional and regulatory capacities, including the hippocampus, hypothalamic-pituitary-adrenal (HPA) axis, and the broader limbic system, undergo substantial growth and engagement with puberty that initiates and directs a program of reorganization and enhanced cortical development (Galvan, 2017). This developmental engagement guides and supports the forming of more secure neural linkages between the subcortical structures and the frontally based neural systems, to facilitate greater top-down cognitive and behavioral control as the need to manage increased challenges with learning and regulation emerges (Blakemore, Burke, & Dahl, 2010; Galvan, 2017; Hunter et al., 2012b).

More specifically, the prefrontal cortex, which has been shown to serve as the principle control center for cognitive and behavioral actions, and has been identified as the slowest-developing region of the brain (i.e., with final myelination proposed to fully complete around the mid-to-latter twenties), emerges as a primary player during the adolescent years (Hunter et al., 2012a). Importantly, the elongated development of the frontal system differs from the enhanced development that occurs in the areas of the brain that manage affective and social responses, the limbic and subcortical regions (Galvan, 2017). This has led to the identification of when some aspects of neural organization are at adult levels, and have an impact on emotional, sexual, and behavior activation circuitry. However, this occurs without the support of a fully mature executive system, that allows for better regulation and impulse management (Blakemore et al., 2010; Galvan, 2017; Hunter et al., 2012b). Hence, protracted organization of the brain during adolescence facilitates a capacity for some aspects of mature cognitive engagement, but without the more mature management that the prefrontal system provides, as it reaches its stable developmental apex (Hunter et al., 2012a, 2012b).

Galvan (2014, 2017) has recently reviewed and synthesized a growing literature that has suggested that "the relatively unstable nature of the prefrontal cortex in adolescents renders it more susceptible to emotional, arousing, or distracting information than in adults" (2014, p. 262). What has come to be understood is that there is a strong contextual pattern with regard to how executive functioning occurs for adolescents (Hackman, Farah, & Meaney, 2010; Hunter et al., 2012a). When confronted by "cold" or less arousing situations, adolescent responses cognitively (and, as a result, behaviorally) are generally consistent with adult-level expectations (Galvan, 2017). In contrast, when engaged with "hot," or more emotionally arousing experiences and situations, adolescent cognitive responses are less mature, and their behavioral reactions are more impulsive and intense (Hunter et al., 2012a, 2012b). Studies have shown that part of the greater tendency toward emotionally intense responses seen during adolescence is a result of this variability in executive control; the reduced capacity for mature regulation of experience leads to a greater degree of reactivity when under stress or challenge (Luna, 2009). This has a strong message regarding how we conceptualize capability and potential response with regard to adolescents. It suggests that we need to directly consider context, and cognitive and behavioral demands placed on adolescents by their differing environments in efforts to assess and make sense of differential vulnerabilities to risk and mental health need (Galvan, 2017; Hackman et al., 2010; Steinberg, 2011; Suleiman & Dahl, 2017).

As noted above, this differential pattern of development allows us to better appreciate how an array of risks plays out for adolescents across teenage and emerging adulthood years. While the underlying neurology readily supports and directs drives toward exploration, risk-taking, and sexual desire, the system that best allows for such drives to be directed and effectively engaged, the executive prefrontal networks, is still immature (Galvan, 2017; Hunter et al., 2012a, 2012b). Hence, as increasingly adult-level feelings and wishes arise, the capacity for thinking through and making sense of these goals and experiences is at times more limited, and at risk for being more impulsively responded to, potentially leading to conflict and challenge educationally, with parents, and with peers (Steinberg, 2011). As adolescence progresses, brakes are stronger on these impulsive choices and responses, however; the exception is when situations are more emotionally arousing and charged (Galvan, 2017), and when they are more directly influenced by underlying risk for psychological distress, like symptoms of depression and anxiety, or when challenged by such difficulties as ADHD (Fine et al., 2018) or a neurodevelopmental disorder like ASD (Wolf, Barton, & Jou, 2018). Youth who experience the sequelae of medical illnesses may also show variabilities in their development during this period (Suleiman & Dahl, 2017). For instance, one of the extended effects for some children who were identified with early cancers and who were treated with chemotherapies is the risk for developing a dysexecutive profile that inhibits effective learning and behavioral regulation as adolescence proceeds (Paltin et al., 2018).

15.3 Considerations Regarding Cross-Cultural Pediatric Neuropsychological Assessment and Implications for Understanding Adolescent Mental Health

Within the USA and other developed Western nations (i.e., Canada, the United Kingdom, Brazil, Mexico, and the western European Union), neuropsychological evaluation has become a more readily available and utilized resource for addressing the challenges that emerge during childhood, adolescence, and adulthood with regard to learning, adaptive functioning, and behavioral and emotional regulation (Elbulok-Charcape et al., 2014; Rivera-Mindt et al., 2010). Initially developed in the latter twentieth century as a downward extension of adult neuropsychological models, pediatric neuropsychology has advanced toward a more explicit approach that is separate from, and more developmentally informed, than adult models of neurocognitive functioning (Baron & Rey-Casserly, 2013; Donders & Hunter, 2010, 2018; Hunter & Donders, 2007; Yeates et al., 2010). As our understanding of developmental neuroscience has progressed, the clinical approach taken with pediatric neuropsychological assessment has evolved, to better capture the organizational efforts that have been found to occur as the brain matures across childhood and through adolescence (Hunter & Sparrow, 2012). This has led to the development of standardized measures as well as scoring approaches that are separate from adult models, and informed by our increasing understanding of how cognition unfolds across time neurodevelopmentally. These tools have assisted in the continued identification of models regarding how the expression of skills and capacities emerges and consolidates into more mature patterns, and when that occurs (Hunter & Sparrow, 2012).

This has allowed for a more effective consideration of the interplay between brain and environment within the discipline, contextual considerations regarding how development unfolds, and an appreciation for the fact that brain development occurs as a response to both genetic (and epigenetic) factors and environmental influences, from gestation through the move into adulthood (Bernstein, 2010; Donders & Hunter, 2018). The understanding of how neurocognitive systems both engage, and then interact neurologically, and how those interactions define the opportunities for learning and behavioral control, has informed how assessment can be best appreciated in its aggregate (Bernstein, 2010). As such, the pediatric neuropsychological evaluation has become a significant tool for making sense of the interplay between what is expected neurodevelopmentally and contextually (Hunter & Sparrow, 2012; Sparrow, 2007, 2012; Spevack, 2006).

Despite these movements forward, there is a significant challenge at play, that has been discussed more readily within the adult neuropsychological literature (Byrd et al., 2008; Elbulok-Charcape et al., 2014; Fujii, 2017; Manly & Echemendia, 2007) but less so with any sophistication in the pediatric neuropsychological literature (see Byrd et al., 2008 and Ries, Potter, & Llorente, 2007). The majority of the measures developed to address neuropsychological functioning in a standardized manner have come from English-speaking countries (e.g., the Wechsler Scales; Byrd et al., 2008; Farmer & Vega, 2010; Fujii, 2017). This is a result of the fact that neuropsychological practice has emerged principally within a Western, and primarily US/Canadian context (Byrd et al., 2008; Elbulok-Charcape et al., 2014; Fujii, 2017). As a result, models are often based on studies conducted on the US culture; and translated versions of measures have remained tied to principally US-published tests as well, relying on structures of measuring cognition that are tied to a framework of learning and knowledge development, as well as behavioral regulation that is culturally narrow and specific, in other words Western hemisphere defined and focused (Byrd et al., 2008; Farmer & Vega, 2010; Fujii, 2017). Efforts are being made regularly to broaden the capacity to utilize neuropsychological measures on a diverse set of individuals more representative of the populations that immigrate to and reside in the USA (and also Australia and Canada, as well as within the Spanish-speaking countries of Mexico and South America; Fujii, 2017). However, what is still being more often considered through assessment methods in the USA is based on a model of development that is situated within a Western framework, and that therefore assesses acculturation to the dominant (i.e., US) culture by evaluating what has been learned through attending a US-based school program. This is opposed to methods that could more readily consider potential differences in capability that may be a product of an individual's foundational cultural experiences (Byrd et al., 2008; Farmer & Vega, 2010; Fujii, 2017; Rivera Mindt et al., 2010).

The failures to consider how measures utilized cross-culturally may assist us in understanding underlying differences that can exist given differing environments and experiences are pronounced. As we begin to consider how addressing alterations in development might have an impact on adolescence, particularly in regard to the interplay of psychopathology and cognition, we are held back in our ability to fully appreciate developmental range and variability based on our continued use of culturally insensitive and biased assessment approaches (Allott et al., 2013; Byrd et al., 2008; Farmer & Vega, 2010; Rivera Mindt et al., 2010). To best appreciate risk, and how one may propose interventions that can alter or ameliorate the impact of that risk in adolescence, it becomes imperative to be able to effectively utilize tools in conjunction with a culturally informed interview approach that facilitates an understanding of underlying developmental status (Byrd et al., 2008; Ries et al., 2007).

Relying on tools that have been developed and utilized as part of a research approach can be informative, but without appropriate normative comparisons, difficulties abound with regard to the identification of cognitive and adaptive differences in comparison with age and education level expectations (Farmer & Vega, 2010). Additionally, as discussed by Farmer and Vega, normative sample development is dependent on the access to and consideration of the breadth of communities that comprise a particular nationally selected sample. In the USA, the emphasis when compiling a Latinx/Hispanic sample is on language most typically, without consideration of regional and national variations in the populations comprising that sample (Farmer & Vega, 2010). Similarly, use of contextually inappropriate or irrelevant standardized tools proves unreliable as well if the goal is to understand adolescents within their environments, and how they differ in their functioning relative to their peers (Byrd et al., 2008). In contrast, if the desire is to compare individuals to the broader context they reside within, such as with families that have immigrated and settled in the USA, then there may be a stronger argument made to utilize the data obtained and effectively identify weaknesses relative to their current context, in other words determining level of acculturation and the impact of English language-based education (Manly & Echemendia, 2007).

15.4 Current Practices in the USA versus China: An Opening for Change

When the author was presenting on the neuropsychological functioning of youth with epilepsy and ASD in Beijing in 2016 and 2017, it became readily apparent that questions asked by Chinese colleagues required a different set of analyses than those typically considered by a Western-oriented pediatric neuropsychologist. In a country with significantly more people than in the USA (i.e., 1,419,408,166 vs. 328,789,078; data obtained from WorldPopulationReview.com on May 13, 2019) and where the availability of resources for intervention and rehabilitation are also more limited depending on where an individual resides (A. S. Chan, Leung, & Cheung, 2010; R. C. K. Chan et al., 2016; Liang, Mays, & Hwang, 2018), a number of differences in approach to assessment and how obtained data are interpreted came into focus. Discussions regarding how assessment is conducted in Beijing, specifically at the Capital Institute of Pediatrics, revealed that the patient load itself, of children and adolescents coming in for evaluations in conjunction with their treatment for seizure disorders, was even more substantial than any program in the USA, Canada, or Australia (i.e., through discussions with colleagues at conferences and meetings; D. Ping, personal communication, November 12, 2017). This has led to a program conducting evaluations across a twenty-four-hour period weekly, as opposed to the typical eight-to-twelve-hour period that is more typical in the USA.

As such, a reliance on the administration of a limited battery of standardized tests was the norm. These included a Chinese version of the Wechsler Intelligence Scale for Children, Revised (WISC-R), a measure first developed and used in the USA in 1974 (Wechsler, 1974; of note, a Mandarin Chinese version of the WISC-4 is used in Taiwan – see Yang et al., 2013), adaptations of tests such as the Tower of Hanoi (Simon, 1975), the Wisconsin Card Sorting Test (Berg, 1948; Heaton et al., 1993), and a number of computer-administered measures taken from cognitive research but not normed clinically. Discussions ensued during this consultation regarding the broader and more comprehensive battery used in a typical US-based clinic, and how this might be balanced with the use of techniques such as quantitative electroencephalography (QEEG; a method of analysis of brain electrical activity that has been applied toward differential diagnosis across both medical and mental health conditions) and neuroimaging (that is commonly utilized to assess structural and some functional information in typically functioning populations and those with neurological conditions).

Both of these are more readily being implemented within the clinical setting in Beijing in comparison to the USA. The emphasis on such biological data as QEEG for the diagnosis of behavioral and cognitive disorders is a likely by-product of the need to utilize potential biomarkers of disease states and disability, and the reality that in China clinicians must assess a large population of patients requiring intervention and support across the full twenty-four-hour day (A. S. Chan et al., 2010; D. Ping, personal communication, November 12, 2017). For example, unlike a typical program in the USA, where between one and four children are seen daily within a hospital-based neuropsychology clinic, with an eight-to-ten-hour norm for clinic scheduling across the work week, in China it was found that assessments were conducted round the clock, six to seven days per week. This process developed because of the need to see thousands of children yearly, versus the hundreds seen by US programs. Importantly, although there is a large research literature regarding the use of neuroimaging and QEEG-based approaches to understand neurodevelopment (Galvan, 2017; Van Horn & Pelphrey, 2015), their applications within the clinical setting, outside neurological diagnosis, still remain under investigation in Western countries. Data supporting their reliability for making clinical diagnoses remain unreliable, and elicit questions regarding the clinical validity as a result (Krull, George, & Strother, 2007).

Additionally discussed, and readily considered, were the challenges regarding how to best appreciate differences in dialect, and how this has an impact on profiles on measures reliant on language skills (see Boone et al., 2007; A. S. Chan et al., 2010; R. C. K. Chan et al., 2016); economic status; implications on such factors as stability of housing, nutrition, and educational opportunity (see Muscatell, 2018); and on the challenge of understanding the impact of developmental psychopathology on cognitive and behavioral functioning within a culture that appreciates emotion and emotional functioning within a very different framework (see A. S. Chan et al., 2010; Ford & Mauss, 2015; Sun & Ryder, 2016). As discussed by Lim (2016):

> In Western or individualist culture, high arousal emotions are valued and promoted more than low arousal emotions. Moreover, Westerners experience high arousal emotions more than low arousal emotions. By contrast, in Eastern or collectivist culture, low arousal emotions are valued more than high arousal emotions. Moreover, people in the East actually experience and prefer to experience low arousal emotions more than high arousal emotions.   (p. 105)

These discussions raised further questions regarding how to best appreciate the interplay of neurodevelopment and profiles of functioning obtained with quantitative versus qualitative measures.

What became apparent from these discussions was a need to better appreciate how effective assessment and determination of functional status in developing individuals requires a multimethod approach (see Bernstein, 2010). To more effectively understand developmental status, particularly with an adolescent population that is vulnerable to significant variability given their unfolding profiles of cognitive and behavioral capability, and their emotion regulatory skill (see Galvan, 2017; Hunter et al., 2012a), the integration of data from both observational and quantitative assessments, and across disciplines involved in working with adolescents, is readily required. Diagnosis and identification of interventions is highly dependent on what can be understood about context and opportunity (Piccolo et al., 2016; Sarsour et al., 2011). For example, to address learning and emotional regulation in a teenager who is affected by both seizures and the effects of the medication used to control epilepsy, the neuropsychologist is encouraged to, at a minimum, gain an understanding of contextual variables like schooling sophistication, social demands and supports, available resources for physical and emotional support, housing stability, and parental and educational staff expectations (Felix & Hunter, 2010). Further, knowledge regarding how this young person is able to meet adaptive demands and what is expected adaptively is also required (Farmer & Vega, 2010; Spevack, 2006).

Risks regarding developmental expectations and how they can be met must also be understood. For instance, an adolescent from a family with substantial resources may be able to more readily receive supports and a balancing of expectations that foster resiliency, versus an adolescent whose family is expecting their adolescent child to balance attending some schooling along with bringing in an income. Hence, addressing how an adolescent is functioning and where support or guidance, let alone more significant intervention, may be helpful within a diverse context, requires a multilayered approach. Cognition and its associated components (e.g., language, attention, memory, perceptual understanding and reasoning, and executive functioning), emotional and behavioral regulation, and current contextual factors all together prove needed, to ensure effective identification and understanding of status (Bernstein, 2010; Sparrow, 2012; Spevack, 2006).

15.5 Where We Can Go Next: A Culturally Informed Model of Pediatric Neuropsychological Assessment

Bernstein (2010) has written about the need to make sense of brain development and the underlying genetics (and epigenetics, the generational variations in risk and resilience that unfold across time) that influence the expression of neural systems and their interactions, and the environment the individual grows up in, when addressing the impact of normative and impacted neurodevelopment. This has become a significant model within pediatric neuropsychology; one that is particularly useful when appreciating and making sense of how adolescents, whose greatest task is to become executively competent as a means of promoting individuation and independence, maturity, and growth, develop and mature. Yet what has become increasingly clear is that a model developed to make sense of normative development for youth who are resourced and growing up within a Western environment is one that is inadequate to appreciate the range of possible trajectories that unfold toward successful adulthood across a more diverse and less financially stable world. Our increased understanding of the underpinnings of neurodevelopment, through current approaches to developmental neuroscience, has allowed us to make sense of the range of interactions and unfolding engagements that take place neurologically to support the move from childhood, through adolescence, into adulthood. However, neuroscience remains young in its capacity to reveal the intricate interactions that underlie cognitive development universally, given the individual and ultimately cultural-level variations that are present, across the interplay of genetics and environment. And testing reflects experience, which is varied among differing settings and opportunities.

Cognitive and behavioral regulation required to support the biological drives and desires that emerge during adolescence that facilitate the promulgation of the human species are sophisticated skills that emerge across time, and not in a necessarily linear manner (Galvan, 2017). As such, understanding the interplay between environmental expectations, in a diverse and increasingly complex world, and how these expectations can be best met given an array of challenges to the system (i.e., psychopathology, learning disorder, mood disorders, injury or illness) requires a clinical approach that is sophisticated in its understanding of differences across cultures, and what they may influence both behaviorally and neurologically. Current models think about what the world requires of adolescents, and what, in turn, can be provided to allow for successful opportunity; these models however are biased toward development in a Western-oriented context (Farmer & Vega, 2010). Moreover, these models are increasingly found to be inadequate for making sense of the reality of our increasingly intersected world, where communications and interactions cross-culturally are more dynamic and movement across settings is more frequent. Bridging these differences requires a process that is intersectional itself; integrating an array of observational, investigational, and quantitative measures and approaches that allow us to make sense of development both within and across contexts (Clauss-Ehlers et al., 2019).

Because a principal developmental task of adolescence is executive control (Hackman et al., 2015; Hunter & Sparrow, 2012; Last et al., 2018; Ursache & Noble, 2016) and the refinement of how emotional and cognitive demands are regulated, it is important to conceptualize assessment during this period as targeted toward identifying both strengths and weaknesses in the areas of attentional shifting, impulse control, and problem-solving. Recognizing that intellectual development is a foundational capacity built upon attentional and executive skills, while also understanding that intelligence itself is not purely executive (Friedman et al., 2006), it is necessary that assessment addresses more than the mere consideration of intelligence. This is particularly important when thinking about how to best support building resilience and autonomy. Identifying how capacities to manage challenge, stress, and independence are unfolding requires a conceptualization that is context-dependent (Sarsour et al., 2011). Determining what the environment an adolescent situates in requires, and addressing expectations placed on the individual sets an initial understanding of what is needed to address where supports or guidance may be required. Such expectations can be identified through a combination of interviewing and gaining access to more direct information (via standardized questionnaires or reports from significant others within the life of the adolescent, be it parents, teachers, and even other clinicians). Learning what expectations are placed on the adolescent sets an initial understanding of what is needed to address where supports or guidance may be required. Understanding culturally what is at play, in terms of educational expectations, goals, and what youth themselves seek to either learn about or take on, also provides guidance about the settings where youth are situated. Recognizing that language, motor, and visuoperceptual demands are often contextually determined (Galvan, 2017), a culturally informed standardized measure or set of measures that guide understanding of the individual's foundational skills become pivotal, if at times quite challenging (Farmer & Vega, 2010; Fujii, 2017). And yet, to best make sense of what autonomy may be present, and how that can be facilitated, requires the examination of developing executive controls. This requirement serves to underscore the work needed ahead, both with regard to standardizing and obtaining a normative profile for youth across diverse cultural settings and environments, and in determining how to develop new measures within evolving technologies that promote a common understanding of development across contexts (Fujii, 2017; Olson & Jacobson, 2014).

15.6 Conclusion

Mental health in adolescence is predicated on a growing capacity for self-regard, self-efficacy, and self-control (Casey & Caudle, 2013; Steinberg, 2011). When depression emerges and becomes severe, or when anxiety increases and is incapacitating for the adolescent, what is often most at issue is not foundational cognitive capabilities, but instead those skills that allow for regulation and problem-solving (Edidin & Hunter, 2012; Marvel & Paradiso, 2004; Sivan, 2010). Executive functioning situates as the domain most at risk at this developmental period (Hackman et al., 2015). As such, the task of the mental health clinician is to work collaboratively with all those providing support for the youth; this includes parents, teachers, coaches, and mentors, in addition to physicians and clinicians, to best assess, across all settings and circumstances for that adolescent, how to best engage and promote increased opportunity for choice and independent decision-making.

When these developing skills are compromised, interventions are required to guide the adolescent toward a more effective capacity to make choices and see one's self as competent. For an adolescent living in a setting where daily community violence is at play and threatens a sense of safety, for instance, engagement in a program of intervention that addresses the trauma experienced and that allows a growing capacity for efficacious choices in response to these challenges can promote more effective outcomes; this is believed in part to be a reflection of enhanced development of executive controls. Hence, collaborative mental health engagement, through interviewing that is culturally sensitive, assessment with appropriate tools given the context within which the adolescent resides and is developing (Eisenberg & Belfer, 2008; Fujii, 2017), and culturally specific considerations to intervention and guidance forward (Clauss-Ehlers et al., 2019), requires a multidisciplinary approach. This multicultural, multidisciplinary approach recognizes the options that are at hand and identifies where opportunity may lie.

References

Achenbach, T. M., & Rescorla, L. A. (2006). *Multicultural understanding of child and adolescent psychopathology: Implications for mental health assessment.* New York: Guilford Press.

Albert, D., Chein, J., & Steinberg, L. (2013). The teenage brain: Peer influences on adolescent decision-making. *Current Directions in Psychological Science, 22* (2), 114–120. doi.org/10.1177/0963721412471347

Allott, K., Proffitt, T., McGorry, P. D., et al. (2013). Clinical neuropsychology within adolescent and young adult psychiatry: Conceptualizing theory and practice. *Applied Neuropsychology: Child, 2*(1), 47–63. doi.org/10.1080/08841233.2012.670566

American Psychiatric Association. (2013). *Diagnostic and statistical manual of mental disorder* (5th ed.; DSM-5). Washington, DC: American Psychiatric Association.

Baron, I. S., & Rey-Casserly, C. (2013). *Pediatric neuropsychology: Medical advances and lifespan outcomes.* Oxford, UK: Oxford University Press.

Berg, E. A. (1948). A simple objective test for measuring flexibility in thinking. *Journal of General Psychology, 39*(1), 15–22. doi.org/10.1080/00221309.1948.9918159

Bernstein, J. H. (2010). Developmental models of pediatric neuropsychology. In J. Donders & S. J. Hunter (Eds.), *Principles and practice of lifespan developmental neuropsychology* (pp. 17–40). Cambridge, UK: Cambridge University Press.

Blakemore, S. J., Burnett, S., & Dahl, R. E. (2010). The role of puberty in the developing adolescent brain. *Human Brain Mapping, 31*(6), 926–933. doi.org/10.1002/hbm.21052

Boone, K. B., Victor, T. L., Wen, J., Razani, J., & Ponton, M. (2007). The association between neuropsychological scores and ethnicity, language, and acculturation variables in a large patient population. *Archives of Clinical Neuropsychology, 22*(3), 355–365. doi.org/10.1016/j.acn.2007.01.010

Burke, J. D., Rowe, R., & Boylan, K. (2014). Functional outcomes of child and adolescent ODD symptoms in young adult men. *Journal of Child Psychology and Psychiatry, 55*(3), 254–272. doi.org/10.1111/jcpp.12150

Byrd, D., Arentoft, A., Scheiner, D., Westerveld, M., & Baron, I. S. (2008). State of multicultural neuropsychological assessment in children: Current research issues. *Neuropsychology Review, 18,* 214–222. doi.org/10.1007/s11065-008-9065-y

Casey, B. J., & Caudle, K. (2013). The teenage brain: Self-control. *Current Directions in Psychological Science, 22*(2), 82–87. doi.org/10.1177/0963721413480170

Casey, B. J., Trainor, R. J., Orendi, J. L., et al. (1997). A developmental functional MRI study of prefrontal activation during performance of a Go-No-Go task. *Journal of Cognitive Neuroscience, 9*(6), 835–847. doi.org/10.1162/jocn.1997.9.6.835

Chan, A. S., Leung, W. W., & Cheung, M. (2010). Clinical neuropsychology in China. In M. Harris-Bond (Ed.), *Oxford handbook of Chinese psychology* (pp. 383–397). Oxford, UK: Oxford University Press.

Chan, R. C. K., Wang, Y., Wang, Y., & Cheung, E. F. C. (2016). Practice, training, and research in neuropsychology in mainland China: Challenges and opportunities. *The Clinical Neuropsychologist, 30*(8), 1207–1213. doi.org/10 .1080/13854046.2016.1217353

Clauss-Ehlers, C. S., Chiriboga, D. A., Hunter, S. J., Roysircar, G., & Tummala-Nara, P. (2019). APA Multicultural Guidelines executive summary: Ecological approach to context, identity, and intersectionality. *American Psychologist, 74*(2), 232–244. doi.org/10.1037/amp0000382

Crone, E., & Dahl, R. E. (2012). Understanding adolescence as a period of social-affective engagement and goal flexibility. *Nature Reviews: Neuroscience, 13*, 636–650. doi.org/10.1038/nrn3313

Donders, J., & Hunter, S. J. (2010). *Principles and practice of lifespan developmental neuropsychology*. Cambridge, UK: Cambridge University Press.

Donders, J., & Hunter, S. J. (2018). *Neuropsychological conditions across the lifespan.* Cambridge, UK: Cambridge University Press.

Edidin, J. P., & Hunter, S. J. (2012). Executive functions in mood and anxiety disorders. In S. J. Hunter & E. P. Sparrow (Eds.), *Executive function and dysfunction: Identification, assessment, and treatment* (pp. 141–148). Cambridge, UK: Cambridge University Press.

Einfeld, S. L., Piccinin, A. M., Mackinnon, A., et al. (2006). Psychopathology in young people with intellectual disability. *Journal of the American Medical Association, 296*(16), 1981–1989. doi.org/10.1001/jama.296.16.1981

Eisenberg, L., & Belfer, M. (2008). Prerequisites for global child and adolescent mental health. *The Journal of Child Psychology and Psychiatry, 50*(1–2), 26–35. doi .org/10.1111/j.1469-7610.2008.01984.x

Elbulok-Charcape, M. M., Rabin, L. A., Spadaccini, A. T., & Barr, W. B. (2014). Trends in neuropsychological assessment of ethnic/racial minorities: A survey of clinical neuropsychologists in the United States and Canada. *Cultural Diversity and Ethnic Minority Psychology, 20*(3), 353–361. doi.org/10.1037/ a0035023

Farmer, T., & Vega, C. (2010). Multicultural considerations in lifespan neuropsychological assessment. In J. Donders & S. J. Hunter (Eds.), *Principles and practice of lifespan developmental neuropsychology* (pp. 55–68). Cambridge, UK: Cambridge University Press.

Felix, L., & Hunter, S. J. (2010). Pediatric aspects of epilepsy. In J. Donders & S. J. Hunter (Eds.), *Principles and practice of lifespan developmental neuropsychology* (pp. 359–370). Cambridge, UK: Cambridge University Press.

Fine, J. G., Marks, D. J., Wexler, D., Dahl, V. M., & Horn, E. P. (2018). Attention-deficit/hyperactivity disorder. In J. Donders & S. J. Hunter (Eds.), *Neuropsychological conditions across the lifespan* (pp. 93–115). Cambridge, UK: Cambridge University Press.

Ford, B. Q., & Mauss, I. B. (2015). Culture and emotion regulation. *Current Opinions in Psychology, 3*, 1–5. doi.org/10.1016/j.copsyc.2014.12.004

Friedman, N. P., Miyake, A., Corley, R. P., et al. (2006). Not all executive functions are related to intelligence. *Psychological Science, 17*(2), 172–179. doi.org/10 .1111/j.1467-9280.2006.01681.x

Fujii, D. (2017). *Conducting a culturally informed neuropsychological evaluation.* Washington, DC: American Psychological Association Press.

Galvan, A. (2014). Insights about adolescent behavior, plasticity, and policy from neuroscience research. *Neuron*, *83*(2), 262–265. doi.org/10.1016/j.neuron.2014.06.027

Galvan, A. (2017). *The neuroscience of adolescence*. Cambridge, UK: Cambridge University Press.

Graham v. *Florida*. (2010). 560 US 48.

Grootens-Wiegers, P., Hein, I. M., van den Broek, J. M., & de Vries, M. (2017). Medical decision-making in children and adolescents: Developmental and neuroscientific aspects. *BMC Pediatrics*, *17*(1), 1–10. doi.org/10.1186/s12887-017-0869-x

Hackman, D. A., Farah, M. J., & Meaney, M. J. (2010). Socioeconomic status and the brain: Mechanistic insights from human and animal research. *Nature Reviews: Neuroscience*, *11*, 651–659. doi.org/10.1038/nrn2897

Hackman, D. A., Gallop, R., Evans, G. W., & Farah, M. J. (2015). Socioeconomic status and executive function: Developmental trajectories and mediation. *Developmental Science*, *18*(5), 686–702. doi.org/10.1111/desc.12246

Hamlat, E. J., Snyder, H. R., Young, J. F., & Hankin, B. L. (2019). Pubertal timing as a transdiagnostic risk for psychopathology in youth. *Clinical Psychological Science*, *7*(3), 411–429. doi.org/10.1177/2167702618810518

Heaton, R. K., Chelune, G. J., Talley, J. L., Kay, G. G., & Curtis, G. (1993). *Wisconsin card sorting test manual: Revised and expanded*. Odessa, TX: Psychological Assessment Resources.

Hunter, S. J., & Donders, J. (2007). *Pediatric neuropsychological intervention*. Cambridge, UK: Cambridge University Press.

Hunter, S. J., Edidin, J. P., & Hinkle, C. D. (2012a). The developmental neuropsychology of executive functions. In S. J. Hunter & E. P. Sparrow (Eds.), *Executive function and dysfunction: Identification, assessment, and treatment* (pp. 17–36). Cambridge, UK: Cambridge University Press.

Hunter, S. J., Hinkle, C. D., & Edidin, J. P. (2012b). The neurobiology of executive functions. In S. J. Hunter & E. P. Sparrow (Eds.), *Executive function and dysfunction: Identification, assessment, and treatment* (pp. 37–64). Cambridge, UK: Cambridge University Press.

Hunter, S. J., & Sparrow, E. P. (2012). Models of executive functioning. In S. J. Hunter & E. P. Sparrow (Eds.), *Executive function and dysfunction: Identification, assessment, and treatment* (pp. 5–16). Cambridge, UK: Cambridge University Press.

Janke, K., & Jacola, L. (2018). Intellectual disability syndromes. In J. Donders & S. J. Hunter (Eds.), *Neuropsychological conditions across the lifespan* (pp. 61–78). Cambridge, UK: Cambridge University Press.

Janke, K., & Klein-Tasman, B. K. (2012). Executive functions in intellectual disability syndromes. In S. J. Hunter & E. P. Sparrow (Eds.), *Executive function and dysfunction: Identification, assessment, and treatment* (pp. 109–122). Cambridge, UK: Cambridge University Press.

Kessler, R. C., Amminger, G. P., Aguilar-Gaxiola, S., et al. (2007). Age of onset of mental disorders: A review of recent literature. *Current Opinions in Psychiatry*, *20*(4), 359–364. doi.org/10.1097/YCO.0b013e32816ebc8c

Kessler, R. C., & Bromet, E. J. (2013). The epidemiology of depression across cultures. *Annual Review of Public Health, 34*, 119–138. doi.org/10.1146/annurev-pub lhealth-031912-114409

Klein-Tasman, B., & Janke, K. (2010). Intellectual disability syndromes across the lifespan. In J. Donders & S. J. Hunter (Eds.), *Principles and practice of lifespan developmental neuropsychology* (pp. 221–238). Cambridge, UK: Cambridge University Press.

Krull, K. R., George, M. R., & Strother, D. (2007). Quantitative electroencephalography and neurofeedback. In S. J. Hunter & J. Donders (Eds.), *Pediatric neuropsychological intervention* (pp. 392–414). Cambridge, UK: Cambridge University Press.

Laceulle, O. M., Vollebergh, W. A. M., & Ormel, J. (2015). The structure of psychopathology in adolescence: Replication of a general psychopathology factor in the TRAILS Study. *Clinical Psychological Science, 3*(6), 850–860. doi.org/10.1177/2167702614560750

Last, B. S., Lawson, G. M., Breiner, K., Steinberg, L., & Farah, M. J. (2018). Childhood socioeconomic status and executive function in childhood and beyond. *PLoS ONE, 13*(8), Article e0202964. doi.org/10.1371/journal.pone.0202964

Liang, D., Mays, V. M., & Hwang, W. (2018). Integrated mental health services in China: Challenges and planning for the future. *Health Policy and Planning, 33*(1), 107–122. doi.org/10.1093/heapol/czx137

Lim, N. (2016). Cultural differences in emotion: Differences in emotional arousal level between the East and the West. *Integrative Medicine Research, 5*(2), 105–109. doi.org/10.1016/j.imr.2016.03.004

Liu, X., Tein, J., & Zhao, Z. (2004). Coping strategies and behavioral/emotional problems among Chinese adolescents. *Psychiatry Research, 126*(3), 275–285. doi.org/10.1016/j.psychres.2004.02.006

Luna, B. (2009). Developmental changes in cognitive control through adolescence. *Advances in Child Development and Behavior, 37*, 233–278. doi.org/10.1016/s0065-2407(09)03706-9

Manly, J. J., & Echemendia, R. J. (2007). Race-specific norms: Using the model of hypertension to understand issues of race, culture, and education in neuropsychology. *Archive of Clinical Neuropsychology, 22*(3), 319–325. doi.org/10.1016/j.acn.2007.01.006

Marvel, C. L., & Paradiso, S. (2004). Cognitive and neurological impairment in mood disorders. *Psychiatric Clinics of North America, 27*(1), 19–36. doi.org10.1016/S0193-953X(03)00106-0

Miller v. *Alabama / Jackson* v. *Hobbs.* (2012). 567 US.

Moleiro, C. (2018). Culture and psychopathology: New perspectives on research, practice, and clinical training in a globalized world. *Frontiers in Psychiatry, 9*, Article 366. doi.org/10.3389/fpsyt.2018.00366

Muscatell, K. A. (2018). Socioeconomic influences on brain function: Implications for health. *Annals of the New York Academy of Sciences, 1428*(1), 14–32. doi.org/10.1111/nyas.13862

Olson, K., & Jacobson, K. (2014). Cross-cultural consideration in pediatric neuropsychology: A review and call to attention. *Applied Neuropsychology: Child, 4*(3), 166–177. doi.org/10.1080/21622965.2013.830258

Paltin, I., Burgers, D. E., Gragert, M., & Noggle, C. (2018). Cancer. In J. Donders & S. J. Hunter (Eds.), *Neuropsychological conditions across the lifespan* (pp. 162–185). Cambridge, UK: Cambridge University Press.

Pardini, D. A., & Fite, P. J. (2010). Symptoms of conduct disorder, oppositional defiant disorder, attention-deficit/hyperactivity disorder, and callous-unemotional traits as unique predictors of psychosocial adjustment in boys: Advancing evidence base for DSM-V. *Journal of the American Academy of Child and Adolescent Psychiatry, 49*(11), 1134–1144. doi.org/10.1016/j.jaac .2010.07.010

Pedraza, O., & Mungas, D. (2008). Measurement in cross-cultural neuropsychology. *Neuropsychology Review, 18*, 184–193. doi.org/10.1007/s11065-008-9067-9

Piccolo, L. R., Arteche, A. X., Fonseca, R. P., Grassi-Oliveira, R., & Salles, J. F. (2016). Influence of family socioeconomic status of IQ, language, memory, and executive functions of Brazilian children. *Psicologia: Reflexao e Critica, 29*, Article 23. doi.org/10.1186/s41155-016-0016-x

Ries, J. K., Potter, B. S., & Llorente, A. M. (2007). Multicultural aspects of pediatric neuropsychological intervention and rehabilitation. In S. J. Hunter & J. Donders (Eds.), *Pediatric neuropsychological intervention* (pp. 47–67). Cambridge, UK: Cambridge University Press.

Rivera Mindt, M., Byrd, D., Saez, P., & Manly, J. (2010). Increasing culturally competent neuropsychological services for ethnic minority populations: A call to action. *The Clinical Neuropsychologist, 24*(3), 429–453. doi.org/10 .1080/13854040903058960

Roper v. *Simmons*. (2005). 543 US 551.

Sarsour, K., Sheridan, M., Jutte, D., et al. (2011). Family socioeconomic status and child executive functions: The roles of language, home environment, and single parenthood. *Journal of the International Neuropsychological Society, 17*(1), 120–132. doi.org/10.1017/S1355617710001335

Simon, H. A. (1975). The functional equivalence of problem solving. *Cognitive Psychology, 7*(2), 268–288. doi.org/10.1016/0010-0285(75)90012-2

Sivan, A. B. (2010). Psychopathological conditions in children and adolescence. In J. Donders & S. J. Hunter (Eds.), *Principles and practice of lifespan developmental neuropsychology* (pp. 449–454). Cambridge, UK: Cambridge University Press.

Sparrow, E. P. (2007). Empirical bases for assessment and intervention. In S. J. Hunter & J. Donders (Eds.), *Pediatric neuropsychological intervention* (pp. 30–46). Cambridge, UK: Cambridge University Press.

Sparrow, E. P. (2012). Assessment and identification of executive dysfunction. In S. J. Hunter & E. P. Sparrow (Eds.), *Executive function and dysfunction: Identification, assessment, and treatment* (pp. 65–89). Cambridge, UK: Cambridge University Press.

Spear, L. (2000). The adolescent brain and age-related behavioral manifestations. *Neuroscience and Biobehavioral Reviews, 24*(4), 417–463. doi.org/10.1016/ s0149-7634(00)00014-2

Spevack, T. V. (2006). A developmental approach to pediatric neuropsychological intervention. In S. J. Hunter & J. Donders (Eds.), *Pediatric neuropsychological intervention* (pp. 6–29). Cambridge, UK: Cambridge University Press.

Steinberg, L. (2011). *Adolescence* (9th ed.). New York: McGraw-Hill.

Steinberg, L., & Morris, A. (2001). Adolescent development. *Annual Review of Psychology, 52*, 83–110. doi.org/10.1146/annurev.psych.52.1.83

Suleiman, A. B., & Dahl, R. E. (2017). Leveraging neuroscience to inform adolescent health: The need for an innovative transdisciplinary developmental science of adolescence. *Journal of Adolescent Health, 60*(3), 240–248. doi.org/10.1016/j.jadohealth.2016.12.010

Sun, J., & Ryder, A. G. (2016). The Chinese experience of rapid modernization: Sociocultural changes, psychological consequences? *Frontiers in Psychology, 7*, Article 477. doi.org/10.3389/fpsyg.2016.00477

Ursache, A., & Noble, K. G. (2016). Socioeconomic status, white matter, and executive function in children. *Brain and Behavior, 6*(10), Article e00531. doi.org/10.1002/brb3.531

Van Horn, J. D., & Pelphrey, K. A. (2015). Neuroimaging of the developing brain. *Brain Imaging and Behavior, 9*(1), 1–4. doi.org/10.1007/s11682-015-9365-9

Yang, P., Cheng, C., Chang, C., et al. (2013). Wechsler Intelligence Scale for Children 4th edition: Chinese version index scores in Taiwanese children with attention-deficit/hyperactivity disorder. *Psychiatry and Clinical Neurosciences, 67*(2), 83–91. doi.org/10.1111/pcn.12014

Yeates, K. O., Ris, M. D., Taylor, H. G., & Pennington, B. F. (2010). *Pediatric neuropsychology: Research, theory, and practice* (2nd ed.). New York: Guilford Press.

Wechsler, D. (1974). *Wechsler intelligence scale for children, revised.* San Antonio, TX: The Psychological Corporation.

Wilson, S., Hicks, B. M., Foster, K. T., McGue, M., & Iacono, W. G. (2015). Age of onset and course of major depressive disorder: Associations with psychosocial functioning outcomes in adulthood. *Psychological Medicine, 45*(3), 505–514. doi.org/10.1017/S0033291714001640

Wolf, J. M., Barton, M., & Jou, R. (2018). Autism spectrum disorder. In J. Donders & S. J. Hunter (Eds.), *Neuropsychological conditions across the lifespan* (pp. 45–60). Cambridge, UK: Cambridge University Press.

World Health Organization. (2005). *Mental health atlas 2005.* Geneva, Switzerland: World Health Organization, Department of Mental Health and Substance Abuse.

World Health Organization. (2014). *Recognizing adolescence.* https://apps.who.int/adolescent/second-decade/section2/page1/recognizing-adolescence.html

Zike, I., Xu, T., Hong, N., & Veenstra-Vanderweele, J. (2017). Rodent models of obsessive-compulsive disorder: Evaluating validity to interpret emerging neurobiology. *Neuroscience, 345*, 256–273. doi.org/10.1016/j.neuroscience.2016.09.012

16 Gowanus Canal and Public Policy

Community Well-Being at a Superfund Site

Beth Bingham and Susan Opotow

In just societies, public policies utilize fair processes to ensure equal access to goods and services that foster the well-being of individuals, families, and groups within the society. Porta and Last (2018) define *public policy* as including the planning, decisions, resource allocations, and actions shaped and executed by elected governmental officials, scientific and technical advisers, public opinion, and advocacy groups. Ideally, this results in enlightened public policies that guide the fair distribution of the goods, services, and opportunities that a society produces.

However, public policies can have negative effects on community well-being when they create barriers for accessing such public goods as quality education, affordable housing, stable employment, and efficient transportation (Coburn, 2004). Public policies can also guide the distribution of harms, often leaving poor communities and communities of color with environmental burdens that include despoiled land, contaminated water, and polluted air (Bullard, 2000; Opotow, 2012, 2018). Public policies fall short when they overburden communities with hazards that undermine individual and collective well-being. This can inadvertently or deliberately exacerbate inequality by excluding individuals, groups, and communities from access to society's goods, including such concrete resources as clean water (e.g., the Flint, Michigan water crisis, 2014–2019), clean air (Opotow & Weiss, 2000), and voice, as a procedural resource in decision-making (Tornblom & Vermunt, 2007). Of concern, public policies throughout the world have increased inequality in subtle and overt ways (Pikkety & Goldhammer, 2014).

This chapter focuses on a public policy. It begins by discussing the critical linkage between policy, zoning, and well-being through the lens of community psychology. We then present a case study of Gowanus, a diverse neighborhood in Brooklyn, New York, the most populous of New York City's five boroughs with an estimated 2.5 million residents (US Census Bureau, 2019). The Gowanus community has struggled with significant historical and contemporary environmental burdens for 150 years. We discuss Gowanus activists' efforts to generate constructive change and promote community well-being via a collaborative process set in motion by the community's Superfund designation in 2009. This designation allowed the community to grapple with its large-scale, historic, and ongoing environmental pollution constructively and collaboratively to envision a better future.

16.1 Public Policy and Community Well-Being

Community well-being, at the center of our analysis, is an ecology that extends to all spheres of community life characterized by "a positive state of affairs, brought about by the simultaneous and balanced satisfaction of diverse objective and subjective needs of individuals, relationships, organizations and communities" (Prilleltensky, 2012, pp. 2–3).

Achieving community well-being requires balancing the welfare of individuals with goals that also serve the collective. When valued personal and collective resources are available, the needs and well-being of individuals and communities can advance simultaneously because each is enriched by the other (Prilleltensky, 2012; Rappaport, 2011). Benevolent public policies, therefore, provide necessary resources for individuals to flourish while also promoting social ties, fostering personal growth, and empowering individuals and communities (Moos, 2003; Schueller, 2009). However, like other resources needed for well-being, community well-being is controlled by policies that are influenced by extant power structures that distribute well-being unevenly across people and groups (Prilleltensky, 2012). As we will describe, advancing the collective well-being at the scale of the neighborhood often means challenging entrenched power structures that have supported systemic inequalities. It also entails improving social and economic conditions and inequalities that are inevitably entwined with environmental conditions (Sarason, 1974).

16.1.1 Community Psychology: Public Policy to Foster Societal Well-Being

Community psychology is a branch of psychology committed to advancing the health of the whole person along with collective well-being. Launched at a 1965 conference in Swampscott, Massachusetts, psychologists in attendance envisaged a new role for psychology in society: working closely with communities, serving as consultants in community affairs, analyzing social systems, and acting as agents of change (Bennett et al., 1966; Bond, 2016; Campbell, 2016). The field's core values – community, citizen participation, and empowerment – encourage community psychologists to foster constructive community and societal change (Case, Todd, & Kral, 2014; Kloos & Duffy, 2012). Linking these professional values to systems that promulgate socially and psychologically sound policies, Bond (2016) has called for community psychologists to support communities by "documenting such challenges and inequities – as well as disparities in access to adequate health care, economic resources, and other supports – [a process that] can be invaluable in focusing our attention on critical social justice issues and in driving important policy decisions" (p. 260).

Thus, from a community psychology perspective, it is essential to critically interrogate systems that influence individual and community well-being because the distribution of resources needed for psychosocial health is subject to political decision-making that can benefit some segments of a community at the expense of others (Bond, 2016; Prilleltensky, 2012).

16.1.2 Zoning and Rezoning: Public Policies, Pollution, and Sacrifice Zones

In many communities, some of the most powerful public policy tools deployed by the state are zoning designations (Bingham & Shapiro, 2020). *Zoning* constitutes a set of policies that segregate land uses, principally dividing up land for industrial, residential, and commercial uses, but it can also result in segregating people (Angotti & Hanhardt, 2001; Pulido, 2000). The regulation of allowable land uses through zoning can influence community well-being in a variety of ways. Zoning determines where activities with noxious effluents that reduce the quality of air, water, or land (e.g., heavy industry or a highway) will be sited. Zoning also determines where public investments in communities (e.g., parkland or a library) will be sited.

Policies that maintain racial, ethnic, and socioeconomic discrimination and housing segregation corral marginalized groups into undesirable neighborhoods. This can result in limited access to key resources (e.g., schools, jobs, medical care, parks, well-stocked and fairly priced stores) that can have cumulative, long-term, harmful effects for individuals and communities (Ruel & Robert, 2009). Policy decisions that permit noxious land uses in communities where people live and work pose a significant threat to individuals' and community health. Communities most at risk of living and working in environments with polluted land, water, and air are people who are poor and people of color (Chavis & Lee, 1987; Checker, 2019; Opotow, 2018). Indeed, in the United States, race is the greatest predictor of where hazardous waste facilities are sited. Checker (2005) observes that "three of every five African Americans and Hispanics and roughly 50 percent of Asian/ Pacific Islanders and Native Americans live in communities containing at least one uncontrolled toxic waste site" (p. 13). Her study of community activism in the face of environmental degradation in the Hyde Park community near Augusta, Georgia, reveals the challenges of a residential community struggling against government indifference while they live amid contaminated land and water that has been despoiled by decades of toxic industrial waste.

As communities change, policies often change along with them. *Rezoning* occurs when existing zoning is challenged in the name of stimulating growth or economic development. It can change the nature of the community as a whole or change specific areas within a community to have significant effects on well-being for people who live and work in areas undergoing zoning change. When zoning designations heap environmental contaminants into the air, water, and ground of already-burdened communities, it results in sites some call *sacrifice zones*, land adjacent to waste disposal and toxic effluents from industry (Bullard, 2000; Lerner, 2010; Opotow, 2018). Typically, sacrifice zones are also designated for low-income residential housing; indeed, public housing is often sited near known environment hazards (Gould & Lewis, 2017).

In recent decades, housing demand in cities sparked interest in using contaminated land for new housing, resulting in an interest and need to clean toxic sites, a process that often changes the community by displacing long-term residents and workers (Angotti & Morse, 2016; Gould & Lewis, 2017). Sam Stein (2019) has argued that zoning and urban renewal are "two policies whose formal *raison d'etre* is to create rational and orderly urban landscapes; in reality, however, these tools are often used to target one racial group for exclusion or expulsion while clearing the way for another's quality of life" (pp. 27–28).

Given this background and these grim examples, this chapter provides a counterexample. In the next section we describe a community in Brooklyn, New York undergoing a federally mandated environmental cleanup as a Superfund site. It offers a promising trajectory that illustrates how chronic and severe environmental pollution can be addressed by an extended collaborative process that endeavors to improve the physical environment and to foster community well-being and social justice.

16.1.3 Case Study: Gowanus Canal Community Advisory Group, Brooklyn, New York

The Gowanus neighborhood, currently in the midst of a significant federal project that seeks to clean up a heavily polluted industrial waterway, is surrounded by several rapidly gentrifying areas (Alexiou, 2015). Through efforts to improve both the physical environment and the social and economic ecology of the community, the work of the Gowanus Canal Community Advisory Group members demonstrates how public policy can strengthen community well-being. Drawing on Beth Bingham's ethnographic fieldwork and an archive of Gowanus Canal Community Advisory Group committee meeting minutes (Gowanus Canal Community Advisory Group, 2019), we sought to understand how the Gowanus Canal Advisory Group, a group of local residents, workers, and business owners, have worked together to shape a large-scale environmental remediation project intended to correct decades of toxic pollution in a community that was designated a Superfund site in 2009.

16.1.4 History of the Gowanus Canal and the Surrounding Neighborhood

In 1849, when Brooklyn was the fastest-growing city in the United States, the New York State Legislature authorized the construction of the Gowanus Canal by dredging the existing Gowanus Creek and hardening the waterway's edges (Gould & Lewis, 2017). Though only two miles long, the Gowanus Canal, surrounded by factories, warehouses, and working-class housing, became a critical hub for Brooklyn's maritime and commercial activities. Much of the brownstone material for which "Brooklyn Brownstones" are known, was shipped from New Jersey and the upper Hudson River to Brooklyn via the canal (Gould & Lewis, 2017).

As Brooklyn developed, heavy industry concentrated on the Gowanus Canal shoreline (including coal gas manufacturers, oil refineries, machine shops, chemical plants, cement makers, sulfur producers, soap makers, and tanneries) discharged untreated waste into the canal (Alexiou, 2015; Gould & Lewis, 2017). The canal and its surrounding land became an unregulated repository for raw sewage from surrounding households and hazardous waste from heavy industrial activity. By the twentieth century, the waterway became so polluted that it was dubbed "Lavender Lake" due to its unnatural hue from a concentration of noxious effluents. Because the industry on the canal's banks was considered critical to the economy of New York City and the region, polluting the estuary and surrounding land was tolerated, which placed the health and well-being of the local workforce and residents at risk (Gould & Lewis, 2017).

In the late 1990s, rising property values in surrounding Brooklyn neighborhoods stirred new interest in the Gowanus area. This, in turn, called into question the water quality classification in place, which allowed high levels of contamination under regulations maintained by the New York State Department of Environmental Quality. Local environmental advocacy during this period included an initiative by the Gowanus Dredgers Canoe Club, which loaned canoes to recreational boaters (Gowanus Dredgers Canoe Club, 2019). This created a new use on the waterway and forced a change in the canal's water quality classification.

In 2006, the Gowanus Canal Conservancy began stewarding several upland sites along the waterfront, leading tours of the canal, and creating opportunities for community volunteers to clear debris and give new life to the toxic land via shoreline plantings (Gowanus Canal Conservancy, 2019).

In 2007, two years prior to the Superfund designation, New York City Mayor Michael Bloomberg proposed a neighborhood-wide rezoning of Gowanus. His proposed changes aligned with real estate interests that sought to transform this historic largely industrial neighborhood with well-known environmental hazards into a Bloombergian vision of New York as a luxury city, attractive to wealthy residents and investors (Angotti & Morse, 2016; Brash, 2010). Bloomberg's rezoning initiative catalyzed the Gowanus neighborhood of working-class and public housing residents, artists, industrial owners, and industrial workers. Community members worked together to challenge the proposed rezoning and demand that the government clean the canal. Based on the hazards in place and a distrust of the City's plan, community activists pursued Superfund designation at the federal level in defiance of the City (Alexiou, 2015).

Bloomberg's rezoning initiative would have brought new residential units onto contaminated land adjacent to the contaminated waterway. The zoning battle that followed was one of many occurring in New York City during this period. Though the rezoning ultimately did not occur because of the Superfund designation (Rice, 2009), the rezoning proposal alone resulted in widespread real estate speculation, displacement of vulnerable residents and businesses throughout the community, and fomented present and future worries about the fate of a neighborhood already burdened by severe environmental degradation.

In 2009, community-led advocacy had been gaining ground for a decade with the formation of several key advocacy groups including the Gowanus Dredgers Canoe Club, Gowanus Canal Conservancy, the Gowanus Canal Community Development Corporation, and the Friends and Residents of Greater Gowanus. Each of these groups sought to focus the attention of governmental leaders and agencies at local, state, and national levels on the toxicity of the canal (Gould & Lewis, 2017). Like other grassroots groups working for environmental justice, the Gowanus activists refused to accept early promises from the City that new housing sited along the waterway would provide a safe place to live. They challenged the City's assurances of environmental safety with their own knowledge, experience, and expertise. They demanded action and, like the aforementioned residents of Hyde Park, Georgia, they "questioned whose representation of the 'truth' is privileged and whose is silenced" (Checker, 2005, p. 186).

Community members hoped that official recognition of the toxicity of their neighborhood would end the plan to rezone and redevelop the neighborhood for luxury housing, and might preserve manufacturing jobs and the extant mixed-use and diverse character of the neighborhood (Alexiou, 2015). Thus, counterintuitively, community activists identified the severity of pollution and pursued a Superfund designation – ordinarily an unwanted encumbrance due to stigmatization associated with this designation – as a procedural resource that might save their neighborhood.

16.1.5 The Superfund Process: From Contamination to Cleanup

After 150 years of heavy industrial use, the Gowanus Canal was designated as a Superfund site in 2009, launching a cleanup that is estimated will take twenty years to complete. The US Environmental Protection Agency (US EPA) describes Superfund sites as follows:

Thousands of contaminated sites exist nationally due to hazardous waste being dumped, left out in the open, or otherwise improperly managed. These sites include manufacturing facilities, processing plants, landfills and mining sites. In the late 1970s, toxic waste dumps such as Love Canal and Valley of the Drums received national attention when the public learned about the risks to human health and the environment posed by contaminated sites. In response, Congress established the Comprehensive Environmental Response, Compensation and Liability Act (CERCLA) in 1980. CERCLA is informally called Superfund. It allows EPA to clean up contaminated sites. It also forces the parties responsible for the contamination to either perform cleanups or reimburse the government for EPA-led cleanup work.   (US EPA, 2018)

To meet a requirement of the cleanup process, the US EPA convened a group of local and regional stakeholders and provided formal facilitation and needed technical resources intended to support and sustain the Community Advisory Group for the duration of the cleanup process. The Gowanus Canal Community Advisory Group (CAG) was created in 2010 to represent a range of interests in the community and to work with the US EPA and with state and local agencies throughout the Superfund process. As this is being written in 2020, volunteers who comprise the CAG have been working together for ten years to support and guide the canal cleanup. The work of the CAG, in turn, is shaping the future of the Gowanus neighborhood.

When the Gowanus Canal CAG was first created, an outside facilitator was hired by the US EPA to convene stakeholders and develop an outreach strategy as a mandated part of the Superfund process. In 2010, the first public meetings called by the US EPA and facilitator were attended by more than two hundred residents, workers, business owners, nonprofit organizations, and real estate developers in Gowanus (Gowanus Canal Community Advisory Group, 2019). The breadth of the initial outreach efforts and the diversity represented by the core group that has remained active for the past ten years reflect the complexity of a community that is inextricable from its surrounding environment (see also Sarason, 1974).

The Gowanus Canal CAG has twenty individual members and thirty organizational representative members (Gowanus Canal Community Advisory Group, 2019) that include resident-advocates, business owners, and organizations active in the community. The CAG represents personal, local, citywide, and regional interests. Some stakeholders clearly have more political power than others. The dynamic present in Gowanus typifies a *contact zone*, a construct that describe how groups with different interests and kinds of power struggle with constructive energy to find common ground (Pratt, 1991; Torre et al., 2008). The Gowanus Canal CAG functions as a contact zone in that a range of groups with diverse accesses to power come together and, in their interactions, struggle for change concerning present and imagined land uses. As a result of these differing and incompatible perspectives among government entities, private developers, and local residents, conflicts that emerge within CAG deliberations can take shape in a variety of ways.

16.1.6 Ongoing Challenges and Working Together

The Superfund designation in 2009 ended Bloomberg's vision to rezone the canal's banks for luxury housing, but several urban planning initiatives in surrounding communities followed. A comprehensive planning process called *Bridging Gowanus*, spearheaded and funded by New York City Council Member Brad Lander, informed a subsequent study undertaken by the NYC Department of City Planning that resulted in a new rezoning proposal made public in 2019.

Interestingly, with each new project and issue that has arisen, many CAG members have begun to support the interests of other community stakeholders, taking a more holistic approach that imagines how planning for the future could benefit more than their own particular interests in the community. In response to each new participatory process concerning rezoning, members of the CAG – as neighborhood stakeholders that include industrial owners/workers and public housing residents – have worked collaboratively to represent community interests. Though Mayor Bill de Blasio's administration is driven by a mandate to create more affordable housing, the rezoning he is proposing is much like Bloomberg's 2007 vision as it would allow upscale and luxury residential development in an industrial zone. As this is being written in 2020, CAG members are continuing their work together to address emerging challenges from a new round of rezoning discussions. Again, the embattled Gowanus community has been catalyzed by the prospect of a city policy that brings new housing into an environment that remains polluted.

16.2 Empowerment, Inclusion, and Tenacity

In her work on moral exclusion and inclusion, Opotow (1990) has examined the social psychological processes that normalize injustice by positioning some groups as outside the boundary in which moral values, rules, and considerations of fairness apply. Excluded groups often lack important public resources, including quality housing, health care, education, worker safety codes, and the availability of fairly paid work. Instead, people positioned as excluded are vulnerable to harm or exploitation that can be normalized as "the way things are" or "the way they ought to be" (Opotow, 2012, p. 416). Inclusionary commitments, in contrast, are characterized by three social justice attitudes: (1) the belief that fairness applies to all, (2) the willingness to share community resources with others, and (3) the willingness to make personal or collective sacrifices to foster the well-being of others (Opotow, 1990, 2012).

Communities, like individuals and groups, can be excluded, exploitable, and expendable, exemplified by despoiled land, air, and water and their designation as dumping grounds for residential and industrial waste (Opotow, 2012). Since the middle of the nineteenth century when the canal and its surrounds became the unregulated repository for industrial waste, the Gowanus area in Brooklyn has exemplified an excluded community where policy drove the concentration of contaminants that polluted the waterway and surrounding land placed residents and local workers at risk (see also Opotow, 2018). Because of this, the challenge of the CAG's efforts has not only been to improve environmental conditions, but also to foster inclusionary processes, policies, structures, and outcomes that can advance community and environmental well-being.

The Gowanus Canal CAG, a group with diverse membership (e.g., residents, business owners, and organizational representatives) that has been brought together by federal policies to steer an environmental cleanup, has grown closer over time. Connected by a political as well as a geographical context, they have formed a *relational community* (Sonn & Fisher, 1996, p. 417). Over the course of a decade, they have developed trust and collaborative skills, enabling members of the Gowanus Canal CAG to work together on individual and shared agendas, fostering connectedness (see also Schueller, 2009). The fifty individual and organizational members of the Gowanus Canal CAG include people with divergent and sometimes conflicting goals for the neighborhood's future. However, as a result of their long-term commitment to working together as volunteers on the Gowanus Canal CAG, they have formed close relationships. Even people and organizations with significantly different agendas work together to ensure that the cleanup of the waterway is comprehensive and good for the community. The important and influential partnerships that have emerged from these collaborative efforts are consistent with Checker's (2005) observation that in environmental justice settings, flexible interpretations of *environment* can operate as an organizing narrative. Thus, the mission of one group can attend to the ecological needs of the natural estuary and another to the workforce needs of manufacturers, but through the CAG they can work together.

Consistent with Deutsch (1975), who observed that the construct, *well-being*, has important psychological, physiological, economic, and social aspects, community psychologists have argued that environmentally sound policies will result from processes and practices that maximize participation by diverse constituencies within the local context to achieve a fair allocation of the societal resources to support community well-being. Deutsch (1973) has also advised that although conflict is an ever-present aspect of social relationships, it is not invariably destructive. Conflict that occurs within a cooperative context, he argues, can surface important issues to foster constructive outcomes. For the Gowanus Canal CAG, conflict has energized individuals, fostered collaborations, and motivated the group to tenaciously pursue positive social and policy changes in the community, though their individual backgrounds, agendas, and expertise are diverse. The members of this group are diverse as well, but they all have a stake in the health and well-being of the Gowanus neighborhood. By acting together, community groups can reduce a community's disproportionate exposure to environmental hazards and burdens (Opotow, 2012). Collaborations that mobilize stakeholders, engage allies, and amplify the public's voice can effectively protest long-standing environmental pollution and obtain access to legal and political power that had been elusive before (Opotow, 2018; Young, 2001).

Bond (2016) has observed that locally, specific issues and practices shape the meaning of diversity within a community. Her work is consistent with environmental justice scholars who have argued that environmental conflicts are best addressed at the local level, which is where they matter most (e.g., Syme et al., 2000). Local people are motivated to resolve issues they face, and their knowledge of the particulars of their community, both physically and socially, can inform environmentally sensitive and sound policy (Chang & Opotow, 2009). As Schueller (2009) observes: "Individuals are best able to reach their potential when their own needs for autonomy, competence and connectedness in the community are met. Empowering communities achieves all of these goals by allowing members and collective organizations the opportunity to define their own agendas, which promotes a sense of competence and connectedness in the community" (p. 931).

16.3 Conclusion

We end with the fundamental question underlying this research: What are the conditions that can foster social justice and moral inclusion while envisioning the remediation and denormalization of exclusionary policy? This longitudinal ethnographic study offers insight into elements and challenges of successful participation. It reveals that conflict, connection, and continuity have served as an important basis for the CAG's accomplishments.

The case of the Gowanus Canal CAG suggests that time is on the side of social justice activist groups. Working together on long-term projects builds relationships, increases knowledge, and the esprit de corps needed to persist (Crane et al., 2018). In this case, the scale and timeframe of the cleanup and the mandated outside facilitation of the CAG resulted in regularly scheduled meetings that fostered timely communication and trust-building over many years.

Opotow (2012) has described the achievement of inclusionary goals as slow, as a process that takes time. In light of that, we view the tenacity of group members, their willingness to continue their work together despite inevitably conflicting interests and priorities as the critically important process of inclusion. Its key elements are valuing diverse perspectives, fostering connectedness, and sustaining the collective determination to correct long-standing, destructive, exclusionary, and unjust policies of the past. And, working together, they draw on local wisdom to envision and realize better policies for the future.

References

Alexiou, J. (2015). *Gowanus: Brooklyn's curious canal*. New York: New York University Press.

Angotti, T., & Hanhardt, E. (2001). Problems and prospects for healthy mixed-use communities in New York City. *Planning Practice & Research, 16*(2), 145–154. doi.org/10.1080/02697450120077352

Angotti, T., & Morse, S. (2016). *Zoned out! Race, displacement, and city planning in New York City*. New York: Terreform, Inc.

Bennett, C. C., Anderson, L. S., Cooper, S., et al. (1966). *Community psychology: A report of the Boston Conference on the Education of Psychologists for Community Mental Health*. Boston: Boston University.

Bingham, B., & Shapiro, J. (2020). Land use regulation for manufacturing. In N. Rappaport (Ed.), *Designing for urban manufacturing* (pp. 203–211). New York: Routledge.

Bond, M. (2016). Leading the way on diversity: Community psychology's evolution from invisible to individual to contextual. *American Journal of Community Psychology, 58*(3–4), 259–268. doi.org/10.1002/ajcp.12083

Brash, J. (2010). *Bloomberg's New York: Class and governance in the luxury city*. Athens, GA: University of Georgia Press.

Bullard, R. (2000). *Dumping in Dixie: Race, class, and environmental quality* (3rd ed.). Boulder, CO: Westview Press.

Campbell, R. (2016). "It's the way that you do it": Developing an ethical framework for community psychology research and action. *American Journal of Community Psychology, 58*(3–4), 294–302. doi.org/10.1002/ajcp.12037

Case, A., Todd, D., & Kral, N. (2014). Ethnography in community psychology: Promises and tensions. *American Journal of Community Psychology, 54*(1), 60–71. doi.org/10.1007/s10464-014-9648-0

Chang, V., & Opotow, S. (2009). Conservation values, environmental identity, and moral inclusion in the Kunene Region, Namibia: A comparative study. *Beliefs and Values, 1*(1), 79–89.

Chavis, B. F., Jr., & Lee, C. (1987). *Toxic wastes and race in the United States*. New York: United Church of Christ Commission for Racial Justice.

Checker, M. (2005). *Polluted promises: Environmental racism and the search for justice in a southern town*. New York: New York University Press.

Checker, M. (2019). Environmental gentrification: Sustainability and the just city. In S. Low (Ed.). *The handbook of anthropology and the city* (pp. 199–213). London and New York: Routledge.

Coburn, D. (2004). Beyond the income inequality hypothesis: Class, neo-liberalism, and health inequalities. *Social Science & Medicine, 58*(1), 41–56. doi.org/10.1016/s0277-9536(03)00159-x

Crane, M., Flynn, K., Lucchini, R., et al. (2018). Health impacts of 9/11. In S. Opotow & Z. B. Shemtob (Eds.), *New York after 9/11* (pp. 145–179). New York: Fordham University Press.

Deutsch, M. (1973). *The resolution of conflict: Constructive and destructive processes.* New Haven, CT: Yale University Press.

Deutsch, M. (1975). Equity, equality, and need: What determines which value will be used as the basis of distributive justice? *Journal of Social Issues, 31*(3), 137–149. doi.org/10.1111/j.1540-4560.1975.tb01000.x

Gould, K., & Lewis, T. L. (2017). *Green gentrification: Urban sustainability and the struggle for environmental justice.* New York: Routledge.

Gowanus Canal Community Advisory Group. (2019). *Home page.* https://gowanuscag.org

Gowanus Canal Conservancy. (2019). *History.* https://gowanuscanalconservancy.org/history/

Gowanus Dredgers Canoe Club. (2019). *History.* https://gowanuscanal.org/gowanus-canal-history

Kloos, B., & Duffy, K. (2012). *Community psychology: Linking individuals and communities* (3rd ed.). Belmont, CA: Wadsworth Cengage Learning.

Lerner, S. (2010). *Sacrifice zones: The front lines of toxic chemical exposure in the United States.* Cambridge, MA: MIT Press.

Moos, R. (2003). Social contexts: Transcending their power and their fragility. *American Journal of Community Psychology, 31*(1–2), 1–13. doi.org/10.1023/A:1023041101850

Opotow, S. (1990). Moral exclusion and injustice: An overview. *Journal of Social Issues, 46*(1), 1–20. doi.org/10.1111/j.1540-4560.1990.tb00268.x

Opotow, S. (2012). Environmental injustice, collaborative action, and the inclusionary shift. In S. Clayton (Ed.), *The Oxford handbook of environmental and conservation psychology* (pp. 414–427). Oxford, UK: Oxford University Press.

Opotow, S. (2018). Social justice theory and practice: Fostering inclusion in exclusionary contexts. In P. L. Hammack (Ed.), *The Oxford handbook of social psychology and social justice* (pp. 41–56). New York: Oxford University Press.

Opotow, S., & Weiss, L. (2000). New ways of thinking about environmentalism: Denial and the process of moral exclusion in environmental conflict. *Journal of Social Issues, 56*(3), 475–490. doi.org/10.1111/0022-4537.00179

Piketty, T., & Goldhammer, A. (2014). *Capital in the twenty-first century.* Cambridge, MA: Harvard University Press.

Porta, M., & Last, J. M. (2018). Public policy. In M. Porta & J. M. Last (Eds.), *A dictionary of public health* (2nd ed.). Oxford, UK: Oxford University Press.

Pratt, M. (1991). Arts of the contact zone. *Profession,* 33–40.

Prilleltensky, I. (2012). Wellness as fairness. *American Journal of Community Psychology, 49*(1–2), 1–21. doi.org/10.1007/s10464-011-9448-8

Pulido, L. (2000). Rethinking environmental racism: White privilege and urban development in Southern California. *Annals of the Association of American Geographers, 90*(1), 12–40. doi.org/10.1111/0004-5608.00182

Rappaport, J. (2011). Searching for OZ: Empowerment, crossing boundaries, and telling our story. In M. S. Aber, K. I. Maton, & E. Seidman (Eds.), *Empowering settings and voices for social change* (pp. 232–237). New York: Oxford University Press.

Rice, A. (2009, October 21). On the waterfront. *The New York Times Magazine*. www .nytimes.com/2009/10/25/magazine/25Key-Gowanus-t.html

Ruel, E., & Robert, S. A. (2009). A model of racial residential history and its association with self-rated health and mortality among black and white adults in the United States. *Sociological Spectrum, 29*(4), 443–466. doi.org/10.1080/02732170902904616

Sarason, S. B. (1974). *The psychological sense of community: Prospects for a community psychology*. San Francisco: Jossey-Bass.

Schueller, S. (2009). Promoting wellness: Integrating community and positive psychology. *Journal of Community Psychology, 37*(7), 922–937. doi.org/10.1002/jcop.20334

Sonn, C. C., & Fisher, A. T. (1996). Psychological sense of community in a politically constructed group. *Journal of Community Psychology, 24*(4), 417–430. doi .org/10.1002/(SICI)1520-6629(199610)24:4<417::AID-JCOP9>3.0.CO;2-Q

Stein, S. (2019). *Capital city: Gentrification and the real estate state*. London, UK: Verso.

Syme, G. J., Kals, E., Nancarrow, B. E., & Montada, L. (2000). Ecological risks and community perceptions of fairness and justice: A cross-cultural model. *Risk Analysis, 20*(6), 905–916. doi.org/10.1111/0272-4332.206083

Tornblom, K., & Vermunt, R. (Eds.). (2007) *Distributive and procedural justice: Research and social applications*. Burlington, VT: Ashgate.

Torre, M. E. & Fine, M. with Alexander, N., Billups, A., Blanding, Y., et al. (2008). Participatory action research in the contact zone. In J. Cammarota & M. Fine (Eds.), *Revolutionizing education: Youth participatory action research in motion* (pp. 23–43). New York: Routledge.

US Census Bureau. (2019). *QuickFacts for Kings County (Brooklyn Borough), New York, 2018*. Retrieved November 28, 2019, from www.census.gov/quickfacts/fact/table/kingscountybrooklynboroughnewyork,US/PST045218

US Environmental Protection Agency. (2018, November 30). *What is a Superfund?* www.epa.gov/superfund/what-superfund

Young, I. M. (2001). Activist challenges to deliberative democracy. *Political Theory, 29*(5), 670–690. doi.org/10.1177/0090591701029005004

17 Family Support Services at Ronald McDonald House Promotes Healing of Seriously Ill Children

Susan Regas, Martha Hernández, John Bakaly, and Ronda Doonan

According to the National Child Traumatic Stress Network (n.d.), childhood injuries and illnesses are common. Five out of a hundred children in the United States are hospitalized for a major acute or chronic illness or injury. Although 11,000 children are diagnosed with new cancers annually, there are approximately 250,000 children who are cancer survivors. More than 1,000 children have organ transplants a year, and thousands are waitlisted. More than 25,000 children are living with a serious illness at any given time in the United States, and nearly 17 million adults are caregivers to a seriously ill child (Kuhlthau et al., 2010).

Children's reactions to medical trauma have more to do with their personal experience of the illness or injury rather than its actual severity. Reactions vary in intensity and can either be adaptive or may negatively impact functioning. Nearly 80% of children and their families suffer some traumatic stress reactions following a life-threatening illness, injury, or painful medical procedure. However, the preponderance of pediatric patients and their families are resilient and do well (National Child Traumatic Stress Network, n.d.).

Given the progress of outpatient care, children who are hospitalized are usually very sick, and unfortunately the best professional to deal with their condition is often not in their local community. Worldwide, specialized pediatric care is concentrated and is highly regionalized (McManus & França, 2019). Therefore, children and families frequently have to travel long distances to receive the help they need, often for long periods of time and sometimes for multiple hospitalizations (Rubin & Franck, 2018). While children may receive the medical care they need, families often find it emotionally and financially challenging. It takes a great deal to be close by their sick child. This chapter describes Family Support Services, a comprehensive psychosocial program to support sick children and their families at a

Acknowledgements: Much appreciation is given to Linda Franck, RN, PhD, FAAN for her help with this chapter.

Ronald McDonald House, which is a "home away from home" while they are involved in the children's treatment.

17.1 Family Centered Care

Caregivers have a compelling desire to be present and share in some or all facets of decision-making and care for their hospitalized child (Power & Franck, 2008). Family-centered care is vitally important in providing health care to children with serious medical conditions. In fact, the American Academy of Pediatrics (2012) has strongly advised a family-centered approach to pediatric health care and encourages families to be present during their child's treatment. The main principles of family-centered care are based on collaboration between the healthcare providers and families, which includes sharing honest information, respecting and honoring family diversity, developing a partnership in healthcare decisions, and caring in the context of family and community (Kuo et al., 2012). When families are involved in their children's hospital care, there are positive psychosocial and clinical outcomes (Davidson et al., 2007; Kuo et al., 2012).

17.1.1 Importance and Challenges of Family Proximity

For families to be involved in their child's health care, they need to be in close proximity to the hospital. Much attention has been placed on family-centered care practices, yet the lack of proximity remains the top concern for families of hospitalized children needing highly specialized care (Davidson et al., 2007; Rubin & Franck, 2018). Often, family participation is both encouraged and expected, yet there are transportation and accommodation uncertainties, challenges, and costs. Understandably, this creates emotional and financial stress on the families (Penchansky & Thomas, 1981). To participate in one child's medical care, many families have to be away from social support systems and their other children, and they incur financial difficulties due to loss of employment (Nabors et al., 2013).

17.2 Ronald McDonald House

The Ronald McDonald House Charities (RMHC) has created facilities and programs that strengthen families throughout their healthcare journeys. Founded in 1974, the mission of RMHC is to keep families of seriously ill or injured children physically and emotionally close to their children who are receiving medical care at leading hospitals worldwide. RMHC has been at the forefront of the family-centered care movement since before the movement was even given a name (Rubin & Franck, 2018). Although RMHC is not a direct healthcare service provider, it provides purpose-built facilities and programs to support families and caregivers of ill and injured children. RMHC has local chapters in more than 64 countries and regions, including 368 Ronald McDonald Houses, 252 Ronald McDonald Family Rooms, and 50 Ronald McDonald Care Mobiles.

A core RMHC program – Ronald McDonald House (RMH) – offers a place for families to call home so they can stay close by their hospitalized child at little to no cost. A diverse population of families whose children are faced with the full range of pediatric acute and chronic illnesses, such as cancer, prematurity, heart conditions, trauma, and organ and tissue transplant, stay at RMH. RMH allows the entire family to participate more actively in health-care decisions and support their child. RMH provides *wraparound* facilities and support to enable family proximity and emotional availability, and this is one of the most important and often cited reasons families are able to be active in their child's hospital care (Rubin & Franck, 2018). RMH provides accommodations, bathrooms, kitchens, meals, playrooms, computer rooms, and laundry facilities, as well as support services.

Hospital leaders worldwide understand that RMH purpose-built accommodations and support for families contribute to high-quality, family-centered care. An international survey of 530 hospital leaders in 16 countries with RMH program affiliations found that the vast majority of these leaders believed that caring for the whole family promoted better health care for pediatric patients. More than 95% of those surveyed testified that their RMH program affiliation enhanced family-centered care. Their responses conveyed the belief that the lodging, food, transportation, and sibling support that RMH provides reduced families' feelings of isolation, provided better sleep, and increased families' ability to cope with stress (Lantz, Rubin, & Mauery, 2015).

17.2.1 Better Hospital Experience

Franck et al. (2015) studied the influence of family accommodations on patient experiences of 5,105 families in 10 US hospitals providing pediatric services. The most common accommodation for families of children who were inpatients involved staying at the bedside (76.8%). For infants in neonatal intensive care, parents were most likely to remain in their own home or at a friend or relative's home (47.2%). Those families who stayed in RMH described significantly more positive experiences for their child's hospital stay and recommended the hospital to family or friends more often compared with parents who stayed elsewhere. They also conveyed that RMH assisted them in being more involved in their child's care. Franck et al. (2015) hypothesized that communal housing that facilitates encouragement from other families having similar experiences, the supportive services at RMH, and the "home away from home" approach may be the reasons for the stronger association with positive hospital experiences. Similarly, in a study of 10 hospitals (1,240 families) in Ontario, Canada, families who stayed at RMH reported that this accommodation type significantly improved their ability to be involved in their child's care (Franck et al., 2017).

17.2.2 Improved Recovery

Families want to stay close when their child is hospitalized, and they believe it improves their child's recovery. Franck, Gay, and Rubin (2013) surveyed two thousand families in six Southern California RMHs and found that families who stayed together at RMH felt that staying close to the hospital provided important benefits for the family experience, and that RMH had an impact on the family's perceptions of their child's recovery. These families believed that medical outcomes improved as a result of being able to stay close to their child. Similarly, Van Horn and Kautz (2007) found that when families – including partners, spouses, and siblings – stay close by the hospital, the child's recovery process is improved. Interestingly, Hispanic/Latinx families believed more strongly than non-Hispanic families that RMH shortened their family stay (Franck et al., 2013).

17.2.3 Improved Sleep

Franck et al. (2014) measured sleep quantity and quality of those that slept at either a United Kingdom RMH or at the bedside of their child while in the hospital. Parents who slept in the child's hospital room had poorer sleep. They had more awakenings and felt less rested after a night's sleep than parents who slept in the RMH. RMH provides parents with a private room, which allows for more restorative sleep. Parents at RMH enjoy better quality of sleep and may be more rejuvenated, which is thought to better able them to tend to their child and work with the medical care team. The parents can be more actively engaged in the child's care and recovery – therefore enhancing the healthcare experience of a seriously ill child. This is in contrast to poor quality of sleep or lack of sleep, which can lead to stress, anxiety, and poor decision-making processes (Franck et al., 2014).

17.2.4 Reduced Anxiety

Between 20% and 30% of parents and 15% and 25% of hospitalized children and siblings experience traumatic stress reactions that negatively impact day-to-day functioning, affect treatment adherence, and hinder recovery (National Child Traumatic Stress Network, n.d.). There are three types of traumatic stress reactions: reexperiencing (thinking a lot about the trauma, even when they wish not to); avoidance (making an effort not to think or talk about the trauma, or anything connected with the illness or treatment); and hyper-arousal (having a "fight or flight response"). Franck et al. (2014) found that more than 25% of parents of hospitalized children experienced significant posttraumatic stress symptoms three months after the children left the hospital.

Wray et al. (2011) evaluated the level of anxiety and stress in the parents of children admitted to a hospital for at least three days and discovered that almost two-thirds of these parents had borderline/clinical levels of anxiety. Moreover, 38% of these parents had this same level of anxiety even three months after their child's discharge.

RMH is helpful in stress management. A study conducted with RMHC Australia found that RMH doesn't just provide accommodations, better sleep, and reduced financial burden, it also reduces stress and anxiety at a very difficult time (Daniel et al., 2013). Similarly, a study in Southern California (Franck et al., 2013) found that since RMH supports a family's ability to stay together when their sick child requires medical treatment, it reduces families' stress and anxiety.

17.2.5 Enhanced Psychological Well-Being

RMH provides important advantages for the family experience and psychological well-being (Franck et al., 2013). Family members expressed the belief that RMH provided networking, emotional support, and stress relief, allowing them to give more time and energy to the care of their child. According to these 2,000 families, their stay at RMH improved psychosocial well-being of caregivers, patient, siblings, and the family as a whole. In another study, 250 families of children being treated for serious illnesses at a hospital in Buenos Aires, Argentina, completed the Health-Related Quality of Life (HRQOL) survey that evaluates how a person's well-being may be affected over time by a medical issue. Sánchez and De Cunto (2014) found that children and their parents who stayed at RMH perceived their quality of life to be better than expected for children with chronic disease. In fact, the children developed strong friendship bonds that increased their social support and quality of life.

17.2.6 Strengthened Coping Abilities

Researchers at the University of Cincinnati and Cincinnati Children's Hospital Medical Center interviewed caregivers staying at RMH. They claimed that support from family and friends was identified as the most important element in developing positive coping strategies. In fact, caregivers found that during their child's hospitalization, support from other families staying at RMH strengthened their coping abilities (Nabors et al., 2013). As a result of staying at RMH, families are able to cope better and focus on the needs of their sick child.

The services provided by RMH have had a positive effect, enabling the family's ability to participate more actively in their child's care. The RMH program represents more than a "home away from home," and the impact on families goes far beyond the basic comforts. However, there can never be too much support for RMH families, and consequently we created the Family Support Services.

17.3 Family Support Services

17.3.1 Needs Assessment

In order to be more deliberate about how RMH actively provides emotional support to the RMH families and the RMH staff and volunteers who care for these families, a needs assessment was done. This assessment took place at four RMHs in Southern California, Stanford RMH, and at Camp Ronald McDonald for Good Times®. Focus groups with RMH families and separate focus groups with RMH staff and volunteers took place at each location.

The results with families were consistent across locations. The families appreciated the private, comfortable, uninterrupted night's sleep that they received and the shared spaces where families found comfort and strength from each other. They believed RMH made the experience of having a sick child more tolerable and helped them be more engaged in their child's care. Although most children and parents were able to cope well, they desired more support and resources. The focus groups identified two main areas for additional support.

First, families wanted comprehensive emotional support for the patient, siblings, caregivers, and families as a whole. They talked about living worried, living with immense responsibilities, and often feeling isolated, although being with the other families in the house helped considerably. They felt anxious and stressed, and they struggled with unhelpful thoughts and painful emotions. At times, they needed help unlocking their own coping resources and unleashing their ability to use them. They discussed wanting skills such as mindfulness, advocacy, coping, communication, and parenting skills.

Second, families wanted to connect with each other and other RMH families to establish a sense of normalcy. They wished to relax, rebuild, and strengthen their family bonds by participating in fun activities that had been put on hold during treatment. They especially wanted to make sure that siblings' concerns about being left out were addressed.

Staff and volunteer focus group analysis was also consistent across locations. RMH staff and volunteers found their work to be both rewarding and enriching, yet at the same time anxiety-producing and stressful. Consistently, RMH volunteers and staff requested training on how to support and manage families of seriously ill children living in a communal setting. They also needed help dealing with their own feelings of loss and grief that got stirred up as a result of working with families with seriously ill children.

17.3.2 Mission of Family Support Services

Based on the findings of the needs assessment and prior research, Family Support Services (FSS) at the RMH-Los Angeles was founded in 2010. The mission of FSS is to provide therapeutic support to the families and children residing in the RMH during a child's illness. The FSS program creates a therapeutic environment that provides (1) wraparound emotional support for the RMH family members that is culturally relevant, strength-based and family-centered (2) therapeutic activities for patients, siblings, caregivers, and families; and (3) aid and training for the RMH staff and volunteers. This is the first comprehensive psychosocial program established at RMHC. FSS is staffed by licensed psychologists and graduate students in training from doctoral-level clinical psychology and master's-level marriage and family therapy programs. These graduate students are referred to as FSS team members. In order to meet the needs of families and staff, the FSS program is staffed 365 days a year, from 9 a.m. to 9 p.m. and on-call during the night for staff and families.

FSS received the 2015 *Hearts and Hands Award* from Global Ronald McDonald House Charities for expanding the reach and impact of RMH. The program was first implemented in Los Angeles (with 75 families living at the house) and has been expanded to other houses in Southern California, including Inland Empire RMH (35 families), Pasadena RMH (14 families), Camp Ronald McDonald House for Good Times®, as well as in Northern California at Stanford RMH (123 families).

17.3.3 Theoretical Framework

FSS is based on a systemic theoretical framework integrating a pediatric psychosocial preventative health model and differentiation. Dealing with children with serious illnesses requires a biopsychosocial systems model (Engel, 1977) versus a model that primarily focuses on the patient. Families are seen as resources as well as in need of help with their own challenges generated by the illness. FSS recognizes the importance of each family member as a powerful psychosocial piece in the recovery process. The needs of all family members, including siblings and extended family, are considered part of the caregiving and healing system.

According to Walsh (2006), when a family faces adversity, family resilience impacts the emotional health of all family members. The support that they have in their lives is an important ingredient in strengthening resilience in families. A family that is secure and functioning well acts as a shock absorber when they face the crisis of having a child with a serious illness (Walsh, 2006).

A well-functioning family is better able to put their energy into dealing with their child and the child's illness, which reduces distress and stress (Barakat et al., 2007). In contrast, a poorly functioning family can reduce resilience and increase parental stress.

17.3.3.1 Pediatric Psychosocial Preventative Health Model

Using a public health framework, the pediatric psychosocial preventative health model (PPPHM) looks at the biopsychosocial needs of all families entering the pediatric healthcare system (Kazak, 2006). PPPHM is helpful in understanding how psychosocial support might be provided to families of seriously ill children that may more likely match their level of need and risk. Kazak (2006) described the three-tier model as a pyramid. She assigned the labels "universal" at the base, "targeted" in the middle, and "clinical" at the top.

Universal represents the largest group of families (59.2%) that enter the pediatric healthcare system and RMH (Kazak et al., 2003). These families are resilient and possess coping abilities that range from acceptable to strong as they deal with their children's unexpected health problem or the exacerbation of an existing condition. They are normal functioning families who are experiencing stress related to their medical experiences. Although there may be other significant life events going on in their lives, these issues do not encroach on their ability to function adequately. The goal of FSS with our RMH families is to support the competence in these families by reinforcing their use of existing resources and to build on their natural resilience. This will aid the family in the present and the future (Kazak, 2006). The therapeutic fun clubs, support groups, and workshops are helpful.

The targeted group (33.6%) in the middle of the pyramid is smaller, but is an important group of families entering the pediatric healthcare system (Kazak et al., 2003). These families are more likely to have ongoing difficulties (Kazak, 2006). They may have patients, siblings, or parents that have preexisting problems, financial issues, employment difficulties, or family problems. Consequently, their coping skills may be challenged and sometimes even exceeded, particularly if there is a deterioration in their child's health or when more intensive medical intervention is necessary. FSS is set up to offer more frequent support services to these families.

The clinical category of families involves an even smaller group (7.2%) of families with ill children, and these families may need even more extensive psychosocial support. There are some factors that indicate high risk for ongoing distress, such as family members' significant anxiety or depression, history of mental health issues, substance abuse, or even legal problems. FSS gives these families much attention. In addition, FSS may make a recommendation for assessment and clinical services outside of RMH.

This prevention model suggests that every child and family receive basic support and information from FSS. Additionally, it enables FSS to be aware of what leads to increased distress in order to provide those children and families with additional and ongoing support and resources (Kazak et al., 2003).

17.3.3.2 Differentiation

FSS utilizes a differentiation-based systems model (Kerr & Bowen, 1988; Regas, 2019; Schnarch & Regas, 2012) in all components of its support and training. Differentiation or emotional maturity is the ability to balance two of humankind's strongest motivational drives: (1) connectedness and togetherness and (2) self-regulation and autonomy. Differentiation involves staying focused on one's own life and values while maintaining clear, open communication with other important people (Kerr & Bowen, 1988). Differentiation is the lifelong process of charting one's own path by means of one's own guidance system rather than looking to other people as a guide. It is a direction in life (Bowen, 1978; Friedman, 2007). Emotional maturity controls how one functions with others and alone.

There has been much research on the importance of differentiation. Differentiation is related to enhanced personal well-being (Jankowski & Sandage, 2011), lower chronic anxiety, and increased psychological adjustment (Solomon et al., 2009), better physical health (Peleg-Popko, 2002), self-regulatory skills (Skowron & Dendy, 2004), relationship satisfaction (Schnarch & Regas, 2012), and family functioning, coping, and optimism (Sahin, Nalbone, & Wetchler, 2010). FSS focuses on the four abilities of differentiation (SAND): **S**olid self in connection, **A**nxiety regulation, **N**onreactivity, and **D**iscomfort for growth (Bowen, 1978; Friedman, 2007; Regas, 2019; Schnarch, 2009; Schnarch & Regas, 2012). (See Figure 17.1.)

Less Differentiation	More Differentiation: SAND
Pseudo self with unclear values	Solid flexible self in connection with clear values
Emotional dysregulation	Anxiety regulation and self-soothing
Reactivity: Locking into arguments and avoiding important people and conversations	Nonreactive
Looking for a quick fix	Discomfort for growth and doing what you need to do

Figure 17.1 *The SAND Model*

Solid Flexible Self. Solid self is the ability to hold onto yourself up close with important people in your life, despite pressure from them to conform or accommodate. Well-differentiated solid individuals are able to hold onto a set of core values and not be influenced by other people or circumstances. People at higher levels of differentiation have well-thought-out beliefs, values, and priorities; however, these individuals are flexible and allow these values to change over time if appropriate. They don't change because of external pressure from others; instead, they decide within themselves based on their well-thought-out inner guidance system.

Those with less differentiation have a pseudo self; to keep the peace, they may do what others want rather than make their own choices (Friedman, 2007; Kerr & Bowen, 1988; Schnarch, 2009). This could be a risk factor for parents with a child with a serious illness. If they desire to be their child's medical advocate and active participant on their child's care team, partners must learn how to bring more of their self to their relationship. Parents must determine their own values, thoughts, and opinions, and share those with each other and the medical team. Instead, those with a pseudo self try hard to be what others want them to be because they are concerned about what people think of them. Needing and seeking approval and validation from others – versus being able to validate oneself – puts a great deal of stress on their relationships.

Anxiety Regulation. The second ability, anxiety regulation through self-soothing, focuses on the ability (1) to generally self-regulate one's own anxiety and (2) to soothe one's own hurt, scared, or angry emotions. Partners with more differentiation are able to soothe their anxiety. Having a nonanxious presence is the ability to contain one's anxiety and not let one's feelings be overwhelming. It is the ability to take care of oneself emotionally. Individuals who can self-soothe and tolerate anxiety in themselves and in others have the ability to remain present, instead of withdrawing from the emotional chaos around them (Kerr & Bowen, 1988). Their nonanxious presence helps reduce the anxiety in their relationships with others.

Nonreactivity. The less differentiated or emotionally mature people are, the more anxiety they experience and the more they work to reduce the anxiety. This is a risk factor for families because this often leads to problems not getting addressed. People with less differentiation are less able to calm their emotional states, regulate their emotions, and control their anxieties. They can feel powerless in the face of emotion. Less differentiated people are often reactive. They overreact to difficult situations or individuals by reflexively arguing or maintaining a fixed position or they keep their reactivity in check by avoiding the people or situations that stir them up (Schnarch & Regas, 2012).

To be nonreactive is the ability to hold on to self with little reactivity to the opinions and behaviors of others. More differentiated individuals have the ability to regulate instincts or automatic responses rather than let the instincts drive them automatically (Friedman, 2007; Kerr & Bowen, 1988; Schnarch, 2009). Anxiety makes the reptilian brain kick in. When this occurs, RMH families and staff may pressure others to take their point of view, get stirred up by those that differ, and get over-involved in others' lives. Less differentiated RMH families or staff may become reactive and lock into power struggles, may blame, or may become reactive by avoiding important conversations or people (Schnarch & Regas, 2012).

Discomfort for Growth. The fourth ability, discomfort for growth, involves tolerating pain for growth. Friedman (2007) suggested that differentiation and growth require tolerating the discomfort of one's anxiety. Most people naturally stay in a "comfort zone" and try to find "quick fixes" for life's dilemmas. The ability to tolerate difficult times and do challenging things distinguishes people who improve their lives and their emotional maturity. This entails getting out of one's "comfort zone," and enduring through disappointment and hardship in order to accomplish one's goals (Bowen, 1978; Schnarch, 2009). Many individuals have a low threshold for pain and a low threshold for others' distress. Conversely, when people are motivated enough to make changes in their lives, their threshold for pain increases.

FSS does not offer quick solutions or give advice. FSS team members are not the experts on RMH families' lives. Instead, team members encourage family members to take full responsibility for making their own decisions. In this way, differentiation supports family members' efforts to embrace their own values. Values are like a compass; they give RMH families a sense of direction (Harris, 2009).

17.4 Components of Family Support Services

There are four components of FSS: (1) training and supervision of FSS team members; (2) psychosocial support of patients, siblings, caregivers, and families; (3) therapeutic fun clubs for parents, families, patients, and siblings; and (4) training for the staff and volunteers.

17.4.1 Training and Supervision of FSS Team Members

All aspects of FSS are based on a theoretical framework that integrates a pediatric psychosocial preventative health model and systems theory. Team members are immersed in this theoretical framework, often learning a different approach than what they are learning in their graduate education. Since

RMHC mandates that RMH family members are not pathologized, the mission of FSS to provide comprehensive therapeutic support for families, staff, and volunteers fits beautifully. The founding faculty and licensed site supervisors seek to provide the most comprehensive training in an innovative approach to working with families with seriously ill children. Supervision and training are extensive; this approach is often different than what mental health graduate students learn in school. All team members spend one day a week in training.

17.4.1.1 Didactics

The emphasis is on these areas: (1) how to create a supportive therapeutic environment at RMH, (2) best practices for supporting RMH families, and (3) how best to integrate FSS into RMH. In addition, a focus on cultural humility and competence is key. Families who stay at RMH come from all over the USA and the world, and from diverse ethnic, religious, and sexual orientations. Each team member receives weekly didactic training and professional development that emphasizes multicultural issues that may impact families' ability to adjust and cope with health-related problems and living in a communal setting. Emphasis is on how age, disability, race, ethnicity, language, immigration status, gender, religion/spirituality, sexual orientation and gender diversity, social class, and their intersectionality have an impact on the family and the healing journey.

17.4.1.2 Individual Supervision

Each house has six to ten FSS team members and at least one licensed psychologist on site; some sites have several supervisors. Team members are either marriage and family therapy graduate students or clinical psychology graduate students. Each team member's contract is for one or two years at twenty hours a week. They each receive one to two hours of individual supervision, where the focus is on the support the team member is providing the families.

Almost 30%–40% of families served by Ronald McDonald Houses in California identify as Latinx, and many are monolingual Spanish speaking. We focus on bridging the language barrier. Therefore, we have created a Spanish training track to provide team members with supervision in Spanish to improve FSS linguistic competence in conducting Spanish support meetings, fun clubs, and workshops.

17.4.1.3 Group Supervision Focused on Self-of-the-FSS-Team-Member (Regas et al., 2017)

The FSS team members are the primary therapeutic tool in our approach. They are the ones that carry out the FSS program. How the FSS team members act in relation to the RMH families is key to promoting a therapeutic environment (Bowen, 1978). Team members must work toward more differentiation: solid self in connection, anxiety regulation, nonreactivity, and discomfort for growth, and implementing those skills at RMH (Regas et al., 2017; Schnarch & Regas, 2012).

Substantial evidence suggests that effectiveness in supporting families under stress depends greatly on the emotional maturity, personality, and degree of self-understanding of the person providing the support (Beutler et al., 2004). Furthermore, the quality of the therapeutic relationship with RMH families is directly affected by the team members' own ability to handle stress, to respond constructively to anxiety, and to think and act autonomously while maintaining meaningful connections with others (Lambert & Friedlander, 2008).

Not only is it imperative that FSS team members become experts at supporting and facilitating resilience and coping of RMH families, but they also need to focus on their own growth, emotional maturity, and relationships (Regas et al., 2017). In group supervision, FSS team members learn to be able to identify their own stumbling blocks and strengths to enhance emotional maturity that affects their work with RMH family members and staff. While self-confrontation and self-awareness are necessary steps toward personal and professional growth, insight put into action is the most important factor in developing emotional maturity (Bowen, 1978). Differentiation is about doing something – not just intellectualizing (Friedman, 2007). FSS team members are asked to engage in systematic self-reflection with the expectation that resolving their issues would improve their support of families at RMH.

17.4.2 Support Meetings with Families

Every family meets with FSS within twenty-four hours of checking in. Although FSS works as a team, the FSS team member assigned to a family will stay in touch with them throughout their health journey. The first meeting, called a Welcome Meeting, allows FSS to introduce the family to the house, hear the family's illness story, learn about their resources and support, and talk about worries they have regarding the illness and treatment, adjusting to communal living, being away from home, or whatever is on their minds. Team members are mindful of general psychosocial factors such as their support system, emotional and financial resources, as well as both strengths and barriers to resilience. A follow-up meeting is held a few days later to see how the family is doing and how they are adapting to communal living and their medical journey. The family can return as often as they want to have meetings with FSS.

Besides meeting with families in a private room, FSS team members are also out and about the house. Families get support while cooking a meal, eating a meal together, in the playroom, computer room, or while walking with FSS to the hospital. FSS is integrated into the RMH environment.

FSS allows families the opportunity to be part of a safe and supportive environment where conversations are welcome. There are many common themes, such as (1) being so absorbed with their sick child that they forget to take care of themselves or be present with the child's siblings; (2) figuring out how to soothe their own anxiety and reactivity, so they are better able to hear what their children are thinking and feeling; and (3) advocating for their child with their medical care team, so they can better understand the illness and subsequent treatment plans. It is thought that this support helps caregivers to be more actively involved in decisions as well as be better able to be present with their children and share important information.

17.4.3 Online Support Community

When the parents return home, they miss the support of RMH and FSS. At the initiative of a former FSS team member and faculty, a RMH online support community was created. Support Community allows families to share their illness story, read others' stories, receive and share important resources, and participate in online computer-mediated support groups as well as lectures and trainings by FSS. The support community encourages the families to maintain the connections that they have gained with other families while living at the house or being at Camp Ronald McDonald House for Good Times®. It also encourages the development of new relationships with RMH families once they return home. Hence, the therapeutic support that was generated through FSS and RMH continues once families return home.

17.4.4 Therapeutic Fun Club

When children are seriously ill, they and their families often experience a loss of control. This can erode confidence, body image, and coping skills. The goal of our daily two-hour and half-day therapeutic fun clubs is to build resilience. There are fun clubs (Figure 17.2) that are oriented toward parents, children, and families.

17.4.4.1 Fun

Fun clubs always revolve around fun and recreation. Each activity is entertaining, to ensure that family members stay involved. Some activities are at a high energy level (carnival games, basketball, obstacle courses), while others may be at a lower energy level (medical play, cooking, arts and crafts). The FSS team works to remove obstacles for participation by adapting activities to fit the RMH culture, including different languages, ages, and mobility. Fun clubs promote cooperation, encouragement, and support – rather than competition between RMH families – and they give families a chance to get to know each other.

Figure 17.2 *Each fun club involves fun, challenge, and self-awareness*

17.4.4.2 Challenge

The aim of each fun club activity is to provide family members the opportunity to try something fun and new. When family members are comfortable with an activity, they are in their comfort zone. When RMH family members are in their growth zone, they get outside their comfort zone enough to try something new. This builds more confidence in oneself and one's ability.

Each fun club is designed to be a series of simple steps, so family members are empowered to move forward with success. Each small success provides the inspiration for the next. This, in turn, enhances confidence in oneself and one's ability. Each therapeutic fun club activity involves a personal challenge. If they would like, family members are encouraged to choose a challenge that fosters growth and development. This may be different for different family members. For example, in a bilingual sing-along fun club, family members may choose to move from sitting and listening to music to (1) singing with the group, (2) singing alone, or (3) leading a song.

17.4.4.3 Self-Awareness

We aim to have all family members learn something about themselves and their abilities. FSS team members facilitate reflective opportunities during the fun clubs to help RMH children and caregivers realize their successes. In addition, they may discover more confidence, self-esteem, autonomy, and friendship with other RMH families.

17.4.5 Staff and Volunteer Training

Individuals who are more differentiated or emotionally mature experience less job-related interpersonal stress than those who are less differentiated. In contrast, RMH staff and volunteers who struggle with the ability to develop a solid self in connection, regulate anxiety, and be nonreactive have more job stress (Cavaiola et al., 2012).

With up to 120 families living worried and facing real challenges under the same roof, anxiety is ever-present at work. Staff tensions may be expressed in different ways: conflict, overinvolvement with families, increased anxiety, or even sick leave. It is natural for caring staff members and volunteers to become overinvolved in a family's life or even develop compassion fatigue. This can be problematic for them, the families, and RMH. Consequently, FSS team members provide support to staff and volunteers as they develop strategies to manage high anxiety issues.

Similar to our training of FSS team members, our staff and volunteer training is designed to build differentiation and emotional maturity into our collective thinking and being. This involves encouraging them to look closely at their own behavior and decision-making at RMH. A major component of functioning well in the workplace, as staff or volunteer, is to monitor one's own behavior at work. Similar to FSS team members, staff and volunteers are encouraged to manage their own anxiety and be nonreactive (Bowen, 1978). Monitoring self means paying attention to which issues, situations, families, or other staff members consume the staff or volunteer attention. They are encouraged to figure out what is making them reactive or anxious, or is pushing them toward overinvolvement. As they become more self-focused, they are better able to look at their own responsibility in the situation. In the same vein, staff and volunteers are asked to consider those problems, issues, families, or staff that they are avoiding. They have to confront themselves on how comfortable they are with people living life differently than they think they should be. Accepting differences is a challenge for most people.

In addition, FSS also offers standard ongoing staff trainings on a variety of topics, such as (1) what RMH families are going through, (2) understanding your role at RMH, (3) how to have flexible boundaries, (4) how to not be too rigid or too overinvolved, (5) being a good empathic listener, (6) being supportive in what you say and *don't* say to families, (7) the impact of dealing with anxiety through gossip, (8) how to handle families in crisis, (9) domestic violence and child abuse, and (10) multicultural training.

17.5 Overall Impact of FSS

There are many benefits to conducting a program evaluation. It serves the best interest of FSS and RMH as well as the children and caregivers that we serve. We have been able to evaluate "what works" and "what does not work" and if RMH families benefit from FSS. The evaluation indicated that both RMH staff and FSS team members believed they had learned the necessary skills and training to deliver services entailed in supporting patients, siblings, and families.

At the end of FSS meetings, all family members fill out a very brief *Meeting Rating Scale* to evaluate if they feel supported and understood and if the meeting helped them to cope better. Team members and supervisors discuss these outcome measures regularly. Parents, guardians, and other family members are also invited at various times to complete a survey about the role of FSS and its impact on their family. Overall, FSS evaluations regarding all aspects of FSS (including welcome meetings, ongoing meetings, fun clubs, workshops, all-house events, and staff trainings) have been excellent. The vast majority strongly agreed that FSS emotionally supported their entire family and helped them to cope better and feel less stress. According to the caregivers, the patient and siblings felt support and FSS helped them to improve their family and relationship functioning. FSS also allowed family members to participate more actively in their sick child's care and improved their child's recovery (Regas, 2017).

17.6 Example of Role of FSS

The Garcías (all identifying information has been changed to protect confidentiality) are a second-generation Mexican American family who resided in the Los Angeles RMH for more than ten months. Josh (fourteen) was diagnosed with leukemia and was successfully treated at a local children's hospital.

While the parents, Josh, and his younger brother stayed at RMH, the FSS team was able to support them in a variety of modalities. Upon arrival, the family had a welcome meeting with the FSS bilingual team member Sylvia who was assigned to take the lead with the García family. The therapeutic focus of this meeting was to create an alliance with each family member. This included (1) welcoming them to RMH; (2) introducing them to the FSS program; and (3) if they shared, listening to their illness story and possibly learning about their resilience and coping strategies.

As the weeks passed, FSS continued to build a relationship with Josh and his family and learned about each family member's experience being at RMH. Josh stayed at the hospital when he was undergoing treatment and at RMH during the off days. What Josh and his brother said they missed the most while at RMH was going to their church campout. Typical for the FSS team, they planned an all-house event aimed at creating a modified campout that was appropriate for RMH. These all-house events, hosted by FSS, have allowed families to come together and participate in group activities and interact with other families, while celebrating customary family experiences they may be missing because they are away from home. FSS invited the seventy-five families staying at RMH to a fun-filled evening that included tents, sleeping bags, roasting marshmallows, pretend fishing in plastic swimming pools, games, and camp songs, all in the RMH courtyard. Although no one slept out overnight, it was a night to remember for all. This has now become a yearly event.

In addition to the all-house events, Josh and his family were able to participate in FSS therapeutic fun clubs. One time when Josh was in the hospital, his brother learned to play "Las Mañanitas," a traditional birthday song played in Mexico on the guitar, and another child strummed a guitar for the first time. Josh's brother and the other children bonded over music, learned a new skill, and prepared to sing "Las Mañanitas" when Josh returned to the house.

While the children were in fun clubs, Josh's parents often attended parent fun clubs. One time at the FSS social hour, while enjoying cheese and crackers, parents began talking about their worries as well as coping strategies. Josh's mother said she believed that her worries about her son's medical condition had become so all-consuming that she struggled to be present with Josh or her other family members. She mentioned she spent endless hours cleaning the family's room at RMH to ensure it was sterile enough for Josh when he stayed at the house between treatments. She acknowledged that the doctors told her that his living space did not need to be like an operating room, but she expressed the fear that she was not doing enough. Another parent in the group agreed that he too had become so focused on his child's treatment that he was ignoring the other siblings. FSS shared strategies for soothing anxiety and becoming more centered and present.

Due to the relationship the family developed with FSS, Josh's parents stopped in to have a meeting with Sylvia in her office. They said they wanted to know what Josh was thinking and feeling about what the doctors had told him about his illness and its treatment, and they wanted FSS to meet with Josh and determine this. Instead of a quick fix and having FSS talk with Josh, Sylvia encouraged his mother to address her fears about talking with Josh. In fact, his mother said she actually wanted to manage her worries and anxiety so that she could be more present with Josh and his brother. In a following meeting with the family, both parents let both Josh and his brother know that they were available and wanted to hear what they were experiencing. Both boys seemed appreciative, but didn't share much because they didn't want their mom to be sad even though she reassured them that she could handle her own pain and wanted to be available for them.

The layout of RMH allowed for Josh and FSS team members to have interactions not typical of an office setting. Sylvia baked cookies with Josh, and another FSS team member made photo albums with the family. A week after watching *The Lion King*, a classic Disney movie in which the father dies and his son, Simba, returns to the land to become the king, Josh asked Sylvia if Simba remembered his dad after he died. Although the doctors had told Josh that they had every reason to believe that his treatment would be successful, the movie led to a discussion about Josh's worries.

Josh said it was lonely not talking about how painful the treatment was, yet he worried that he would make his parents sad if he talked to them about it. Sylvia wondered aloud if he might want to share his thoughts and feelings with his parents since they seemed to want to hear about his experience. Josh agreed that he would like his mother's support. Courageously, he took it upon himself to share his thoughts during a family meeting. Although it was hard for his mom to hear, she listened intently.

Periodically, Josh talked more to his parents. Josh learned that his parents were able to hear about his fears, and his brother discovered that his parents were able to understand how he felt left out. They were able to do this yet still care for themselves. This is differentiation. When they left RMH, they stayed involved in the online support community.

17.6.1 Self-of-the-FSS-Team-Member

Sylvia, the FSS team member, had worries and concerns about being able to support all the various subsystems of the family. She struggled with thoughts that she would be unable to do enough. This was similar to how the parents felt. At first, Sylvia found herself wanting to be involved in trying to solve the child's and family's problems in an effort to reduce their and her distress. At other times, she wanted to withdraw since it was painful to see. In individual and group supervision, Sylvia explored her role as an FSS team member. She focused on soothing her own anxiety and being more present and available for Josh and the family so they could make their own decisions about what would be best for them. At the beginning of her stay, Silvia also supported the RMH staff member who was getting reactive when mom's panic led her to frequently dismiss cleaning equipment as not adequate to sterilize her guest room. FSS and RMH staff had to understand PPPHM and know that all families cope with their child's illness differently, depending on who they are and what stage of the treatment they are experiencing, and staff members should not take it personally. As the FSS team and RMH team worked together, Josh and his family felt supported and cared for, and the team members found that supporting them was professionally meaningful and growth-producing.

17.7 Summary

This chapter described FSS, a comprehensive psychosocial program to support seriously sick and injured children and their families, which was designed after a needs assessment of California RMHs. This program provides intensive training for mental health professionals and RMH staff and volunteers in order to provide emotional support for families, taking into account PPPHM and utilizing a differentiation-based model (SAND).

What we have learned these past ten years is that support means many different things to RMH families. Some families prefer private meetings in the FSS office. A family may prefer to attend therapeutic fun clubs, while others may like sharing what they are going through with FSS as they are walking to the hospital or while making dinner. There are also family members that prefer to participate in the online support community. Providing a range of services that meet these varying support needs and preferences is of critical importance for RMH.

In addition to the wraparound facilities and support that RMH provides families so that they can be active in their children's hospital care (Rubin & Franck, 2018), FSS provides a well-thought-out psychosocial program for families and staff 365 days a year. FSS evaluations indicate we have created a supportive environment that adds to the services and care already offered at RMH. By using varied and innovative ways to support families under stress, RMH and FSS together have allowed families to focus on healing their children and maintaining strong connections among family members.

References

American Academy of Pediatrics. (2012). Policy statement: Family centered care and pediatrician's role. *Pediatrics, 129*(2), 394–404. doi.org/10.1542/peds.2011-3084

Barakat, L. P., Patterson, C. A., Tarazi, R. A., & Ely, E. (2007). Disease-related parenting stress in two sickle cell disease caregiver samples: Preschool and adolescent. *Families, Systems, & Health, 25*(2), 147–161. doi.org/10.1037/1091-7527.25.2.147

Beutler, L. E., Malik, M. L., Alimohamed, S., et al. (2004). Therapist variables. In M. J. Lambert (Ed.), *Bergin and Garfield's handbook of psychotherapy and behavior change* (pp. 227–306). New York: Wiley.

Bowen, M. (1978). *Family therapy in clinical practice.* Northvale, NJ: Jason Aronson.

Cavaiola, A., Peters, C., Hamdam, N., & Lavender, N. (2012). Differentiation of self and its relation to work stress and work satisfaction. *Journal of Psychological Issues in Organizational Culture, 3*(1), Article 20. doi.org/10.1002/jpoc.20092

Daniel, G., Wakefield, C. E., Ryan, B., et al. (2013). Accommodation in pediatric oncology: Parental experiences, preferences and unmet needs. *Rural and Remote Health, 13*(2), Article 2005.

Davidson, J. E., Powers, K., Hedayat, K. M., et al. (2007). Clinical practice guidelines for support of the family in the patient-centered intensive care unit: American College of Critical Care Medicine Task Force 2004–2005. *Critical Care Medicine, 35*(2), 605–622. doi.org/10.1097/01.CCM.0000254067.14607.EB

Engel, G. L. (1977). The need for a new medical model: A challenge for biomedicine. *Science, 196*(4286), 129–136. doi.org/10.1126/science.847460

Franck, L. S., Ferguson, D., Fryda, S., & Rubin, N. (2015). The child and family experience: Is it influenced by family accommodation? *Medical Care Research and Review, 72*(4), 419–437. doi.org/10.1177/1077558715579667

Franck, L. S., Ferguson, D., Fryda, S., & Rubin, N. (2017). The influence of family accommodation on pediatric hospital experience in Canada. *BMC Health Services Research, 17*(1), Article 561. doi.org/10.1186/s12913-0-17-2529-0

Franck, L. S., Gay, C. L., & Rubin, N. (2013). Accommodating families during a child's hospital stay: Implications for family experience and perceptions of outcomes. *Families, Systems and Health, 31*(3), 294–306. doi.org/10.1037/a0033556

Franck, L. S., Wray J., Gay, C., et al. (2014). Where do parents sleep best when children are hospitalized? A pilot comparison study. *Behavioral Sleep Medicine, 12*(4), 307–316. doi.org/10.1080/15402002.2013.801347

Friedman, E. H. (2007). *A failure of nerve: Leadership in the age of the quick fix*. New York: Seabury Books.

Harris, R. (2009). *ACT made simple: An easy-to-read primer on acceptance and commitment therapy*. Oakland, CA: New Harbinger.

Jankowski, P. J., & Sandage, S. J. (2011). Meditative prayer, hope, adult attachment, and forgiveness: A proposed model. *Psychology of Religion and Spirituality, 3*(2), 115–131. doi.org/10.1037/a0021601

Kazak, A. (2006). Pediatric psychosocial preventative health model (PPPHM): Research, practice, and collaboration in pediatric family systems medicine. *Families, Systems, & Health, 24*(4), 381–395. doi.org/10.1037/1091-7527.24.4.381

Kazak, A. E., Cant, M. C., Jensen, M. M., et al. (2003). Identifying psychosocial risk indicative of subsequent resource use in families of newly diagnosed pediatric oncology patients. *Journal of Clinical Oncology, 21*(17), 3220–3225. doi.org/uk10.1200/JCO.2003.12.156

Kerr, M. E., & Bowen, M. (1988). *Family evaluation*. New York: W. W. Norton.

Kuhlthau, K., Kahn, R., Hill, K. S., Gnanasekaran, S., & Ettner, S. (2010). The well-being of parental caregivers of children with activity limitations. *Maternal Child Health Journal, 14*(2), 155–163. doi.org/10.1007/s10995–008-0434-1

Kuo, D. Z., Houtrow, A. J., Arango, P., et al. (2012). Family-centered care: Current applications and future directions in pediatric health care. *Maternal and Child Health Journal, 16*(2), 297–305. doi.org/10.1007/s10995-011-0751-7

Lambert, J. E., & Friedlander, M. (2008). Relationship of differentiation of self to adult clients' perceptions of the alliance in brief family therapy. *Psychotherapy Research, 18*(2), 160–166. doi.org/10.1080/10503300701255924

Lantz, P. M., Rubin, N., & Mauery, D. R. (2015). Hospital leadership perspectives on the contributions of Ronald McDonald Houses: Results from an international survey. *Journal of Health Organization and Management, 29*(3), 381–392. doi.org/10.1108/JHOM-09-2013-0194

McManus, M., & Franca, U. (2019). Visualizing patterns in pediatric and adult hospital care. *Hospital Pediatrics, 9*(5), 398–401. doi.org/10.1542/hpeds.2018-0259

Nabors, L. A., Kichler, J. C., Brassell, A., et al. (2013). Factors related to caregiver state anxiety and coping with a child's chronic illness. *Families, Systems, &*

Health: The Journal of Collaborative Family Healthcare, 31(2), 171–180. doi
.org/10.1037/a0031240

National Child Traumatic Stress Network. (n.d.). *Medical events and traumatic stress
in children and families.* Retrieved January 2, 2019, from www.nctsn.org/
resources/medical-events-and-traumatic-stress-children-and-families

Peleg-Popko, O. (2002). Bowen theory: A study of differentiation of self, social anxiety,
and physiological symptoms. *Contemporary Family Therapy: An
International Journal, 24*(2), 355–369. doi.org/10.1023/A:1015355509866

Penchansky, R., & Thomas, J. W. (1981). The concept of access: Definition and
relationship to consumer satisfaction. *Medical Care, 19*(2), 127–140. doi
.org/10.1097/00005650-198102000-00001

Power, N., & Franck, L. (2008). Parent participation in the care of hospitalized
children: A systematic review. *Journal of Advanced Nursing, 62*(6), 622–641.
doi.org/10.1111/j.1365-2648.2008.04643.x

Regas, S. (2017). *Family Support Services at Ronald McDonald House:
A comprehensive program and manual to support families of seriously ill
children.* Unpublished manuscript.

Regas, S. (2019). Infidelity, self-differentiation, and intimacy: The mindful differentiation model of couple therapy. In P. Pitta & C. Datchi (Eds.), *Integrative
couple and family therapies* (pp. 71–90). Washington, DC: American
Psychological Association.

Regas, S. J., Kostick, K. M., Bakaly, J. W., & Doonan, R. L. (2017). Including the
self-of-the-therapist in clinical training. *Couple and Family Psychology:
Research and Practice, 6*(1), 18–31. doi.org/10.1037/cfp0000073

Rubin, N., & Franck, R. N. (2018). *Ronald McDonald House Charities® is Keeping
Families Close®: A unique role in family-centered care* [Position paper].

Sahin, Z., Nalbone, D. P., & Wetchler, J. L. (2010). The relationship of differentiation,
family coping skills, and family functioning with optimism in college-age
students. *Contemporary Family Therapy, 32*(3), 238–256. doi.org/10.1007/
s10591-1010-9116-4

Sánchez, C., & De Cunto, C. (2014). Health-related quality of life in children with
chronic conditions lodged at a comprehensive accommodation in the City of
Buenos Aires. *Archivos Argentinos de Pediatria, 112*(3), 231–238. doi.org/10
.5546/aap.2014.231

Schnarch, D. (2009). *Passionate marriage: Love, sex, and intimacy in emotionally
committed relationships.* New York: W. W. Norton.

Schnarch, D., & Regas, S. (2012). The crucible differentiation scale: Assessing differentiation in human relationships. *Journal of Marital and Family Therapy, 38*
(4), 639–652. doi.org/10.1111/j.1752-0606.2011.00259.x

Skowron, E. A., & Dendy, A. K. (2004). Differentiation of self and attachment in
adulthood: Relational correlates of effortful control. *Contemporary Family
Therapy: An International Journal, 26*(3), 337–357. doi.org/10.1023/B:COFT
.0000037919.63750.9d

Solomon, Z., Dekel, R., Zerach, G., & Horesh, D. (2009). Differentiation of the self
and posttraumatic symptomatology among ex-POWs and their wives.
Journal of Marital and Family Therapy, 35(1), 60–73. doi.org/10.1111/j
.1752-0606.2008.00102

Van Horn, E. R., & Kautz, D. (2007). Promotion of family integrity in the acute care setting: A review of the literature. *Dimensions of Critical Care Nursing, 12*(3), 101–107. doi.org/10.1097/01.DCC.0000267803.64734.c1

Walsh, F. (2006). *Strengthening family resilience* (2nd ed.). New York: Guilford Press.

Wray, J., Lee, K., Dearmun, N., & Franck, L. (2011). Parental anxiety and stress during children's hospitalization: The Stay Close study. *Journal of Child Health Care, 15*(3), 163–174. doi.org/10.1177/1367493511408632

18 Community Psychology and a Fresh Look at Faith Healing Camps

Experiences in Ghana

Angela Ofori-Atta, Seth Asafo, Kwadwo Obeng, and Robert Rosenheck

18.1 Introduction

Ghana, a country of almost 28 million people, has 3 psychiatric hospitals operating about 1,500 beds, 6 psychiatric units of 10–20 beds each in several regional general hospitals, and 36 active psychiatrists. In contrast there are thousands of faith healers across the country in both urban, rural, and remote locations.

For the purposes of this chapter, faith healers are church pastors of primarily Pentecostal Christian background who use prayer, fasting, biblical teaching, holy oils, holy water, and other aids to perform healing. They are trained as regular pastors to lead churches, to preach the gospel, and if they are perceived to have the gift of healing, to heal the sick through the laying on of hands, etc. (Arias et al., 2016). The selection process to healing ministries varies according to each church's criteria. In the faith healing camps, the leader has absolute power and authority, which are seen to come from God.

Faith healing camps are considered places of refuge and healing. There is usually a head pastor, prophet, or healer, supported by junior pastors and/or hired attendants. Prayer camps tend not to begin as such but become established as churches grow and pastors find themselves challenged to heal the sick who come via their own free will or who are brought to church by their despairing relatives. As a result, on the basis of numbers alone, access to care for people with psychiatric illnesses in Ghana is far more available from faith healers than from conventional health professionals (Ae-Ngibise et al., 2010).

Faith healing has evolved in communities in response to urgent need for the provision of care to people with severe, disabling mental illnesses that do not lend themselves to rapid recovery. Perhaps most importantly in the Ghanaian cultural context, severe mental illness is not easily explicable, for example, in the same way that germ theory explains infections, especially among people steeped in old traditional beliefs of illness causation (Arias et al., 2016). In such circumstances, complex understandings based on faith in spirits or

367

divinities are the most readily available accounts. These accounts clarify and give meaning to the long periods of dysfunction and distress, offering understandings that help with coping and, perhaps, survival itself. In these circumstances, faith healing can become the only alternative (Kpobi & Swartz, 2018; Ofori-Atta & Linden, 1995).

This chapter is about prayer camps and comprises a brief description of the extent of the need for mental health services in Ghana, of the limited, existing "Western-style" psychiatric facilities and mental health services, and of the services provided by faith healers. We will discuss the results of a qualitative study on religious and cultural beliefs of illness causation in a prayer camp, present a summary of a randomized control study in the same camp, a trial which integrated Western psychiatry and faith healing, and present our recommendations for future policies for prayer camps under the guidance of Ghana's Mental Health Law, Act 846 (Mental Health Law, 2012).

18.2 The Need for Mental Health Services in Ghana

Global mental health statistics suggest that approximately 10.4% of the burden of all diseases is attributable to mental illness (including neuropsychiatric and neurological disorders), a burden that outweighs that associated with malaria or HIV/AIDS (Whiteford et al., 2013). Considerable epidemiological research suggests that approximately 0.9%–1.0% of adults worldwide suffer from schizophrenia, a severe and disabling lifelong illness. This would lead us to estimate that approximately 280,000 Ghanaians over the age of eighteen may suffer from schizophrenia. If we further assume that approximately 15% of the adult population suffers from depression or another mental illness (Ferrari et al., 2013), one could reasonably estimate that an additional 420,000 need mental health services. However, in 2017, a report by the Ghana Mental Health Authority (Mental Health Authority of Ghana, 2018) stated that only 142,000 patients received any services from the outpatient departments of all mental health facilities in the country and only 5,560 were admitted to inpatient facilities in that year.

Indeed, in a national survey of psychological distress in Ghana, almost one in five Ghanaians reported moderate to severe psychological distress on the Kessler 10 scale (Canavan et al., 2013). In addition, the researchers reported an average of three days of work lost out of every thirty days for reasons of emotional distress. This, they said, translated to economic loss of approximately 7% of Ghana's gross domestic product attributable to psychological distress.

These rough estimates suggest that at a minimum, there are more than half a million people in need of mental health services in Ghana. The disparity between need and access to services is indeed startling, as will be apparent in the rest of the chapter.

18.3 Mental Health Care in Ghana

Most Ghanaians needing mental health care visit a variety of types of healers and facilities: herbalists, fetish priests, faith healing or prayer camps, as well as state hospitals (Appiah-Poku et al., 2004; Quinn, 2007). Herbalists are healers who prescribe and produce plant medicines whose recipes have been passed down from generations. Fetish priests are traditional priests whose healing practices are rooted in the ancient spiritual beliefs and plant medicine knowledge of their communities. Their practices comprise the use of herbs, drumming and incantations, trance states, rituals to counter anxiety, etc. (Kpobi, Swartz, & Ofori-Atta, 2018). Although they too may be classified as faith healers, the difference is that their faith is not Christian based.

Unfortunately, there appear to be human rights abuses in many community-grown places of healing, including prayer camps (Arias et al., 2016). One stark example is the use of chains or shackles to restrict patient movement. Another is lack of access to previously prescribed medications for chronic physical and mental illness, thus putting lives in jeopardy. Stigma is strong in many locations and patients are subject to both physical and emotional abuse, and in some places, the lack of even minimal housing leaves people with serious mental illness at significant physical health risks from exposure to the elements whilst in the prayer camps (Arias et al., 2016).

In this situation of extensive unmet need, it is worth considering the optimal recommended mix of services as per the World Health Organization (WHO) standards of care, as illustrated in the pyramid in Figure 18.1. We can use this as a framework against which to benchmark current service availability.

18.4 Self-Care

At the base of the pyramid where the largest numbers of community members are located, mental health needs can be adequately met by community members having access to information which enables them to take care of themselves; for example, information on healthy behaviors such as eating right, getting enough sleep, avoiding substances of abuse, and understanding the risk of addictions. At this level, there should be ready access to information on the causes and treatment of mental illness, as well as advice to avoid unnecessarily stressful life styles, for example, through encouragement to pay careful attention to traffic patterns, providing employment for most community members, good education for children, and strict adherence to laws that protect the public from harmful medications, from traumatic exposure to crime, and interpartner violence (e.g., Sipsma et al., 2013). In Ghana, the District Health Management Teams (DHMTs) of the Ghana Health Service are responsible for ensuring public health education at the community level. Unfortunately, they have been more focused on infectious disease

Figure 18.1 *Optimal mix of mental health services*
Source: Adapted from World Health Organization (2005, p. 18)

prevention, especially HIV and malarial and diarrheal diseases, as well as mother and child care in obstetrics and gynecology. This can be seen in the fact that approximately no more than 2% of the Ghana Health budget is apportioned to mental health services; in 2011, mental health spending from central government on the three psychiatric hospitals was only 1.4% of the total health budget (Roberts, Mogan, & Asare, 2014). The year before this, in 2010, a minimum of 1.3% was spent on mental health services, likely on the three psychiatric hospitals. This is very low when compared to the (global) estimate of 13% of total burden of disease attributable to mental, neurological, and substance use disorders (Eaton & Ohene, 2016).

From our lived experiences in Ghana, there are many cultural practices that are associated with self-care at the community level. These include various rites of passage among our different ethnic groups. For example, pregnant women return to the homes of their parents until after the birth of their children, thereby reducing the risk of domestic violence and antenatal depression. Naming ceremonies, which are called "outdooring," typically occur on the seventh day after childbirth. These and the elaborate care provided by grandmothers to new mothers and newborns reduce the incidence of maternal fatigue and postpartum depression. At a later age, there are community dances in the moonlight and festivals that encourage fraternizing among families in most small communities. The resolution of conflicts at dawn is common among the Akan. To mention one additional example, well-known puberty rites among the Krobo educate youth about their bodies, their sexuality, and customary laws of acceptable intimate behavior.

Unfortunately, with urbanization, some of these practices are no longer available to many. When people move to cities, they often leave critical social rituals and natural supports behind. In internal migration as in external migration to another country altogether, people are vulnerable to distinctive psychological stresses including mental illnesses, in large measure because processes of cultural self-care erode (Rousseau & Frounfelker, 2019).

It is also important to note that not all rites of passage are good for mental health. Female genital mutilation has been banned for the terrible pain it causes and potential detrimental effects on health (Sipsma et al., 2012). And while many widowhood rites are filled with symbolism that allow the remaining spouse to grieve and move on healthily, others add stress to an already difficult time in life (Immigration and Refugee Board of Canada, 2002).

18.5 Informal Community Care

When an individual's distress is not adequately reduced or prevented by self-care, the second step of the pyramid of services, informal community care, becomes increasingly important. What examples do we have of informal community care? Prayer support from church pastors is a critical source of help for many while secular ethnic membership groups assist many people living far away from their native communities and homes. There is also a tier of informal community services that buffer unavoidable sources of existential angst (Lamensdorf, 1990). These are the healers and spiritualists who offer protection from illness and evil spirits, who have developed prayer camps by adding a residential component to their churches (Arias et al., 2016; Fosu, 1995; Ofori-Atta et al., 2018; Sorketti, Zainal, & Habil, 2012). Often the ceremonies are uplifting and serve a healing function, but not uncommonly, they include caning for the exorcism of evil spirits and forced fasts that may make hallucinations worse among those with serious mental illness. Some healers encourage separation from family for long periods of time in camps with poor hygiene, or even forced chaining to trees or fences, with exposure to the elements in all kinds of weather. Whether they ever had a healing effect or not, these particular camps have fallen into the category of human rights abusers and have been condemned by international human rights groups (US Department of State: Bureau of Democracy, Human Rights, and Labor, 2019). Faith healing camps often begin as conventional prayer centers and churches for the general public and develop adjunct units to care for the severely mentally ill who are brought to them by their relatives for healing. As the numbers have grown, and without the necessary resources, knowledge, and infrastructure for the ethical management of people living with mental illness, prayer camps or centers have come to use more and more physical barriers such as shackles to keep the mentally ill from leaving the camps.

Where the faith healers have ethical practices, they provide adequate shelter, have forbidden physical abuse, and provide access to medication through the services of visiting community psychiatric nurses (Arias et al., 2016). These positive developments raise the question of "Why use chains at all?". The Mental Health Law, Act 846, recognizes that where patients are agitated or where there is a chance of self-harm or harm of others, there is the need for some form of restraint, but requires the use of least forms of physical restraints (Mental Health Law, 2012).

The law also requires that people needing such care must be sent to hospitals within forty-eight hours, although there has been little enforcement of this aspect of the law. This may be because neither the police, community leaders, nor the faith healers are very conversant with this law, or because there are few alternatives of places of healing, or because of people's beliefs of the spiritual being associated with illness causation.

Many conventional churches, recognizing the use of excessive restraint, have closed down their prayer camps to avoid being in contravention of the law and human rights. Those who have remained open may have done so because there is an unmet need for services for the mentally ill, and there has not been adequate enforcement of the law.

18.6 Mental Health Care through Primary Healthcare Services

In the next step of the services pyramid (WHO, 2005) primary health care becomes the central medium through which formal mental health services are obtained. The Ghana Health Service trains and hires community psychiatric nurses (CPNs), medical assistants in psychiatry (MAPs), and medical officers in more than half the districts in the country. This model of care was thought to have raised the standards and access to services in many low- and middle-income countries including Uganda (The Mental Health and Poverty Project, 2010).

In an attempt to merge informal community care, primary health care, and mental healthcare services within one prayer camp, we conducted a demonstration project with a rigorous evaluation component that introduced psychologists and senior psychiatry residents from the University of Ghana Medical School to one of the largest prayer camps in Ghana (Ofori-Atta et al., 2018). There were between 120 and 140 people resident in the sanatorium (as it was called) at any given time. The sanatorium comprised four blocks of dormitories for men and three for women. In these there were various levels of freedom of movement with some dorms being more restrictive than others. As residents' health improved, they were graduated out to a semi-completed structure where they had full autonomy over their own movements. There were other residents in the camp who were not part of the sanatorium but who were there for prayer and healing. These may have been simply people of faith retreating to worship and pray. In an earlier study with a traditional healer, Lamensdorf (1990) reported that reasons given for consultation fell into the category of general anxiety and mood-related complaints (a sense of insecurity), as well as stress related to responsibilities outside of one's usual role. Lamensdorf concluded that healers thus provided services that helped to maintain good mental health among people with mild to moderate stress. In this prayer camp, the faithful and those with possible mild to moderate symptoms rented one-bedroom apartments on the same large compound, removed from the sanatorium, and owned by the church. They attended church services held two to three times each week, as well as visiting with the prophet for laying on of hands, rituals associated with healing. Mentally ill patients from the sanatorium were also taken to the prophet in a group for the laying on of hands, and also attended church services, if there was no risk associated with absconding.

The goal of this clinical project was to link the effectiveness of formal psychiatric care, especially medications, with the cultural acceptability of informal faith healing. In addition, a research component was introduced to rigorously evaluate the impact of medication on health outcomes for adults with serious mental illnesses in the prayer camp. The goal of research was to (1) change the beliefs of the staff around illness causation and medical treatment and (2) demonstrate the effectiveness of linking models of care across different cultures and belief systems.

In this initiative, residents of the prayer camp with schizophrenia and mood disorders were randomly assigned to receive prescribed medication with nurse supervision along with usual prayer camp activities (prayers and fasting) ($N = 71$) or prayer camp activities alone ($N = 68$). There were no significant differences between individuals in the experimental and control group except for the use of prescribed medication in the experimental group. That is, individuals who were in the experimental arm of the study were given medication and had a better health outcome than individuals who were not on medication. Ethics approval was sought from and granted by the Institutional Review Board of the Noguchi Memorial Institute for Research (NMIR IRB). Regular reports were submitted to the NMIR IRB and permissions granted over the course of the two years of the study. Consent was granted by patients who were able to give consent, or else consent was sought from their next of kin or close family member who had brought them to the prayer camp. If a patient chose not to participate, this did not affect the nature of their treatment in the camp. Similarly, if they chose to drop out of the study, this also did not affect their lives in the prayer camp, and they were informed about this right at the beginning. There were six cases that were crossed over from the control to the experimental group as their symptoms had so deteriorated that they clearly needed medication. At the end of the study, the control group patients were given the choice of medication. If they agreed, the prescribed medication was administered daily. All patients on medication continued on it after the study was over, through the services of a community health nurse under supervision from the district psychiatric nurse and district hospital. All diagnoses and prescriptions were made by senior residents in psychiatry (i.e., qualified doctors in specialist training).

Psychologists blind to the intervention group of participants assessed change in symptoms through the Brief Psychiatric Rating Scale (BPRS), which is commonly used to measure symptoms such as depression, anxiety, hallucinations, and psychotic behavior. BPRS outcomes were taken every two weeks for six weeks. At the end of the study period, the total BPRS symptoms were significantly lower in the experimental group ($p = 0.003$) than in the control group, with a moderate effect size (Cohen's d -0.48). The two groups also differed significantly on subscales of BPRS documenting thought disorder and hostility. This is exactly the effect observed in Western trials of such medications. There was, however, no significant difference in the number of days spent in chains between groups. The decision of whether to have a patient remain in chains or not was that of the prayer camp staff to make, and largely at the discretion of the prophet (as he was called) in charge of the camp. Our theory of change had been that medication would reduce illness symptoms, improve health outcomes, and therefore lead to a significant reduction in days spent in chains. The medications used in the trial were the tried and tested antipsychotics and antidepressants on the essential medication list of the Ghana Health Service.

The results showed that although as expected, the medication group did substantially better in symptom improvement, the days out of chains did not significantly change, unfortunately, perhaps reflecting the short, six-week duration of the trial. In addition, we used a retrospective measure of days in chains going back two weeks. We believe now that we should have measured this daily. However, the explanation offered by prayer camp staff was that without the needed security at their camp, their fear was that patients would abscond and may never be found again. According to them, given the stigma associated with mental illness, the patient could be at risk of harm outside the camp. The camp would then be held responsible. We had assumed that the patient's primary diagnosis, often of psychosis, schizophrenia, or bipolar disorder, was the major reason for their being chained. This however did not take full cognizance of the impact of the other comorbidities on the behavior of the patient, and by extension that of their caregivers. As such, there were patients who exhibited disruptive behavior after improvement in their psychotic symptoms that were due to personality disorders. There were other patients that had histories of leaving the camp without permission to procure and use psychoactive substances due to various substance use disorders. These two groups of patients were kept in chains after their psychotic symptoms had resolved s the caregivers feared that their actions may have resulted in harm to hemselves or to others.

We also qualitatively assessed the impact of viewing the changes in patients after use of medication on beliefs of caregivers at the camp. We nterviewed seven caregivers pre- and postintervention and analyzed the hange in perception and beliefs about illness causation. The seven inter-iewees were assistants of the faith healer (who were hired to take care of he daily needs of patients) and the interviews were centered on their understandings of mental illness, symptomatology, and methods of allevi-tion of these ailments. The NMIR IRB approved this part of the study as well. Staff were informed about the purpose of the study and were given the hoice to participate or not. Time spent with each individual was about hirty minutes.

Three main themes emerged from the interviews in comparing respondent perceptions before and after the intervention: perceptions of causality, of the ffectiveness of medication, and of the reasons for the experimental collabor-tion (Table 18.1). Each is described in the following sections.

18.7 Theme 1: Perceptions of the Causes of Mental Illness

This theme describes the opinions of the staff of the prayer camp with egards to the causes of mental illness and treatment. All respondents ($N = 7$)

Table 18.1 *Summary of derived themes*

Themes	Description
Theme 1 Beliefs regarding illness causation	This theme typifies the beliefs of the staff with regards to causes of mental illness and treatment: possession by evil spirits, curses for going against social norms and taboos, and the effects of psychoactive substances and stress.
Theme 2 Perceptions of effectiveness of medications	This theme encompasses the perceptions of respondents on the efficacy of psychotropic medication in the treatment of patients at the camp. Generally, they reported that medications made patients lively and sociable, brought self-awareness, and promoted sleep and appetite.
Theme 3 Recognition of the value of the collaborative trial	This theme described respondents' recognition that conventional and nonconventional mental health professionals may work together; such collaboration being possible because there are both physical and spiritual aspects of mental illness.

were of the view that the primary cause of mental illness rested in a spiritual or supernatural basis and therefore a spiritual remedy was required. Some responses were as follows:

> Mental illness is caused by demons and curses ... prayer takes care of the spiritual aspects of the illness. (Respondent 1)

> Mental illness is caused by evil spirits ... fasting and prayers fight these evil spirits. (Respondent 2)

> Prayer and fasting breaks curses and anointing drives away evil spirits. (Respondent 3)

Interestingly, the respondent below moves a step further to state that drinking and smoking are also causes of mental illness but qualifies specifically that those behaviors are also essentially spiritual attacks. This is exemplified in the extracts below.

> Illness is caused by witches, breaking taboos and wronging gods, smoking and drinking are all spirit attacks ... Bible teachings change mind-sets, prayer and fasting heals mental illness. (Respondent 4)

> Demons and witches can also cause mental illness, prayer solves the spiritual part and medication the physical part. (Respondent 6)

Respondents also expressed the belief that mental illness could arise as punishment or consequence from going against social norms, for example:

> Mental illness is caused by curses ... you see when you and some powers make an agreement and you break it, they can punish you with mental illness. (Respondent 1)

> You see when for example, you follow someone's wife or husband, as a punishment you can be cursed and you get mad. (Respondent 6)

> Illness is caused by breaking taboos ... for example some places have rules against sleeping with another man's wife so you can get mad when you go against it. (Respondent 7)

After the randomized trial had been in process for six months, the interviews were repeated. The analyses revealed a more varied perception about the cause of mental illness than as exclusively spiritual. Four respondents again claimed a spiritual causality but had expanded their views, stating that other factors could also account for the onset of mental illness. There was a general consensus about the role of extreme stress in life as a cause of mental illness (e.g., a sudden shock, sustained emotional and/or physical pain as a result of a tragic event, loss of a loved one, and betrayal were all implicated). The following narratives exemplify this perspective:

> Mental illness is caused by disappointment ... for example, a lady here got mad because a certain man who promised to marry her, married another lady. (Respondent 1)

> There is one guy here who sold his things to pay for a visa connection, the connection man run away with the money. On hearing the news, he just went crazy.   (Respondent 3)

> Mental illness is caused by putting your trust in people too much.   (Respondent 6)

> A man I know lost the wife and two children in an accident, the pain was too much for him he took to drinking and now his mind is gone.   (Respondent 7)

In another variation, two other respondents mentioned that some people had developed mental illness because someone in their family may also have had it. This dimension seemed to imply belief in a genetic component of mental illness, as follows:

> Some doctor has mentioned to me that some people are born with it [mental illness] and it makes me remember how in the past before you marry, your family will warn you that there is madness in a certain family so you should not go there ... I think it is true.   (Respondent 3)

The respondent above not only accepts the genetic aspect of mental illness but also describes what that means socially with regards to marriage. Another respondent talks about how it is possible for mental illness to run in families when he says,

> If it were just curses or spiritual attacks, then how would a little child who knows nothing, come into the world and have mental illness? They have wronged no one nor committed any crime ... maybe the mother has it in her blood.   (Respondent 4)

18.8 Theme 2: Perceptions of the Effectiveness of Medications

A significant point that supports change in beliefs as a result of the exposure of prayer camp staff to the trial is reflected in the expression of belief in the effectiveness of medication. Prayer camp staff ($N = 5$) came to recognize the efficacy of psychotropic medication by observing the trial. Prayer camp staff observed changes in mood as a direct effect of medicating patients in the sanatorium. Supporting extracts are as follows:

18.8.1 Theme 2a: Makes Patients Lively and Sociable

> Medicines make patients who did not want to talk, talk. For example, one guy brought here had not spoken but after he was given an injection, I could even go and sit with him and chat.   (Respondent 1)

> Medication takes away dullness and energizes the patients.   (Respondent 3)

The respondent below noticed that one of the changes was that a patient had become able to appreciate a joke and even respond to it after the onset of medication:

> Medication takes away dullness from the patients so they talk more as compared to when they started taking the medicine ... for example, one of my patients even laughs when I make a joke.   (Respondent 5)

> Because of the medicine, you can chat with them and even send them small small ...   (Respondent 6)

> Some patients on medication start getting close to other patients, they even go to the church on their own and watch television with other colleagues.   (Respondent 7)

18.8.2 Theme 2b: Brings Self-Awareness

Respondents ($N = 4$) described some of the effects of medication as helping patients gain insight and becoming aware of their surroundings. Supporting extracts are as follows:

> Medicines make the patients want to be clean ... they complain of the way other patients in their ward are dirty or smelling. (Respondent 5)

> Medication makes patients want to bathe and brush their teeth and also wear clothes. (Respondent 6)

> Medication makes patients see when they are dirty ... I have sometimes heard them complain to the doctors that caregivers do not give them chance to bath everyday.   (Respondent 7)

18.8.3 Theme 2c: Promotes Sleep and Appetite

Another significant effect of medications as described by respondents ($N = 4$) was of a physical nature that could be observed directly. In their opinion, these were indices that showed patients were getting better. Sleep and appetite were particularly discussed, as described below:

> For some patients when the illness starts, they cannot sleep ... the medicines make them sleep and when they wake up, they are hungry...   (Respondent 3)

> Medicine makes patients eat and sleep well ...   (Respondent 5)

18.9 Theme 3: Recognition of the Value of the Collaborative Trial

Six of the seven respondents were of the opinion that it would be useful for conventional mental health professionals and members of the faith community to work together because there are both physical and spiritual causes of mental illness, a view that differed from their previously held perceptions, as one respondent stated:

> Prophet and pastors need to do their part before the doctors' methods will work ... Bible teachings also will bring faith in the patient to be able to overcome. (Respondent 5)

Another said:

> You see the Bible even warns that we wrestle not against flesh and blood ... so the illness has a spiritual aspect which we need spiritual means to fight and that's why we fast as well as the patients ... we then have power to fight the demons or witches ... (Respondent 6)

What we conclude from these interviews is that prayer camp staff began with a predominant belief in the spiritual causes of illness and, over a six-month period, as the medication trial proceeded, their beliefs became more comprehensive and incorporated both biological and social causes of illness into their worldview. We are hoping that this change in worldview will translate into less stigma and more humane arrangements.

18.10 Ethical Considerations

Some may consider it unethical to conduct research in prayer camps and other community settings in which unethical practices such as chaining are followed (Patel, 2018). However, we argue that on the one hand researchers must, themselves, follow all laws and ethical rules that govern their professional practice, in resource-poor settings as in affluent settings. However, if they do not work in such places, how can they possibly bring about evidence-based change? How could we possibly impact policy without evidence? The University of Ghana follows the strictest rules for the protection of human subjects, believes in the principles of justice/utility, respect for the autonomy of competent others, beneficence and nonmaleficence. Our research participants were informed that they could drop out of the research at any time and still ask for treatment if they so elected. Control participants were given the opportunity to participate in the experimental arm of the study if they chose to after the six-week period in the control group. Fasting was not permitted during the trial so that all research participants had access to meals as we deemed it unhealthy otherwise and had negotiated with the prophet for this. Although one of our theories of change had been that the chains would be removed once people got better, we had little or no authority over this. Prayer camp staff removed chains when they were comfortable that patients would not be aggressive toward other patients and would not run away. Their uncertainty was particularly strong with patients who also had addictive disorders as the cravings associated with drug use would drive patients out of the camp in search of the next hit. We believe that it was the constraints of infrastructure, more than beliefs of illness, which made it difficult for staff to remove chains within the admittedly brief six-week duration of the trial for individual participants.

Although the research design was a randomized control trial, the partnership approach employed was also community-based participatory research. The prophet himself was a strong advocate of the demonstration and the research, and this support was the critical ingredient without which nothing would have occurred. We met regularly with staff, and with the prophet, to discuss the stages of our research, and also addressed the difficulties faced by prayer camp staff through workshops. Workshop themes included the importance of maintaining boundaries with one's patients, the importance of hygiene (with staff permission, we invited the district health management team to visit and disinfect the camp), side effects of medications, the natural cycles of episodic illness, navigating and working with the healthcare system, discharge planning, and helping patients with dual diagnoses of substance abuse, the mental health law and its stand on the use of chains, etc. The staff at the camp were the first to be given the results of the study and discussions held about the findings. There were discussions about the use of chains, the need to hospitalize some patients for physical care, and a plan to turn the prayer camp into a recovery center post hospitalization in a psychiatric hospital. This, it was agreed, would eliminate the use of chains.

In community-based participatory research, the power inequality between researchers and community can often stand in the way of getting to agreements (Small, 2015) and with hindsight, we wished we had signed some kind of memorandum of understanding at the beginning that would have allowed us more power to insist on when chains would be removed. We also wished that we could have mustered resources to make the buildings safer for patients so that the use of chains could be eliminated. We wished we could have dialogued until we had reached agreement on how to turn the prayer camp into a recovery center. On the other hand, had we insisted on such conditions, the research, and its positive message, may not have taken place at all.

In the end, what was achieved? Patients did get better on medication. Staff learned about the important gains with medication and how it could make life easier for their patients and for themselves. They moved closer to holding a worldview of mental illness that was not so steeped in the spiritual and we learned that injection of resources (financial, educational, and health) into prayer camps would most certainly change circumstances for the better. We therefore believe that the demonstration effect of the use of medication in a prayer camp served to change the views of staff. The use of medication continues in the camp today, four years later.

18.11 Long-Term Stay Facilities and Specialist Hospitals

At the very peak of the pyramid (WHO, 2005) are long-term stay facilities for the most severely disabled. There are, in fact, no formal long-term stay medical/psychiatric facilities in Ghana. The three psychiatric hospitals are often, by default, used as long-stay medical facilities, which has had the unfortunate consequence that in the past, many patients stayed for very extended periods of time, unnecessarily. The three psychiatric facilities are state-owned and are all placed in the southern part of the country, immediately pointing to a skewed distribution of services. Originally large with more than a thousand-bed capacity each, they have currently reduced occupancy to between four hundred and six hundred apiece. Thankfully, there are no shackles used in these facilities and there tend to be trained medical personnel (psychiatrists, residents, medical officers, psychiatric nurses, etc.). However, there are unethical practices associated with these hospitals as well. Resource availability does not match that of regular hospitals and this may partly be because of the stigma associated with mental illness (Ofori-Atta et al., 2018). There often are medication shortages, and the surroundings are dilapidated and depressing. The framework is predominantly biomedical without psychosocial interventions since the state hospitals tend not to have psychologists. The teaching hospitals, on the other hand, have begun to provide specialized psychiatric services within the teaching hospital setting, with some psychosocial support (cognitive behavioral therapy and other forms of psychotherapy, community mental health home visits, etc.) and young psychiatrists in training. The care settings are more friendly, and the standard of care is better. There is also less stigma attached.

Currently psychiatric hospitals attempt to stabilize patients as quickly as possible and discharge them to follow up with community care teams, an imperative fueled by the limited resources available. A community care team is typically based in a district hospital and comprises a mix of community psychiatric nurses, community mental health officers, and/or medical assistants in psychiatry. These cadres of staff are trained to identify and manage mental disorders to varying degrees of expertise, often managing small inpatient psychiatric units. They are also trained and equipped to follow up on their clients at their homes and within their communities. They are often backed by primary healthcare doctors in district and regional hospitals.

In the absence of long-term and assisted living facilities for people with severe mental illness, prayer camps have filled the gap.

18.12 Discussion

18.12.1 Recommendations for Policy Change

The legal instrument for bringing about change is available in Ghana in the Mental Health Law (2012), Act 846, a rights-based body of legislation.

Given that the staff of the camp we studied changed their attitudes toward mental illness and medication during the brief trial described previously, we believe it would be possible to change the culture of care in most camps, using a training and research approach, backed by law if adequate resources were made available.

18.12.1.1 Bringing the Law into Informal, Community Models of Care for Detaining People Involuntarily

As Ae-Ngibise et al. (2010) describe, whether human rights are violated or not, people will go to prayer camps because it is the best alternative available to them, and it is consonant with their deeply held religious beliefs. However, Section 51 of the mental health law forbids any nonaccredited institutions from treating any mentally ill patients involuntarily. This means that, by law, prayer camps can no longer detain any mentally ill patients against their will and must restrict their activities to patients voluntarily seeking assistance. In accordance with this, all patients, violent or otherwise, being brought to the camp against their will by relatives or unrelated people must be referred to the nearest medical facility. Section 48 (3) of the law allows acutely ill patients to be detained in a nonaccredited institution in an emergency situation and only for a limited time set at forty-eight hours. This is only permitted if it is not practically possible to offer involuntary care in an accredited facility. The involuntary treatment of people suffering from mental illness, under Section 42, has to be ordered by the court, and only if two medical practitioners declare that the patient poses a threat to himself or herself or to other people, or there is a substantial risk of the patient's condition deteriorating rapidly.

18.12.1.2 Managing People Who Want to Be in Prayer Camps

Section 57 of the law mandates that people suffering from mental illness are entitled to the same quality of bedding, sanitation, food, and buildings that they would get if they were treated for a physical condition. In line with this requirement, patients in prayer camps cannot, by law, be made to lie on the bare floor, be without access to basic sanitation, or be without adequate protection from the environment, including mosquito control. Patients are also legally entitled to regular meals each day unless they choose to fast, in other words fasting cannot be forced.

The need for prayer camps to deal with aggressive patients who require physical restraint should be drastically reduced, as camps should stop admitting or managing involuntary patients. Those remaining calmer voluntary patients should be able to be cared for using the existing sanitary facilities available in the camp and actual beds should be made available. Mosquito nets must also be made available for the patients in the camp.

18.12.1.3 Future Role of Prayer Camps

By law, therefore, prayer camps in Ghana can no longer manage involuntary patients, in other words no patient should be chained under any circumstances or forced to do anything he or she does not want to do, including fasting. This provision of the law is not currently being enforced as the relevant authorities have not yet adopted a model of enforcement that caters for the large number of people currently being involuntarily managed in these camps.

It would logically fall to the DHMTs to ensure that the living conditions for all patients in prayer camps are improved to the level of care provided in hospital or community clinics as soon as is feasible. New involuntary admissions to camps should thus be halted altogether and a drive to empty camps of all involuntarily admitted patients should be initiated. This drive could feasibly be supervised and enforced by DHMTs and the Mental Health Authority, the body which manages all matters on mental health nationally.

Existing psychiatric hospitals are already overburdened with inpatients, with some of them operating above their maximum bed capacity. The psychiatric hospitals are, therefore, not likely to be able to take up the large number of adults currently being involuntarily held in prayer camps. These patients may be released from the camps as their mental health improves with appropriate treatment. The release of patients as they get better, coupled with a cessation of new admissions, should eventually result in the end of involuntary detentions in camps. The Mental Health Authority has closed down some camps and is currently monitoring others and giving them the opportunity to make their practices more ethical.

The treatment model used in the study "Joining Psychiatric Care and Faith Healing in a Prayer Camp in Ghana: A Randomized Trial" (Ofori-Atta et al., 2018) could be adopted as a way of treating people to allow them to be discharged out of the camps. This model would require a regular supply of psychotropic medication and regular outpatient visits from a professional treatment team. We thus recommend a step-by-step model of change where the DHMTs:

1. engage faith healers in drawing up a road map of change from involuntary care for some patients to a voluntary recovery model of care for all patients;
2. arrange for teams of medics, nurses, and psychologists to decongest existing prayer camps by sending involuntary patients for care in hospitals, or by initially providing psychiatric care within camps until no patients need physical restraints. Then the camp switches to a recovery model with only voluntary patients;
3. help camps to design psycho-social-spiritual recovery programs for patients, including for addictive disorders;
4. provide some infrastructure support for camps to make them safer, more hygienic, and provide oversight to ensure the abuses are a thing of the past.

The supply of medications was a challenge during the study, and this was reflective of the challenges faced by many district community psychiatric units in Ghana. The national central supply of medications is often erratic or unpredictable, forcing units to either not supply medications or purchase medications from private sector pharmacies. Medications sourced from the private sector tend to be more expensive and their cost is prohibitive for some families with a severely mentally ill family member. The DHMT will have to take an active role in securing psychotropic medications and in the regularization and stabilization of the medication supply to medical teams that service prayer camps.

Prayer camps with oversight by DHMTs could also be accredited as sites for rotations in community medicine so residents in family medicine and psychiatry could thus participate in the professional multidisciplinary teams and contribute to desperately needed workforce development. The project to empty prayer camps of involuntary patients may be approached as a joint demonstration project between all the concerned institutions and severely ill patients transferred to the closest hospitals for care. The District Assembly should pay for the treatment of these patients whilst they are on admission to hospital. The District Assembly of the district in which a person living with mental illness resides, is mandated under the Mental Health Law, Act 846 73 (4) to address the needs of that person. The District Assembly can use funds derived from the disability fund to provide needed care. People living with mental illness can decide on their next course of action once they have been stabilized and can receive care on a voluntary basis. These patients may choose to live with their families or may choose to return to the prayer camp for more spiritual interventions.

There are likely to be some patients who are stable, but who do not have identifiable social support systems, thus making it difficult to send them home at the end of their initial treatment. There may be others who suffer from cognitive deficits that are not reversed with treatment. These groups of patients may choose to stay in the camp voluntarily once they have been stabilized. The local assembly should pay for the cost of their continued care in the camp, with money from the disability fund.

Ghanaians are very religious people and naturally seek spiritual assistance when they or their family members fall ill. The prayer camp will still be a likely major point of call for many families seeking assistance for an acutely mentally ill family member, although some will go to hospitals directly. Acutely ill patients who are referred to a psychiatric hospital would return to the prayer camp after their acute care needs are met and would be discharged to deal with the spiritual aspect of their illness in the prayer camp setting, with needed medical support. Patients discharged from psychiatric hospitals may require an intermediate environment, where people understand their needs and their deficits, before being returned home.

Prayer camp staff can facilitate the referral of acutely ill patients that report there as the first point of call. The experience of taking a relative to a psychiatric hospital can be a daunting one for families and they may appreciate the help of a religious figure who is also familiar with the psychiatric health services. The prayer camp staff may be able to facilitate the transport of the patient to the medical facility, facilitate the interaction between the clinical staff and the family, provide accommodation for relatives who wish to stay near the patient (particularly in the first seventy-two hours during which newly admitted patients are often detained for observation pending a final decision on whether they are to have prolonged hospital stays or not), provide religious services to the patient and family members during the admission process, and participate in discharge planning.

Patients discharged from psychiatric hospitals often require an intermediate environment before being returned home. Some of these patients may still be adjusting to the idea of suffering from a mental illness and are not yet ready to engage with their regular lives. Some families have difficulty adjusting either to the fact that a family member has a mental illness, or to the fact that the mental illness has been managed and the person is now stable (Gerson & Rose, 2012; Solomon, Beck, & Gordon, 1988). Some families are not able to provide the kind of stable home environment that is desirable for somebody recovering from mental illness. Some patients are discharged when they are relatively stable but not yet fully recovered. Patients discharged in this manner require more assistance than stable patients and some families are not able to provide the level of assistance required. These categories of patients and their families will be looking for an environment where people understand their needs and their deficits, and which may also provide spiritual guidance.

Within camps, healthcare teams may help streamline admission procedures for voluntary patients and also provide standards of safety to be followed by camp staff.

When camps say they offer spiritual care, then they must be held accountable for this. There must be a written description of these services that is followed regularly since it is the reason patients are there.

In addition to these services, members of Ghana's "Psych Corps" (fresh graduates in psychology who have studied community or clinical psychology and who are trained to give psychological first aid), with supervision from psychologists and community psychiatric nurses, may also use manuals written on scripture-based psychological interventions to assist in the recovery of patients. These services may include narcotics and alcoholics anonymous groups, insight therapy, family therapy (including the recovery model and their role in it), and resilience-building (De Jong et al., 2019; Goldstein & Miklowitz, 1995; Kaskutas, 2009).

The Psych Corps was created as a task-shifting measure to provide psychological interventions in communities given the gap in psychosocial services across the country (Ofori-Atta, Bradley, & Nyonator, 2013; Ofori-Atta, Ketor. & Bradley, 2014). Psychology undergraduates who express interest are given training in basic clinical community interventions that aid people in mental health crisis situations. On graduation, these Psych Corps are posted to work mainly with community-based psychiatric nurses and medical doctors. The CPN, who is the link between the professional team and the camp staff, will be able to monitor the patient's day-to-day progress whilst monitoring their adherence to prescribed medications and looking out for the development of drug reactions.

These interventions should be conducted as a closely monitored demonstration project to gain knowledge that may serve as a basis for both further improvement of the model and for a national drive to make faith-based institutions compliant and consistent with the goals of the mental health law.

18.13 Conclusion

The policy suggestion here is that provision and oversight of community mental health services are the purview of local government providers, in other words DHMTs in Ghana, and they are not to cede this responsibility to prayer camps. DHMTs should sustain active involvement in setting and maintaining the same standards of humane care as are expected in community places of physical healing. The constitution of the country and the mental health law require respect of the human rights of all people and although these are explicitly granted to everyone in the constitution of Ghana, at present there is no government agency that guarantees these rights through enforcement to people with mental illness, especially at vulnerable times of acute decompensation. Our experience is that many health professionals are deeply religious and have spiritual beliefs about illness causation (Ighodaro et al., 2015; Stefanovics et al., 2016) that make them uncomfortable confronting the abuses in prayer camps with the rigor prescribed by the law. However, this confrontation is necessary and may be the only way to safeguard the well-being of the majority of people living with mental illness in Ghana.

In this chapter we have described a comprehensive picture of mental health care in Ghana from the most informal self-care to the most restrictive institutional care, identifying the important, often constructive, contributions to care, but acknowledging also unacceptable human rights violations in prayer camps and faith healing. We have described a path through which we believe prayer camps can and should be transformed into places of uncompromised healing and teaching of medical practice and culture, of assisted living, of spiritual exercise, and deepening of faith in accordance with local beliefs and traditions. This is a great opportunity to grow a culturally evolved practice into twenty-first-century holistic care.

References

Ae-Ngibise, K., Cooper, S., Adiibokah, E., et al. (2010). 'Whether you like it or not people with mental problems are going to go to them': A qualitative exploration into the widespread use of traditional and faith healers in the provision of mental health care in Ghana. *International Review of Psychiatry, 22*(6), 558–567. doi.org/10.3109/09540261.2010.536149

Appiah-Poku, J., Laugharne, R., Mensah, E., Osei, Y., & Burns, T. (2004). Previous help sought by patients presenting to mental health services in Kumasi, Ghana. *Social Psychiatry and Psychiatric Epidemiology, 39*(3), 208–211. doi.org/10.3109/09540261.2010.536149

Arias, D., Taylor, L., Ofori-Atta, A., & Bradley, E. H. (2016). Prayer camps and biomedical care in Ghana: Is collaboration in mental health care possible? *PLoS ONE, 11*(9), Article e0162305. doi.org/10.1371/journal.pone.0162305

Canavan, M. E., Sipsma, H. L., Adhvaryu, A., et al. (2013). Psychological distress in Ghana: Associations with employment and lost productivity. *International Journal of Mental Health Systems, 7*(1), Article 9. doi.org/10.1186/1752-4458-7-9

De Jong, S., Van Donkersgoed, R. J. M., Timmerman, M. E., et al. (2019). Metacognitive reflection and insight therapy (MERIT) for patients with schizophrenia. *Psychological Medicine, 49*(2), 303–313. doi.org/10.1017/S0033291718000855

Eaton, J., & Ohene, S. (2016). Providing sustainable mental health care in Ghana: A demonstration project. In Forum on Neuroscience and Nervous System Disorders, Board on Health Sciences Policy, Board on Global Health, et al. *Providing sustainable mental and neurological health care in Ghana and Kenya: Workshop summary* (pp. 183–232). Washington, DC: National Academies Press.

Ferrari, A. J., Charlson, F. J., Norman, R. E., et al. (2013). Burden of depressive disorders by country, sex, age, and year: Findings from the Global Burden of Disease Study 2010. *PLoS Medicine, 10*(11). doi.org/10.1371/journal.pmed.1001547

Fosu, G. B. (1995). Women's orientation toward help-seeking for mental disorders. *Social Science & Medicine, 40*(8), 1029–1040. doi.org/10.1016/0277-9536(94)00170-X

Gerson, L. D., & Rose, L. E. (2012). Needs of persons with serious mental illness following discharge from inpatient treatment: Patient and family views. *Archives of Psychiatric Nursing, 26*(4), 261–271. doi.org/10.1016/J.APNU.2012.02.002

Goldstein, M. J., & Miklowitz, D. J. (1995). The effectiveness of psychoeducational family therapy in the treatment of schizophrenic disorders. *Journal of Marital and Family Therapy, 21*(4), 361–376. doi.org/10.1111/j.1752-0606.1995.tb00171.x

Ighodaro, A., Stefanovics, E., Makanjuola, V., & Rosenheck, R. A. (2015). An assessment of attitudes towards people with mental illness among medical students and physicians in Ibadan, Nigeria. *Academic Psychiatry, 39*, 280–285. doi.org/10.1007/s40596-014-0169-9

Immigration and Refugee Board of Canada. (2002, May 7). *Ghana Ashanti widow rituals, steps required, whether the widow can refuse to participate, whether she would be required to marry her husband's relative, and consequences for refusal* (Document GHA38600.E). www.refworld.org/docid/3df4be3520.html

Kaskutas, L. A. (2009). Alcoholics Anonymous effectiveness: Faith meets science. *Journal of Addictive Diseases, 28*(2), 145–157. doi.org/10.1080/10550880902772464

Kpobi, L., & Swartz L. (2018). "That is how the real mad people behave": Beliefs about and treatment of mental disorders by traditional medicine men in Accra, Ghana. *International Journal of Social Psychiatry, 64*(4), 309–316. doi.org/10.1177/0020764018763705

Kpobi, L., Swartz, L., & Ofori-Atta, A. L. (2018). Challenges in the use of the mental health information system in a resource-limited setting: Lessons from Ghana. *BMC Health Services Research, 18*(1), 1–8. doi.org/10.1186/s12913-018-2887-2

Lamensdorf, A. M. (1990). Socio-economic development and mental health in Ghana. In S. Arnold & A. Nitechi (Eds.), *Culture and development in Africa* (pp. 203–210). Trenton, NJ: Africa World Press Inc.

Mental Health Authority of Ghana. (2018). *2017 annual report*. Accra, Ghana: Bayuti Enterprise.

Mental Health Law. (2012). *Act 846*. www.refworld.org/pdfid/528f243e4.pdf

Ofori-Atta, A., Attafuah, J., Jack, H., Baning, F., Rosenheck, R., & Joining Forces Research Consortium. (2018). Joining psychiatric care and faith healing in a prayer camp in Ghana: Randomised trial. *The British Journal of Psychiatry, 212*(1), 34–41. doi.org/10.1192/bjp.2017.12

Ofori-Atta, A., Bradley, E., & Nyonator, F. (2013). *Increasing access to primary mental health care through task shifting: Embracing a new cadre of graduates in psychology in primary health care in Ghana*. Paper presentation, Scientific Conference, Centre for Global Mental Health, Institute of Psychiatry, London. Also presented at the 3rd Annual Joint Conference of the Departments of Psychiatry and Psychology.

Ofori-Atta, A., Ketor, R., & Bradley, R. (2014). *Positioning a new cadre of community workers into the mental health system of a low resourced country: The case of Ghana*. Presented at the 2014 Annual Convention of the South African Society of Psychiatrists, Durban.

Ofori-Atta, A., & Linden, W. (1995). The effect of social change on causal beliefs of mental disorders and treatment preferences in Ghana. *Social Science & Medicine, 40*(9), 1231–1242. doi.org/10.1016/0277-9536(94)00248-R

Patel, V. (2018). Commentary on joining psychiatric care and faith healing in a prayer camp in Ghana: Randomized trial. *British Journal of Psychiatry, 212*(1), 34–41. doi.org/10.1192/bjp.2017.12

Quinn, N. (2007). Beliefs and community responses to mental illness in Ghana: The experiences of family carers. *International Journal of Social Psychiatry, 53*(2), 175–188. doi.org/10.1177/0020764006074527

Roberts, M., Mogan, C., & Asare, J. B. (2014). An overview of Ghana's mental health system: Results from an assessment using the World Health Organization's Assessment Instrument for Mental Health Systems

(WHO-AIMS). *International Journal of Mental Health Systems*, *8*, Article 16. doi.org/10.1186/1752-4458-8-16

Rousseau, C., & Frounfelker, R. L. (2019). Mental health needs and services for migrants: An overview for primary care providers. *Journal of Travel Medicine*, *26*(2). doi.org/10.1093/jtm/tay150.

Sipsma, H., Chen, P., Ofori-Atta, A., et al. (2012). Female genital cutting: Current practices and beliefs in West Africa. *WHO Bulletin*, *90*(2), 120–127. doi.org/10.2471/blt.11.090886

Sipsma, H., Ofori-Atta, A., Canavan, M., et al. (2013). Poor mental health in Ghana: Who is at risk? *BMC Public Health*, *13*(1), Article 288. doi.org/10.1186/1471-2458-13-288

Small, M. L. (2015). De-exoticizing ghetto poverty: On the ethics of representation in urban ethnography. *City & Community*, *14*(4), 352–358. doi.org/10.1111/cico.12137

Solomon, P., Beck, S., & Gordon, B. (1988). Family members' perspectives on psychiatric hospitalization and discharge. *Community Mental Health Journal*, *24*(2), 108–117. doi.org/10.1007/BF00756653

Sorketti, E. A., Zainal, N. Z., & Habil, M. H. (2012). The characteristics of people with mental illness who are under treatment in traditional healer centres in Sudan. *International Journal of Social Psychiatry*, *58*(2), 204–216. doi.org/10.1177/0020764010390439

Stefanovics, E., He, H., Tavares Cavalcanti, M., et al. (2016). Witchcraft and biopsychosocial causes of mental illness: Attitudes and beliefs about mental illness among health professionals in five nations. *Journal of Nervous and Mental Diease*, *204*(3), 169–174. doi.org/10.1097/nmd.0000000000000422

The Mental Health and Poverty Project. (2010). *Mental health policy development and implementation in four African countries* (HD6). https://assets.publishing.service.gov.uk/media/57a08af9e5274a31e00008b2/MHaPP_Final_Report_forR4D.pdf

US Department of State: Bureau of Democracy, Human Rights, and Labor. (2019). *Country reports on human rights practices for 2018: Ghana 2018 human rights report*. www.state.gov/wp-content/uploads/2019/03/Ghana-2018.pdf

Whiteford, H. A., Degenhardt, L., Rehm, J., et al. (2013). Global burden of disease attributable to mental and substance use disorders: Findings from the Global Burden of Disease Study 2010. *The Lancet*, *382*(9904), 1575–1586. doi.org/10.1016/S0140-6736(13)61611-6

World Health Organization. (2005). *Mental health policy and service guidance package: Human resources and training in mental health*. Geneva, Switzerland: World Health Organization.

19 Community Impact of Social Media

Carlos Storck-Martinez, Cara Lomaro, Grace Koguc, and Caroline S. Clauss-Ehlers

19.1 Introduction: Defining Community Psychology and Social Media

19.1.1 Community Psychology

The concept and application of community psychology is ever evolving. Specifically, this concept holds true in the use of community psychology in social media networks. On the Internet, complex relationships are made using various social media outlets that are continually updated to better serve users. The way in which individuals choose to communicate can have many implications. More profound even, is the effect that various outlets of communication may have on relationships within and outside of one's own physical community.

19.1.2 Social Media

The specific link between community psychology and social media has not been heavily researched. Further research would benefit the field and give community psychology a current edge, particularly as community psychology can affect social learning, self-image, and social comparison.

19.1.2.1 Social Media Timeline

The idea of a sense of community developed by social media has developed over time as demonstrated by the social media timeline presented in Figure 19.1.

The social media frenzy of the late twentieth to the early twenty-first century revolutionized the modern world. The impact of social media in its "current form" (e.g., social media platforms) has had an enduring and ever-evolving impact on the way that individuals interact in social settings.

By the 1980s personalized computers became more popular and common-place in homes. These devices were vastly inferior to the computers of today,

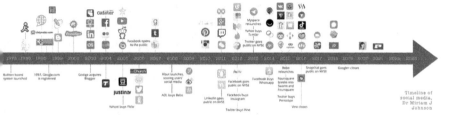

Figure 19.1 *Social media timeline*
Source: Miriam, J. (2019). Timeline of social media, 2019. *Retrieved June 23,
2021 from www.booksaresocial.com/social-media-timeline-2019/. Copyright for this
article is retained by the author(s), with first publication rights granted to the
journal. This is an open-access article distributed under the terms and conditions
of the Creative Commons Attribution license (http://creativecommons.org/licenses/
by/4.0/)*

with very limited capabilities and functionality. For example, simple games
with basic graphics could be run on these devices, along with simple programs
used to enable the user to paint and process words.

It wasn't until the 1990s when the World Wide Web was created that users
were able to connect with others (Andrews, 2019). This is where the modern
concept of social media and connecting through the Internet began
(Hendricks, 2013).

In the early 2000s MySpace and LinkedIn started. Users had the ability to
connect from around the world and share ideas from their daily experiences.
Another commonly used website today, YouTube, started in 2005. This
website changed the way that individuals shared content given that users could
post videos of their choosing. This meant that now Internet users could use a
range of ways to connect with one another. Video postings allowed for new
creativity and the introduction of people presenting themselves on YouTube
as YouTubers with individualized platforms. This social media through the
Internet allowed for connections and creative expression across the globe.

By 2006, both Facebook and Twitter were live. Facebook allows users to
connect with other users by adding "friends," with each user being able to
reach out to other users through messages and posts on one's homepage and
via comments and private messages. Twitter is similar, allowing users to post
limited texts with no more than 280 characters.

In 2007 a large shift was seen toward what can be considered modern social
media, or social media that resembles the platforms still used today. Users
from around the world were beginning to connect to relatives, friends, and
complete strangers with new and exciting insights about the world around us.
In places like Egypt, large social movements such as the "Kefaya" movement
were able to use sources like blogging to communicate under an oppressive
government. The group's ultimate goal was to have the public band together

against an unjust government. Younger generations began to use social media sites such as Facebook to protest and rally against similar injustices in Egypt (Lim, 2012).The protest on January 25, 2011 in Egypt shows a more modern context of the role that social media can have on the well-being of a large-scale community. Social media websites were once again used to orchestrate protest dates and spread information. Social media platforms were able to gather the support of roughly eighty thousand people. Other protests stemmed from these, making the overall impact of social media in this instance immeasurable. Even after the government temporarily shut down the Internet, the movement continued as everything was put on display for the world to see (Lim, 2012).

Instagram is a photo-sharing application that began in 2010. It allows users to post pictures to a feed, a list of images posted in order of submission that continually updates. Their followers can comment and like the pictures. Snapchat, a social media app that began in 2011, allows users to send pictures and videos with or without filters to other users, or a collection of photos and videos (to one's story), for a specified time. Afterwards there is an option for the picture to be more or less deleted.

19.1.3 Crowdfunding

19.1.3.1 Reward-Based Crowdfunding

Examples of reward-based crowdfunding can be seen as early as 2003, with the website ArtistShare (Freedman & Nutting, 2015). While this was a basic website, it set up the format for most crowdfunding websites today as users were able to interact with the website and decide which contributions to make with various levels of commitment.

The history of crowdfunding closely mirrors the evolution of social media, with more involvement and more user-friendly platforms coming later in time. ArtistShare was one of the first crowdfunding sources, specifically targeted toward record labels and musicians to fund their creative projects. Donations that went toward these projects sometimes even offered rewards for donors, such as the artist crediting individuals on the finished product (Freedman & Nutting, 2015). Other platforms later emerged with a broader focus, including Indiegogo in 2008 and Kickstarter in 2009. Instead of just focusing on art, both sites were open to raising money for many different categories, such as community, environment, and business, among other areas.

19.1.3.2 Debt-Based Crowdfunding

This form of crowdfunding relies on person-to-person loans. It is generally used for refinancing debt at high interest rates with high risk for lenders

(Freedman & Nutting, 2015). Lenders use websites such as LendingClub, a website that formulates the rates of loans and informs lenders of the risk level of the borrower (Freedman & Nutting, 2015).

19.1.3.3 Donation-Based Crowdfunding

Online donations were not a new concept to large charities but they spread in the early 2000s to be used more widely by individuals for their own personal goals (Freedman & Nutting, 2015). By 2010 crowdfunding websites for charitable donations were in full effect, with examples like GoFundMe starting (Freedman & Nutting, 2015). GoFundMe is a donation-based crowdfunding website where individuals or groups can raise donations for any specified charity or event.

As previously shown, crowdfunding is rooted in social media-like platforms, sharing similar starting dates to earlier social media websites and being revitalized in new forms just as social media websites continually have to do.

19.1.4 Connection between Sense of Community and Social Media

The previous examples show the depth of the connection between one's sense of community and social media throughout the past twenty-plus years. Social media use has increased in prevalence and with it a possible reconstruction of what a community may be for an individual. As the definition of what one's community is changes, so too may the implementation of outreach programs that are designed to enact change within a community and observe the reciprocal effect that one person can have on their community and the impact that one's community can have on them. To better serve a community, the relationship between one's self and one's community must be better understood. The timeline suggests that there are many more avenues where community psychology can be used to promote social justice and a greater sense of global community through social media.

19.2 Positive and Negative Impact of Social Media

Social media can have negative effects on mental health but can also provide resources and support. Research shows that online communities can have both positive and negative effects on individuals (Bibby & Stead, 2017; Branley & Covey, 2017; Chun & Lee, 2017; Cyberbullying Research Center, 2017; Marino et al., 2018; Nickolaou, 2017; Young et al., 2017).

With regard to the positive aspects, there are individuals who may actually prefer using the Internet as a source of social connection, due to specific factors such as time constraints, social anxiety, and distance, to name a few.

A recent example of a time where people have been forced to use social media as a means of interaction has been during the COVID-19 global pandemic, where individuals from all parts of the world were asked to quarantine and not engage in direct person to person communication. Users may receive support when turning to social media for personal issues they do not wish to speak to family and friends about. They may find solace in finding others with similar issues. These groups receive input from others with the same issues, along with support outside of their everyday networks. The number of friends on social media has been found to be positively associated with perceived support (Jung Oh, Ozkaya, & LaRose, 2014). Having positive Internet relationships has been found to have a positive correlation with perceived companionship support, appraisal support, and life satisfaction (Jung Oh et al., 2014).

With regard to the negative impact of social media, concerns often center on issues of being able to access material on the Internet, potential lack of parental supervision of internet access, a relationship between depression and social media usage, and concerns about social skill development, among other areas (Lin et al., 2016). For instance, building effective interpersonal skills is important for the workplace, the development and maintenance of friendships, relationships with peers, collaboration with teachers and mentors, and parent–child relationships.

There is no social experience as genuine as person-to-person relations; the brain can tell the difference (Dumas et al., 2010). While this connection cannot be ignored, it can introduce a detrimental cost: time. In a fast-paced world, individuals struggle with finding balance – an existential dilemma many face daily. The question here becomes: Are individuals tricking themselves into believing that the social media experience is the apex of communication when interacting with communities not physically in front of them, or are they simply accepting the realities of the world and its limitations?

Use of social media and the Internet can raise other concerns such as seeking medical advice not necessarily posted by a qualified provider. Without proper evidence and qualifications, information can be misleading, with nuances not captured by overgeneralized medical descriptions.

In reference to forums that allow input from many users, one may seek out medical advice in reference to a particular set of symptoms or drug combinations. Some websites allow users to discuss any topic – with users asking the forum if mixing certain drugs, legal or not, is "safe," to which other users will often give personal testimony. The obvious issue with examples as previously noted is that no two individuals are alike. As a result, mixing drugs/medications may not lead to immediate negative side effects in one person, whereas another may exhibit more severe side effects. The fields of medicine and mental health are very complex. A large forum should not take the place of professional health and mental healthcare advice; in certain situations this can be very dangerous. Humans have a tendency to pay far more attention to personal narrative, and avoid statistical analyses and data that healthcare professionals might rely upon (Kida, 2009). In summation, an online community can provide advice and support, but certain issues are far too complex and require professional support.

In terms of social support and impact on the overall well-being of individuals attempting to deal with physical and/or mental health issues that may or may not be pertinent, online forums may not be the answer. Of course, it cannot be said that the concept only has negative connotations. Realistically, when individuals need social support, having others who have gone through similar experiences and who are in the same place can be very comforting (Eysenbach et al., 2004). The difference is the impact and role of the advisor's and other users' opinions on the situation (De Choudhury & De, 2014). At one end of the spectrum, individuals receive social support from others with similar circumstances who lend a listening ear (as indicated by posts). At the other, are individuals seeking advice for complicated matters, such as medications and more serious medical questions. Here an issue is that the quality of information may vary and often be inconsistent (Moorhead et al., 2013).

Despite positive and negative attributes of social media, such as those described above, social media platforms continue to be utilized and accessed throughout our global society. This is particularly apparent in examples such as Facebook that went from 1.94 billion users in March 2017 to 2.07 billion in June 2017 (Kallas, 2019). Such growth indicates the presence and impact of social media outlets.

We have also seen the role of social media in promoting social justice and equity. For example, there are instances in the United States where individuals capture and share footage of police brutality. Here social media helps individuals document injustice and demand higher standards from their local, state, and federal governments. Some of the results that came from broadcasting police brutality in recent years through social media sites like Facebook and YouTube include large-scale protests and riots (Steijns, 2017). In part, this process has prompted many police departments to work toward lessening biases associated with the police and build better relationships with the public through outreach programs (US Department of Justice, n.d.). Darnella Frazier, the teen who recorded George Floyd's murder on her smartphone in May 2020 underscores the role that social media can play in promoting social justice. Her documentation (which she uploaded onto Facebook) led to worldwide protests. Ultimately, Derek Chauvin was convicted of George Floyd's murder (Peters, 2021).

19.3 Major Concepts Defined

Having introduced some of the complexities associated with social media, this literature review will examine how it influences community psychology. For this review, we are defining community psychology as "a branch of psychology that encourages the development of theory, research, and practice relevant to the reciprocal relationships between individuals and the social systems that constitute the community context. It intersects with other branches of psychology (e.g., social psychology) and with other disciplines, such as sociology and public health" (American Psychological Association [APA], 2020a). We are defining social media as any online platform that allows users to interact and maintain the following seven characteristics, as noted by (Kietzmann et al., 2011): identity, conversation, sharing, presence, relationships, reputation, and groups.

Popular and well-recognized social media platforms include Facebook, Instagram, Snapchat, and Twitter. Communication via such platforms can occur on computers, mobile phones, and tablets. Through social media, users with accounts can create a profile about themselves, connect with others through their profiles, and engage in online dialogue and communication. "It has been suggested that social media is a change from a unidirectional model of communication to a multidirectional model of communication" (Evers et al., 2013). This multidirectional model of communication speaks to the interconnected ways that social media users connect via their participation in various social media platforms.

19.4 Community Psychology and Social Media: Gaps in the Literature

19.4.1 Community Health

Community health has been affected by social media in the form of blogging and social media profiles dedicated to fitness and healthy eating. Instagram is a hub for healthy recipes, diet recommendations, fitness motivation, exercise regimens, and detox solutions from sponsored and accredited sources. In addition, in recent times, applications such as Instagram and Snapchat have been at the forefront of body positivity campaigns, sharing images of beauty from different nationalities and backgrounds and sizes. Apps designed for health benefits and weight loss allow individuals to set goals and create profiles in an app community that allows people to see one's progress, others' progress, give positive feedback, and make suggestions for success. Chat rooms in these types of apps may allow for a sense of community within personal journeys with people trying to obtain similar goals.

Social media may also allow people to find healthy community activities to participate in. For instance, many healthy activities going on within the Rutgers University community, where coauthors are either students or faculty members, are posted and promoted through the use of Facebook pages, such as the annual Mud Run and activities held for the first week of freshman year.

To avoid health hazards, social media also aids the Rutgers community by posting notices about school closings, traffic issues, and crime alerts, both on campus as well as in the New Brunswick community. Community health and well-being has been affected by the introduction of social media, but studies have not been done to prove how these forms of social media aid or hinder the community overall.

19.4.2 Social Media and One's Own Sense of Community

In addition, the relationship between social media and one's own sense of community has not been heavily analyzed. Social media may allow people to become aware of disparities within their communities. In addition, people may use social media to ask for assistance or show the realities of their conditions through accounts such as Facebook. It seems through observation that many people are more comfortable talking to members of their community over social media. Social media may also let members of high-income nations see what it is like to live in low- and middle-income communities, potentially gaining support for other communities, and having a greater appreciation of their own (Clauss-Ehlers et al., 2020).

In recent times, public facilities, such as community centers and libraries, have offered computers for personal use. On the web, support groups exist for all types of disorders or diagnoses, such as depression, cancer, mental health issues, and reference group identification, among others. Internet use has allowed citizens across nations to communicate their struggles and offer advice. Blogging, video chatting, posting inspirational or motivational pictures on social media, and joining chat rooms are all examples of how those seeking communal support can find solace through the use of technology. Websites have been created for people to discuss depression, grief, anorexia, sexual violence, bipolar, transgender issues, postpartum depression, and being considered overweight, to name a few. Many of these resources feature small chat rooms and video sessions for an intimate and specific community experience.

With access to technology in the home, therapy and support can be offered in the comfort of people's personal spaces. In addition, help can be given on the go, with the use of laptops and smartphones, for those who have busy schedules but need reassurance throughout the day. In a study conducted in 2010 by Horgan and Sweeney (Horgan & Sweeney, 2010), it was concluded through a questionnaire that participants who would use social media for mental health believed that this form of help offered anonymity, privacy, and confidentiality. As well, participants claimed that social media offered accessibility, speed, and low cost. In addition, participants believed that they would not be judged, and that it would be easier to express themselves. This new form of communication and online sense of community needs to be further studied to determine how useful it can be within a community context, as well as how reliable these forms of assistance are.

19.4.3 Crowdfunding

"Crowdfunding allows founders of for-profit, artistic, and cultural ventures to fund their efforts by drawing on relatively small contributions from a relatively large number of individuals using the internet, without standard financial intermediaries" (Mollick, 2014, p. 1). Crowdfunding via social media platforms depends on one's social network. Therefore, the more "friends" or "followers" one has, the more likely one is to reach one's fundraising goals. This can have different implications depending on which crowdfunding platform is used (Gerber et al., 2014; Wash & Solomon, 2014). For example, Kickstarter.com uses the All-or-Nothing Model. If users do not raise their goal amount of money, it is returned to those who donated. Other platforms such as Indiegogo allow users to keep any money that was raised (Hui, Greenberg, & Gerber, 2014; Wash & Solomon, 2014).

There are issues that may emerge in the crowdfunding arena. First, spelling out a specific project and requesting funds for it, does not necessarily protect against others replicating/copying that project. A second related concern is that, while the person requesting funding is in need of resources, others interested in replicating the proposed idea may have those very resources to implement the other person's ideas before the person proposing them is able to do so (Valanciene & Jegeleviciute, 2013).

A third factor concerns making remote donations. For instance, someone may learn about the project through an online platform, be moved by it, and decide to donate to it. While the project platform may state that donations will be allocated towards the project, the individual making the donation may not necessarily be certain that the funds are being put to the stated use in the platform (Valanciene & Jegeleviciute, 2013; Zenone & Snyder, 2018).

19.5 Current Status of Research

As discussed in this chapter, research indicates a range of outcomes associated with social media usage. Such strengths and weaknesses need to be considered within a context that recognizes the pervasive use of social media usage in people's lives (Marino et al., 2018). The paragraphs that follow discuss cyberbullying and the Fear of Missing Out (FOMO) as two such experiences that have an impact on social media users. More research is needed to explore the impact of these experiences among young people. This research is important given the potential for negative mental health outcomes among young people related to social media use (USDHHS, 2017). Research can also explore how parents, educators, and communities can foster media literacy among those engaged in social media platforms (Clauss-Ehlers et al., 2020).

19.6 Cyberbullying

Bullying is defined by the USDHHS as any "unwanted, aggressive behavior among school aged children that involves a real or perceived power imbalance" (USDHHS, 2017). The USDHHS defines cyberbullying as "bullying that takes place over digital devices like cell phones, computers, and tablets. Cyberbullying can occur through SMS, Text, and apps, or online in social media, forums, or gaming where people can view, participate in, or share content. Cyberbullying includes sending, posting, or sharing negative, harmful, false, or mean content about someone else. It can include sharing personal or private information about someone else causing embarrassment or humiliation. Some cyberbullying crosses the line into unlawful or criminal behavior" (USDHHS, n.d.). According to the National Center for Education Statistics (NCES), in 2019, approximately 15.7% of 9th to 12th grade youth reported being electronically bullied in the past year (NCES, 2021).

Cyberbullying is particularly hard to detect and prevent because of the nature of the act. Perpetrators have the option to be anonymous or create a fake persona. Online communication is not face-to-face, therefore making it easier to spread information without having to directly see the outcome. The use of smartphones or computers influences the way we view decisions with moral dilemmas. In a study about moral judgments in digital contexts, it was concluded that "using a Smartphone rather than a PC has a reliable impact on moral judgments only when dilemmas or scenarios have high emotional content" (Barque-Duran et al., 2017, p. 187). The study tested how subjects would respond to a moral dilemma. In three different trials, participants were asked to respond using smartphones or computers. Those who used smartphones were found to make more utilitarian decisions based off of rational thought rather than deontological decisions based off of intuition and emotion. This implies that smartphones may act as a barrier to emotional perceptions of a scenario (Barque-Duran et al., 2017).

The effects of cyberbullying are well-known, implied by the anti-cyberbullying laws implemented across the United States. Forty-eight out of the fifty states include cyberbullying or online harassment in their generic bullying legislation; some even have criminal sanctions against it (Cyberbullying Research Center, 2017). Cyberbullies attack their victim's reputation and image online. This feels most devastating to young people, who often use this image to measure their social status in school.

When you are young and developing an identity, social status contributes to self-perception that in turn is used to inform self-worth. In a study done on adolescent cyberbullying, victims were twice as likely to show symptoms of social anxiety and depression than those who had not experienced online harassment (Fahy et al., 2016). While most of the young people affected had shown risk factors for depressive symptoms prior to the study, almost none of them had shown signs of being socially anxious. The bullying they had experienced both exacerbated depression and produced anxiety. Taking it even further, rates of suicide have increased with cyberbullying. In 2011, suicide was in the top three leading causes of death for adolescents. Victims of cyberbullying are 14.5% more likely to have suicidal thoughts and are 8.7% more likely to attempt suicide (Nikolaou, 2017). News coverage not only brings to light the issue, but also describes and spreads it. While the news stories centered around cyberbullying were especially alarming toward the beginning of the rise of social media, they also provided the details of the incidents. The Werther Effect describes the phenomenon of copycat suicides, and commonly occurs after a popular public figure ends their life (Jack, 2014). The same can be said of these news coverages. For instance, news stories that describe how an individual has taken one's life can have a negative impact among adolescents and others. There are several factors that have been found to more strongly contribute to the Werther Effect. The Werther Effect is more likely to happen if specific details of the suicide are described, victims are described, the case is presented as part of an epidemic, or the case is described as only having one cause – in this case, online harassment (Young et al., 2017). Presenting the deaths as being a direct causation of cyberbullying undermines other areas of a victim's life and the intermediate mental health concerns that arise beforehand.

19.7 Fear of Missing Out

The fear of missing out, most commonly known as FOMO, is "a pervasive apprehension that others might be having rewarding experiences from which one is absent, [and] is characterized by the desire to stay continually connected with … others" (Przybylski et al., 2013, p. 1841). Users who experience FOMO tend to feel less personal satisfaction. Cyclically, these users tend to have high rates of Facebook usage, since they constantly feel the need to be included or informed of what others are doing (Błachnio & Przepiórka, 2018). The social comparison from Facebook use has been linked to a decrease in psychological well-being, namely increased instances of anxiety and depression. Facebook users, both male and female, tend to self-objectify and body shame (Hanna et al., 2017). Commonplace with all social media usage, users tend to compare their realities to the tailored realities of their peers on the Internet. Most people forget that what they are viewing on another's profile are the highlights that a particular person chose to share, and not their everyday life. In turn, FOMO has been linked to an increased use of social media for young people (Bibby & Stead, 2017). Social media, in this case, is used to feel more socially connected to others and alleviate the feeling that one is separate from those whose ideal lives they are viewing.

19.8 Youth and Adolescent Social Learning

Video streaming is another new concept with the age of the Internet. YouTube is the most popular video streaming service, providing a platform for anyone to upload their work. Although the site has specific guidelines, YouTube allows viewers access to everything its users circulate. This could have negative effects on communities and young people, depending on what is shared (Ahern et al., 2015). For instance, the romanticization of smoking is an issue for impressionable youth. While there are programs in place for them in schools and certain communities to prevent smoking and other drug use, the imagery of tobacco and cigarettes in online photos and videos presents the idea to an impressionable group who are not yet aware of its dangers. In popular culture, especially in music videos, smoking is often romanticized, showing the act in conjunction with happy, beautiful, young people. The same can be said for alcohol. One study found that videos containing depictions of intoxication were more likely to be "liked" by their child and adolescent viewers (Ahern et al., 2015).

Psychoactive substances can also be portrayed positively in videos, more explicitly in first-hand experiences. While music videos and party scenes from movies are popular, people also record themselves and their personal experiences using substances. These videos depict users giving a "review" of their psychoactive experience, describing the effects they felt from the use of their drug. Often, the experiences are portrayed in a good light and encourage others to experiment with their use as well, which could influence young people to experiment with substances without a comprehensive awareness of any negative effects.

In terms of mental health, YouTube can be a dangerous platform for those at risk of developing mental illness. YouTube provides access to all sorts of videos of self-harm, whether that be cutting, burning, choking, or purging. These portrayals influence young viewers by teaching them new ways to self-harm as well as normalizing the actions. This is especially problematic if a viewer is already struggling with mental illness or similar self-injurious behaviors.

Social media also provides incentives for youth to engage in risky behavior through different challenges. Since 2011, the Cinnamon Challenge has been circulating around the Internet, encouraging people of all ages to ingest a tablespoon of dry cinnamon in less than a minute. This is dangerous and could lead to severe consequences such as choking, irritation, asthma attacks, and lung damage (Grant-Alfieri, Schaechter, & Lipshultz, 2013). Some of these attempts have concluded with hospitalization and medical attention, especially if the person had asthma or any other pulmonary issues. Because cinnamon does not break down or dissolve in the lungs, it can cause burning in the nose and throat, bleeding from the nasal cavity, vomiting, tightness in the chest, or collapse of the lungs (Bosmia & Leon, 2015).

Media displays of women especially have contributed to developing a new "beauty standard" that defines a standard way to look (Brooks & Hebert, 2006). Magazine and television portrayals are one thing, but the widespread use of editing throughout social media paints false and unrealistic pictures of what people should look like. Using filters on photos allows people to contour their face and body how they want and may be linked to an increase in cosmetic surgery (Chen et al., 2019). On social media sites, images can be selected particularly for aesthetic purposes that allows users to avoid portraying the parts of their lives and appearance they do not want others to see. People also have the option to "share" other people's photos or information as well.

This information can come in the form of encouragement and motivation; and while some of it is helpful in promoting a healthy lifestyle (e.g., nutrition, exercise tips), it can also potentially activate eating disorders, whether intentionally or unintentionally. For instance, certain accounts, often found on picture-focused platforms such as Tumblr, Pinterest, and Twitter, will promote themselves as "pro-ana" or "pro-mia," which are accounts that promote anorexic and bulimic behaviors (Bert et al., 2016). Such accounts may provide tips on how to avoid eating, conceal efforts to overexercise, and/or ease the pain of "purging," or self-inflicted vomiting.

These accounts tend to promote this information as if eating disorders are a choice to be made and not a mental illness (Branley & Covey, 2017). They provide pictures of extremely thin people as motivation, and romanticize being underweight by portraying it as fashionable and avoiding other effects of the disorder such as thinning hair or weakness. Images often portray protruding bones in a sexually suggestive way, further equating the idea of being thin with being desirable or attractive (Ghaznavi & Taylor, 2015). The promotion of disordered eating especially endangers teenage girls, who are the most affected by such illnesses, that have a higher rate of mortality compared to other mental illnesses (Arcelus et al., 2011; National Eating Disorder Association, 2018).

19.9 Health: Access to Resources

Social media and social networking services, or SNS, present ways for people to learn more about health and access health information (Evers et al., 2013). For instance, a study conducted by Evers and colleagues (2013) examined the relationship between young people in Australia, SNS, social media, and sexual health communication, and found that "information seeking on sexual health issues online was most common outside of social media and SNS" (p. 267). From their findings, Evers and colleagues (2013) state the importance of supporting online and social media sexual health communication with resources and accurate knowledge. For instance, they state: "From this pilot study we have learned that sexual health communication with young people involving social media and SNS-based health communication needs to be supported with adequate resources to allow for ongoing moderation and ongoing provision of content. Time and funding will be required to develop resources, foster technical skills, and manage support in the way of permission, policy, and risk management" (p. 272). Among the LGBTQ+ community, social media can present important tools for social and sexual identity development, social support, and building community (Rhodes et al., 2016).

19.10 Perceived Social Support

Social support refers to

> the provision of assistance or comfort to others, typically to help them cope with biological, psychological, and social stressors. Support may arise from any interpersonal relationship in an individual's social network, involving family members, friends, neighbors, religious institutions, colleagues, caregivers, or support group. It may take the form of practical help (e.g., doing chores, offering advice), tangible support that involves giving money or other direct material assistance, and emotional support that allows the individual to feel valued, accepted, and understood.   (APA, 2020b)

This perceived social support, in turn, is found to be a significant factor in increasing one's perceived sense of power/control over one's environment. Perceived sense of power/control refers to the feeling of having control over resources and the ability to influence others (Galinsky, Gruenfeld, & Magee, 2003). This may then trigger individuals to act once people consider themselves to possess enough social ties and resources by interacting with those who have shared similar viewpoints (Bullers, 2001). On social media, individuals tend to find a group of people who share similar opinions and interests through online comments and may perceive social support from others' comments, leading to a stronger sense of control or empowerment to express their opinions (Lee & Chun, 2016). Thus, it could be said that perceived social support may be positively associated with perceived sense of power/control. Perceived opinion congruency will also have an indirect effect on willingness to speak out within one's online social networks mediated by perceived social support, followed by perceived sense of power/control (Chun & Lee, 2017). "In a recent report, SNS users perceived a greater level of emotional support and companionship than did general internet users (Hampton et al., 2011), at a level that was almost equivalent to the amount that married or cohabiting Americans normally perceive from their live-in partners" (Oh et al., 2014, p. 70). The feeling of sense of control allows people to conduct better lifestyles, whether they are dealing with something like depression, or trying to lose weight.

19.11 Implications for Sense of Community Driven by Social Media

As is very clear by the diversity of apps/websites under the term "social media," there is incredible variety in the ways in which individuals choose to express themselves and connect with others. Although some of these sites vary to a slight degree, they all serve the same purpose: to connect users from around the world. Individuals who use the most common forms of social media often have accounts on all or most of the most popular social media websites and apps, with the average person having about seven accounts (Mander, 2017).

The attraction of social connectivity through the Internet lies in the ability to broaden one's sense of community and feel as though one is part of something bigger than oneself (Clauss-Ehlers, 2008). Online communities can open up and shrink, in the sense that anyone can be a part of a community, as long as they can stay connected and plugged in. In a setting that allows for cultural exchange, individuals may broaden their minds to new communities and branch out in larger groups, allowing acceptance and understanding where there may have not been previously.

An important aspect of community psychology is in reference to its social effects on the international/macro level. The macro level at which social media can make an impact and influence a sense of community and connection can have a profound impact on one's everyday life.

Social media has the ability to diminish the biases associated with a lack of "contact hypothesis" (Schiappa, Gregg, & Hewes, 2005). The Contact Hypothesis refers to the recognition of similarities between what individuals consider to be "in-groups" and "out-groups" with an increase in contact. The Contact Hypothesis states that an increase in exposure to out-groups may lead to a decrease in anxiety and prejudice when dealing with others who are not easily associated with the in-group (Schiappa et al., 2005). In reference to social issues within a country, the increased awareness of specific social issues may lead to large groups banding together in support or defense of that issue via social media websites and forums. When political issues, oppressive governments, global climate issues, and scientific discoveries reach the public we see an outpouring of opinions and ideas from all over the world. Such examples are listed in Section 19.12.

19.12 Modern-Day Case Examples

When famines and natural disasters strike we can see an outpouring of aid from around the world. Many companies will even place ads and different opportunities for donations through social media platforms. Branching out to the community and allowing platforms for crowdfunding may increase the ability, and the responsibility, that one may feel for helping others outside one's "physical" community. The objective of crowdfunding "is to collect money for investment; this is generally done by using social networks, in particular through the Internet (Twitter, Facebook, LinkedIn and different other specialized blogs). The crowd-funders (those who provide the money) can at times also participate in strategic decisions or even have voting right" (Belleflamme, Lambert, & Schwienbacher, 2010, p. 1). We next present two examples that illustrate how social media contributed to a sense of community and social justice among groups experiencing inequity.

19.12.1 Case Example 1: Hurricane María and Puerto Rico

On September 20, 2017, Hurricane María, a Category 5 hurricane that was described as the "worst natural disaster" had a devastating impact on Saint Croix, Dominica, and Puerto Rico (Milman, 2017). This brief case study will focus on the experience of Puerto Rico in the face of Hurricane María. The devastation of Hurricane María was a major humanitarian crisis for Puerto Rico. There was an immense lack of resources, power outages for months, and flooding (Giusti, 2018). There was an ongoing controversy regarding mortality in Puerto Rico due to Hurricane María. Initially, for instance, the government put the death toll rate at 64 people (Florido, 2019; Telemundo PR, 2017). However, a study published by The George Washington University's Milken Institute of Public Health, in partnership with the University of Puerto Rico Graduate School of Public Health, "estimated post-hurricane mortalities at 2, 975" (Baldwin & Begnaud, 2018; Milken Institute School of Public Health, 2018). Another study published by the Harvard T.H. Chan School of Public Health estimated "a total of 4645 excess deaths" with excess deaths referring to "deaths that would not have occurred if the island hadn't been plunged into a prolonged disaster following the devastating storm" (Harris, 2018; Kishore, et al., 2018). Despite the enormity of this devastation, the government was slow and inactive in response to the crisis in Puerto Rico. This inactive response was devastating given 3.5 million Puerto Rican residents lacked electricity and communications (Hispanic Federation, n.d.).

Social media platforms were widely used to reach out and support efforts to promote social change along with voicing complaints about the US government's inactivity and lack of presence in Puerto Rico months later. Although Puerto Rico is considered a US territory it lacks the authenticity of being a state and thus doesn't have a vote in Congress. The fact that Puerto Rico is not on the "mainland" may be the cause of the inactivity in reference to the time it took to waive legislation that continually hindered the rebuild. Puerto Rico received much support from outside communities. For example, the Hispanic Federation set up a hurricane relief fund called "Unidos." Through this fund, people were able to donate through text, through the Hispanic Federation website, or in person (Hispanic Federation, n.d.). A large global crowdfunding community, GlobalGiving, raised more than twelve million dollars in aid for Puerto Rico (GlobalGiving, n.d.).

Students raised money as well. For instance, Rosana Guernica, a student at Carnegie Mellon University, raised more than $250,000, mostly through crowdfunding, that paid for relief trips that brought supplies, as well as to evacuate people (Rea & Mattera, 2018). The outpouring of support on social media platforms shown in this example portrays the impact that social media can have on an individual's sense of community and compassion for their distant community members.

19.12.2 Case Example 2: Transgender Individuals and the Military

A case in which social media afforded mass communication to support social movements can be seen in the following example. There was a social uproar after President Trump tweeted the following statements on July 26, 2017: "After consultation with my Generals and military experts, please be advised that the United States Government will not accept or allow Transgender individuals to serve in any capacity in the U.S. Military" (Miller, 2017) and "Our military must be focused on decisive and overwhelming … victory and cannot be burdened with the tremendous medical costs and disruption that transgender in the military would entail. Thank you" (Thompson, 2019). Celebrities and politicians flooded Twitter with their opinions, with a majority condemning the president, with hashtags such as "#transrightsarehumanrights" or "#ProtectTransTroops" (Cirisano, 2017). Around the USA there were organized riots to protest the president's tweets and the ban of transgendered individuals from joining the military (Allen, 2017). President Biden repealed this ban in January 2021 as one of his first executive orders.

These two examples demonstrate the power that social media has on addressing social injustice and promoting equity. Users were able to provide their own insight and opinions in broadcasts to the entire world. Such sites also aided in the organization process, as dates and places for protests were announced and decided upon. For many users, social media can be considered a more personal and honest source of news in comparison to how issues are portrayed in mainstream media outlets (Lopes, 2014).

19.13 Conclusion

This chapter has examined the community impact of social media. A definition of social media is provided along with a timeline of events that indicate the development of various platforms. Positive and negative outcomes that can stem from social media are presented. These strengths and weaknesses address the tension between a sense of community and support that many gain through social media vs. experiences of cyberbullying or the Fear of Missing Out such as when one sees online posts of others engaged in fun activities that the person has not been invited to participate in.

Two case studies demonstrate the political power that social media can engender. Through the communication tools provided by online platforms, community members and organizations organized to provide support for those impacted by Hurricane María. For instance, crowdfunding efforts provided support for Puerto Rican residents in the face of a government that was inactive and slow to respond to the humanitarian crisis. With regard to President Trump's tweets banning transgender individuals from the military, social media provided a way for people to collectively protest the ban.

More research is needed to examine the negative vs. positive impact of social media. Future studies can further explore topics such as the impact of social media usage on mental health, the role of parents in media literacy, skill development training in effective and safe social media usage, and how social media platforms specifically contribute to a sense of community.

References

Ahern, N. R., Sauer, P., & Thacker, P. (2015). Risky behaviors and social networking sites: How is YouTube influencing our youth? *Journal of Psychosocial Nursing and Mental Health Services, 53*(10), 25–29. doi.org/10.3928/02793695-20150908-01

Allen, K. (2017, July 27). *Protests erupt nationwide following Trump's transgender military ban announcement.* ABC News. abcnews.go.com/US/protesters-rally-trumps-transgender-military-ban/story?id=48876355

American Psychological Association. (2020a). Community psychology. In *American Psychological Association dictionary.* https://dictionary.apa.org/community-psychology

American Psychological Association. (2020b). Social support. In *American Psychological Association dictionary.* https://dictionary.apa.org/social-support

Andrews, E. (2019, October 28). *Who invented the Internet?* www.history.com/news/who-invented-the-internet

Arcelus, J., Mitchell, A., Wales, J., & Nielsen, S. (2011). Mortality rates in patients with anorexia nervosa and other eating disorders: A meta-analysis of 36 studies. *Archives of General Psychiatry, 68*(7), 724–731. doi.org/10.1001/archgenpsychiatry.2011.74

Baldwin, S. H., & Begnaud, D. (August 28, 2018). *Hurricane María caused an estimated 2,975 deaths in Puerto Rico, new study finds.* CBS News. https://web.archive.org/web/20180828152629/https://www.cbsnews.com/news/hurricane-maria-death-toll-puerto-rico-2975-killed-by-storm-study-finds/

Barque-Duran, A., Pothos, E. M., Hampton, J. A., & Yearsley, J. M. (2017). Contemporary morality: Moral judgments in digital contexts. *Computers in Human Behavior, 75,* 184–193. doi.org/10.1016/j.chb.2017.05.020

Belleflamme, P., Lambert, T., & Schwienbacher, A. (2010). *Crowdfunding: An industrial organization* [Working paper]. https://economix.fr/uploads/source/doc/workshops/2010_dbm/Belleflamme_al.

Bert, F., Gualano, M. R., Camussi, E., & Siliquini, R. (2016). Risks and threats of social media websites: Twitter and the proana movement. *Cyberpsychology, Behavior, and Social Networking, 19*(4), 233–238. doi.org/10.1089/cyber.2015.0553

Bibby, P. A., & Stead, H. (2017). Personality, fear of missing out and problematic internet use and their relationship to subjective well-being. *Computers in Human Behavior, 76,* 534–540. doi.org/10.1016/j.chb.2017.08.016

Błachnio, A., & Przepiórka, A. (2018). Facebook intrusion, fear of missing out, narcissism, and life satisfaction: A cross-sectional study. *Psychiatry Research, 259,* 514–519. doi.org/10.1016/j.psychres.2017.11.012

Bosmia, A., & Leon, K. (2015). Lung injury and the cinnamon challenge: College students should beware this internet dare. *Journal of Injury and Violence Research, 7*(1), 41–42. doi.org/10.5249/jivr.v7i1.541

Branley, D. B., & Covey, J. (2017). Pro-ana versus pro-recovery: A content analytic comparison of social media users' communication about eating disorders on Twitter and Tumblr. *Frontiers in Psychology, 8,* Article 1356. doi.org/10.3389/fpsyg.2017.01356

Brooks, D. E., & Hebert, L. P. (2006). Gender, race, and media representation. In B. J. Dow (Ed.), *Gender and communication in mediated contexts* (pp. 297–317). Thousand Oaks, CA: SAGE Publications.

Bullers, S. (2001). The mediating role of perceived control in the relationship between social ties and depressive symptoms. *Women & Health, 31*(2–3), 97–116. doi.org/10.1300/j013v31n02_05

Chen, J., Ishii, M., Bater, K., et al. (2019). Association between the use of social media and photograph editing applications, self-esteem, and cosmetic surgery acceptance. *JAMA Facial Plastic Surgery, 21*(5), 361–367. doi.org/10.1001/jamafacial.2019.0328

Chun, J. W., & Lee, M. J. (2017). When does individuals' willingness to speak out increase on social media? Perceived social support and perceived power/control. *Computers in Human Behavior, 74,* 120–129. doi.org/10.1016/j.chb.2017.04.010

Cirisano, T. (2017, July 26). *Celebrities react to Trump banning transgender people from U.S. military service.* Billboard. www.billboard.com/articles/news/politics/7881047/trump-transgender-military-ban-celebrity-reactions-twitter

Clauss-Ehlers, C. S. (2008). Sociocultural factors, resilience, and coping: Support for a culturally sensitive measure of resilience. *Journal of Applied Developmental Psychology, 29*(3), 197–212. doi.org/10.1016/j.appdev.2008.02.004

Clauss-Ehlers, C. S., Guevara Carpio, M., & Weist, M. D. (2020). Mental health literacy: A strategy for global adolescent mental health promotion. *Adolescent Psychiatry, 10*(2), 73–83. doi.org/10.2174/2210676610666200204104429

Clement, J. (2019). Facebook: Number of monthly active users worldwide 2008–2019. *Statista.* Retrieved March 7, 2020, from www.statista.com/statistics/264810/number-of-monthly-active-facebook-users-worldwide/

Cyberbullying Research Center. (2017). *Bullying laws across America* [Interactive map]. https://cyberbullying.org/bullying-laws

De Choudhury, M., & De, S. (2014, May). Mental health discourse on Reddit: Self-disclosure, social support, and anonymity. *Eighth International AAAI Conference on Weblogs and Social Media, 8*(1).

Dumas, G., Nadel, J., Soussignan, R, et al. (2010). Inter-brain synchronization during social interaction (interacting brains synchronize). *PLoS ONE, 5*(8), Article e12166. doi.org/10.1371/journal.pone.0012166

Evers, C. W., Albury, K., Byron, P., & Crawford, K. (2013). Young people, social media, social network sites and sexual health communication in Australia: 'This is funny, you should watch it'. *International Journal of Communication, 7*(1), 263–280.

Eysenbach, G., Powell, J., Englesakis, M., Rizo, C., & Stern, A. (2004). Health related virtual communities and electronic support groups: Systematic review of the effects of online peer to peer interactions. *BMJ, 328*(7449), 1166. doi.org/10.1136/bmj.328.7449.1166

Fahy, A. E., Stansfeld, S. A., Smuk, M., et al. (2016). Longitudinal associations between cyberbullying involvement and adolescent mental health. *Journal of Adolescent Health, 59*(5), 502–509. doi.org/10.1016/j.jadohealth.2016.06.006

Florido, A. (2019, September 24). 2 years after Hurricane María hit Puerto Rico, the exact death toll remains unknown. NPR. www.npr.org/2019/09/24/763958799/2-years-after-hurricane-maria-hit-puerto-rico-the-exact-death-toll-remains-unkno

Freedman, D., & Nutting, M. R. (2015). *A brief history of crowdfunding including rewards, donation, debt, and equity platforms in the USA.* www.freedmanchicago.com/ec4i/History-of-Crowdfunding.pdf

Galinsky, A., Gruenfeld, D., & Magee, J. (2003). From power to action. *Journal of Personality and Social Psychology, 85*(3), 453–466. doi.org/10.1037/0022-3514.85.3.453

Gerber, E., Muller, M., Wash, R., et al. (2014). Crowdfunding: An emerging field of research. *CHI'14 Extended Abstracts on Human Factors in Computing Systems,* 1093–1098. doi.org/10.1145/2559206.2579406

Ghaznavi, J., & Taylor, L. D. (2015). Bones, body parts, and sex appeal: An analysis of #thinspiration images on popular social media. *Body Image, 14*, 54–61. doi.org/10.1016/j.bodyim.2015.03.006

Giusti, C. (2018, June 18). *Puerto Rico issues new data on Hurricane María deaths.* NBC News. www.nbcnews.com/health/health-news/puerto-rico-issues-new-data-hurricane-maria-deaths-n882816

Global Giving. (n.d.). *Puerto Rico & Caribbean hurricane relief fund.* www.globalgiving.org/projects/hurricane-maria-caribbean-relief-fund/

Grant-Alfieri, A., Schaechter, J., & Lipshultz, S. (2013). Ingesting and aspirating dry cinnamon by children and adolescents: The "cinnamon challenge." *Pediatrics, 131*(5), 833–835. doi.org/10.1542/peds.2012-3418

Hampton, K. N., Goulet, L. S., Rainie, L., & Purcell, K. (2011). *Social networking sites and our lives* (Vol. 1). Washington, DC: Pew Internet & American Life Project. http://pewinternet.org/Reports/2011/Technology-and-social-networks.aspx

Hanna, E., Ward, L. M., Seabrook, R. C., et al. (2017). Contributions of social comparison and self-objectification in mediating associations between Facebook use and emergent adults' psychological well-being.

Cyberpsychology, Behavior, and Social Networking, 20(3), 172–179. doi.org/10.1089/cyber.2016.0247

Harris, R. (2018, May 29). *Study puts Puerto Rico death toll from Hurricane María near 5000*. NPR. www.npr.org/sections/health-shots/2018/05/29/615120123/study-puts-puerto-rico-death-toll-at-5-000-from-hurricane-maria-in-2017

Hendricks, D. (2013, May 8). *Complete history of social media: Then and now*. Small Business Trends. smallbiztrends.com/2013/05/the-complete-history-of-social-media-infographic.html

Hispanic Federation (n.d.). *"Unidos": A hurricane relief fund for Hurricane María victims in Puerto Rico*. Hispanic Federation. https://hispanicfederation.org/media/press_releases/a_hurricane_relief_fund_for_hurricane_maria_victims_in_puerto_rico/

Horgan, Á., & Sweeney, J. (2010). Young students' use of the Internet for mental health information and support. *Journal of Psychiatric and Mental Health Nursing, 17*(2), 117–123. doi.org/10.1111/j.1365-2850.2009.01497.x

Hui, J., Greenberg, M., & Gerber, E. (2014). Understanding the role of community in crowdfunding work. *Proceedings of the 17th ACM Conference on Computer Supported Cooperative Work & Social Computing*, 62–74. doi.org/10.1145/2531602.2531715

Jack, B. (2014) Goethe's *Werther* and its effects. *The Lancet Psychiatry, 1*(1), 18–19. doi.org/10.1016/S2215-0366(14)70229-9

Jung Oh, H., Ozkaya, E., & LaRose, R. (2014). How does online social networking enhance life satisfaction? The relationships among online supportive inter-action, affect, perceived social support, sense of community, and life satisfac-tion. *Computers in Human Behavior, 30*(C), 69–78. doi.org/10.1016/j.chb.2013.07.053

Kallas, P. (2019, September 2). Top 15 most popular social networking sites and apps. *Dreamgrow*. www.dreamgrow.com/top-15-most-popular-social-networking-sites/

Kida, T. E. (2009). *Don't believe everything you think: The 6 basic mistakes we make in thinking*. Blue Ridge Summit, PA: Prometheus Books.

Kietzmann, J. H., Hermkens, K., McCarthy, I. P., & Silvestre, B. S. (2011). Social media? Get serious! Understanding the functional building blocks of social media. *Business Horizons, 54*(3), 241–251. doi.org/10.1016/j.bushor.2011.01.005

Lee, M. J., & Chun, J. W. (2016). Reading others' comments and public opinion poll results on social media: Social judgment and spiral of empowerment. *Computers in Human Behavior, 65*, 479–487. doi.org/10.1016/j.chb.2016.09.007

Lim, M. (2012). Clicks, cabs, and coffee houses: Social media and oppositional movements in Egypt, 2004–2011. *Journal of Communication, 62*(2), 231–248. doi.org/10.1111/j.1460-2466.2012.01628.x

Lin, L., Sidani, J., Shensa, A., et al. (2016). Association between social media use and depression among U.S. young adults. *Depression and Anxiety, 33*(4), 323–331. doi.org/10.1002/da.22466

Lopes, A. R. (2014). The impact of social media on social movements: The new opportunity and mobilizing structure. *Journal of Political Science Research, 4*(1), 1–23.

Mander, J. (2017, June 9). *Internet users have average of 7 social accounts*. Global Web Index. https://blog.globalwebindex.com/chart-of-the-day/internet-users-have-average-of-7-social-accounts/

Marino, C., Gini, G., Vieno, A., & Spada, M. M. (2018). The associations between problematic Facebook use, psychological distress and well-being among adolescents and young adults: A systematic review and meta-analysis. *Journal of Affective Disorders, 226*, 274–281. doi.org/10.1016/j.jad.2017.10.007

Milken Institute School of Public Health, The George Washington University in collaboration with the University of Puerto Rico Graduate School of Public Health. (2018). *Ascertainment of the excess mortality from Hurricane María in Puerto Rico*. https://publichealth.gwu.edu/sites/default/files/downloads/projects/PRstudy/Acertainment%20of%20the%20Estimated%20Excess%20?Mortality%20from%20Hurricane%20Maria%20in%20Puerto%20Rico.pdf

Miller, Z. J. (2017, August 25). President Trump has taken a key step to implement his transgender military ban. *Time*. time.com/4916871/donald-trump-transgender-military-ban/

Milman, O. (2017, November 9). Six weeks after Hurricane María, Puerto Ricans still waiting for help from Fema. *The Guardian*. www.theguardian.com/world/2017/nov/09/six-weeks-after-hurricane-maria-puerto-ricans-still-waiting-for-help-from-fema

Mollick, E. (2014). The dynamics of crowdfunding: An exploratory study. *Journal of Business Venturing, 29*(1), 1–16. doi.org/10.1016/j.jbusvent.2013.06.005

Moorhead, S. A., Hazlett, D. E., Harrison, L., et al. (2013). A new dimension of health care: Systematic review of the uses, benefits, and limitations of social media for health communication. *Journal of Medical Internet Research, 15*(4). doi.org/10.2196/jmir.1933

National Center for Education Statistics. (2021). *Bullying at school and electronic bullying*. https://nces.ed.gov/programs/coe/indicator/a10

National Eating Disorder Association. (2018). *Common health consequences of eating disorders*. www.nationaleatingdisorders.org/health-consequences

Nikolaou, D. (2017). Does cyberbullying impact youth suicidal behaviors? *Journal of Health Economics, 56*, 30–46. doi.org/10.1016/j.jhealeco.2017.09.009

Peters, J. (2021, June 11). *Darnella Frazier, who documented George Floyd's murder, receives Pulitzer Prize citation*. The Verge. https://nces.ed.gov/programs/coe/indicator/a10

Przybylski, A., Murayama, K., Dehaan, C., & Gladwell, V. (2013). Motivational, emotional, and behavioral correlates of fear of missing out. *Computers in Human Behavior, 29*(4), 1841–1848. doi.org/10.1016/j.chb.2013.02.014

Rea, S., & Mattera, J. (2018, April 2). Dietrich College student named one of "Larry's Hometown Heroes." Carnegie Mellon University, Dietrich College of Humanities and Social Sciences. www.cmu.edu/dietrich/news/news-stories/2018/april/rosana-guernica-honored.html

Rhodes, S. D., Bachmann, L. H., Mccoy, T. P., et al. (2016). Using social media to increase HIV testing among gay and bisexual men, other men who have sex with men, and transgender persons: Outcomes from a randomized community trial. *Clinical Infectious Diseases, 62*(11), 1450–1453.

Schiappa, E., Gregg, P. B., & Hewes, D. E. (2005). The parasocial contact hypothesis. *Communication Monographs*, *72*(1), 92–115. doi.org/10.1080/0363775052000 342544

Shaban, H. (2019, February 7). Twitter reveals its daily active user numbers for the first time. *The Washington Post*. www.washingtonpost.com/technology/2019/02/07/twitter-reveals-its-daily-active-user-numbers-first-time/

Sigar, K. (2012). Fret no more: Inapplicability of crowdfunding concerns in the internet age and the JOBS Act's safeguards. *Administrative Law Review*, 473–506.

Steijns, J. (2017). "The Cincinnati effect" to "the Ferguson effect": Media's growing involvement in police brutality against Black citizens. *Journal of Psychiatric and Mental Health Nursing*, *17*(2), 117–123.

Telemundo PR. (2017, December 9). Aumentan a 64 muertes certificados por María. *NBCUniversal Media*, LLC. www.telemundopr.com/noticias/puerto-rico/aumentan-a-64-las-muertes-por-el-huracan-maria/10690/

Thompson, M. (2019, January 14). How to spark panic and confusion in three tweets. *The Atlantic*. www.theatlantic.com/politics/archive/2019/01/donald-trump-tweets-transgender-military-service-ban/579655

US Department of Health and Human Services. (2017). *What is bullying*. www .stopbullying.gov/what-is-bullying/index.html

US Department of Health and Human Services. (n.d.). *What is cyberbullying?* www .stopbullying.gov/cyberbullying/what-is-it

US Department of Justice. (n.d.). *Importance of police-community relationships and resources for further reading* (File No. 836486). www.justice.gov/crs/file/836486/download

Valancienė, L., & Jegeleviciūtė, S. (2013). Valuation of crowdfunding: Benefits and drawbacks. *Economics and Management*, *18*(1), 39–48. doi.org/10.5755/j01 .em.18.1.3713

Wash, R., & Solomon, J. (2014). Coordinating donors on crowdfunding websites. *Proceedings of the 17th ACM Conference on Computer Supported Cooperative Work & Social Computing*, 38–48. doi.org/10.1145/2531602.2531678

Young, R., Subramanian, R., Miles, S., Hinnant, A., & Andsager, J. L. (2017). Social representation of cyberbullying and adolescent suicide: A mixed-method analysis of news stories. *Health Communication*, *32*(9), 1082–1092. doi.org/10.1080/10410236.2016.1214214

Zenone, M., & Snyder, J. (2018). Fraud in medical crowdfunding: A typology of publicized cases and policy recommendations. *Policy & Internet*, *11*(2). doi .org/10.1002/poi3.188

20 Supporting Communities through Educational Access

Lynn Pasquerella

20.1 The Growing Economic and Racial Segregation in Higher Education

In their groundbreaking report, *Separate and Unequal: How Higher Education Reinforces the Intergenerational Reproduction of White Racial Privilege*, Anthony Carnevale and Jeff Strohl (2013) detail a growing economic and racial segregation in American higher education. While more students of color and economically disadvantaged students are attending college, elite private colleges and universities continue to be dominated by White students in the wealthiest quarter of the population. At the same time, the percentage of White, wealthy students at public community colleges has decreased, as those at the lowest socioeconomic rungs, African American, Latinx, and Native American students are funneled to open-access, under-resourced institutions. The authors point to this disparity in resources as a major contributor to the significantly higher graduation rates from more selective colleges (Carnevale & Strohl, 2013).

Carnevale and Strohl's (2013) findings were reinforced by the 2018 *Indicators of Higher Education Equity in the United States* report, issued by the Pell Institute for the Study of Higher Education and the Alliance for Higher Education and Democracy at the University of Pennsylvania (Cahalan et al., 2018). According to the study, though the number of Pell eligible students increased from 32% in 2001 to 45% in 2015, there was no comparable increase in their representation at elite private colleges. Indeed, the needle only moved one percentage point, from 15% to 16% during that span of time (Cahalan et al., 2018).

A further study by Raj Chetty, John Friedman, and Nathaniel Hendren reveals that students from families who earn more than $630,000 a year, constituting the top 1%, are seventy-seven times more likely to attend an Ivy League School than students whose families make less than $30,000 a year. Moreover, these researchers revealed that thirty-eight elite colleges have more students from the top 1% than from the bottom 60%, representing families with a yearly income of less than $65,000 (Chetty et al., 2020). The promise of social mobility offered by higher education is undermined by a system that perpetuates class divides through social reproduction, and these statistics signal the extent to which the most well-

413

resourced institutions function as gated communities, excluding the underserved and thereby failing to mitigate intergenerational poverty.

Today, almost half (49%) of students enrolled in four-year colleges and universities start in community colleges. However, a 2019 report from the Jack Kent Cook Foundation entitled *Persistence: The Success of Students Who Transfer from Community Colleges to Selective Four-Year Institutions* (Glynn, 2019) indicates that the most selective colleges and universities enroll community college transfer students at a substantially lower rate. At these institutions, only 5% of the 14% of transfer students come from community colleges, despite success rates equal to those who transfer from other four-year institutions, including public, private, selective, and open-access colleges and universities (Camera, 2019). In addition, high school students from the top academic quartile were much more likely to attend community college if they were in the lowest socioeconomic quartile than those from the top quartile who had similar grades and test scores (Camera, 2019).

Given research showing that low-income students attending elite colleges have a greater than 50% chance of rising to the top 20% socioeconomically upon graduation, redressing the economic and racial segregation in higher education is critical to ensuring that all students have access to the American Dream (Cahalan et al., 2018). Nevertheless, a 2016 report from the Community College Research Center at Columbia University, *Tracking Transfer: New Measures of Institutional and State Effectiveness in Helping Community College Students Attain Bachelor's Degrees*, noted that of the 1.1 million students who enroll annually in community colleges, 80% have the goal of transferring to a four-year institution, yet only 14% of those earn a bachelor's degree within six years (Jenkins & Fink, 2016). The reasons range from the lack of articulation agreements between two- and four-year colleges, the unavailability of general education courses needed to transfer, prerequisites requiring developmental preparation, and inadequate advising around transfer options to rising tuition at both public and private colleges, alongside limited financial aid, making a four-year degree unattainable. If low-income students are denied the opportunity to gain access to the colleges and universities most able to invest in student completion and success, higher education will itself perpetuate the structural inequities it seeks to redress.

20.2 Advancing Student Success through Guided Pathways

Understanding the urgency of promoting equity and social justice in our society by increasing the number of college graduates, Thomas Bailey, Shanna Smith Jaggars, and Davis Jenkins argue for a fundamental redesign of community college education in their book *Redesigning America's Community Colleges: A Clearer Path to Student Success* (2015). The authors detail findings from their intensive study of community colleges over an eight-year period, providing the foundation for targeted reforms and institutional restructuring around the creation of guided pathways. The Guided Pathways Project that emerged is centered on building institutional capacity to define clear and coherent pathways for degree completion, while ensuring that students are achieving specific learning outcomes. The four main practice areas, or pillars, within the Guided Pathways Framework involve (1) mapping pathways to student end goals, (2) helping students choose and enter a program pathway, (3) keeping students on the path, and (4) ensuring that students are learning (Association of American Colleges & Universities [AAC&U], 2019a).

Guided Pathways is an integrated, institution-wide approach to student success at community colleges that is designed to promote structured educational experiences from the first to final semester. Students are provided with coherent program maps that entail course sequences, progress milestones, and specific learning outcomes aligned to requirements at four-year institutions and the job market. In 2019, AAC&U entered a collaboration with the Center for Community College Student Engagement (CCCSE) at the University of Texas-Austin, seeking to enhance an emphasis on the fourth pillar of the Guided Pathways model – ensuring that students are learning – through the creation of active and culturally responsive learning environments.

With support from the Bill & Melinda Gates Foundation and the Ascendium Education Group, AAC&U and CCCSE developed "Strengthening Guided Pathways and Career Success by Ensuring Students Are Learning" (AAC&U, 2019a). With special attention to closing persistent gaps for historically underserved students, the initiative calls for the use of culturally responsive teaching practices. These practices go beyond engaging students in active learning and foster a sense of agency by empowering students to relate coursework to their backgrounds and experiences.

A call for proposals resulted in the selection of twenty community colleges committed to focusing on "'the development of a scalable faculty-led teaching, learning, and assessment model that promotes the completion of high-quality degrees and credentials that will fully prepare students for lifelong and career success,' [said] Tia Brown McNair, AAC&U's vice president for Diversity, Equity, and Student Success" (AAC&U, 2019c). Through institutes and webinars, institutional participants from across the country are brought together to collaborate and exchange best practices around strengthening designs for "project-based and applied learning experiences, and to assess student achievement of learning outcomes to advance equity and student success goals along guided pathways" (AAC&U, 2019b).

Colleges were selected for participation based on their capacity to demonstrate success with the first three pillars and readiness to focus on student learning and assessment. Criteria included the ability to provide essential baseline data regarding learning outcomes, particularly the ability to disaggregate data by race/ethnicity, first generation, gender, low-income status, and age; and the capacity to carry out direct and indirect assessment activities fundamental to the project, such as preparedness to gather direct evidence from courses, to organize data for uploading and analysis, and to identify project-based learning experiences (AAC&U, 2019a).

Divided into the processes of planning, implementation, and evaluation, guided pathways require strong leadership, a commitment to using data, and understanding where institutions are to prepare for change, while committing to pathways for the long run that encompass all students. Large-scale transformation mandates a number of essential conditions, including strong change leadership throughout the institution; faculty and staff engagement; a technology infrastructure, alongside a commitment to and the capacity for using data; a dedication to student success and equity; professional development; and favorable policies at all levels, combined with board support. During the planning phase, institutional participants must understand where they are, prepare for change, and build awareness, simultaneously ensuring that the pathways are both sustainable and available to all students. This requires engaging stakeholders; developing an implementation plan; building partnerships with K-12 schools, business and industry, other universities, and employers; developing flowcharts of how students choose, enter, and complete programs; and establishing a baseline for key performance indicators (Pathways, 2019).

Box 20.1   Guided pathways and high impact practices

The long-term sustainability of guided pathways and their impact necessitates leveraging technology to support the redesigned student experience; integrating pathways into hiring and evaluation processes; redefining the roles of faculty, staff, and administrators where needed, and providing corresponding professional development; reallocating resources; and engaging students. A successful implementation process will include mapping all curricular programs to transfer and career outcomes, identifying core courses and sequences, requirements, credentials, and progress milestones. High Impact Practices (HIPs) such as first-year experiences, career exploration, and integrated academic support, as well as intrusive advising, are critical for keeping students on their pathways (Pathways, 2019).

The latter is a proactive approach to advising that involves intentional, faculty-initiated intervention designed to increase academic motivation and persistence. Intrusive advising uses the specific strategy of frequent contact to establish a caring relationship demonstrating faculty interest in the student. The goal is to educate students on available options and engage in preemptive decision-making before there is a crisis. This is particularly important for first-generation and low-income students who may not have the confidence, due to a lack of social and cultural capital, to approach a professor and ask for advice. Advising relationships have proven to be a key factor in retention and completion and long-term success after college (Drake, Jordan, & Miller, 2013).

Finally, there is an equity imperative that requires embracing a paradigm shift from ranking and sorting students to ensuring that all students benefit from the most powerful forms of learning. Inclusive excellence involves: "Taking direct aim at educational disparities and patterns of systemic disadvantage, especially those resulting from historical and contemporary effects of racism" (Pasquerella, 2020, p.12). Student success depends not on the "college readiness" of individual students, but rather on the readiness of the institution to welcome and support all students and to respond to the changing needs of an increasingly diverse society.

Quality assessment entails the evaluation of applied learning experiences, centered on student agency. Assignments should be transparent, making clear the learning objectives, and be scaffolded in a way that moves toward engaging students in increasingly complex work. The best evidence of student gains in proficiency is found not in the results of standardized tests but rather in the actual work they produce across their diverse learning pathways; the most promising assessment approach evaluates samples of such authentic student work using scoring guides, or rubrics. Authentic forms of assessment also yield actionable evidence of the effectiveness of teaching and learning practices. Therefore, faculty, staff, and administrators must work together to identify the institutional structures, policies, and programs that create barriers to this type of assessment and act by making changes in the curriculum and in current practices.

A new impetus for moving away from standardized tests and developing more equitable forms of assessment has emerged as a result of the COVID-19 pandemic and its impact on higher education. The need for social distancing to prevent the spread of coronavirus caused SAT and ACT testing centers to shut down and led to a flurry of top-ranked national liberal arts colleges and universities, including Harvard and Cornell, waiving their standardized test requirements for the fall of 2021 and beyond (Vigdor & Diaz, 2020). While the College Board has announced that it is developing a digital SAT test that can be taken at home, the sudden pivot to remote and online learning necessitated by COVID-19 unveiled the expanse of the digital divide among students, along with food and shelter insecurity issues that would negatively impact those forced to take the test at home. These factors compound concerns over standardized tests related to allegations of discrimination related to race, class, and disability status. Indeed, increased attention to the lack of availability of expensive test preparation; stereotype threat, which raises self-doubt and increases anxiety for those who are negatively stereotyped; and the myth of meritocracy revealed by the Varsity Blues scandal, in which wealthy parents paid to have their children's test scores changed, issued forth a lawsuit against the University of California system. The plaintiffs called for the elimination of the SAT or ACT requirement, claiming the tests are biased and not an accurate predictor of academic success (Elsessor, 2019). The trend toward more equitable assessment in the admission process and throughout a student's education carries potential for contributing positively to completion rates of low-income students at elite institutions and to their social mobility.

20.3 Colleges and Universities as Anchor Institutions

In addition, to increase the number of underserved students at the most well-resourced colleges and universities, all colleges and universities must position themselves as anchor institutions, grounded in their localities in a way that demonstrates their success as intertwined with the health, welfare, education, and economic opportunities of those in the surrounding community. When serving as an anchor institution is central to the institutional mission, a sense of collective responsibility and interdependence emerges that fosters civic engagement in collaboratively addressing issues of public concern.

An understanding of populism and privilege, power and pluralism in the academy needs to start on our own campuses and within our own communities. Critical service-learning pedagogy, by definition, is aimed at engaging students in the identification and evaluation of systemic sources of inequality and redressing reinforcing mechanisms of oppression. Destabilizing the influence of propaganda and ideological power at the basis of populist appeals and replacing it with pluralism's focus on coexistence and cooperation despite differing principles and sources of authority necessitates true campus–community partnerships. For this reason, when AAC&U began the initiative to establish truth, racial healing, and transformation (TRHT) campus centers (AAC&U, 2020) designed to jettison a belief in the hierarchy of human value, we required the identification of community partners. Campuses across the country, from Duke, the Citadel, University of Maryland-Baltimore County, Rutgers-Newark, and Millsaps to Hamline University, the University of Hawaii, Austin Community College, Spelman College, and Brown University have adopted an equity-minded lens, evaluating how racial differences and inequalities manifest and reify inequities on their own campus alongside the communities within which they are situated (AAC&U, 2020).

Such undertakings hold the promise of helping to restore the democratic structures that have been dismantled. There are other examples, as well. Wagner College, Kingsborough Community College, and California State University-Chico have been particularly thoughtful in how they have engaged community leaders in underserved areas and how they have supported a diversity of community-engaged experiences, including town hall events and public debates that expose students to what it means to connect learning with civic issues and dialogue across difference.

Beyond taking advantage of local epistemologies and establishing true partnerships with K-12 schools, business, industry, and a broad range of organizations and associations, reward systems, including the tenure and promotion process within the academy, need to change by recognizing the critical work of those dedicated to providing the broadest access to higher education – practice that reaches beyond the gates. Faculty should work through their own professional organizations and disciplinary societies to question why peer-reviewed journal articles continue to have currency over all else, how community engagement work can be held in equal esteem, and why professors of practice are often excluded from the tenure track.

20.4 Proposed Policy Changes Regarding Federal Financial Aid

College and university leaders must also encourage their local and national legislators to increase access to opportunity for those most economically disadvantaged. Several policy changes should be implemented related to access to federal financial aid. Federal Pell grants have failed to keep pace with the rising costs of a college degree. For instance, in 1980, Pell grants covered 68% of the average costs of attending college, whereas now they cover only 25% (Cahalan et al., 2018). Further, the policies and conditions for granting Pell awards have not evolved with a changing college demographic. The amount of aid offered is determined on the basis of eligibility under the Free Application for Federal Student Aid (FAFSA) form and is derived from a consideration of the cost of attendance and one's status as a full- or part-time student. Yet, this calculus does not account for the changing demographic within higher education. In the 1980s and 1990s, most college students were between the ages of eighteen and twenty-four and attended full-time. By 2018, of the more than 19 million Americans who enrolled in college, 6.7 million were part-time students and almost half were listed as independent students, not listed on their parents' income taxes (National Center for Education Statistics, 2019). Students are automatically categorized as independent if they are twenty-four years of age or older, married, have a dependent, are an orphan, in foster care or legally emancipated, or are a veteran.

Currently, every $10,000 increase in parental earnings reduces a student's eligibility for need-based aid by approximately $3,000. When it comes to independent students, including a nineteen-year old parent or a homeless veteran, every $10,000 increase in salary results in a $5,000 decrease in eligibility. The impact is far-reaching. "For example, students who qualify for subsidized direct loans based on their income are not required to pay interest ...while enrolled and for six months after completion of their educational programs" (Pasquerella & Oates, 2020). With the 2018–2019 interest rate of 5.05%, not increasing one's debt while applying for jobs is a substantial economic advantage for the poorest students (Pasquerella & Oates, 2020). Therefore, policies should be reformed to make the impact of additional income the same for independent and dependent students by increasing the eligibility for independent students for federal aid.

Second, to qualify currently for financial aid, students must be registered at least part-time. Most colleges and universities require students to be enrolled for twelve credits to be considered full-time and six credits for part-time status. According to Higher Learning Advocates, of the students enrolled in 2018, 38% were over twenty-five years old, 26% were parents, 40% were attending part-time, and 58% were working more than twenty-five hours per week (Peller, 2018). Allowing students to take advantage of federal financial aid, even when taking one course at a time, would decrease burdens on adult students who are attempting to balance work and family obligations. This policy should be implemented while examining the impact on student retention and academic success.

The length of eligibility for Pell grants should also be extended. Pell grants of up to a maximum of $6,095 were awarded in 2018–2019 to students who had the most limited financial resources. Prior to 2008, there were no limits on Pell eligibility other than continued financial need until earning a bachelor's degree. "The 2008 reauthorization of the Higher Education Act imposed a lifetime limit (https://fas.org/sgp/crs/misc/R45418.pdf) of 18 semesters. This was reduced even further by the Consolidated Appropriations Act of 2012, which placed a limit of 12 semesters on full-time students and 24 semesters on part-time students. At a time when rapidly changing technology means rapid obsolescence and the jobs of the future have not yet been invented, the opportunity for lifelong learning and training is more critical than ever. Increasing eligibility to 16 semesters or more would enable many low-income working adults to continue their education and job training" in ways that will advance social mobility (Pasquerella & Oates, 2020).

Finally, changes should be made to existing requirements regarding Satisfactory Academic Progress (SAP). In order to qualify for Pell grants and federal loans, students must maintain a minimum academic average of 2.0 and have a ratio of completing two out of three classes. However, many of the more than thirty-one million Americans with some college credit but not a degree and who are seeking better jobs were disqualified from eligibility based on performance five, ten, or twenty years ago. Expunging the record for adults who have worked for three to five years has the potential to increase academic completion and promote economic security by making Pell grants and Direct Loans available again to students committed to completing their education (Pasquerella & Oates, 2020).

20.5 Restoring Public Trust in Higher Education

A final piece of creating access to higher education and redressing economic segregation in colleges and universities calls for academics to pay attention to the growing mistrust in higher education among the general public. Though college graduates can still expect to earn more than 80% more than those with only high school diplomas, a poll released by Gallup in December 2019 reveals that only 51% of US adults now consider a college education to be very important, down from 70% in 2013. Bolstered by concerns ranging from the high costs of college and the belief that campuses are bastions of liberal progressivism to the belief that institutions of higher education are failing to provide students with twenty-first-century skills, the most jarring statistic from the Gallup survey was that younger adults, between the ages of eighteen and twenty-nine, were more likely than those from other age groups to question the value of a college degree (Marken, 2019).

Public confidence in higher education varies based on race, as well. A 2015 Pew poll reveals that Hispanic and Black parents are significantly more likely than White parents to view earning a college degree as either "extremely important" or "very important." A total of 86% of Hispanic and 79% of Black parents of children under the age of eighteen regard a college degree as central to social mobility at the heart of the American Dream and a requirement for being a member of the middle class. By contrast, only 67% of White parents, who have greater representation in the middle class, agreed (Stepler, 2016).

On October 4, 2018, the author gave a presentation that was part of the theme titled *The Integration of the Humanities and Arts with Sciences, Engineering and Medicine in Higher Education: Branches from the Same Tree* (Pasquerella, 2018; Skorton & Bear, Eds., 2018):

"To restore public trust in higher education and destabilize the cultural attitudes at the basis of proposals that devalue liberal education, we need reframe the narrative, highlighting the fact that in the global knowledge economy, employer demand for graduates with a liberal education is growing. This was part of the impetus behind AAC&U's most recent round of employer research, "Fulfilling the American Dream: Liberal Education and the Future of Work." The survey, conducted on behalf of AAC&U by Hart Research Associates, included the perspectives of both business executives and hiring managers, with the goal of assessing the extent to which each group believes that a college education is important and worthwhile, identifying the learning outcomes they believe are most important for success in today's economy, and discerning how prepared these different audiences perceive recent college graduates to be in these areas.

The 501 business executives at private sector and nonprofit organizations and 500 hiring managers, whose current job responsibilities include recruiting, interviewing, and hiring new employees, express higher satisfaction with colleges and universities than does the American public as a whole. Sixty-three percent noted having either "a lot of confidence" or "a great deal of confidence" in American higher education. Business executives and hiring managers also agree upon the value of college, maintaining it is an essential and worthwhile investment of time and money. In addition to the potential for increased earnings, both executives and hiring managers cited the benefits of the accumulation of knowledge, the development of critical and analytical skills, and the pursuit of … goals as especially meaningful" (Pasquerella, 2018, pp. 7–8). However, their focus was not on what students have already learned but rather on the potential to learn new things throughout their careers.

The author continued as follows:

"Further, consistent with findings from six earlier surveys commissioned by AAC&U as part of its ongoing Liberal Education and America's Promise (LEAP) initiative, employers overwhelmingly endorse broad learning and cross-cutting skills as the best preparation for long-term career success. The college learning outcomes that executives and managers rate as most important are oral communication, critical thinking, ethical judgment, working effectively in teams, written communication, and the real-world application of skills and knowledge. They also rated highly the skills of locating, organizing and evaluating information from multiple sources, analyzing complex problems, working with people from different backgrounds, being innovative and creative, and staying current on technologies.

Internships and apprenticeships were deemed particularly valuable, with 93 percent of executives and 94 percent of hiring managers indicating that they would be more likely to hire a recent graduate who has held an internship or apprenticeship with a company or organization. Similarly, employers at non-profits say they are much more likely to hire recent graduates who have community-based or service learning experience. This is not surprising given that only 33 percent of executives and 39 percent of hiring managers believe that recent graduates are "very well prepared" to apply knowledge and skills in real-world settings" (Pasquerella, 2018, pp. 8–9).

20.6 Conclusion

Colleges and universities have an obligation to educate students to become productive citizens, undoubtedly including an education that leads to financial security. Any institution that fails to incorporate ways for students to think about careers, gain workplace experience, and apply their learning is doing a disservice to those we seek to educate. "A liberal education for the 21st century mandates the acceleration of integrative, high-impact learning opportunities that engage every student in solving unscripted, real-world problems across all types of institutions, within the context of the workforce, not apart from it" (Pasquerella, 2018, p. 10).

Moreover, at a time of increasing polarization and partisanship, incivility and misinformation, the knowledge, skills, and dispositions at the foundation of a liberal education are more critical than ever. A liberal education offers a collaborative model of problem-solving that demonstrates the value of expertise applied in service to community. Freedom of inquiry and expression is essential to a liberal education, which exposes students to the challenge and discomfort that can result from engagement with values and beliefs, ideas and opinions that differ from their own. In contrast to illiberal education that discourages freedom of thought and promotes unquestioned acceptance of authority and susceptibility to manipulation and prejudice, liberal education frees students to think for themselves, provides them with the knowledge and skills required for responsible participation in self-governance, and disposes them to civic involvement and the creation of a more just and inclusive society. It offers an unparalleled means to the democratic end of universal access to opportunity, to fulfilling the promise of social mobility, and to unleashing the potential of those otherwise most likely to be excluded from full participation in civic and economic life.

References

Association of American Colleges & Universities. (2018, July). *Fulfilling the American Dream: Liberal education and the future of work*. Hart Research Association. www.aacu.org/sites/default/files/files/LEAP/2018EmployerResearchReport.pdf

Association of American Colleges & Universities. (2019a). *Strengthening guided pathways and career success by ensuring students are learning*. www.aacu.org/strengthening-guided-pathways

Association of American Colleges & Universities (2019b, May 14). *AAC&U announces twenty institutions in new Guided Pathways Project*. Author. https://www.aacu.org/press/press-releases/aacu-announces-twenty-institutions-new-guided-pathways-project

Association of American Colleges & Universities (2019c, February 14). *AAC&U's new Guided Pathways Project champions student learning, career preparation, and completion*. Posted on spaces4learning, Impacting K-12 & higher-education environments. https://spaces4learning.com/articles/2019/02/14/aacu-guided-pathways-project.aspx

Association of American Colleges & Universities. (2020). *Truth, racial healing and transformation campus centers*. www.aacu.org/trht-campus-centers

Bailey, T., Smith Jaggars, S., & Jenkins, D. (2015). *Redesigning America's community colleges: A clearer path to student success*. Cambridge, MA: Harvard University Press.

Cahalan, M., Perna, L. W., Yamashita, M., Wright, J., & Santillan, S. (2018, May). *Indicators of higher education equity in the United States*. Pell Institute & the Alliance for Higher Education and Democracy at the University of Pennsylvania. http://pellinstitute.org/downloads/publications-Indicators_of_Higher_Education_Equity_in_the_US_2018_Historical_Trend_Report.pdf

Camera, L. (2019, January 15). *Community college transfer students: Underenrolled, overachieving*. US News and World Report. www.usnews.com/news/education-news/articles/2019-01-15/community-college-transfer-students-underenrolled-overachieving

Carnevale, A., & Strohl, J. (2013, July). *Separate and unequal: How higher education reinforces the intergenerational reproduction of white racial privilege*. Georgetown Public Policy Institute. https://1gyhoq479ufd3yna29x7ubjn-wpengine.netdna-ssl.com/wp-content/uploads/SeparateUnequal.FR_.pdf

Chetty, R., Friedman, J. N., Saez, E., Turner, N., & Yagan, D. (2020). Income segregation and intergenerational mobility across colleges in the United States. *The Quarterly Journal of Economics, 135*(3), 1567–1633. doi.org/10.1093/qje/qjaa005

Drake, J. K., Jordan, P., & Miller, M. A. (Eds.). (2013). *Academic advising approaches: Strategies that teach students to make the most of college*. San Francisco: Jossey-Bass.

Elsesser, K. (2019, December 11). Lawsuit claims SAT and ACT are biased – here's what research says. *Forbes*. www.forbes.com/sites/kimelsesser/2019/12/11/lawsuit-claims-sat-and-act-are-biased-heres-what-research-says/

Glynn, J. (2019, January). *Persistence: The success of students who transfer from community colleges to selective four-year institutions*. Jack Kent Cooke Foundation. www.jkcf.org/wp-content/uploads/2019/01/Persistance-Jack-Kent-Cooke-Foundation.pdf

Jenkins, D., & Fink, J. (2016, January). *Tracking transfer: New measures of institutional and state effectiveness in helping community college students attain bachelor's degrees*. Community College Research Center. https://ccrc.tc.columbia.edu/publications/tracking-transfer-institutional-state-effectiveness.html

Marken, S. (2019, December 30). *Half in U.S. now consider college education very important*. Gallup. www.gallup.com/education/272228/half-consider-college-education-important.aspx

National Center for Education Statistics. (2019). *Back to school statistics*. https://nces.ed.gov/fastfacts/display.asp?id=372

Pasquerella, L. (2018, October 4). *The integration of the humanities and arts with sciences, engineering, and medicine in higher education: Branches from the same tree*. Presentation given at the Seattle Marriott Waterfront.

Pasquerella, L. (2020, September 17). Higher education's racial reckoning. *Diverse Issues in Higher Education, 37*(15), 12.

Pasquerella, L., & Oates, J. (2020, April 6). *Federal student aid policy must be reformed to make college affordable for low-income students*. Inside Higher Ed. www.insidehighered.com/views/2020/04/06/federal-student-aid-policy-must-be-reformed-make-college-affordable-low-income

Pathways. (2019, October). *Guided pathways: Planning, implementation, evaluation*. www.pathwaysresources.org/wp-content/uploads/2020/01/PathwaysGraphic-10-23-19.pdf

Peller, J. (2018, June 22). *New higher education campaign launches to highlight changing experiences of today's students through their stories*. PR Newswire. www.prnewswire.com/news-releases/new-higher-education-campaign-launches-to-highlight-changing-experiences-of-todays-students-through-their-stories-300670906.html

Skorton, D. J., & Bear, A. (2018). *The integration of the humanities and arts with sciences, engineering, and medicine in higher education: Branches from the same tree*. The National Academies Press.

Stepler, R. (2016, February). *Hispanic, Black parents see college degree as key for children's success*. Pew Research Center. www.pewresearch.org/fact-tank/2016/02/24/hispanic-black-parents-see-college-degree-as-key-for-childrens-success/

Vigdor, N., & Diaz, J. (2020, May 21). More colleges are waiving SAT and ACT requirements. *The New York Times*. www.nytimes.com/article/sat-act-test-optional-colleges-coronavirus.html

21 Psychological Impact of Climate Change on Communities

Zachary Foley, Carlos Storck-Martinez, Grace Koguc, Maria Guevara Carpio, Cara Lomaro, and Caroline S. Clauss-Ehlers

21.1 Introduction

Mounting scientific evidence has supported the fact that the Earth's temperature is rising (Rahmstorf, 2010; Solomon et al.. 2007; Vermeer & Rahmstorf, 2009). Human activity has caused a depletion of the ozone layer and natural resources (National Aeronautics and Space Administration [NASA], 2020). This affects weather patterns, infrastructure, and health trends (NASA, 2020). Scientific publications have been greatly debated among politicians. Beliefs and actions regarding climate change have become polarized despite recorded changes in sea levels, temperature, and weather events (Dunlap & McCright, 2008).

Storms and public health shifts have created the need for newer and greater resources in the healthcare system, housing, infrastructure, and energy usage; however, not everyone has equal access to what they need (Cavallo, Powell, & Becerra, 2010). A focus on sustainable practices has garnered attention from environmentally conscious movements that developed toward the end of the last century (Ben-Eli, 2018). In this chapter, we focus on the wide-reaching consequences of the Earth's rising temperatures. We begin with a discussion of the parameters of climate change and then move to look at polarization and education around this issue. From there we discuss climate change as a social justice issue and provide several examples to illustrate this connection. The chapter concludes with recommendations for sustainability efforts moving forward.

21.2 History of Environmental Movements

The late twentieth century brought about an awareness of environmental issues because of the increasing rapidity of climate change and human contribution to environmental degradation. Most of the economic growth over the past few centuries has occurred specifically after 1820 and the Industrial Revolution. This new era of production increased not only the global Gross Domestic Product (GDP) and population size, but also the human use of natural resources and their subsequent emissions (McNeill, 2001). The 1960s through the 1970s were decades filled with movements and protests. In 1962, Rachel Carson published *Silent Spring*. In this book she talked about the dangerous use of pesticides and their impact on the environment (Carson, 1962). She called for people to be mindful of the planet and encouraged them to question government practices regarding the environment. This work prompted environmental reform and the organization of the first Earth Day (Gaard, 2011; The Energy and Resources Institute, 2014). Senator Gaylord Nelson of Wisconsin was focused on the environment and environmental change. His efforts led to the organization of the first Earth Day on April 22, 1970 (The Energy and Resources Institute, 2014). Soon after, in July 1970, the Environmental Protection Agency was formed.

The United States created the Environmental Protection Agency and passed the Clean Air Act (Clean Air Act, 1970), Clean Water Act (Clean Water Act, 1972), and Endangered Species Act (Endangered Species Act, 1973) to legally ensure protective measures for the environment (Freeman, 2002; The Energy and Resources Institute, 2014). Earth Day protests ranged in motive, with some targeting corporations, some targeting overpopulation, and some targeting everyday practices. Demonstrations included picking up trash and dropping it on the steps of a courthouse, dumping oil in the reflecting pools of standard oil, and making plastic molds of babies to symbolize an overgrowing population. People boycotted cars, airplanes, pesticides, having animal fur on clothing, and nuclear power plants (Lowenthal, 1970).

Earth Day helped to support recycling across the globe. It laid the groundwork that inspired the 1992 United Nations Earth Summit in Rio de Janeiro. This conference sought to transform the practices of governments and corporations to promote eco-efficiency and the health of the planet. A total of 172 governments participated and 2,400 NGO representatives attended. They focused on environmental concerns as a consequence of economic inequality. The main points emphasized cleaner methods of production, alternative energy use, increased public transportation, and water scarcity awareness (United Nations Sustainable Development, 1992). A follow-up to the Stockholm Conference of 1972, the Earth Summit resulted in Agenda 21 that outlines actions of the UN agencies for sustainable development (United Nations Sustainable Development, 1992). Earth Day 2000 globally united activists in the pursuit of clean energy, shifting the focus specifically to climate change (American Institute of Physics, 2016).

One main theme from the first Earth Day was an emphasis on individual actions. The media framed the environmental movement as a collective responsibility, emphasizing individual actions to have fewer children and conserve resources, rather than recognizing nuanced causes of pollution among different groups of people (Dunaway, 2008). This seemed to be an effective tool, as collective guilt has been found to motivate action against climate change (Ferguson & Branscombe, 2010). However, this approach did not fully and accurately address the full scope of harm. For example, pesticides have more of an effect on farmers working in the fields than those who consume their produce (Dunaway, 2008). This focus ignores the macro-level influence of large corporations by diverting blame. While legislation was passed to reduce environmental pollutants and individuals did their part to reduce and reuse, there was less of a focus on dealing with the consequences of the pollutants already present. In another example, while lead levels were a topic of concern, there was no agenda to protect inner-city children who were most exposed to lead paint (Dunaway, 2008).

Individual responsibility takes many different forms. For instance, since 2012, the interest in a vegan diet and lifestyle has quadrupled. Companies such as McDonalds, Tyson Foods, Ben and Jerry's, and Starbucks have all added vegan alternatives to their everyday products (The Vegan Society, 2018). People present a variety of reasons to switch, but a common rationale has to do with the environment. Those who follow a vegan lifestyle list concerns with resource scarcity, deforestation, and sustainable agriculture (Janssen et al., 2016). For instance, animal agriculture contributes a larger carbon footprint compared to vegetable production. The meat industry causes 88% of the global water footprint, 15% of all greenhouse gas emissions, and 65%–70% of the total Amazon rainforest deforestation (Martinelli & Berkmanienė, 2018).

It is also important to note how people are affected by climate issues from an international perspective. Ecofeminism, coined in the 1980s, is the idea that women have a unique relationship with the Earth and environment (Gaard, 2011). Susan Griffin's (1980) *Woman in Nature* explored how nature was seen as feminine, and therefore inferior to the man-made and male-dominated order (Gaard, 2011). At the same time, rural women and women in the Global South are most vulnerable to the effects of climate change. For example, in these regions, women primarily take care of the resources for the home. If these resources such as wood or water are scarce, they must travel longer distances to retrieve them. In terms of natural disasters, women experience higher rates of mortality, greater domestic workload, risk of sexual harassment, and decreased access to services and infrastructure that would alleviate these problems (Pearse, 2017).

Historically left out of popular media coverage and international treaty negotiations, Indigenous climate activists have long been advocating for sustainable land practices across the globe (Powless, 2012; Roosvall & Tegelberg, 2016). Much of their livelihood and existence is dependent on the earth, and so they are also disproportionately impacted by climate change. The International Indigenous Climate Movement (IICM) focuses on recognizing Indigenous groups as having collective right to land (Powless, 2012). Similarly to ecofeminism, the IICM criticizes domination over the earth and exploitation of resources (Powless, 2012; Warren & Jackson, 2003). If we are to consider alternative and sustainable ways of life for the future, we must acknowledge and turn to Indigenous activists who hold traditional ecological knowledge.

21.3 Parameters of Climate Change

Global temperature is expected to rise about 3–4°C in this decade (New et al., 2011). With a 4°C increase, sea-level rise is expected to reach 0.5–2 m by 2100 (Nicholls et al., 2011). Crop yields will ultimately become less stable, as increases in adverse weather conditions will lead to higher risk of landslides and erosion (Schmidhuber & Tubiello, 2007). This is of particular concern in regions where food is already scarce and homes are built poorly. Landslides are particularly dangerous in developing nations, because homes are poorly built making them collapse more easily when there is heavy rainfall. Crop yields will initially increase with a raise in carbon dioxide, but eventually some cereals and forage crops will yield less protein (Schmidhuber & Tubiello, 2007). Some regions in Central America are located in the dry corridor (e.g., El Salvador, Guatemala, Honduras, and Nicaragua), a region that has seen extreme drought and weather patterns so severe that the agricultural sector is unsustainable causing large migrations (Blitzer, 2019). Overall, an increase in temperature will lead to a decrease in crop yields in most regions in the United States, Central America, Africa, Australia, and many Asian countries (Wheeler & von Braun, 2013, p. 510). Furthermore, production and supply markets will be adversely affected by climate change, with an expected increase in cost of crops (Wheeler & von Braun, 2013, p. 512).

There is irrefutable evidence that global weather patterns are becoming more severe. In terms of tropical cyclones, the intensity of such cyclones is expected to increase from 2% to 11% by 2100 (Knutson et al., 2010). Islands in the Caribbean are particularly prone to damage from cyclones, due not only from the precariousness of their location, but their vulnerability to increased rainfall. As storms grow in strength, a projected 20% increase in rainfall within 100 km of storm centers is expected in the coming years (Knutson et al., 2010). Global warming is the problem, since hurricanes and tropical cyclones increase in frequency as temperatures rise. Human-induced greenhouse gases are the reason behind the Earth's warming (Knutson et al., 2010). Over the past few years weather patterns have become increasingly dangerous, especially in the hurricane belt, where aggressive hurricanes are expected to prevail in the next two to three decades (Pielke Jr. et al., 2003, p. 103).

The heating of the globe is the beginning of the problem. Vulnerable regions become more vulnerable as global temperatures rise, as a warming climate leads to an increase in catastrophic weather events. From the year 1880 to 2000 the climate warmed by 0.6°C (Anderson, Hawkins, & Jones,

2016). Similarly, CO_2 release in the atmosphere has shown a positive correlation with global temperatures (Anderson et al., 2016). Thus, the increase in global temperatures can be attributed largely to the first world, with countries like the United States contributing to a large portion of the CO_2: 15% in 2015 (Union of Concerned Scientists, 2020). The heating of the globe and higher CO_2 in the atmosphere has led to more prevalent and severe weather systems (Intergovernmental Panel on Climate Change [IPCC], 2014, p. 7). Unfortunately, the countries that contribute the least to the problem are the ones that suffer the consequences. According to the National Coordination of Food Security, drought severely impacted the agricultural sector in Haiti, with 60%–80% production loss from February to August 2016 (Janvier, 2016).

The heating of the globe also leads to rising sea level, which is of particular concern for islands. There are many speculations in reference to how high the sea will rise in the coming years, but it is of concern now for islands like Haiti as the sea level has risen 0.19 m between 1901 to 2010 (IPCC, 2014, p. 42). Islands with dense populations such as Haiti are more vulnerable to risks of flooding and hurricanes. Regions with a dense population are usually associated with poverty, poor infrastructure, and poor governance. These influences add to the precarity in underdeveloped countries.

The oceans have also become warmer, with a combined land and ocean surface of 0.65–1.06°C between 1880 and 2012 (IPCC, 2014, p. 2). As previously noted, warmer water leads to hurricanes, a particularly salient fact for Haitians who have to deal with a combination of natural disasters. Hurricanes have begun to change for the worst, with higher frequencies and aggression seen since 1970 (IPCC, 2014, p. 53).

Heavy downpours are also more frequently occurring as the weather variability has become more extreme, a direct influence from the increased greenhouse gases in the environment (Trenberth, 1999). From heavy downpours comes flooding, which leads to two disastrous effects, mainly in poor countries. Flooding can lead to landslides, which can be deadly; specifically Haiti has dealt with such losses. Another major problem with heavy downpours is the spread of diseases (Hunter, 2003). Both waterborne disease and vector-borne diseases spread easier with sitting water (Hunter, 2003). Vector-borne diseases are perpetuated as sitting water allows mosquitos to lay eggs and facilitates populations of disease-spreading bugs.

21.4 Polarization of Climate Change

Despite efforts made to support climate change, a distinct divide exists between those who believe that climate change is a reality and those who do not. For many who do not believe in climate change, they do not believe that climate change is anthropogenic, meaning that it's the result of human action (Webb & Hayhoe, 2017). Social psychologists have been studying increasing trends of in-group identification and authoritarian tendencies as a result of climate change (Fritsche et al., 2012; Hamilton, 2011). The goal of these researchers is to discover why people are so reluctant to accept the scientific consensus that climate change is occurring and anthropogenic in nature.

A promising result of this research reveals that the heuristics, or quick mental processes that cause individuals to form opinions and develop a stance on climate science, may result from the complexity and multitude of climate change science and information that bombards the knowledge-seeker (Valdez, Peterson, & Stevenson, 2018). Heuristics cause people to readily accept information from sources they trust and share similar ideas with (Kahan et al., 2012). As a result, knowledge is selectively acquired and information that contradicts the individual's beliefs is often ignored. This phenomenon of selectively processing and searching for information that adheres to the norms of a community and the individual's beliefs, while paying no mind to contradicting information, is known as *motivated cognition* and often results in an increasing divide between ideologies (Plutzer & Hannah, 2018).

The culmination of selective processing and becoming more extreme in one's beliefs in relation to a larger group is referred to as "group polarization" (Kahan et al., 2012; Hamilton, 2011). According to the *APA Dictionary of Psychology* (American Psychological Association, 2007), group polarization is defined as

> the tendency for members of a group discussing an issue to move toward a more extreme version of the positions they held before the discussion began. As a result, the group as a whole tends to respond in more extreme ways than one would expect given the sentiments of the individual members prior to deliberation. Polarization is sustained by social comparison, by exposure to other members' relatively extreme responses, and by groups' implicit social decision schemes.

Ideologically polarized beliefs about climate change revolve around the skepticism of whether or not climate change is actually occurring and if it is anthropogenic in nature. However, according to NASA's climate consensus (NASA, 2020), it has long been established by scientists and years of research that climate change is in fact occurring and is the result of anthropogenic influence (NASA, 2020).

The issue and scope of climate change is too extensive to include a thorough explanation of its origins within this chapter. However, the paragraphs that follow attempt to present evidence as to why scientists have established that climate change is occurring and anthropogenic "since before the turn of the 20th century" (Rich, 2018, p. 1).

To begin our analysis, the US EPA (1979) shared a statement about the impact of fossil fuels on the environment, stating that "the continued use of fossil fuels might, within two or three decades, bring about 'significant and damaging' changes to the global atmosphere" (Rich, 2018, p. 2). Here the government acknowledges that the human use of fossil fuels had been affecting the world's climate through its impact on the atmosphere. It had even made predictions based upon the occurring trends of atmospheric damages at that time.

Climate Central (2012) found that "the *pace* of warming in *all* regions accelerated dramatically starting in the 1970s." A 1957 Humble Oil study discussed "the enormous quantity of carbon dioxide" that contributed to the atmosphere since the Industrial Revolution "from the combustion of fossil fuels" (Rich, 2018, p. 6). The emission of carbon dioxide into the atmosphere traps the sun's energy closer to the Earth's surface while acting as a barrier for this energy to leave the atmosphere. This increases the Earth's average temperature over time and is one of the biggest concerns regarding climate change (The Climate Reality Project, 2018). The disequilibrium arises when the surface heat cannot escape the atmosphere at a rate that allows for normal planetary cooling (NASA, 2020; Rich, 2018). The result of the greenhouse effect is an increase in average temperature. The current rise in temperature in the USA is a warming of 1.3°F over the past one hundred years. Climate Central (2012) provides a brief history of the warming trend:

> Since 1970, warming began accelerating everywhere. The speed of warming across the lower 48 more than tripled, from 0.127°F per decade over the 100-year period, to 0.435°F per decade since 1970, while the gap between the fast and slowly warming states narrowed significantly; the 10 fastest warming states heated up just twice as fast, not 60 times as fast as the 10 slowest warming states (0.60°F vs. 0.30°F per decade). Over the past 42 years 17 states warmed more than half a degree F per decade.

Group membership refers to the specific group to which an individual identifies and agrees with and thus perpetuates the beliefs and values associated with the group as a whole (Masson & Fritsche, 2014). In a 2008 study on political party affiliation and climate change belief in the United States, it was found that 76% of Democrats agreed that global warming was occurring compared to only 41% of Republicans (Dunlap & McCright, 2008). The tendency for polarization and group membership to perpetuate group beliefs is depicted by the increase in percentage of Democratic agreement of global warming from 47% in 1998 to 76% in 2008 and Republican decrease in climate consensus from 46% to 41% during the same timeframe (Dunlap & McCright, 2008). The timeframe may have allowed for more group members to become invested in the group values, as well as time for climate change science and popularity to increase and become a more salient phenomenon.

Group membership can become increasingly important for people when a perceived threat is present. For instance, when under threat, people may become defensive and more supportive of their in-groups, increasing likeliness to act on in-group norms (Giannakakis & Fritsche, 2011). The "threat" studied in much of the current literature on group theories is the perceived threat of climate change (Fritsche et al., 2012, p. 2). Climate change acts as a threat because its predicted environmental impact will directly affect quality of life, living conditions, and even mitigate the satisfaction of psychological needs (Fritsche et al., 2012). In a recent 2019 Pew Research Center survey, 90% of Democrats (including Independents who "lean to the Democratic Party") said the government needed to do more regarding climate change issues. Republicans appeared divided in responses, with differences reflecting ideology, age, and gender. For instance, a "majority of moderate or liberal Republicans (65%, including GOP-leaning independents) say the federal government is doing too little to reduce the effects of climate change....only about one-quarter of conservative Republicans (24%) say the same, while about half (48%) think the government is doing about the right amount and another 26% say it is doing too much" (Funk & Hefferon, 2019). With regard to age and gender, a majority of younger Republicans supported further looking into alternative energies, with Republican women believing developing alternative energy was more important than fossil fuel expansion, a view also shared by a smaller proportion of Republican men (Funk & Hefferon, 2019).

These perceived climate change threats that conflict the predisposed ideologies of group members may cause a phenomenon known as authoritarian tendencies. Authoritarian tendencies are defined as acting in accordance or obedience with what is presented as a superior entity or system, and the administration of those beliefs through oppression or aggression toward an insubordinate. Authoritarian tendencies are a major contributor when solidifying membership within a group, as they allow group consensus to comfort any perceived ideological threat of clashing information (Fritsche et al., 2012). Authoritarian tendencies comfort such threats through the collaboration of in-group members' efforts in reaffirming the common beliefs held by the group populace through communication of intragroup members, and demonizing or ignoring the triggering information. As posited by Fritsche et al. (2012), "individuals' concern for maintaining or establishing normative consensus in groups is assumed to motivate individual authoritarian attitudes, such as acting in line with ingroup norms (conventionalism), obeying people or institutions that promote norm compliance (authoritarian submission) and punishing those who are breaking the norms of the ingroup (authoritarian aggression)" (p. 1).

The desire to remain within the group consensus may cause people to behave in ways that maintain group norms. When prompted with notions that conflict with the norms, group members may lash out against deviants in an effort to bolster their sense of belonging and further perpetuate the way the group functions in its beliefs and values. In a study conducted on German university students, it was found that when thinking about climate change threat, participants became more aggressive in thought toward groups that go against society (e.g., punishment of criminals, deviating groups) and other general authoritarian attitudes (Fritsche et al., 2012). This implies that climate change is a very emotionally stimulating subject matter that can indeed elicit aggressive response and adherence to the norm, or general group, to which the individual belongs. This can contribute to furthering polarization through aggressive perpetuation and enforcing group norms.

21.5 Group Membership and Education

Climate education aims to instruct learners of the science behind climate change in the hope that this knowledge will create a well-informed populace that agrees with the scientific consensus and establishes pro–climate change behaviors amongst learners (Hamilton, 2011). However, climate science education is under scrutiny by researchers who are attempting to analyze deficits in current pedagogical approaches to climate change. According to the National Survey of Science Teachers, 57% of teachers have had no prior exposure to climate change science (Plutzer & Hannah, 2018). Because the majority of teachers have had no formal education on climate science themselves, they must resort to self-education measures such as obtaining information from online media, news sources, and reviewing material that they will teach to their students (Hamilton, 2011; Plutzer & Hannah, 2018). This becomes problematic when teachers' desire for group approval causes them to include predisposed ideological and political beliefs of the group to which they belong in their search for climate information. Educators' biased climate knowledge can then affect whether they emphasize the scientific consensus in class or embrace inquiry and debate about established science (Plutzer & Hannah, 2018).

One survey found that "a large majority of American science educators embrace inquiry and debate on empirically settled scientific questions" (Plutzer & Hannah, 2018, p. 313). Although inquiry methods are extremely effective in engaging learners with coursework, one school of thought says that it is of utmost importance to emphasize the scientific consensus rather than encouraging debate as this leads to the students questioning established science (Plutzer & Hannah, 2018). Furthermore, teaching climate science in a manner that may arouse concern and leaves room for skepticism could result in perceived threat and increase the likelihood that the learner will search for sources of anti-climate change "evidence" that ease their fears through reaffirming the learner's beliefs (Masson & Fritsche, 2014; Plutzer & Hannah, 2018). These types of motivated sources, that can influence and bolster group beliefs, may lead to learners believing and spreading "false science" (e.g., scientific statements that lack evidence to support claims), that may influence how the learner views and understands climate change-related science (Hamilton, 2011; Kahan et al., 2012). Education and awareness about climate change and global warming presents complications and limitations (Kahan et al., 2012; Valdez et al., 2018). Much of the knowledge and information people receive about climate change is from the Internet and various media outlets (Hamilton, 2011). These sources may reflect a particular political viewpoint connected with climate change or present false science (Hamilton, 2011). As a result, such Internet sources may further contribute to a lack of information and awareness, or people seeking out websites that present information that supports their views. Such websites may allow for the reinforcement of individuals with misinformed ideologies to find comfort in similar-minded informative knowledge outlets and create a polarization of education and information. States Hamilton (2011): "The politicization of what was originally a scientific question has not been accidental. Polarization reflects the opposition between conservative campaigns promoting the views of a small number of "skeptical" or contrarian scientists to argue against greenhouse gas reductions, on the one hand, . . .and publications of the wider scientific consensus (such as the IPCC) supported by liberal and environmental activists (such as Al Gore, with *An Inconvenient Truth*) on the other."

Hamilton (2011) conducted a study to test the interaction between education/information and political orientation, with data from two regional surveys, one in Michigan, the other in New Hampshire. Two key questions about global warming were presented in both surveys. One of the questions focused on understanding (e.g., "Next, thinking about the issue of global warming, sometimes called the 'greenhouse effect,' how well do you feel you understand this issue–would you say very well, fairly well, not very well, or not at all?") and the other focused on threat (e.g., "Do you think that global warming will pose a serious threat to you or your way of life in your lifetime, or not?"; Hamilton, 2011).

For both surveys, Hamilton (2011) found "interaction effects" for "*interaction* hypotheses involving education (or information) and political orientation." For instance, the research found that "Among Democrats, the better they think they understand the issue, the more likely they are to perceive it as a threat... Among Republicans, however, the better they think they understand the issue, the *less* likely they are to perceive a threat."

Furthermore, it was found that informal learning, or learning without a formal teacher, holds more weight in predicting climate change attitude and belief than the traditional accumulation of knowledge. In a study conducted on middle school adolescents in the United States, for instance, a surprising 14.5% of students had actually never discussed climate change in the classroom (Valdez et al., 2018). New forms of education involving schoolwide presentations and assemblies are being tested to account for both the lack of proper in-class climate change lessons, the impact informal learning has on students, and to inspire constructive dialogue outside of class among students' peers and friends.

This form of education is known as edutainment, which involves a mixture of education with entertaining platforms. In one case study, a one-hour presentation on climate change conducted by the Alliance for Climate Education explored whether such a presentation would prove effective in increasing positive attitudes toward climate change among high school students (Flora et al, 2014). The study was quite effective. After a four-week follow-up, for instance, results proved significant in improving students' attitudes and behaviors toward climate change (Flora et al., 2014). This presents a promising new model for inspiring students and improving beliefs about climate change.

21.6 Climate Change as a Social Justice Issue: Connections with Community Psychology

"Social justice involves concern for wellness of all persons and the inclusive vision of community and a recognition of human diversity" (Kloos et al., 2012, p. 30). Equity has been defined in the literature as "social justice or fairness; it is an ethical concept, grounded in principles of distributive justice" or the absence of systematic disparities (Braveman & Gruskin, 2003, p. 254). Compared to equality, equity concerns itself with getting the resources needed for certain groups, rather than giving the same amount of resources to every group. As climate change causes changes and devastation to communities, the gaps and disparities between communities become apparent.

Community psychology focuses on the well-being of the community. With regard to climate change and the environment, community psychology examines the impact of the environment on communities, including prevention strategies and plans to decrease destruction. One prevention example is to build sturdy community infrastructures (e.g., houses, schools, office buildings) that are designed to remain intact should there be a natural disaster (Beatley, 2009). In addition, "Strengthening social networks will make a community more resilient but will also result in richer human relationships, a stronger sense of community, and potentially greater meaning in life, all things that are intrinsically valuable" (Beatley, 2009, p. 5).

The ecological levels discussed in community psychology originally created by Bronfenbrenner, help us to understand how different systems interact with each other, to devise plans for interventions with the ultimate goal of having a thriving community, and to understand that a problem has multiple causes (Clauss-Ehlers et al., 2019; Kloos et al., 2012, p. 18). Bronfenbrenner's ecological model (Bronfenbrenner, 1994) allows us to recognize that local, organizational, and macro institutions have a major impact on systems that run our everyday lives, access to needs during times of difficulty, and how a community fares after a natural disaster or flooding that results from climate change.

For instance, there are some coastal communities that will not fare as well as others as climate change continues to progress. The concept of social vulnerability analysis has been defined as "the relationship between social characteristics and biophysical vulnerability to climate change stressors and other environmental hazards, as well as the distribution of tangible and intangible impacts on particular subpopulations or communities" (Foster et al., 2019, p. 129). Foster and colleagues (2019) identified factors that have an impact on social vulnerability and its analysis that include the nature of governance, the structure of available housing, networks of support, and healthcare access. Communities at a disadvantage in these areas are far more likely to be ill-equipped to deal with the aftermath of climate change disasters or floods, and less likely to receive timely or effective aid, making climate change an issue of equity (Foster et al., 2019). "Within the climate change literature, elements of distributional equity include recognition of inequalities in social vulnerability to climate change; inequalities in the capacity to adapt or influence mitigation of climate change; inequalities in benefits associated with adaptation policies; and inequalities and unintended consequences of adaptation and mitigation efforts" (Foster et al., 2019, p. 128). When a disaster hits an entire state, there will be communities within a larger scope that will struggle far more than those who can afford to evacuate, those who have insurance, and those who are seen as important to the government.

A recent example of the immense gap in resources and equity was the response to Hurricanes Irma and María that demolished Puerto Rico, compared to Hurricanes Harvey and Irma that hit mainland United States, affecting Texas and Florida. In Texas the Federal Emergency Management Agency (FEMA) had prepositioned supplies and resources before Hurricane Harvey made landfall and President Trump made a major disaster declaration that allowed thirty-one thousand government employees to be immediately deployed to the area, making the response one of the largest responses in FEMA history (FEMA, 2017). In contrast, his response in Puerto Rico was much different. The island was hit with a stronger "high-end" level 4 hurricane but initially only received ten thousand federal employees. One month later, the maximum of nineteen thousand federal employees was reached (Willison et al., 2019). Furthermore, the island received comparable economic aid four months after the hurricane, whereas two months after both Florida and Texas were given recovery aid (Willison et al., 2019).

Direct deaths are defined by the National Oceanic and Atmospheric Administration (NOAA) as "'[d]eaths occurring as a direct result of the forces of the tropical cyclone.' These would include individuals who drowned in storm surge, rough seas, rip currents and freshwater floods. Indirect deaths are defined as, '[d]eaths occurring from such factors as heart attacks, house fires, electrocutions from downed power lines, vehicle accidents on wet roads, etc.'" (Cangialosi, Latto, & Berg, 2018; Willison et al., 2019). Communities deserved attention and funds, but the government response to the situation for the people of Puerto Rico was slow, inadequate, and unsupportive.

Even in the most affluent coastal areas, there are laws that make having affordable housing available, and around the globe many coastal communities represent a lower socioeconomic status. Thus, communities experience different outcomes and hardships when it comes to climate change and possible relocation.

The community impact of another issue, flooding, is highlighted in the following statements: "as the oceans warm, seawater expands and raises sea level. Melting ice adds more water to the ocean, further raising sea level" (US EPA, 2016, p. 1). "Whether or not storms become more intense, coastal homes and infrastructure will flood more often as sea level rises, because storm surges will become higher as well. Rising sea levels are likely to increase flood insurance rates, while more frequent storms could increase the deductible for wind damage in homeowner insurance policies" (US EPA, 2016, p. 2). Living in vulnerable areas becomes more expensive as the climate becomes less predictable, and could possibly drive people out of their homes. Coastal areas that have been affected by flooding need to repair homes, raise taxes, and increase insurance rates, all of which can cause families to leave or be deterred from living in such communities. The following paragraphs present examples of linkages between social justice considerations and climate change with regard to Syria, Tuvalu, Haiti, and Central America.

21.6.1 Forced Migration: Syria

Climate/environmental refugees are

> persons who can no longer gain a secure livelihood in their traditional homelands because of environmental factors of unusual scope, notably drought, desertification, deforestation, soil erosion, water shortages and climate change, also natural disasters such as cyclones, storm surges and floods. In face of these environmental threats, people feel they have no alternative but to seek sustenance elsewhere, whether within their own countries or beyond and whether on a semi-permanent or permanent basis. (Myers & Kent, 1995, pp. 18–19)

Syria presents an example of how climate change issues give rise to environmental refugees. The Syrian civil war that began in 2011 left more than 2.3 million people displaced in 2013 (Acarturk et al., 2015). The cause of the civil war was rooted in climate change, where severe droughts had lasted roughly five years, the worst drought in the history of the area. This in turn led to internal migration that fueled civil unrest (Selby et al., 2017). Increased global temperatures lead to more precipitation, which leads to a loss in natural water availability (Van Lanen, Tallaksen, & Rees, 2007).

Another notable factor that led to the Syrian civil war was the increased pricing of wheat from China and Russia, where rising temperatures led to higher pricing as wheat yields declined (Selby et al., 2017). This led to further unrest as the prices of basic supplies were inflated (Selby et al., 2017). The stress of not being able to acquire basic needs is surely enough to cause separation between upper and lower social classes, and later rioting and chaos.

The outcome in Syria is a warning for other countries as climate stressors become more severe. The large emigration from Syria has led to a group of immigrants who potentially suffer from various mental illnesses related to threats associated with living in a conflict area. These include death, torture, starvation, serious injury, death or disappearance of family members, separation from family members, and prior trauma (Selby et al., 2017). Given these experiences, refugees are at higher risk for PTSD (Kazour et al., 2017). As the climate worsens it is highly probable that other developing countries will be susceptible to similar outcomes as access to basic necessities such as crops and clean water are already insecure.

21.6.2 Tuvalu

Tuvalu consists of 9 islands in the Pacific Ocean. With 11,000 people, it's the world's fourth smallest country. Rising sea levels and an eroding coast related to climate change mean that Tuvalu faces flooding and going under water (Farbotko & Lazrus, 2012). The trauma of this situation is further underscored by the concern that this is irreversible, with predictions that Tuvalu will no longer be a place to live (Farbotko & Lazrus, 2012). The island has seen coastal erosion, coral bleaching, lessening of the fish population, and a lack of production in the agricultural sector (Farbotko & Lazrus, 2012). Mitigation efforts have predominantly been underdeveloped in this region, as maintaining ecosystems has been the predominant focus (Farbotko & Lazrus, 2012). If mitigation efforts stay the same globally, forced migration will be the only chance for Tuvaluans, leading to a potential loss of cultural connection that the population has with its homeland.

21.6.3 Haiti

The 2010 earthquake that hit Haiti was a magnitude 7.2 earthquake causing enormous destruction and loss for the country. The Disaster Emergency

Committee (DEC, n.d.) reported that "3,500,000 people were affected by the quake, 220,000 people estimated to have died, 300,000+ people were injured...4,000 schools were damaged or destroyed, 25% of civil servants in Port au Prince died, [and] 60% of Government and administrative buildings...were destroyed or damaged." At one point, 1.5 million people were living in camps (DEC, n.d.). The economic loss for Haiti due to the earthquake was estimated at being between US$7.2 billion and US$13.9 billion, accounting for roughly 120.6% of the nominal GDP (Cavallo et al., 2010; Hou & Shi, 2011).

A hurricane landfall is "The intersection of the surface center of a tropical cyclones with a coastline" (National Hurricane Center and Central Pacific Hurricane Center, n.d.). This is significant because "the strongest winds in a tropical cyclone are not located precisely at the center, it is possible for a cyclone's strongest winds to be experienced over land even if landfall does not occur. Similarly, it is possible for a tropical cyclone to make landfall and have its strongest winds remain over the water" (National Hurricane Center and Central Pacific Hurricane Center, n.d.). Haiti is vulnerable to hurricanes given it is located in the center of a hurricane belt (PAHO, n.d.), has 1,100 miles of coastline, encompasses a small area (e.g., 10,714 square miles; United Press International, 1988) with 11,544,173 million people (Worldometer, 2021), and has an underdeveloped infrastructure (PAHO, n.d.).

Hurricanes have begun to change for the worst, with higher frequencies and aggression seen since 1970 (IPCC, 2014). For islands in the Caribbean this is a disaster, specifically for the island of Haiti, which has a 10% chance of a hurricane making landfall every year (Pielke Jr. et al., 2003). To assume that the data suggesting that hurricanes will happen more often and be more aggressive are true, is to assume that on average Haiti will be hit with one or more aggressive hurricanes each year and that this pattern will continually worsen. A country cannot mitigate damages if every year brings at least one devastating cyclone. The problem is mitigating the adverse effects from a government standpoint, where Haiti does not have the economic power to effectively mitigate damage that has and will happen.

Before the earthquake that hit in 2010, hurricanes were a huge problem in Haiti, but one that was front and center on the government's agenda. For example, before 2010, many houses and buildings were generally made of concrete, a great structure that will hold up to the high winds of a hurricane, but a disaster for dealing with earthquakes (Hou & Shi, 2011). When houses are made of concrete they crumble when earthquakes hit, creating a trap in which those who were in the house cannot escape (Hou & Shi, 2011). Related issues with flooding in Haiti are the landslides and likelihood of disease spreading. One example of the detrimental nature of landslides includes Haiti's 2018 landslide where three people died, one went missing, one was injured, and fifteen houses were destroyed or damaged (Davies,

2018). Landslides are frequent and deadly in Haiti; the sitting water created from these events allows mosquitos to breed and further circulate diseases that spread rapidly in developing countries where health care is poor (Ammar et al., 2012).

21.6.4 Central America

What is known as the Dry Corridor region of Central America includes the following countries: Guatemala, El Salvador, Honduras, and Nicaragua. The Dry Corridor region is "home to some ten million people, it is defined by its susceptibility to droughts, tropical storms, landslides, and flash floods; more than half of the residents in the region are subsistence farmers, and at least two million of them have gone hungry in the last decade because of extreme weather" (Blitzer, 2019). Climate change is leading to the loss of crops, ultimately forcing Central Americans north. A 10% decrease in crop yield is expected to force 2% of the population towards the United States border (Feng, Krueger, & Oppenheimer, 2010). This is currently being seen: As of December 2018 to February 2019 there was an 85% increase in arrests at the US/Mexican border over the previous year (Flaherty, 2019).

21.6.5 COVID-19 Global Impacts

Developing research around the novel coronavirus and climate change shows important interactions between the virus, public health measures, and the environment. Since this research is fairly new the data has yet to be analyzed, but initial findings are showing positive effects on rates of pollution and animal activity, and a decrease in human environmental impact. These sources are found mainly from news coverage. Therefore, these findings will need further analysis to validate and analyze any lasting impacts.

One of the first important things to note when talking about climate change and disease is how an unhealthy environment can actually exacerbate existing inequalities. COVID-19 is particularly dangerous to those who have preexisting medical conditions, lack access to proper health care, and live in more polluted areas (Moore, 2020; Zaru, 2020). A Harvard study has also found that even a small increase in exposure to polluted air increases the death rate of coronavirus by 15% (Wu et al., 2020). These factors disproportionately impact marginalized communities. Environmental racism is the concept that environmental hazards such as air pollution or waste disposal sites are unequally distributed around factors such as race or class (Cole & Foster, 2000). This is what causes disproportionate levels of disease in certain communities. For example, while the African American community only makes up about 30% of Chicago's population, African Americans constitute more than 50% of coronavirus cases and more than 70% of fatalities (Moore, 2020).

Disparities in health due to the environment, as well as unequal access to health care or other resources, are responsible for these trends.

The public's response to the pandemic has also had an impact on the Earth's atmosphere and overall environment. Recent observations have shown a decrease in air pollution in just a year's difference. From March 2019 to March 2020, pollution in New York City decreased 50% (Henriques, 2020). Travel restrictions and widespread shutdowns led to a decrease in the amount of nitrogen dioxide (NO_2) emissions (Gardiner, 2020; Georgiou, 2020; Holcombe & O'Key, 2020). Nitrogen dioxide is produced from burning fossil fuels particularly from vehicles (cars, planes, buses, trucks, etc.) and industrial facilities (power plants and water treatment plants, etc.) (Georgiou, 2020; Holcombe & O'Key, 2020). Carbon emissions are also likely to follow in the recession that the pandemic is causing (Georgiou, 2020). The projected decline in carbon emissions is based on trends from previous global economic recessions, where energy-intensive activities (one major example being travel for leisure) decreased (Georgiou, 2020). Similar patterns have been found in China, Italy, Spain, and the United States (Henriques, 2020). These reductions mainly follow the paths of main traffic corridors, which supports the fact that human activity creates climate change. These observations can help guide humanity into a more sustainable future. While the rates of pollution are low now, they will eventually increase as travel is permitted and widely accepted across the country and around the globe again. Since pollution reflects the amount of human activity at a certain point, we need to consider how to move into the future using cleaner energy sources.

21.7 Conclusion: Climate Change and a New Definition of Sustainability

Climate change is a vast social, public health, and mental health issue with many factors that affect communities differently. It is possible, however, to diminish the negative impact of climate change by focusing on a behavioral approach that includes education, psychology, sustainability, and the environment.

This chapter section advocates for the undertaking of a new perspective when discussing climate change and sustainability. This new perspective incorporates a worldview that includes people's behaviors, their understanding of climate change within the context of their environments, and how this relates to sustainable behaviors. However, it is important to clarify that this chapter does not use the conventional definition of "sustainability."

According to the United States Environmental Protection Agency's website (US EPA, 2016), "to pursue sustainability is to create and maintain the conditions under which humans and nature can exist in productive harmony to support present and future generations." Even though this definition satisfies and appropriately utilizes the meaning of the word "sustainability," "Since it is difficult to establish economic utility values for future generations, it remains vague" (Ben-Eli, 2018, p. 1338). For policies and change to be effective, definitions and goals need to be clear and specific, thus a vague definition can present a challenge (Ben-Eli, 2018). Hence, this chapter uses Ben-Eli's (2018) view on sustainability as a system state, meaning "the result of the interaction of identifiable, specific variables" (Ben-Eli, 2018, p. 1340). In conclusion, this chapter defines sustainability as:

> A dynamic equilibrium in the process of interaction between a population and the carrying capacity of its environment such that the population develops to express its full potential without producing irreversible adverse effects on the carrying capacity of the environment upon which it depends.   (Ben-Eli, 2018, p. 1340)

Environmental uncertainty, regarding the importance of climate change or what actions or policy measures are needed, is large. In addition, people's perception of others' self-control and efficacy is low (Lange, Joireman, & Milinski, 2018). Moreover, there is a lack of resources and methods to promote pro-environmental behavior. One of the definitions for pro-environmental behavior is what people do to protect and do not damage the environment (Steg & Vlek, 2009). A clear example is the United States, where even though approximately 70% of the population is aware that global warming is happening, there is research that shows only 36% of people discuss climate change occasionally, and only 22% of the population hears about global warming in the news at least once a week (Mildenberger et al., 2018). Consequently, for society to combat climate change and transition to a sustainable economy, researchers and politicians need to begin looking at climate change as a holistic and informed understanding of people's behaviors, experiences, and responses to climate change (Bradley & Reser, 2017). To accomplish this new cognizance of climate change, there needs to be a higher comprehension of the contribution of social and environmental psychology to promote pro-environmental behaviors and sustainability (Bradley & Reser, 2017).

The research of Spence and Pigeon (2009) presents the hopeful idea "that when provided with information, people will change their behaviors in an environmentally beneficial way" (Spence & Pidgeon, 2009, p. 10). However, achieving effective communication to incentivize individuals into action is more complex and often contains subtle factors (Spence & Pidgeon, 2009). In addition, there are other external factors affecting human behavior in the context of sustainability and climate change. These include age, groups, and individual dynamics, trust between citizens and politicians or their government policies (Fischer et al., 2011). Hence, dialogue focused on climate change can be considered within an ecological perspective. These "emphasize certain aspects of an issue and de-emphasize others," hence organizing and defining a compound topic (Spence & Pidgeon, 2009, p. 11). Since the media is one of the current most used ways of communication, perhaps, it is important to analyze the frames that it utilizes to create effective pro-environmental communication campaigns (Spence & Pidgeon, 2009).

As discussed in Section 21.1 and from other sources, individuals in Western cultures tend to perceive climate change as a relevant issue. One popular method that the media uses to incentivize individuals is to portray climate change through "fear framing" (Spence & Pidgeon, 2009, p. 11). Fear framing displays climate change in catastrophic and emotive terms. Research suggests that viewing things in a catastrophic way can be motivating. However, such findings also state that a critically motivating factor that influences a sense of action, is to feel one is in control. Nonetheless, when there is a lack of control, denial can minimize fear, thus decreasing the chances of a person acting (Spence & Pidgeon, 2009). Consequently, Spencer and Pidgeon advise a better way to exercise "fear framing." They recommend that people "frame emotive messages alongside positive, credible steps which people themselves can take" (Spence & Pidgeon, 2009, p. 11).

Economic interests can prompt behaviors that go against supporting the environment (Spence & Pidgeon, 2009). One possible solution is to attach economic incentives to behaviors that support the environment. An example of financial incentives that motivate people to engage in such behaviors is seen in a study implemented by Bradley and Reser (2017). This study, conducted in Australia, found that 89% of participants recycled, 83% used energy saving lightbulbs, and 80% engaged in efforts to reduce water and electricity usage (Bradley & Reser, 2017). When asked why they engaged in these behaviors, 17% of participants stated it was due to their economic benefit.

Engaging in behaviors that support the environment may also be impeded by systemic factors. A lack of educational outreach about the realities of climate change may result in limited awareness about the impact of environmentally unsupportive behaviors. A dearth of political action to address climate change can interfere with behavioral change on many levels (Bradley & Reser, 2017).

Trust (and relatedly, hope) are other factors that have an impact on climate change. Here trust refers to the extent that someone believes others will act in ways that address climate change (Fischer et al., 2011). For instance, a qualitative study in European countries (Hungary, Germany, Scotland, the Czech Republic, and the Netherlands) found that research participants had a lack of hope in others: "[H]uman ability for cooperation based on insight, morals or voluntary agreements was regarded as limited" (Fischer et al., 2011, p. 1033). People may struggle with trying to adjust their behavior to support a healthy climate if they see that others around them are not committed. This could be a barrier to change (Spence & Pidgeon, 2009). Furthermore, the interviewees found "top-down approaches that restrained behavior such as regulations, increased prices and educational campaigns organized by the government to shape the behavior of the younger generations" as most effective to achieve large-scale behavioral change (Fischer et al., 2011, p. 1033). This is an example of how a lack of political action can become a social barrier to promoting sustainable behaviors in the context of climate change.

References

Acarturk, C., Konuk, E., Cetinkaya, M., et al. (2015). EMDR for Syrian refugees with posttraumatic stress disorder symptoms: Results of a pilot randomized controlled trial. *European Journal of Psychotraumatology*, *6*(1), 1–9. doi.org/10.3402/ejpt.v6.27414

American Institute of Physics. (2016). Earth Day. *Physics Today*. https://physicstoday.scitation.org/do/10.1063/PT.5.031205/full/

American Psychological Association. (2020). Group polarization. In *APA dictionary*. https://dictionary.apa.org/group-polarization

Ammar, S. E., Kenawy, M. A., Abdelrahman, H. A., Gad, A. M., & Hamed, A. F. (2012). Ecology of the mosquito larvae in urban environments of Cairo Governorate, Egypt. *Journal of the Egyptian Society of Parasitology*, *42*(1), 191–202. doi.org/10.12816/0006307

Anderson, T. R., Hawkins, E., & Jones, P. D. (2016). CO_2, the greenhouse effect and global warming: From the pioneering work of Arrhenius and Calendar to today's Earth System Models. *Endeavour*, *40*(3), 178–187. doi.org/10.1016/j.endeavour.2016.07.002

Beatley, T. (2009). *Planning for coastal resilience: Best practices for calamitous times*. Washington, DC: Island Press.

Ben-Eli, M. U. (2018). Sustainability: Definition and five core principles, a systems perspective. *Sustainability Science*, *13*(5), 1337–1343. doi.org/10.1007/s11625-018-0564-3

Blitzer, J. (2019, April 3). How climate change is fueling the US border crisis. *The New Yorker*. www.newyorker.com/news/dispatch/how-climate-change-is-fuelling-the-us-border-crisis

Bradley, G., & Reser, J. (2017). Adaptation processes in the context of climate change: A social and environmental psychology perspective. *Journal of Bioeconomics*, *19*(1), 29–51. doi.org/10.1007/s10818-016-9231-x

Braveman, P., & Gruskin, S. (2003). Defining equity in health. *Journal of Epidemiology & Community Health*, *57*(4), 254–258. doi.org/10.1136/jech.57.4.254

Bronfenbrenner, U. (1994). Ecological models of human development. *Readings on the Development of Children*, *2*(1), 37–43.

Cangialosi, J. P., Latto, A. S., & Berg, R. (2018). *National Hurricane Center tropical cyclone report: Hurricane Irma*. Washington, DC: National Hurricane Center. www.nhc.noaa.gov/data/tcr/AL112017_Irma.pdf

Carson, R. (1962). *Silent spring*. Boston: Houghton Mifflin.

Cavallo, E., Powell, A., & Becerra, O. (2010). Estimating the direct economic damages of the earthquake in Haiti. *The Economic Journal, 120*(546), 298–312. doi .org/10.1111/j.1468-0297.2010.02378.x

Clauss-Ehlers, C. S., Chiriboga, D. A., Hunter, S. J., Roysircar, G., & Tummala-Narra, P. (2019). APA Multicultural Guidelines executive summary: Ecological approach to context, identity, and intersectionality. *American Psychologist, 74*(2), 232–244. doi.org/10.1037/amp0000382

Clean Air Act. (1970). 42 USC §§ 7401 et seq.

Clean Water Act. (1972). 33 USC §1251 et seq.

Climate Central. (2012, June 23). *The heat is on: U.S. temperature trends.* www .climatecentral.org/news/the-heat-is-on/

Cole, L., & Foster, S. (2000). *From the ground up: Environmental racism and the rise of the environmental justice movement.* Albany, NY: New York University Press.

Davies, R. (2018, May 8). *Caribbean – 4 dead after floods and landslides hit Jamaica, Haiti and Dominican Republic.* Floodlist. http://floodlist.com/america/carib bean-floods-jamaica-haiti-dominican-republic-may-2018

Disaster Emergency Committee (n.d.). *Haiti earthquake facts and figures.* www.dec.org .uk/article/haiti-earthquake-facts-and-figures

Dunaway, F. (2008). Gas masks, pogo, and the ecological Indian: Earth Day and the visual politics of American environmentalism. *American Quarterly, 60*(1), 67–95. doi.org/10.1353/aq.2008.0008

Dunlap, R. E., & McCright, A. M. (2008). A widening gap: Republican and Democratic views on climate change. *Environment: Science and Policy for Sustainable Development, 50*(5), 26–35. doi.org/10.3200/ENVT.50.5.26-35

Endangered Species Act. (1973). 16 USC ch. 35 § 1531 et seq.

Farbotko, C., & Lazrus, H. (2012). The first climate refugees? Contesting global narratives of climate change in Tuvalu. *Global Environmental Change, 22* (2), 382–390. doi.org/10.1016/j.gloenvcha.2011.11.014

Federal Emergency Management Agency. (2017, September 22). *Historic disaster response to hurricane Harvey in Texas (HQ-17-133).* US Department of Homeland Security. www.fema.gov/news-release/2017/09/22/historic-disas ter-response-hurricane-harvey-texas

Feng, S., Krueger, A. B., & Oppenheimer, M. (2010). Linkages among climate change, crop yields and Mexico–US cross-border migration. *Proceedings of the National Academy of Sciences, 107*(32), 14257–14262. doi.org/10.1073/pnas.1002632107

Ferguson, M., & Branscombe, N. (2010). Collective guilt mediates the effect of beliefs about global warming on willingness to engage in mitigation behavior. *Journal of Environmental Psychology, 30*(2), 135–142. doi.org/10.1016/j .jenvp.2009.11.010

Fischer, A., Peters, V., Vávra, J., Neebe, M., & Megyesi, B. (2011). Energy use, climate change and folk psychology: Does sustainability have a chance? Results from a qualitative study in five European countries. *Global Environmental Change, 21*(3), 1025–1034. doi.org/10.1016/j.gloenvcha.2011.04.008

Flaherty, A. (2019, February 8). *Border arrests up 85 percent over same period last year: US Customs and Border Protection.* ABC News. https://abcnews.go.com/ Politics/border-arrests-85-percent-period-year-us-customs/story?id=60939312

Flora, J., Saphir, M., Lappé, M., et al. (2014). Evaluation of a national high school entertainment education program: The Alliance for Climate Education. *Climatic Change, 127*(3), 419–434. doi.org/10.1007/s10584-014-1274-

Foster, S., Leichenko, R., Nguyen, K., et al. (2019). New York City Panel on Climate Change 2019 report chapter 6: Community-based assessments of adaptation and equity. *Annals of the New York Academy of Sciences, 1439*(1), 126–173. doi.org/10.1111/nyas.14009

Freeman, A. M. (2002). Environmental policy since Earth Day I: What have we gained? *Journal of Economic Perspectives, 16*(1), 125–146. doi.org/10.1257/0895330027148

Fritsche, I., Cohrs, J. C., Kessler, T., & Bauer, J. (2012). Global warming is breeding social conflict: The subtle impact of climate change threat on authoritarian tendencies. *Journal of Environmental Psychology, 32*(1), 1–10. doi.org/10.1016/j.jenvp.2011.10.002

Funk, C., & Hefferon, M. (2019, November 25). U.S. public views on climate and energy. *Pew Research Center.* www.pewresearch.org/science/2019/11/25/u-s-public-views-on-climate-and-energy/

Gaard, G. (2011). Ecofeminism revisited: Rejecting essentialism and re-placing species in a material feminist environmentalism. *Feminist Formations, 23*(2), 26–53. doi.org/10.1353/ff.2011.0017

Gardiner, B. (2020, April 8). Pollution made COVID-19 worse. Now, lockdowns are clearing the air. *National Geographic.* www.nationalgeographic.com/science/2020/04/pollution-made-the-pandemic-worse-but-lockdowns-clean-the-sky/#close

Georgiou, A. (2020, March 24). Coronavirus is having a major impact on the environment, with reduced CO_2, better air quality, and animals roaming city streets. *Newsweek.* www.newsweek.com/coronavirus-major-impact-environment-co2-air-quality-animals-1493812

Giannakakis, A. E., & Fritsche, I. (2011). Social identities, group norms, and threat: On the malleability of ingroup bias. *Personality and Social Psychology Bulletin, 37*(1), 82–93. doi.org/10.1177/0146167210386120

Griffin, S. (1980). *Woman and nature: The roaring inside her.* New York: Harper & Row.

Hamilton, L.C. (2011). Education, politics and opinions about climate change evidence for interaction effects. *Climatic Change, 10*(4), 231–242. 10.1007/s10584-010-9957-8.

Henriques, M. (2020, March 27). *Will Covid-19 have a lasting impact on the environment?* BBC. www.bbc.com/future/article/20200326-covid-19-the-impact-of-coronavirus-on-the-environment

Holcombe, M., & O'Key, S. (2020, March 23). *Satellite images show less pollution over the US as coronavirus shuts down public places.* CNN. www.cnn.com/2020/03/23/health/us-pollution-satellite-coronavirus-scn-trnd/index.html

Hou, L., & Shi, P. (2011). Haiti 2010 earthquake: How to explain such huge losses? *International Journal of Disaster Risk Science, 2*(1), 25–33. doi.org/10.1007/s13753-011-0003-x

Hunter, P. R. (2003). Climate change and waterborne and vector-borne disease. *Journal of Applied Microbiology, 94*(1), 37–46. doi.org/10.1046/j.1365-2672.94.s1.5.x

Intergovernmental Panel on Climate Change. (2014). *Climate change 2014 synthesis report summary for policymakers (fifth assessment report)*. United Nations. www.ipcc.ch/site/assets/uploads/2018/02/AR5_SYR_FINAL_SPM.pdf

Janssen, M., Busch, C., Rodiger, M., & Hamm, U. (2016). Motives of consumers following a vegan diet and their attitudes towards animal agriculture. *Appetite, 105*(1), 643–651. doi.org/10.1016/j.appet.2016.06.039

Janvier, R. (2016, January 25). *Drought and climate change in Haiti*. Church World Service. https://cwsglobal.org/drought-and-climate-change-in-haiti/

Kahan, D. M., Peters, E., Wittlin, M., et al. (2012). The polarizing impact of science literacy and numeracy on perceived climate change risks. *Nature Climate Change, 2*(10), 732–735. doi.org/10.1038/nclimate1547

Kazour, F., Zahreddine, N. R., Maragel, M. G., et al. (2017). Post-traumatic stress disorder in a sample of Syrian refugees in Lebanon. *Comprehensive Psychiatry, 72*, 41–47. doi.org/10.1016/j.comppsych.2016.09.007

Kloos, B., Hill, J., Thomas, E., Wandersman, A., & Elias, M. J. (2012). *Community psychology: Linking individuals and communities* (3rd ed.). Belmont, CA: Wadsworth Cengage Learning.

Knutson, T. R., McBride, J. L., Chan, J., et al. (2010). Tropical cyclones and climate change. *Nature Geoscience, 3*(3), 157–163. doi.org/10.1038/ngeo779

Lange, P. A., Joireman, J., & Milinski, M. (2018). Climate change: What psychology can offer in terms of insights and solutions. *Current Directions in Psychological Science, 27*(4), 269–274. doi.org/10.1177/0963721417753945

Lowenthal, D. (1970). Earth Day. *Area, 2*(4), 1–10.

Martinelli, D., & Berkmanienė, A. (2018). The politics and the demographics of veganism: Notes for a critical analysis. *International Journal for the Semiotics of Law – Revue Internationale de Sémiotique Juridique, 31*(3), 501–530. doi.org/10.1007/s11196-018-9543-3

Masson, T., & Fritsche, I. (2014). Adherence to climate change-related ingroup norms: Do dimensions of group identification matter? Adherence to climate change-related ingroup norms. *European Journal of Social Psychology, 44*(5), 455–465. doi.org/10.1002/ejsp.2036

McNeill, J. R. (2001). *Something new under the sun: An environmental history of the twentieth-century world* (Global Century series). New York: W. W. Norton & Company.

Mildenberger, M., Marlon, J., Howe, P., & Leiserowitz, A. (2018). Correction to: The spatial distribution of Republican and Democratic climate opinions at state and local scales. *Climatic Change, 147*(1), 355–358. doi.org/10.1007/s10584-017-2128-4

Moore, N. (2020, April 6). In Chicago, COVID-19 is hitting the Black community hard. *National Public Radio.* www.npr.org/sections/coronavirus-live-updates/2020/04/06/828303894/in-chicago-covid-19-is-hitting-the-black-community-hard

Myers, N., & Kent, J. (1995). *Environmental exodus: An emergent crisis in the global arena*. Washington, DC: Climate Institute.

National Aeronautics and Space Administration. (2020, February). *Causes of climate change*. Global Climate Change: Vital Signs of the Planet. https://climate.nasa.gov/causes/

National Hurricane Center and Central Pacific Hurricane Center. (n.d.). *Glossary of NHC terms*. www.nhc.noaa.gov/aboutgloss.shtml

New, M., Liverman, D., Schroder, H., & Anderson, K. (2011). Four degrees and beyond: The potential for a global temperature increase of four degrees and its implications. *Philosophical Transactions of the Royal Society A, 369*(6), Article 19. doi.org/10.1098/rsta.2010.0303

Nicholls, R. J., Marinova, N., Lowe, J. A., et al. (2011). Sea-level rise and its possible impacts given a "beyond 4 C world" in the twenty-first century. *Philosophical Transactions of the Royal Society A: Mathematical, Physical and Engineering Sciences, 369*(1934), 161–181. doi.org/10.1098/rsta.2010.0291

Pan American Health Organization. (n.d.). *Haiti: Haiti's vulnerability to natural disasters*. www.paho.org/english/DD/PED/reginfohaiti.htm

Pearse, R. (2017). Gender and climate change. *Wiley Interdisciplinary Reviews: Climate Change, 8*(2), Article 451. doi.org/10.1002/wcc.451

Pielke Jr, R. A., Rubiera, J., Landsea, C., Fernández, M. L., & Klein, R. (2003). Hurricane vulnerability in Latin America and the Caribbean: Normalized damage and loss potentials. *Natural Hazards Review, 4*(3), 101–114. doi.org/10.1061/(ASCE)1527-6988(2003)4:3(101)

Plutzer, E., & Hannah, A. L. (2018). Teaching climate change in middle schools and high schools: Investigating STEM education's deficit model. *Climatic Change, 149*(3–4), 305–317. doi.org/10.1007/s10584-018-2253-8

Powless, B. (2012). An Indigenous movement to confront climate change. *Globalizations: Global Movement, 9*(3), 411–424. doi.org/10.1080/14747731.2012.680736

Rahmstorf, S. (2010). A new view on sea level rise. *Nature Reports Climate Change, 4*(4), 44–45. doi.org/10.1038/climate.2010.29

Rich, N. (2018, August 1). Losing earth: The decade we almost stopped climate change. *The New York Times*. www.nytimes.com/interactive/2018/08/01/magazine/climate-change-losing-earth.html

Roosvall, A., & Tegelberg, M. (2016). Natural ecology meets media ecology: Indigenous climate change activists' views on nature and media. In G. Heike (Ed.), *Environment in the age of the Internet* (pp. 75–104). Cambridge, UK: Open Book Publishers. doi.org/10.11647/OBP.0096.04

Schmidhuber, J., & Tubiello, F. N. (2007). Global food security under climate change. *Proceedings of the National Academy of Sciences, 104*(50), 19703–19708. doi.org/10.1073/pnas.0701976104

Selby, J., Dahi, O. S., Fröhlich, C., & Hulme, M. (2017). Climate change and the Syrian civil war revisited. *Political Geography, 60*, 232–244. doi.org/10.1016/j.polgeo.2017.05.007

Solomon, S., Qin, D., Manning, M., et al. (2007). *Climate change 2007: The physical science base*. Intergovernmental Panel on Climate Change. www.ipcc.ch/site/assets/uploads/2018/05/ar4_wg1_full_report-1.pdf

Spence, A., & Pidgeon, N. (2009). Psychology, climate change & sustainable bahaviour. *Environment: Science and Policy for Sustainable Development, 51*(6), 8–18. doi.org/10.1080/00139150903337217

Steg, L., & Vlek, C. (2009). Encouraging pro-environmental behaviour: An integrative review and research agenda. *Journal of Environmental Psychology, 29*, 309–317. doi.org/10.1016/j.jenvp.2008.10.004

The Climate Reality Project. (2018, July 30). *What is the greenhouse effect?* www.climaterealityproject.org/blog/what-greenhouse-effect

The Energy and Resources Institute. (2014). Earth Day: The history of a moment. *TerraGreen, 7*(2), 8–9.

The Vegan Society (2018). *Statistics.* www.vegansociety.com/news/media/statistics

Trenberth, K. E. (1999). Conceptual framework for changes of extremes of the hydrological cycle with climate change. *Climatic Change, 42*(1), 327–339. doi.org/10.1023/A:1005488920935

Union of Concerned Scientists. (2020, August 12). *Each country's share of CO_2 emissions.* www.ucsusa.org/global-warming/science-and-impacts/science/each-countrys-share-of-co2.html

United Nations Sustainable Development. (1992, June). *Agenda 21.* UN Conference on Environment and Development – Rio de Janeiro. https://sustainabledevelopment.un.org/content/documents/Agenda21.pdf

United Press International. (1988). *Area: 10,714 square miles Capital: Port-au-Prince History – Columbus landed...* www.upi.com/Archives/1988/06/20/Area-10714-square-milesCapital-Port-au-Prince-History-Columbus-landed/3133582782400/

United States Environmental Protection Agency. (1979, January). *On administration of the Marine Protection, Research, and Sanctuaries Act of 1972, as amended (P.L. 92-532) and implementing the international London dumping convention.* Washington, DC: US EPA. https://cfpub.epa.gov/si/si_public_record_Report.cfm?Lab=OWOW&dirEntryID=58602

United States Environmental Protection Agency. (2016, October). *Learn about sustainability.* www.epa.gov/sustainability/learn-about-sustainability#what

Valdez, R. X., Peterson, M. N., & Stevenson, K. T. (2018). How communication with teachers, family and friends contributes to predicting climate change behaviour among adolescents. *Environmental Conservation, 45*(2), 183–191. doi.org/10.1017/S0376892917000443

Van Lanen, H. A., Tallaksen, L., & Rees, G. (2007). *Droughts and climate change.* Commission of the European Communities. www.geo.uio.no/edc//downloads/droughts_and_climate_change_2007.pdf

Vermeer, M., & Rahmstorf, S. (2009). Global sea level linked to global temperature. *Proceedings of the National Academy of Sciences of the United States of America, 106*(51), 21527–21532. doi.org/10.1073/pnas.0907765106

Warren, K. B., & Jackson, J. E. (2003). *Indigenous movements, self-representation, and the state in Latin America.* Austin: University of Texas Press.

Webb, B., & Hayhoe, D. (2017). Assessing the influence of an educational presentation on climate change beliefs at an Evangelical Christian college. *Journal of Geoscience Education, 65*(3), 272–282. doi.org/10.5408/16-220.1

Wheeler, T., & von Braun, J. (2013). Climate change impacts on global food security. *Science, 341*(6145), 508–513. doi.org/10.1126/science.1239402

Willison, C., Singer, P., Creary, M., & Greer, S. (2019). Quantifying inequities in US federal response to hurricane disaster in Texas and Florida compared with

Puerto Rico. *BMJ Global Health*, *4*(1), e001191. doi.org/10.1136/bmjgh-2018-001191

Worldometer. (2021). *Haiti population (live)*. www.worldometers.info/world-population/haiti-population/

Wu, X. Nethery, R. C., Sabath, M. B., Braun, D., & Dominici, F. (2020). Exposure to air pollution and COVID-19 mortality in the United States. *Harvard T. H. Chan School of Public Health*. https://projects.iq.harvard.edu/files/covid-pm/files/pm_and_covid_mortality.pdf

Zaru, D. (2020, April 28). T.I. says coronavirus health disparities in black communities expose "systemic institutionalized racism." *ABC News*. https://abcnews.go.com/US/ti-coronavirus-health-disparities-black-communities-expose-systemic/story?id=70365101

22 Optimal Local Government and Public Service Provision

Joseph Drew

22.1 An Old, Old Problem

"One of the most enduring questions in the theory and practice of public administration" is the quest for "optimum organisational size for the delivery of public services" (Andrews & Boyne, 2009, p. 739). Indeed, Aristotle examined this problem in the fourth century BCE and one sometimes wonders whether we have really progressed much since this time (Dahl, 1990). For Aristotle (1992) the question of size was not one of merely the number of citizens contained within a given geographical boundary, but rather the "quality" of the citizens and the ability of the association (for him the state, for us in this present discussion the local government) to carry out the functions necessary for the citizens to be able to live the good life. Of course, Aristotle lived in very different conditions to those that prevail today and his discussion of the quality of citizens (that incidentally excluded foreigners, slaves, women, and children) – for example, having too many mechanics and not enough heavily armed soldiers – seems peculiar to modern-day readers. However, he was right in drawing attention to the fact that mere numbers of persons was an insufficient criterion; that the needs of citizens and their ability to contribute to the common good was of perhaps greater import (a fact lost on many modern scholars). Not unsurprisingly, Aristotle (1992) examined the two extremes of government size and advocated for the mean position (consistent with his golden mean philosophy). His objection to a small state was that it would not have sufficient resources and autonomy to carry out its functions.

On the other hand, a state that was too large was asserted to be too difficult to manage – the town criers would not be able to project their voice far enough (hardly a problem for us given amplifiers, television, and email) and people would not be able to really get to know one another well enough (which still seems to be a substantial limitation). Aristotle (1992) also fretted about the lack of transparency in a large government – in particular, he was worried about foreigners consuming public goods that they were not entitled to. The modern-day equivalent is the economic idea of free-riders who consume public goods and services to which they have not contributed adequately – a problem that still tends to disturb the carefully laid plans of modern local government boundary policy architects.

In more recent times, the political luminary Robert A. Dahl (1967, 1990) has also tackled the question of the optimal size of government (but with greater emphasis on its ability to satisfy democratic ideals, rather than merely satisfy the need for public goods and services). In similar vein to Aristotle, Dahl considers the two extremes of size (too small or too large) and uses this to advocate for city governments of between fifty thousand and two hundred thousand persons. Dahl's (1967) population floor is dictated by the need for government to be self-rule (the people have a meaningful voice in influencing policy and public services), as well as the need to also be able to act autonomously. He argues that many problems extend well beyond the boundaries of the village and thus require larger entities to manage effectively. For instance, effective management of river systems requires that a single body can act with a free hand (autonomy from other local governments and higher tiers of government) to manage both the catchments and the ultimate estuarine outflow.

Similarly, crime prevention requires a coordinated approach that covers an area large enough to contain most of the interactions of people as they go about their normal life activities – it is no good one village having a highly responsive police force if people regularly commute between it and its close neighbor where chaos reigns. On the other hand, Dahl shares Aristotle's concern that government that is too large might become too remote from its citizens and thus curtail any chance of the people having a direct say in the decisions made over critical elements of their lives. Dahl (1967, p. 960) summarizes his position in the declaration that "at one extreme [in large government] people vote but do not rule, at the other [small government] they rule but have nothing to rule over." Notably, Dahl places considerably less emphasis (than did Aristotle) on the type of person constituting governments and is generally representative of a more modern tendency to focus heavily on population size benchmarks rather than the needs and capacity of people.

Recent local government amalgamation debates[1] have tapped into many of the themes raised by Aristotle and Dahl respectively. For instance, it has been strongly argued that local government needs to be of adequate scale in order for it to have strength, capacity and autonomy for regional planning, legitimacy as a partner for higher tiers of government, ability to attract suitably qualified staff, and greater political competition (and hence a higher calibre of politician; Drew, 2018). Like I noted earlier, things really have not progressed an awful lot in more than 2,300 years.

---

[1] Local government amalgamation refers to the construction of a new local government entity from two or more extant local governments (or parts thereof). Generally, amalgamation is a politically divisive issue and often amalgamations can be forced, against the will of the local governments, through legislation by higher tiers of government. Proponents of amalgamation often point to potential improvements to efficiency and effectiveness. Opponents worry about loss of local identity, disenfranchisement, and loss of control relating to local planning. Readers are referred to Drew (2018) for a thorough account of contemporary amalgamation debates.

The problem with capacity arguments (that is, arguments that assert that a certain size is required to deal with widespread problems), of course, is that it is never possible to entirely eliminate spillover effects (gains or losses to persons outside of the local government boundaries as a result of actions executed by the local government in question) and hence guarantee autonomy. Indeed, it seems always possible to come up with a prima facie compelling example of a public good or service that is beyond the capacity of any government smaller than the entire planet earth (Dahl, 1990). For instance, defense can't be addressed by local government – which is why it is a function ordinarily assigned to nation states (Oates, 1999). But modern experience has also shown us that even a nation state has often insufficient capacity to be able to assure the protection of its citizens (hence military alliances such as NATO [North Atlantic Treaty Organization] and security organizations such as the United Nations).

Another example is environmental protection – climate change seems to require a coordinated global effort. But surely a local government the size of the globe (the size required to take autonomous action on climate change) would be too remote, and we certainly would not be able to have a direct say in the decisions about what sort of public environmental goods and services should be provided (and how this might be done). Otherwise stated, the functional scale and capacity argument of Aristotle (and later Dahl) is far from definitive – it is riddled with exceptions and does not provide a precise "scientific" optimal size for government. Surely, one might ask, given our "great" accomplishments in the last 2,300 years – for example, our ability to create weapons of mass destruction the likes of which the ancient Greeks could not have dreamt of – we should be able to employ a much more sophisticated approach to the question of the optimal size of government for the provision of public goods and services?

22.2 Solutions to the Problem of Optimal Government Size: Efficiency in Our Times

In the late eighteenth century the Scottish philosopher (and some would say the father of free market economic theory) Adam Smith published his seminal work *The Wealth of Nations* in which he describes, in some detail (among many other matters), the benefits of specialization in production of goods. To be specific, Smith (2014, p. 5) takes a "trifling manufacture" of haberdashery pins to illustrate his point that having a number of workers specializing in just one or two of the multitude of tasks apparently required to produce a haberdashery pin was eminently more efficient than having just one person create the entire pin. Indeed, Smith (2014, pp. 5–6) claims that where one man could ordinarily "have made twenty, perhaps not one pin in a day" ten men specializing in different parts of the production could make "a tenth part of 48,000 pins" or 4,800 per person. I suspect that Smith might have gotten a little carried away in his enthusiasm for the modern marvel of specialization (although without having ever sat down to make a haberdashery pin I am reticent to accuse Smith of deliberate misrepresentation), but certainly the idea that "economies of scale" (derived principally from specialization) could be harnessed for more efficient production functions is now staple fare for any secondary school economics student and a treasured concept in the study of public administration (Schachter, 2007).

Indeed, there is probably no more pervasive notion, when it comes to reform of local government with the aim of optimizing size for the most efficient production of public goods and services, than economies of scale. To be precise, economies of scale refers to the neoclassical economic concept whereby it is expected that the average total costs of some production functions will initially decrease as output expands. Where economies of scale do occur, the typical pattern is that they become exhausted at some stage, after which point an extensive domain of constant returns to scale dominate. If production is expanded beyond this domain, then diseconomies of scale (increased average total costs) might be expected to emerge (for a detailed discussion of economies and diseconomies of scale in local government production see Grant & Drew, 2017). The initial savings associated with some production functions are said to arise mainly as a result of increased opportunities for specialization, but also better use of excess capacity in capital equipment, and greater buying power. Diseconomies of scale emerge generally as a result of lower levels of transparency (recall Aristotle feared this), which makes it difficult to identify poorly performing staff and staff taking unwarranted perquisites, as well as difficulty coordinating large numbers of staff. Figure 22.1 plots the association between average total costs and output size expected for some functions.

No doubt our astute readers have noticed my somewhat labored use of the qualifying term "some" when describing local government production functions. This is because not all local government functions exhibit evidence consistent with economies of scale. For instance, in a thorough review of the eleven functions performed by local government in New South Wales, Australia, just four functions were found to exhibit evidence consistent with theory, and then economies of scale were typically exhausted at relatively low scales (Fahey, Drew, & Dollery, 2016). This is not entirely unexpected because public goods and services are far from the "trifling manufacture" that Adam Smith (2014, p. 5) considers – that is, it is often impossible to introduce a high degree of specialization when performing local government services. To take an admittedly extreme example, I am sure you would be unimpressed to find that the local government nuisance animal catching service involved one person to drive the car, another to catch large dogs, a different person to catch small dogs, yet another to catch cats, another to fill in the paperwork, another to load the animal into the car...

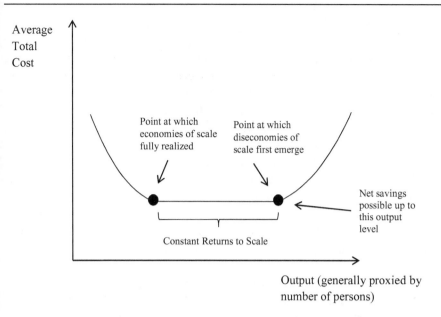

Average
Total
Cost

Point at which
economies of scale
fully realized

Point at which
diseconomies of
scale first emerge

Net savings
possible up to
this output
level

Constant Returns to Scale

Output (generally proxied by
number of persons)

Figure 22.1 *Economies of scale in public goods and services production*

Moreover, local governments don't produce haberdashery pins (well mine, in Tamworth, Australia, doesn't anyhow), but rather a considerably more diversified and complex basket of public goods and services that, in theory at least, are tailored to the needs of the citizen (Grant & Drew, 2017). Introducing people and their complex needs into the optimal public service provision equation considerably complicates matters. For example, not all people derive the same utility from any given public good (yet economists must assume this is the case), and complex goods and services may be difficult to measure or not responsive to economies of scale. In addition, how one defines the outputs of a local government production function can significantly alter one's assessment of whether a production function is evaluated as being efficient or not (Schachter, 2007). For instance, harking back to Adam Smith's example I am reasonably certain that I could make more than twenty haberdashery pins a day, but I am equally certain that any of our readers who use pins for clothing alterations and the like would be appalled at the quality of the pins I would produce. Thus, it can be seen that if one includes a desired quality in production equations then the assessment of efficiency can change markedly. In addition, the purpose of the production process might significantly affect our appraisal of its "efficiency" – for instance, if the pin was produced by a sheltered workshop which as a "by-product" also produced self-esteem and essential life skills, then the quantity (or indeed the quality) of the pins produced might be of relatively less importance.

Returning to the specific challenges faced in providing public goods and services for local government it is also apparent that the context for how we specify the output also radically alters our evaluation of the efficiency of a public good or service. For example, in the case of local government response to natural disasters pecuniary considerations are likely to only factor in marginally (if at all) – responding to a flood or bushfire will undoubtedly require extra staff resources and long hours (and concomitant high overtime charges), paying top dollar to have supplies provided as quickly as possible, and other nonbudgeted expenses. But would anyone seriously suggest that a local government should slow down its response in order to seek out the cheapest provider of supplies or minimize overtime expenses? Clearly in situations such as this other values take precedence over technical efficiency (which economists define as the optimal conversion of inputs [staff and money] into outputs [generally proxies for the quantity (notably not quality) of local government goods and services produced]) – in this particular case "effectiveness" and "timely response to need" seems to trump pecuniary considerations hands down. Indeed, running elections and paying elected representatives a stipend is prima facie terribly inefficient (for instance, compulsory sortition would be much cheaper), unless one values democracy. Other values that are held as closely, if not more closely than pecuniary efficiency, include due process (calling and responding to tenders, for example, adds additional expense that would be frowned upon by anybody concerned entirely with maximizing the input–output criterion), transparency (publishing and compiling statistics, annual reports, and financial statements is only "efficient" if we value open government), redistribution initiatives and needs-based funding (which can only be justified if we are concerned with equity) (see Goodin & Wilenski, 1984).

Indeed, if one pauses and interrogates the efficiency rhetoric that often accompanies local government reforms aimed at optimizing the size of local government for efficient service provision one is immediately struck by the fact that efficiency is generally presented in purely pecuniary terms and merely assumed (rather than argued) to be ipso facto good (Drew, Razin, & Andrews, 2018b). However, as we have noted, efficiency defined in this way ignores many of the values that citizens hold most dear (such as democracy and effectiveness). It also fails to highlight that pecuniary efficiency is no more than a means to satisfying other wants. So, if money is saved – for example by amalgamating local governments, thus potentially reaping economies of scale in public service provision – then inevitably the rhetoric paints a picture of lower local government taxation or new/additional local government infrastructure or services.

Otherwise stated, some wants (more effective democratic participation through smaller government, or the wants of the local government staff whose jobs are sacrificed in the pursuit of economies of scale) are traded in for other wants (lower taxation, new services, or new infrastructure). When analyzed in these terms – that is, efficiency as merely a means to satisfying wants – there is nothing particularly ipso facto good about pecuniary efficiency at all. It is hard to see how or why the pursuit of some wants should be preferenced over other wants. Moreover, the whole preoccupation with pecuniary efficiency in public service provision seems to lose sight of the very reason that people come together to form government in the first place.

22.3 Optimizing Local Government Service Delivery for Human Dignity and the Common Good

The Principle of Subsidiarity has its roots in the Natural Law philosophical tradition (which harks back to at least Aristotle), which asserts that right behavior can be discerned from the observation of the nature of things as well as the use of practical reason (Finnis, 2013).[2] At the heart of the philosophy is the person (Natural Law philosophers are careful to never refer to individuals in view of the fact that the fourth "good" of Thomas Aquinas was the natural inclination to live in community), who it is argued is a creature uniquely able to perceive and pursue its existential ends ("the perfection of man's [sic] being"; Messner, 1952, p. 20). According to the Principle of Subsidiarity, this ability to put aside mere reaction and animal instinct sets the person apart from the rest of creation (that is, nature). Further, the Principle of Subsidiarity asserts an ontology (a set of given concepts that might be said to truly exist) of plural social forms (that is, many different types of "societies," of which the most foundational is the family), which it is argued is necessary for the person to flourish (achieve their existential ends). This acknowledgment of the need for plural associations sets up a tension between human dignity (the right of the person to pursue their existential ends) and the common good (the help accruing to persons as a result of their cooperation) (Drew & Grant, 2017).

Subsidiarity resolves this tension (between the right of a person to pursue their existential ends and the need to draw from and contribute to the common good), by both prohibiting larger associations from subsuming the legitimate remit of persons and persons in lesser association, and also by establishing a positive obligation for the greater association to provide help in the case of bona fide need (according to strict conditions that we relate below). Under this conception of local government the concerns regarding capacity, size, or pecuniary efficiency take a back seat to ensuring that the services provided by local government do not impinge on the dignity of persons and lesser associations. Otherwise stated, the institution of local government ceases to

---

[2] There are also a number of strands of Natural Law philosophy that have been adapted to the three monotheistic faiths. In these instances, the ordinance of G-d is also invoked as a way to discern good conduct (see Emon, Levering, & Novak, 2014).

be the focus and is replaced instead by a preoccupation with the need and capacity of the person.

The two overriding criteria for the legitimate provision of public services in response to need, according to the Principle, is that said services must (1) lie within the proper mandate of the association (in our case local government) and (2) be delivered in a manner consistent with the concept of *subsidium* (defined as help delivered for bona fide need in a manner designed to make it superfluous as quickly as possible; Messner, 1952). The proper mandate of government, according to the Natural Law tradition, is the provision of goods and services that cannot be provided by the person themselves or persons in lesser (smaller) associations – this would include many (but by no means all) public goods and services but is unlikely to ever include private goods and services (which are sometimes produced by local governments). Economists define public goods and services as items that are both nonexcludable (persons cannot be prevented somehow from availing themselves of the goods) and nonrival (one person's consumption does not have a material effect of the ability of others to consume) (Grant & Drew, 2017).

Private goods, on the other hand, are both excludable and rival in consumption. The Principle of Subsidiarity states that it is an "injustice ... grave wrong ... and a disturbance of right order" for government to subsume the function of providing goods and services that the person or a lesser association is capable of producing for themselves (Pius XI, 1931, paragraph 80). Indeed, doing so is compared to the theft of a person's property by the State. It is argued that exceeding government's mandate fosters a state of dependency (at odds with the core concern for human dignity), reduces moral proximity (moral accountability between donors and recipients is difficult to establish in larger associations), threatens to undermine critical mediating structures (such as the family, required to reduce alienation, provide meaning, and transmit values), threatens the financial sustainability of government (which could be "overwhelmed and crushed by infinite tasks and duties" [Pius XI, 1931, paragraph 78]), and reduces the capacity for spontaneous reaction to need and opportunity (the wheels of government are said to turn slowly) (Drew & Grant, 2017). Of particular importance is the idea of the collaborative good that is the side effect of production by smaller associations that establishes "a principled limit to the power of the State as well as to the subcontracting (or 'outsourcing') mentality characteristic of markets" (Hittinger, 2003, p. 280).

Even if the good or service falls within the legitimate mandate of local government, the Principle insists that another criteria must be met – the good or service must be delivered in a manner consistent with the concept of *subsidium*. The etymology of the term is instructive – it is a term used to describe Roman auxiliary troops that were held in reserve during major battles so that they could be deployed to address weaknesses that might develop in the battle line. These reserve units would be deployed as a temporary measure to address critical need, with a view to withdrawal as soon as possible so that they would also be available for future needs that might emerge. The Principle of Subsidiarity views help afforded to lesser associations in similar terms – that it should be deployed for critical bona fide need, but with a view to making it superfluous as quickly as possible both so that the resources can be redeployed if necessary but also to ensure that the help does not foster a state of dependency (which erodes human dignity; Messner, 1952).

Not all public goods provided by local government represent a response to critical need. For instance, the local government area in which I reside has just announced plans to build a skate park costing A$1.7 million, to replace the existing one across the road from the proposed site (Craig, 2018). To put this announcement in perspective this rural local government area of sixty-one thousand residents is not able to afford sealed roads, potable water supply, sewer services, and rubbish removal for its residents who live outside the main town area. Moreover, by its own reckoning in the audited financial statements the quantum required to bring its assets up to a merely satisfactory standard is A$7.8 million (Tamworth Regional Council, 2018). It is therefore hard to argue that an A$1.7 million skate park is a bona fide need – a want certainly (moreover a want accessible to a very small part of the population in a local government area spanning 988,435 hectares), but *not* a need. Because of the likelihood of political capitalization (the tendency of democratically elected representatives to seek to provide concentrated benefits for defined groups of voters in order to enhance their chances at future elections), local governments often respond to "wants" instead of "needs" (Buchanan, 2000). Doing so creates a taxation obligation on the majority for the benefit of the minority, which is difficult to defend on moral grounds – certainly for discretionary public goods when considered through the lens of the Principle of Subsidiarity (Sirico, 1997).

Sometimes a naive (thin ontological) interpretation of Subsidiarity is made that merely asserts that services should be provided by the lowest tier of government that has the capacity to do so. This trickling down of authority approach totally ignores the important principles of legitimate mandate and *subsidium* for bona fide need, and hence is not a true reflection of Subsidiarity because it does little to strike the balance between human dignity and the common good (for a commonly cited thin ontological interpretation see Oates, 1999). The Principle is also often invoked by those seeking to avoid local government amalgamation as a supposed moral constraint on higher tiers forcing consolidations – but this similarly is a poor reflection of Subsidiarity, denuded of its Natural Law foundations (Golemboski, 2015). In truth, Subsidiarity imposes a negative obligation on subsuming the legitimate function of persons and persons in association that goes far beyond refereeing turf wars between the various tiers of government.

The Principle also imposes positive obligations on greater associations (in our case local government) that are often neglected by scholars. Subsidiarity is not about local government vacating important functions and thereby leaving its citizens without the help that they need to pursue their existential ends. Instead, the Principle imposes a duty on government to help, encourage, and even establish lesser associations where a task is more appropriately located with said lesser association (Messner, 1952). So, in the case of our cited examples, local government might provide help and support for skateboard enthusiast groups and assist them in achieving their ends (instead of merely subsuming these duties). Action of this type is dignity-enhancing and community-building (and probably even more difficult than a local government simply taking over the role) and thus promises to produce sustainable public services in the most optimal manner for persons to achieve fulfillment of their ends.

Otherwise stated, a Subsidiarity approach to optimizing the role of local government for the provision of public services brings the needs and capacity of persons and persons in association to the fore and thus offers a refreshing alternative to the dominant approaches of population size targets or pecuniary efficiency equations.

22.4 How Local Government Is Upsized or Downsized and the Effect of Doing So on Public Services

Public policy architects that believe population is an appropriate (and indeed the principal) criteria for optimizing local government service delivery may be keen to manipulate boundaries to engineer whatever target size they believe to be ideal. In Australia, public policy architects clearly hold strongly to the population size argument as evidenced by mass forced amalgamation programs that occur every few years in the country (Grant & Drew, 2017). Indeed, the number of local governments in Australia has fallen from 1,067 in 1910 to just 538 in 2018 and the average size of Australian local government (46,280 persons; Australian Bureau of Statistics, 2018) is more than four times the Organisation for Economic Co-operation and Development (OECD) average (9,693), and more than seven times the European average (5,887) (OECD, 2018). Australia has also suffered a number of deamalgamations (reversing earlier amalgamations) including one in Victoria (Delatite Shire deamalgamated in 2002) and four in Queensland in 2014 (Cairns, Rockhampton, Sunshine Coast, and Tablelands). In fact, Australia may cement its position as the deamalgamation capital of the world after the New South Wales (NSW) state political opposition pledged to allow reversals of a recent controversial mass forced amalgamation program, should they win government in the future.

We first take a brief look at the rhetoric, stated objectives and unintended consequences arising from Australia's most recent forced amalgamation program (in NSW in 2016) before briefly considering the difficulties, opportunities, and outcomes of pursuing deamalgamations (with reference to the former Delatite Shire, in rural Victoria, Australia, because it provides us with a unique record of the implications for citizens living in the area).

22.4.1 Amalgamations Down Under

The most recent forced amalgamation program[3] in Australia occurred in NSW in 2016 after a tortuous four-year consultation process. Originally conceived as an evidence-based and voluntary inquiry to enhance the "ability [of local government] to support the current and future needs of local communities," it morphed over time into a forced amalgamation program (Independent Local Government Review Panel [ILGRP], 2013, p. 9). In the final analysis NSW local governments were reduced from 152 down to just 128, although many more amalgamations were initially planned (but were abandoned after legal contest, and heavy political casualties – loss of bi-elections, and the resignation of the premier and deputy premier; see Drew et al., 2018b).

The stated justification for the forced amalgamations was "to ensure that ratepayers get value for money and the services and infrastructure they *deserve*" (emphasis added to highlight the justification according to entitlement arguments rather than need; Baird, 2015). The argument employed by amalgamation proponents was that bigger councils would capture economies of scale and that the resultant pecuniary efficiency would put downward pressure on local government taxation and be used to provide more and better quality services (Grant & Drew, 2017). Indeed, the ILGRP (2013) that first raised the specter of amalgamations was devoted to population targets and asserted that the "great majority of [rural] councils should have populations close to or greater than 10,000" (p. 111) and that most of the Sydney local governments should be amalgamated with a view to creating "a local government of considerably greater stature and capacity ... its population would reach about 670,000 by 2031" (p. 100). Notably, the claims of the public policy architects were not supported by empirical evidence, failed to even acknowledge the possibility of diseconomies of scale, and entirely neglected the fact that various local governments operated in widely disparate contexts (thus suggesting that rule of thumb population targets were inappropriate). Despite these problems, both pecuniary efficiency and population size arguments were prominent in the rhetoric of this amalgamation program – like we have noted a few times now, not much has changed over the centuries.

What was largely absent from the amalgamation debate, however, were the needs of the person and person in association. There is a human cost to

---

[3] When a number of amalgamations are pursued at once, it is referred to as an amalgamation program. Generally, massed forced amalgamations have been pursued in Australia, rather than isolated single cases. Presumably this is administratively convenient and may also be intended to ensure political pain is not drawn out over an extended period through a series of divisive amalgamations.

amalgamation that is for the most part neglected by public policy architects, but nevertheless has weighty implications for people's lives and the ethical conduct of government. For instance, the pecuniary efficiencies arising from amalgamations mostly come about as a result of eliminating duplication – which is a nice way of saying that senior staff and political representatives will lose their jobs the moment that the governor's proclamation is read (this often happens mid-term and with little warning, as was the case in NSW; Drew, Grant, & Fisher, 2017). It is also the case that the act of amalgamating local governments almost always involves transfers of wealth between citizens of the consolidated entities. This occurs because the new entity arising from the amalgamation inherits the debts of the constituent local governments. So for instance if two councils of similar size are merged where one local government has no net debt but the other carries a net debt of say A$200 million, then the residents of the former local government will effectively have A$100 million of debt transferred to them (that must ultimately be repaid through local government taxation). The contention that persons should have substantial debt transferred to them, without having had a say in the matter and often for public services that have already been fully consumed by their neighbors, is not morally licit (Drew et al., 2017). In addition, amalgamation effectively dilutes the voice of the citizen (one vote has even less value), and reduces the capacity for citizens to truly know each other and have sufficient moral proximity required for transparency between donors and recipients of the common good (Dahl, 1967; Messner, 1952).

However, amalgamation is not all bad news. There is the potential for amalgamation to enhance regional equity given that service levels are often harmonized following consolidation (Kwon & Feiock, 2010). This generally means that citizens from constituent local governments who had lower levels of services than their neighbors typically have services upgraded following amalgamation (it would seem a bold political move to reduce services down to the lowest standard of constituent councils). Of course, this is only good news for the citizens who hark from the relatively poorer serviced local government area, and it might also be noted that the harmonized service levels have to be paid for (generally through higher local government taxation).

The human cost of local government amalgamation, along with the sense of being deprived of meaningful voice in what is meant to be self-rule, results in amalgamations being hotly contested in Australia. Moreover, resentment at having a "solution" to the problem of sustainable local government *imposed* on citizens tends to lead to sustained political activism and in some instances deamalgamation.

22.4.2 Deamalgamation

It is not surprising that state political opposition parties will often pledge to allow deamalgamations should they be successful at the next election (the only surprise to my mind is that this pledge is not made more frequently). Essentially this is a way for political opposition parties to accrue significant political capital at no cost to themselves (the convention in Australia is that the local government seeking to break away from amalgamation bears the entire cost of doing so; Grant & Drew, 2017). However, actually delivering on the promise is often much harder than it seems.

The most imposing problem faced by communities (apart from the cost of deamalgamation itself that often runs to upwards of A$10 million) is how to untangle the combined assets and liabilities of the consolidated local government. How these spoils of victory are divided essentially dictates which community (the breakaway local government or the residual entity) will prosper (Drew & Dollery, 2014). The second big problem faced by those seeking to extricate themselves from earlier amalgamations is what to do about the standard of public services for the new entity – if services were harmonized upward following amalgamation then failure to renegotiate service standards with the community will mean that the old business model (levels of taxation and fees) may no longer prove financially viable. Indeed, case studies have shown that breakaway local governments that concentrate on eliminating discretionary public services and reducing service standards to base levels have experienced extraordinary success (Drew & Dollery, 2015).

22.5 Case Study of the Australian Mansfield Shire

One such case was the creation of Mansfield Shire following the deamalgamation of Delatite Shire in 2002. A forensic case study by Drew and Dollery (2015) showed that the breakaway council's strategy of reducing service levels to base standard, coupled with its good fortune in not being allocated fixed assets (that required considerable maintenance) or artwork (that was written down substantially in sequent financial periods) contributed to its fiscal success. Moreover, the breakaway council experienced extraordinary success in terms of citizen satisfaction. Victoria is one of the few jurisdictions in Australia where consistent and robust citizen satisfaction surveys have been conducted annually over an extended period and the deamalgamation of Delatite in Victoria therefore presents an ideal opportunity to glean some understanding of the effect of boundary change on citizens.

Table 22.1 reproduces data from Drew, Dollery, and Kortt (2014) that demonstrates that satisfaction increased substantially in the breakaway local government following deamalgamation despite the significant reduction in service levels that we noted earlier. In the residual Benalla Shire (where service levels were not altered) satisfaction also increased, but not to quite the same extent. What is particularly interesting here is that the higher satisfaction persisted for at least three years after the deamalgamation. One explanation for this data is that people were expressing satisfaction with a smaller-sized

Table 22.1 *Overall satisfaction (%) following deamalgamation of Delatite Shire*

Local Government	2001	2002	2003	2004	2005
Delatite	55	58			
Benalla (after deamalgamation)			62	64	60
Mansfield (after deamalgamation)			66	71	65
Mean satisfaction all local governments	65	65	65	65	65

Source: Drew et al. (2014)

local government. However, the fact that the council that stripped service levels down to the bare necessities experienced a more significant improvement in overall satisfaction seems to hint that providing common good support for only bona fide need, as prescribed by the Principle of Subsidiarity, may also sit well with the average citizen within this context.

Of course, this is far from definitive, but it is the best indication we have at present that what we hear when we talk to residents (that they want local governments to concentrate on delivering core services at low cost to the local taxpayer) may actually be the case. I am constantly bemused by the claim one often hears from political representatives and their peak bodies, that local governments are under fiscal stress as a result of responding to acute resident need – because I am yet to meet anyone who *needs* (for example) a A$1.7 million skate park. I am sure there are people who *want* a skate park – however, I believe them to be in the absolute minority (and the Principle of Subsidiarity tells us clearly that imposing on others to pursue *wants* is not only contrary to Natural Law principles of distributive justice but also denies lesser associations the opportunity to pursue their ends). No doubt we will gain further insights after what appears to be a high likelihood of more deamalgamations in NSW in the future. Unfortunately, deamalgamation has attracted far less scholarly attention than amalgamation, but given the cost of unscrambling the egg (and the sheer economic vandalism of spending upwards of A$20 million to amalgamate only to return to the preamalgamation position a few years later) it is certainly an area worthy of future analysis.

22.6 Conclusion: A Better Way?

Population size approaches – upsizing or downsizing – to optimizing local government public service delivery are mostly likely to end in abject failure because they perceive individuals as merely proxies for output, rather than as persons who have needs and capacities to draw from, or contribute to, the common good. Approaches such as these – typically advocated by those still caught up in the postprogressive-era fixation on pecuniary efficiency (that is, those who believe economic efficiency can be an overriding goal of government) but also, to a lesser degree, population benchmark proponents (such as Dahl) – merely paper over the cracks in the financial sustainability of public service provision for a limited time, and entirely neglect whether or not the foundation of local government is stable. Otherwise stated, marginal reductions to unit cost that *might* be able to be made by changes to the population size of local government are likely to pale into insignificance when set against the cost (both pecuniary and social) of providing public services that do not respect the dignity of donors or recipients of the common good.

Moreover, if extant local government size is not considered sufficient for autonomous and competent service provision in specific functions, then cooperation with neighboring local governments may well prove a more efficacious approach. This is particularly clear when one acknowledges both that different local government functions are associated with different optimal scales, and that in most jurisdictions local government population size is constantly evolving through internal and external migration as well as organic growth. Otherwise stated, boundaries engineered to optimize scale now may well prove redundant after only a few years as a result of population growth. By way of contrast, local governments banding together to help one another to achieve their ends (broadly consistent with the Principle of Subsidiarity) is a much more flexible arrangement that can be tailored to specific functions, capabilities, needs, and dynamic changes in circumstances (see Drew, McQuestin, & Dollery, 2018a).

However, a local government-centric application of the Principle – despite being a great advancement on the blunt public policy tool of amalgamation and deamalgamation – will not support the full realization of balancing human dignity and the common good. This can only be achieved by carefully examining, and relaying if necessary, the foundations of local government. Only when one returns to consider the fundamental questions regarding why persons and persons in association come together to form associations in the first place does one begin to understand the ultimate deleterious effect (to both donors and recipients) of governments overstepping their mandate, as well as the propensity of local government to become "overwhelmed and crushed by infinite tasks and duties" (Pius XI, 1931, paragraph 78) if they do so – as occurred in 2013 at Detroit, Michigan in the United States of America (which was the largest municipal bankruptcy in history; Murphy, 2018) and Central Darling Shire (NSW in remote Australia, which was Australia's first case of government financial failure in 2013; Grant & Drew, 2017) and countless other jurisdictions around the world where local governments have slept-walked into financial failure.

Over the course of this chapter we have done quite a bit of nonlinear time travel: We started with Aristotle, then went through the postprogressive scientific approach to maximizing technical efficiency and then back to the late nineteenth-century Principle of Subsidiarity that can be said to have some origins in Aristotle's Natural Law. Unfortunately, our public policy architects seem to be stuck firmly in the population size and technical efficiency paradigms and fixated on government and government size rather than the needs of persons and persons in association. I believe that a focus on persons and persons in association is the best path forward for stronger communities, and more sustainable public services that are delivered in response to bona fide need and in an equitable manner. One hopes that scholars will not find themselves despairing of the fact that my arguments have not been progressed in another 2,300 years' time – but sadly I suspect this will be the case.

References

Andrews, R., & Boyne, G. (2009). Size structure and administrative overheads: An empirical analysis of English local authorities. *Urban Studies, 46*(4), 739–759. doi.org/10.1177%2F0042098009102127

Aristotle. (1992). *The politics.* New York: Penguin Classics.

Australian Bureau of Statistics. (2018). *National regional profile.* Canberra, Australia: ABS. http://stat.abs.gov.au/itt/r.jsp?databyregion#/

Baird, M. (2015). *Fit for the future: $2 billion community windfall by merging unfit councils* [Press Release]. www.olg.nsw.gov.au/news/ministerial-media-release-fit-future-2-billion-community-windfall-merging-unfit-councils

Buchanan, J. (2000). *The limits of liberty: Between anarchy and Leviathan.* Indianapolis, IN: Liberty Fund.

Craig, H. (2018, March 9). Tamworth's Viaduct Park to be home to new $1.7m skatepark. *The Northern Daily Leader.* www.northerndailyleader.com.au/story/5274373/skate-city-17m-new-skatepark-near-tamworth-cbd-video/

Dahl, R. (1967). The city in the future of democracy. *American Political Science Review, 61*(4), 953–970. doi.org/10.2307/1953398

Dahl, R. (1990). *After the revolution?* London, UK: Yale University Press.

Drew, J. (2018). How losers can turn into winners in disputatious public policy: A heuristic for prospective herestheticians. *Australian Journal of Political Science, 54*(1), 1–16. doi.org/10.1080/10361146.2018.1520195

Drew, J., & Dollery, B. (2014). Separation anxiety: An empirical evaluation of the Sunshine Coast regional council de-amalgamation. *Public Money & Management, 34*(3), 213–220. doi.org/10.1080/09540962.2014.908032

Drew, J., & Dollery, B. (2015). Breaking up is hard to do: The de-amalgamation of Delatite Shire. *Public Finance and Management, 15*(1), 1–23.

Drew, J., Dollery, B., & Kortt, M. (2014). Can't get no satisfaction. *Australian Journal of Public Administration, 75*(1), 65–77. doi.org/10.1111/1467-8500.12117

Drew, J., & Grant, B. (2017). Subsidiarity: More than a principle of decentralisation – a view from local government. *Publius, 47*(4), 522–545. doi.org/10.1093/publius/pjx039

Drew, J., Grant, B., & Fisher, J. (2017). Re-evaluating local government amalgamations: Utility maximisation meets the principle of double effect. *Policy & Politics, 45*(3), 379–394. doi.org/10.1332/030557316X14539914690045

Drew, J., McQuestin, D., & Dollery, B. (2018a). Good to share? The pecuniary implications of moving to shared service production for local government services. *Public Administration, 97*(1), 1–15. doi.org/ 10.1111/padm.12575

Drew, J., Razin, E., & Andrews, R. (2018b). Rhetoric in municipal amalgamations: A comparative analysis. *Local Government Studies, 45*(5), 1–20. doi.org/10 .1080/03003930.2018.1530657

Emon, Q., Levering, M., & Novak, D. (2014). *Natural law: A Jewish, Christian and Islamic trialogue.* Oxford, UK: Oxford University Press.

Fahey, G., Drew, J., & Dollery, B. (2016). Merger myths: A functional analysis of economies of scale in New South Wales municipalities. *Public Finance and Management, 16*(4), 362–382.

Finnis, J. (2013). *Human rights and common good.* Oxford, UK: Oxford University Press.

Golemboski, D. (2015). Federalism and the Catholic principle of subsidiarity. *Publius, 45*(4), 526–551. doi.org/10.1093/publius/pjv005

Goodin, R., & Wilenski, P. (1984). Beyond efficiency: The logical underpinnings of administrative principles. *Public Administration Review, 44*(6), 512–517. doi .org/10.2307/3110413

Grant, B., & Drew, J. (2017). *Local government in Australia: History, theory and public policy.* Singapore: Springer Palgrave.

Hittinger, R. (2003). *The first grace: Rediscovering the natural law in a post-Christian world.* Wilmington, DE: ISI Books.

Independent Local Government Review Panel. (2013, October). *Revitalising local government.* Final report. Sydney, Australia: ILGRP. www.localgovernmentreview .nsw.gov.au/documents/LGR/Revitalising%20Local%20Government%20-% 20ILGRP%20Final%20Report%20-%20October%202013.pdf

Kwon, S., & Feiock, R. (2010). Overcoming barriers to cooperation: Intergovernmental service agreements. *Public Administration Review, 70*(6), 876–884. doi.org/10.1111/j.1540-6210.2010.02219.x

Messner, J. (1952). *Social ethics: Natural law in the modern world* (J. Doherty, Trans.). St. Louis, MO: Herder Book Co.

Murphy, A. (2018). Bond pricing in the biggest city bankruptcy in history: The effects of state emergency management laws on default risk. *International Review of Law and Economics, 54*, 106–117. doi.org/10.1016/j.irle.2017.12.001

Oates, W. (1999). An essay on fiscal federalism. *Journal of Economic Literature, 37*(3), 1120–1149. doi.org/10.1257/jel.37.3.1120

Organisation for Economic Co-operation and Development. (2018). *Subnational governments in OECD countries: Key data.* Paris: OECD.

Pius XI. (1931). *Quadragesimo anno.* Vatican City: The Holy See.

Schachter, H. (2007). Does Frederick Taylor's ghost still haunt the halls of government? A look at the concept of government efficiency in our time. *Public Administration Review, 67*(5), 800–810. doi.org/10.1111/j.1540-6210.2007 .00768.x

Sirico, R. (1997). Subsidiarity, society and entitlements: Understanding and application. *Notre Dame Journal of Law, Ethics & Public Policy, 11*, 549–579.

Smith, A. (2014). *The wealth of nations.* Middletown, DE: Shine Classics.

Tamworth Regional Council. (2018). *Audited financial statements 2017–18.* Tamworth, Australia: Tamworth Regional Council.

23 A Public Health Approach to Delinquency and Incarceration

A Case Study

Elizabeth Jensen, Kimberly Fazio-Ruggiero, and David Belsham

23.1 Introduction

Utilizing the lens of a public health approach delves into examining the situation from a societal level and establishes measures for how the overall health of the public can be improved with respect to the delinquency rates in a population. This methodology is hinged upon accurate problem recognition, assessment of risk and protective factors, and the implementation of evidence-based prevention strategies at the individual and systemic level. Applying this lens to incarceration in the criminal justice system provides new insight to a system originally designed to solely protect society by removing and separating those people who imposed a threat to the public (Claborn & McCarthy, 2011). Throughout the world, more than eleven million people are imprisoned at any time, and more than thirty million people navigate the prison system per year (Kouyoumdjian et al., 2015). Dumont et al. (2012) discussed the surge in incarceration in the United States beginning in the 1970s that led to the phrases "mass incarceration" and "hyperincarceration." This was mainly fueled by "tough on crime" politics and the "war on drugs," which disproportionately impacted non-Whites. More contemporary approaches are considering "decarceration" to address the problems of overpopulation (Smith & Rynne, 2014). These alternatives to incarceration do not represent a weakening on crime (Prenzler, 2009), and enjoy community support (Palk, Hayes, & Prenzler, 1998). However, it is difficult to imagine that diversionary paths are a panacea for incarceration for those who commit serious offenses and must take a different form for individuals already imprisoned. Imprisonment itself includes a range of punitive actions, from incarceration aimed at the deprivation of liberty, to the death penalty in certain jurisdictions (Claborn & McCarthy, 2011).

International data suggests people who experience imprisonment have overall poorer health compared to the general population, with higher rates of communicable and noncommunicable diseases, substance use, and mental health issues (Stürup-Toft, O'Moore, & Plugge, 2018). Wildeman and Wang (2017) reported that people who are incarcerated during their lives are "disproportionately in poor health both before, during, and after their incarceration" (p. 1464). Incarceration rates can both be related to deficits in public health, as compensatory mechanisms for a lack of adequate community-based mental health care and drug treatments, as well as have an impact on the health of society (Dumont et al., 2014). As Stürup-Toft et al. (2018) observed, the socioeconomic determinants of both crime and health are broadly similar. They argued that increasingly this can be seen in mortality rates in incarcerated populations, as while suicide remains the highest internationally, "natural" causes of death via noncommunicable disease is the biggest killer in English and Welsh prisons, which may be related to aging populations as well as other factors that in a community context we would consider a public health problem (Stürup-Toft et al., 2018).

Dumont et al. (2012) noted that compared to the community, African American inmates' mortality rate is lower, whereas for Caucasian inmates it is slightly higher or the same, but "the protective effect of incarceration is revealed to be illusory by the surge in mortality in the weeks following release" (p. 329). They explained that former inmates who were recently released from prison are at much greater risk for death from a drug overdose than others in the community. This increased rate of death also reflects the instability in their lives upon release and access to resuming previous risky behaviors. Given the similarity of determinants between incarceration and deficient health, a prison may offer a potential intervention point for both the individual and the community (Stürup-Toft et al., 2018).

By far the most pressing manifestation of this problem is occurring in the United States of America, which currently imprisons more individuals than any other country (2.2 million individuals) (Stürup-Toft et al., 2018). According to Wildeman and Wang (2017), the US rate of incarceration was 312 per 100,000 in 1985 and up to 743 per 100,000 in 2005. For a global comparison, they noted the country with the next highest rate in 2005 was New Zealand (173 per 100,000), followed by Luxembourg (159 per 100,000) and Spain (140 per 100,000). In this context, the troubling reality is that the United States' rate of incarceration is approximately twice that of comparable nations. As of May 2019, the rate in the USA decreased to 655, New Zealand was up to 214, Luxembourg dropped to 107, and Spain decreased to 127 (all per 100,000 people) (Duffin, 2019).

The international trend, based on United Nations data, suggests the world prison population is 144 per 100,000, and varies by region, with the Americas and Oceania being significantly higher than the global 20% increase since the year 2000 (increasing at 40% and 60% respectively, against population expansion of 18% in the same period) (Stürup-Toft et al., 2018). The question must therefore be asked, given these escalating numbers, could a public health approach to prisons in the United States and Australia be applied? This would shift the focus to providing opportunities for health care, education programs, and appropriate services upon release (Kouyoumdjian et al., 2015). Such

interventions could benefit the health of those incarcerated while simultaneously decreasing cost, improving recidivism rates and therefore public safety
(Kouyoumdjian et al., 2015). Thus, the conceptualization of individuals who
are incarcerated can be simultaneously viewed as an issue of both criminal
justice and public health.

23.2 Case Illustration

The following is a case study of an incarcerated individual that
elucidates the relationship between public health factors and incarceration.
The case has been deidentified to protect confidentiality. Edgar "Ed" M. is
currently serving a 240-month sentence for armed robbery, possession with
intent to distribute heroin, and possession of a firearm by a felon. The severity
of these actions and sentence duration suggest an intractable problem for
correctional services concerned with rehabilitation targeting recidivism. The
case is presented to highlight that any postsentence intervention is necessarily
symptom reduction. For Ed, the response must be so. However, as his case
reveals, continuing to treat a symptom while allowing causes to go unchal-
lenged not only results in overwhelming current correctional systems but
suggests that the abatement of worsening trends is not occurring despite clear
evidence of their existence. Thus, Ed represents an opportunity to highlight
issues indicative of later delinquency and attempt to address them through a
more proactive paradigm, that of public health.

Ed was born in the 1980s in an impoverished and violent area of Los
Angeles, California. His parents, both members of the popular gang in the
area, were still teenagers when Ed was born and already had a daughter. They
went on to have two more children together after Ed. His parents frequently
verbally fought and would often throw or break objects in the home when
arguing. On occasion, those verbal clashes would escalate to physical alterca-
tions. Ed now understands that alcohol use escalated these conflicts as well.
Eventually, tensions regarding infidelities led to Ed's parents separating. He
remembers being about kindergarten age when this happened. When his
mother left the area, he and his older sister were initially cared for by his
paternal great-aunt, as his father could not handle the children on his own. His
younger siblings stayed with another relative. Ed's great-aunt had several
other young children in the small home. Ed relayed that times were tough,
money was tight, and he vividly recalls picking chunks out of his milk for his
cereal in the mornings, and often wearing dirty clothes to school. His father
would occasionally stay in the home but during this time was also in and out
of jail for drug offenses or would be staying with other members of his gang.

Ed recalled he was about eight years old when he and his siblings went to
live with his father. While this resulted in increased financial stability, he also
witnessed his father and associates sell and use drugs. Ed expressed that his

father did not act like a parent, and he felt he was treated more like an "amigo de la pandilla" (friend from the gang) than a son. On the one hand, he noted he and his siblings could do whatever they wanted, but if their father decided one of them did something meriting punishment, they were all punished for the one's actions. Ed noted if his father found out one of them got into a fight at school, he would beat the others if he found out they did not fight too in defense of their sibling. Both in home and at school, Ed expressed he was always seen as "the bad kid" or "alborotador" (troublemaker). Even if he was the victim of assault, the teachers treated him as the guilty party, and his response was to retaliate against the aggressor and "make them regret it." He also fought teachers, and later correctional staff, as he was first incarcerated at age twelve. Ed says he has felt angry for as long as he can remember. Discussing it, he presents as regretful and states this is not the person he wanted to be, acknowledging he has "a chip on my shoulder." Being self-reliant and not asking for help has been a long-standing point of pride as well, many times to his detriment.

Ed was exposed to gang life from early childhood. Both of Ed's parents and many relatives were heavily involved and were active from both inside and outside of prison. Gang members were a powerful entity, and as a child, it was exciting for Ed to be accepted and allowed into their world. By nine years old, he began running errands for them, suggesting swift acculturation to these practices. He would socialize with them and watch his older cousins and friends "get drunk, get high, and get with girls." At an impressionable age he observed their relative wealth, seemingly constant inebriation, and quick inclination to violence. It was not long before he tried alcohol and marijuana himself.

Ed was eager for acceptance and he rose through the ranks quickly, attaining status in the gang lifestyle. Associated with this was spending multiple years of his adolescence in residential facilities, both correctional and treatment oriented. He never completed his education, and to date, has not attained his High School Equivalency Certificate. Accompanying this is the diagnosis of various mood and behavioral disorders, as well as attention deficit hyperactivity disorder (ADHD). While Ed has denied ever attempting to take his own life, he has engaged in reckless actions that could have resulted in his death and stated he had accepted death as a possible outcome from early on.

At age sixteen, Ed fathered a son of his own, Arturo (a pseudonym). Although he has been incarcerated for most of Arturo's life, Ed has expressed gratitude that his son's mother raised him and said he does not want him to have the same life he has. Despite this, he worries as Arturo has spent the last two years on probation after being suspended from school for assault. Arturo currently spends the majority of his time smoking marijuana with friends and is not employed nor working toward a high school diploma. He exhibits violent behaviors that Ed recalls engaging in just like his son at that age.

To Ed, Arturo appears to be very clearly following his path. He believes his mother has good intentions, but little control of Arturo.

For Ed, trying to be a parent both from across the country and behind bars is extremely challenging, as he can only make phone calls in fifteen-minute increments (up to a total of five hours a month), and still can only make as many as he can afford with his twenty cents per hour work assignment. Aside from the logistical difficulty of making phone calls, Ed's distance and limited contact results in Arturo controlling these interactions. This means that Ed has limited capacity to advise his son, as Arturo is likely to hang up and may not accept calls for several weeks if he perceives any criticism. If Ed has enough time, Arturo will often remain on the line long enough to tell Ed he is in no position to tell him what to do. Perceiving his son as being disrespectful, Ed will become defensive and the communication gap continues to stretch further apart. There has not been a visit in years.

The strained relationship with Arturo is only one of Ed's concerns. Several years ago, with hopes to set a better example for his son and to live a life outside of prison, Ed made the tough decision to leave his gang. This decision puts his life at risk, meaning Ed needs to be vigilant in the situations he puts himself in for the rest of his life. Many people in his situation choose to relocate after prison, which is a decision he still must make.

Moreover, without the support and structure of the organization, Ed essentially must start from nothing when he is released from prison in what he considers old age. He struggles with feeling embarrassed that when he is released he will not have the things he feels he is expected to, such as a home, a wife and children, a vehicle, and an established career. He wonders about whether he will be a desirable partner as he tries to develop new relationships. He worries about how much time it will take him to establish himself, and whether he will be too late for certain things, such as more children, as he races against the clock. He is unsure whether he will be able to live up to the standards of society, and whether it is worth it. For Ed, the challenges of life upon release present many anxiety-provoking scenarios. The comparative familiarity of his previous gang lifestyle presents simpler solutions to these issues. His relationships with friends, family, and society, were structured by the rules of this affiliation. Perhaps even more complex is that his self-worth was based on the respect and admiration from others due to his affiliation with the gang. Without membership in the gang, his self-worth is deficient and unstable.

Accordingly, Ed experiences tension related to what he is supposed to do: how he is supposed to comport himself; the appropriate demeanor; the acceptable ways to respond to threat, challenge, or conflict; and which and how much emotion to show. The last thing he wants is to seem weak. The tension creates anxiety and doubt, as he frequently perceives he is being challenged. This perception of being challenged could stem from a staff member "hassling" him or a lower-status inmate making jokes he would not have tolerated before. Ed's hypervigilance often results in aggression. He noted he says to himself, "Let's see who can go harder." He has come to recognize that his reputation and demeanor contribute to a cyclical pattern of interactions with others. He would like to be able to socialize "normally" but feels he often cannot relate.

"Stressed, depressed, and miserable" is how Ed describes being in prison; he says he is eager to get out and move on with his life. Given he still has significant time to serve, he has to push against thoughts he refers to as "institutionalization." He explained inmates have "messed up thinking" that "regular" people do not, such as "this is my space, my chair, my TV" and often will go to great lengths to defend what is not really theirs at significant risk to their lives and freedom. We do not yet know whether Ed will make it out of prison, and if so, what impact he will have on society. A question looms: *Will he leave prison in a healthier state than he entered?* Will he be rehabilitated? His ongoing difficulties suggest a guarded prognosis. What is of great concern still is that Arturo is potentially already following in his father's footsteps. It is in the community interest to prevent this.

23.3 Risk Factors for Delinquency

Delinquency is an issue of social importance to multiple stakeholders (Borg, Hermann, & Bilsky, 2017). Social scientists, researchers, criminologists, psychologists, advocates, practitioners and others theorize explanations regarding delinquent behaviors and how individuals become implicated within this subculture (Clinkinbeard et al., 2011; Dembo et al., 2011; Dumont et al., 2014; Rocque, Welsh, & Raine, 2012). Risk factors and behavioral cues that manifest early in life are important to identify as areas amenable to prevention programming before the onset of violent behavior. Reaching those youth before they become entrenched in the justice system will not only help the individual(s) but also assist in preserving community public health.

To better understand the etiology of delinquency, researchers have uncovered numerous risk factors that span across various domains, such as the individual and their family system, associated peer groups, educational setting, and environmental/community factors (Dembo et al., 2011; Newsome & Sullivan, 2014; Wasserman et al., 2003). Research makes a distinction specifying *long-term* risk factors to include factors such as impulsivity, poor social skills, inadequate parental supervision, and low academic performance (Van der Laan, Blom, & Kleemans, 2009). Although no single risk factor leads one child into delinquency, the likelihood of early offending is associated with multiple risk factors and the absence of protective factors (parental involvement, abstinence from drugs and substance abuse, abstaining from dropping out of school, healthy social relationships, refraining from joining gangs, etc.) (Van der Laan et al., 2009; Wasserman et al., 2003; Zagar, Busch,

& Hughes, 2009a). There is an interrelationship of substance abuse, mental health disorders, and delinquency, where the research provides evidence of significant relationships among these domains (Dembo et al., 2011). As such, when examining delinquency in youth, risk factors may overlap domains and youth may suffer from multiple factors concurrently, like using alcohol and/or marijuana and a diagnosis of ADHD that could lend to the involvement in delinquent behaviors. This complex relationship between youth's substance use and mental health history may contribute or exacerbate delinquent behavior over time (Dembo et al., 2011).

Zagar et al. (2009b) discuss the socio-neuro-economic developmental theory of violent delinquency. This theory is based on empirical studies surrounding the risk trajectory from infants to adults and the later offense of homicide. Studies showed that significant risk can be associated with events occurring as early as gestation (such as fetal substance exposure), perinatal difficulties, and a violent and/or abusive family. Factors such as poor executive functioning, instability in the home, and missing and/or antisocial parents, can impede on success within the school, socially, or within the neighborhood (Zagar et al., 2009b). This early, maladaptive development, coupled with other risk factors (e.g., antisocial peers, gang affiliation, substance abuse, absentee parents) lends to the poor choices made by youth mired with these tribulations. Preventing problem behavior in adolescence can be enhanced by reducing early risk factors and increasing protective processes (Arthur et al., 2002). This is key to early prevention and identifying areas where support or intervention could be implemented. For example, in the case illustration, Ed's parents were teenagers when they had him and grew up in a low socioeconomic status. Ed witnessed domestic violence within the household and eventually went to live with his great-aunt when his parents separated. This early development, paired with other risk factors, such as early introduction to gang life, a father figure who was involved in selling drugs and encouraged violence, an incomplete high school education, incarceration at age twelve, and a diagnosis of ADHD all contribute to areas where proactive prevention treatment could have been implemented. There is no one risk factor that was solely responsible for Ed's tumultuous journey that resulted in incarceration. Instead, there were a multitude of opportunities for intervention.

When focusing on child risk factors, increasingly personal individual factors emerge, such as birth complications, hyperactivity, low academic achievement, depression, temperamental issues, impulsiveness, and sensation-seeking (Defoe, Farrington, & Loeber, 2013; Van der Laan et al., 2009; Wasserman et al., 2003). A child's behavior is the result of an amalgam of these bio-psycho-social factors that are frequently interrelated. For example, Newsome and Sullivan's (2014, p. 1081) research suggests approximately half of anti-social behaviors may be related to genetic factors. These neurological deficiencies and cognitive impairments, including impulsiveness, and antisocial behaviors and favorable attitudes toward violence, have been linked to violent behaviors (Reingle, Jennings, & Maldonado-Molina, 2012). Research studies have indicated one of the best predictors of later juvenile delinquency is the onset of early antisocial behavior, which ranges from aggression to rule defiance (including fighting, theft, and property damage) (Loeber & Farrington, 2001; Wasserman et al., 2003). Having witnessed and/or having been a victim of violence was identified as a risk factor for perpetrating violence by Weaver, Borkowski, and Whitman (2008). Belknap and Holsinger (2006) found incarcerated juveniles believed their own victimization was related to their own offending. Family factors, akin to parental criminal behaviors, such as parental substance abuse issues, poor parenting skills, inadequate parental supervision, maltreatment/abuse, divorce, teenage parenthood, and family violence can also have a negative impact on the child and increase the risk of delinquency (Loeber & Farrington, 2001; Van der Laan et al., 2009). Arthur et al. (2002) cited risk factors in the familial domain, including poor monitoring, unclear expectations, and inconsistency of punishment and reward as variables that increase the risk for delinquency including drug use and violence. Reviews indicated children of incarcerated parents are at an increased risk for criminality and disrupted home environments (Dawson, Jackson, & Nyamathi, 2012; Loeber & Farrington, 2001).

In Belknap and Holsinger's (2006) study of institutionalized delinquent youth, two-thirds of their sample reported a parent had been incarcerated. They found 14% of girls and 9% of boys stated they would rather reside at the institution than at home (Belknap & Holsinger, 2006). According to the National Resource Center on Children & Families of the Incarcerated (2014), one in twenty-eight American children have an incarcerated parent and suffer shame and stigma. Further, this adverse experience is racially disproportionate and represents one in nine among African Americans, one in twenty-eight among Latina/Latino Americans, and one in fifty-seven among Whites/White Americans in the United States. Incarcerated individuals have less access to, and contact with, their children. This suggests an intergenerational cycle of incarceration, which, in combination with the "revolving door" of recidivism, implies complex entrenchment of families within prisons. Research has demonstrated insufficient parental supervision and involvement are linked to deviant behaviors, and a poor relationship between parent and child. This lack of parental involvement lends to the child forming associations with delinquent peers (Cheng & Li, 2017), further ingraining the problem in the community. Aaron and Dallaire (2010) noted significant strain of a parent's current and prior incarceration on other family members stating that "recent parental incarceration influenced family conflict, which, along with family victimization, predicted children's delinquency better than parental incarceration" (p. 1481). As evidenced in Ed's situation in the case illustration, his parents were both teenagers when they had him and his father was in and out of prison. His father was a poor role model who endorsed selling and using drugs and would engage in domestic violence within the home. Ed's parents separated and he had inadequate supervision, specifically a father who acted more like a friend. The cycle of incarceration was generational, as exemplified by Arturo's experience with the criminal justice system and probation.

An individual's delinquency often occurs in the presence of peer groups demonstrating similar behaviors. A consistent finding within the research is that adolescents who commit offenses often do so in groups, as they encourage the committing of offenses, wish to gain respect or acceptance within the group, or remain loyal to group members (Van der Laan et al., 2009). A robust finding in the crime and delinquency research purports one's own delinquency is related to the delinquency of one's peers (Morris & Johnson, 2014) due to conforming to the deviant norms of the group (Borg et al., 2017). One study conducted by Cheng and Li (2017) revealed findings that youth affiliations with delinquent peers was positively correlated with their own delinquent behaviors (p. 208). Case (2017) summarized earlier data that indicated once youths feel stigmatized or negatively labeled, they have a hard time developing friendships outside those with similar labels, and then have a greater likelihood of future problematic behaviors as a result of their association with those peers. Some studies suggest those who have more delinquent friends reported a greater risk of committing violent behaviors and more involvement with the criminal justice system (Cheng & Li, 2017; Morris & Johnson, 2014).

Borum and Verhaagen (2006) discussed how males traditionally are involved in the criminal justice system at much higher rates than females, but since the mid-1980s girls' violence has increased, and not decreased as much as boys' has since the mid-1990s. They noted girls have been increasingly involved with gangs. They reviewed the research and cited that, "not surprisingly, gang affiliation or membership appears to increase risk of violence and delinquency even beyond the general risk associated with delinquent peers" (Borum and Verhaagen, 2006, p. 42). They noted that killings related to gang activity account for 40% of juvenile homicide, and the killers typically come from neighborhoods plagued by high crime and high drug use. Barkan (2001) discussed sociological theories on delinquent gangs and noted how being in a gang socialized lower-class boys into embracing values such as rejecting authority, being tough, believing in luck and fate (versus outcomes of one's efforts), seeking excitement, outwitting others, and avoiding being outwitted oneself. It is apparent such values relate to unlawful behavior and delinquency. As in Ed's case, early gang affiliation resulted in greater exposure to violence, delinquency, and rejection of authority.

Once involved in the criminal justice system, this increases the opportunity for additional interaction with peers who have a negative influence on behavior, potentially through the normalization of deviant acts, with less opportunities to socialize with nondeviant peers. Brook et al. (1997) found family conflict, peer modeling of specific behaviors, and tolerance of deviance affected youths' delinquency and drug use more so than school environment and street culture, which also had an impact. In 2007, the Task Force on Community Preventative Services evaluated research related to whether there was an impact on violent behavior related to facilitating the transfer of individuals from the juvenile justice system into the adult system. It recommended against transferring juveniles into adult systems, concluding it did not deter subsequent criminality, and may increase it (Centers for Disease Control and Prevention, 2007).

Adolescents who engage in delinquent behaviors are also more likely to find themselves involved in other high-risk activities, such as alcohol and drug use, carrying a firearm, discontinuing education, gang involvement, and high-risk sexual activity (Reingle et al., 2012). Substance abuse research in the United States has found positive relationships between alcohol, marijuana, and other drug use and delinquent behaviors stemming from various research studies (Dembo et al., 2011). Being under the influence of alcohol or drugs may cause a loss of inhibitions and an increase in the probability of offending (Van der Laan et al., 2009).

In the educational domain, indicators of later delinquency include poor performance and a weak attachment to school (Van der Laan et al., 2009). This failure to engage in education may lead to delinquent behaviors later (Wasserman et al., 2003). Unnever, Cullen, and Barnes (2016) found African American students engaged in less externalizing behaviors (e.g., fighting, lying or cheating, making threats of harm) when they were more significantly attached to their instructors, schools, and committed to educational pursuits. They also found that the stronger the bond the students had with their mothers, the stronger their attachment was to the educational institution. Furthermore, a meta-analysis of approximately a hundred studies on the relationship between delinquency and poor academic performance found that poor academic performance is related to the onset, frequency, and seriousness of delinquency (Wasserman et al., 2003). Delinquency during education can be related to underachievement, truancy, and interventions with the disciplinary team (that might include suspensions or expulsion; Zagar et al., 2009a), leading to a cyclical pattern of behavior.

Environmental factors also influence delinquency. As aptly put by deVuono-Powell et al. (2015), "incarceration is both a predictor and a consequence of poverty" (p. 11). Youth who live in low-income urban communities are exposed to social factors that increase their risk (Case, 2017). Contributing factors include concentrated poverty, unemployment, and violence (Wasserman et al., 2003). For example, underresourced neighborhoods are often prevalent for delinquent peer groups and gangs that engage young people into criminal activity and high-risk activities through exposure to norms that are favorable to crime (Wasserman et al., 2003). Poverty or low incomes within the family place chronic stress on juveniles, who may eventually display delinquency (Cheng & Li, 2017). It was apparent from early childhood that Ed felt the strain of his family's limited resources. When Ed saw older youths and young adults living more comfortably as a result of income from crime, this greatly appealed to him.

Concentrated areas of poverty within a community may also lead residents to be disinclined to intervene when young people are engaging in delinquent acts (Wasserman et al., 2003). Such factors that exist within the community level include racial dispersion, which is a measure of the racial heterogeneity in the neighborhood. When all members of the community are of the same racial group, racial dispersion is zero (Reingle et al., 2012). When a neighborhood has a high level of racial heterogeneity, there is a greater exposure to racial tension that is linked to violent behavior and racism (Kaufman, 2005; Reingle et al., 2012).

Research has identified risk factors that are predictive of delinquency. These risk factors may fall in various domains (i.e., individual, family, peer groups, educational, and environmental). Depending on the level and the amount of risk factors a person is exposed to will impact their involvement in delinquent behaviors (Williams et al., 1999). When reviewing the risk factors that Ed was exposed to in Table 23.1, it is apparent that multiple domains and risk factors are evident.

23.4 Protective Factors for Delinquency

Examining protective factors that reduce the risk of delinquency is an important part of identifying interventions. Protective factors are those that reduce occurrences of problematic behavior or influence exposure to risk factors (Arthur et al., 2002). For example, violence and delinquent behaviors may be mitigated through encouraging abstinence from alcohol and drug use during pregnancy among urban women (Zagar et al., 2009a). It is also important to keep youth engaged with education, and desist from substance abuse and gang membership (Zagar et al., 2009a). Common protective factors identified in the research are parental involvement, strong cognitive abilities, and prosocial behaviors.

Parental involvement and attachment to parents has been identified as a protective factor from violence. As such, studies have found that parental monitoring and disapproval communications are effective for decreasing peer associations with deviant adolescents (Tilton-Weaver et al., 2013). Unnever et al. (2016) found less exhibition of externalizing behaviors in minors that were highly attached to their mothers or fathers. In addition, a good relationship with one parent, observed by warmth and absence of severe criticism, may have a significant protective feature against later delinquency and antisocial behavior (Yoshikawa, 1995).

Strong cognitive abilities are recognized as a protective factor against delinquency. Better success in the academic realm is developed through cognitive capacities and associated social skills in childhood interactions (Zagar et al.,

Table 23.1 *Risk factors for delinquency*

Domain Level	Risk Factor	Present for Ed as a Youth
Individual	Impulsivity	Yes
	Sensation-seeking	Yes
	Poor social skills	Yes
	Substance abuse	Yes
	Mental illness/depression	Yes
	Maltreatment/abuse	Yes
	Hyperactivity	Yes
	Perinatal difficulties	Unknown
	Fetal substance exposure	Unknown
	Birth complications	Unknown
	Temperamental issues	Unknown
	Early onset of aggression	Yes
	Early onset of rule defiance	Yes
Family /	Inadequate parental supervision	Yes
Peer Group	Missing and/or antisocial parents	Yes
	Weak attachment to parents	Yes
	Instability in the home	Yes
	Low SES	Yes
	Violent/abusive family	Yes
	Poor parenting skills and unclear expectations/inconsistency of punishment and reward	Yes
	Teenage parenthood	Yes
	Parental substance use	Yes
	Parental incarceration	Yes
	Peer modeling of delinquent behavior	Yes
	Delinquent and/or antisocial peers	Yes
	Gang affiliation	Yes
Education	Low academic performance	Yes
	Weak attachment to school/instructors	Yes
Community	Concentrated poverty	Yes
	Neighborhood violence	Yes
	High unemployment	Yes
	Presence of delinquent peer groups	Yes
	Racism	Unknown

Note: As an individual exists in multiple domains, these factors are interrelated, and exert influence on one another.

2009a). A longitudinal study of 837 children on the Hawaiian island of Kauai reported how age-appropriate language attainment at ages two and ten years served as a protective factor among children against later delinquency (Yoshikawa, 1995). Another longitudinal study from New Zealand included

1,037 children with results that indicated deficits in the Intelligence Quotient (IQ) preceded the development of serious antisocial behaviors. Further, the effects of low IQ on these behaviors occurred independently of associated variables like academic attainment, socioeconomic status, motivation, and ethnicity (Yoshikawa, 1995). Unnever et al. (2016) noted less externalizing behavior in youths whose main caregiver was a high school graduate.

Adolescents and youth who are able to remain prosocial when faced with various life problems and adverse situations display resiliency (Newsome & Sullivan, 2014). Resiliency has been studied extensively since the 1970s due to the protective factors relevant to youth. Research has found the presence of prosocial behaviors among adolescents, as rated by teachers, served as a protective factor, specifically among those who have been identified to have risk factors for committing crimes before the age of thirteen (Wasserman et al., 2003). Thus, the research substantiates that deficiencies in areas that may lead an individual to a path of delinquency are also those that may ultimately be targeted for intervention. Unfortunately, this may only occur following behaviors that result in incarceration.

23.5 Incarceration

A consequence of delinquent behavior for many is involvement with the criminal justice system, which may include being incarcerated, or confined to a correctional institution for a period of time. There are significant differences in types of incarceration. A primary distinction is made between prisons and jails. Typically, jails house individuals awaiting trial or sentencing or serving relatively short sentences of usually less than one year but up to two in some jurisdictions (Welch, 2004). Jails may be inappropriately used as default holding places for individuals with substance abuse issues, mental illness, and for those without shelter (Welch, 2004). Prisons, however, hold inmates who are sentenced for longer lengths of time. Aside from prisons and jails, people who have not committed crimes may also be incarcerated in secure facilities or detention centers related to immigration status.

The literature illuminates several ways in which community public health deficits can affect incarceration. Dumont et al. (2012) pointed out that inmates have greater rates of mental and physical illnesses than individuals in the community and are often from areas already medically underserved. The role of these institutions as mental health providers is largely not disputed. Cook County Jail in Chicago, for instance, has been acknowledged as the largest mental health provider in the United States (Ford, 2015).

Correctional institutions vary widely in the quality and quantity of mental health services offered to inmates. In the United States, Magaletta and Boothby (2003) suggested that the legal mandate for providing mental health services in jails and prisons was established with *Estelle* v. *Gamble* in 1976. Emerging from the case was a ruling that it is an Eighth Amendment violation to deny inmates medical treatment. Thus, correctional facilities are already acting as public health providers. However, given the deleterious effect that imprisonment itself can have on mental health it must be asked if they are the appropriate places to do so? In practice, correctional mental health providers operate much differently than they would if providing community-based care.

There are multiple aspects of incarceration that affect the provision of psychological services. Issues of privacy and stigma are heightened in these contexts. As Magaletta and Boothby (2003) noted, providing mental health services is not the primary mission of such facilities and frequent challenges are presented for the clinician. In the correctional setting, there are several additional limitations to confidentiality, as safety and security have clear contextual issues in correctional facilities. Mental health providers must consider the disclosure of information that may be relevant to other correctional staff members.

Arguably, incarceration can protect broader community public health by confining individuals who have been determined to pose a risk and providing rehabilitation prior to release. However, the majority of people in prison are not incarcerated due to high-profile offenses. Sawyer and Wagner (2019) highlighted that on any given day, there are approximately 451,000 people who are in correctional facilities for nonviolent drug offenses. In the US federal prison population, drug offenses accounted for 45.3% as of June 8, 2019 (Bureau of Prisons, 2019). Additionally, Sawyer and Wagner (2019) further noted 540,000 inmates in the United States are in pretrial detention, meaning that they have not yet been convicted of the crime(s) for which they are accused. The pretrial population of the federal system consists of 51,000 individuals (Sawyer & Wagner, 2019).

Moreover, many jail inmates would not be there if they could afford their bail (Sawyer & Wagner, 2019). Welch (2004) further distinguished that jail cells are used for people with lower incomes and lower socioeconomic status and those who spend time in jail are more likely to be unemployed than the general public. He outlined how being jailed can harm the fragile social ties and disrupt the lives of those already seen by society as disreputable. When compounded by the conditions of incarceration (inadequate phone or computer access) the ability to make arrangements with employers, landlords, and other financial contacts is drastically reduced. Also, many prison and jail inmates are incarcerated for violations of supervised release (Sawyer & Wagner, 2019). Violations of postincarceration supervision conditions may be as severe as committing a new criminal offense, but also include conduct such as possessing a weapon, failing to notify of a change in address or employment, failing to report to one's probation officer in a timely fashion, engaging in unauthorized communication with a felon, or failing to register as a sex offender (Administrative Office of the US Courts, n.d.).

For the justice-system-involved people, prior to incarceration, and in between periods of incarceration (for those individuals for whom incarceration has become recurrent in their lives), it is not surprising that their lifestyles are likely not optimal for maintaining good health. Richardson (2003) explained many offenders' lives are characterized by unhealthy environments, such as alcohol and other drug use, which when combined with limited health care, may cause age-related illnesses to develop faster in comparison to individuals in the community. However, the reverse may also be true, as Richardson (2003) discussed Goetting's (1983) assertion that elderly offenders may in some ways fare better in prison than in free society as their basic needs are met. Welch (2004) explained that for people coming from urban ghettos, in prison the housing, food, medical treatment (even more so for inmates with HIV/AIDS), education, vocational training, and substance abuse treatment are better than what is available at home. Thus, depending on one's personal circumstances, being incarcerated may or may not improve one's health. As Richardson (2003) advised, people with greater medical and mental health needs are likely to have greater difficulty coping with incarceration and incur more disciplinary infractions. According to Hogenboom (2018), facts of prison life, such as being apart from loved ones or subjected to potentially traumatizing events like searches or placement in solitary confinement, can make existing problems worse. Families that were able to remain connected, in spite of the often-prohibitive costs of calls and visitation, were able to buffer their loved one from incarceration's adverse effects on health (deVuono-Powell et al., 2015).

Illicit substance use is far from absent in correctional facilities, as many inmates have substance use disorders. Fazel, Yoon, and Hayes (2017), following a meta-analysis, outlined the high prevalence of alcohol and drug disorders among incarcerated individuals worldwide. They reported pooled estimates of 24% of inmates meeting criteria for an alcohol use disorder, and 51% with a drug use disorder, compared to 8.7% and 4.6% of nonincarcerated men and women respectively, in the USA, and 1.5% and 0.3% of nonincarcerated men and women globally having an alcohol use disorder. For drug use disorder, they reported community rates of 3.4% of males and 1.9% of females in the USA and 0.8% of males and 0.4% of females globally (Fazel et al., 2017). A public health approach views psychoactive substance misuse as disease and acknowledges the negative impacts on one's health, strain on healthcare systems, strain on families, and strain on employment. Public health approaches may favor the decriminalization of substance abuse and reallocating the significant funding spent on incarceration toward treatment in the community as well as programs to reduce harm such as decreasing the instance of people sharing needles, and providing more accurate comprehensive information about psychoactive substances to the public (Welch, 2004).

Moreover, engaging in substance use while incarcerated may represent a greater risk of harm than in the community. For example, by consuming alcohol made covertly, individuals have contracted botulism, which can lead to paralysis and death (Adams et al., 2015; McCrickard et al., 2017). In Adams et al.'s (2015) study, it was noted inmates do not trust prevention information about illicit alcohol safety from the correctional institution and disregard warnings. Inmates also abuse substances differently than what they may have used in the community such as ingesting K2/spice or synthetic cannabinoids rather than marijuana due to availability and greater ability to conceal. News outlets from across the United States cautioned of the dangers of these substances, including escalating rates of inmate deaths (Blaskey, 2018; Kirkland, 2018; Lammers, 2018; Ruland, 2018). They explained that inmates smuggle in or create such intoxicants from a variety of chemicals that are hazardous to humans, including insecticide and rodent poison (Blaskey, 2018; Ruland, 2018). According to the National Institute on Drug Abuse (2018), noted effects of using synthetic cannabinoids include extreme anxiety, paranoia, confusion, hallucinations, violent behavior, and suicidal thoughts. A desire to avoid being sanctioned for disciplinary infractions may prevent inmates from seeking help for current substance use or abuse.

A paradox of prison life is that it is both monotonous and routine, yet unpredictable at the same time. Daily routines can be repetitive, but with very little notice, an individual could be transferred to a different institution. Thus, per Jarrett (2018) prison life could be thought of both as structured and simultaneously socially threatening, given the lack of free choice, privacy, stigma, and fear. Jarrett (2018) described interviews with prisoners who reported difficulty with relationships and trusting others, feeling more emotionally numb and distanced from others, and reported impaired decision-making skills. Those he queried noted a need to conceal and suppress emotional expression (Jarrett, 2018). Increased impulsiveness and decreased ability to focus one's attention were noted as well even after short terms of incarceration. As many believe rehabilitation is, or should be, a primary aim of incarceration, this uncertainty must play a component role when preparing for release. Similarly, it is predictable that those incarcerated may be highly homogeneous. As Wildeman and Wang (2017) asserted, an incarcerated individual is typically male, of low socioeconomic status, and with low educational attainment. Couloute (2018) noted that 25% of former inmates do not have a GED (General Educational Development) or high school diploma, and the unemployment rate for those individuals is even worse than the 27% rate for the formerly incarcerated overall. He stated that people of color, and especially Black women, had the most difficulty securing employment after release.

Rehabilitation, delivered at the point of incarceration, largely focuses on recidivism as a measurable outcome. Nowhere is this more evident than in the Australian criminal justice system. The increasing incarceration of Indigenous peoples is a trend that has been evident for some time, and is getting worse with the Australian Bureau of Statistics reporting as of June 30, 2018,

Aboriginal and Torres Strait Islander prisoners accounted for 28% of the overall prison population, despite representing approximately only 2% of the Australian community aged eighteen and over. As the Law Council of Australia (2018) made clear, this translates to an imprisonment rate 12.5 times higher for Aboriginal and Torres Strait Islander people, and a staggeringly high 25 times higher for juvenile offenders. If recidivism is the metric for rehabilitation, then the outcome of 55% reincarceration within two years, at a faster rate than non-Indigenous counterparts (Willis & Moore, 2008), suggested efforts were not working. The Law Council of Australia (2018) suggested that "Closing the Gap" Justice Targets are required to coordinate action and maintain accountability, in the context of multiple reports observing these trends in Indigenous incarceration.

High levels of disparity in incarceration appear to co-occur with markers of social deprivation for Indigenous Australians. The "Closing the Gap" initiative has been in operation for a decade and derives its name from the attempt to reduce inequality between Indigenous and non-Indigenous Australians in multiple areas relating to education, employment, and health. This program emerged from the Council of Australian Governments' acknowledgment in 2008 of the need to address systemic disadvantage. Progress and modification of targets is ongoing and regularly reported upon, with the most recent report from the Commonwealth of Australia, Department of the Prime Minister and Cabinet (2019) making clear of the current seven targets only two are on track. Failure to meet these goals is significant given that the seven areas include: to halve child mortality (which has declined 10% since 2008, but as the non-Indigenous rate has fallen faster the gap has not closed); to increase school attendance (attendance rates have not improved and are currently at 82%, below the non-Indigenous figure of 93%); and to increase life expectancy (which has improved by 2.5 and 1.9 years for Indigenous males and females respectively). While targets in early childhood education and Year 12 attainment are being met, the *Closing the Gap* report (Commonwealth of Australia, Department of the Prime Minister and Cabinet, 2019) cites insufficient data to update progress since 2018, meaning that reading and numeracy targets are not on track, nor is the aim to halve the gap in employment. Thus, considerable disadvantage still exists in measures of socioeconomic standing of Indigenous Australians when contrasted with their non-Indigenous counterparts. By these markers of social deprivation, Indigenous Australians are suffering. A notable target in the domain of justice is to address the overrepresentation of Indigenous people in the criminal justice system, and specifically, reducing youth detention by 11%–19% by 2028.

Recognizing Indigenous Australians are overrepresented in the criminal justice system is an understatement. Since the 1991 Royal Commission into Aboriginal Deaths in Custody, it has been widely acknowledged Indigenous Australians are overrepresented in correctional facilities (Dawes et al., 2017). A notable problem is preexisting strategies are not resulting in change. An indicator of concern is that on discharge from prison, three in five Indigenous inmates report a health improvement, including mental health (with half reporting a decrease in the suicidal thoughts they had while in prison), suggesting access to services while incarcerated is enhanced over community availability (Muhunthan, Eades, & Jan, 2016). Thus, in contrasting jurisdictions with alternative healthcare models, it appears the question of rehabilitation becomes a question of public health, by which the underlying social deprivation needs to be addressed.

23.6 Prevention Efforts as Part of a Public Health Approach

As Ax (2003) noted, a public health model "implies a global perspective, a vital component because neither crime nor pathogens respect national boundaries and because migration patterns are increasingly a factor in American society and prisons" (p. 305). Furthermore, Ax instructed that in order for a public health intervention to be effective in preventing and/or reducing incarceration, prisoners and others involved in the justice system must be viewed as a part of the community as opposed to separate from it. It is heartening that global delinquency prevention efforts are being made. As part of the 2030 Agenda, the United Nations Office on Drugs and Crime (n.d.) has set out to help prevent youth crime, via the promotion of peace, using sports as a means to encourage respect, tolerance, and empowerment. It also noted sports can help youth develop life skills to manage adversity in a healthier way.

In Walters' (1990) discussion of the criminal lifestyle, he noted that for meaningful change to occur, the offender has to be sufficiently reinforced by noncriminal activities and experiences, such as work, interpersonal relationships, and freedom from legal supervision. He noted that the capacity and willingness to accept responsibility for one's criminal actions and challenge criminal thinking patterns is essential. He explained that several factors in one's environment serve to mitigate or protect against engagement in crime, or exacerbate or increase risk of such by way of increasing or decreasing one's options. He cautioned against a narrow perspective on criminality, saying that "offenders cannot legitimately use social injustice as an excuse for their criminal actions, neither can we as a society realistically escape our responsibilities by putting everything off on the offender" (p. 178). The etiology of criminal behavior is complex and multifaceted, and is best understood by appreciating an individual's unique experience. From Ed's perspective, he was immersed in a criminal lifestyle from his early childhood. He was rewarded for engaging in actions that were unlawful, both directly and indirectly. Currently, he must participate in the therapeutic interventions at the prison and challenge his own thinking patterns to prepare for life outside of prison bars.

But if through the lens of a public health approach, the aim is to reach at-risk youth before any offenses occur, therapeutic intervention and programs should be tactful and purposeful. Targeting such youth prior to the delinquent actions is the best way to mitigate risks (Zagar et al., 2009a). According to the US government, research has shown that the most effective (and cost-effective) time to intervene in preventing juvenile delinquency is as early as possible (youth.GOV, n.d.). Early intervention has been substantiated to positively affect delinquency outcomes (Zagar et al., 2009a).

Such intervention efforts strive to alter the life course of at-risk youth and steer them toward prosocial life choices, attending school, away from violence, and choosing to be sober. Per the US government, types of prevention programs recommended by the Office of Juvenile Justice and Delinquency Prevention consist of comprehensive community interventions, bullying prevention, after-school recreation, mentoring, classroom and behavior management, other school organization programs, and school curriculums focused on promoting social competence, conflict resolution, and violence prevention (youth.GOV, n.d.).

Within the early childhood developmental period, one way to decrease overall delinquency rates among youth may be direct prevention efforts prior to any contact with the criminal justice system (Yoshikawa, 1995). One such effort is predicated in bolstering parental behavior to combat the development of delinquent traits and attitudes among adolescents and children. Research out of the Oregon Social Learning Center has proposed and developed supportive evidence "for a model of how parenting behavior can lead to antisocial behavior in children" (Yoshikawa, 1995, p. 53). The programs they have developed involve interventions to reduce coercive interactions within the parent–child dyad and follow-up studies report a decrease in antisocial behaviors up to 4.5 years after treatment (Yoshikawa, 1995). Another program aimed at intervention during prenatal or early childhood is supported by Olds et al. (1998): Prenatal Infancy Nurse Home Visits. The program targets pregnant, teenaged mothers younger than nineteen years old with an annual income of less than $18,000 and supports the mother during pregnancy and their infants up to twenty-four months old. The program's main intervention aspects include nurse visits, training for the mother, antidrug training, and nutritional/diet assistance. Outcomes of the program resulted in less welfare utilization, fewer arrests, fewer subsequent pregnancies, and fewer doctor visits.

Furthermore, multiple risk factors for delinquency may have an impact on a child at any given moment in their life trajectory. As a result, early childhood prevention programs that target more than one risk factor would be more successful in preventing delinquency among youth and adolescents. These programs should aim to enhance parental support through education and training, and foster positive familial interactions within the family system. Direct intervention through parental training and home visitation is successful in infant and child abuse prevention (Zagar et al., 2009a).

Another facet of a prevention program should aim to facilitate early cognitive development among those children at risk for later delinquency. Early cognitive and social skill development has been successful in higher achievement in school (Zagar et al., 2009a). Case (2017) demonstrated how developing "key youth assets ... lead to favorable outcomes" (p. 517) with minority youth who were at risk for delinquency in his exploration of the Peer Ambassadors program. He noted the benefits of fostering supportive relationships and social skills that led to behavioral accountability, increased confidence, and sense of self-worth and self-efficacy. Furthermore, the youth were provided opportunities to develop social skills that also increased their confidence and allowed them to think of themselves in more positive ways. They experienced feeling they were important and could challenge the idea they were destined to live a criminal lifestyle.

Related to self-efficacy beliefs, Hardie-Williams (2018) discussed ways one can help a youth develop resilience, which she noted includes supporting them developing an internal locus of control, or the belief that they are in charge of their lives, rather than their circumstances. She expressed that children are much less likely to have their emotional development disrupted by trauma if there is even just one supportive and responsive adult in their lives. Youth need opportunities to develop skills in adapting to stress in their environments. They should be supported in trying to solve problems independently and monitoring their emotions, with the adult providing guidance as needed (Hardie-Williams, 2018). She noted that witnessing adults model these behaviors facilitates the development of resilience as well.

Garces, Thomas, and Currie (2000) presented as optimistic about the benefits of Head Start, a public preschool designed to be nurturing and provide services such as nutrition and preventative medical care. They observed Black individuals who participated in Head Start were significantly less likely to have been criminally charged or convicted versus nonparticipating siblings. The researchers also noticed positive spillovers from older youth who attended the program to their younger siblings, especially regarding criminal behavior.

Zagar et al. (2009a) professed another key aspect in reduction of offenses is best achieved by utilizing treatment modalities that have been empirically supported to reduce delinquency rates over time. The outcomes of the treatment programs must deliver meaningful results (e.g., better functioning of youth after treatment as measured by specific variables) and are applicable to multiple geographic locations with high violent crime. Research purports the most effective treatment modalities are "multimodal, carefully monitored, and closely supervised by researchers, are applied in 100 or more contact hours delivered in two or more contacts per week, for six months or longer" (Zagar et al., 2009a, p. 284). Certain interventions, such as supervision for youth and parental training, may help to reduce the number of delinquents and violent criminals, which are the most expensive to society (up to $2 million per violent offender). The return on investment for society will be billions of dollars in savings due to the associated costs of incarceration, adjudication, decreased crime and victimization (Zagar et al., 2009a). Another benefit of treatment is that over time, these programs will disrupt the cyclical nature of crime and delinquency that continues throughout generations. As observed with Ed and Arturo, Ed can already see how his son is following the same path he took, which is why it is imperative to aim prevention efforts at those high-risk populations as early as possible.

23.7 Conclusion

As exemplified throughout this chapter, public health, delinquency, and incarceration have overlapping areas of interest to various stakeholders. When operating from a public health approach, consideration for each citizen's rights must be built into the system to protect against unjust deprivation of freedoms (Claborn & McCarthy, 2011). The impact on the larger community must also be considered. As such, incarcerating individuals costs the community a significant sum of money, which many would argue could be better spent on treatment. In the USA, the 2015 average annual per-inmate cost was $33,274, although some states' costs were as high as $69,355 or as low as $14,780 (Mai & Subramanian, 2017). At the time of Mai and Subramanian's data collection, there were 1.33 million individuals incarcerated in state prison systems in the United States. Federal inmates, on average, cost $36,299.25 yearly to house in jails and prisons in 2017, and $32,209.80 in residential reentry centers (Hyle, 2018). Bushnell (2017) provided the figure of A$109,500 as the 2014 per year cost to incarcerate someone in Australia, which he noted was quite high in comparison to similar countries.

McLaughlin et al. (2016) noted that for each dollar cited as part of the cost of incarceration in correctional facilities, several dollars in social costs are not acknowledged. They reported the "aggregate burden of incarceration to be one trillion dollars ... eleven times larger than corrections spending" (p. 4). Costs other than those directly related to incarceration are those to the inmate, his or her family, and society at large.

Overall, the causes of incarceration are multidetermined. Societal, community, and familial factors have effects. Finally, individuals make choices based upon the range of options available to them. For some that range is narrower than others. These factors serve to increase or decrease one's risk of being incarcerated, which in turn affects their health and well-being and the health and well-being of their communities. The fabric of society is affected by having large segments of its population at a time segregated via incarceration, especially when certain segments are disproportionately impacted by it. While a full exploration is beyond the scope of this chapter, the public health is undoubtedly affected via the impact of incarceration on those who work in corrections, in addition to the impact on those who are incarcerated.

In Ed's case, factors in his early environment shaped his beliefs related to crime and the instability contributed to poor emotional control and problematic behavior. At this time, he has spent almost as much time locked up as he has free, and he has about seven more years to serve. While it is a difficult path not free from obstacles, he has taken steps to change his behavior. Ed presented as honest in therapy and motivated to seriously examine his emotions and thought processes. He noted he was never open to this when younger. This presents an interesting potential avenue for intervention as we relate his case to other juveniles at risk for delinquency – what would help them be open to help? Perhaps hearing about life choices from someone like Ed, who has been in their shoes? Currently, he has good relationships with his parents, who have since left the gang lifestyle and stopped abusing substances. This gives us hope for Ed. Of his siblings, his sister was never involved in the criminal justice system, his younger brother was released from prison and is now doing well for himself, and the other brother will be incarcerated for decades due to a gang-related attempted murder. Ed's story is not over, and neither is Arturo's; as they continue to learn, we may learn from them.

As a community we are charged with finding ways to intervene to prevent individuals from engaging in criminal behavior and being incarcerated, to reduce rates of recidivism and the impact these acts have on those around them. Conceptualizing delinquency as an issue of public health provides prevention opportunities at early stages of offending and even prior to it. As the case presented illustrates, proactive strategies, in combination with reactive responses, may provide the best overall response to juvenile delinquency.

References

Aaron, L., & Dallaire, D. H. (2010). Parental incarceration and multiple risk experiences: Effects on family dynamics and children's delinquency. *Journal of Youth and Adolescence, 39*(12), 1471–1484. doi.org/10.1007/s10964-009-9458-0

Adams, L. E., Yasmin, S., Briggs, G., et al. (2015). Alcohol production, prevention strategies, and inmate knowledge about the risk for botulism from pruno consumption in a correctional facility – Arizona, 2013. *Journal of Correctional Healthcare, 21*(4), 335–342. doi.org/10.1177/1078345815599763

Administrative Office of the US Courts. (n.d.). *Overview of probation and supervised release conditions.* www.uscourts.gov/services-forms/overview-probation-supervised-release-conditions

Arthur, M. W., Hawkins, J. D., Pollard, J. A., Catalano, R. F., & Baglioni Jr., A. J. (2002). Measuring risk and protective factors for substance use, delinquency, and other adolescent problem behaviors: The Communities That Care Youth Survey. *Evaluation Review, 26*(6), 575–601. doi.org/10.1177/0193841X0202600601

Australian Bureau of Statistics. (2018). *Prisoner characteristics, Australia*. www.abs
.gov.au/ausstats/abs@.nsf/Lookup/by%20Subject/4517.0~2018~Main%
20Features~Prisoner%20characteristics,%20Australia~4

Ax, R. K. (2003). A viable future for correctional mental health care. In T. J. Fagan &
R. K. Ax (Eds.), *Correctional mental health handbook* (pp. 303–327).
Thousand Oaks, CA: SAGE Publications.

Barkan, S. E. (2001). *Criminology: A sociological understanding* (2nd ed.). Upper
Saddle River, NJ: Prentice Hall.

Belknap, J., & Holsinger, K. (2006). The gendered nature of risk factors for delinquency.
Feminist Criminology, 1(1), 48–71. doi.org/10.1177/1557085105282897

Blaskey, S. (2018, August 22). This drug is turning Florida inmates into "zombies." It's
fueling a record death toll. *Miami Herald*. www.miamiherald.com/news/
special-reports/florida-prisons/article215642855.html

Borg, I., Hermann, D., & Bilsky, W. (2017). A closer look at personal values and
delinquency. *Personality and Individual Differences, 116*, 171–178. doi.org/10
.1016/j.paid.2017.04.043

Borum, R., & Verhaagen, D. (2006). *Assessing and managing violence risk in juveniles*.
New York: The Guilford Press.

Brook, J. S., Whiteman, M., Balka, E. B., & Cohen, P. (1997). Drug use and delinquency: Shared and unshared risk factors in African American and Puerto
Rican adolescents. *The Journal of Genetic Psychology, 158*(1), 25–39. doi.org/
10.1080/00221329709596650

Bureau of Prisons. (2019, June 8). *Offenses*. www.bop.gov/about/statistics/statistics_
inmate_offenses.jsp

Bushnell, A. (2017). *Australia's criminal justice costs: An international comparison*.
Institute of Public Affairs. https://ipa.org.au/wp-content/uploads/2017/08/IPA-
Report-Australian-Criminal-Justice_Costs-An-International-Comparison.pdf

Case, A. D. (2017). A critical-positive youth development model for intervening with
minority youth at risk for delinquency. *American Journal of Orthopsychiatry,
87*(5), 510–519. doi.org/10.1037/ort0000273

Centers for Disease Control and Prevention. (2007, November 30). Effects on violence
of laws and policies facilitating the transfer of youth from the juvenile to the
adult justice system: A report on the recommendations of the Task Force on
Community Preventive Services. *MMWR: Morbidity and Mortality Weekly
Report, 56*(RR-9), 1–11. www.cdc.gov/mmwr/PDF/rr/rr5609.pdf

Cheng, T. C., & Li, Q. (2017). Adolescent delinquency in child welfare system:
A multiple disadvantage model. *Children and Youth Services Review, 73*,
205–212. doi.org/10.1016/j.childyouth.2016.12.018

Claborn, D., & McCarthy, B. (2011). Incarceration and isolation of the innocent for
reasons of public health. *The Journal of the Institute of Justice & International
Studies, 11*, 75–86.

Clinkinbeard, S. S., Simi, P., Evans, M. K., & Anderson, A. L. (2011). Sleep and
delinquency: Does the amount of sleep matter? *Journal of Youth and
Adolescence, 40*(7), 916–930. doi.org/10.1007/s10964-010-9594-6

Commonwealth of Australia, Department of the Prime Minister and Cabinet. (2019).
Closing the gap: Report 2019. www.niaa.gov.au/sites/default/files/reports/
closing-the-gap-2019/sites/default/files/ctg-report-20193872.pdf

Couloute, L. (2018, October). *Getting back on course: Educational exclusion and attainment among formerly incarcerated people* [Press release]. www.prisonpolicy.org/reports/education.html

Dawes, G., Davidson, A., Walden, E., & Isaacs, S. (2017). Keeping on country: Understanding and responding to crime and recidivism in remote Indigenous communities. *Australian Psychologist, 52*(4), 306–315. doi.org/10.1111/ap.12296

Dawson, A., Jackson, D., & Nyamathi, A. (2012). Children of incarcerated parents: Insights to addressing a growing public health concern in Australia. *Children and Youth Services Review, 34*(12), 2433–2441. doi.org/10.1016/j.childyouth.2012.09.003

Defoe, I. N., Farrington, D. P., & Loeber, R. (2013). Disentangling the relationship between delinquency and hyperactivity, low achievement, depression, and low socioeconomic status: Analysis of repeated longitudinal data. *Journal of Criminal Justice, 41*(2), 100–107. doi.org/10.1016/j.jcrimjus.2012.12.002

Dembo, R., Briones-Robinson, R., Barrett, K., et al. (2011). Mental health, substance use, and delinquency among truant youth in a brief intervention project: A longitudinal study. *Journal of Emotional and Behavioral Disorders, 21*(3), 176–192. doi.org/10.1177/1063426611421006

deVuono-Powell, S., Schweidler, C., Walters, A., & Zohrabi, A. (2015). *Who pays? The true cost of incarceration on families.* Oakland, CA: Ella Baker Center, Forward Together, Research Action Design. http://whopaysreport.org/

Duffin, E. (2019). *Incarceration rates in OECD countries as of 2019.* Statista. www.statista.com/statistics/300986/incarcreation-rates-in-oecd-countries/

Dumont, D. M., Brockmann, B., Dickman, S., Alexander, N., & Rich, J. D. (2012). Public health and the epidemic of incarceration. *Annual Review of Public Health, 33*, 325–329. doi.org/10.1146/annurev-publhealth-031811-124614

Dumont, D. M., Wildeman, C., Lee, H., et al. (2014). Incarceration, maternal hardship, and perinatal health behaviors. *Maternal and Child Health Journal, 18*(9), 2179–2187. doi.org/10.1007/s10995-014-1466-3

Fazel, S., Yoon, I. A., & Hayes, A. J. (2017). Substance use disorders in prisoners: An updated systematic review and meta-regression analysis in recently incarcerated men and women. *Addiction, 112*(10), 1725–1739. doi.org/10.1111/add.13877

Ford, M. (2015, June 8). America's largest mental hospital is a jail. *The Atlantic.* www.theatlantic.com/politics/archive/2015/06/americas-largest-mental-hospital-is-a-jail/395012/

Garces, E., Thomas, D., & Currie, J. (2000). *Longer term effects of Head Start.* (National Bureau of Economic Research [NBER] Working Paper No. 8054). www.nber.org/papers/w8054.pdf

Goetting, A. (1983, August). *The elderly in prison: Issues and perspectives.* Paper presented at the annual meeting of the American Sociological Association, Detroit, MI.

Hardie-Williams, K. (2018, May 4). *How can we help children become more resilient?* www.goodtherapy.org/blog/how-can-we-help-children-become-more-resilient-0504184

Hogenboom, M. (2018, April 16). *Locked up and vulnerable: When prison makes things worse.* BBC. www.bbc.com/future/article/20180411-locked-up-and-vulnerable-when-prison-makes-things-worse

Hyle, K. (2018, April 30). *Federal Register notice: Annual determination of average cost of incarceration* (FR Document No. 2018-09062). www.federalregister.gov/documents/2018/04/30/2018-09062/annual-determination-of-average-cost-of-incarceration

Jarrett, C. (2018, May 1). *How prison changes people.* BBC. www.bbc.com/future/article/20180430-the-unexpected-ways-prison-time-changes-people

Kaufman, J. M. (2005). Explaining the race/ethnicity–violence relationship: Neighborhood context and social psychological processes. *Justice Quarterly, 22*(2), 244–251. doi.org/10.1080/07418820500088986

Kirkland, T. (2018, September 18). *Synthetic marijuana use among inmates a 'disaster waiting to happen,' expert says.* Fox News. www.foxnews.com/us/synthetic-marijuana-use-among-inmates-a-disaster-waiting-to-happen-expert-says

Kouyoumdjian, F. G., Schuler, A., Hwang, S. W., & Matheson, F. I. (2015). Research on the health of people who experience detention or incarceration in Canada: A scoping review. *BMC Public Health, 15*, 1–8. doi.org/10.1186/s12889-015-1758-6

Lammers, T. (2018, September 25). *Prisons around the country face a growing K2 problem.* Fox61. www.fox61.com/article/news/local/outreach/awareness-months/prisons-around-the-country-face-a-growing-k2-problem/

Law Council of Australia. (2018, August). *The justice project final report: Introduction and overview.* www.lawcouncil.asn.au/files/web-pdf/Justice%20Project/Final%20Report/Introduction%20and%20Overview.pdf

Loeber, R., & Farrington, D. P. (2001). *Child delinquents: Development, intervention, and service needs.* Thousand Oaks, CA: SAGE Publications.

Magaletta, P., & Boothby, J. (2003). Correctional mental health professionals. In T. J. Fagan & R. K. Ax (Eds.), *Correctional mental health handbook* (pp. 21–37). Thousand Oaks, CA: SAGE Publications.

Mai, C., & Subramanian, R. (2017, May). *The price of prisons: Examining state spending trends, 2010–2015.* Vera Institute of Justice. https://storage.googleapis.com/vera-web-assets/downloads/Publications/price-of-prisons-2015-state-spending-trends/legacy_downloads/the-price-of-prisons-2015-state-spending-trends.pdf

McCrickard, L., Marlow, M., Self, J. L., et al. (2017). Notes from the field: Botulism outbreak from drinking prison-made illicit alcohol in a federal correctional facility – Mississippi, June 2016. *MMWR: Morbidity and Mortality Weekly Report, 65*(52), 1491–1492. www.cdc.gov/mmwr/volumes/65/wr/mm6552a8.htm

McLaughlin, M., Pettus-Davis, C., Brown, D., Veeh, C., & Renn, T. (2016). *The economic burden of incarceration in the U.S.* (Working Paper No. CI072016). https://advancingjustice.wustl.edu/SiteCollectionDocuments/TheEconomicBurdenofIncarcerationintheUS.pdf

Morris, R. G., & Johnson, M. C. (2014). Sedentary activities, peer behavior, and delinquency among American youth. *Crime & Delinquency, 60*(6), 939–968. doi.org/10.1177/0011128710386205

Muhunthan, J., Eades, A., & Jan, S. (2016). UN-led universal periodic review highly critical of Australia's record on human rights and health for Indigenous Australians. *BMJ Global Health, 1*(1), 1–5. doi.org/10.1136/bmjgh-2015-000018

National Institute on Drug Abuse. (2018, February). *Synthetic cannabinoids (K2/ spice).* www.drugabuse.gov/publications/drugfacts/synthetic-cannabinoids-k2spice

National Resource Center on Children & Families of the Incarcerated. (2014). *Children and families of the incarcerated 2014 fact sheet.* https://nrccfi.camden.rutgers.edu/files/nrccfi-fact-sheet-2014.pdf

Newsome, J., & Sullivan, C. (2014). Resilience and vulnerability in adolescents: Genetic influences on differential response to risk for delinquency. *Journal of Youth and Adolescence, 43*(7), 1080–1095. doi.org/10.1007/s10964-014-0108-9

Olds, D., Henderson, C. R., Cole, R., et al. (1998). Long-term effects of nurse home visitation on children's criminal and antisocial behavior: 15-year follow-up of a randomized trial. *Journal of the American Medical Association, 280*(14), 1238–1244. doi.org/10.1001/jama.280.14.1238

Palk, G., Hayes, H., & Prenzler, T. (1998). Restorative justice and community conferencing: Summary of findings from a pilot study. *Current Issues in Criminal Justice, 10*(2), 138–155. doi.org/10.1080/10345329.1998.12036123

Prenzler, T. (2009). *Ethics and accountability in criminal justice: Towards a universal standard.* Bowen Hills, Australia: Australian Academic Press.

Reingle, J. M., Jennings, W. G., & Maldonado-Molina, M. M. (2012). Risk and protective factors for trajectories of violent delinquency among a nationally representative sample of early adolescents. *Journal of Youth Violence and Juvenile Justice, 10*(3), 261–277. doi.org/10.1177/1541204011431589

Richardson, L. (2003). Other special offender populations. In T. J. Fagan & R. K. Ax (Eds.), *Correctional mental health handbook* (pp. 199–216). Thousand Oaks, CA: SAGE Publications.

Rocque, M., Welsh, B. C., & Raine, A. (2012). Biosocial criminology and modern crime prevention. *Journal of Criminal Justice, 40*(4), 306–312. doi.org/10.1016/j.jcrimjus.2012.05.003

Ruland, S. (2018, September 7). What you need to know about K2 – The synthetic marijuana that triggered Pa. prison lockdown. *York Daily Record.* https://eu.ydr.com/story/news/2018/09/05/k-2-synthetic-marijuana-weed-caused-pennsylvania-prison-lockdown-what-you-need-know/1192337002/

Sawyer, W., & Wagner, P. (2019, March 19). *Mass incarceration: The whole pie 2019.* Prison Policy Initiative. www.prisonpolicy.org/reports/pie2019.html

Smith, C., & Rynne, J. (2014). Corrections. In H. Hayes & T. Prenzler (Eds.), *An introduction to crime and criminology* (pp. 309–322). Melbourne, Australia: Pearson.

Stürup-Toft, S., O'Moore, E. J., & Plugge, E. H. (2018). Looking behind the bars: Emerging health issues for people in prison. *British Medical Bulletin, 125*(1), 15–23. doi.org/10.1093/bmb/ldx052

Tilton-Weaver, L. C., Burk, W. J., Kerr, M., & Stattin, H. (2013). Can parental monitoring and peer management reduce the selection or influence of delinquent peers? Testing the question using a dynamic social network approach. *Developmental Psychology, 49*(11), 2057–2070. doi.org/10.1037/a0031854

United Nations Office on Drugs and Crime. (n.d.). *Crime prevention through sports.* www.unodc.org/dohadeclaration/en/topics/crime-prevention-through-sports.html

Unnever, J. D., Cullen, F. T., & Barnes, J. C. (2016). Racial discrimination, weakened school bonds, and problematic behaviors: Testing a theory of African-American offending. *Journal of Research in Crime and Delinquency, 53*(2), 139–164. doi.org/10.1177/0022427815610794

Van der Laan, A. M., Blom, M., & Kleemans, E. R. (2009). Exploring long-term and short-term risk factors for serious delinquency. *European Journal of Criminology, 6*(5), 419–438. doi.org/10.1177/1477370809337882

Walters, G. D. (1990). *The criminal lifestyle: Patterns of serious criminal conduct.* Newbury Park, CA: SAGE Publications.

Wasserman, G. A., Keenan, K., Tremblay, R. E., et al. (2003, April). *Risk and protective factors of child delinquency.* Office of Juvenile Justice and Delinquency Prevention (Child Delinquency Bulletin Series), 1–15.

Weaver, C. M., Borkowski, J. G., & Whitman, T. L. (2008). Violence breeds violence: Childhood exposure and adolescent conduct problems. *Journal of Community Psychology, 36*(1), 96–112. doi.org/10.1002/jcop.20219

Welch, M. (2004). *Corrections: A critical approach* (2nd ed.). New York: McGraw Hill.

Wildeman, C., & Wang, E. A. (2017). Mass incarceration, public health, and widening inequality in the USA. *The Lancet, 389*(10077), 1464–1474. doi.org/10.1016/S0140-6736(17)30259-3

Williams, J. H., Ayers, C. D., Abbott, R. D., Hawkins, J. D., & Catalano, R. F. (1999). Racial differences in risk factors for delinquency and substance use among adolescents. *Social Work Research, 23*(4), 241–256. doi.org/10.1093/swr/23.4.241

Willis, M., & Moore, J. P. (2008). *Reintegration of Indigenous prisoners* (Research and Public Policy Series No. 90). Canberra: Australian Institute of Criminology. www.aic.gov.au/publications/rpp/rpp90

Yoshikawa, H. (1995). Long-term effects of early childhood programs on social outcomes and delinquency. *The Future of Children, 5*(3), 51–75.

youth.GOV. (n.d.). *Prevention & early intervention.* https://youth.gov/youth-topics/juvenile-justic/prevention-and-early-intervention

Zagar, R. J., Busch, K. G., & Hughes, J. R. (2009a). Empirical risk factors for delinquency and best treatments: Where do we go from here? *Psychological Reports, 104*(1), 279–308. doi.org/10.2466/PR0.104.1.279-308

Zagar, R. J., Isbel, S. A., Busch, K. G., & Hughes, J. R. (2009b). An empirical theory of the development of homicide within individuals. *Psychological Reports, 104*(1), 199–245. doi.org/10.2466/PR0.104.1.199-245

24 Public Service Organizations and Community Empowerment

A Toolkit to Develop the School–Family–Community Connection at an Urban Middle School

Meghan F. Oppenheimer and Elizabeth W. Miller

Public service organizations, by design, are positioned to serve the public. In many instances, and across many different sectors in many different settings, such organizations are not only serving individuals, but supporting and empowering communities as well. From government agencies to not-for-profit organizations, public service organizations are engaged in meaningful support and collaboration within a wide spectrum of communities. For the purpose of this chapter, we will specifically focus on the potential impact that public schools have on the growth and empowerment of students and families, and the communities wherein they reside. A toolkit to enhance community development and the school–family–community connection will be presented, and further explored through a case study.

While many public service organizations are in a position to support communities, few have the level of access to youth and families in communities as schools. Specifically, in the United States, students spend approximately thirty to thirty-five hours at school each week. This results in approximately fifteen thousand school hours by the time students graduate from high school (Rutter & Maughan, 2002). While much of this time is devoted to developing students' academic knowledge and abilities, it is also imperative for children to utilize the school setting to foster healthy and positive relationships, develop character and life skills to overcome challenges, build resiliency, and learn to navigate the world outside of school. Students should be taught to become independent thinkers and increasingly develop their decision-making skills. They should also be encouraged to strengthen personal skills and engage in self-advocacy efforts. When students are encouraged to speak up and voice their opinions, they are more likely to participate and take responsibility in school decisions. This participation "enhances self-awareness and social achievement, improves mental health and academic performance, and reduces rates of dropping out of school, delinquency, and substance abuse" (Morse & Allensworth, 2015, p. 786). In short, schools are encouraged to function to empower students.

In addition to empowering students, it is also vital to empower the parents/guardians that students live with by providing them with information and resources related to effective schooling and educational factors that may have an impact on student academic or social-emotional development (Holcomb-McCoy & Bryan, 2010; Kim, Fletcher, & Bryan, 2018). For the purposes of this chapter, when we refer to parents/guardians, we are including parents, stepparents, caregivers, legal guardians, and foster parents. We are also aware that other family members may have important caregiving roles within the family system including those of sibling, godparent, grandparent, and family friend, among others. It is similarly important to empower parents/guardians with the awareness of systemic obstacles and provide them with the skills to push for change when educational institutions do not meet expectations (Kim & Bryan, 2017; Kim et al., 2018). Empowering parents/guardians results in positive outcomes for both parents/guardians (e.g., increased knowledge of resources, improved advocacy skills) as well as students, as parent empowerment is linked to improvement in students' mental health (e.g., decreased risk factors related to suicide; Toumbourou & Gregg, 2002) and increased academic achievement (Holcomb-McCoy & Bryan, 2010; Jasis & Ordonez-Jasis, 2004; Kim & Bryan, 2017; Nieto, 2000).

As Pstross et al. (2016) stated, "Helping parents to empower themselves with the necessary knowledge and skills to frame the education of their child can have a transformative impact on the future of that child" (p. 651). Holcomb-McCoy (2007) similarly stated, "The key to increase student achievement and to ensure more equitable practices in schools is to increase parent and community involvement" (p. 66). Ultimately, the goal of parent/guardian empowerment is to shift them from a position of passive recipient of decisions related to their child's education and well-being to the role of active advocate (Connor & Cavendish, 2018). By making this shift, "parents not only have equal voice but also participate in the decision making, planning, and implementation of solutions to problems affecting their children"(Bryan & Henry, 2012, p. 410).

Efforts to connect with and empower families should be an essential component of all schools. This is especially important in underserved communities where resources can be scarcer, both in and out of the school. In addition to reduced access to resources, low-income, underrepresented, and immigrant parents/guardians can view schools as unwelcoming and isolating (Bemak, Chung, & Siroskey-Sabdo, 2005; Bryan, 2005; Holcomb-McCoy & Bryan, 2010; Kim et al., 2018). By way of example, this is also true of African American families, as "the value of school-family-communities partnerships to African American children's academic achievement cannot be understated ... partnerships may serve as a protective factor that supports educational resilience in children and thus reduces the negative effects of stress and sociocultural inequities that sometimes plague the lives of African American families" (Moore-Thomas & Day-Vines, 2010, p. 54). Therefore, utilizing a public service organization as a means of connecting individuals to those resources can be particularly beneficial.

Fostering the development of a school–family–community connection can also be useful in overcoming additional challenges of schools in underserved communities. These challenges might include the impact of poverty, community violence and trauma, and the culmination of multiple stressors faced by families, which can often make it difficult for them to engage fully with schools and school supports. Research has shown that "experiencing trauma, such as maltreatment and abuse, can have negative effects on a child's brain and learning. These effects can range from differences in children's cognitive development to their social-emotional and behavioral development" (Hartman et al., 2016, p. 405). Additionally, "children who experience mistreatment often struggle in school settings, leading to concerns with behavior, inattention, or falling academic achievement" (Hartman et al., 2016, p. 405). Therefore, a collaborative approach between schools and communities is required to ensure positive outcomes for children and adolescents (Hartman et al., 2016).

24.1 Toolkit to Foster Empowerment

Given the importance of the school–family–community partnership, we will now shift our focus to the implementation of practices to promote this partnership through increased empowerment of those involved, at the individual, family, and community level. Specifically, we will share a series of interventions developed to maximize the reach of schools to support and empower those in and around the community. Taken together, these interventions form a toolkit from which other schools, or public service organizations, can pull to develop the right combination to support the unique makeup of their school, students, families, and community (see Table 24.1).

24.1.1 School Overview

The school in which these specific interventions have been developed and implemented is a middle school in a large metropolitan area in the northeast USA. The school is located in one of the poorest Congressional districts in the country with 48% of district youth living below the poverty line (as cited in Oppenheimer, Miller, & Clauss-Ehlers, n.d.; US Census Bureau, 2016). The median household income in the district is roughly $28,000 per year while the US average is $60,336, and the per capita income is $15,566 per year while the US average is $32,397 (US Census Bureau, 2016). However, what the district lacks in financial wealth is countered by the wealth of diversity within the community, where more than 67% of residents identify as Hispanic/Latinx and 28% identify as Black/African American (US Census Bureau, 2016). Additionally, 67% of residents speak a language other than English at home, which is more than three times the national average of 21%, and 37% of residents are foreign-born (as cited in Oppenheimer et al., n.d.; US Census Bureau, 2016). The school's student body is similarly diverse, with 59% of students identifying as Hispanic/Latinx and 37% identifying as Black/African

Table 24.1 *Toolkit to develop the school–family–community partnership*

	Components of Toolkit	Goals
Part I: School-Level Interventions	Trauma and attachment sensitive approach	To provide a safe environment where all students can grow
	Advisory program	To promote school connectedness To provide academic and behavioral supports
	Character program	To support students in identifying and developing character strengths
	School-wide initiatives	To increase awareness of social issues and foster connectedness to others
	Community service projects	To develop a sense of responsibility within the community
	Counseling	To provide students' social-emotional health and functioning
Part II: Family-Level Interventions	ESL classes	To increase parents' access to resources
	Parent dinners	To promote a sense of connectedness between parents/guardians and provide them with resources
Part III: Community-Level Interventions	Community partnerships	To provide connections and supports for students and families to thrive in the community, and to promote growth within the community

American, and with students hailing from countries all over the world. In many ways, this diversity enriches the academic environment by opening awareness to the many differences that exist between school members. However, it also comes with some challenges, including finding services to support the school to communicate with families in their native languages, or differing beliefs regarding educational or discipline practices. The school sets out to work with families to remedy these challenges and, in the process, school policies often evolve to become more productive and inclusive.

24.1.2 Toolkit Part I: School-Level Interventions

A vast majority of the interventions in the proposed toolkit occur at the school level. At this level, there are a multitude of actions that can be taken to empower students. In this section, we will discuss several interventions that have been useful in supporting students within the middle school described above. We will start by proposing interventions at a school-wide level. This tier of interventions are proactive and preventative, and include a trauma and attachment sensitive focus, school-wide advisory and character programs, and other community events and initiatives. Next, we will explore the programs limited to a subset of students, most notably the community service project that eighth grade students are required to complete (Kiner, 1993). Finally, the intervention at the individual level will be discussed, which involves the provision of comprehensive mental health services, including individual and small group services, for students.

24.1.2.1 Trauma and Attachment Sensitive Approach

At the foundation of the school's work with students and families is a trauma and attachment sensitive approach. As the school is located in an area marked by high rates of poverty and community violence, many of the students have faced at least one, if not more than one, adverse childhood experiences. For some students, these adverse experiences have not had a significant impact on functioning, while for others, these experiences have had a negative impact on their ability to self-regulate, focus, and learn. A trauma and attachment sensitive approach allows the school to support students with known trauma histories as well as those without trauma histories or with trauma histories that will never be known (Oppenheimer et al., n.d.).

In attempting to establish this environment, the school first provides a series of professional developments to staff in which they are provided with information related to the effects of trauma and ways to work with trauma in the school setting. The lessons from these trainings are further integrated into the school through classroom observations completed by the psychological intervention team. During these observations, team members seek to identify key components of a trauma-sensitive environment, including, but not limited to, clear expectations, consistent structures, affirming language, and positive body language and tone.

In addition to the implementations of trainings and observations, other components of the school's structure, most notably its discipline practices, also contribute to the establishment of a trauma and attachment sensitive approach. In a systematic restructure, the school's discipline department shifted to fall under the guidance program. This ensures that the school's approach and response to behavior is aligned with the trauma and attachment sensitive environment. Accordingly, the school has shifted its focus from addressing misbehaviors to identifying and praising positive behaviors. This subtle, but high-impact shift has helped staff members become less reactive and more proactive in managing student behavior.

Along the same lines, there has been a shift from punitive consequences to restorative practices. Students are provided with the opportunity to repair with others when misbehaviors and conflicts arise. These repairs are structured to allow students and staff to take responsibility for misbehaviors or mistakes, and ultimately promote positive relationships. This process can give students the chance to revise their understanding of relationships and can be particularly useful for individuals with histories of attachment-related trauma. This is helpful because it builds trust between students and adults, and gives students the understanding that even when two people disagree, they can come together to resolve their differences. It also allows students to see that adults make mistakes, too. It can be healing for students when adults own up to those mistakes and even apologize for them. Ultimately, in establishing a trauma and attachment sensitive school environment, the school seeks to create a supportive space in which all students are able to learn and grow.

24.1.2.2 Advisory

One program that was created as a benefit to both children and parents/guardians was the advisory program. According to the Association for Middle Level Education, an advisory program promotes school connectedness, which is linked to higher grades, higher test scores, and lower dropout rates, regardless of students' socioeconomic status (Shulkind & Foote, n.d.). The goal of the advisory program at this school is to provide academic and behavioral support in a smaller setting. More specifically, the goal is for each student to have at least one staff member in the building who knows them on a more personal level. Another goal is for scholars to feel comfortable with a small group of students, sharing information and getting to know their peers in a unique way.

At this school, advisory classes meet once a week for forty minutes. Advisories have between six and ten students in each group, led by a staff member at the school. Group sizes are smaller than regular classes to ensure each child has the chance to develop a connection with peers in the advisory as well as the advisor. The curriculum includes classes that solely focus on checking grades to make sure students stay on track, to other classes that discuss family traditions connected to different holidays. Advisors are encouraged to share their own personal stories to help establish a sense of connection and trust with the students. In this way, advisors take on a different role than a normal classroom teacher and students are able to see their teachers/advisors in a different light.

In addition to the academic, behavioral, and social benefits the advisory group provides students, advisory groups also serve as a benefit to parents/guardians. Advisors serve as the contact person for families and parents/guardians are always welcome to call with any questions or concerns they have about their child. Similarly, advisors are encouraged to call home as often as they would like, so the parent/guardian ideally should also be establishing a strong connection with someone in their child's school. Since the school has many families whose primary language is not English, Spanish-speaking advisors were paired with children who came from Spanish-speaking homes, so parents/guardians could be contacted in their native language (Oppenheimer et al., n.d.). Advisors are also required to call home about upcoming events, such as parent–teacher conferences, in hopes of increasing parent/guardian participation. This outreach has shown to be successful, with more than 70% of parents/guardians attending parent–teacher conferences. This is a stark jump from the 30% of parents/guardians who attended prior to the formal start of the advisory program.

24.1.2.3 Character

The school also implemented a school-wide character program, which was designed to help students identify and develop positive character strengths, and to use these character strengths to help navigate challenges in and out of school. The twenty-four character strengths that are the focus of the program are classified under the virtues of wisdom, courage, humanity and justice, temperance, and transcendence, and include the strengths of humor, fairness, and perseverance, among others (Peterson & Seligman, 2004). All students and teachers found out the order of their character strengths by taking the VIA Survey, a 240-item self-report questionnaire designed to identify a person's most common strength (Peterson & Seligman, 2004). Among adults, the most common character strengths are kindness, fairness, and honesty (Park & Peterson, 2006), while among children, the most prevalent strengths are gratitude, humor, and love (Park & Peterson, 2008). Research has found the use of character strengths to be linked to increased ability to overcome challenges, improved relationships, and enhanced health and overall well-being (VIA Institute on Character, n.d.). Accordingly, as character strengths can act as a buffer against the negative effects of trauma, the character program is "in line with the school's trauma and attachment sensitive approach" (Oppenheimer et al., n.d., p. 11).

The program is designed to have students engage in one character class per week throughout the academic year. In its current form, the curriculum is designed to promote the study of one of the twenty-four character strengths each week, coinciding with an external holiday or event, when possible. For instance, the strength of gratitude is studied around Thanksgiving, bravery is explored around Veteran's Day, leadership is examined around Martin Luther King, Jr. Day and love is discussed around Valentine's Day. During National Bullying Prevention Awareness month in October, kindness and open-mindedness are explored (Oppenheimer et al., n.d.). Similarly, in the weeks leading up to high-stakes testing, the strengths of perseverance, creativity, curiosity, love of learning, and prudence are studied. The program also includes practices "that promote increased self-regulation and emotional safety among scholars," as well as skills related to communication, organization, critical thinking, and teamwork (Oppenheimer et al., n.d., p. 11).

Instead of the psychological intervention team or guidance counselors, the character class is purposely taught by classroom teachers. This design component reflects the school's attempt to have character strengths infused within the greater school culture. Teachers are encouraged to integrate the lessons from character class into academic instruction. This, in turn, can further motivate students to engage with and develop the strengths that are important to them, and ultimately, to empower students to overcome challenges in both the school and community settings.

24.1.2.4 School-Wide Initiatives

Throughout the year, there are a few school-wide initiatives all grades participate in, with the purpose of coming together as a community for the greater good. For instance, the school participated in No One Eats Alone Day (Beyond Differences, n.d.), a national effort that strived to inform kids about (and subsequently work together to end) social isolation. Two students from each homeroom were assigned the role of "ambassadors" and were responsible for teaching their peers about social isolation. Starting at the beginning of the week and going for the next four days, the ambassadors would start each morning in the homeroom with a presentation about social isolation, answering any questions from their classmates. In addition to the presentation, there was also an all-school activity, which was an art installation on display in the hallway. Students made a tree with leaves, branches, and flowers, and each reflected on how they would end social isolation. After four days of presentations, the week culminated in the main event: At lunchtime, all students made sure that no one ate alone and included new peers in conversation and free time. The school also had staff participate, so teachers, deans, and administrators all ate lunch with a group of students.

An additional city-wide initiative this school participated in was Respect For All (RFA) week, the aim of which was to promote respect for diversity and focus on preventing bullying, intimidation, and harassment (www .schools.nyc.gov/school-life/school-environment/respect-for-all). The week consisted of learning about bullying and kindness and having students participate in different activities together. Similarly to No One Eats Alone Day, the students made a mural for the school, where each student wrote a response to the prompt, "What can you do to make this a more respectful school?" Another activity included having each scholar select a "Random Act of Kindness" from a jar and being challenged to complete the act by the end of the school day. A separate day had each homeroom do the "Stand Up" activity, the point of which was to show that all students have both similarities and differences, and even with our differences, everyone can choose to be kind to each other and work together as a class. In participating in these large-scale events, students were able to work toward a common goal with youth outside of their immediate community. This sense of connectedness and teamwork lead to increased levels of empowerment among students, evident through observations.

24.1.2.5 Community Service

To graduate, the school requires every eighth grade student to complete a community service project. This project is designed to engage students in an exploration of the needs in various communities, and address these needs through purposeful actions. In the process, students are encouraged to reflect on their personal responsibility in servicing their community. Students propose, plan, implement, and present a project that they feel will serve a need in their community. Examples of goals include increasing awareness, raising money, informing others, or advocating on behalf of someone else. Past community service projects have included toy drives for kids with cancer, raising money to help stray animals, or tutoring younger students in a nearby elementary school.

In reflecting upon their experience, most students report that they enjoy completing their project as it is often the first time they are participating in service activity. By investigating, planning, and carrying out this project, either individually or in a small group, students are learning many different skills they might not otherwise learn in their middle school classes, such as research and thinking skills, self-management and time-management skills, and communication and social skills. While students work with a supervisor who oversees the project and makes sure they are on track, students, for the most part, have to complete the various steps on their own. For example, if they do a toy drive for a local hospital, they are required to personally deliver the toys to the hospital.

Over the years, the school has established many relationships with places in the community where the kids can be of service. Local hospitals, animal shelters, and even gardens have opened their doors and gates to these students. Students learn the importance of helping others and giving back to their communities. They also learn how much a little can go a long way and it is the school's hope that a philanthropic belief carries with them in the future.

24.1.2.6 Counseling

While there are many school-wide initiatives to help support and empower students, there are also individual and small group interventions aimed at achieving the same goal. One such intervention is counseling. While 7% of the student body receives counseling services in accordance to their Individual Education Plans (IEPs), an additional 23% of the student body participates in voluntary, at-risk counseling. This totals 30% of the student body participating in counseling on a weekly basis. The students who participate in at-risk counseling most frequently enter counseling through a self-referral process, but can also be identified through a school-wide social-emotional health assessment, a parent/guardian referral, or a staff referral. Students who are in the midst of crises can also elect to utilize counseling services as walk-ins, and approximately five to ten students choose to engage with these supports each day. Outside of the school setting, potential barriers to treatment include challenges related to limited resources, financial means to pay for services, language barriers, distrust of a system, and treatment that is not culturally competent (Becker, Greenwald, & Mitchell, 2011). By offering counseling services to students within the school setting, these potential barriers to treatment are removed.

24.1.3 Toolkit Part II: Family-Level Interventions

There are also interventions in the toolkit structured to extend support and connectedness to the family level. In this section, we discuss two interventions that have been useful in supporting families of students within the school setting, including English language classes and parent dinners.

24.1.3.1 English as a Second Language Classes

Research shows how important an integrative approach is when it comes to students' academics, behaviors, and their social-emotional well-being, and the more that schools, families, and communities can come together, the better supported the child will be. As previously discussed, the school has a very diverse population, with many parents speaking a language other than English. At no cost to the families, the school offers an English as a Second Language (ESL) class to any parent/guardian who is interested. The class is offered on Saturdays as most parents work during the week and cannot take time off. With parents/guardians learning English, the hope is that they can get more involved in their child's classes and help with schoolwork, as well as opening them up to more jobs in the community that are not limited to Spanish-speaking roles.

24.1.3.2 Parent Dinners

The school also offers monthly parent-to-parent (PTP) dinners to all parents/guardians who wish to attend. The dinners, led by the psychological intervention team, cover a range of social and emotional health topics, mostly chosen by the parents/guardians. Topics have included peer pressure, substance use and abuse, social media, bullying, and relationships, to name a few. The goal of the dinners is to have parents/guardians interact with each other and normalize any issues they may be having with their teenage child. It is also a chance for parents/guardians to connect to the psychological intervention team, and building this relationship with parents/guardians can only help make families feel more supported in the school setting.

Since the school understands that many factors may get in the way of parents/guardians participating, the school tries to eliminate these impediments as much as possible. For one, the dinners are in the evening, giving parents/guardians a chance to get home from work. Second, dinner is offered to the entire family as the school knows childcare may be an issue. Lastly, a Spanish-speaking staff member is always present to translate so that no one is excluded from conversations and workshops.

24.1.4 Toolkit Part III: Community-Level Interventions

In addition to working with students and families, the school has also worked to develop community partnerships. The goal of these partnerships is to provide connections and supports for students and families to thrive within the community, while simultaneously promoting growth and development within the community. For instance, the school partnered with a local community center to provide students with a safe space to learn and grow after school hours. Students can spend up to four hours at the center after school each day, engaging in a wide range of activities including basketball, cooking, dance, and homework help. Students are provided with supervision, food, and a space to learn and grow each day, while parents/guardians, who are often working or managing other responsibilities, are provided with the peace of mind that their child is cared for after school. The school has also established partnerships with the local police department and local hospitals, which provide supports in the way of sexual health courses for students, access to free preventative health care, and parent workshops, among other things. Taken together, these community partnerships have supported students and families by connecting them to resources, while simultaneously building a greater sense of community within these outside organizations.

24.1.5 Case Study: Kierra

Kierra is a fourteen-year-old, African American female in the eighth grade.[1] She was born and raised in New York City, and currently lives with her mother, stepfather, and five-year-old brother. She reports being in close contact with her maternal grandmother. There is no known history of mental illness in her mother's family, although Kierra's description of her mother suggests a history of mood dysregulation and difficulty managing anger. Little

---

[1] This is a composite, deidentified case that is meant to reflect possible stressors faced by urban middle school adolescents.

is known about Kierra's father or paternal family history. Kierra's stepfather has a history of substance abuse. There is an extensive history of domestic violence, with Kierra often witnessing this violence, in the relationship between Kierra's mother and stepfather. In school, Kierra is an average student who gets along well with both peers and staff members. She has formed several close relationships marked by trust, care, and mutual respect. Despite her ability to create and maintain close relationships, she has had a few relational conflicts that escalated to verbal arguments and, on one occasion, a physical altercation with a peer. Kierra enjoys participating in enrichment activities, including step dance and softball.

In pulling from the toolkit, there are several interventions that have been implemented in an attempt to empower and support Kierra during her three years of middle school, including a trauma and attachment sensitive approach, engagement in the advisory and character programs, completion of the community service project, at-risk counseling services, parental engagement through the parent dinners, and connecting her to the local community center (Oppenheimer et al., n.d.).

24.1.5.1 Trauma and Attachment Sensitive Approach

Kierra's trauma history includes exposure to domestic violence, exposure to substance abuse, and at times when her mother is angry, excessive corporal punishment for perceived misbehaviors. Kierra has reported that her home life is often chaotic and unpredictable. Utilizing the trauma-sensitive approach, the school is able to create a structured setting for Kierra where staff members set out to clearly and concisely articulate expectations around academic work and behaviors, as well as clear and logical consequences should those expectations not be met. Additionally, staff members are encouraged to be thoughtful about the body language, volume, and tone and they use in interactions with Kierra and her classmates. They also set out to provide Kierra with positive praise and, when needed, help coach her in managing her emotions. Taken together, the approach provides a well-structured, safe environment where Kierra has been able to grow and, at times, flourish.

24.1.5.2 Advisory and Character Programs

The advisory and character programs have provided Kierra a small group setting to connect with staff members and peers. In Advisory, Kierra can often be observed engaging in meaningful conversations with her close-knit group. These discussions range from the high school application process to stressors related to social issues within the school. With the help of her advisor, she also uses the program to set personal and academic goals for herself. The advisor regularly checks her grades, which keeps Kierra focused on her goals. If help is needed, or the advisor notices that a grade is slipping, he immediately makes a plan with Kierra to get her back on track.

Kierra similarly utilizes character to engage in meaningful conversations about topics, including bullying prevention. As she continues to develop her own voice, Kierra has become an ally for students who are bullied, and can often be seen advocating for these individuals to school staff and administration. This behavior is in line with her signature character strengths of kindness, love, teamwork, and creativity. Kierra embraces these strengths in her daily interactions, and has continued to practice and develop these strengths during her time in middle school. It is the hope of the psychological intervention team that as these strengths grow, Kierra will employ these strengths to overcome challenges in high school and beyond.

24.1.5.3 Community Service Project

For her community service project, Kierra set out to serve individuals affected by substance abuse. Given her own experience with her stepfather's substance abuse, this was a cause that invigorated Kierra. Accordingly, Kierra connected with a community center focused on providing substance abuse prevention programs to local youth. For several weeks, she visited the program and spent time interacting with the children. In reflecting on the project, Kierra felt grateful to work with this population and provide children with a healthy, positive social experience. When asked to describe her experience at the center, she simply used the word, "fun." Although she successfully met the threshold for service hours required for graduation, Kierra expressed plans to regularly return to the center to provide additional support and outreach.

24.1.5.4 Counseling

Throughout the past three years, Kierra has been seen in weekly, individual counseling with the same provider. Kierra requested counseling herself when she started sixth grade, and has asked for it each year since. Because of Kierra's sometimes chaotic home life, it is important to keep to the structured time and day of counseling. Kierra never misses a session, and if, for some reason, the provider is unable to keep the regularly scheduled time, Kierra immediately asks when the session will be rescheduled.

Each week, Kierra primarily utilizes her counseling time to express her thoughts and feelings related to her home life, peer conflicts, relationships, and academics. She is open and honest, and has become increasingly insightful over the past few years. She has learned coping techniques to use at home when she needs them, including deep breathing and journaling, and has significantly decreased her peer conflicts at school. She has also shown tremendous growth and maturity by coming to the psychological intervention team when she feels someone else is at risk. If she hears a friend or acquaintance talking about self-harm or other concerning issues, she will immediately disclose it for her peer to receive the necessary help.

24.1.5.5 Parent Dinners

Although she did not attend in sixth grade, Kierra's mother started coming to the parent-to-parent dinners in seventh grade and has been coming every month since. While she was a bit reserved at first, she is now one of the most outspoken parents in the group, sharing personal stories of the trials and tribulations of raising a teenager. She also immediately formed connections with other parents who attend, which makes her feel like part of the community. Recently, Kierra was not getting along with a student in her class, but as this student's mother also regularly attends the dinners, the two mothers collaborated to help the students come to a resolution. Because of their strong connection, the two students no longer have any issues with each other. From observations and informal feedback, it is clear the parent dinners benefit both Kierra's mom and Kierra.

24.1.5.6 Community Partners

As previously discussed, Kierra has witnessed domestic violence and her stepfather has a known substance abuse problem. Because of these stressors, Kierra often does not want to go home after school. While she sometimes stays at the school for softball practice, the local community center offers longer hours where Kierra can go when softball gets out. The center not only offers her activities such as cooking, dance, and homework help, but it also offers her a community of supports, from peers her age to the staff that work there. They all look out for each other and provide a safe space for a few extra hours each day after school. Kierra often states she does not know what she would do without the center and is extremely grateful to be connected to such a safe place within the community.

24.2 Conclusion

Given what is known about the ways in which family and community engagement and empowerment can lead to positive outcomes for youth, it is no longer acceptable for schools to function in isolation and focus solely on students' academic achievement. Instead, the school–family–community connection can and should be constantly nurtured and further developed. While this chapter proposed a toolkit for interacting on the student, family, and community levels, individual schools will need to evaluate these interventions to determine which, if any, will work for their unique student body in their current form, or if the interventions should be modified to better fit their setting. It is through purposeful interventions that students and families will be empowered, and in turn, bask in the positive outcomes associated with such empowerment.

References

Becker, J., Greenwald, R., & Mitchell, C. (2011). Trauma-informed treatment for disenfranchised urban children and youth: An open trial. *Child and Adolescent Social Work Journal, 28*(4), 257–272. doi.org/10.1007/s10560-011-0230-4

Bemak, F., Chung, R. C. Y., & Siroskey-Sabdo, L. A. (2005). Empowerment groups for academic success: An innovative approach to prevent high school failure for at-risk, urban African American girls. *Professional School Counseling, 8* (5), 377–389.

Beyond Differences. (n.d.). *No one eats alone: A Beyond Differences initiative.* www.nooneeatsalone.org

Bryan, J. (2005). Fostering educational resilience and achievement in urban schools through school-family-community partnerships. *Professional School Counseling, 8*(3), 219–227.

Bryan, J., & Henry, L. (2012). A model for building school-family-community partnerships: Principles and process. *Journal of Counseling & Development, 90*(4), 408–420. doi.org/10.1002/j.1556-6676.2012.00052.x

Connor, D. J., & Cavendish, W. (2018). Sharing power with parents: Improving educational decision making for students with learning disabilities. *Learning Disabilities Quarterly, 41*(2), 79–84. doi.org/10.1177/0731948717698828

Hartman, S. L., Stotts, J., Ottley, J. R., & Miller, R. (2016). School-community partnerships in rural settings: Facilitating positive outcomes for young children who experience maltreatment. *Early Childhood Education Journal, 45* (3), 403–410. doi.org/10.1007/s10643-016-0796-8

Holcomb-McCoy, C. (2007). *School counseling to close the achievement gap: A social justice approach.* Thousand Oaks, CA: Corwin Press.

Holcomb-McCoy, C., & Bryan, J. (2010). Advocacy and empowerment in parent consultation: Implications for theory and practice. *Journal of Counseling & Development, 88*(3), 259–268. doi.org/10.1002/j.1556-6678.2010.tb00021.x

Jasis, P. M., & Ordonez-Jasis, R. (2004). *Convivencia* to empowerment: Latino parent organizing at La Familia. *The High School Journal, 88*(2), 32–42. doi.org/10.1353/hsj.2004.0023

Kim, J., & Bryan, J. (2017). A first step to a conceptual framework of parent empowerment: Exploring relationships between parent empowerment and academic performance in a national sample. *Journal of Counseling & Development, 95,* 168–179. doi.org/10.1002/jcad.12129

Kim, J., Fletcher, K., & Bryan, J. (2018). Empowering marginalized parents: An emerging parent empowerment model for school counselors. *Professional School Counseling, 21*(1b), 1–9. doi.org/10.1177/2156759X18773585

Kiner, R. (1993). Community service: A middle school success story. *The Clearing House: A Journal of Educational Strategies, Issues and Ideas, 66*(3), 139–140. doi.org/10.1080/00098655.1993.9955952

Moore-Thomas, C., & Day-Vines, N. L. (2010). Culturally competent collaboration: School counselor collaboration with African American families and communities. *Professional School Counseling, 14*(1), 53–63. doi.org/10.1177/2156759X1001400106

Morse, L. L., & Allensworth, D. D. (2015). Placing students at the center: The whole school, whole community, whole child model. *Journal of School Health, 85*(11), 785–794. doi.org/10.1111/josh.12313

Nieto, S. (2000). *Affirming diversity: The sociopolitical context of multicultural education.* New York: Longman.

Oppenheimer, M., Miller, E., & Clauss-Ehlers, C. (n.d.). *Psychological intervention in a middle school located in a high poverty area: An advocacy-based social-emotional health model* [Unpublished manuscript].

Park, N., & Peterson, C. (2006). Moral competence and character strengths among adolescents: The development and validation of the Values in Action Inventory of Strengths for Youth. *Journal of Adolescence, 29*(6), 891–910. doi.org/10.1016/j.adolescence.2006.04.011

Park, N., & Peterson, C. (2008). Positive psychology and character strengths: Application to strengths-based school counseling. *Professional School Counseling, 12*(2), 85–92. doi.org/10.1177/2156759X0801200214

Peterson, C., & Seligman, M. E. P. (2004). *Character strengths and virtues: A handbook and classification.* New York: Oxford University Press & Washington, DC: American Psychological Association.

Pstross, M., Rodriguez, A., Knopf, R. C., & Paris, C. M. (2016). Empowering Latino parents to transform the education of their children. *Education and Urban Society, 48*(7), 650–671. doi.org/10.1177/0013124514541464

Rutter, M., & Maughan, B. (2002). School effectiveness findings, 1979–2002. *Journal of School Psychology, 40*(6), 451–475. doi.org/10.1016/S0022-4405(02)00124-3

Shulkind, S. B., & Foote, J. (n.d.). *Creating a culture of connectedness through middle school advisory programs.* www.amle.org/BrowsebyTopic/WhatsNew/WNDet/TabId/270/ArtMID/888/ArticleID/279/Culture-of-Connectedness-through-Advisory.aspx

Toumbourou, J. W., & Gregg, M. E. (2002). Impact of an empowerment-based parent education program on the reduction of youth suicide risk factors. *Journal of Adolescent Health, 31*(3), 277–285. doi.org/10.1016/s1054-139x(02)00384-1

US Census Bureau. (2016). *American Community Survey 1-year estimates.* Retrieved from Census Reporter Profile page for Congressional District 15, NY. https://censusreporter.org/profiles/50000US3615-new-york-congressional-district-15/

VIA Institute on Character. (n.d.). *Why do character strengths matter?* www.viacharacter.org

25 Women and Immigration

Pratyusha Tummala-Narra, Laura D. Gonzalez,
and Helen P. Hailes

While the social forces and contexts of migration have shifted across the centuries, the movement of individuals and communities around the world has always influenced human society. The International Organization for Migration (IOM, 2019) defines migration as any person or group of persons moving across or within international borders for any length of time as a result of any cause, including refugees and internally displaced persons (IDPs). Now, perhaps more than ever, migration affects the lives and well-being of many: According to the United Nations Department of Economic and Social Affairs (2017), there were more than 257 million migrants world-wide in 2017, with more than 49 million arriving to the United States alone, predominantly from Mexico, China, India, and the Philippines. Approximately half of those migrants, both worldwide and in the USA, were women and girls. Although psychologists have studied the mental health implications of migration for decades (American Psychological Association [APA], 2012), it is important to consider the specific context of women and girls as they migrate. The present chapter seeks to discuss the experience of immigration for women.

In the mid-1900s, the typical migrant to the United States was perceived to be a male head-of-household migrating, sometimes seasonally, to secure employment and send remittances to his family in his country of origin. By the 1980s, this perception began to shift due to research indicating that women had in fact been migrating in significant and increasing numbers to the United States over the course of the twentieth century (Donato et al., 2011). As women's experiences of migration are shaped by contextual and systemic factors, in subsequent decades, researchers began to explore gendered aspects of migration (Suárez-Orozco & Qin, 2006). For example, scholars (Chammartin, 2002) investigated women's search for employment, and related shifts in positions of power within their families. At the same time, research findings note the increased risk of migrating without documentation that can leave women more vulnerable to abuse and violence (Simmons, Menjívar, & Téllez, 2015). These factors, among others, highlight the importance of studying the unique impact of migration on women and girls.

This chapter provides an overview of salient factors that have an impact on migrant women through an ecological framework, emphasizing the role of stressors and supports. The ecological framework in the context of immigration recognizes the dynamic interaction of multiple layers of context and development, including the influence of sociopolitical climate on mental health and access to appropriate resources (APA, 2012; Clauss-Ehlers et al., 2019). We highlight various aspects of immigrant women's ecological contexts and their influence on stress and resilience. Further, while the chapter includes a review of literature concerning refugees, IDPs, asylum seekers, and other migrants, it is not intended to be a comprehensive review of the literature regarding any single group. Although the chapter is relevant to the experiences of immigrant women in different world regions, we focus primarily on experiences of immigrant women in the United States. A case study illustrates the role of some significant risk and protective factors in women's experiences.

25.1 Reasons and Circumstances of Migration

The decision to migrate is a complex and difficult one for migrants, including reasons to leave their country of origin (i.e., push factor) and migrate to a particular country (i.e., pull factor) (Mejía, Pizurki, & Royston, 1979). The push factors that lead to migration out of a country may include forced displacement or voluntary migration. Pull factors may include the hope for securing physical safety, the search for economic and educational opportunities, and family reunification. Some common reasons for forced migration include displacement due to natural disasters, war, conflict, persecution, and trafficking. In cases of voluntary migration, the search for family reunification, employment and education are common reasons driving relocation (APA, 2012).

25.1.1 Natural Disasters

As climate change contributes to increasing numbers of natural disasters, its influence on migratory patterns continues to grow. Most weather-related events result in internal displacement, with 18.8 million displaced people in 2017 due to some form of natural disaster (Internal Displacement Monitoring Centre, 2018). Despite the likelihood of internal displacement, one review of thirty-eight cases of environmental migration found that interstate migration occurred in half of the weather-related events (Reuveny, 2007). Research indicates an increase in depressive symptoms in those fleeing natural disasters, particularly earthquakes, after relocation (Kiliç et al., 2006). Studies have also found that women and girls are especially vulnerable to death in the aftermath of a natural disaster because of preexisting gender inequalities (e.g., men being prioritized for rescue) (Neumayer & Plümper, 2007). Further, women and girls are particularly at risk for climate change-induced migration (Chindarkar, 2012).

25.1.2 Violence and Persecution

In addition to disaster-related displacement, the link between violence and migration has been well documented (Lozano-Gracia et al., 2010). In 2017, the amount of people worldwide who were newly internally displaced due to conflict and violence nearly doubled from the previous year to 11.8 million, with Syria, the Democratic Republic of the Congo, and Iraq accounting for half of the displacement (Internal Displacement Monitoring Centre, 2018). There were another 25 million refugees and 3 million asylum seekers in the same year fleeing some type of violence and persecution (United Nations High Commissioner for Refugees, 2018). Within Latin America, growing economic and political instability in Venezuela since 2014 has resulted in the migration of approximately 4.5 million Venezuelans (with a marked increase since 2019), one of the largest forced displacements in the Western hemisphere (United Nations High Commissioner for Refugees, 2019). Literature has documented the complex decision-making process involved in fleeing violence. For instance, at lower levels of violence, people are more likely to remain in the safety of their home environment. However, as the violence becomes more extreme, people are prompted to flee given the increased threat of staying (Bohra-Mishra & Massey, 2011).

25.1.3 Trafficking

Although human trafficking is not always viewed as a reason for migration, international human trafficking results in a vulnerable person being removed from one's country of origin and taken to a new country, often with the false promise of securing employment opportunities. Human trafficking includes any labor or commercial sex act that is obtained using force, fraud, or coercion (National Institute of Justice, 2019). The National Human Trafficking Hotline reported having 10,949 cases of human trafficking in 2018, within the United States, marking a 25% increase since 2017 (Polaris, 2019). In fact, the hotline identified more than 23,000 survivors, with more than 15,000 of these survivors being female, and the racial backgrounds of the majority of survivors as Latinx, Asian, and African, African American, or Black. Recent migration or relocation was identified as the top risk factor for trafficking among these survivors (Polaris, 2019).

Logan, Walker, and Hunt (2009) reviewed nine reports on human trafficking and noted similar risk factors, indicating that extreme poverty, particularly among immigrants in their countries of origin, leaves people vulnerable to trafficking. They noted that the majority of people trafficked are immigrants and that these reports linked human trafficking particularly to undocumented status. Traffickers, for instance, may lure migrants to the United States with promises of better jobs and a higher quality of life. Additional risk factors identified for immigrants in their country of origin include civil unrest, lack of opportunities for women, a culture of female subservience, corruption in local government, lack of education, isolation, racism, and being young and/or a female (Bryant-Davis & Tummala-Narra, 2017; Logan et al., 2009). These risk factors make it more likely that immigrants may be deceived in their country of origin into believing a trafficker's promise for high-paying jobs and a better life in America. Even if not recruited into trafficking in the home country, the large fees associated with voluntary migration to the United States make trafficking victims more likely to be held in debt bondage (Schauer & Wheaton, 2006).

25.1.4 Search for Family Reunification, Work, and Education

In addition to forced migration and displacement, many women choose to migrate to another country. As the patterns of migration have shifted to reflect an increase in women, transnational motherhood has become a familiar experience for many families. Children are often left behind in the mother's country of origin and cared for by extended family members (Dreby, 2015), which can lead to significant negative sequelae in the children (Cortes, 2015). As children get older and mothers save more money, mothers may send for their children to migrate and reunite with them in the United States (Dreby, 2007). A study with documented immigrants in the United States found that nearly a third of immigrant youth had been separated from at least one parent for two or more years (Gindling & Poggio, 2009). Further, research with both documented and undocumented immigrant youth indicates a significantly higher rate of family separation, with 85% reporting separating from parents at one point during the migration process (Suárez-Orozco, Todorova, & Louie, 2002). Notably, rates of family separation and patterns of reunification varied widely depending on the migrants' country of origin and the migration patterns for that group (Suárez-Orozco et al., 2002). Once families have been reunited in the United States, the issue of family reunification is not completely in the past. The threat of deportation may be ever-present, as 16.6 million people lived in mixed-status families with at least one undocumented member in 2010 (Taylor et al., 2011). If a family member is deported, parents often migrate again to reunite with their children. Among both documented and undocumented migrants, family separation has been identified as the most important factor in the decision to remigrate over economic factors (Berger Cardoso et al., 2016).

Finally, many individuals choose to emigrate in search of work and/or educational opportunities. As globalization has increased, so has the number of women migrating to find work in other countries (Browne & Braun, 2008). Notably, women are migrating as primary wage earners for their families and seeking work in the United States (United Nations, 2005). Many of these women view migration as a means of economic advancement (Dreby, 2015) and are able to send remittances back home to family in their home country

(García, 2018; Moran-Taylor, 2008). Women with university degrees also migrate in order to gain particular job experiences that will open up opportunities in the United States and their countries of origin (Cuban, 2018). Access to better educational opportunities has also been identified as a primary reason for migrating to the United States among some subgroups of Asian immigrants (Chen et al., 2009). Mothers may also migrate to the United States to gain access to resources that will advance their children's educational opportunities in their home country (Moran-Taylor, 2008).

Overall, the decision to emigrate from one's home country is a complex one influenced by various factors (e.g., natural disasters, political conflict, poverty, family reunification, search for work). This decision is further shaped by the specific sociopolitical forces at play in each country.

25.2 Key Stressors

Once women arrive in the United States, they face numerous stressors that shape their lives in their new country as they adjust to a new environment. Common stressors include those related to acculturation, traumatic experiences, discrimination, poverty, and separation from family and friends.

25.2.1 Acculturation

Acculturation to life in the United States can be a significant challenge for those whose experiences in their home countries differ from that of the dominant norms in the United States. In particular, language difficulties pose large barriers that impact numerous domains of life for immigrants. Extant literature has tied limited English skills to barriers finding employment (García, 2018), deceased self-esteem, difficulty developing new and meaningful relationships (Sin, 2015), greater symptoms of depression (Aroian, Uddin, & Blbas, 2017), and difficulty navigating tasks of daily life (e.g., enrolling children in school). Additionally, adapting to different cultural practices and traditions can be a source of stress (Ahmad et al., 2005; Akhtar, 2011). For example, Araújo Dawson (2009) found that both high and low levels of acculturation were significantly related to stress in a sample of Dominican immigrant women. She suggested that this may be due to a loss of support and cultural connections to their home culture in those with low acculturation, while those with high levels of acculturation may have lost cultural protective factors.

Regardless of the level or degree of acculturation, it is clear that this process of adaptation is often a source of stress in the lives of many immigrant women. Further, scholars have noted the importance of recognizing differences in acculturation and cultural value conflicts between immigrant women (first generation) and immigrant-origin women born in the new country (second generation) (Inman, 2006). For example, first- and second-generation women may have different worldviews concerning sex or gender roles and responsibilities in relation to men, sexual expression, and dating relationships (Inman, 2006; Tummala-Narra, 2016). It is also important to note that acculturation is a life-long, dynamic process that interacts with developmental and contextual factors in shaping women's experiences, and that acculturation is experienced uniquely both across and within ethnic groups and immigrant generations (Akhtar, 2011; APA, 2012; Clauss-Ehlers et al., 2019).

25.2.2 Interpersonal Violence

Many immigrants experience significant trauma, such as interpersonal violence and community violence, before arriving in the United States (Comas-Díaz, 2012). Though premigration trauma may contribute to the decision to migrate, migrants also face trauma during and after migration to the United States. In a study of Latina immigrant women (Kaltman et al., 2011), almost 90% of the women had experienced at least one form of violence in their lifetime. Many of these women reported political, community, and interpersonal violence in their countries of origin. Violence during migration depended heavily on the means of immigration (e.g., flying to the USA versus arrival on foot), and women who had prolonged journeys on land reported traumatic and sometimes life-threatening experiences. Upon arrival to the United States, intimate partner violence was the most common form of trauma and was often tied to increased alcohol consumption by a male partner. Further, transwomen migrants face additional stressors and trauma, as they are often targets for abuse in both their countries of origin and in the United States (Cerezo et al., 2014).

Intimate partner violence (IPV) is a particularly notable stressor upon arrival. Numerous studies have documented the experiences of IPV among immigrant women from different national origins (Alvarez et al., 2018; Kaltman et al., 2011; Raj & Silverman, 2002). One study found that abuse by a partner was actually worse for some women after immigrating to the United States (Alvarez et al., 2018). The stressors and barriers women face upon arrival, such as limited knowledge of the US legal system, gender role inequities, and limited English skills, may facilitate the abuse, as the perpetrator gains increased economic, social, and interpersonal power (Kaltman et al., 2011; Raj & Silverman, 2002). Additionally, in some cases, women may live in a continual fear of deportation. Deportation may be used as a threat by their partners (Reina, Lohman, & Maldonado, 2014) or may keep women from reporting IPV to the police for fear that they or their partner will be deported (García, 2018).

Additionally, an emerging area of research has documented the negative impact of sexual violence on immigrant women's well-being. Most research concerning sexual violence among immigrant communities has focused on sexual violence occurring in the context of IPV. However, a recent study with South Asians in the USA indicated that more than one-quarter of participants reported sexual abuse in childhood (Robertson, Nagaraj, & Vyas, 2016). Research further suggests that psychologists should attend to the problem of stigma and silence around sexuality and sexual violence within immigrant communities in the USA, as these factors can exacerbate traumatic stress and limit access to adequate resources (Tummala-Narra et al., 2019). Further, sexual violence can transform identity and perceptions of one's social position, as there are various ecological conditions that impact the ways in which immigrant women and girls experience violence and are responded to by others within their families, ethnic and religious communities, and broader society. The negative impact of sexual trauma can also be compounded by sexism, racism, homophobia, and other forms of discrimination.

25.2.3 Discrimination

Identity-based discrimination can pose a significant stressor for immigrant women due to their multiple marginalized identities. Immigrant women of various ethnic, racial, and religious backgrounds experience racism, xenophobia, and stereotypes (Araújo Dawson, 2009; Muñoz, 2013; Panchanadeswaran & Araújo Dawson, 2011). For example, since the 9/11 terrorist attacks in the USA, there has been a rise of Islamophobia and hate crimes committed against Muslims and those perceived as Muslim, Middle Eastern, or South Asian. Immigrant, Muslim women in the USA and other parts of the world, particularly those wearing visible markers such as the hijab, have been profiled, targeted, harassed, and assaulted (Abu-Ras & Abu-Bader, 2008; Sirin & Fine, 2008). The current anti-immigrant sentiment in the USA, where immigrants are labeled as "terrorists," "rapists," and "criminals," has further triggered harassment and violence against immigrants, particularly Black and Brown women and men. Racial minority immigrant children and adolescents face ongoing racial discrimination at schools, in neighborhoods, and on social media, where they receive derogatory messages from peers and adults about their racial, ethnic, and religious backgrounds (García Coll & Marks, 2009; Suárez-Orozco & Qin, 2006; Tummala-Narra & Sathasivam-Rueckert, 2016). Such experiences have been linked to higher levels of mental health symptoms, including depression, anxiety, and suicidal ideation, and to lower self-esteem (Araújo Dawson, 2009; Panchanadeswaran & Araújo Dawson, 2011; Sirin & Fine, 2008; Tummala-Narra, Alegria, & Chen, 2012).

Sexism and gender-based discrimination can compound experiences of racism or xenophobia for immigrant women. Purkayastha (2005) noted that women arriving in the United States encounter sex-segregated jobs and sexism that limit their career opportunities, leading women to work in less prestigious roles. Moreover, immigrants may migrate to the United States with different expectations of gender roles than the mainstream American culture. The increased opportunities for women in the United States can challenge these gender roles as women secure employment and develop social networks. Research has indicated that this break from traditional gender roles can leave women at increased risk for violence and cause conflict between women and their partners (Alvarez et al., 2018; Raj & Silverman, 2002). Additionally, immigrant women experience gendered racism (Essed, 1991). Specifically, racial stereotypes are gendered such that subgroups of immigrant women and girls are perceived as exotic, passive, hypersexual, or animalistic (Capodilupo & Forsyth, 2014; Smart & Tsong, 2014). Multiracial women may experience marginalization based on stereotypes rooted in gendered racism within multiple racial and ethnic communities. It is important to note that these stereotypes marginalize racial minority immigrant women in ways that are distinct from those marginalizing immigrant men.

In addition to gender-based and race-based discrimination, immigrants who identify as LGBTQ (lesbian, gay, bisexual, transgender, or queer) also face a range of stressors throughout the immigration process. The decision to migrate to the United States may be due to persecution due to their LGBTQ status in one's country of origin (APA, 2012). For some, the United States is viewed as a safe place to live openly and safely (Cerezo et al., 2014). However, immigrants are faced with rejection, violence, harassment, and discrimination based on their sexual orientation and gender identity both in the general public and among their ethnic and/or immigrant communities (Cerezo et al., 2014). The lack of access to culturally sensitive services that acknowledge the needs of LGBTQ migrants poses an additional barrier to an already marginalized group (Chávez, 2011).

We further note that immigrant women with disabilities face a number of systemic challenges related to discrimination. Specifically, immigrants with disabilities experience discrimination both in school and workplace settings, and tend to have less access to resources (APA, 2012; Xiang et al., 2010). There is also a higher risk for interpersonal violence among women and girls with disabilities, both within and outside of their ethnic and religious communities, compounding the effects of disableism on safety (APA, 2012). Estimates of violence against women with disabilities vary, with one review indicating that 26%–90% of women with disabilities experience some type of abuse (e.g., physical, sexual) during their lifetime (Hughes et al., 2011).

25.2.4 Poverty

Foreign-born individuals in the United States have higher rates of poverty than native-born individuals (Jargowsky, 2009), which can be a downward shift in social mobility from their status in their country of origin (Ahmad et al., 2005). For many immigrants, the issue of poverty intersects with traditional gender roles accorded to women. Specifically, women are forced to contend with the decision to stay home to raise their children in the midst of financial hardship or work outside the home to gain greater financial means (Goodkind et al., 2008). Yet, many women struggle to find employment that is appropriate for their skill level while receiving fair compensation (Goodkind et al., 2008). The stress posed by poverty is compounded by documentation status for a subset of immigrants. In some instances, undocumented immigrant women are confronted with the fear that the family's primary earner will be deported, leaving the family with greater economic insecurity (García, 2018). Undocumented immigrants also face policy barriers that restrict their access to certain benefits, such as federal financial aid, internships, and employment (Dreby, 2015; Muñoz, 2013).

25.2.5 Separation from Family and Friends

A common experience for immigrant women is the separation they experience from their family and friends due to migration. For some subgroups of immigrant women, reuniting with loved ones in the USA can be especially daunting. For example, transwomen face challenges with sponsoring their partners, even in cases where they have had sex reassignment surgery and legally married (Chávez, 2011). These separations and losses can have a significant impact on immigrant women. For example, the loss of one's social network and ties to extended family members has been linked to depression, loneliness, and decreased physical health (Ahmad et al. 2005; Garcini et al., 2019). Even when family members are together in the United States, the fear that they or a loved one will be deported is a constant stressor. In fact, the threat of deportation has been found to be the most significant stressor for undocumented women (García, 2018). The connection to one's family and ethnic and/or religious communities has been thought to be an essential source of support in the acculturation process, and as such, separation of family members is a key stressor that shapes psychological health and adjustment to the new country (Akhtar, 2011). Further, recent policies in the USA that separate undocumented immigrants from family members, particularly children and adolescents from their parents and caregivers, imposes systemic abuse of immigrant families, contributing to long-term traumatic stress for parents and children.

Overall, the stressors that immigrant women face upon arrival to the United States are manifold. Some may be expected before migration (e.g., challenges related to acculturation), while others (e.g., discrimination, poverty) may be newly encountered upon arrival. Traumatic stress may be experienced at varying points in the migration process (premigration, during the journey, through displacement, and postmigration). While each of these stressors presents its own set of challenges to women, many migrants also arrive in the United States with a myriad of strengths and supports that may foster resilience in the face of such challenges (APA, 2012).

25.3 Key Sources of Support

Though immigrant women face a range of challenges upon arrival in the United States, research has also documented some of the key sources of support that many women rely upon to cope with the stressors they encounter. While the literature has identified strength and resilience among immigrant women in many forms, the following summary highlights five particularly prominent sources of support: family and friends, safe spaces for women, education, financial resources, and social or political engagement.

25.3.1 Family and Friends

One of the single biggest sources of support that immigrant women have identified in the literature is their relationships and connections with close loved ones, both inside and outside of the family context. Within the family, relationships with spouses or romantic partners can be essential to an immigrant woman's support system. One study of Latina immigrants in an ESL program found that social support from a significant other was associated with a greater sense of meaning in life for both women and men (Dunn & O'Brien, 2009). In another study, Mexican immigrant mothers identified supportive husbands as critical for emotional well-being as well as support in financial and household matters (Ornelas et al., 2009). Research with refugee and undocumented women in the USA found that romantic partners were important sources of support for resilience in the face of trauma (Goodman et al., 2017). Along with romantic partners, immigrant women from diverse national origins have identified family more generally as a key support (Donnelly et al., 2011). For some women, the support of female family members is particularly important (Ornelas et al., 2009). For others, maintaining connection with kin in countries of origin or other countries provides an important support network (Akhtar, 2011). There has also been increased online engagement with the Internet and social media that allows for more frequent contact with family and friends who live far away.

Outside of the family, immigrant women from various national origins have also identified friendships as a key source of social, emotional, and material support (APA, 2012). Further, research indicates that immigrant women rely in particular on other women (Callister, Beckstrand, & Corbett, 2011), and studies of Latina women with postpartum depression, women from China and Sudan, and refugee and undocumented women have found that social supports are particularly valuable within one's own ethnic and/or religious communities (Callister et al., 2011; Donnelly et al., 2011; Goodman et al., 2017). Common bonds that fostered social support included shared ethnicity, language, or country of origin. While there is stigma and silence concerning issues of interpersonal violence among many immigrant communities and families, the role of support and advocacy within families and ethnic and religious communities is especially important for survivors' well-being (Tummala-Narra et al., 2019).

25.3.2 Safe Spaces for Women

Supportive relationships for immigrant women may develop organically and informally through family and community networks. However, some research also suggests that there may be an additional value of formalized groups and safe spaces for immigrant women to meet, share, and support one another. These spaces seem particularly critical for women seeking safety and support around issues of domestic violence. For instance, in a study of domestic violence support groups for Mexican immigrant women, participants found the groups empowering (Marrs Fuchsel & Hysjulien, 2013) and, similarly, a culturally informed program for Latina immigrant women focused on self-esteem and domestic violence increased participants' self-esteem and personal growth and led to a greater sense of empowerment in relationships (Marrs Fuchsel, 2014). Not only can support groups for immigrant women increase empowerment and self-esteem, but they have also been shown to help women build relationships and support networks that may carry on outside of the designated safe space (Molina et al., 2009). It is worth noting that in some cases, immigrant women's informal groups and collectives transform over time to more formal resources. For example, Saheli is a women's group in the Boston area that was initiated by a group of Indian immigrant mothers who sought to engage in discussions about their families' adjustment to US society. Over the past two decades, Saheli developed into a formal group that provides advocacy for South Asian survivors of domestic violence and economic empowerment for South Asian women. These types of women's groups are critical sources of support for immigrant women and their families.

25.3.3 Education

Along with social support, access to education can be an important factor in the coping and well-being of immigrant women. While immigrant women may arrive in the United States with a wide range of educational backgrounds and experiences, one common obstacle that many face upon arrival is English-language learning. In a study with Vietnamese refugee and immigrant women in the USA, English-language proficiency was correlated with better mental health outcomes (Brown, Schale, & Nilsson, 2010), and in a study with immigrant women in Canada, participants identified taking English classes as one of the central tasks of settling into their new country (Dlamini, Anucha, & Wolfe, 2012). Studies of both Mexican immigrant mothers and of refugee women living in the United States have found that accessing free English classes in the community or through refugee resettlement agencies is a key strategy for maintaining emotional health (Goodman et al., 2017; Ornelas et al., 2009). In addition to learning English, immigrant women caregivers from China and from South Asia have identified other education opportunities, including parenting classes and professional education programs, as valuable supports (Neufeld et al., 2002).

25.3.4 Financial Resources

One reason why education and English-language proficiency can be essential to coping and adjusting to life in the United States is that these can be limiting factors in finding employment outside of the home. Diverse groups of immigrant women, including Mexican immigrant women with a history of domestic violence and elderly Indian immigrant women, have discussed financial independence and the ability to have control over personal finances as an important coping strategy (Acharya & Northcott, 2007; Kim et al., 2017). For some immigrant women, working outside of the home is both a source of economic and social freedom and also as a method of achieving higher status within their own household (Dlamini et al., 2012). Immigrant and refugee women have also shared that engagement in classes or jobs can serve as a welcome distraction from some of life's difficulties and hardships (Goodman et al., 2017).

Along with seeking employment and striving for financial independence and stability, immigrant women have also reported receiving financial or material support from services and resources provided by refugee resettlement agencies, NGOs, government programs, and even through their children's schools (Goodman et al., 2017; Ornelas et al., 2009). These kinds of formal support programs can provide necessary tangible resources to promote not only financial stability but also other related outcomes, such as housing and food security. Unsurprisingly, stable housing has been found to be critical for the mental health of immigrant women, and finding a place to live is a top priority of many (Dlamini et al., 2012).

25.3.5 Social and Political Engagement

Another critical source of coping and support for immigrant women is engagement in social, cultural, and religious/spiritual communities and political action. While it is not possible here to review the many forms of such engagement, we highlight women's involvement in religious communities and community activism. Immigrant women of various religious backgrounds endorse the use of religious or spiritual coping for emotional suffering and trauma (Donnelly et al., 2011; Dunn & O'Brien, 2009), and religious activities such as praying and fasting can serve as an important source of cultural connection (Acharya & Northcott, 2007). Additionally, immigrant women describe religious communities as sources of support. For instance, in one study of Mexican immigrant women, the Catholic Church provided a community of informal supports during experiences of domestic violence (Marrs Fuchsel, 2012). Another study found that immigrant Latina mothers used churches as a way to meet other Latina mothers and experienced priests as a source of advice and comfort (Ornelas et al., 2009). These findings parallel those in other research with immigrant women from different religious and spiritual backgrounds, such as Muslim, Hindu, Buddhist, and Jewish women (Sirin & Fine, 2008; Tummala-Narra, 2016).

Immigrant women may also find a sense of community, purpose, and political engagement by participating in grassroots activism movements. For example, one study of grassroots organizing among Mexican immigrant women in the United States found that involvement in activism helped immigrant women to develop a greater political consciousness and a sense of community (Jiménez, 2010). Another study focused on racialized immigrant women in Canada and indicated that involvement in activism played a role in women's overall well-being (MacDonnell et al., 2017). In particular, engagement in activism increased immigrant women's resilience and contributed to a greater sense of agency.

While facing challenges in their adjustment to a new country, immigrant women carry remarkable strength, resilience, and creativity in coping. The interpersonal and material supports discussed above represent many but not all of the key sources of support that immigrant women engage and rely upon as they build communities and lives away from their countries of origin. While these supports promote well-being, mental health concerns among immigrant women are important to consider.

25.4 Mental Health Concerns

Immigrant women experience a wide range of mental health concerns, such as depression, anxiety, post-traumatic stress disorder (PTSD), substance abuse, eating disorders, bipolar disorder, psychosis, and suicidal ideation (APA, 2012). Migration and displacement can shape not only psychological processes (e.g., identity, self-esteem) but also psychological distress and mental health problems. Despite evidence noting the prevalence of mental health distress among immigrants and their children, immigrants underutilize mental health services (Sue et al., 2012). Further, immigrant women tend to rely more on family and community structures, religious practices, and healing practices consistent with their heritage culture (APA, 2012; Chávez, 2011; Da Silva et al., 2017). At the same time, mental health problems are often unrecognized by others within families and communities, posing risk to women's health. It is also important to note that a majority of studies concerning differences in prevalence of mental health problems such as depression and anxiety across immigrant generation indicate that second and later generation racial minority immigrant-origin individuals (individuals born and raised in the USA) experience worse mental health outcomes when compared with racial minority first-generation immigrants (individuals who arrived to the USA as adults) (García Coll & Marks, 2009). These findings, marking what has come to be known as the "immigrant paradox" (Alegria et al., 2008), do not suggest that first-generation immigrants are not experiencing mental health symptomology. Rather, they indicate that second and later generations may be at particular risk for psychological distress, and that distress may be experienced uniquely across immigrant generations (APA, 2012).

25.4.1 Mental Health in the Immigrant Context

Although there are shared biological, psychological, interpersonal, and systemic factors that contribute to mental health concerns among women across different sociocultural backgrounds, there are some unique features of the immigrant context that shape the experience of mental health concerns among racial minority immigrant women. Generally, mental health concerns in the immigrant context have been thought to be rooted in three major forms of stress, including acculturation, discrimination, and trauma (APA, 2012). Psychological distress may be rooted in or compounded by acculturative stress, as immigrant women negotiate a new cultural and linguistic environment, shifts in gender role expectations, and norms concerning expressions of sexuality (Awad, Martinez, & Amer, 2013). There may also be significant changes in family structure and dynamics, which along with acculturative stress, contributes to intergenerational conflict among older and younger members within the family (Lui, 2015). For example, parents and children may have divergent views of friendships, dating, and career choices due to distinct acculturative processes experienced by each member of the family. Immigrant parents may wish to retain heritage cultural and religious traditions, as they cope with separation from family and a familiar environment in the country of origin, while children may wish to engage more fully in mainstream social context. It is important to note that acculturative stress experienced by parents and children tends not to be spoken about explicitly within families, and yet contributes to feelings of distress and disconnection among family members (Tummala-Narra, 2016).

With regard to stress related to discrimination, it is important to note that cumulative experiences of discrimination based on gender, race, ethnicity, immigration status, religion, sexual orientation, disability, and social class can have lasting consequences to mental health, identity, and relational life. Both overt and subtle discrimination, stereotypes, and microaggressions (verbal and/or behavioral slights and invalidating experiences, based in stereotypes and prejudice, directed against individuals and groups, such as racial, ethnic, religious, and sexual minorities and women) in addition to shaping mental health, have consequences for a sense of belonging in the new country, as immigrants cope with psychological isolation (APA, 2012; Sue et al., 2007).

Undocumented women are especially vulnerable to racial profiling, discrimination, trafficking, exposure to gangs, and deportation (APA, 2012; Garcini et al., 2019). Many immigrant women and girls further struggle with marginalization within their homes and ethnic and religious communities, which further compounds psychological distress (Tummala-Narra, 2016). As mentioned earlier, traumatic stress rooted in interpersonal violence, community violence, trafficking, and political trauma often contributes to depression, post-traumatic stress and other types of anxiety disorders, substance abuse, and suicidal ideation and behavior.

25.4.2 Barriers to Seeking and Receiving Help

Mental health concerns based in these ecological conditions are often unrecognized by others as a result of several factors. From a systemic perspective, many immigrant women face discrimination and a lack of access to culturally informed assessment, psychotherapy, and other forms of intervention. In fact, many Black women immigrants in the USA experience an overdiagnosis of psychotic disorders, indicating a lack of understanding of the role of social and contextual stressors in their lives (Nicolas & Smith, 2013). Undocumented women, due to fear of their own deportation or that of loved ones, may not seek the help of mental health professionals, as it is unclear in many mental health and legal settings whether their documentation status will be reported to authorities (Yoshikawa, 2011). Immigrant women also face limitations in mental health service settings in accessing providers who speak their heritage language (APA, 2012). Further, in many clinical settings, a Western, Eurocentric theoretical framework continues to guide formulation and intervention, contributing to clinicians' bias with regard to views on psychopathology and resilience (Tummala-Narra, 2016).

The lack of access to culturally informed providers and systems of care contributes to women's reluctance to seek help, as they are aware that they may face further marginalization within mental healthcare settings. It is important to note disparities that exist in access to health care and mental health care among immigrant communities in the USA. Specifically, there is a high degree of unmet mental health needs among lower-income immigrant communities, and among communities where there is little access to English-language learning. For example, in a study indicating significant health disparities experienced by Bangladeshi immigrant women in New York City, almost half of the participants reported receiving incomes that were at or below the federal poverty level, and more than 90% of women had limited English proficiency (Patel, Rajpathak, & Karasz, 2012).

Immigrant women may also not report psychological distress within their families and communities due to stigma and concern that they may burden others. This appears to be especially poignant for women experiencing interpersonal violence, and women marginalized due to their sexual orientation, gender identity, and disability (APA, 2012). Relatedly, definitions of mental illness and psychological distress vary significantly across cultural contexts, and although women may report experiences consistent with depression, anxiety, or other types of stress categorized in US diagnostic systems, the ways in which they experience and express psychological distress may be distinct from that which is familiar to a mental health professional (Collier, Munger, & Moua, 2012; Tummala-Narra, 2016). For example, an immigrant, Korean American woman may express her feelings of sadness through somatic symptoms such as headaches. She may experience this particular form of expression as more culturally congruent with the ways in which distress is communicated to others in her family and in her Korean and Korean American communities.

25.5 Critical Issues in Interventions

The current Multicultural Guidelines of the American Psychological Association (Clauss-Ehlers et al., 2019) offer a broad framework through which clinical and community-based interventions with immigrant women can be formulated and implemented. The Guidelines draw on Bronfenbrenner's (1979) ecological model, including emphasis on various layers of an individual's ecological context: (1) the *microsystem* (family, friends, teachers, and institutions); (2) the *mesosystem* (relationships and social entities in the microsystem); (3) the *exosystem* (societal and cultural forces, such as immigration policy); (4) the *macrosystem* (cultural context, values, and norms); and (5) the *chronosystem* (passage of time, developmental transitions, historical context). This framework suggests that interactions within and across these different layers of one's ecological context are dynamic in nature, affecting individuals' and communities' psychological experiences, well-being, and identity (Clauss-Ehlers et al., 2019). As ecological conditions shape immigrant women's experiences with migration, displacement, and acculturation in unique ways, it is important that interventions consider the impact of these conditions on mental health.

Additionally, the ecological model supports a contextual understanding of women's resilience in the face of challenges related to migration and cultural adjustment. Specifically, resilience should be understood through closely examining how any single woman may define resilience and how her heritage cultural context and her new cultural context shape her views. It is also important to recognize that immigrant women may experience any given context as both a source of stress and resilience. For example, a woman who is divorced or separated from her spouse may draw a sense of meaning and purpose through engaging in her spiritual community, and at the same time feel marginalized and isolated when members of her spiritual community denigrate divorce. As such, psychologists' recognition of resilience as culturally embedded is critical to developing appropriate assessment and intervention (APA, 2012; Harvey, 2007).

25.5.1 Psychotherapy

Consistent with the ecological model, feminist and multicultural scholars have developed approaches to working with immigrant women in clinical settings that emphasize women's empowerment and well-being with attunement to the challenges faced by immigrant women. Feminist, multicultural scholars have established therapeutic approaches that recognize diversity of backgrounds and intersectionality of identities and social locations among women of color (Comas-Díaz, 2012). For example, for many women of color, a specific type of discrimination, such as racism, may be more salient in a particular context, more so than another type of discrimination, such as homophobia. At the same time, their experiences of homophobia may become more salient within a different context, or during a different developmental period. Therefore, it is important that clinicians integrate an understanding of the complexity of immigrant women's experiences, which encompasses but is not limited to experiences of gender, race, sexual identity, social class, immigration status, religion, and disability. Further, definitions of feminism and related constructs vary significantly across and within cultural contexts (Tummala-Narra, 2016). For example, how the concept of assertiveness is conceptualized in one cultural context can diverge from that of another context. For some immigrant women, assertiveness may manifest in expressing their personal needs nonverbally rather than stating their needs verbally, which is often a premise of interventions in the USA, such as assertiveness training.

Feminist and multicultural psychotherapy approaches have also been integrated with other frameworks, such as psychodynamic, humanistic, and cognitive-behavioral theories, emphasizing women's experiences in relation to their sociocultural contexts (Chang et al., 2016; Crane, 2013). These integrative approaches stress the importance of the therapist's development of knowledge of the client's sociocultural background and context, and reflection of the impact of their own sociocultural histories on the therapeutic relationship (Hays, 2016; Tummala-Narra, 2016). Over the past two decades, scholars have also proposed Womanist and Mujerista perspectives that emphasize women's cultural and spiritual narratives as critical to empowerment and therapeutic change (Bryant-Davis & Comas-Díaz, 2016). It is important to consider that these emerging perspectives on psychotherapy with women of color and immigrant women call for increased attention to the unique needs of specific immigrant communities and to subgroups of women within these communities (e.g., sexual minorities, women with disabilities, undocumented women, multiracial women). Further, it is sometimes necessary to modify traditional models of psychotherapy to include helpful traditional healing practices and the client's significant others, such as family, friends, and religious or spiritual figures, when these individuals can provide support necessary for the healing process (Comas-Díaz, 2012).

Trauma-focused psychotherapy approaches are also increasingly integrating understandings of sociocultural context, including experiences of premigration context, transit to new country and displacement process, and postmigration context (Amri & Bemak, 2013; Comas-Díaz, 2012). Specifically, stress related to interpersonal violence, political violence, and discrimination is conceptualized with the recognition of the complexities of the immigration and acculturation processes. Regardless of the clinician's particular theoretical perspective, we emphasize the importance of using a strength-based approach to understand the challenges faced by immigrant women and their families. We also recommend that therapists examine the linguistic and cultural needs of clients in psychotherapy, as defined within the client's sociocultural context and experience, and consider how the cultural narratives of the therapist interplay with that of the client (Clauss-Ehlers et al., 2019; Tummala-Narra, 2016).

25.5.2 Community-Based Intervention

Community-based intervention can be particularly effective in addressing psychological distress related to mental health issues, discrimination, and trauma experienced by immigrant women. Outreach efforts that involve culturally informed psychoeducation can be especially helpful and can address some gaps in access to mental health services. For example, school-based interventions can promote an awareness of the impact of interpersonal violence and discrimination in the lives of adolescent girls, and community-based health fairs can improve mental health literacy and, specifically, understandings about the impact of mental health distress on women's overall well-being (Na, Ryder, & Kirmayer, 2016). Further, research indicates that family-based interventions can also be used effectively to raise awareness of mental health problems (e.g., depression, anxiety, traumatic stress, suicidal ideation) faced by immigrant women (Fang & Schinke, 2013). These interventions should develop through collaboration with stakeholders within families and communities, and recognize the linguistic or other communication needs of all members. Family and community-based interventions can take a number of different forms in addressing mental health issues, such as education aimed at preventing and responding to sexual violence, discussion related to how individuals within a family or community can address stigma accorded to mental illness, and dialogue concerning dilemmas of parenting in a new cultural context and negotiating shifts in gender roles (Lau, Fung, & Yung, 2010).

Community-based intervention can also include ongoing education and training of professionals in mental health and legal settings focused on developing knowledge of the specific experiences and needs of immigrant women and their families, and the impact of immigration policies on the daily lives of women (e.g., undocumented women) (Garcini et al., 2019). Training of law enforcement officials is also critical to develop more trust among survivors of violence and trauma who make attempts to seek help. There can also be increased collaboration between mental health professionals, medical professionals, policymakers, and law enforcement officials such that immigrant women can access a network of individuals who can support them, rather than engender fear and mistrust of systems that may otherwise be able to provide resources (Sabri, Simonet, & Campbell, 2018). Finally, education and outreach are increasingly conducted online, and are particularly important for subgroups of immigrant women who have little access to information regarding issues such as the impact of immigration, trauma, discrimination, and acculturation on mental health, and available resources. Some of these subgroups include women who are undocumented, experience financial hardship, trauma, language and cultural barriers, identify as a sexual or gender minority, have a disability, or have been victimized through trafficking. Therefore, community-based interventions should be formulated and implemented in ways that can be accessed by immigrant women who are especially vulnerable due to these conditions and/or social locations.

25.6 Case Vignette: Adina

Please note that the identifying information for this client has been modified to protect confidentiality.

Adina is a twenty-nine-year-old cisgender woman who emigrated from Bangladesh to the USA soon after she married. She was referred to a psychologist by her cousin, after experiencing increasing anxiety and sadness, and an inability to concentrate at her workplace. When Adina first met her therapist, she was overwhelmed by sadness related to her separation from her husband who had been physically and psychologically abusive to her since the beginning of their marriage. Although the couple do not have children together, Adina had hoped to become a mother and came to believe that this was no longer a possibility in her life due to her separation. Adina reported that she met her husband through a family friend in Bangladesh, and that she fell in love with her husband the first time she met him. She knew little about her husband or his family who resided in the USA, but based on her family friend's recommendation, she agreed to get married. A few months later, the couple were married and they resided in a suburban area in the USA with his parents and younger brother and his younger brother's wife. Adina, who is fluent in English, completed a bachelor's degree in Bangladesh, and after moving to the USA, worked part-time in a retail store.

Several weeks after moving to the USA, Adina was shocked and devastated when her husband began to hit her. The physical violence led to emotional abuse, where he would insult her appearance and her family for apparently being from a lower middle-class background. His family compounded her stress by ignoring her pleas for help. Over the course of several weeks and months, Adina resigned to the idea that her marriage would not last, and she contacted her parents who encouraged her to seek help from a distant cousin who lived in close proximity to her, but discouraged her from returning to Bangladesh due to stigma of marital separation and divorce for women.

She maintained frequent contact with her mother who prayed with her, and encouraged her to find a mosque where she could "pray for an answer" to her marriage. In the coming weeks, Adina made the decision to seek her cousin's help and moved to her home. While staying with her cousin, although she did not feel threatened by her husband, she and her cousin were targeted by a neighbor who sent them notes stating that they "should go back to their country" and others stating "No Muslims in the USA." Although Adina had not experienced explicit forms of racism prior to these incidents, she did experience Islamophobia when some people in her neighborhood made negative statements about Muslims, stereotyping them as terrorists. She noted to her therapist that she and her cousin may have been targeted by more overt racism since her cousin wears a hijab.

Adina's anxiety and sadness related to her abuse and betrayal by her husband and subsequent separation from him became overwhelming as she faced hostility in the USA toward Muslims and immigrants. She was grateful for the support she received from her cousin who encouraged her to seek medical and mental health care as a first step in coping with her trauma, and gradually forming decisions about her marriage.

In psychotherapy, Adina's work focused on managing her symptoms of anxiety and depression, and eventually her traumatic stress (e.g., flashbacks, nightmares, difficulty sleeping, trouble concentrating). Adina told her therapist that she feels "lost" without a home in the USA or in Bangladesh. She may further face deportation if she decides not to remain in the marriage. She has been exploring the possibility of seeking asylum, but in the current political climate she does not feel as though this is a viable option. When her therapist inquired about where she would prefer to live, Adina stated that she wished she could return to Bangladesh, but she worried about bringing shame to her parents and her siblings, due to the stigma faced by divorced women in her community. She recognized that her parents love her and want her to be safe, and yet, at the same time, they fear for her safety in both Bangladesh and in the USA.

Adina's case illustrates the complexity of women's experiences of immigration and adjustment to living in a new country, within the context of interpersonal violence. Adina's traumatic stress and immigration experience are intertwined in that she negotiates her marriage, relationships with family members, her new cultural environment, and separation from loved ones within a traumatic context. She receives support and affirmation from her family of origin, and at the same time experiences constraints that are embedded in both her US and Bangladeshi contexts. We highlight the unique ways in which immigrants draw on sources of resilience (e.g., family, spirituality in Adina's case) in making challenging decisions in a hostile and demeaning climate.

It is critical that her therapist create a space in which Adina can both receive support in managing her stress, and explore her experiences of trauma and immigration in a way that fully recognizes the complexity of her dilemma regarding where to live. It is also important that the therapist collaborate with Adina to identify and expand sources of support outside of her family such that she can access appropriate legal help that can help guide her decisions in the future.

25.7 Conclusion

Immigrant women experience a range of different challenges and opportunities in adapting to a new country. The reasons for migrating are greatly varied, as are experiences of the premigration context, migration or displacement, and postmigration context. In this chapter, we have identified a number of important sources of stress and support that shape the acculturation process. There is a clear need for improved access to culturally informed interventions that recognize the influence of multiple layers of women's ecological contexts on their well-being. We have also emphasized that psychologists should attend to the unique experiences of subgroups of immigrant women whose individual histories, identities, social locations, and ecological conditions interact to influence mental health and access to appropriate resources. We call for increased attention to the nuances of formulation and implementation of psychological interventions that consider stress and resilience faced by immigrant women, their families, and their communities.

References

Abu-Ras, W., & Abu-Bader, S. (2008). The impact of the September 11, 2001 attacks on the well-being of Arab Americans in New York City. *Journal of Muslim Mental Health, 3*(2), 217–239. doi.org/10.1080/15564900802487634

Acharya, M. P., & Northcott, H. C. (2007). Mental distress and the coping strategies of elderly Indian immigrant women. *Transcultural Psychiatry, 44*(4), 614–636. doi.org/10.1177/1363461507083901

Ahmad, F., Shik, A., Vanza, R., et al. (2005). Voices of South Asian women: Immigration and mental health. *Women & Health, 40*(4), 113–130. doi.org/10.1300/j013v40n04_07

Akhtar, S. (2011). *Immigration and acculturation: Mourning, adaptation, and the next generation.* New York: Jason Aronson.

Alegria, M., Chatterji, P., Wells, K., et al. (2008). Disparity in depression treatment among racial and ethnic minority populations in the United States. *Psychiatric Services*, *59*(11), 1264–1272. doi.org/10.1176/appi.ps.59.11.1264

Alvarez, C., Lameiras-Fernandez, M., Holliday, C. N., Sabri, B., & Campbell, J. (2018). Latina and Caribbean immigrant women's experiences with intimate partner violence: A story of ambivalent sexism. *Journal of Interpersonal Violence*. doi.org/10.1177/0886260518777006.

American Psychological Association. (2012). *Crossroads: The psychology of immigration in the new century – Report of the APA Presidential Task Force on Immigration*. Washington, DC: American Psychological Association. www.apa.org/topics/immigration/immigration-report.pdf

Amri, S., & Bemak, F. (2013). Mental health help-seeking behaviors of Muslim immigrants in the United States: Overcoming social stigma and cultural mistrust. *Journal of Muslim Mental Health*, *7*(1), 43–63. doi.org/10.3998/jmmh.10381607.0007.104

Araújo Dawson, B. (2009). Discrimination, stress, and acculturation among Dominican immigrant women. *Hispanic Journal of Behavioral Sciences*, *31*(1), 96–111. doi.org/10.1177/0739986308327502

Aroian, K., Uddin, N., & Blbas, H. (2017). Longitudinal study of stress, social support, and depression in married Arab immigrant women. *Health Care for Women International*, *38*(2), 100–117. doi.org/10.1080/07399332.2016.1253698

Awad, G. H., Martinez, M. S., & Amer, M. M. (2013). Considerations for psychotherapy with immigrant women of Arab/Middle Eastern descent. *Women & Therapy*, *36*(3–4), 163–175. doi.org/10.1080/02703149.2013.797761

Berger Cardoso, J., Hamilton, E. R., Rodriguez, N., Eschbach, K., & Hagan, J. (2016). Deporting fathers: Involuntary transnational families and intent to remigrate among Salvadoran deportees. *International Migration Review*, *50*(1), 197–230. doi.org/10.1111/imre.12106

Bohra-Mishra, P., & Massey, D. S. (2011). Individual decisions to migrate during civil conflict. *Demography*, *48*(2), 401–424. doi.org/10.1007/s13524-011-0016-5

Bronfenbrenner, U. (1979). *The ecology of human development: Experiments by nature and design*. Cambridge, MA: Harvard University Press.

Brown, C., Schale, C. L., & Nilsson, J. E. (2010). Vietnamese immigrant and refugee women's mental health: An examination of age of arrival, length of stay, income, and English language proficiency. *Journal of Multicultural Counseling and Development*, *38*(2), 66–76. doi.org/10.1002/j.2161-1912.2010.tb00115.x

Browne, C. V., & Braun, K. L. (2008). Globalization, women's migration, and the long-term-care workforce. *The Gerontologist*, *48*(1), 16–24. doi.org/10.1093/geront/48.1.16

Bryant-Davis, T., & Comas-Díaz, L. (2016). *Womanist and Mujerista psychologies: Voices of fire, acts of courage*. Washington, DC: American Psychological Association.

Bryant-Davis, T., & Tummala-Narra, P. (2017). Cultural oppression and human trafficking: Exploring the role of racism and ethnic bias. *Women & Therapy, Special Issue on Trafficking*, *40*(1–2), 152–169. doi.org/10.1080/02703149.2016.1210964

Callister, L. C., Beckstrand, R. L., & Corbett, C. (2011). Postpartum depression and help-seeking behaviors in immigrant Hispanic women. *Journal of Obstetric, Gynecologic & Neonatal Nursing, 40*(4), 440–449. doi.org/10.1111/j.1552-6909 .2011.01254.x

Capodilupo, C. M., & Forsyth, J. M. (2014). Consistently inconsistent: A review of the literature on eating disorders and body image among women of color. In M. L. Miville & A. D. Ferguson (Eds.), *Handbook of race-ethnicity and gender in psychology* (pp. 343–359). New York: Springer.

Cerezo, A., Morales, A., Quintero, D., & Rothman, S. (2014). Trans migrations: Exploring life at the intersection of transgender identity and immigration. *Psychology of Sexual Orientation and Gender Diversity, 1*(2), 170–180. doi.org/10.1037/sgd0000031

Chammartin, G. (2002). *The feminization of international migration.* International Migration Programme: International Labour Organization, 37–40. https:// library.fes.de/pdf-files/gurn/00072.pdf

Chang, D. F., Hung, T., Ng, N., et al. (2016). Taoist cognitive therapy: Treatment of generalized anxiety disorder in a Chinese immigrant woman. *Asian American Journal of Psychology, 7*(3), 205–216. doi.org/10.1037/aap0000052

Chávez, K. R. (2011). Identifying the needs of LGBTQ immigrants and refugees in Southern Arizona. *Journal of Homosexuality, 58*(2), 189–218. doi.org/10 .1080/00918369.2011.540175

Chen, J., Gee, G. C., Spencer, M. S., Danziger, S. H., & Takeuchi, D. T. (2009). Perceived social standing among Asian immigrants in the US: Do reasons for immigration matter? *Social Science Research, 38*(4), 858–869. doi.org/10 .1016/j.ssresearch.2009.06.003

Chindarkar, N. (2012). Gender and climate change-induced migration: Proposing a framework for analysis. *Environmental Research Letters, 7*(2), 025601. doi .org/10.1088/1748-9326/7/2/025601

Clauss-Ehlers, C., Chiriboga, D., Hunter, S. J., Roysircar-Sodowsky, G., & Tummala-Narra, P. (2019). APA Multicultural Guidelines executive summary: Ecological approach to context, identity, and intersectionality. *American Psychologist, 74*(2), 232–244. doi.org/10.1037/amp0000382

Collier, A. F., Munger, M., & Moua, Y. K. (2012). Hmong mental health needs assessment: A community-based partnership in a small mid-western community. *American Journal of Community Psychology, 49*(1–2), 73–86. doi.org/10 .1007/s10464-011-9436-z

Comas-Díaz, L. (2012). *Multicultural care: A clinician's guide to cultural competence.* Washington, DC: American Psychological Association.

Cortes, P. (2015). The feminization of international migration and its effects on the children left behind: Evidence from the Philippines. *World Development, 65,* 62–78. doi.org/10.1016/j.worlddev.2013.10.021

Crane, L. S. (2013). Multiracial daughters of Asian immigrants: Identity and agency. *Women & Therapy, 36*(3–4), 268–285. doi.org/10.1080/02703149 .2013.797776

Cuban, S. (2018). "Any sacrifice is worthwhile doing": Latina au pairs migrating to the United States for opportunities. *Journal of Immigrant & Refugee Studies, 16* (3), 235–254. doi.org/10.1080/15562948.2016.1263775

Da Silva, N., Dillon, F. R., Verdejo, T. R., Sanchez, M., & De La Rosa, M. (2017). Acculturative stress, psychological distress, and religious coping among Latina young adult immigrants. *The Counseling Psychologist*, *45*(2), 213–236. doi.org/10.1177%2F0011000017692111

Dlamini, N., Anucha, U., & Wolfe, B. (2012). Negotiated positions: Immigrant women's views and experiences of employment in Canada. *Affilia*, *27*(4), 420–434. doi.org/10.1177/0886109912464479

Donato, K. M., Alexander, J. T., Gabaccia, D. R., & Leinonen, J. (2011). Variations in the gender composition of immigrant populations: How they matter. *International Migration Review*, *45*(3), 495–526. doi.org/10.1111% 2Fj.1747-7379.2011.00856.x

Donnelly, T. T., Hwang, J. J., Este, D., et al. (2011). If I was going to kill myself, I wouldn't be calling you. I am asking for help: Challenges influencing immigrant and refugee women's mental health. *Issues in Mental Health Nursing*, *32*(5), 279–290. doi.org/10.3109/01612840.2010.550383

Dreby, J. (2007). Children and power in Mexican transnational families. *Journal of Marriage and Family*, *69*(4), 1050–1064. doi.org/10.1111/j.1741-3737.2007 .00430.x

Dreby, J. (2015). US immigration policy and family separation: The consequences for children's well-being. *Social Science & Medicine*, *132*, 245–251. doi.org/10 .1016/j.socscimed.2014.08.041

Dunn, M. G., & O'Brien, K. M. (2009). Psychological health and meaning in life: Stress, social support, and religious coping in Latina/Latino immigrants. *Hispanic Journal of Behavioral Sciences*, *31*(2), 204–227. doi .org/10.1177/0739986309334799

Essed, P. (1991). *Understanding everyday racism*. Newbury Park, CA: SAGE Publications.

Fang, L., & Schinke, S. P. (2013). Two-year outcomes of a randomized, family-based substance use prevention trial for Asian American adolescent girls. *Psychology of Addictive Behaviors*, *27*(3), 788–798. doi.org/10.1037/a0030925

García, S. J. (2018). Living a deportation threat: Anticipatory stressors confronted by undocumented Mexican immigrant women. *Race and Social Problems*, *10*(3), 221–234. doi.org/10.1007/s12552-018-9244-2

García Coll, C., & Marks, A. K. (2009). *Immigrant stories: Ethnicity and academics in middle childhood*. New York: Oxford University Press.

Garcini, L. M., Galvin, T., Pena, J. M., et al. (2019). "A high price paid": Migration-related loss and distress among undocumented Mexican immigrants. *Journal of Latinx Psychology*, *7*(3), 245–255. doi.org/10.1037/lat0000127

Gindling, T. H., & Poggio, S. (2009). *Family separation and the educational success of immigrant children* [Policy Brief]. Baltimore: University of Maryland.

Goodkind, J. R., Gonzales, M., Malcoe, L. H., & Espinosa, J. (2008). The Hispanic Women's Social Stressor Scale: Understanding the multiple social stressors of US-and Mexico-born Hispanic women. *Hispanic Journal of Behavioral Sciences*, *30*(2), 200–229. doi.org/10.1177/0739986308316178

Goodman, R. D., Vesely, C. K., Letiecq, B., & Cleaveland, C. L. (2017). Trauma and resilience among refugee and undocumented immigrant women. *Journal of Counseling & Development*, *95*(3), 309–321. doi.org/10.1002/jcad.12145

Harvey, M. R. (2007). Towards an ecological understanding of resilience in trauma survivors. *Journal of Aggression, Maltreatment & Trauma, 14*(1–2), 9–32. doi .org/10.1300/J146v14n01_02

Hays, P. A. (2016). *Addressing cultural complexities in practice: Assessment, diagnosis, and therapy*. Washington, DC: American Psychological Association.

Hughes, R. B., Lund, E. M., Gabrielli, J., Powers, L. E., & Curry, M. A. (2011). Prevalence of interpersonal violence against community-living adults with disabilities: A literature review. *Rehabilitation Psychology, 56*(4), 302–319. doi.org/10.1037/a0025620

Inman, A. G. (2006). South Asian women: Identities and conflicts. *Cultural Diversity and Ethnic Minority Psychology, 12*(2), 306–319. doi.org/10.1037/1099-9809.12.2.306

Internal Displacement Monitoring Center. (2018). *Global report on internal displacement 2018*. www.internal-displacement.org/publications/2018-global-report-on-internal-displacement

International Organization for Migration. (2019). *Who is a migrant?* www.iom.int/ who-is-a-migrant

Jargowsky, P. A. (2009). Immigrants and neighbourhoods of concentrated poverty: Assimilation or stagnation? *Journal of Ethnic and Migration Studies, 35*(7), 1129–1151. doi.org/10.1080/13691830903006150

Jiménez, H. (2010). Unidos Por La Justicia and Mujeres Fuertes: Grassroots groups shaping Mexican immigrant women's activism in San José, California. *Latino Studies, 8*(4), 442–462. doi.org/10.1057/lst.2010.46

Kaltman, S., Hurtado de Mendoza, A., Gonzales, F. A., Serrano, A., & Guarnaccia, P. J. (2011). Contextualizing the trauma experience of women immigrants from Central America, South America, and Mexico. *Journal of Traumatic Stress, 24*(6), 635–642. doi.org/10.1002/jts.20698

Kiliç, C., Aydin, İ., Taşkıntuna, N., et al. (2006). Predictors of psychological distress in survivors of the 1999 earthquakes in Turkey: Effects of relocation after the disaster. *Acta Psychiatrica Scandinavica, 114*(3), 194–202. doi.org/10.1111/j .1600-0447.2006.00786.x

Kim, T., Draucker, C. B., Bradway, C., Grisso, J. A., & Sommers, M. S. (2017). Somos Hermanas Del Mismo Dolor (We are sisters of the same pain): Intimate partner sexual violence narratives among Mexican immigrant women in the United States. *Violence against Women, 23*(5), 623–642. doi .org/10.1177/1077801216646224

Lau, A. S., Fung, J. J., & Yung, V. (2010). Group parent training with immigrant Chinese families: Enhancing engagement and augmenting skills training. *Journal of Clinical Psychology, 66*(8), 1–15. doi.org/10.1002/jclp.20711

Logan, T. K., Walker, R., & Hunt, G. (2009). Understanding human trafficking in the United States. *Trauma, Violence, & Abuse, 10*(1), 3–30. doi.org/10.1177/ 1524838008327262

Lozano-Gracia, N., Piras, G., Ibáñez, A. M., & Hewings, G. J. (2010). The journey to safety: Conflict-driven migration flows in Colombia. *International Regional Science Review, 33*(2), 157–180. doi.org/10.1177/0160017609336998

Lui, P. P. (2015). Intergenerational cultural conflict, mental health, and educational outcomes among Asian and Latino/a Americans: Qualitative and meta-analytic review. *Psychological Bulletin, 141*(2), 404–446. doi.org/10.1037/a0038449

MacDonnell, J. A., Dastjerdi, M., Khanlou, N., Bokore, N., & Tharao, W. (2017). Activism as a feature of mental health and wellbeing for racialized immigrant women in a Canadian context. *Health Care for Women International*, *38*(2), 187–204. doi.org/10.1080/07399332.2016.1254632

Marrs Fuchsel, C. L. (2012). The Catholic Church as a support for immigrant Mexican women living with domestic violence. *Social Work and Christianity*, *39*(1), 66–87.

Marrs Fuchsel, C. L. (2014). Exploratory evaluation of Sí, Yo Puedo: A culturally competent empowerment program for immigrant Latina women in group settings. *Social Work with Groups*, *37*(4), 279–296. doi.org/10.1080/01609513.2014.895921

Marrs Fuchsel, C. L., & Hysjulien, B. (2013). Exploring a domestic violence intervention curriculum for immigrant Mexican women in a group setting: A pilot study. *Social Work with Groups*, *36*(4), 304–320. doi.org/10.1080/01609513.2013.767130

Mejía, A., Pizurki, H., & Royston, E. (1979). *Physician and nurse migration: Analysis and policy implications* [Report on a WHO study]. https://apps.who.int/iris/bitstream/handle/10665/37260/9241560592.pdf

Molina, O., Lawrence, S. A., Azhar-Miller, A., & Rivera, M. (2009). Divorcing abused Latina immigrant women's experiences with domestic violence support groups. *Journal of Divorce & Remarriage*, *50*(7), 459–471. doi.org/10.1080/10502550902970561

Moran-Taylor, M. J. (2008). When mothers and fathers migrate north: Caretakers, children, and child rearing in Guatemala. *Latin American Perspectives*, *35*(4), 79–95. doi.org/10.1177/0094582X08318980

Muñoz, S. M. (2013). "I just can't stand being like this anymore": Dilemmas, stressors, and motivators for undocumented Mexican women in higher education. *Journal of Student Affairs Research and Practice*, *50*(3), 233–249. doi.org/10.1515/jsarp-2013-0018

Na, S., Ryder, A. G., & Kirmayer, L. J. (2016). Toward a culturally responsive model of mental health literacy: Facilitating help-seeking among East Asian immigrants to North America. *American Journal of Community Psychology*, *58*(1–2), 211–225. doi.org/10.1002/ajcp.12085

National Institute of Justice. (2019). *Human trafficking.* www.nij.gov/topics/crime/human-trafficking/pages/welcome.aspx

Neufeld, A., Harrison, M. J., Stewart, M. J., Hughes, K. D., & Spitzer, D. (2002). Immigrant women: Making connections to community resources for support in family caregiving. *Qualitative Health Research*, *12*(6), 751–768. doi.org/10.1177/10432302012006003

Neumayer, E., & Plümper, T. (2007). The gendered nature of natural disasters: The impact of catastrophic events on the gender gap in life expectancy, 1981–2002. *Annals of the Association of American Geographers*, *97*(3), 551–566. doi.org/10.1111/j.1467-8306.2007.00563.x

Nicolas, G., & Smith, L. (2013). Adjusting to life in the United States: Therapy with Haitian immigrant women. *Women & Therapy*, *36*(3–4), 150–162. doi.org/10.1080/02703149.2013.797850

Ornelas, I. J., Perreira, K. M., Beeber, L., & Maxwell, L. (2009). Challenges and strategies to maintaining emotional health: Qualitative perspectives of Mexican immigrant mothers. *Journal of Family Issues*, *30*(11), 1556–1575. doi.org/10.1177/0192513X09336651

Panchanadeswaran, S., & Araújo Dawson, B. A. (2011). How discrimination and stress affects self-esteem among Dominican immigrant women: An exploratory study. *Social Work in Public Health*, *26*(1), 60–77. doi.org/10.1080/10911350903341069

Patel, V. V., Rajpathak, S., & Karasz, A. (2012). Bangladeshi immigrants in New York City: A community based health needs assessment of a hard to reach population. *Journal of Immigrant Minority Health*, *14*(5), 767–773. doi.org/10.1007/s10903-011-9555-5

Polaris. (2019). *2018 hotline statistics.* https://polarisproject.org/wp-content/uploads/2019/09/Polaris_National_Hotline_2018_Statistics_Fact_Sheet.pdf

Purkayastha, B. (2005). Skilled migration and cumulative disadvantage: The case of highly qualified Asian Indian immigrant women in the US. *Geoforum*, *36*(2), 181–196. doi.org/10.1016/j.geoforum.2003.11.006

Raj, A., & Silverman, J. (2002). Violence against immigrant women: The roles of culture, context, and legal immigrant status on intimate partner violence. *Violence Against Women*, *8*(3), 367–398. doi.org/10.1177/10778010222183107

Reina, A. S., Lohman, B. J., & Maldonado, M. M. (2014). "He said they'd deport me": Factors influencing domestic violence help-seeking practices among Latina immigrants. *Journal of Interpersonal Violence*, *29*(4), 593–615. doi.org/10.1177/0886260513505214

Reuveny, R. (2007). Climate change-induced migration and violent conflict. *Political Geography*, *26*(6), 656–673. doi.org/10.1016/j.polgeo.2007.05.001

Robertson, H. A., Nagaraj, N. C., & Vyas, A. N. (2016). Family violence and child sexual abuse among South Asians in the US. *Journal of Immigrant and Minority Health*, *18*(4), 921–927. doi.org/10.1007/s10903-015-0227-8

Sabri, B., Simonet, M., & Campbell, J. C. (2018). Risk and protective factors of intimate partner violence among South Asian immigrant women and perceived need for services. *Cultural Diversity and Ethnic Minority Psychology*, *24*(3), 442–452. doi.org/10.1037/cdp0000189

Schauer, E. J., & Wheaton, E. M. (2006). Sex trafficking into the United States: A literature review. *Criminal Justice Review*, *31*(2), 146–169. doi.org/10.1177/0734016806290136

Simmons, W. P., Menjívar, C., & Téllez, M. (2015). Violence and vulnerability of female migrants in drop houses in Arizona: The predictable outcome of a chain reaction of violence. *Violence against Women*, *21*(5), 551–570. doi.org/10.1177/1077801215573331

Sin, M. K. (2015). A qualitative analysis of stress and coping in Korean immigrant women in middle-age and older-adulthood. *Issues in Mental Health Nursing*, *36*(1), 52–59. doi.org/10.3109/01612840.2014.942447

Sirin, S. R., & Fine, M. (2008). *Muslim American youth: Understanding hyphenated identities through multiple methods.* New York: New York University Press.

Smart, R., & Tsong, Y. (2014). Weight, body dissatisfaction, and disordered eating: Asian American women's perspectives. *Asian American Journal of Psychology, 5*(4), 344–352. doi.org/10.1037/a0035599

Suárez-Orozco, C., & Qin, D. B. (2006). Gendered perspectives in psychology: Immigrant origin youth. *International Migration Review, 40*(1), 165–198. doi.org/10.1111/j.1747-7379.2006.00007.x

Suárez-Orozco, C., Todorova, I. L., & Louie, J. (2002). Making up for lost time: The experience of separation and reunification among immigrant families. *Family Process, 41*(4), 625–643. doi.org/10.1111/j.1545-5300.2002.00625.x

Sue, D. W., Capodilupo, C. M., Torino, G. C., et al. (2007). Racial microaggressions in everyday life: Implications for clinical practice. *American Psychologist, 62* (4), 271–286. doi.org/10.1037/0003-066X.62.4.271

Sue, S., Cheng, J. K. Y., Saad, C. H., & Chu, J. P. (2012). Asian American mental health: A call to action. *American Psychologist, 67*(7), 532–544. doi.org/10 .1037/a0028900

Taylor, P., Lopez, M. H., Passel, J. S., & Motel, S. (2011). *Unauthorized immigrants: Length of residency, patterns of parenthood.* Washington, DC: Pew Hispanic Center.

Tummala-Narra, P. (2016). *Psychoanalytic theory and cultural competence in psychotherapy.* Washington, DC: American Psychological Association.

Tummala-Narra, P., Alegria, M., & Chen, C. (2012). Perceived discrimination, acculturative stress, and depression among South Asians: Mixed findings. *Asian American Journal of Psychology, Special Issue: Secondary analysis of the National Latino and Asian American Study (NLAAS) Dataset – Part I, 3* (1), 3–16. doi.org/10.1037/a0024661

Tummala-Narra, P., Gordon, J., Gonzalez, L. D., et al. (2019). Breaking the silence: Perspectives on sexual violence among Indian American women. *Asian American Journal of Psychology, 10*(4), 293–306. doi.org/10.1037/aap0000159

Tummala-Narra, P., & Sathasivam-Rueckert, N. (2016). The experience of ethnic and racial group membership among immigrant-origin adolescents. *Journal of Adolescent Research, 31*(3), 299–342. doi.org/10.1177/0743558415592178

United Nations. (2005). *2004 world study on the role of women in development: Women and international migration.* New York: UN Department of Economic and Social Affairs.

United Nations Department of Economic and Social Affairs. (2017). *Trends in international migrant stock: The 2017 revision* [Data file]. www.un.org/en/development/desa/population/migration/data/estimates2/estimates17.asp

United Nations High Commissioner for Refugees. (2018). *Global trends: Forced displacement in 2017.* www.unhcr.org/5b27be547.pdf

United Nations High Commissioner for Refugees. (2019). *Venezuela situation.* www .unhcr.org/en-us/venezuela-emergency.html

Xiang, H., Shi, J., Wheeler, K., & Wilkins, J. R. (2010). Disability and employment among U.S. working-age immigrants. *American Journal of Industrial Medicine, 53*, 425–434. doi.org/10.1002/ajim.20802

Yoshikawa, H. (2011). *Immigrants raising citizens: Undocumented parents and their children.* New York: Russell Sage Foundation.

26 Community-Based Transition Interventions for Adolescents and Young Adults with Neurodevelopmental Disabilities

Alexa Stern, Elicia C. Wartman, Megan N. Scott, and Scott J. Hunter

26.1 Introduction: Identifying the Problem: Transition-Related Issues

For many adolescents and young adults (AYAs), transitioning to adulthood and becoming an independent and contributing member of their communities are important developmental milestones. This transition is a complex process that involves multiple, simultaneous changes across and within various systems, including education, employment, housing, health care, community engagement, and recreation. Transition is not a one-size-fits-all process, and this is particularly true for individuals with neurodevelopmental disabilities, due to the heterogeneity of their conditions. Neurodevelopmental disabilities are chronic, lifelong conditions that require the coordination and continuous provision of services. Neurodevelopmental conditions occur early in fetal or child development and impact the brain, the etiology of which often results from a complex interaction of genetic, individual, and environmental factors. This class of disabilities may include difficulties across different cognitive and behavioral skills, including language, attention, learning, memory, problem-solving, and social functioning. Individuals with a neurodevelopmental disability can demonstrate a wide range of functioning, with some individuals requiring constant caregiving and lifelong support and others requiring minimal support.

Effective transitions to adulthood are critical to youth with neurodevelopmental disabilities, who face unique challenges navigating this process (Nguyen et al., 2018). As an increasing number of children with complex disabilities are surviving into adulthood, greater emphasis is being placed on understanding this transition process among youth with special needs (Antosh et al., 2013).

Like early childhood, emerging adulthood is another developmental period during which individuals with neurodevelopmental disorders are particularly vulnerable. Indeed, the benefits of early intervention for infants and toddlers with neurodevelopmental disabilities are clear, as research evaluating these programs has shown marked improvements in adaptive, academic, and social outcomes (Goode, Diefendorf, & Colgan, 2011). From a developmental perspective it is also important to consider which age-appropriate supports are needed later in life during the critical transition to adulthood. However, in contrast to the early years of life, during emerging adulthood there is often decreasing institutional and family support alongside increasing agency (Kim & Turnbull, 2004). In fact, for AYAs with neurodevelopmental disabilities, this marks a point at which they often lose access to high-quality intervention services and struggle to maintain continuity of care (McKenzie et al., 2017; Nguyen et al., 2018).

Typically developing youth may have less difficulty negotiating the transition to adulthood, while those with developmental disabilities may lack the skills to navigate these hurdles independently. Such individuals are at risk for poor outcomes such as failure to live independently, obtain full-time employment, participate in the community, and engage in postsecondary education (Bellin et al., 2011; Lee & Carter, 2012; Wagner et al., 2005). Further, youth with comorbid medical conditions may experience gaps in health care during this transitional period, resulting in negative health outcomes (Davis et al., 2014; Seeley & Lindeke, 2017).

Despite progress in the recognition and provision of services for AYAs with neurodevelopmental disabilities, such youth experience persistent disparate inequities compared to typically developing peers in outcomes related to postsecondary education enrollment, employment, and rates of independent living (Bouck, 2012). Due to their often complex medical presentations, they often require additional healthcare needs that can further complicate the transition to adult healthcare systems. This chapter aims to provide an overview of evidence-based assessments and community interventions related to the transition process for AYAs with neurodevelopmental disabilities. This chapter will utilize a developmental approach while incorporating a global perspective by highlighting transition programs in different countries. Based on existing literature we will also identify and discuss developmentally appropriate guidelines within a community context to facilitate a successful transition to adulthood for this population. Further, we discuss how these interventions promote the inclusion of individuals with neurodevelopmental disabilities into their communities, as well as how program developers must take an ecological systems perspective and facilitate the interaction of providers across systems to help these interventions be successful.

26.2 Transition among Youth with Neurodevelopmental Disabilities

Before existing community intervention services for transition-aged youth with disabilities is discussed, it is important to review the recognized components of the transition process. These components address the social, community, independent living, and healthcare domains of transition. From a social perspective, the transition to adulthood includes individuating from the family, negotiating new roles, and navigating and establishing more complex, intimate relationships with peers. In the USA and many other countries, AYAs must transition out of secondary education by age twenty-two into postsecondary education or employment. The transition process may also include transitioning from living with family into living in the community. This involves not only navigating housing, finances, and transportation, but also establishing ties within one's community.

As previously noted, AYAs with developmental disabilities must transition from pediatric to adult healthcare providers and subspecialists as part of their transition to adulthood. These individuals often require providers across multiple subspecialties. In the pediatric healthcare system, care is family-centered and coordinated among different providers, while adult health care can be impersonal and disjointed. As a result, in the adult health system it is incumbent upon the patient to coordinate care. Navigating the adult healthcare system also requires more self-advocacy on behalf of the patient. In particular, for individuals with neurodevelopmental disabilities, an additional challenge may be educating providers about their condition. Adult healthcare providers often lack the specific knowledge about developmental conditions, as well as the specific training in providing care to individuals who have the types of behavioral and communication challenges associated with such conditions (Crane, 2013). In summary, navigating these components of transition requires the mastery of many skills that such youth with neurodevelopmental disabilities often struggle to obtain, including those related to self-care, self-determination, problem-solving, and adaptive functioning.

26.3 Providing Context: An Overview of Selected Neurodevelopmental Disabilities

For the purposes of this chapter, neurodevelopmental disabilities refer to spina bifida, autism spectrum disorder, and intellectual disability. The following section will describe these conditions and highlight relevant neuro-psychological, adaptive, and medical complications that may impede the transition process. Spina bifida (SB) occurs when the neural tube (i.e., the embryonic structure that later develops into the brain, spine, and spinal cord) fails to close completely in the first trimester and is the most common congenital birth defect compatible with life. Worldwide prevalence rates are estimated at one in a thousand births (Copp et al., 2015). SB has an impact on the brain and spinal cord, and is associated with cognitive, neurological, physical and psychosocial difficulties. It is a heterogeneous disorder, and the level of impairment differs based on the lesion level in the spine. Youth with

SB often require assistive devices to ambulate. SB is associated with hydro-cephalus (i.e., excessive fluid on the brain). Given their medically complex presentation, youth with SB have intensive healthcare needs. Treatment is focused on symptom reduction and can involve multiple surgeries, adhering to medication regimens, management of bowel and bladder programs for incontinence, monitoring for shunt infections, diet and exercise modifications, and conducting skin checks for pressure injuries.

Neurocognitively, individuals with SB experience challenges with executing functioning, attention, problem-solving, verbal comprehension, and pragmatic aspects of language and social skills. As a result, they are at risk for delayed autonomy, particularly in those with comorbid hydrocephalus (i.e., excess fluid in the brain), which can lead to brain damage if left untreated (O'Hara & Holmbeck, 2013). AYAs with SB have demonstrated lower rates of employment and independent living, lower likelihood of achieving adult milestones, and increased isolation in communities compared to other adolescents with chronic health conditions, due in part to their cognitive challenges (Beal et al., 2016; Bellin et al., 2011; Zukerman, Devine, & Holmbeck, 2010).

Autism spectrum disorder (ASD) is a developmental disability characterized by impairments in social relationships, difficulties with communication, deficits with sensory integration, repetitive behaviors, and/or restricted interests (Lee & Carter, 2012). Current prevalence rates estimate that one in fifty-three children in the USA are diagnosed with ASD, with approximately one-third being identified as having a comorbid intellectual disability (Center for Disease Control and Prevention, 2018). Youth with ASD may exhibit a broad range of cognitive abilities. Neuropsychologically, they experience deficits in executive functioning across multiple domains (i.e., cognitive flexibility, working memory, theory of mind, and planning), social-emotional perception, social knowledge, sustained attention, motor coordination skills and behavioral rigidity (Zwick, 2017). ASD can co-occur with intellectual disability, attention deficit hyperactivity disorder (ADHD), epilepsy, speech-language delays, and psychiatric disorders (i.e., anxiety and depression). These challenges have a particular impact on trajectories of transition-related outcomes, such that AYAs with ASD demonstrate difficulties obtaining employment, maintaining friendships, completing postsecondary education, and living independently (Lee & Carter, 2012; Lord et al., 2018).

Regarding employment, AYAs with ASD work fewer hours, make less money, and receive fewer benefits than typically developing peers (Lee & Carter, 2012; Newman et al., 2011; Ruble et al., 2018). Moreover, some may perceive higher-functioning individuals with ASD as needing fewer services, which may prevent them from accessing formal transition- or employment-related services and supports provided by public schools, agencies, or organizations (Lee & Carter, 2012).

Intellectual disability (ID) is characterized by limitations in cognitive abilities and adaptive behavior. This condition must originate in childhood before the age of eighteen. International prevalence rates of individuals with ID range from 0.22% to 1.55% (McKenzie et al., 2016). Cognitive abilities are typically assessed through intelligence testing. Individuals with ID exhibit significantly lower scores of intelligence, at least two standard deviations below the normative average cognitive capacity of their peers. Individuals with ID also exhibit deficits in adaptive behaviors, which are conceptualized as behaviors that help a person interact with and function daily within their environment. These include the development of life skills such as activities of daily living (e.g., self-care, eating, and toileting), autonomy (e.g., awareness of money and its use), and independence (e.g., transportation use). AYAs with ID often experience higher rates of emotional and behavioral problems, as well as higher rates of comorbid medical conditions such as epilepsy (Foley et al., 2016). Given their limitations in adaptive behavior and the frequency of comorbid conditions, individuals with ID may struggle to transition from an entitlement system (i.e., traditional elementary and secondary school, where supports are directly built in to assist them) to a system more reliant on self-promotion and determination, such as college or the workforce. In 2009, only 52% of individuals with ID who graduated high school were engaged in postgraduate activities such as jobs or advanced education. In fact, AYAs with ID have the lowest rates of education, employment attainment, and work preparation compared to peers with other disabilities (Hartman, 2009). Additionally, there are more opportunities available to those with other types of disabilities (e.g., learning disabilities) and those with chronic medical conditions than there are for those with ID (Hartman, 2009). While those with ID have access to services within high school, they often receive fewer services outside of formal schooling. Given their unique strengths and weaknesses, researchers have identified a need for specialized transition-related programming for individuals with ID (Hartman, 2009).

26.4 Evidence-Based Transition Interventions

In this section we will discuss evidence-based transition interventions and existing guidelines for AYAs with neurodevelopmental disabilities. The World Health Organization (WHO, 2001, 2007) has developed the International Classification of Functioning, Disability and Health (ICF), which is an ecological model for understanding and defining disability. This framework focuses on functional ability (ability to engage in activities of daily living and community living skills) and highlights how the reciprocal interactions among one's health conditions, individual factors, and environmental influences relate to their level of disability and ability to participate in different areas of life (WHO, 2007). Importantly, this classification system is designed to be used across service systems (WHO, 2007). In other words, this classification system acknowledges the physical, social, and psychological characteristics that influence functioning in youth with disabilities and aligns with a biopsychosocial perspective, which implies the need for a holistic and interdisciplinary approach to transition planning and interventions (Nguyen et al., 2018).

Researchers have made a case for applying this framework to transition research, as this comprehensive method has the potential to identify gaps in needed services for AYAs (Nguyen et al., 2018). To better understand how community-based transition programs are couched within social policy, while promoting the empowerment and inclusion of individuals with neurodevelopmental disabilities at the community level, a brief overview of transition-related legislation within the United States will be provided. Upon review of the current literature pertaining to such programming, it was evident that individual programs focused on employment and/or education transition outcomes separate from health-related transition outcomes. As such, the programs will be discussed by country and then transition outcome.

26.4.1 United States of America

In the United States, federal legislation has primarily driven transition-related services for youth with disabilities. The Individuals with Disabilities Education Act (IDEA, 2004) mandated that for youth with disabilities, transition planning must be incorporated into a student's Individualized Education Program (IEP) and begin by age sixteen. IDEA allows students to stay in high school until they turn twenty-two years old or earn a high school diploma. In addition, this policy requires a multi-informant assessment to identify the strengths and transition needs of the student. Other US legislation, such as Section 504 of the Rehabilitation Act of 1973 (US Department of Health, Education, and Welfare. Office of Civil Rights, 1978) was intended to promote equal access to education as well as funding for state and local government programs for people with disabilities. This act also offers pre-employment services through state vocational rehabilitation agencies. The Americans with Disabilities Act (ADA) of 1990 further promoted equal access to postsecondary education opportunities and prohibited discrimination based on disability/ability status. The Higher Education Opportunity Act (2008) offered postsecondary education, transition programs, and other services for students specifically with intellectual disability. While IDEA seeks to tailor the child's educational services to meet their individuals needs and promote success, other initiatives (ADA and Section 504) ensure equal access to educational opportunities. As a result, students with disabilities at the postsecondary education level must undertake responsibility for identifying their needs, requesting accommodations, and proving documentation needed for such accommodations. This discrepancy in federal services at the high school versus postsecondary level has shaped the current transition services for AYAs with disabilities.

Carter and Bumble (2018) found support for the Community Conversations Approach as a promising tactic to promoting transition among AYAs with developmental disabilities that capitalized on a community's local assets. Designed to be implemented at the community level, this solution-focused approach consists of a two-hour event that involves multiple rounds of conversations centered on a particular transition-related issue. Local stakeholders (e.g., employers, educators, family members, and individuals with disabilities) are included to discuss different perspectives based on their priorities, expertise, and preferences. This can be an iterative process. Carter and Bumble (2018) identified 113 empirically evaluated community conversation events that utilized this approach to address transition topics such as promoting integrated employment, facilitating school and community involvement, providing inclusive recreation, and improving school and transition services for youth with neurodevelopmental disabilities. These events occurred across multiple different states and found success within rural, suburban, and urban settings. Community-based conversations illustrate how professionals from different systems can collaborate to form a supportive network for individuals with disabilities.

Community-based transition interventions have also been found to be effective in supporting employment among AYAs with severe disabilities, including individuals with lower-functioning ASD and ID (Carter et al., 2009). Carter and colleagues (2009) developed a multicomponent set of interventions that utilized both broad (i.e., community conversations and resource mapping), as well as highly individualized strategies (i.e., summer-focused planning, community connectors, and employer liaisons), that led to significantly higher rates of community-based participation among AYAs with severe neurodevelopmental disabilities.

Another approach involved a community-based transition program (CBTP) for 18- to 22-year-olds with intellectual disabilities to plan and guide their postgraduate transition in Virginia (Hartman, 2009). This program utilized a teacher who had specialized training in transition consulting and a job coach to assist in goal planning with the individual and the individual's family. They also provided communication, social, and collaboration skills within the students' natural environment outside of a classroom (Hartman, 2009). Their CBTP was conveniently located in the public library, and afforded student access to a local kitchen and shopping center at which they could practice independence skills (Hartman, 2009).

Project SEARCH is a business-led transition model for graduation-eligible high schoolers with disabilities. This model is based on collaborations among families, schools, vocational rehabilitation agencies, and local businesses, and involves setting a goal of obtaining competitive employment and three separate, immersive internship opportunities in the student's desired career setting. Project SEARCH has been successfully adapted for youth with ASD by providing additional supports such as social skills training, behavioral reinforcement, and increased structure and schedules (Wehman et al., 2013).

JobTIPS is an internet-based employment training program designed for AYAs with high-functioning ASD that provides skills throughout different stages of the employment process (e.g., career determination, interview steps, job maintenance; Strickland, Coles, & Southern, 2013). In addition to the use of embedded visual resources to supplement the skills training, JobTIPS includes a virtual reality component to allow individuals to practice their skills. Research has shown that this program significantly improved perspective-taking and job interviewing skills among AYAs with ASD (Strickland et al., 2013).

Other interventions have focused on the transition process relating to postsecondary education. The Collaborative Model for Promoting Competence and Success (COMPASS; Ruble et al., 2018) is a manualized, in-school treatment for AYAs with ASD. This comprehensive intervention (described in Ruble et al., 2012) involved an initial parent–special education teacher consultation and completion of questionnaires to identify appropriate IEP goals for postsecondary education, isolate barriers to goals, and develop targeted plans for each goal. Following the consultation session, multiple teacher-led coaching sessions with the parents and AYAs were used to implement the plans and reassess progress for their desired goals. A randomized controlled trial evaluating COMPASS found that students with ASD who participated in this program met a significantly greater number of their IEP and postsecondary goals than those who had not participated (Ruble et al., 2018).

Beyond high school, an intensive, manualized week-long summer program has demonstrated success in helping young adults with ASD transition and adjust into college settings (Summer Transition Program [STP2]; Hotez et al., 2018). STP2 used a strengths-based, participatory approach, in which college students with ASD play an integral role in developing and administering the program. In this intervention, college students with and without ASD served as mentors and taught incoming students with ASD self-advocacy and self-determination skills, in addition to social and classroom readiness skills. This pilot intervention was found to be feasible and suggests the importance of including individuals with disabilities in the design and implementation of transition programs (Hotez et al., 2018). By actively engaging individuals with disabilities in the decision-making process, STP2 exemplifies community-based participatory research and demonstrates one way by which individuals with disabilities can gain greater self-determination and advocacy skills while forging relationships that benefit the members within their college community.

Similarly, the Stepped Transition in Education Program for Students with ASD (STEPS) focused on facilitating the transition into college settings for AYAs with ASD by improving self-determination and self-regulation (White et al., 2017). This intervention consists of a two-part curriculum. It also used a participatory approach by involving emerging adults with ASD and their families in the design process. This program has separate interventions for youth enrolled in high school and those who were actively transitioning into postsecondary education. It included one-on-one counseling, community-based outings to practice skills, an immersion experience for students who have enrolled in a postsecondary education institution, and online content over multiple weeks. Importantly, this intervention was developmentally sensitive, as parents were less actively involved in sessions once the student matriculated to promote independence. Feedback from preliminary studies has been positive, and transition-related outcomes (i.e., college adjustment, academic performance, and independent living) are currently being evaluated in a randomized controlled trial (White et al., 2017).

Programs designed to support the transition to adult health care for youth with neurodevelopmental disabilities have focused on those with additional complex medical needs, such as SB. The Transition Care Coordination (TCC) pilot study involved training resource nurses in care coordination for youth and families with SB. TCC was a family-centered approach where nurses met face-to-face or contacted patients and their families monthly to promote realistic self-management and independence goals with regard to their healthcare tasks. This pilot study found improvements in transition readiness scores, suggesting the coordination program was successful in preparing adolescents to be more autonomous with their health care (Seeley & Lindeke, 2017).

A Spina Bifida Transition Program (SBTP) was developed based on best-practice information (Sawin et al., 2015). SBTP implemented pretransition supports as key elements to the transition process, including a meeting with an advanced nurse at the patient's existing children's hospital, a summary of the adolescent's medical history, a tour of the chosen adult healthcare clinic, coordinated transfer of medical records to the adult provider, and multiple visits at the adult clinics (Sawin et al., 2015). AYAs with SB and their parents who participated in this program rated their medical transition process to be a positive experience. They found that the comprehensive preparation led to a clearer understanding of the differences between pediatric and adult healthcare systems (Sawin et al., 2015).

26.4.2 Canada

We will highlight two transition programs related to healthcare for AYAs with disabilities that draw on community supports in Canada, where the government supports universal health care for all individuals. The Developmental Disabilities Primary Care Initiative (Sullivan et al., 2018) is a tool designed to provide resources for caregivers of AYAs with intellectual and developmental disabilities (IDD) as they transition to the adult healthcare system. This initiative emphasizes the role of using the AYA's primary care physician to facilitate the transition process (Ally et al., 2018). Advantages of involving community-based family physicians in this process include their contributions to creating individualized transition plans for

AYAs with IDD, knowledge of the AYA's unique developmental needs, and helping the family to engage with the appropriate community agencies and services (Ally et al., 2018).

For youth with neurodevelopmental disabilities and complex medical needs, an interagency transition model has demonstrated effectiveness among youth with SB (Lindsay et al., 2016). This model was developed through a partnership between a pediatric hospital and an adult community healthcare center to provide coordinated, continuous, developmentally appropriate, and patient-centered care to AYAs with SB. The transition team involved an adolescent medicine specialist, transition-focused nurse practitioner, peer mentors, and transition-focused life skills coach to help with independence skills and postsecondary education supports (Lindsay et al., 2016). AYAs with SB were involved in this program from age fourteen to twenty-five. Patients were connected with several resources, including adult primary care, adult sub-specialists, rehabilitation services, and social services. Importantly, a nurse practitioner and life skills coach were cross-appointed at both the pediatric and adult healthcare centers to ensure a smooth transition. Compared to AYAs with SB who did not participate in the program, participants felt significantly more supported during their transition and reported their health care to be more continuous (Lindsay et al., 2016). Another benefit that families noted was the encouragement to gradually transfer health responsibilities from parents to the AYA, alongside the broader transition process. Families who lived in rural areas reported a need for more support (Lindsay et al., 2016).

26.4.3 United Kingdom

Project SEARCH, the workplace training program for transition-age youth with disabilities that relies on partnerships with local businesses, has found some success among AYAs with ID in the United Kingdom (Kaehne, 2016). One variation between the programs in the UK and Canada was that Project SEARCH UK involved not only leading, local businesses, but also local authorities who could help foster employment opportunities in the community. This study demonstrated strong support for the program, in that employment rates of participants were higher (~50%) than estimates of those with IDs traditionally in the UK (~12%; Kaehne, 2016). A supported employment project that was based off of a peer support model has also been tested among AYAs with IDs (Youth Supported Employment Program; Kaehne & Beyer, 2013). This intervention drew on the social support of typically developing youth to partner with students with IDs during twelve-month part-time work placements. Youth and their parents rated the peer mentors highly and employers gave positive feedback about the AYAs' work performance. However, despite the positive response, families noted that they continued to face barriers in developing pathways to employment for their AYAs and employers were not more likely to hire participants after the program finished.

26.4.4 Australia

An effective program designed to transition individuals from the school to work environment was successfully implemented for youth with disabilities in Australia. The Transition to Work Program is a two-year government-sponsored program targeting students with disabilities who are leaving school and transitioning to employment. To help prepare participants for the workplace, staff provided training on social skills and adaptive functioning (Wilson & Frawley, 2016). Many students had success with this program and found full- or part-time, open or supported employment (Wilson & Frawley, 2016). This program provided practical preemployment services such as education, training, connection with local job opportunities and community services, and job experience placements (Wilson & Frawley, 2016).

BOOST-A^{TM} is an online transition planning program for AYAs with autism that is based on self-determination theory, and utilizes a strengths-based approach while incorporating technology into the intervention (Hatfield et al., 2017). This web-based program consists of four online modules to assist AYAs with autism in their transition from school to desired tertiary education or career goals. As part of the first module, participants completed an autism-specific, strengths-based assessment that was used to determine their learning style and needs, which were then used to promote engagement in the program. The program guides the adolescent and their family in choosing a team to provide additional support, which included teachers, local government coordinators, occupational therapists, speech pathologists, and support workers. Participants in this program rated it to be feasible, acceptable, and viable (Hatfield et al., 2017). Further iterations of this pilot study incorporated participant feedback to make the program more usable (e.g., inclusion of visual supports; Hatfield et al., 2017).

In summary, several exemplars of programs designed to facilitate the transition to adulthood have been developed specifically for AYAs with neurodevelopmental disabilities, including ASD, intellectual disabilities, and SB. As discussed in the Conclusion section (Section 26.6), the success of the program was dependent upon the ability of the intervention developers to meet the unique needs of the youth, as well as their ability to draw upon the support of community stakeholders, such as local educational institutions, businesses, and peers. While these interventions generally received positive feedback from participants, the degree to which they were successful in improving outcomes related to independent living, higher education, employment, and health care are less well known and require more rigorous implementation and dissemination research.

26.5 Illustrating the Importance of Transition Services: Case Studies

The following is a case study that illustrates how obtaining appropriate support services may lead to positive transition outcomes for youth with developmental disabilities. Jane is a fourteen-year-old Mexican adolescent with spina bifida. She ambulates using a wheelchair. She and her family recently immigrated to the USA to receive specialized health care and comprehensive support for her condition. When Jane initially presented to the interdisciplinary healthcare clinic, her mother had primary responsibility for managing her health-related tasks, which included management of her bowel program, catheterization, and daily medication regimen. At her previous school in Mexico, Jane spent much of her time alone and had difficulty navigating the facilities as they were not wheelchair-accessible. She reported feeling isolated from peers in her community due to her urological and bowel issues and felt ostracized at school due to her learning difficulties. She spent most of her recreational time at home and was not involved in extracurricular activities. At her initial appointment, she presented with secondary health conditions related to poor regimen adherence, including pressure wounds, recurrent urinary tract infections, and bowel incontinence.

As part of the interdisciplinary clinic, Jane and her family were seen by multiple providers, which included a social worker, psychologist, orthopedist, neurologist, urologist, dietician, and nurse. A social worker assigned as a transition coordinator assisted Jane and her family with establishing realistic goals for independence. She received a comprehensive neuropsychological evaluation, which revealed average intelligence with a specific learning disability in math and deficits in attention and executive functioning. The social worker and neuropsychologist helped Jane's family work with the school special education team to establish an IEP that advocated for appropriate educational and environmental supports, including specific accommodations and interventions to address her learning disability and neurocognitive concerns (e.g., working with a math specialist and a coach regarding her executive functioning needs). Jane was referred to a child psychiatrist to address her attentional needs, to assess whether medication was an option. As part of the neuropsychologist's and social worker's recommendations, Jane initiated weekly individual psychotherapy at the hospital to address concerns with self-esteem, social functioning, and adjusting to life in the United States. The psychologist connected Jane's family with a state-sponsored association for individuals with disabilities, which provided Jane with a scholarship to attend a summer camp for youth with SB. Here, she met other adolescents with SB, learned about her medical condition, and was given opportunities to practice her medical care independently.

Two years later, at age sixteen, Jane presented for her annual visit with the interdisciplinary clinic. She reported maintaining friendships with peers at school and her church. She was attending a youth group at her church and had become involved in an adaptive sports group in her community. In preparation for her yearly IEP meeting, the social worker introduced options for postsecondary education and employment. She continued to see a therapist and had made gains in her self-esteem. She had recently started a therapy group for adolescents with developmental disabilities that focuses on social skills. She was managing her urinary and bowel programs independently. After expressing interest in increased independence for her medical care, Jane was supported by the psychologist and social worker in developing a plan with her family to gradually attain more autonomy for her SB-related and personal responsibilities. As a result, Jane and her parents agreed that she would spend a portion of her doctors' visits alone. Additionally, Jane began meeting with a driver's rehabilitation specialist to learn how to drive with adaptive equipment.

At age eighteen, Jane was enrolled at a local community college, where she majored in early education. In line with her family's cultural expectations, she lived at home with her parents. She underwent a second neuropsychological evaluation to obtain updated recommendations for accommodations in college; results highlighted a continued need for supports around aspects of independent decision-making and problem-solving, and offered recommendations regarding ongoing executive skills and adaptive functioning coaching. Through her college program, she obtained a part-time paid position at a daycare center. During her annual clinic visit, the social worker educated Jane and her family on local, state, and federal services for adults with disabilities, including life skills, financial planning, and social security benefits. She learned about accessible transportation options. Her medical team had more involved conservations with Jane and her parents about preparing to transition to adult healthcare services. Based on recommendations from the social worker, her parents opened a joint checking account in Jane's name to house her social security and job payment, and she was now responsible for paying for her recreational activities. She began attending a group at her community center to learn more about adaptive skills, including cooking and cleaning.

When nearing age twenty-two, Jane was preparing to graduate from her community college program in early education when she met with her care team. She had already participated in the hospital's healthcare transition program, facilitated through the support of the social worker and nurse coordinator. With this program, Jane learned about her insurance benefits; she became more knowledgeable about the options she had under the plan she had continued with as a college student still living with her parents and began to look at independent options for health insurance needs postgraduation. The nurse coordinator helped Jane and her parents identify adult subspecialty providers in her community. She attended initial, introductory visits with the adult providers while maintaining care at her pediatric interdisciplinary clinic, fostering opportunities for more effective communication between providers. The coordinator assisted Jane in scheduling her medical appointments and connected her pediatric and adult providers so that they could smoothly transfer her medical care. Jane expressed her interest to her psychologist about moving out of her parents' home, but shared that she had reservations about living independently. She was connected with an accessible, assisted living center built for adults with disabilities; she visited this program with her parents and decided to add her name to the waiting list for an apartment. Jane also received employment coaching at a local community center.

At age twenty-five, Jane had successfully completed her medical transition to the adult healthcare system and was well managing her SB in conjunction with her adult care team. She had not had a secondary medical complication in several years, and felt proud about her capacity to meet medical goals and demands effectively. She was offered an apartment in the accessible assisted living center, which she accepted, and moved out of her parents' home. She reported that she enjoyed the greater independence she had with her new home, and had developed good relationships with other tenants with disabilities living with her. She worked full-time as an early education teacher's aide in her neighborhood, at a program that was accessible by bus. Jane remained involved in her community by volunteering at her church. She continued to work with a community-based psychologist who specializes in working with adults with disabilities, whom she met with weekly. Therapy provided continued to provide support for her transition to adulthood, including guiding her toward continued opportunities for training in complex activities of daily living, self-advocacy skills for her employment setting, and social skills related to navigating intimate relationships.

Our next case addresses an individual with ASD who experienced a lack of appropriate transition services that led to negative transition outcomes; the challenge is further complicated by his comorbid ID. Jamal is a seventeen-year-old African American male, with ASD and comorbid mild ID. He has limited verbal ability and communicates through vocalizations and gestures. Jamal recently underwent formal neuropsychological testing, indicating a developmental age of about eight years old. He was attending public school and was in a self-contained special education high school program. In addition, he received services through an IEP including speech-language therapy, occupational therapy, and behavioral supports. He lived with his mother and younger brother. Jamal's mother worked full time and shared caregiving responsibilities with her younger son. Due to her work schedule and inflexibility with her employment administration, she was unable to take part in most parent–teacher meetings. Further, she missed opportunities to meet with the school social worker and behavior specialist. At a parent–teacher meeting that was able to take place, Jamal's mother reported feeling overwhelmed and worried about caring for him as an adult. The school social worker recommended resources and support groups for parents and adolescents. These groups were located in a nearby city and due to transportation barriers they were unable to attend. Jamal had no major health complications and saw a pediatrician annually for wellness visits.

At age nineteen, Jamal was enrolled in a transition program for students with developmental disabilities who have IEPs. Jamal was eligible to participate in this program until twenty-one years of age. This transition program focused on activities of daily living, community participation, and recreation and leisure activities. At that time, his mother continued to help him with his morning routine. He received assisted transportation from his home to the education building daily. Jamal enjoyed learning basic workplace skills while interacting with same-aged peers. He continued to receive speech-language therapy, occupational therapy, and social work services throughout his time in the program. Jamal had a particular interest in zoology and expressed interest in working with animals. The vocational program partnered with a pet store to provide Jamal with a volunteer opportunity and coordinated transportation to and from the facilities.

Jamal graduated from the vocational transition program and received a high school diploma at age twenty-one. After his graduation, he was no longer eligible to receive services through the public education system; he was supposed to have had a transition plan developed and in place, but the difficulties with coordinating appropriate meetings with his mother, who had been identified as his legal guardian, led to his graduating without a plan being in place. Without the assisted transportation, Jamal could not continue his volunteer position at the pet store. Further, without the psychosocial supports provided through his program within the public education system, he was unable to obtain postsecondary employment. Given the lack of scheduled activities and structured support, he spent the majority of his time at home playing with electronics. He briefly attended a vocational training program at his local community center. Jamal had difficulty participating in many of the activities due to his intellectual challenges. Jamal's mother was initially excited for him to be a part of this community program. However, after several weeks and no observed progress she felt concerned he was not being stimulated and pulled him from the program. She attempted to enroll him in other state- and federal-sponsored programs for adults with disabilities; however, such attempts were met with placement on increasingly long waitlists and inadequate services for Jamal's unique needs. At his annual visit with his pediatrician, his mother received a notice that he would need to find an adult healthcare provider as he had aged out of the practice.

Over the next few years Jamal's behavior and social skills regressed. His brother left home to attend college, leaving his mother to assume primary care for Jamal. She became overwhelmed balancing Jamal's care with her full-time job and she subsequently developed depression. Due to the lack of support surrounding his healthcare transition he never transferred providers and had not seen a doctor since the last visit with his pediatrician.

As exemplified in the above cases, transition services are integral in supporting an adolescent with a complex neurodevelopmental disability as he or she approaches adulthood. Comprehensive planning to understand the AYA's unique pattern of strengths and weaknesses, as well as effective communication among providers and between the care team and the family, are critical. With the appropriate supports, Jane was able to maximize her potential and has successfully negotiated her changing role within her family and her wider community. Further, the medical team took a culturally sensitive approach to balance Jane's cultural needs with her desire to be autonomous. Thus, Jane was able to attend community college while living at home. Unfortunately, Jamal's case demonstrates how the transition to adulthood is a highly vulnerable period for youth with disabilities, and how an abrupt drop-off in supports puts them at risk for not meeting developmental milestones or even regressing functionally. Complicated by a lack of financial resources and social support, his case shows the barriers that many families of youth with disabilities face as they try to navigate this process without access to adequate services.

26.6 Conclusion

This chapter has reviewed the transition from adolescence to young adulthood for individuals with neurodevelopmental disabilities, and community interventions designed to facilitate this process. It is apparent that this complex, multifaceted transition involves changes across multiple systems and requires support from various stakeholders to ensure success. Furthermore, transition outcomes vary based on individual needs, goals for the future, and available community resources. We have seen these variations reflected in the different transition interventions available across and within countries. In other words, the transition services that a community can provide are constrained by the supports available at local, state, and federal levels. For typically developing AYAs, the transition to adulthood mirrors growth in autonomy and life skills, which is reflected in the transfer of responsibilities and decision-making from the caregivers to the child. However, for individuals with neurodevelopmental disabilities, there is a continued need for external supports. This review has demonstrated that with adequate programming, the balance of some of these necessary supports can be successfully shifted from the family environment to the broader, community context, thus promoting interdependence for this vulnerable population.

In the limited portion of communities where there are available resources to implement transition-related interventions, outcomes are generally favorable. The literature discussed in this chapter shows that AYAs with disabilities and their families rated many transition-related programs to be feasible, acceptable, and helpful. In the few studies that tested intervention efficacy, participation in these programs was related to positive outcomes, including increased self-determination, involvement in postsecondary education, and fruitful connections with local employers. Common strengths among the programs we reviewed included tailoring the intervention to the individual's unique set of strengths, preferences, and needs; specifying appropriate and clear transition-related goals; a developmental approach; use of an interdisciplinary team; continued parental involvement; and an emphasis on drawing on the natural resources of the community.

We have also seen the significance of technology, as demonstrated by web-based and virtual reality programming. Building off the inclusion of available community resources, some interventions utilized a community participatory approach. The inclusion of local stakeholders, especially those individuals with neurodevelopmental disabilities, in the development and refinement of these transition interventions is invaluable, because they provide perspectives and advocacy beyond that of university-based researchers.

However, it is apparent that only those with access to these evidence-based programs receive the associated benefits. While a thorough review of these interventions is beyond the scope of this chapter, indeed our review of community interventions globally revealed that formal transition programs for AYAs with neurodevelopmental disabilities were more prominent in regions within the United States, Canada, Australia, and the United Kingdom, and less visible in other areas such as South America, Africa, or Asia. On a community level, several possible explanations for these discrepancies can include insufficient funding, culturally laden stigma related to disability, lack of access to services and facilities, and inadequate training for professionals. On a broader scale, poor economic resources, policies that do not promote the inclusion of those with disabilities, and lack of evidence-based research in developing countries may contribute to barriers related to creating and implementing high-quality transition programs (see World Report on Disability; WHO, 2011). As a result, community-based transition programs for individuals with disabilities may already be occurring in developing countries, but efforts to examine such interventions on a global scale may prove difficult due to challenges with research evaluating the efficacy of such programs. However, discrepancies in access to services are still evident even within developed countries, including the United States. National policies in the United States have set the tone for increased inclusion and funding for individuals with disabilities, but these policies may fall short in reaching individuals with complex disabilities, leaving the ultimate responsibility for dissemination and implementation at the local level.

While many AYAs with intellectual and developmental disabilities hope to pursue higher education or work after secondary education, they continue to report difficulty with achieving these goals (Shogren & Plotner, 2012). One study found that less than 10% of young adults with such disabilities were accessing integrated employment (Butterworth & Migliore, 2015). It is highly possible that many of these individuals lack the access to or knowledge of such recommended services. Relatedly, the majority of programs were developed and tested at academic medical centers or universities, but less is known about how these programs translate into rural settings, where tangible supports may be less available. While best practices for transition services exist and hold promise for youth with disabilities, future work is needed to close the research-to-practice gap.

26.7 Additional Considerations: Importance of Culture

It should be noted that both the concepts of transition and disability are culturally constructed. As such, a "successful" transition to adulthood for an adolescent with an intellectual or developmental disability may be conceptualized differently based on familial, religious, or societal values. Many of the interventions included in this chapter are grounded in Western values, where independence is idealized. However, it is important not to blindly impose these values when developing targets for transition and assessing transition-related needs. A focus group conducted with Latina mothers of young adults with developmental disabilities revealed different perspectives about transition goals that may not fit with a traditionally Western emphasis on productivity, individualism, and autonomy (Rueda et al., 2005). These mothers perceived themselves as experts on decision-making for their children compared to professionals, expressed wanting a greater emphasis placed on training for life skills over future employment, and viewed having their child respected and well-cared for as more important than living independently (Rueda et al., 2005). Moreover, their perspectives differed from that of the institutions that served their families.

In a qualitative study, British South Asian young adults with disabilities described how their gender, ethnic, racial, and religious minority statuses interacted with disability/ability status in terms of negotiating transitions with their families and community agencies (Hussain, 2003). Indeed, disability is only one aspect of an individual's identity. Cultural humility (i.e., a process through which providers address the differential power dynamic with clients of diverse backgrounds by acknowledging and engaging in self-reflection about the layers of cultural identity, attitudes, and biases they bring to the provider–client relationship; Fisher-Borne, Cain, & Martin, 2015) and awareness are critical tools for any clinician when developing or implementing transition services.

26.8 Additional Considerations: Future Directions

Empirical research on transition models is converging on the need for holistic, person-centered, and developmentally oriented services that foster communication among professionals and families across different fields related to transition (e.g., health, education), rather than treating them separately within silos. Interestingly, we found that the majority of current literature on such models is comprised of descriptive studies or discussion papers providing frameworks for designing and delivering transition services. The next wave of research should focus on evaluating the effectiveness of community-based interventions with greater methodological rigor, including the use of randomized controlled trials. Research is also needed to evaluate a potential systems-level approach to transition planning and programs, given the pervasive impact of neurodevelopmental disabilities. Cross-site collaborations could be helpful in this regard.

Further, while the studies reviewed focused on outcomes related to transitioning across health, education, employment, and community contexts, AYAs with disabilities have identified additional needs that must be addressed, but continue to receive scant attention (Fair et al., 2016). These include issues related to mental health, social networking, sexuality, quality of life, health insurance, safety, and transportation needs. Future research should seek to incorporate these aspects of transition into existing interventions. Finally, while this chapter focused on the critical transition from adolescence to adulthood, it should be noted that neurodevelopmental disabilities are lifelong, chronic conditions. As such, continued programming within communities designed to support individuals with disabilities across the lifespan (e.g., geriatric) warrant greater consideration.

From a social justice perspective, individuals with disabilities may face multiple social inequities as they transition to adulthood. The programs we reviewed demonstrate that such individuals, when given the appropriate opportunities and resources, can make meaningful contributions to not only their own personal transition, but also the communities in which they live. With the support of mental health professionals, solution-focused interdisciplinary collaborations, and an ecological understanding of the multiple contexts in which AYAs with disabilities live in, we can include and empower individuals with neurodevelopmental disabilities as they navigate this developmental period.

References

Ally, S., Boyd, K., Abells, D., et al. (2018). Improving transition to adulthood for adolescents with intellectual and developmental disabilities: Proactive developmental and systems perspective. *Canadian Family Physician, 64*(Suppl. 2), S37–S43.

Americans with Disabilities Act. (1990). 42 USC 12101 et seq.

Americans with Disabilities Amendments Act. (2008, September 25). Public Law 110-325.

Antosh, A. A., Blair, M., Edwards, K., et al. (2013, April). *A collaborative interagency, interdisciplinary approach to transition from adolescence to adulthood.* Silver Spring, MD: Association of University Centers on Disabilities.

Beal, S. J., Riddle, I. K., Kichler, J. C., et al. (2016). The associations of chronic condition type and individual characteristics with transition readiness. *Academic Pediatrics, 16*(7), 660–667. doi.org/10.1016/j.acap.2016 .06.007

Bellin, M. H., Dicianno, B. E., Levey, E., et al. (2011). Interrelationships of sex, level of lesion, and transition outcomes among young adults with myelomeningocele. *Developmental Medicine & Child Neurology, 53*(7), 647–652. doi.org/10.1111/j.1469-8749.2011.03938.x

Bouck, E. C. (2012). Secondary students with moderate/severe intellectual disability: Considerations of curriculum and post-school outcomes from the National Longitudinal Transition Study-2. *Journal of Intellectual Disability Research, 56*(12), 1175–1186. doi.org/10.1111/j.1365-2788.2011.01517.x

Butterworth, J., & Migliore, A., (2015). Trends in employment outcomes of young adults with intellectual and developmental disabilities, 2006–2013. University of Massachusetts Boston, Institute for Community Inclusion.

Carter, E. W., & Bumble, J. L. (2018). The promise and possibilities of community conversations: Expanding opportunities for people with disabilities. *Journal of Disability Policy Studies, 28*(4), 195–202. doi.org/10.1177/1044207317739408

Carter, E. W., Trainor, A. A., Ditchman, N., Swedeen, B., & Owens, L. (2009). Evaluation of a multicomponent intervention package to increase summer work experiences for transition-age youth with severe disabilities. *Research and Practice for Persons with Severe Disabilities, 34*(2), 1–12. doi.org/10.2511/ rpsd.34.2.1

Center for Disease Control and Prevention. (2018). *Data and statistics on autism spectrum disorder.* Division of Birth Defects, National Center on Birth Defects and Developmental Disabilities, Centers for Disease Control and Prevention. www.cdc.gov/ncbddd/autism/data.html

Copp, A. J., Adzick, N. S., Chitty, L. S., et al. (2015). Spina bifida. *Nature Reviews Disease Primers, 1,* 15007. doi.org/10.1038/nrdp. 2015.7

Crane, S. (2013). *The transition to adulthood for youth with ID/DD: A review of research, policy and next steps* [Policy Brief]. Autistic Self Advocacy Network. https://autisticadvocacy.org/policy/briefs/healthcare-transition/

Davis, A. M., Brown, R. F., Taylor, J. L., Epstein, R. A., & McPheeters, M. L. (2014). Transition care for children with special health care needs. *Pediatrics, 134*(5), 900–908. doi.org/10.1542/peds.2014-1909

Fair, C., Cuttance, J., Sharma, N., et al. (2016). International and interdisciplinary identification of health care transition outcomes. *JAMA Pediatrics, 170*(3), 205–211. doi.org/10.1001/jamapediatrics.2015.3168

Fisher-Borne, M., Cain, J. M., & Martin, S. L. (2015). From mastery to accountability: Cultural humility as an alternative to cultural competence. *Social Work Education, 34*(2), 165–181. doi.org/10.1080/02615479.2014.977244

Foley, K. R., Taffe, J., Bourke, J., et al. (2016). Young people with intellectual disability transitioning to adulthood: Do behaviour trajectories differ in those with and without Down syndrome? *PLoS ONE, 11*(7), Article e0157667. doi .org/10.1371/journal.pone.0157667

Goode, S., Diefendorf, M., & Colgan, S. (2011). *The importance of early intervention for infants and toddlers with disabilities and their families.* The National Early

Childhood Technical Assistance Center. https://files.eric.ed.gov/fulltext/ED522123.pdf

Hartman, M. A. (2009). Step by step: Creating a community-based transition program for students with intellectual disabilities. *Teaching Exceptional Children, 41*(6), 6–11.

Hatfield, M., Murray, N., Ciccarelli, M., Falkmer, T., & Falkmer, M. (2017). Pilot of the BOOST-A™: An online transition planning program for adolescents with autism. *Australian Occupational Therapy Journal, 64*(6), 448–456. doi.org/10.1111/1440-1630.12410

Higher Education Opportunity Act. (2008, August 14). Public Law 110-315.

Hotez, E., Shane-Simpson, C., Obeid, R., et al. (2018). Designing a summer transition program for incoming and current college students on the autism spectrum: A participatory approach. *Frontiers in Psychology, 9*, Article 46. doi.org/10.3389/fpsyg.2018.00046

Hussain, Y. (2003). Transitions into adulthood: Disability, ethnicity and gender among British South Asians. *Disability Studies Quarterly, 23*(2), 100–112. doi.org/10.1111/jar.12207

Individuals with Disabilities Education Act. (2004). 20 U.S.C. § 1400.

Kaehne, A. (2016). Project SEARCH UK: Evaluating its employment outcomes. *Journal of Applied Research in Intellectual Disabilities, 29*(6), 519–530. doi.org/10.1111/jar.12207

Kaehne, A., & Beyer, S. (2013). Supported employment for young people with intellectual disabilities facilitated through peer support: A pilot study. *Journal of Intellectual Disabilities, 17*(3), 236–251. doi.org/10.1177/1744629513495265

Kim, K. H., & Turnbull, A. P. (2004). Transition to adulthood for students with severe intellectual disabilities: Shifting toward person-family interdependent planning. *Research and Practice for Persons with Severe Disabilities, 29*(1), 53–57.

Lee, G. K., & Carter, E. W. (2012). Preparing transition-age students with high-functioning autism spectrum disorders for meaningful work. *Psychology in the Schools, 49*(10), 988–1000. doi.org/10.1002/pits.21651

Lindsay, S., Cruickshank, H., McPherson, A. C., & Maxwell, J. (2016). Implementation of an inter-agency transition model for youth with spina bifida. *Child Care, Health and Development, 42*(2), 203–212. doi.org/10.1111/cch.12303

Lord, C., Elsabbagh, M., Baird, G., & Veenstra-Vanderweele, J. (2018). Autism spectrum disorder. *The Lancet, 392*(10146), 508–520. doi.org/10.1016/S0140-6736(18)31129-2

McKenzie, K., Milton, M., Smith, G., & Ouellette-Kuntz, H. (2016). Systematic review of the prevalence and incidence of intellectual disabilities: Current trends and issues. *Current Developmental Disorders Reports, 3*(2), 104–115. doi.org/10.1007/s40474-016-0085-7

McKenzie, K., Ouellette-Kuntz, H., Blinkhorn, A., & Démoré, A. (2017). Out of school and into distress: Families of young adults with intellectual and developmental disabilities in transition. *Journal of Applied Research in Intellectual Disabilities, 30*(4), 774–781. doi.org/10.1111/jar.12264

Newman, L., Wagner, M., Knokey, A. M., et al. (2011). *The post-high school outcomes of young adults with disabilities up to 8 years after high school: A report from* the *National Longitudinal Transition Study-2 (NLTS2)* (NCSER 2011-3005). National Center for Special Education Research.

Nguyen, T., Stewart, D., Rosenbaum, P., et al. (2018). Using the ICF in transition research and practice? Lessons from a scoping review. *Research in Developmental Disabilities, 72*, 225–239. doi.org/10.1016/j.ridd.2017.11.003

O'Hara, L. K., & Holmbeck, G. N. (2013). Executive functions and parenting behaviors in association with medical adherence and autonomy among youth with spina bifida. *Journal of Pediatric Psychology, 38*(6), 675–687. doi.org/10.1093/jpepsy/jst007

Ruble, L. A., Dalrymple, N. J., & McGrew, J. H. (2012). *Collaborative model for promoting competence and success for students with ASD*. New York: Springer Science & Business Media.

Ruble, L. A., McGrew, J. H., Toland, M., et al. (2018). Randomized control trial of COMPASS for improving transition outcomes of students with autism spectrum disorder. *Journal of Autism and Developmental Disorders, 48*(10), 3586–3595. doi.org/10.1007/s10803-018-3623-9

Rueda, R., Monzo, L., Shapiro, J., Gomez, J., & Blacher, J. (2005). Cultural models of transition: Latina mothers of young adults with developmental disabilities. *Exceptional Children, 71*(4), 401–414. doi.org/10.1177/001440290507100402

Sawin, K. J., Rauen, K., Bartelt, T., et al. (2015). Transitioning adolescents and young adults with spina bifida to adult healthcare: Initial findings from a model program. *Rehabilitation Nursing, 40*(1), 3–11. doi.org/10.1002/rnj.140

Seeley, A., & Lindeke, L. (2017). Developing a transition care coordination program for youth with spina bifida. *Journal of Pediatric Health Care, 31*(6), 627–633. doi.org/10.1016/j.pedhc.2017.04.015

Shogren, K. A., & Plotner, A. J. (2012). Transition planning for students with intellectual disability, autism, or other disabilities: Data from the National Longitudinal Transition Study-2. *Intellectual and Developmental Disabilities, 50*(1), 16–30. doi.org/10.1352/1934-9556-50.1.16

Strickland, D. C., Coles, C. D., & Southern, L. B. (2013). JobTIPS: A transition to employment program for individuals with autism spectrum disorders. *Journal of Autism and Developmental Disorders, 43*(10), 2472–2483. doi.org/10.1007/s10803-013-1800-4

Sullivan, W. F., Diepstra, H., Heng, J., et al. (2018). Primary care of adults with intellectual and developmental disabilities: 2018 Canadian consensus guidelines. *Canadian Family Physician, 64*(4), 254–279.

US Department of Health, Education, and Welfare, Office of Civil Rights. (1978). *Section 504 of the Rehabilitation Act of 1973: Fact sheet – Handicapped persons rights under Federal law*. Washington, DC: Dept. of Health, Education, and Welfare, Office of the Secretary, Office of Civil Rights.

Wagner, M., Newman, L., Cameto, R., Garza, N., & Levine, P. (2005). *After high school: A first look at the postschool experiences of youth with disabilities*. A report from the National Longitudinal Transition Study-2 (NLTS2). Menlo Park, CA: SRI International. www.nlts2.org/reports/2005_04/nlts2_report_2005_04_complete.pdf

Wehman, P., Schall, C., McDonough, J., et al. (2013). Project SEARCH for youth with autism spectrum disorders: Increasing competitive employment on transition from high school. *Journal of Positive Behavior Interventions, 15*(3), 144–155. doi.org/10.1177/1098300712459760

White, S. W., Elias, R., Capriola-Hall, N. N., et al. (2017). Development of a college transition and support program for students with autism spectrum disorder. *Journal of Autism and Developmental Disorders, 47*(10), 3072–3078. doi.org/10.1007/s10803-017-3236-8

Wilson, N. J., & Frawley, P. (2016). Transition staff discuss sex education and support for young men and women with intellectual and developmental disability. *Journal of Intellectual & Developmental Disability, 41*(3), 209–221. doi.org/10.3109/13668250.2016.1162771

World Health Organization. (2001). *International classification of functioning, disability and health: ICF.* Geneva, Switzerland: World Health Organization.

World Health Organization. (2007). *International classification of functioning, disability and health: Children and youth version (ICF-CY).* Geneva, Switzerland: World Health Organization.

World Health Organization. (2011). *World report on disability.* Geneva, Switzerland: World Health Organization.

Zukerman, J. M., Devine, K. A., & Holmbeck, G. N. (2010). Adolescent predictors of emerging adulthood milestones in youth with spina bifida. *Journal of Pediatric Psychology, 36*(3), 265–276. doi.org/10.1093/jpepsy/jsq075

Zwick, G. P. (2017). Neuropsychological assessment in autism spectrum disorder and related conditions. *Dialogues in Clinical Neuroscience, 19*(4), 373–379. doi.org/10.31887/DCNS.2017.19.4/gzwick

27 Mental Health on College Campuses

Michele M. Tugade, Tse Yen Tan,
Louise S. Wachsmuth, and Elizabeth H. Bradley

27.1 Introduction

College years are a critical part of development as students move from adolescence to young adulthood, with the attendant challenges of navigating new opportunities and new risks. The prevalence of mental health problems among college students is substantial (Hunt & Eisenberg, 2010; Pedrelli et al., 2015). The most recent data from the World Health Organization World Mental Health Surveys indicate that at least 27% of US college students suffered from one or more mental disorders in the previous twelve months, with one in three first-year students reporting a mental health disorder (Auerbach et al., 2018). More than 80% of mental health disorders reported in college have begun prior to college matriculation and continue to persist during college (Auerbach et al., 2018; Kessler et al., 2007). Experts suggest that attending college may exacerbate episodes tied to psychopathology that onset in childhood (Pedrelli et al., 2015). Much attention is given to the beginning of this college transition, particularly first-year experiences, which can be particularly challenging (Bruffaerts et al., 2018). First-year students face the challenge of moving to new environments and acclimating to new social structures, and the challenges continue beyond the first year. Fourth-year students have been reported to have even higher rates of mental health concerns, for instance, compared to students in the first three years of college (Beiter et al., 2015). It is increasingly important to examine the mental health patterns associated with this period, as the college years represent a distinct period for development and transition (Auerbach et al., 2018).

The most prevalent type of mental health disorder, affecting about 25% of US college students, has been documented as anxiety according to the American College Health Association (ACHA) *National College Health Assessment* (NCHA) survey (ACHA, 2019). Peak onset for post-traumatic stress disorder (PTSD) occurs at sixteen to seventeen years old (Cusack et al., 2019), and obsessive-compulsive disorder (OCD) peaks at nineteen years old (Vaingankar et al., 2013), while generalized anxiety disorder is believed to peak at about the age of twenty (Pedrelli et al., 2015; Vaingankar et al., 2013). Depression is also common among college students, although prevalence estimates vary markedly across studies. A recent review suggests a broad range of prevalence (10%–85%) with a weighted mean prevalence of 30.6% based on extant literature (Ibrahim et al., 2013).

Other disorders include eating disorders, reported by just less than 10% of students (Eisenberg, Nicklett, et al., 2011) and more common among females, with peaking onset at college age (Eisenberg, Nicklett, et al., 2011; Stice et al., 2009), as well as attention deficit hyperactivity disorder (ADHD) with estimates of 2%–8% of students having ADHD (DuPaul et al., 2009). Schizophrenia and autism spectrum disorders (ASD) are both found to be far less prevalent at 1%–2% of the college population (Pedrelli et al., 2015).

Unsafe health behaviors are also common among college students. Suicide is the third leading cause of death for young adults, and estimates indicate that about 11% of students experienced suicide ideation in the last four weeks (Mortier et al., 2018). In a study of first-year college students from several countries including the USA, about 1% of students reported at least one suicide attempt in the last twelve months (Mortier et al., 2018). Studies report that 20% of college students meet criteria for alcohol use disorder (AUD) (Slutske, 2005) and about 40% had engaged in heavy drinking (five or more drinks in a row) in the last two weeks (O'Malley & Johnson, 2002). Alcohol use is associated with a host of other health risks including motor vehicle accidents, unsafe sex, sexual assault, and accidental injuries – as well as poor academic performance (Pedrelli et al., 2015). Data from the National Survey on Drug Use and Health reported that 24% of college men and 16% of college women are current marijuana users (Substance Abuse and Mental Health Services Administration [SAMHSA], 2013), 10% reported nonmedical use of pain relievers in the past (Pedrelli et al., 2015), and other studies have found that 5%–35% of college students report misusing stimulants (Wilens et al., 2008) – with about one-third using tobacco (Rigotti, Lee, & Wechsler, 2000).

Several risk factors for mental health problems among the college population have been identified, many of which are largely consistent with risk factors for the broader population. Female students are more likely than male students to report depression and anxiety while male students are more likely than female students to attempt suicide (Eisenberg, Gollust, et al., 2007). Having low income is also a risk factor for mental health issues among college students (Eisenberg, Gollust, et al., 2007; Hunt & Eisenberg, 2010). Social exclusion is another risk factor for mental illness for those in marginalized groups of individuals feeling injustice and social disadvantage (Reicher & Matischek-Jauk, 2018). In addition to sociodemographic risk factors, environmental and social climate risk factors are also important. Students who have a poorer social support network (Hefner & Eisenberg, 2009) – as may be experienced by students of color in predominantly White institutions (Barry et al., 2017; Corona et al., 2017) first-generation students, bisexual, and transgender students (Liu et al., 2019), and students with disabilities (Coduti et al., 2016) – are at higher risk of mental health disorders. These data suggest that multifaceted and multimodal approaches for diagnosis, treatment, and intervention are needed.

Despite the prevalence of mental health problems on college campuses, many students fail to receive the mental health services they need (Bruffaerts et al., 2018, Hunt & Eisenberg, 2010). Mental health counselors and therapists on college campuses are working at or beyond capacity, with treatment needs far exceeding available resources. Several studies (ACHA, 2009; Eisenberg, Golberstein, & Gollust, 2007) have suggested that less than half of students (in some cases only 20%) who have screened positive for depression or anxiety disorders received treatment in the prior year. As reviewed by Hunt and Eisenberg (2010), barriers include lack of time, stigma, privacy concerns, lack of emotional readiness, perceived financial constraints, being unaware of services or insurance coverage, skepticism about whether treatment will help, and lack of perceived need for help.

Despite the extensive literature on both the prevalence and risk factors for mental health disorders among college students, evidence about the effects of interventions to address these issues remains sparse. Many colleges and universities are experimenting with models of mental health care as part of efforts to improve the sense of belonging on campus and to help students be successful through college graduation and beyond. Nevertheless, preintervention research – including community-based participatory research with college students – as well as postintervention research to evaluate what works has yet to be reviewed and integrated. Such integration of what is known and what remains unknown in this area is paramount to advancing the field for researchers, educators, and college and university leadership.

Accordingly, the remaining part of this chapter seeks to present the latest data on trends in the prevalence of mental health disorders and on use of mental health services by college students, discuss several barriers to treatment, and highlight current innovations in treatment and harm reduction efforts. We conclude with a set of recommendations for future directions to address the pressing problem of mental health across college campuses in the United States.

27.1.1 Trends in Prevalence of Mental Health Disorders and Use of Mental Health Services

Using data from the American College Health Association (ACHA), the prevalence of mental health concerns among college students in the United States has increased from about 17% in 2010 to 26.1% in 2015 to 32.9% in 2019 (ACHA, 2019; see Figure 27.1). Similarly, colleges are also reporting increases in the number of students seeking mental health services (ACHA, 2019; see Figure 27.4), particularly for depression and anxiety (Kruisselbrink Flatt, 2013; Pedrelli et al., 2015; Prince, 2015). A recent report from the Center for Collegiate Mental Health (CCMH, 2021) indicated that the top five presenting concerns among college students receiving mental health services were anxiety (reported by 62.7% of students receiving mental health services),

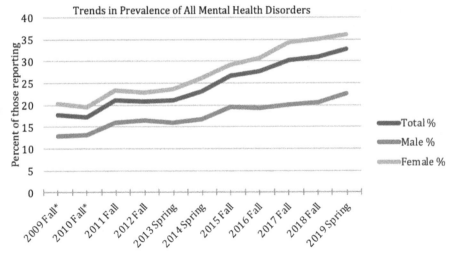

Figure 27.1 *Proportion of college students reporting diagnosis or treatment of any mental health disorder in the last twelve months*
Note: * The data reported are from the surveys by the American College Health Association–National College Health Assessment: ACHA–NCHA II (Fall 2009–Fall 2010); ACHA–NCHA IIb (Fall 2011–Spring 2014); ACHA–NCHA IIc (Fall 2015–Spring 2019). Source: Data from ACHA, 2019

depression (reported by 49.3%), stress (reported by 43.6%), family (reported by 30.7%), and academic performance (reported by 24.2%).

27.1.1.1 Anxiety among College Students

Anxiety is the most common mental health concern in college students (CCMH, 2020) and the reported prevalence has increased from 9.2% in 2010 to 17.7% in 2015 to 24.0% in 2019 (ACHA, 2019; see Figure 27.2). In addition, the ACHA survey found that 29% of students responding reported that anxiety had affected academic performance, defined as having "received a lower grade on an exam, or an important project; received a lower grade in the course; received an incomplete or dropped the course" (ACHA, 2019, p. 5). Anxiety-related concerns without a diagnosis or treatment are even more common: A large portion of all college students responding to the survey reported feeling overwhelmed (88.0%), feeling lonely (67.4%), feeling exhausted (85.0%), feeling hopeless (57.5%), or having experienced overwhelming anxiety (66.4%) while in school (ACHA, 2019).

Academic performance pressures contribute to college student anxiety. Some of the main sources of academic stress include a focus on grades and evaluation pressures, test-taking, and time-management (Crocker & Luhtanen, 2003). Anxiety is related to student attrition, while depression is associated with lower grade point average (GPA) and the likelihood of withdrawing (Eisenberg, Golberstein, & Hunt, 2009), which can produce a

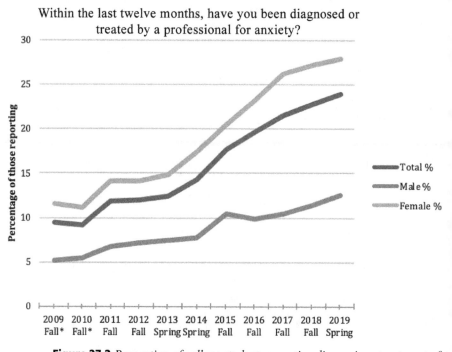

Figure 27.2 *Proportion of college students reporting diagnosis or treatment of anxiety in the last twelve months*
*Note: * The data reported are from the surveys by the American College Health Association–National College Health Assessment: ACHA–NCHA II (Fall 2009– Fall 2010); ACHA–NCHA IIb (Fall 2011–Spring 2014); ACHA–NCHA IIc (Fall 2015–Spring 2019). Source: Data from ACHA, 2019*

downward spiral of creating even greater anxiety and subsequent decreases in academic GPA (Stallman, 2010).

"Financial stress is also a major contributor that both directly and indirectly impacts student anxiety" (Jones et al., 2018, p. 2). Of incoming first-year students, 33.7% report a major concern over financing their college education, and 64.6% report having either some concern or major concerns about their ability to finance college (Stolzenberg et al., 2019). Some researchers have noted parallels between the increasing financial strain (funding cutbacks in scholarships and loans) over the past several decades and an increase in student mental health needs (Kitzrow, 2003).

27.1.1.2 Depression among College Students

Depression on college campuses is a significant public health concern. Based on findings from ACHA's NCHA report, the rates of students "diagnosed or treated" with depression have increased from 10.3% in 2000, to 8.3% in 2010, to 20.0% in Spring 2019 (ACHA, 2019; see Figure 27.3). The consequences of depression are significant. State Mackenzie and colleagues (2011):

Within the past twelve months, have you been diagnosed or treated by a professional for depression?

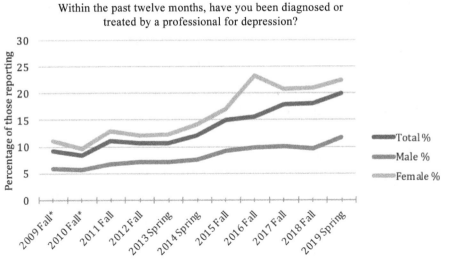

Figure 27.3 *Proportion of college students reporting diagnosis or treatment of depression in the last twelve months*
*Note: * The data reported are from the surveys by the American College Health Association–National College Health Assessment: ACHA–NCHA II (Fall 2009– Fall 2010); ACHA-NCHA IIb (Fall 2011–Spring 2014); ACHA–NCHA IIc (Fall 2015–Spring 2019). Source: Data from ACHA, 2019*

"Depression and anxiety are consistently listed among the top 10 factors impairing academic performance in the past 12 months on the NCHA (ACHA, 2008). Diagnosed depression was associated with a 0.49 decrease in student GPA, and treatment was associated with a 0.44 protective effect (Hysenbegasi, Hass, & Rowland, 2005)."

Beyond academic concerns, depression is related to a host of student concerns. Depression is a risk factor for self-injury (Gollust, Eisenberg, & Golberstein, 2008) and suicide behavior (talking about, attempting, or taking actions related to ending one's life; Kisch, Leino, & Silverman, 2005). Depressive symptoms have been associated with a host of adverse health and behavioral risk factors, including poor relationships and polyvictimization (i.e., partner violence, physical, psychological, or sexual victimization; Sabina & Straus, 2008), as well as maladaptive health behaviors (e.g., tobacco use, alcohol consumption, physical inactivity) (Strine et al., 2015).

Depression has been consistently identified as a major risk factor for suicide in teens and young adults (ACHA, 2019; Brody, Pratt, & Hughes, 2018; Cukrowicz et al., 2011), and according to recent data from the Centers for Disease Control and Prevention (2019), suicide is the second leading cause of death for youth and young adults aged ten years (Brody et al., 2018). In addition, of full-time college students (18–24 years), 8% have had suicidal thoughts, 2.4% have made a suicide plan, 0.9% have made a suicide attempt, and 0.3% received medical attention after a suicide attempt (Brody et al.,

2018). Suicide ideation (thinking, considering, or planning suicide) among college students is marked by a number of factors unique to the developmental adjustments that occur during the college years. This transitional stage is often marked by changes in family and social support structures, as well as increased financial and academic pressures. Taken together, suicide prevention programs can benefit from a focus on the emotional, social, and behavioral challenges that arise during the college years.

27.1.1.3 Use of Mental Health Services

Research on treatment utilization over time shows steady increases in the number of students utilizing off-campus mental health care (counselor, therapist, psychologist), ranging from 29.4% of total students reporting in 2010 to 42.6% in 2019 (ACHA, 2019; see Figure 27.4). Students also showed an increase in use of on-campus mental health services, ranging from 10.4% in 2010 to 21.3% in 2019 (ACHA, 2019; see Figure 27.5).

Of deep concern for many college campuses is the fact that many students suffer in silence. Undiagnosed or untreated symptoms can worsen and increase in severity, making it challenging for everyday coping and personal and social functioning. Research shows that 73% of students with behavioral concerns (social isolation, failing courses, not showing up to class) may

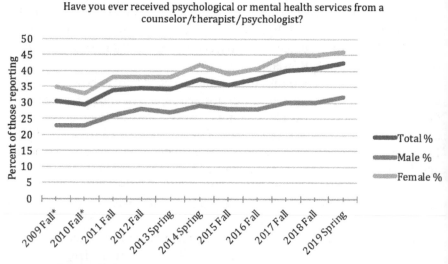

Figure 27.4 *Use of any mental health service: prevalence of students reporting having received mental health services through a counselor, therapist, or psychologist.*
*Note: * The data reported are from the surveys by the American College Health Association–National College Health Assessment: ACHA–NCHA II (Fall 2009–Fall 2010); ACHA-NCHA IIb (Fall 2011–Spring 2014); ACHA–NCHA IIc (Fall 2015–Spring 2019). Source: Data from ACHA, 2019*

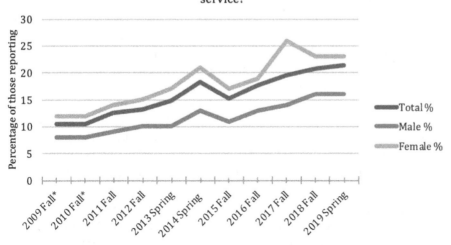

Figure 27.5 *Use of college/university mental health service: prevalence of students reporting having received psychological or mental health services at their college/university counseling center.*
*Note: * The data reported are from the surveys by the American College Health Association–National College Health Assessment: ACHA–NCHA II (Fall 2009– Fall 2010); ACHA-NCHA IIb (Fall 2011–Spring 2014); ACHA–NCHA IIc (Fall 2015–Spring 2019). Source: Data from ACHA, 2019*

experience a mental health crisis, and 64% of students who withdraw from college report having behavioral health concerns (De Luca et al., 2016). Integrated healthcare systems (physical health care, mental health services, academic support) are critical for institutions of higher education to help identify high-risk students who may not self-identify and provide essential resources for students in need of treatment.

27.2 Who Seeks Treatment?

Although use of mental health services has increased over the last decade (ACHA, 2019; see Figures 27.4 and 27.5), recent evidence suggests substantial treatment gaps persist (ACHA, 2019; Gallagher, 2015). According to the Healthy Minds 2018–2019 study, which examines mental health and related issues in college populations (Eisenberg et al., 2019), only 43% of undergraduates who screened positive for depression or anxiety received treatment or counseling from a health professional. Treatment gaps may be exacerbated for communities on campus who face microaggressions and added stress (Meyer, 2003), racial fatigue (Franklin,

2019), stigmatization (Cheng, Kwan, & Sevig, 2013), and transitional difficulties (Stephens, Markus, & Phillips, 2014) as they encounter the day-to-day academic challenges that come with college life as well. Some of these communities include LGBTQ (lesbian, gay, bisexual, transgender, or queer) students (Kulick et al., 2017), ethnic minorities including American Indian/Alaska Native American (Yang, Byers, & Fenton, 2006) and African American students (Smith, Hung, & Franklin, 2011), and international students (Williams, Case, & Roberts, 2018).

The literature reports that students who are female and students who are White have more positive attitudes toward seeking help for mental health issues compared with male students and students of color (Eisenberg, Hunt, et al., 2011; Masuda et al., 2009; Masuda et al., 2005; Twentyman, Frank, & Lindsey, 2017). In a nationwide study surveying mental health and treatment among college students, Asian/Asian American students were found to have the lowest treatment rates, with only 20% of students with apparent mental health conditions receiving treatment. Additionally, Asians/Asian Americans who sought treatment had the highest rates of distress at intake (Lipson, Kern, Eisenberg, & Breland-Noble, 2018).

The 2018–2019 Healthy Minds survey largely of US college students identified additional barriers to treatment: 23% of respondents cited financial reasons as a barrier to help-seeking, 27% said they would "prefer to deal with the issues on my own or with support from family/friends," 10% responded that they were "not sure where to go," and 23% cited a lack of time (Eisenberg et al., 2019). Barriers for international students, who may lack extensive social support networks, may additionally include language difficulties, cultural differences, and lack of culturally appropriate counseling services (Williams et al., 2018). Furthermore, depending on the degree of cultural differences between a student's culture of origin and host culture, international students might experience greater acculturative stress entering their new college environment (Wu, Garza, & Guzman, 2015). Additionally, international students may be unaware of or unfamiliar with the mental health services provided by the college, since such treatment may not be available in their native countries (Lee et al., 2014).

27.3 Treatment

Early intervention, tailored to college students' needs and context, can provide individuals with tools to understand and lessen the destructive impact of untreated mental health issues. While college years can bring new stress that may trigger or exacerbate mental health issues, the college environment also provides opportunities to maximize the impact of preventative and treatment strategies. Colleges can be particularly well-suited to provide an environment with multiple layers and networks of support, which can include educators, peers, student-life staff (e.g., residential life staff, academic deans, professors), and health practitioners (Downs et al., 2018).

A variety of services are available for college students. Only 45%–55% of colleges and universities have some psychiatric services that prescribe medication (although almost all schools provide mental health services of some kind, such as cognitive behavioral therapy (CBT) or group therapy) with larger and private institutions more likely to have more extensive services, and rural colleges more likely to have more limited access to care (Downs et al., 2018). College counseling centers can provide a variety of services to the campus community including consultation, prevention, outreach, clinical services, and training (Downs et al., 2018). Mental health center staff have been found to devote approximately 60% of their time on direct service delivery – psychotherapy, assessment, crisis intervention, and case management – while the other 40% of staff time is directed to prevention through outreach and education, direct training and education, and collaboration with other schools and professionals and with other campus departments (Brunner et al., 2014). The most common therapies provided by mental health staff on college campuses are CBT, interpersonal/dialectical behavior therapy, and mindfulness therapy (Downs et al., 2016).

Many colleges offer both individual and group therapy. Group therapy may help centers manage demand while still providing adequate care to students. Studies show that there is little to no difference between individual and group therapy in terms of reducing symptoms of anxiety and depression (Fawcett et al., 2020). In a study of university students, although individual therapy was rated higher than group therapy by students, both group and individual therapy created positive attitudes toward therapy in general (Fawcett et al., 2020). Ideally, whether group or individual therapy is concerned, counseling centers use team-based and student-centered approaches, which stress the importance of multidimensional and comprehensive initial assessments (e.g., evaluating client preferences in counseling type or therapist style), as well as ongoing follow-up. Comprehensive assessment information as well as the therapeutic alliance serve as the basis for all other interactions and can help an individual's attitude toward receiving care (Downs et al., 2016).

Individual therapy or counseling is a process where a student works one-on-one with a trained mental health specialist in a safe and caring environment. Together, the student and counselor develop goals for growth and improvement in coping skills and well-being practices. The therapy sessions promote the opportunity for each student to receive support while they identify aspects of their lives that they would like to change or understand.

Group counseling is a type of psychotherapy that involves meeting with a group of individuals who all face similar concerns. Group sessions involve sharing experiences and listening to other's experiences. Some of the groups are focused on a particular theme (e.g., grief and loss, eating issues, creating healthy relationships, managing anxiety) or the group may be targeted to a specific group of individuals (e.g., women, men, or nontraditional students). Group counseling provides a supportive environment to discuss problems and concerns and to work toward student goals (Denton, Gross, & Wojcik, 2017). Group counseling can be an effective treatment modality for a variety of students and presenting issues. State Denton and colleagues (2017): "A recent meta-analysis by Burlingame, Fuhriman, and Mosier (2003) found that 72% of individuals who received group therapy showed some form of improvement, with counseling centers being the primary provider of group services (ahead of other institutions such as correctional facilities and mental health clinics). Groups may have equal utility outside the realm of treating student psychopathology; students' decision-making abilities regarding career selection can improve with participation in a career counseling group (Rowell, Mobley, Kemer, & Giordano, 2014) while grief groups allow bereft students to more effectively cope with the loss of a loved one (Janowiak, Mei-tal, & Drapkin, 1995; O'Neill & Fry, 2013; Prior, 2015). Stress management groups have become particularly relevant offerings in counseling centers over recent years" (p. 542).

The most effective form of intervention is widely debated, and some suggest that no single model for counseling is superior; rather the quality not the format of service delivery, is most important (Downs et al., 2016). Recognizing the limited empirical data-evaluating services on campus, the literature suggests that evaluations must contextualize services and care within the specific campus environment, recognizing difference in student populations, campus cultures, available resources, and administrative reporting structures (Downs et al., 2018). The limited evidence that does exist has found that college mental health services can positively influence student mental health and that the creation of positive therapist–client relationships is vital to facilitate positive outcomes (Locke et al., 2012).

Additional research examining the advantages and drawbacks of different organizational models of care (singular versus collaborative) is warranted. Some institutions have switched to using collaborative models of care that combine primary care, health promotion, psychiatry, and counseling with the hope of providing holistic and easily accessible care. In fact, in a survey of 621 counseling centers at colleges and universities, approximately 56% collaborated with health services centers most of the time or "when it makes sense to do so" (LeViness, Bershad, & Gorman, 2017, p. 63). The benefits of these integrated models include the opportunity to provide more holistic care, emphasize wellness, improve the continuity of care, streamline resources, potentially save costs, and create a "no wrong door" approach for students to reduce barriers to treatment and increase access to mental health care. This "no wrong door" approach means that students can seek care from a variety of different sources and be directed to the appropriate services regardless of where they begin. These approaches, however, come with challenges such as administrative coordination and combining of two or more separate systems (health services and mental health services), allocation and adequacy of resources, and effective communication between different offices and services. While empirical evidence remains limited, data have suggested that integrated support services are important to meeting student needs, making timely referrals, and creating more efficient use of services (Downs et al., 2018). Even integrating physical and mental health services in smaller ways can be helpful. For example, implementing a brief mental health survey/screening process during a student's health center visit can increase awareness of mental health professionals and improve treatment decision-making for both students and clinicians (Alschuler, Hoodin, & Byrd, 2008).

Providing mental health treatment opportunities for students is especially important in the midst of national and global crises, such COVID-19. College students may be especially vulnerable to increased mental health concerns due to fears about their own and their families' health, new economics pressures, a loss of important "rite of passage" milestones (e.g., senior week, graduation), uncertainty about the future, and a loss of autonomy. The disruption in their college peer experiences can compromise opportunities for emotional, behavioral, and identity development. Separated from their peers, students miss the chance to engage in the behaviors and vulnerabilities that characterize this developmental stage and provide opportunities for growth and exploration.

In the midst of the global crisis of COVID-19 in particular, colleges and universities may adopt a digital strategy that can include telehealth psychotherapy, allowing therapy and care to continue despite requiring social distancing to limit spread of the coronavirus. Telehealth psychotherapy is an online system that allows a therapist to collect data that monitor progress in client behaviors and use these data to inform the treatment, a strategy that has been shown to lead to effective treatment outcomes (Lewis et al., 2018). Telehealth psychotherapy may also increase use of mental health services in rural and other areas where there is a scarcity of providers. Furthermore, telehealth psychotherapy allows clinicians to access more detailed and nuanced information about their patients by observing their lives at home, which offers the opportunity to evaluate the change process during treatment. With telehealth psychotherapy, clinicians can observe the patient's behavior as it occurs, and give immediate feedback. In many ways, innovative telehealth therapies may illuminate new and more effective treatment during times of social distancing and isolation.

27.4 Prevention

Mental health issues in college students may arise or worsen because of various pressures and stressors. Therefore, it is vital that colleges and universities develop various prevention strategies instead of only focusing on treatment programs. Prevention programs differ based on the behavior or mental health problem they seek to prevent. Evidence shows that prevention programs are most helpful when they are personalized and individualized programs in one-on-one or small group settings either via computer or face-to-face (Reavley & Jorm, 2010).

Preventative programs largely fall under two categories: psychoeducational strategies and skills training (Conley, Durlak, & Kirsch, 2015).

Psychoeducational programs inform students about the sorts of pressures and stressors they are likely to face and discuss various healthy coping strategies to help students deal with these challenges and reduce the level of stress they experience. Ideally, this type of information will motivate students to act and employ these coping strategies in order to prevent negative outcomes. Skill training programs focus on teaching and practicing strategies such as cognitive restructuring, mindfulness, relaxation, conflict resolution, effective communication, and other skills. Such programs that seek to teach certain behavioral skills may help prevent negative outcomes (Conley et al., 2015). In an analysis of six different categories of skills-based or psychoeducational-based interventions, Conley and colleagues (2015) found that skill-based training programs with supervised practice were more effective than psychoeducational programs and were helpful across in a variety of different outcomes such as reduction of anxiety, stress, and depression, improving social-emotional skills, self-perceptions, and academic adjustment. Psychoeducation, on the other hand, resulted in limited changes in anxiety and stress reduction, as well as limited improvements in academics and self-perceptions; however, the programs did not reduce depression or improve social-emotional skills, or interpersonal relationships (Conley et al., 2015).

Psychoeducational programs can help to lessen the barrier of lack of information about mental health care, enhance willingness to seek help, and increase intention to use mental health services. In 2018, 664 university students participated in internet-based personalized feedback based on their self-reported symptoms and symptom severity in mental health issues including depression, anxiety, suicidal thoughts and behaviors, substance use, and self-injury (Ebert et al., 2018). This survey then provided students with psychoeducational information tailored to their symptom profile and information on university mental health services offered in this context. The students who participated in this intervention (compared with the control group) reported significantly higher intentions to seek help and to utilize mental health services in the next semester (Ebert et al., 2018). This study suggests that providing students with personal, tailored information on their own mental health profiles and, importantly, concrete information on help-seeking options available to them may encourage students to reach the decision to seek help.

Another potential strategy for prevention of a variety of mental health issues is providing gatekeeper training (GKT) and peer/authority support. GKT involves educating nonprofessionals to identify at-risk individuals and offer support. Lipson and colleagues (2018) found that the majority of students of color who face mental health issues seek nonclinical sources for support, such as friends and family. Further literature (Rickwood, Deane, & Wilson, 2007) also suggests a growing number of students of all backgrounds seek support from informal sources such as the Internet. Such findings suggest that it may be beneficial for institutions to help provide gatekeeper trainers to other students so they may act as effective sources of support and aid in referring students to mental health services. In terms of mental health, GKT programs are not new in the field; for instance, the Mental Health First Aid (MHFA) GKT program is employed in many colleges. Such programs aim to equip nonprofessionals that are in frequent contact with others in their communities with skills and resources to improve mental health and increase service utilization (Lipson et al., 2014). Reliable gatekeepers, however, must first be identified and trained. Professors, administrative staff, and residential assistants tend to be frequently targeted as seemingly ideal gatekeepers; however, in exploring the effectiveness of GKT, Lipson and colleagues (2014) found limited evidence that GKT for authority figures increased help-seeking within the community, although GKT was found to encourage the trainees (the gatekeepers themselves) to seek professional mental health services for themselves.

While the 2014 study by Lipson and colleagues had notable limitations, as discussed by Reid (2015), it does suggest some possible means to increase the efficacy of GKT. Targeting peers may be a useful strategy. Studies suggest that individuals who receive GKT to facilitate peer counseling demonstrate better social functioning, empowerment, and problem-focused coping strategies (Kirsch et al., 2014). Such programs may operate with principles akin to Sexual Health Peer Education (SHPE) workshops, which have been successful in disseminating basic information to help students recognize symptoms of sexually transmitted disease and encourage help-seeking behaviors in a youth-friendly and cost-effective manner (Francis et al., 2016). From a practical standpoint, it may also be effective to develop and offer peer-counseling services, given the finite financial resources and clinical pressures exerted on the college from the student population. Such training may also be useful for the trainees themselves by providing guidance for them to become aware of their own possible prejudices toward individuals with mental health problems and the campus climate they perpetuate (Scantlebury et al., 2018). Since campus climate plays such a large role in the proliferation of mental health issues as well as the encouragement/discouragement of help-seeking behaviors, increased awareness about students' own biases may aid in the mental well-being of the college population.

27.5 Recommendations and Future Directions

Exploring ways to reduce the mental health concerns among college students has become increasingly important. New and innovative approaches to normalize mental health struggles may help address the treatment gap on college campuses. We recommend that colleges prioritize programs and practices that make mental health and wellness a part of everyday life. This culture change may be achieved through approaches involving positive psychology and digital technology.

27.5.1 Positive Psychology

Positive psychology goes hand-in-hand with traditional mental health interventions. As a complement to clinical psychology, practices based on positive psychology principles help individuals discover and build personal strengths (e.g., courage, kindness, compassion) to navigate their relationships with others and maintain positive mental health (Parks & Layous, 2016). Interventions that promote resilience, self-compassion, empathy, mindfulness, gratitude, and forgiveness can be practiced daily to help maintain well-being in the midst of trying times (Fredrickson, 2001; Parks & Layous, 2016). Used in conjunction with trained counselors or therapists, positive psychology interventions have been shown to relieve symptoms of depression, reduce suicide ideation, increase social connectedness, and increase subjective well-being (Stone & Parks, 2018).

27.5.2 Technology

Although the use of technology can have some detriments to mental health (e.g., Twenge, Martin, & Campbell, 2018), the same technologies can also offer a number of opportunities for the enhancement of mental health and the treatment of mental illness. One example of a relatively new way to reach students can be found at the University of Michigan. This university has focused its outreach efforts on providing mental health events and activities and on a YouTube channel focusing on mental health, which has more than seventy thousand views (Gibbons et al., 2019). Outreach and treatment based on online or social media platforms can be very useful. In fact, online help-seeking is one of the most common information-gathering and help-seeking strategies used by young adults including college students (Fox, 2011). Similarly, in a survey of 6,034 students, 60% reported willingness to use online mental health services (Dunbar et al., 2018). Online forms of creative outreach to students can help students easily receive information regarding mental health, promote healthy coping strategies, potentially improve the campus climate surrounding mental health, and, importantly, promote help-seeking behaviors among students.

27.5.3 Digital Mental Health

Digital mental health refers to online mental health interventions (i.e., information, psychoeducation, training) that are presented to users through the

Web or mobile handheld devices (smartphones, smartwatches, tablets, Web-based applications). This method of mental health delivery can be especially useful for college students who have unmet mental health needs. Digital mental health may also be especially valuable for students when traditional face-to-face treatment is unavailable (e.g., during a global pandemic, natural disasters). Research shows that college students hold favorable attitudes toward digital technology and online services, and a majority indicate that they would be willing to use online mental health services (Dunbar et al., 2018; March et al., 2018).

Given that smartphone ownership is prolific among college students today (86% of undergraduates reported owning a smartphone in a 2014 report by EDUCAUSE [Dahlstrom & Bichsel, 2014]), it is thus important to consider the efficacy of technology-based interventions. The benefits of utilizing technology to reach the college-aged population are numerous: Web-based apps are more accessible and convenient, especially when the cost of counseling services are prohibitive (Olfson et al., 2000); likewise, intervention apps may be useful to address the stigma associated with mental health treatment among populations, who might be reluctant to access in-person services initially (Corrigan, 2004). Furthermore, due to the increased digital literacy among millennials (born 1980–1995) and Gen-Zers (born 1996–2015), it is unsurprising that studies have found younger patients to prefer mobile methods of treatment and monitoring (Matthews et al., 2008).

The benefits of digital mental health programs are many. Literally at one's fingertips, digital mental health support is easy to access and use, it is quick, and it is efficient. Such technology may be especially effective in crisis situations; when students need immediate support, they can send a text to a crisis center, which often offers twenty-four-hour support. Furthermore, digital mental health services are generally affordable, and can offer an easy and anonymous entryway to treatment for many who may have avoided mental health services due to perceived stigma or cultural sensitivity concerns (National Institute of Mental Health, 2019).

A digital strategy for mental health can be especially valuable for crisis management in the midst of COVID-19. Short-term digital interventions may provide accessible support during mental health crises. Psychologists recommend that brief, short-term interventions in the midst of COVID-19 can be helpful (Gruber et al., 2020). Single-session interventions require a brief meeting with a trained counselor or therapist to provide immediate care. Such sessions can reduce symptoms of psychopathology in young adults, and have been shown to be effective for treating self-harm, depression, and conduct problems (Schleider et al., 2020). In the midst of social-distancing requirements, sessions can be conducted remotely via the Web or telephone with a therapist or via the Web without a therapist present (Schleider et al., 2020). The accessibility of this approach may have valuable public health benefits to communities.

Digital technology can also be packaged with wearable devices for ambulatory assessment of needs (e.g., activity trackers, wireless medical devices). With new third-party apps, a device's built-in sensors can track changes in one typical behavior pattern. Sensors can unobtrusively monitor keyboard dynamics (e.g., typing speed and rhythm, error corrections via backspace and autocorrect), which can assess the onset of mental health disorders. For instance, digital phenotypes can be used to track patterns for bipolarity, as keystrokes can reflect behavioral patterns of depression and mania (Zulueta et al., 2018). Wearable sensors can track real-time physiological data, such as galvanic skin response, skin temperature, or heart rate (Smets et al., 2018). Accelerometers can track mobility patterns and social environment, and voice recordings can detect speech and vocal markers of mood, which can be used to predict an anxiety or panic episode (Torous, Onnela, & Keshavan, 2017). When changes in behavior are detected by these apps, a signal can be sent immediately, signaling a potential crisis to a therapist, peer counselor, or other mental healthcare professional. Other apps are important in providing games that engage users to develop cognitive skills that improve memory and cognitive performance.

27.5.4 Digital Positive Psychology Interventions

Researchers have used digital mental health interventions grounded in principles of positive psychology to increase resilience, happiness, and well-being (Parks et al., 2018; Schueller & Parks, 2012, Tan et al., 2019; Wachsmuth et al., under review). Interventions aimed at cultivating positive emotions and positive behaviors can decrease symptoms of depression (Sin & Lyubomirsky, 2009), improve physical health in diseased populations (Lamers et al., 2012), improve coping skills, and reduce depression in patients with chronic illness (Cohn et al., 2014). Other research has examined the "person–activity fit" that is important when users seek guidance for deciding amongst the array of available digital interventions (Munoz et al., 2018). These studies have examined which types of activities may be most useful, for whom (Parks et al., 2012, as well as the number and variety of interventions that are most beneficial for promoting well-being (Schueller & Parks, 2012). Digital positive psychology interventions can be useful in decreasing treatment barriers (increasing mental health equity) by reaching a number of individuals who may need support, but who may otherwise have limited access to mental health services (Munoz et al., 2018; Wang et al., 2005).

In one study, a randomized, controlled design was conducted to evaluate the efficacy of using an app to improve emotional well-being. The app uses evidence-based, clinically validated interventions grounded in the fields of positive psychology (building on personal strengths, such as gratitude, kindness and compassion; Schueller & Parks, 2012), CBT (learning awareness of situations that elicit emotions and thoughts) (Beck, 2011), and mindfulness-based stress reduction (focused on mindful breathing and emotional regulation) (Kabat-Zinn, 2013). Findings revealed that participants using the app with the recommended usage (two to three activities per week) over an eight-week period showed post-intervention decreases in anxiety and depression and increases in resilience, compared with an online psychoeducational comparison group (Parks et al., 2018). This study demonstrates how recommended usage of digital mental health can help individuals develop new skills to manage stress and adversity, especially in the context of their daily life. As new technologies are developed over time, research will be required to evolve accordingly to assess the effectiveness of such interventions.

27.5.5 Internet-Based Cognitive Behavioral Therapy

Another digital mental health treatment modality that provides accessible and affordable care is internet-based cognitive behavioral therapy (iCBT) (Jolstedt et al., 2018). Participants complete self-guided exercises via the Internet (problem-solving strategies and behavioral activation techniques to understand the connection between one's thoughts and emotions). The exercises are taught and completed without an in-person therapist, but with guidance from a therapist or counselor. Guidance is offered in a variety of ways, including weekly automated emails, moderated online discussion forums, brief therapist phone calls that offer support and clarification of exercises, and longer therapist sessions that are aimed at building rapport, addressing concerns, and motivating participants to continue with their exercises (Burns et al., 2011).

Empirical evidence for digital mental health interventions is growing. Recent meta-analyses have evaluated the efficacy of iCBT programs as compared to face-to-face CBT (Andersson & Cuijpers, 2009; Davies, Morriss, & Glazebrook, 2014; Spek et al., 2006). Randomized controlled trials demonstrate that iCBT and traditional face-to-face CBT have equivalent efficacy outcomes (Andrews et al., 2018; Carlbring et al., 2005; Carlbring et al., 2018; Davies et al., 2014; Hedman et al., 2011). Furthermore, iCBT is more effective than no treatment. Together, the accumulation of data suggests that iCBT can be a viable means to provide mental health services to treat disorders like depression (Webb, Rosso, & Rauch, 2017) and anxiety (Hedman et al., 2011) thereby addressing barriers to treatment. Nevertheless, additional research that compares the efficacy of digital mental health to both traditional mental health services as well as to no treatment among college students is warranted. Furthermore, understanding how the features of digital mental health can be tailored to different groups of college students to improve access and engagement would be helpful to meet the growing expectations of students and their families.

27.6 Conclusion

Normalizing and destigmatizing mental health concerns likely requires a college-wide prevention and treatment program that involves all facets of the college (residential life, academic advising coursework, faculty involvement). Approaches aimed at greater inclusiveness should match mental health treatments and services to meet student needs (Lindley, 2012), as a sense of belonging can buffer against mental illness (Treichler & Lucksted, 2018). New and innovative approaches are necessary especially in the midst of the COVID-19 global pandemic, which will likely change the face of mental health services in the future. Psychologists are predicting a severe "mental health curve" that will also need flattening (Gruber et al., 2020). With the world facing the worst pandemic since 1918, and forecasts of more pandemics to come with the changing climate, the melting of the Arctic permafrost, and the human encroachment on rainforests and other natural boundaries, innovative strategies for mental health treatment and prevention are paramount.

Creative approaches to enhance public awareness about mental health can improve knowledge about mental illness: Students, faculty, and staff can recognize relevant symptoms of pathology; help identify who may be at risk; and help reduce any treatment barriers. The implementation of social media, workshops, and college-wide conversations can make information about mental health concerns accessible to all (Gibbons et al., 2019). Such programs may go a long way toward a culture shift toward acceptance of mental health service use and availability when and where students need such support.

In summary, a community-wide approach to treatment and prevention can provide important opportunities to address growing mental health challenges for college students. A digital strategy to mental health can be useful when social distancing limits the possibility of in-person treatment, thereby minimizing the gap between treatment needs and access to care. Community efforts to address mental health might also involve laypersons to provide support. As shown in some global models to mental health care, community leaders, religious groups, and cultural elders can deliver effective and sensitive care for a variety of mental health concerns (Chibanda et al., 2016; Singla et al., 2017). Broadening the scope of treatment and prevention strategies can transform mental health practices for college students, with the support of community efforts and continued global mental health conversations.

References

Altschuler, K., Hoodin, F., & Byrd, M. (2008). The need for integrating behavioral care in a college health center. *Health Psychology, 27*(3), 388–393. doi.org/10.1037/0278-6133.27.3.388

American College Health Association. (2009). American College Health Association–National College Health Assessment Spring 2008 reference group data report (abridged): The American College Health Association. *Journal of American College Health, 57*(5), 477–488. doi.org/10.3200/JACH.57.5.477-488

American College Health Association. (2019, Spring). *American College Health Association – National College Health Assessment II: Undergraduate student executive summary*. Silver Spring, MD: American College Health Association. www.acha.org/documents/ncha/NCHA-II_SPRING_2019_UNDERGRADUATE_REFERENCE%20_GROUP_EXECUTIVE_SUMMARY.pdf

American College Health Association. (2008, Fall). *National college health assessment: Reference group executive summary*. Baltimore, MD: Author.

Andersson, G., & Cuijpers, P. (2009). Internet-based and other computerized psychological treatments for adult depression: A meta-analysis. *Cognitive Behavioral Therapy, 38*(4), 196–205. doi.org/10.1080/16506070903318960

Andrews, G., Basu, A., Cuijpers, P., et al. (2018). Computer therapy for the anxiety and depression disorders is effective, acceptable and practical health care: An updated meta-analysis. *Journal of Anxiety Disorders, 55*, 70–78. doi.org/10.1016/j.janxdis.2018.01.001

Auerbach, R. P., Alonso, J., Axinn, W. G., et al. (2018). WHO World Mental Health Surveys International College Student Project: Prevalence and distribution of mental disorders. *Journal of Abnormal Psychology, 127*(7), 623–638. doi.org/10.1037/abn0000362

Barry, A., Jackson, Z., Watkins, D., Goodwill, J. R., & Hunt, E. R. H. (2017). Alcohol use and mental health conditions among Black college males: Do those attending postsecondary minority institutions fare better than those at primarily White institutions? *American Journal of Men's Health, 11*(4), 962–968. doi.org/10.1177/1557988316674840

Beck, J. S. (2011). *Cognitive behavior therapy: Basics and beyond* (2nd ed.). New York: Guilford Press.

Beiter, R., Nash, R., McCrady, M., et al. (2015). The prevalence and correlates of depression, anxiety, and stress in a sample of college students. *Journal of Affective Disorders, 173*, 90–96. doi.org/10.1016/j.jad.2014.10.054

Brody, D. J., Pratt, L. A., & Hughes, J. P. (2018). Prevalence of depression among adults aged 20 and over: United States, 2013–2016. *NCHS Data Brief, 303*, 1–8. www.ncbi.nlm.nih.gov/pubmed/29638213

Bruffaerts, R., Mortier, P., Kiekens, G., et al. (2018). Mental health problems in college freshmen: Prevalence and academic functioning. *Journal of Affective Disorders, 225*, 97–103. doi.org/10.1016/j.jad.2017.07.044

Brunner, J. L., Wallace, D. L., Reymann, L. S., Sellers, J.-J., & McCabe, A. G. (2014). College counseling today: Contemporary students and how counseling centers meet their needs. *Journal of College Student Psychotherapy, 28*(4), 257–324. doi.org/10.1080/87568225.2014.948770

Burlingame, G. M., Fuhriman, A., & Mosier, J. (2003). The differential effectiveness of group psychotherapy: A meta-analytic perspective. *Group Dynamics: Theory, Research, and Practice, 7*(1), 3–12. doi.org/10.1037/1089-2699.7.1.3

Burns, N. M., Beagle, M., Duffecy, J., et al. (2011). Harnessing context sensing to develop a mobile intervention for depression. *Journal of Medical Internet Research, 13*(3), 1–17. doi.org/10.2196/jmir.1838

Carlbring, P., Andersson, G., Cuijpers, P., Riper, H., & Hedman-Langerlöf, E. (2018). Internet-based vs. face-to-face cognitive behavior therapy for psychiatric and somatic disorders: An updated systematic review and meta-analysis. *Cognitive Behavioral Therapy, 47*(1), 1–18. doi.org/10.1080/16506073.2017.1401115

Carlbring, P., Nilsson-Ihrfelt, E., Waara, J., et al. (2005). Treatment of panic disorder: Live therapy vs. self-help via the Internet. *Behavior Research and Therapy, 43*(10), 1321–1333. doi.org/10.1016/j.brat.2004.10.002

Center for Collegiate Mental Health. (2021, January). *2020 annual report* (Publication No. STA 21-045). https://ccmh.psu.edu/assets/docs/2020%20CCMH%20Annual%20Report.pdf

Centers for Disease Control and Prevention. (2019). *National Vital Statistics System – mortality data for via CDC WONDER.* https://wonder.cdc.gov/controller/saved/D76/D91F023

Cheng, H., Kwan, K. K., & Sevig, T. (2013). Racial and ethnic minority college students' stigma associated with seeking psychological help: Examining psychocultural correlates. *Journal of Counseling Psychology, 60*(1), 98–111. doi .org/10.1037/a0031169

Chibanda, D., Weiss, H. A., Verhey, R., et al. (2016). Effect of a primary care-based psychological intervention on symptoms of common mental disorders in Zimbabwe. *JAMA, 316*(24), 2618–2626. doi.org/10.1001/jama.2016.19102

Coduti, W. A., Hayes, J. A., Locke, B. D., & Yoon, S. J. (2016). Mental health and professional help-seeking among college students with disabilities. *Rehabilitation Psychology, 61*(3), 288–296. doi.org/10.1037/rep0000101

Cohn, M. A., Pietrucha, M. E., Saslow, L. R., Hult, J. R., & Moskowitz, J. T. (2014). An online positive affect skills intervention reduces depression in adults with type 2 diabetes. *Journal of Positive Psychology, 9*(6), 523–534. doi.org/10 .1080/17439760.2014.920410

Conley, C. S., Durlak, J. A., & Kirsch, A. C. (2015). A meta-analysis of universal mental health prevention programs for higher education students. *Prevention Science, 16*(4), 487–507. doi.org/10.1007/s11121-015-0543-1

Corona, R., Rodriguez, V., McDonald, S., et al. (2017). Associations between cultural stressors, cultural values, and Latina/o college students' mental health. *Journal of Youth and Adolescence, 46*(1), 63–77. doi.org/10.1007/s10964-016-0600-5

Corrigan, P. (2004). How stigma interferes with mental health care. *American Psychologist, 59*(7), 614–625. doi.org/10.1037/0003-066X.59.7.614

Crocker, J., & Luhtanen, R. K. (2003). Level of self-esteem and contingencies of self-worth: Unique effects on academic, social, and financial problems in college students. *Personality and Social Psychology Bulletin, 29*(6), 701–712. doi.org/10.1177/0146167203029006003

Cukrowicz, K. C., Schlegel, E. F., Smith, P. N., et al. (2011). Suicide ideation among college students evidencing subclinical depression. *Journal of American College Health, 59*(7), 575–581. doi.org/10.1080/07448481.2010.483710

Cusack, S. E., Hicks, T. A., Bourdon, J., et al. (2019). Prevalence and predictors of PTSD among a college sample. *Journal of American College Health, 67*(2), 123–131. doi.org/10.1080/07448481.2018.1462824

Dahlstrom, E., & Bichsel, J. (2014, October). *ECAR study of undergraduate students and information technology.* Louisville, CO: ECAR. www.educause.edu/ecar

Davies, E. B., Morriss, R., & Glazebrook, C. (2014). Computer-delivered and Web-based interventions to improve depression, anxiety, and psychological well-being of university students: A systematic review and meta-analysis. *Journal of Medical Internet Research, 16*(5), Article e130. doi.org/10.2196/jmir.3142

De Luca, S. M., Franklin, C., Yueqi, Y., Johnson, S., & Brownson, C. (2016). The relationship between suicide ideation, behavioral health, and college academic performance. *Community Mental Health Journal, 52*(5), 534–540. doi .org/10.1007/s10597-016-9987-4

Denton, L., Gross, J., & Wojcik, C. (2017). Group counseling in the college setting: An international survey of center directors. *International Journal of Group Psychotherapy, 67*(4), 540–564. doi.org/10.1080/00207284.2016.1260458

Downs, N., Alderman, T., Schneiber, K., & Swerdlow, N. R. (2016). Treat and teach our students well: College mental health and collaborative campus communities. *Psychiatric Services, 67*(9), 957–963.

Downs, N., Galles, E., Skehan, B., & Lipson, S. K. (2018). Be true to our schools: Models of care in college mental health. *Current Psychiatry Reports, 20*(9), Article 72. doi.org/10.1007/s11920-018-0935-6

Dunbar, M. S., Sontag-Padilla, L., Kase, C. A., Seelam, R., & Stein, B. D. (2018). Unmet mental health treatment need and attitudes toward online mental health services among community college students. *Psychiatric Services, 69* (5), 597–600. doi.org/10.1176/appi.ps.201700402

DuPaul, G. J., Weyandt, L. L., O'Dell, S. M., & Varejao, M. (2009). College students with ADHD: Current status and future directions. *Journal of Attention Disorders, 13*(3), 234–250. doi.org/10.1177/1087054709340650

Ebert, D. D., Franke, M., Kählke, F., et al. (2018). Increasing intentions to use mental health services among university students: Results of a pilot randomized controlled trial within the World Health Organization's World Mental Health International College Student Initiative. *International Journal of Methods in Psychiatric Research, 28*(2), Article e1754. doi.org/10.1002/mpr.1754

Eisenberg, D., Golberstein, E., & Gollust, S. E. (2007). Help-seeking and access to mental health care in a university student population. *Medical Care, 45*(7), 594–601. doi.org/10.1097/MLR.0b013e31803bb4c1

Eisenberg, D., Golberstein, E., Hunt, J. B. (2009). Mental health and academic success in college. *The B. E. Journal of Economic Analysis & Policy, 9*(1), 1–35. doi.org/10.2202/1935-1682.2191

Eisenberg, D., Gollust, S. E., Golberstein, E., & Hefner, J. L. (2007). Prevalence and correlates of depression, anxiety, and suicidality among university students. *American Journal of Orthopsychiatry, 77*(4), 534–543. doi.org/10.1037/0002-9432.77.4.53

Eisenberg, D., Hunt, J., Speer, N., & Zivin, K. (2011). Mental health service utilization among college students in the United States. *Journal of Nervous and Mental Disorders, 199*(5), 301–308. doi.org/10.1097/NMD.0b013e3182175123

Eisenberg, D., Lipson, S. K., Ceglarek, P., et al. (2019). *The Healthy Minds study: 2018–2019 data report.* Healthy Minds Network. https://healthymindsnetwork .org/wp-content/uploads/2019/09/HMS_national-2018-19.pdf

Eisenberg, D., Nicklett, E. J., Roeder, K., & Kirz, N. E. (2011). Eating disorder symptoms among college students: Prevalence, persistence, and correlates, and treatment-seeking. *Journal of American College Health, 59*(8), 700–707. doi.org/10.1080/07448481.2010.546461

Fawcett, E., Neary, M., Ginsburg, R., & Cornish, P. (2020). Comparing the effectiveness of individual and group therapy for students with symptoms of anxiety and depression: A randomized pilot study. *Journal of American College Health, 68*(4), 430–437. doi.org/10.1080/07448481.2019.1577862

Fox, S. (2011). *Health topics: 80% of internet users look for health information online.* Pew Internet & American Life Project. www.pewresearch.org/science

Francis, C., Bradley, J., Bass, C., Scipio, K., & Braithwaite, R. (2016). Black college women sexual health peer education at Clark Atlanta University. *Journal of the Georgia Public Health Association*, 6(2), 223–230. doi.org/10.21633/jgpha .6.2s07

Franklin, J. D. (2019). Coping with racial battle fatigue: Differences and similarities for African American and Mexican American college students. *Race Ethnicity and Education*, 22(5), 589–609. doi.org/10.1080/13613324.2019.1579178

Fredrickson, B. L. (2001). The role of positive emotions in positive psychology: The broaden-and-build theory of positive emotions. *American Psychologist*, 56(3), 218–226. doi.org/10.1037//0003-066x.56.3.218

Gallagher, R. P. (2015). *National survey of college counseling centers 2014 (9V)*. University of Pittsburg. http://d-scholarship.pitt.edu/28178/

Gibbons, S., Trette-Mclean, T., Crandall, A., et al. (2019). Undergraduate students survey their peers on mental health: Perspectives and strategies for improving college counseling center outreach. *Journal of American College Health*, 67 (6), 580–591. doi.org/10.1080/07448481.2018.1499652

Gollust, S. E., Eisenberg, D., & Golberstein, E. (2008). Prevalence and correlates of self-injury among university students. *Journal of American College Health*, 56(5), 491–498. doi.org/10.3200/JACH.56.5.491-498

Gruber, J., Prinstein, M. J., Clarke, L. A., et al. (2020). Mental health and clinical psychological science in the time of COVID-19: Challenges, opportunities, and a call to action. *American Psychologist*. doi.org/10.1037/amp0000707

Hedman, E., Andersson, G., Ljótsson, B., et al. (2011). Internet-based cognitive behavior therapy vs. cognitive behavioral group therapy for social anxiety disorder: A randomized controlled non-inferiority trial. *PLoS ONE*, 6(3), Article e18001. doi.org/10.1371/journal.pone.0018001

Hefner, J., & Eisenberg, D. (2009). Social support and mental health among college students. *American Journal Orthopsychiatry*, 79(4), 491–499. doi.org/10.1037/ a0016918

Hunt, J., & Eisenberg, D. (2010). Mental health problems and help-seeking behavior among college students. *Journal of Adolescent Health*, 46(1), 3–10. doi.org/10 .1016/j.jadohealth.2009.08.008

Hysenbegasi, A., Hass, S. L., & Rowland, C. R. (2005). The impact of depression on the academic productivity of university students. *The Journal of Mental Health Policy and Economics*, 8(3), 145–151. https://pubmed.ncbi.nlm.nih .gov/16278502/

Ibrahim, A., Kelly, S., Adams, C. E., & Glazebrook, C. (2013). A systematic review of studies of depression prevalence in university students. *Journal of Psychiatric Research*, 47(3), 391–400. doi.org/10.1016/j.jpsychires.2012.11.015

Janowiak, S. M., Mei-tal, R., & Drapkin, R. G. (1995). Living with loss: A group for bereaved college students. *Death Studies*, 19(1), 55–63. doi.org/10.1080/ 07481189508252713

Jolstedt, M., Ljótsson, B., Fredlander, T., et al. (2018). Implementation of internet-delivered CBT for children with anxiety disorders in a rural area: A feasibility trial. *Internet Interventions*, 12, 121–129. doi.org/10.1016/j.invent.2017.11.003

Jones, P. J., Park, S. Y., & Lefevor, G. T. (2018). Contemporary college student anxiety: The role of academic distress, financial stress, and support. *Journal of College Counseling*, 21(3), 252–264. https://doi.org/10.1002/jocc.12107

Kabat-Zinn, J. (2013). *Full catastrophe living: How to cope with stress, pain and illness using mindfulness meditation* (Rev. ed.). New York: Hachette.

Kessler, R. C., Chiu, W. T., Demler, O., Merikangas, K. R., & Walters, E. E. (2005). Prevalence, severity, and comorbidity of 12-month DSM-IV disorders in the National Comorbidity Survey Replication. *Archives of General Psychiatry*, *62* (6), 617–627. doi.org/10.1001/archpsyc.62.6.617

Kirsch, D. J., Pinder-Amaker, S. L., Morse, C., et al. (2014). Population-based initiatives in college mental health: Students helping students to overcome obstacles. *Current Psychiatry Reports*, *16*(525), 1–8. doi.org/10.1007/s11920-014-0525-1

Kisch, J., Leino, E. V., & Silverman, M. M. (2005). Aspects of suicidal behavior, depression, and treatment in college students: Results from the Spring 2000 National College Health Assessment Survey. *Suicide and Life-Threatening Behavior*, *35*(1), 3–13. doi.org/10.1521/suli.35.1.3.59263

Kitzrow, M. (2003). The mental health needs of today's college students: Challenges and recommendations. *NASPA Journal*, *41*(1), 167–181.

Kruisselbrink Flatt, A. (2013). A suffering generation: Six factors contributing to the mental health crisis in North American higher education. *College Quarterly*, *16*(1), Article EJ1016492.

Kulick, A., Wernick, L. J., Woodford, M. R., & Renn, K. (2017). Heterosexism, depression, and campus engagement among LGBTQ college students: Intersectional differences and opportunities for healing. *Journal of Homosexuality*, *64*(8), 1125–1141. doi.org/10.1080/00918369.2016.1242333

Lamers, S. M., Bolier, L., Westerhof, G. J., Smit, F., & Bohlmeijer, E. T. (2012). The impact of emotional well-being on long-term recovery and survival in physical illness: A meta-analysis. *Journal of Behavioral Medicine*, *35*(5), 538–547. doi.org/10.1007/s10865-011-9379-8

Lee, E.-J., Ditchman, N., Fong, M. W. M., Piper, L., & Feigon, M. (2014). Mental health service seeking among Korean international students in the United States: A path analysis. *Journal of Community Psychology*, *42*(6), 639–655. doi.org/10.1002/jcop.21643

LeViness, P., Bershad, C., & Gorman, K. (2017). *The Association for University and College Counseling Center Directors annual survey*. www.aucccd. org/assets/ documents/Governance/2017% 20aucccd% 20surveypublicapr26.Pdf

Lewis, C. C., Boyd, M., Puspitasari, A., et al. (2018). Implementing measurement-based care in behavioral health: A review. *JAMA Psychiatry*, *76*(3), 324–335. doi.org/10.1001/jamapsychiatry.2018.3329

Lindley, E. (2012). Inclusive dialogue: The way forward in anti-stigma mental health education? *Journal of Public Mental Health*, *11*(2), 77–87. DOI:10.1108/ 17465721211236426

Lipson, S. K., Kern, A., Eisenberg, D., & Breland-Noble, A. M. (2018). Mental health disparities among college students of color. *Journal of Adolescent Health*, *63*(3), 348–356. doi.org/10.1016/j.jadohealth.2018.04.014

Lipson, S. K., Speer, N., Brunwasser, S., Hahn, E., & Eisenberg, D. (2014). Gatekeeper training and access to mental health care at universities and colleges. *Journal of Adolescent Health*, *55*(5), 612–619. doi.org/10.1016/j .jadohealth.2014.05.009

Liu, C. H., Stevens, C., Wong, S. H. M., Yasui, M., & Chen, J. A. (2019). The prevalence and predictors of mental health diagnoses and suicide among U.S. college students: Implications for addressing disparities in service use. *Depression and Anxiety*, *36*(1), 8–17. doi.org/10.1002/da.22830

Locke, B., Bieschke, K. & Castonguay, L., & Hayes, J. (2012). The Center for Collegiate Mental Health: Studying college student mental health through an innovative research infrastructure that brings science and practice together. *Harvard Review of Psychiatry*, *20*(4), 233–245. doi.org/10.3109/10673229.2012.712837

Mackenzie, S., Wiegel, J. R., Mundt, M., Brown, D., Saewyc, E., Heiligenstein, E., Harahan, B., & Fleming, M. (2011). Depression and suicide ideation among students accessing campus health care. *The American Journal of Orthopsychiatry*, *81*(1), 101–107. https://doi.org/10.1111/j.1939-0025.2010.01077.x

March, S., Day, J., Ritchie, G., et al. (2018). Attitudes toward e-mental health services in a community sample of adults: Online survey. *Journal of Medical Internet Research*, *20*(2), Article e59. doi.org/10.2196/jmir.9109

Masuda, A., Anderson, P. L., Twohig, M. P., et al. (2009). Help-seeking experiences and attitudes among African American, Asian American, and European American college students. *International Journal for the Advancement of Counseling*, *31*(3), 168–180. doi.org/10.1007/s10447-009-9076-2

Masuda, A., Suzumura, K., Beauchamp, K. L., Howells, G. N., & Clay, C. (2005). United States and Japanese college students' attitudes toward seeking professional psychological help. *International Journal of Psychology*, *40*(5), 303–313. doi.org/10.1080/00207590444000339

Matthews, M., Doherty, G., Coyle, D., & Sharry, J. (2008). Designing mobile applications to support mental health interventions. In J. Lumsden (Ed.), *Handbook of research on user interface design and evaluation for mobile technology* (pp. 635–656). Hershey, PA: IGI Global.

Meyer, I. H. (2003). Prejudice, social stress, and mental health in lesbian, gay, and bisexual populations: Conceptual issues and research evidence. *Psychological Bulletin*, *129*(5), 674–697.

Mortier, P., Auerbach, R., Alonso, J., et al. (2018). Suicidal thoughts and behaviors among first-year college students: Results from the WMH-ICS project. *Journal of the American Academy of Child and Adolescent Psychiatry*, *57*(4), 263–273. doi.org/10.1016/j.jaac.2018.01.018

Munoz, R. F., Chavira, D. A., Himle, J. K., et al. (2018). Digital apothecaries: A vision for making health care interventions accessible worldwide, *mHealth*, *4*(18). doi.org/10.21037/mhealth.2018.05.0

National Institute of Mental Health. (2019). *Technology and the future of mental health treatment.* www.nimh.nih.gov/health/topics/technology-and-the-future-of-mental-health-treatment/index.shtml

Olfson, M., Guardino, M., Struening, E., et al. (2000). Barriers to the treatment of social anxiety. *The American Journal of Psychiatry*, *157*(4), 521–527. doi.org/10.1176/appi.ajp.157.4.521

O'Malley, P. M., & Johnson, L. D. (2002). Epidemiology of alcohol use and other drug use among American college students. *Journal of the Study of Alcohol, Supplement*, *14*, 23–29. doi.org/10.15288/jsas.2002.s14.23

O'Neill, D., & Fry, M. (2013). The grief group: A university and hospice collaboration. *Journal of College Student Development*, *54*(4), 430–432. doi.org/10.1353/csd.2013.0064

Parks, A. C., Della Porta, M. D., Pierce, R. S., Zilca, R., & Lyubomirsky, S. (2012). Pursuing happiness in everyday life: The characteristics and behaviors of online happiness seekers. *Emotion*, *12*(6), 1222–1234. doi.org/10.1037/14861-023

Parks, A. C., & Layous, K. (2016). Positive psychological interventions. In J. C. Norcross, G. R. VandenBos, D. K. Freedheim, & R. Krishnamurthy (Eds.), *Handbook of clinical psychology: Applications and methods* (pp. 439–449). Washington, DC: American Psychological Association.

Parks, A. C., Williams, A. L., Tugade, M. M., et al. (2018). Testing a scalable web and smartphone based intervention to improve depression, anxiety, and resilience: A randomized controlled trial. *International Journal of Wellbeing, 8*(2), 22–67. doi.org/10.5502/ijw.v8i2.745

Pedrelli, P., Nyer, M., Yeung, A., Zulauf, C., & Wilens, T. (2015). College students: Mental health problems and treatment considerations. *Academic Psychiatry, 39*(5), 503–511. doi.org/10.1007/s40596-014-0205-9

Prince, J. P. (2015). University student counseling and mental health in the United States: Trends and challenges. *Mental Health & Prevention, 3*(1–2), 5–10. doi.org/10.1016/j.mhp.2015.03.001

Prior, A. (2015). A guide to setting up a college bereavement group: Using monologue, soliloquy, and dialogue. *Journal of College Student Psychotherapy, 29*(2), 111–119. doi:10.1080/87568225.2015.1008366

Reavley, N., & Jorm, A. F. (2010). Prevention and early intervention to improve mental health in higher education students: A review. *Early Intervention in Psychiatry, 4*(2), 132–142. doi.org/10.1111/j.1751-7893.2010.00167.x

Reicher, H., & Matischek-Jauk, M. (2018). Depressive adolescents at risk of social exclusion: The potentials of social-emotional learning in schools. *Improving Schools, 22*(1), 43–54. https://doi.org/10.1177/1365480218763845

Reid, A. M. (2015). Do NOT close the gate on gatekeeper training at universities and colleges. *Journal of Adolescent Health, 56*(3), 360. doi.org/10.1016/j.jadohealth.2014.11.014

Rickwood, D. J., Deane, F. P., & Wilson, C. J. (2007). When and how do young people seek professional help for mental health problems? *The Medical Journal of Australia, 187*(7), S35–S39. doi.org/10.5694/j.1326-5377.2007.tb01334.x

Rigotti, N. A., Lee, J. E., & Wechsler, H. (2000). US college students' use of tobacco products: Results of a national survey. *Journal of the American Medical Association, 284*(6), 699–705. doi.org/10.1001/jama.284.6.699

Rowell, P. C., Mobley, A. K., Kemer, G., & Giordano, A. (2014). Examination of a group counseling model of career decision making with college students. *Journal of College Counseling, 17*(2), 163–174. doi.org/10.1002/j.2161-1882.2014.00055.x

Sabina, C., & Straus, M. A. (2008). Polyvictimization by dating partners and mental health among college students. *Violence and Victims, 23*(6), 667–682. doi.org/10.1891/0886-6708.23.6.667

Scantlebury, A., Parker, A., Booth, A., McDaid, C., & Mitchell, N. (2018). Implementing mental health training programmes for non-mental health trained professionals: A qualitative synthesis. *PLoS ONE, 13*(6), Article e0199746. doi.org/10.1371/journal.pone.0199746

Schleider, J. L., Dobias, M. L., Sung, J. Y., & Mullarkey, M. C. (2020). Future directions in single-session youth mental health interventions. *Journal of Clinical Child and Adolescent Psychology, 49*(2), 264–278. doi.org/10.1080/15374416.2019.1683852

Schueller, S. M., & Parks, A. C. (2012). Disseminating self-help: Positive psychology exercises in an online trial. *Journal of Medical Internet Research, 14*(3), Article e63. doi.org/10.2196/jmir.1850

Sin, N. L., & Lyubomirsky, S. (2009). Enhancing well-being and alleviating depressive symptoms with positive psychology interventions: A practice-friendly meta-analysis. *Journal of Clinical Psychology, 65*(5), 467–487. doi.org/10.1002/jclp.20593

Singla, D. R., Kohrt, B. A., Murray, L. K., et al. (2017). Psychological treatments for the world: Lessons from low-and middle-income countries. *Annual Review of Clinical Psychology, 13*, 149–181. doi.org/10.1146/annurev-clinpsy-032816-045217

Slutske, W. S. (2005). Alcohol use disorders among US college students and their non-college-attending peers. *Archives of General Psychiatry, 62*(3), 321–327. doi .org/10.1001/archpsyc.62.3.321

Smets, E., Rios, V. E., Schiavone, G., et al. (2018). Large-scale wearable data reveal digital phenotypes for daily-life stress detection. *NPJ Digital Medicine, 1*, Article 67. doi.org/10.1038/s41746-018-0074-9

Smith, W. A., Hung, M., & Franklin, J. D. (2011). Racial battle fatigue and the miseducation of black men: Racial microaggressions, societal problems, and environmental stress. *Journal of Negro Education, 80*(1), 63–82. www.jstor .org/stable/41341106

Spek, V., Cuijpers, P., Nyklícek, I., et al. (2006). Internet-based cognitive behaviour therapy for symptoms of depression and anxiety: A meta-analysis. *Psychological Medicine, 37*(3), 319–328. doi.org/10.1017/S0033291706008944

Stallman, H. M. (2010). Psychological distress in university students: A comparison with general population data. *Australian Psychologist, 45*(4), 249–257. doi .org/10.1080/00050067.2010.482109

Stephens, N., Markus, H. R., & Phillips, L. T. (2014). Social class culture cycles: How three gateway contexts shape selves and fuel inequality. *Annual Review of Psychology, 65*, 611–634. doi.org/10.1146/annurev-psych-010213-115143

Stice, E., Nathan Marti, C., Shaw, H., et al. (2009). An 8-year longitudinal study of the natural history of threshold, subthreshold, and partial eating disorders from a community sample of adolescents. *Journal of Abnormal Psychology, 118*(3), 587–597. doi.org/10.1037/a0016481

Stolzenberg, E. B., Eagan, M. K., Aragon, M. C., et al. (2019). *The American freshman: National norms Fall 2017*. Los Angeles: Higher Education Research Institute, UCLA.

Stone, B. M., & Parks, A. C. (2018). Cultivating subjective well-being through positive psychological interventions. In E. Diener, S. Oishi, & L. Tay (Eds.), *Handbook of well-being*. Salt Lake City, UT: Noba Scholars.

Strine, T. W., Mokdad, A. H., Balluz, L. S., et al. (2015). Depression and anxiety in the United States: Findings from the 2006 Behavioral Risk Factor Surveillance System. *Psychiatric Services, 59*(12), 1383–1390. doi.org/10.1176/ps.2008.59 .12.1383

Substance Abuse and Mental Health Services Administration. (2013). *Results from the 2012 National Survey on Drug Use and Health: Summary of national findings* [NSDUH Series H-46, HHS Publication No. (SMA) 13-4795]. Rockville, MD: Substance Abuse and Mental Health Services Administration. www.samhsa .gov/data/sites/default/files/NSDUHresults2012/NSDUHresults2012.pdf

Tan, T. Y., Wachsmuth, L. S., & Tugade, M. M. (2019). Resilience. In F. Maggino (Ed.), *Encyclopedia of quality of life and well-being research* (2nd ed.). New York: Springer.

Torous, J., Onnela, J.-P., & Keshavan, M. (2017). New dimensions and new tools to realize the potential of RDoC: Digital phenotyping via smartphones and connected devices. *Translational Psychiatry, 7*(3), e1053. doi.org/10.1038/tp.2017.25

Treichler, E. B. H., & Lucksted, A. A. (2018). The role of sense of belonging in self-stigma among people with serious mental illnesses. *Psychiatric Rehabilitation Journal, 41*(2), 149–152. doi: 10.1037/prj0000281

Twenge, J. M., Martin, G. N., & Campbell, W. K. (2018). Decreases in psychological well-being among American adolescents after 2012 and links to screen time during the rise of smartphone technology. *Emotion, 18*(6), 765–780. doi.org/10.1037/emo0000403

Twentyman, J., Frank, M., & Lindsey, L. (2017). Effects of race and ethnicity on mental health and help-seeking amongst undergraduate university students. *Journal of Undergraduate Ethnic Minority Psychology, 3*, 6–15.

Vaingankar, J. A., Rekhi, G., Subramaniam, M., et al. (2013). Age of onset of life-time mental disorders and treatment contact. *Social Psychiatry and Psychiatric Epidemiology, 48*(5), 835–843. doi.org/10.1007/s00127-012-0601-y

Wachsmuth, L. S., Tan, T. Y., & Tugade, M. M. (under review). Examining life as it is lived: Experience sampling methodology for positive psychology intervention research.

Wang, P. S., Lane, M., Olfson, M., et al. (2005). Twelve-month use of mental health services in the United States: Results from the National Comorbidity Survey Replication. *Archives of General Psychiatry, 62*(6), 629–640. doi.org/10.1001/archpsyc.62.6.629

Webb, C. A., Rosso, I. M., & Rauch, S. L. (2017). Internet-based cognitive-behavioral therapy for depression: Current progress and future directions. *Harvard Review of Psychiatry, 25*(3), 114–122. doi.org/10.1097/HRP.0000000000000139

Wilens, T. E., Adler, L. A., Adams, J., et al. (2008). Misuse and diversion of stimulants prescribed for ADHD: A systematic review of the literature. *Journal of the American Academy of Child Adolescent Psychiatry, 47*(1), 21–31. doi.org/10.1097/chi.0b013e31815a56f1

Williams, G., Case, R., & Roberts, C. (2018). Understanding the mental health issues of international students on campus. *Educational Research: Theory and Practice, 29*(2), 18–28.

Yang, R. K., Byers, S. R., & Fenton, B. (2006). American Indian/Alaska Native students' use of a university student support office. *Journal of American Indian Education, 45*(1), 35–48.

Wu, H. P., Garza, E., & Guzman, N. (2015). International students' challenge and adjustment to college. *Education Research International*, 1–9. doi.org/10.1155/2015/202753

Zulueta, J., Piscitello, A., Rasic, M., et al. (2018). Predicting mood disturbance severity with mobile phone keystroke metadata: A BiAffect digital phenotyping study. *Journal of Medical Internet Research, 20*(7), e241. www.jmir.org/2018/7/e241/

28 LGBTQ+ Communities

Confronting Discrimination and Gaps in Community Supports

Erica R. Garagiola, Scott J. Hunter, Mary Ann Villarreal, Richard L. Renfro, and Caroline S. Clauss-Ehlers

28.1 Introduction

Gender and sexuality have come to be understood on a continuum (Savin-Williams, 2005, 2016a, 2017). Savin-Williams' (2016b) "continuum-based perspective regarding the nature of sexual orientation for both women and men," explains "potential implications for investigating the prevalence of nonheterosexuals, sexual-orientation differences in gender nonconformity, causes of sexual orientation, and political issues" (p. 37). The LGBTQ+ population is a community that has come to include lesbian, gay, bisexual, transgender, queer, nonbinary, gender-fluid, gender-neutral, gender-nonconforming (GNC), and pansexual individuals, along with many other identifications. The "+" is symbolic of the spectrum of gender and sexuality that cannot be categorized neatly and, instead, is continuously added to and explored. Discrete categorization has become an outdated approach to gender and sexuality identity, with a shift to an emphasis on fluidity (Gold, 2018; Morgan, 2013). This perspective sets the framework for this chapter.

The LGBTQ+ population has historically faced significant discrimination and adversity (Jones et al., 2020). LGBTQ+ communities have fought for basic human rights and protections for decades, and although headway has been made, the fight is hardly over. Due to chronic, compounded stressors unique to LGBTQ+ individuals, this population is at an elevated risk for adverse mental and physical health conditions (McConnell et al., 2018). This reality is explained by Minority Stress Theory, which postulates that minority groups express the cumulative toll of stress due to discrimination and stigmatization through negative physical and mental health outcomes (McConnell et al., 2018; Smith, Cunningham, & Freyd, 2016). Ilan H. Meyer formulated the Minority Stress Model in 1995 as being composed of three processes: internalized homophobia (e.g., internalized negative beliefs with regard to one's orientation due to sexual prejudice); perceived stigma (e.g., increased expectations and fears of rejection or exclusion in social settings due to one's orientation); and an experience of discriminatory events (Meyer, 1995). Eight years later, in 2003, Meyer added a fourth component: identity concealment that refers to hiding one's orientation due to fear of harm (Forenza, 2017; Mereish & Poteat, 2015; Meyer, 2003; Morandini et al., 2015). An experience of these stressors puts LGBTQ+ individuals, notably LGBTQ+ youth, at significant risk for maladaptive behaviors and thought processes including, but not limited to, decreased self-esteem, avoidant coping strategies, suicidal ideation, and depression (Bearss, 2013; Forenza, 2017; Jones et al., 2020).

28.2 Prevalence Data: A Contextual Approach to Concerns and Stressors

Horn, Koswic, and Russell (2009) opt for an understanding of the experiences of LGBTQ+ communities not from an at-risk point of view, but rather with regard to considering how LGBTQ+ communities can engage in coping behaviors. When utilizing this framework, there is evidence of a significant discrepancy between what has been readily gained, specifically in the United States, but also over the broader world: marriage equality, access for many LGBTQ+ parents to opportunities for parenthood, and greater acceptance in selected communities. More so, over the last two decades, increased media visibility of LGBTQ+ individuals, from Ellen DeGeneres ("Yep, I'm Gay," 1997) to Brian Michael Smith (Milan, 2017), has led to a misperception that visibility equals changed attitudes broadly.

However, this is not fully the case, as many communities experience significant prejudice regarding sexual minority and gender minority individuals. From disputes over bathroom usage, to flagrant bigotry within the broader media toward transgender women (i.e., the 2020 arguments regarding bigotry expressed by author J. K. Rowling [Conley, 2020]), to efforts being made in the United States under the Trump administration to attempt to claw back greater equality for sexual minority individuals, there is a substantial daily reminder that not being heteronormative is unacceptable. This challenges the capacity for feeling secure as an LGBTQ+ person. As a result, greater visibility has brought to the forefront the gaps in our attention to the spectrum of experiences across LGBTQ+ identities. The literature is clear: LGBTQ+ people have a dearth of support concerning their welfare, and physical and psychological health at every life stage. Interventions across all domains of life must take into account the diversity of socially imposed constructions of gender identity.

When assessing the LGBTQ+ population as a whole, several stressors and concerns come to light. The marginalization, discrimination, stigmatization, and victimization of LGBTQ+ people are attributed to several factors that can be classified into two categories: proximal and distal stressors (Mereish & Poteat, 2015). Proximal stressors refer to internal stress caused by negative beliefs and attitudes regarding one's orientation. Examples experienced by LGBTQ+ individuals include, but are not limited to, internalized homophobia, concealment and chronic secrecy, stigma consciousness, rejection sensitivity, and expectations of experiencing distal stressors (McConnell et al., 2018; Morandini et al., 2015). Concealment and internalized homopho-bia, specifically, are linked with lack of pursuing close relationships for fear of rejection and discrimination. This can lead to poor social support, avoidant coping strategies, risky sexual behavior, depression, and suicidal ideation (McConnell et al., 2018; Mereish & Poteat, 2015; Winderman, Martin, & Smith, 2018). Distal stressors refer to external stress exuding from society (Mereish & Poteat, 2015). Examples include, but are not limited to, prejudice, discrimination, verbal or physical harassment, sexual assault, taunting, microaggressions, structural oppression, hate crimes, lack of civil rights and protections, and anti-gay violence/gay-bashing (Mereish & Poteat, 2015; Morandini et al., 2015).

The experience of distal and proximal stressors is associated with poor mental and physical health, as well as difficulties with adjustment (Mereish & Poteat, 2015). It is important to note that intersectional minorities (i.e., LGBTQ+ people of color) can experience these effects to a greater degree (Advocates for Youth, n.d.; Clauss-Ehlers et al., 2019; McConnell et al., 2018). Several consequences arise from such stress that can seep into every aspect of LGBTQ+ individuals' lives. With regard to mental health outcomes, proximal and distal stressors can lead to low self-esteem, a lack of self-love and self-care, feelings of low self-worth, hopelessness, depression, suicidality, and low perception of control (Forenza, 2017; McConnell et al., 2018; Smith et al., 2016; Soohinda et al., 2019).

LGBTQ+ individuals are 2.5 times more likely to have attempted suicide compared to their heterosexual counterparts; it is estimated that one in four LGBTQ+ individuals have attempted suicide at some point in their life, compared to 4%–15% of heterosexual individuals (Rutherford et al., 2012; Smith et al., 2016). A total of 33% of LGBTQ+ youth report suicidal ideation and 40% report depressive symptoms (Wehse et al., 2018). LGBTQ+ individuals are at higher risk for being diagnosed with anxiety disorders, depressive disorders, panic disorder, post-traumatic stress disorder (PTSD), and sub-stance abuse disorders (Pachankis et al., 2020; Smith et al., 2016; Snapp et al., 2015). In fact, LGBTQ+ individuals are 1.5 times more at risk for depression and anxiety disorders compared to the rest of the population (Rutherford et al., 2012).

From a physical health standpoint, proximal and distal stressors lead to several problems including weight issues; chronic health concerns; sexual risk-taking, leading to a higher instance of sexually transmitted diseases; and substance abuse (Advocates for Youth, n.d.; Snapp et al., 2015). LGBTQ+ individuals also have a significantly higher risk of experiencing sexual harassment and sexual assault compared to their heterosexual counterparts: 85% of bisexual and lesbian women and 20% of bisexual and gay men report being sexually assaulted at some point during their lives; this only exacerbates mental health outcomes, such as developing PTSD (Smith et al., 2016). In addition to sexual assault, LGBTQ+ people are also at an elevated risk for experiencing interpersonal trauma, such as violence from family members or physical violence from peers (Smith et al., 2016).

LGBTQ+ individuals experience several structural stressors with regard to employment, healthcare access, and housing, all of which disadvantage them further and have a negative impact on overall well-being and health (Gowin et al., 2017). It is estimated that one in five LGBTQ+ individuals do not go to the doctor when needed because they cannot afford it, 17% lack healthcare coverage, and one in five individuals live in poverty (Human Rights Campaign [HRC], 2018a). Additional sources of stress specific to the LGBTQ+ community include disclosure stress, which refers to stress associated with "coming out"; social isolation, rejection, and exclusion, brought about due to stigmatization or invalidation of individuals' LGBTQ+ status; and relationship dissatisfaction, related to others undermining the legitimacy of LGBTQ+ relationships (McConnell et al., 2018; Soohinda et al., 2019).

Transgender individuals have stressors unique to their community that the rest of the LGBTQ+ community does not necessarily experience, namely in the medical realm. A total of 25% of transgender individuals report problems accessing health care; 55% report being denied surgical care; 33% report discrimination and verbal or physical harassment in healthcare settings; 50% report having to teach their healthcare provider some aspect of their health needs as transgender individuals due to systemic undereducation of LGBTQ + health in medical school; and many report being denied transition-related health care, such as hormone replacement therapy or gender reassignment surgeries (Rutherford et al., 2012; Valentine & Shipherd, 2018; Wehse et al., 2018). Transgender individuals often receive the least amount of acceptance societally (White Hughto, Reisner, & Pachankis, 2015). Studies have found that 40% of transgender individuals have attempted suicide at least once in their lifetime, with 92% of attempts occurring before the age of twenty-five (Wehse et al., 2018). The rate of suicide among the transgender population is nine times higher in comparison to the rest of the population (Wehse et al., 2018). The following sections build upon these realities, presenting gaps in support for LGBTQ+ communities and ways in which they can be addressed.

28.3 Community Gaps and Interventions

Community psychology is a branch of psychology that examines social, cultural, academic, economic, political, and environmental factors that have an impact on community experiences (Society for Community Research and Action, n.d.). Community psychology in the United States of America (USA) developed during the civil rights movement and at a time of deinstitutionalization from state hospitals to community mental health centers. Its origins sought to address concerns that psychology at that time was too focused on individual consultation and not concerned enough with larger societal issues including social action, empowerment, and advocacy.

Amid this backdrop, it is important to acknowledge many of the recent policy changes in support of LGBTQ+ communities. In 1982, Wisconsin became the first state to ban discrimination based on sexual orientation (Politico Staff, 2013). In 1993, President William Clinton signed legislation where those applying to the military could not be asked about their sexual orientation. This was later coined as the "Don't Ask, Don't Tell" bill by Charles Moskos. While still discriminatory, this legislation was a stepping-stone nonetheless, paving the way for the Obama administration to overturn the legislation and legalize LGBTQ+ individuals joining the military openly in 2011 (Politico Staff, 2013). In 2004, Massachusetts became the first state in the USA to legalize same-sex marriage; nine years later in 2013, the Supreme Court voted five to four to legalize same-sex marriage nationwide (Politico Staff, 2013).

While these changes demonstrate greater societal acceptance and support of the LGBTQ+ community, there are still significant gaps leaving this already vulnerable community at high risk for adverse outcomes. These gaps especially fail LGBTQ+ youth and LGBTQ+ people of color (Bearss, 2013; Jones et al., 2020). The following sections examine gaps in responsiveness to LGBTQ+ communities with regard to academic, legislative, religious, economic, medical, social, and social-environmental realms. While it is beyond the scope of this chapter to go into each realm in great detail, key realities are presented to give the reader an overall sense of critical gaps in community support as well as considerations for intervention.

28.3.1 Academic Community Gaps and Community Interventions

28.3.1.1 Academic Gaps

Navigating middle and high school can already be a difficult transitional time in adolescents' lives; LGBTQ+ youth especially struggle through these formative years as they can face discrimination and social stigmatization that can leave them with lower self-esteem and a lack of social support (Bearss, 2013). LGBTQ+ youth spend much of their time in educational settings that often pose threats of bullying that can lead to suicide and long-term damaging social relationships. High school age LGBTQ+ youth face several distal stressors throughout their school career. For instance, the Human Rights Campaign (HRC) Youth Report shows that LGBTQ+ youth are twice as likely to report verbal harassment at school (HRC, 2012). Only 26% of LGBTQ+ high school students report feeling safe in a classroom and reports show that 70% experience bullying at school related to their LGBTQ+ identity. A more recent 2018 HRC report highlights how LGBTQ+ youth struggle to gain access to counselors who provide services for bullying, stress, sexual abuse, and depression (HRC, 2018e).

One challenge is connecting those who want to help with youth; thus, making it important to elevate and increase the visibility of programs and resources available to LGBTQ+ youth. In April 2018, journalist Emelina Minero wrote in *Edutopia* that a disconnect existed between what educators wanted to do and what actual protections were provided by districts and states. As of 2018, there were thirty-two states that did not have legislation prohibiting bullying (Minero, 2018). The GLSEN 2016 survey report, *From Teasing to Torment: School Climate Revisited*, found that more than 80% of teachers wanted to intervene in school LGBTQ+ bullying, but did not do so because they did not know what to do or believed that they would not be supported (Greytak et al., 2016). Other issues arise in terms of inclusion in curriculum; many schools do not openly discuss the LGBTQ+ community in school settings such as in sexual education classes (HRC, 2018e). This lack of education is detrimental to LGBTQ+ youth, as it can make them feel excluded, exacerbates oppression of their identity, and withholds important health-related information. For instance, the HRC surveyed LGBTQ+ youth and found that only 12% received relevant safe-sex information related to being an LGBTQ+ individual (HRC, 2018e).

Reports show that less than a third of school-aged transgender youth feel they can express themselves as the gender they identify with, more than half can never use the bathroom they identify with in school, only 33% are called their preferred name, and only 20% are referred to with their preferred pronouns (HRC, 2018e).

Once LGBTQ+ youth reach higher education, stressors unfortunately continue. Institutions of higher education can perpetuate an environment of intolerance and discrimination against the LGBTQ+ community through a process called *institutional betrayal*. Institutional betrayal entails "wrong-doings perpetrated by an institution upon individuals dependent on that institution, including failure to prevent or respond supportively to wrong-doings committed within the context of the institution" (Smith et al., 2016, p. 352). Prominent examples include the failure of institutions to respond appropriately to sexual assault allegations reported by LGBTQ+ individuals; this betrayal exacerbates the negative outcomes associated with such trauma and leaves the person more susceptible to anxiety, depression, PTSD, and dissociation (Smith et al., 2016). Institutional betrayal incites psychological distress and can leave LGBTQ+ individuals feeling as if they are undervalued members of the institution and less valued than their heterosexual counterparts (Smith et al., 2016).

28.3.1.2 Academic Interventions

Interventions in school settings require a multipronged approach that is not heteronormative, but assumes a wide audience and uses language specifically focused on LGBTQ+ youth (Earnshaw et al., 2017). In a high school setting, the sexual education curriculum must be reformed to include information relevant to the LGBTQ+ community as they enter puberty and navigate sex and sexuality. Further interventions are needed regarding bullying and creating a safe space. Schools that implement programs, such as gay–straight alliances, "have seen marked reductions in homophobic bullying and increases in students' perceptions of safety, tolerance, and respect toward sexual minority students" (Smith et al., 2016, p. 352). In addition to inclusive programs, schools must be more accepting of transgender students and strive to use correct pronouns and names. Other interventions for transgender students can include creating gender-neutral bathroom spaces.

With regard to higher education, the creation of a resource center is central to building a collaborative environment on college and university campuses, particularly given that LGBTQ+ students often arrive on campuses having had a negative experience during their high school years. Creating an affirming and safe environment in the classroom and on campus must be included in all discussions about campus safety and efforts to support well-being across university settings. Further, Derek Siegel (2019) writes that campus climate surveys are not enough. Rather, he advocates for microclimate studies. While institutions may provide opportunities to change preferred names, a checked-box approach is not enough to serve transgender students. Siegel's (2019) conclusions make clear that only via deep-dive climate assessments can institutions offer specific interventions that serve transgender students at both the individual and group level (Siegel, 2019).

A recent study by Flores and Sheely-Moore offers examples of how Relational-Cultural Theory (RCT)-based interventions can address the gap of intersectional experiences, specifically with regard to race and gender identity. The authors write, "One RCT approach that can assist clients in the reformulation of relational images is through growth-fostering relationships within the therapeutic alliance and beyond" (Flores & Sheely-Moore, 2020, p. 73). This approach weaves together an ecosystem that connects LGBTQ+ students to the campus, reinforcing a sense of belonging and validation.

28.3.2 Legislative Community Gaps and Community Interventions

28.3.2.1 Legislative Gaps

Several medieval laws still exist that violate human rights and equal protections with regard to the LGBTQ+ community that must be abolished (Soohinda et al., 2019). The political sphere has made progress in the past decade; however, harmful and discriminatory legislation is still in place in several states such as anti-transgender bathroom bills, conversion therapy, and legislation allowing the denial of services based on an individual's LGBTQ+ identity (Advocates for Youth, n.d.; Platt, Wolf, & Scheitle, 2018; Wehse et al., 2018). Additionally, in some states it is legal to use the

Gay/Trans Panic Defense in court cases, in which a defendant may plead not guilty with the defense that "the shock of the victim coming out as gay or transgender warranted an excessively violent reaction, including murder" (Wehse et al., 2018, p. 4).

The LGBTQ+ community needs more protection under the law; only nineteen states and the District of Columbia fully prohibit discrimination based on sexual orientation and gender identity (Keith & Gagliano, n.d.). On March 23, 2018, the Trump administration announced a new policy that bans most transgender people from serving in the military; after several court battles, the Supreme Court allowed the ban to go into effect in January 2019 (CNN Editorial Research, 2020). The harmful rhetoric spewed by political leaders sets the tone for the attitudes of the masses by setting societal norms. This example of prejudice emanating from the Oval Office serves to show that there are still several interventions needed to create true political equality.

Not only must policy change, but police reform is needed. This population is at an increased risk for experiencing harassment, assault, and intimidation, while at the same time receiving decreased responsiveness and redress from police (Advocates for Youth, n.d.). The LGBTQ+ community receives unequal and inadequate protections under the law and that must change. Studies focused on LGBTQ+ youth make clear that this population is disproportionately homeless and make up 20%–40% of the homeless youth population. McCandless' study of LGBTQ+ youth who are homeless and police interaction highlights how common police stereotypes of LGBTQ+ individuals as overly sexual beings perpetuates a more hostile environment for them in detention centers and leaves them with little protection (McCandless, 2018). A repeated form of intervention is education; in this case police need to be educated about how to interact with LGBTQ+ youth (McCandless, 2018). LGBTQ+ youth and the homeless need social service interventions, rather than policing, especially if they cannot return home.

28.3.2.2 Legislative Interventions

Slowly progress is being made in the form of policy change and repealing harmful legislation. The June 2020 decision of the Supreme Court of the United States that extended the civil rights law to LGBTQ+ employees is perhaps the most impactful political intervention since the Supreme Court ruled on marriage equality in 2015, allowing same-sex couples to legally marry (Totenberg, 2020). The June 2020 Supreme Court ruling prohibits discrimination in the workplace based on sexual orientation, such as unlawful firing (Jenkins, 2020; Totenberg, 2020). In 2017, the District of Columbia became the first place in the USA to allow residents to select a gender-neutral option on their driver's licenses (CNN Editorial Research, 2020). In 2019, New York Governor Andrew Cuomo banned the Gay/Trans Panic Defense (CNN Editorial Research, 2020).

Further political strides have been made with regard to representation. In 1973, Congressman Gerry Studds was the first openly gay congressman to be elected. This prompted increasingly greater LGBTQ+ representation in the political sphere (Politico Staff, 2013). In 2018, Jared Polis was elected governor of Colorado; the first openly gay governor to win this office (CNN Editorial Research, 2020). LGBTQ+ individuals are running for office in higher numbers. For instance, in the 2018 US midterm elections, it was estimated that 559 openly LGBTQ+ individuals secured offices (Ramgopal, 2018).

As for LGBTQ+ and police relations, Gregory Herek, an anti-LGBTQ+ hate crime expert who is retired from the University of California, Davis, said, "the responding officer and the quality of his or her LGBTQ cultural-competency training can have a direct effect on whether a bias crime is properly recorded" (Keith & Gagliano, 2018). Police officers need higher volumes and more relevant training pertaining to the LGBTQ+ community to respond sensitively and effectively. In 2012, the New Orleans Police Department began making progressive policy changes to address the gap in protections such as "refraining from aggressive frisk procedures – which had involved patting down transgender suspects' genitals to confirm their sex – and adopting gender-affirming language, such as addressing people by their chosen name, title and pronoun" (Keith & Gagliano, 2018). Police departments of other major cities such as Baltimore and Newark slowly began following this lead to improve treatment of LGBTQ+ individuals (Keith & Gagliano, 2018). Some police departments created liaison positions to increase and maintain trust between police officers and the LGBTQ+ community (Keith & Gagliano, 2018).

28.3.3 Religious Community Gaps and Community Interventions

28.3.3.1 Religious Gaps

Religious communities may be more conservative and can come into direct conflict with LGBTQ+ ideas. Mediating the conflict within oneself between religious and LGBTQ+ identities can be a cause of significant stress for those with overlapping identities. The burden of conflicting identities can take a toll on the well-being and mental health of such individuals, leaving them more vulnerable to stressors. This interpersonal conflict, in conjunction with a lack of support and being ostracized from one's religious community, can lead to feelings of shame, guilt, personal hatred, depression, and suicidal ideation (Shilo, Yossef, & Savaya, 2016).

28.3.3.2 Religious Interventions

In recent years, many religious institutions have put out statements officially welcoming LGBTQ+ individuals into their communities (HRC, n.d.b). Within

the Roman Catholic Church, the Vatican has stated "homosexual tendencies …
must be accepted with respect, compassion, and sensitivity. Every sign of unjust
discrimination in their regard should be avoided" (HRC, 2018b). In 2018, the
Presbyterian Church, a sect of Christianity, voted unanimously on a resolution
stating "religious freedom is not a license for discrimination against any of God's
people, and cannot justify the denial of secular employment or benefits, healthcare, public or commercial services or goods, or parental rights to persons based
on race, ethnicity, sex, gender, sexual orientation, gender identity, religion or
gender expression" (HRC, 2018c). Several sects of Judaism have shared similar
remarks, such as the Religious Action Center of Reform Judaism that stated:
"Each of us, created in God's image, has a unique talent, with which we can
contribute to the high moral purpose of tikkun olam, the repair of our world.
Excluding anyone from our community lessens our chance of achieving this goal
of a more perfect world" (HRC, 2018d).

Religious platforms that share accepting views that are in solidarity with the
LGBTQ+ community can mitigate stigmatization, but do not completely
eradicate the internal conflicts within individuals experiencing aforementioned
conflicting identities. Proposed interventions for congregations to close the
gap in the LGBTQ+ religious community include expanding social activities
and opportunities for religious sexual minorities, providing a safe and supportive environment to cultivate a coexisting combination of religious faith
and sexual identity, and enabling LGBTQ+ people to maintain their faith and
the religious rituals that promote mental health among believers (Shilo et al.,
2016). The HRC (n.d.b) has a Faith Positions webpage that presents the
position of various faith communities with regard to LGBTQ+ people
and experiences.

28.3.4 Economic Community Gaps and Community Interventions

28.3.4.1 Economic Gaps

The LGBTQ+ community faces a higher degree of socioeconomic disadvantages compared to the community's heterosexual counterparts (Gowin et al.,
2017). These disadvantages can be seen through the percentage of LGBTQ+
individuals living in poverty, as well as rates of homelessness, namely
among LGBTQ+ youth. According to information compiled by the HRC,
20% of the LGBTQ+ community lives in poverty and 40% of homeless youth
identify as LGBTQ+ (HRC, 2018a).

Additionally, LGBTQ+ individuals face increased career indecision due to
a phenomenon known as the bottleneck effect. Essentially, the bottleneck
effect refers to stress placed on LGBTQ+ individuals, due to their sexual
minority status, that takes up a large degree of inner resources, depleting them
of the ability to explore career options and academic interests in a normative
way (Winderman et al., 2018). This disadvantage expresses itself through a

number of adverse outcomes such as psychological distress, decreased well-being, decreased academic performance, and dissatisfaction with career choices (Winderman et al., 2018).

28.3.4.2 Economic Interventions

The medical well-being of LGBTQ+ communities has a financial toll, especially in more recent years with increasing medical costs and political battles over access. In 2016, the Affordable Care Act (ACA) prohibited insurers from discriminating based on gender identity or denying coverage due to preexisting conditions, including gender dysphoria (Tomita, 2019; Wang, Kelman, & Cahill, 2016). This helped level the playing field in terms of medical financial gaps.

Impoverished and homeless LGBTQ+ individuals can be immediately aided through LGBTQ+ specific homeless shelters or outreach programs. In terms of long-term, systemic change, steps outlined by The National Coalition for the Homeless include ensuring schools are a safe haven for homeless LGBTQ+ youth, recognition of LGBTQ+ homeless individuals' unique needs, and expanding housing options specific to the needs of LGBTQ+ communities (National Coalition for the Homeless, n.d.). With regard to the bottleneck effect, combatting career indecision entails providing networks of support for LGBTQ+ individuals throughout K–12 education and college such as career counseling offered by career centers or opportunities for professional development.

28.3.5 Medical and Mental Health Community Gaps and Community Interventions

28.3.5.1 Medical and Mental Health Gaps

Inequality and prejudice in the medical community is one of the most dangerous forms of discrimination the LGBTQ+ community faces. A total of 19% of LGBTQ+ individuals report being refused medical care on the basis of their identity and 28% report experiencing verbal harassment in a medical setting (Rutherford et al., 2012). The outright refusal of care is detrimental to the physical and psychological well-being of LGBTQ+ communities. For instance, LGBTQ+ individuals may be denied transition-related health care in several states, such as hormone replacement therapy or gender-reassignment surgeries (Wehse et al., 2018). In addition to the denial of care, individuals often struggle to make changes to legal documents, such as birth certificates in the case of transgender individuals (Wehse et al., 2018).

The failure of the medical community starts in medical school, with 34% of deans of medical education at universities rating their LGBTQ+ curriculum as "very poor" (Rutherford et al., 2012). Furthermore, 40% of medical residents surveyed in 2002 reported receiving "inadequate education" on issues relevant to gay men's health and 68% felt they received "inadequate education" on issues relevant to health among the lesbian community (Rutherford et al., 2012). A more recent 2018 survey of 658 medical students showed no improvements have been made in the last two decades; for instance, an estimated 80% of respondents reported they did not feel competent in "medical treatment of gender and sexual minority patients" (Cohen, 2019).

Medical inequalities are not only seen in the realm of physical health, but also in mental health. Psychology and psychiatry historically have over-pathologized LGBTQ+ individuals, leaving many reluctant to seek professional help (Platt et al., 2018; Valentine & Shipherd, 2018). The *Diagnostic and Statistical Manual of Mental Disorders* (DSM) listed homosexuality as a disorder until 1973 (American Psychiatric Association, 1973), and the current edition still contains gender identity disorder, which perpetuates stigmatization of this group (Rubinstein, 1995; Rutherford et al., 2012). Additionally, some clinicians practice conversion therapy (Platt et al., 2018; see case illustration below in Section 28.5). Moreover, as seen with physical health, few clinicians specialize and have the proper background education in LGBTQ+ specific care. The lack of training and expertise reflects a failure of medical and mental health communities in providing appropriate and sensitive care to the LGBTQ+ community leading to higher levels of dissatisfaction with mental health resources in comparison to heterosexual counterparts (Platt et al., 2018; Rutherford et al., 2012).

28.3.5.2 Medical and Mental Health Interventions

Interventions within the medical community must include health services that are affirming and inclusive. This includes making preferred names, pronouns, sexual orientation, and gender identity fields accessible in healthcare software for patients and for staff to collect; welcoming images in offices; and well-established, inclusive intake forms (Valentine & Shipherd, 2018). It is critical for medical interventions to include services for transgender teens and youth, including puberty blockers, gender-affirming hormones, and care for mental and emotional health (Kim et al., 2019).

The impact of inclusive health practitioners on mental health is astonishing. Transgender patients who reported having LGBTQ+ inclusive healthcare experiences were less likely to report symptoms of depression – 38% compared to 54%; anxiety – 51% compared to 57%; and suicidal ideation – 29% compared to 48% (Valentine & Shipherd, 2018). Medical interventions such as gender-affirming surgeries or hormone therapy are linked with lower levels of anxiety, depression, suicidality, substance abuse, and stress and connected to higher levels of social support (Valentine & Shipherd, 2018). With regard to healthcare access, in 2016 the ACA was signed into law, preventing insurers from turning away individuals due to their sexual orientation (Wang et al., 2016).

In terms of medical school, biases truly start in the classroom. Medical students need a more comprehensive and inclusive curriculum educating them on LGBTQ+ matters such as "basic LGBT-related terminology, appropriate interview questions to facilitate the disclosure of sexual orientation and gender identity, information regarding the health impact of heterosexism and homophobia, and specific health care needs of sexual and gender identity minority people" (Rutherford et al., 2012, p. 903). The last decade has seen a greater emphasis placed on more affirmative training with regard to medical education; this has been largely supported by the increased presence of LGBTQ+ candidates for medical training, as well as increased attendings coming out to their peer physicians, nurses, and trainees. Nonetheless, a recognition of healthcare disparities for LGBTQ+ persons remains a principal focus within medical training programs and academic medical centers.

Concerning mental health interventions, in July 2020, Virginia became the twentieth US state to ban conversion therapy for minors (Sopelsa, 2020). The District of Columbia is the only US territory with a ban on conversion therapy for all individuals, not just minors (The Trevor Project, 2019). It is "estimated that 10,000 LGBTQ youths 13 to 17 had been protected from conversion therapy because of state bans" (Sopelsa, 2020). This is certainly a step in the right direction, but additional progress can be made through a nationwide ban and more comprehensive, ongoing training for mental health practitioners. The focus must be on educating, training, and continued training through ongoing participation in workshops, conferences, and continuing professional education courses, as well as continued self-awareness and cultural humility (Clauss-Ehlers et al., 2019; Rutherford et al., 2012).

28.3.6 Social Community Gaps and Community Interventions

28.3.6.1 Social Gaps

Studies have shown that low levels of social support and a decreased sense of community belongingness are linked to poor mental and physical health outcomes. Societal norms play a large role in the social community gaps facing the LGBTQ+ community. Social gaps can be dissected through parents, extended family, and the workplace.

With regard to parental interaction and support, or lack thereof, a global study conducted across all seven continents reported that 68% of the world's population – 78% Africa, 77% Asia, 64% Americas, 61% Europe, 44% Oceania – would be either "very" or "somewhat" upset if their child were to be in love with someone of the same sex (Carroll & Itaborahy, 2015). Lack of parental support exacerbates negative mental health outcomes, making suicide attempts 8.4 times more likely, depression 5.9 times more likely, and substance abuse or risky sexual behavior 3.4 times more likely among LGBTQ+ youth and young adults facing parental rejection (Snapp et al.,

2015). Additionally, 67% of LGBTQ+ youth across the USA reported hearing their families making negative remarks with regard to LGBTQ+ individuals (HRC, 2018e). Another 48% of youth who are out to their parents claim their family makes them feel bad about identifying as LGBTQ+ (HRC, 2018e). Many LGBTQ+ youth do not come out to parents out of fear of being disowned, kicked out of the home, or forced into conversion therapy (HRC, 2018e).

The extended family and nuclear family can contribute to stressors differently among LGBTQ+ individuals. Grandparents and other members of one's extended family may have more traditional and conservative ideas regarding gender roles and sexuality (HRC, n.d.a.). Studies of disclosure patterns reveal that individuals come out much later to extended family than other populations such as friends, nuclear family, and coworkers; additionally, the lowest percentage of individuals come out to their extended family (Soohinda et al., 2019). While one can hope for an accepting and progressive extended family, often at least one member of the extended family perpetuates discrimination through microaggressions, using incorrect pronouns/misgendering, or other offensive acts, and refuses to change, which can be harmful to the LGBTQ+ individual's self-esteem, lead to ostracization, and strain familial relationships (HRC, n.d.a).

The workplace is another problematic social arena for many LGBTQ+ individuals. Some 25% of LGBTQ+ workers "report experiencing discrimination based on sexual orientation or gender identity in the past year – half of whom said it negatively impacted their work environment" (Movement Advancement Project, n.d., p. 2). Studies suggest around 50% of LGBTQ+ workers remained closeted in the workplace out of fear of being "stereotyped or jeopardizing professional connections" (Movement Advancement Project, n.d., p. 2). Many times, LGBTQ+ individuals "obscure details" regarding their sexual orientation when applying to jobs (Movement Advancement Project, n.d.). Such concealment may be detrimental to the mental health of these individuals, as seen through the Minority Stress Theory's fourth component: identity concealment (Forenza, 2017). From 2016 to 2017, 27% of transgender workers report "being fired, not hired, or denied promotions" due to their sexual identity (Movement Advancement Project, n.d.). Some 35% of LGBTQ+ individuals responding to the General Social Survey (GSS) reported being harassed at work and 58% reported "hearing derogatory comments about sexual orientation and gender identity in their workplaces" (Pride at Work, 2017). A further 15% were verbally harassed, physically attacked, or sexually assaulted in the workplace (Pride at Work, 2017).

There is also a strong intersectional component in the workplace, with LGBTQ+ people of color reporting two times "more discrimination based on sexual orientation" (Movement Advancement Project, n.d., p. 2). LGBTQ+ workers of color are among the most disadvantaged groups in

America, with extremely high rates of poverty and unemployment "due to discrimination coupled with a lack of workplace protections, unequal job benefits and taxation, and unsafe, under-resourced U.S. schools" (National LGBTQ Task Force, 2013).

Additional discrimination can be seen when examining companies' policies on paid family leave for LGBTQ+ workers. Data show that only one out of five US companies offer paid family leave for their LGBTQ+ workers (Movement Advancement Project, n.d.). Other workplace gaps can be seen through inaccessible and unsafe bathrooms for transgender individuals: 59% of transgender individuals reported avoiding bathrooms at work and around 33% reported limiting food and drink intake in order to avoid using public restrooms at work (Pride at Work, 2017).

28.3.6.2 Social Interventions

Parental support is a strong predictor of positive life outcomes for LGBTQ+ individuals, increasing self-esteem and general well-being (Snapp et al., 2015). Family acceptance during adolescence is especially important for LGBTQ+ youth to form confidence in their identity and mitigate possible adverse mental health outcomes that family stigma may cause (Snapp et al., 2015). Family interventions entail "promot[ing] tolerance and foster[ing] strong relationships between parents and their LGBTQ children," which could be done through activities such as a parent attending a community meeting with their LGBTQ+ child (Parker et al., 2018, p. 385). Education and open dialogue are needed for parents and family members to develop understanding and acceptance for the LGBTQ+ community (Parker et al., 2018). Additionally, it is important for parents to not dismiss their child's LGBTQ+ identity as "just a phase" as it belittles and takes recognition away from the child.

With regard to extended family, sometimes the best intervention is simply distance. Distancing oneself from the family member who is unaccepting may be the best option for the mental health of the LGBTQ+ individual (HRC, n. d.a). Obviously, this is not always possible and, in such instances, reminding family members of proper terminology, educating them on LGBTQ+ matters, and "cultivating allies" among other family members may help with extended family discrimination (HRC, n.d.a).

When examining the workplace it is important to note the Supreme Court's decision to end workplace discrimination in June of 2020. This decision effectively banned discrimination based on sexual and gender identity in the workplace and was a crucial win in legislative and social arenas for LGBTQ+ individuals (Jenkins, 2020). Many companies implement "anti-discrimination policies and employee resource groups (ERGs) ... to better establish a more inclusive environment" (Raynor, 2020). Other interventions include mentoring programs, an inclusive dress code, diversity and inclusion training, targeted recruiting programs, and education on inclusive language (Raynor, 2020).

In addition to parents, extended family, and the workplace, the Internet and social media have become a promising form of social intervention in recent years as LGBTQ+ individuals turn to online sources for information and community. Media has become a great source of educational resources, social support, and identity development (Wehse et al., 2018). The anonymity behind a computer screen may help an LGBTQ+ individual explore a deeper understanding about their identity in a safe space, meet others, and talk in easier ways than in-person (Paceley et al., 2015). A study conducted by Craig et al. in 2015 found that media could foster positive coping mechanisms and resilience for LGBTQ+ youth (Forenza, 2017). Social media has also been an excellent avenue for advocacy, as seen with the viral #WeJustNeedToPee campaign created to fight back on harmful bathroom bills for transgender individuals (Wehse et al., 2018). In addition, feelings of camaraderie and community that are fostered through online connections or online role models can be invaluable to the mental health and identity development of LGBTQ+ individuals (Wehse et al., 2018).

28.3.7 Social-Environmental Community Gaps and Community Interventions

28.3.7.1 Social-Environmental Gaps

The environment exerts influences on LGBTQ+ acceptance, namely with regard to urban versus rural localities. The experience of LGBTQ+ individuals varies greatly depending on which environment they live in. LGBTQ+ individuals living in rural areas are more susceptible to minority stress, report significantly higher levels of concealment, higher concerns regarding disclosure, decreased sense of community, fewer friendships and weaker social support, and higher levels of internalized homophobia when compared with their urban counterparts (Morandini et al., 2015). LGBTQ+ individuals residing in rural areas often face less acceptance due to a smaller LGBTQ+ population in comparison to urban areas that often have larger LGBTQ+ communities (Morandini et al., 2015). As a result, these individuals face more hostile environments, higher degrees of social exclusion and rejection, and increased experiences of distal stressors, all of which leave this population more susceptible to depression, substance abuse, and suicidal ideation, with the largest impact occurring among LGBTQ+ rural youth (Mereish & Poteat, 2015; Morandini et al., 2015).

The home is among the most harmful environments for many LGBTQ+ youth as they risk parental rejection or living in silence, leaving little room for them to explore their identities in healthy formats, be connected to services that provide diverse avenues of support, and develop positive interactions with communities that inform their development through "concurrent influences of personal characteristics (e.g., race/ethnicity, gender nonconformity" (Snapp et al., 2015, p. 426).

28.3.7.2 Social-Environmental Interventions

It is clear that social experiences among members of the LGBTQ+ community may take a toll on mental well-being from an early age as evidenced by research that demonstrates a lack of family acceptance, bullying, and isolation in social circles growing up (Mereish & Poteat, 2015). While research has centered on the preventative, Gahagan and Colpitts (2017) argue that these methods are "problematized, measured, and defined using a cisnormative, heteronormative, and biomedical framing" (p. 103). Potential interventions from these methods produce few viable options as they do not address the target audiences effectively. Instead they offer a framework based on a strength-based perspective that makes "visible the diverse experiences of LGBTQ populations" (Gahagan & Colpitts, 2017, p. 103). Quite simply, the intervention changed the frame of the questions to center the experiences and lives of LGBTQ+ people reinforcing that idea that models must center LGBTQ+ experiences as the norm, not at the margins of the heteronormative experience.

When examining differences in experiences and resources available to LGBTQ+ individuals based on geographical location and community closeness, it becomes evident that rural and suburban localities are disadvantaged compared to urban locations. Proposed interventions may include creating community centers, also known as Gender and Sexual Minority Centers (GSMs). These centers successfully provide a myriad of social supports for LGBTQ+ individuals including concrete, emotional, financial, and informational support. Such centers provide outreach and education, support groups, social/recreational groups, health/wellness services, drop-in hours, and leadership development for sexual minority communities (Paceley et al., 2015).

Regarding the home environment, Snapp and colleagues (2015) identify family interventions as one source to mitigate the tensions between silence and forced silence of shaming and disdain. Research shows that greater "tailored" family interventions are needed (Snapp et al., 2015). Newcomb et al. (2019) state that parents need specific guidance and education on how to support their child, but first they may need help figuring out how to respond to their child's needs while going through their own anxieties. They offer examples of targeted interventions for LGBTQ+ youth that are tailored to specific issues, "e.g. sexual health promotion, mental health, and violence prevention" (Newcomb et al., 2019, p. 143). They also note that the challenge for creating successful interventions based on existing studies is stymied by the lack of coordination among datasets.

28.4 How Community Psychology Can Support LGBTQ+ Individuals

As defined earlier, community psychology emerged within professional psychology as a recognition of the need to consider the individual within the array of environments and experiences they have throughout development. It also recognized that our psychological well-being is predicated on our experiences within our social world, and that determinants of self-efficacy, self-esteem, and the capacity to engage effectively and meet developmental goals are deeply influenced by how the community is capably functioning and supporting human growth (Angelique & Culley, 2007). By recognizing intersectional influences on personhood and engaging the social, educational, and vocational contributions to identity and community participation, community psychological approaches to understanding human effectiveness have served to influence how a broader understanding of opportunity for a satisfactory participation in life can occur.

Born out of a goal of building awareness and recognition of how individuals are not sole actors, determining their lives separate from their environments, community psychological professionals emphasize the engagement of a social justice approach to addressing means for building and promoting resilience. For LGBTQ+ individuals, as we have discussed, this has increasingly, particularly since the Stonewall riots, emphasized the reality that sexual and gender differences are a prominent part of human life. Despite political challenges that have served to challenge the opportunities of LGBTQ+ persons, there has been a strong reliance on the capacity for advocacy and promotion of a belief in both self and community integrity, to foster greater opportunity and safety.

As an example of how community psychological perspectives regarding supporting and advocating for the humanity and efficacy of LGBTQ+ persons have strongly influenced current thinking regarding policy and practice in professional psychology, the American Psychological Association (APA) has been one such professional organization promoting significant advocacy. APA strongly emphasized, since the removal of the term homosexuality and, more recently, transgender identity as indications of mental illness, a proactive approach for education, training, and practice with regard to professional support for and advocacy regarding sexual and gender minorities. Through the development of both the *Guidelines for Psychological Practice with Lesbian, Gay, and Bisexual Clients* (APA, 2011), which superseded the initial guidelines approved and published in 2000 (and which are presently being revised again for review and approval by the APA Board of Directors and Council in 2021), and the *Guidelines for Psychological Practice with Transgender and Gender Nonconforming People* (APA, 2015b), there has been a broad transformation in how LGBTQ+ individuals are regarded psychologically, and as part of their engagement with professional psychological practice (across education, clinical and counseling services, research participation, and when engaged during consultation). Each iteration of the guidelines, as they have been developed and presented, has widened the lens by which professional psychology is advised and guided toward a clearer community-oriented participation and practice, to embrace cultural humility and the awareness of what is developmentally appropriate regarding sexual and gender minority status, and the relevant needs for treatment, education, and consultation. While providing aspirational guidance, these guidelines also reflect the transformation within APA over the past twenty years toward a more community-engaged advocacy, that is directly informed by social justice, to insure that there is greater attention paid to the ways in which persons of minority status are better understood, considered in the context of professional practices, and supported in developing resilience and self-determination. Particularly relevant to our discussion are the *Guidelines for Psychological Practice with Transgender and Gender Nonconforming People* (APA, 2015b), which reflect the consideration that is required of society, and more specifically psychological practitioners who are addressing mental health care, to reassess and transform their efforts at working with and building forward the lives of persons with gender variance. By providing a strong foundation for understanding the ways in which transgender persons come to understand their gender identity developmentally, the current understanding of transgender identity from a biopsychosocial perspective, and how this influences their capacity for being accepted within their social environments, and accepting themselves, through language, culture, and regard, the guidelines support psychologists across multiple means of work to integrate a holistic and intersectional regard for the lives of trans clients, students, research subjects, and consultees.

By framing transgender and gender nonconforming persons' lives within a community framework, whereby educational experience, peer relationships, and opportunities to develop within an accepting environment are key considerations, efforts to advocate for the appropriate training required to support this from within professional psychology are required. Recognizing how bias and misunderstanding both contribute to failures of engagement, misgendering, and disrespect, and understanding how, developmentally, processes of coming out as a sexual or gender minority serve to facilitate growth, or lead to trauma, professional psychology has come to see that it holds a substantial role in guiding efforts toward acceptance and integration.

More directly, the engagement and promotion of approaches affirming gender and sexuality to professional psychology has meant direct partnerships with advocacy and legal organizations supporting the rights of transgender and sexual minority individuals to live full lives within their communities. Through the filing of amicus briefs regarding persons who are transgender being discriminated against in employment (Abrams, 2019), or with regard to the lesbian and gay marriage rights (Mills, 2015), the APA, as well as the American Psychiatric Association and the National Association of Social Workers, have together emphasized the strong need for a consistent level of recognition and acceptance of individuals who are sexual and gender minorities. Efforts by these mental health professional organizations, together with those of groups like Lambda Legal, the

American Civil Liberties Union, and the Transgender Legal Defense and Education Fund, in tandem with myriad community, counseling, clinical, and social psychological researchers and scholars, have provided significant legal and academic support for the work of community-based programs that directly influence and assist persons of sexual and gender minority status as they seek to live their daily lives effectively (cf. Abrams, 2019). Research regarding the success of such community-directed programs for transgender persons in particular has shown that it provides a means for becoming more self-accepting and engaged with the social environment, which then leads to greater acceptance within their communities, schools, and work settings (Dentato, Craig, & Smith, 2010; Gelaude et al., 2013). As a specific example, youth who have been supported in their transitions within their social communities (i.e., school and neighborhoods), by both parents and teachers, have been shown to demonstrate no elevations in depression and mild elevations in anxiety relative to age expectations (Olson, Durwood, & McLaughlin, 2016). Similarly, multiple studies have shown how acceptance of sexual minorities as members of the community lead to greater cohesion within that community and foster more stable lives (Flores & Park, 2018; Frost & Meyer, 2013).

28.5 Case Illustration: Nathaniel, A Survivor of Conversion Therapy

28.5.1 Nathaniel, A Survivor of Conversion Therapy

Nathaniel, age twenty-two, a recent college graduate, appears reluctant to talk with you in therapy. It is his first session, and you learn he was referred by a friend who assured him you could be trusted. Nathaniel is upfront in sharing that he feels uncomfortable seeing you, but feels he has no alternative but to seek help. He is tired all the time, can barely get out of bed in the morning, and has an intense job opportunity starting at the end of the summer as an investment banker. Nathaniel shares he is excited about this new position, but worries that his emotional state is fragile to the point of not being able to function. He is hoping that he can regain momentum and motivation during June and July. He again shares with you that he is concerned that you will judge him and not support who he is.

As therapy progresses, you are attuned to Nathaniel's concern with being able to trust you in your role as a mental health professional. After several weeks of working with you, Nathaniel begins to open up about his adolescent experience of conversion therapy. He talks about how, growing up in a small rural community in southern Virginia, he always felt different – feelings that accelerated when Nathaniel reached his teenage years. Nathaniel shares how at that time his guy friends were "hooking up" with girls and started having romantic relationships. In the context of this hook-up culture, Nathaniel was increasingly aware that he was attracted to other males. In light of increasing pressure from his guy friends to date girls and invite someone to the junior prom, Nathaniel felt alone and as though he had nowhere to turn. He decided to tell his parents about his feelings. He was fifteen at the time this event occurred.

Nathaniel recalls for you how his parents listened quietly when he told them about his attraction to other males. They did not say much immediately, but Nathaniel stated that he could tell that they were upset and, even worse, disappointed in him. Nathaniel recounts his surprise when following his sharing this information, his parents simply left the room. They said absolutely nothing to him; they did not share either approval or disapproval, nor did they offer him any physical or emotional consideration, not a hug or even expressed anger. They instead did nothing, and left him alone with his feelings.

As the therapy with Nathaniel continues, you learn how about two weeks after coming out to his mom and dad, Nathaniel's parents asked to speak with him. They shared that they had found a person they wanted him to talk to – "an expert," they said. "This is someone who can help you – and us – with your problem," said Nathaniel's mom. "It's someone who you can talk to about how to change your feelings, how to correct yourself, so that you're attracted to girls instead of boys. It's called conversion therapy."

In an effort to please his parents and with the hope that somehow this expert would help him feel less alone, Nathaniel agreed to participate. But his feelings of isolation were only amplified as the conversion therapy treatment unfolded. The therapist encouraged Nathaniel to visualize being with girls. He shared social skills exercises where Nathaniel had to practice "being a man" in interactions with girls at school – and was expected to show his heterosexual guy friends that "he's one of them."

Nathaniel reported that during this process of therapy, he felt very uncomfortable and depressed. He tried the interventions – but they did not work. He was unable to think about his female peers sexually, and felt like a failure, often wondering what was wrong with him. He felt increasingly more strongly that there was never going to be a way he could be accepted for who he is. He felt that he was damaged and unlike the boy his parents and peers expected him to be. As conversion therapy progressed, Nathaniel started to think about ending his own life. He more frequently felt that there was no point in going on if people could not accept him for who he is, and that because he could not change and become attracted to girls, he was unfit to remain living among his family and peers. He shared that on many occasions he had no sense of who he even was anymore. Sensing his increasingly depressed mood, the conversion therapist suggested to Nathaniel's parents that he join one of the conversion therapy support groups the therapist ran regularly for boys Nathaniel's age.

Nathaniel shares that he felt terrified by this recommendation. He told his parents that he was too busy with school to go to therapy anymore, and became more active in sports, in an effort to signal to his parents that "he's OK." Nathaniel's parents were reportedly thrilled that he began to be more engaged in sports, as this was something they equated with a traditional male identity and an expression of heterosexual masculinity. They assumed the conversion therapy had "cured" their son, however, Nathaniel never talked again with them about his feelings regarding his sexuality or his masculinity.

As Nathaniel continues to work with you in therapy, he shared that he felt he needed to speak with someone more urgently, and at the suggestion of his trusted friend who referred him to you, when Virginia's law changed regarding the practice of conversion therapy in the state. Following the passage of House Bill (HB) 386 on July 1, 2020, Virginia banned the practice of conversion therapy in the state for anyone under the age of eighteen. Nathaniel shares that the passing of this law made him feel both relieved and angry. He stated that he is relieved that this law protects youth from having to go through what he did, but he acknowledges feeling angry about being robbed of his identity, and having to survive being told by an expert and others that who he is was not acceptable; that he had to be someone he was not able or capable of being.

Nathaniel shares that his anger is also related to his feelings of confusion the conversion therapy process brought up for him, including the feelings of guilt and shame given his belief that something was in fact wrong with him, as stated to him by his parents and the conversion therapist. The passing of HB 386 was validating for Nathaniel ultimately, as it affirmed that the practice of conversion therapy was discriminatory and harmful, because it served to deny that being a person attracted to same gender peers was something acceptable and normal. The passage of the bill affirmed for Nathaniel that it is okay to be who he is, and that there is no acceptable process for changing that. He also shared regret that it had not been considered and passed many years earlier, so that he would not have had to go through something so unaffirming and harmful to his sense of himself as a man.

28.5.2 Policy Implications That Emerge from Nathaniel's Story

Nathaniel's story and experience speak to the need for policies that protect LGBTQ+ communities. Conversion therapy is a practice whereby the therapist works individually with a client, or with individuals in a group context, with a focus on changing one's sexual orientation from LGBTQ+ to being heterosexual. While currently in the United States conversion therapy techniques primarily involve talk therapy, social skills, and visualization, they have included chemical castration, lobotomies, electric shock treatment, and many other aversive interventions (Drescher et al., 2016). Conversion therapy once held a degree of respect within the mental health community, when it was believed that a heterosexual and cisgender identity were the normative standard. In 2003, Robert Spitzer published research where he claimed that the subjects in his study reported changing from having an attraction to primarily same-sex partners to being primarily attracted to partners of the opposite sex. It was later revealed that this study lacked peer review – and Spitzer himself ultimately stated it was not possible "to judge the credibility of subject reports of change in sexual orientation" (Spitzer, 2012, p. 757).

Substantial research done in the past thirty years has challenged views such as Spitzer's (2003). Currently, the majority of medical and mental health professional organizations and the scientific community have come to a shared agreement, based on these studies, that conversion therapy is both ineffective and harmful. These organizations have together, with LGBTQ+ advocacy organizations, pressured many governments across the world to recognize that conversion therapy holds no evidence of efficacy and to ban its practice.

Supporting these efforts is the clear understanding that there are no data to support the belief that sexual orientation can be changed. For instance, the American Medical Association supports state and federal governmental efforts to ban conversion therapy (Fitzsimons, 2019), the American Psychiatric Association supports a ban on conversion therapy, sharing that same-sex orientations do not need to be changed (American Psychiatric Association, 2018), and the American Psychological Association supports a ban on conversion therapy, advocating for acceptance of one's sexual orientation rather than pathologizing it (APA, 2015a). Such efforts are further supported by the American Academy of Pediatrics and the American Medical Association. These are but a few of the many professional organizations that have spoken out against conversion therapy.

As can be seen through Nathaniel's experience, conversion therapy is harmful. It sends the message that people cannot accept themselves for who they are. It makes people feel that there is something wrong with them rather than supporting their development. For Nathaniel, this increased his feelings of isolation. Given conversion therapy's ineffectiveness and harm, some states and territories have started to ban it. On April 8, 2015, President Barack Obama called for an end to conversion therapies that aimed to "change" LGBTQ+ youth to have a heterosexual orientation. President Obama's statement was delivered in response to the death of Leelah Alcorn, a seventeen-year-old who committed suicide after her parents took her out of school and put her in conversion therapy as an effort to change her sexual orientation (Reuters Staff, 2015).

On July 1, 2020, approximately five years and three months after President Obama's statement, Virginia was the twentieth state, and the first Southern state in the USA, to ban conversion therapy – and did so for youth under the age of eighteen. Other states that have banned conversion therapy include New Jersey, California, Illinois, Oregon, Connecticut, Vermont, New Mexico, Utah, Maine, Colorado, New York, Massachusetts, New Hampshire, Maryland, Hawaii, Nevada, Washington, Delaware, and Rhode Island. The District of Columbia banned conversion therapy – and is the only US territory that has done so for adults as well as youth under eighteen years of age. Puerto Rico also banned conversion therapy.

Nathaniel's feelings of relief that Virginia banned conversion therapy, coupled with anger as to why this ban took so long and occurred after he had to survive it, speaks to the outrage of a system that has been unable to fully condemn this practice. At the time of this writing, for instance, only three countries have effectively led a nationwide ban on conversion therapy: Brazil, Ecuador, and Malta (Savage, 2020). How is it that policy cannot result from science, for example, the science that shows conversion therapy is harmful and ineffective? How is it that nations are unable to address this concern? While data about the practice of conversion therapy globally may be sparse, reports have indicated that eighty countries have shared that it is being practiced within their borders (Savage, 2020). A study conducted by the University of Southern California's Williams Institute indicates that 698,000 adults in the USA had conversion therapy (Mallory, Brown, & Conron, 2019). How many more people, and particularly young people, will undergo conversion therapy before it is banned?

28.6 Conclusion

The lives of sexual and gender minority individuals in many countries have improved significantly in many ways over the last forty years, following movement towards greater acceptance and engagement. Legal and political changes have taken place, given the significant contributions of community-based research and advocacy, with a lead taken within the community psychology realm in particular. Through engagement across organizations and professionals committed to advocacy for LGBTQ+ persons, particularly within the past twenty years, and in response to a sea change in understanding the humanity of gender and sexual variation, persons who in the near past would have been forced to continue to hide their true selves and their needs, and who were directed toward unsafe and detrimental practices within professional psychology, such as conversion therapies and other denigrating forms of therapy, are now more fully living their lives.

And yet, there remain large pockets of unacceptance, shaming, and rejection that still take place; persons who are LGBTQ+ continue to be at high risk for substance abuse, depression and anxiety, trauma, interpersonal violence, and suicide. Daily, youth who are sexual or gender minorities become homeless due to family rejection. And there remain countries around the world that have made being a sexual or gender minority a crime, with substantial punishments allocated if identified and arrested.

Community psychology as a field of practice is one of the particular domains that has taken on assertive advocacy toward removing stigma and embracing the humanity of LGBTQ+ persons. As we have discussed, much has improved toward promoting resiliency and engagement within the social structures that facilitate self-regard and genuine acceptance of one's differences for LGBTQ+

individuals. But much remains necessary to ensure that full lives are possible, across all domains of experience and opportunity. Addressing mental and physical health needs, educational and vocational opportunities, and the capacity to live full lives, as partners, parents, and community members remains a substantial goal. It is the continued work, through alliances between the practitioners of community psychology, their professional organizations, the voices of the LGBTQ+ community and supporters, and legal and social advocacy organizations, to influence the political structures, that will foster change and increase societal acceptance.

References

Abrams, Z. (2019, October 25). *Taking psychological science to the high court.* APA News. www.apa.org/news/apa/2019/lgbt-discrimination-supreme-court

Advocates for Youth. (n.d.). *LGBTQ health and rights.* https://advocatesforyouth.org/issue/lgbtq-health-and-rights/

American Psychiatric Association. (1973). *DSM-II 6th printing change: Elimination of homosexuality as a mental disorder and substitution of the new category sexual orientation disturbance.* Arlington, VA: American Psychiatric Association.

American Psychiatric Association. (2018, November 15). *APA reiterates strong opposition to conversion therapy.* www.psychiatry.org/newsroom/news-releases/apa-reiterates-strong-opposition-to-conversion-therapy

American Psychological Association. (2011). *Guidelines for psychological practice with lesbian, gay, and bisexual clients.* Washington, DC: American Psychological Association. www.apa.org/pi/lgbt/resources/guidelines

American Psychological Association. (2015a, April 9). *American Psychological Association applauds President Obama's call to end use of therapies intended to change sexual orientation.* APA News. www.apa.org/news/press/releases/2015/04/therapies-sexual-orientation

American Psychological Association. (2015b). Guidelines for psychological practice with transgender and gender nonconforming people. *American Psychologist, 70*(9), 832–864. doi.org/10.1037/a0039906

Angelique, H. L., & Culley, M. R. (2007). History and theory of community psychology: An international perspective of community psychology in the United States: Returning to political, critical, and ecological roots. In S. M. Reich, M. Riemer, I. Prilleltensky, & M. Montero (Eds.), *International community psychology* (pp. 37–62). Boston: Springer.

Bearss, N. (2013). Working with lesbian, gay, bisexual, and transgender youth in schools. In C. S. Clauss-Ehlers, Z. N. Serpell, & M. D. Weist (Eds.), *Handbook of culturally responsive school mental health* (pp. 89–105). New York: Springer.

Carroll, A., & Itaborahy, L. P. (2015). *State-sponsored homophobia: A world survey of laws: Criminalisation, protectionand recognition of same-sex love* (10th ed.). ILGA.

Clauss-Ehlers, C. S., Chiriboga, D., Hunter, S. J., Roysircar, G., & Tummala-Narra, P. (2019). APA Multicultural Guidelines executive summary: Ecological approach to context, identity, and intersectionality. *American Psychologist*, *74*(2), 232–244. doi.org/10.1037/amp0000382

CNN Editorial Research. (2020, June 17). *LGBTQ rights milestones fast facts.* Retrieved July 12, 2020, from www.cnn.com/2015/06/19/us/lgbt-rights-mile stones-fast-facts/index.html

Cohen, R. D. (2019, January 20). *Medical students push for more LGBT health training to address disparities.* NPR. www.npr.org/sections/health-shots/2019/01/20/ 683216767/medical-students-push-for-more-lgbt-health-training-to-address-disparities

Conley, G. (2020, July 8). *CNN Opinion: J.K. Rowling's bigotry is painful and maddening.* www.cnn.com/2020/07/07/opinions/jk-rowling-conversion-ther apy-transphobia-conley/index.html

Craig, S. L., McInroy, L., McCready, L. T., & Alaggia, R. (2015). Media: A catalyst for resilience in lesbian, gay, bisexual, transgender, and queer youth. *Journal of LGBT Youth*, *12*(3), 254–275. doi.org/10.1080/19361653.2015.1040193

Denato, M., Craig, S., & Smith, M. (2010). The vital role of social workers in community partnerships: The alliance for gay, lesbian, bisexual, transgender, and questioning youth. *Child and Adolescent Social Work Journal*, *27*(5), 323–334. doi.org/10.1007/s10560–010-0210-0

Drescher, J., Schwartz, A., Casoy, F., et al. (2016, June 1). The growing regulation of conversion therapy. *Journal of Medical Regulation*, *102*(2), 7–12. https:// meridian.allenpress.com/jmr/article/102/2/7/80848/The-Growing-Regulation-of-Conversion-Therapy

Earnshaw, V. A., Reisner, S. L., Juvonen, J., et al. (2017, October 1). LGBTQ bullying: Translating research to action in pediatrics. *Pediatrics*, *140*(4), e20170432. doi.org/10.1542/peds.2017-0432

Fitzsimons, T. (2019, November 21). *American Medical Association backs nationwide conversion therapy ban.* NBC News. www.nbcnews.com/feature/nbc-out/ameri can-medical-association-backs-nationwide-conversion-therapy-ban-n1088731

Flores, A., & Park, A. (2018). *Examining the relationship between social acceptance of LGBT people and legal inclusion of sexual minorities.* Los Angeles: UCLA School of Law Williams Institute.

Flores, C. A., & Sheely-Moore, A. I. (2020, April 14). Relational-cultural theory–based interventions with LGBTQ college students. *Journal of College Counseling*, *23*(1), 71–84. doi.org/10.1002/jocc.12150

Forenza, B. (2017). Exploring the affirmative role of gay icons in coming out. *Psychology of Popular Media Culture*, *6*(4), 338–347. doi.org/10.1037/ ppm0000117

Frost, D. M., & Meyer, I. H. (2013). Measuring community connectedness among diverse sexual minority populations. *Journal of Sex Research*, *49*(1), 36–49. doi.org/10.1080/00224499.2011.565427

Gahagan, J., & Colpitts, E. (2017). Understanding and measuring LGBTQ pathways to health: A scoping review of strengths-based health promotion approaches in LGBTQ health research. *Journal of Homosexuality*, *64*(1), 95–121. doi.org/ 10.1080/00918369.2016.1172893

Gelaude, D. J., Sovine, M. L., Swayzer, R., & Herbst, J. H. (2013). HIV prevention programs delivered by community based organizations to young transgender persons of color: Lessons learned to improve future program implementation. *International Journal of Transgenderism, 14*(3), 127–139. doi.org/10.1080/15532739.2013.824846

Gold, M. (2018, June 21). The ABCs of L.G.B.T.Q.I.A.+. *The New York Times.* www.nytimes.com/2018/06/21/style/lgbtq-gender-language.html

Gowin, M., Taylor, E., Dunnington, J., Alshuwaiyer, G., & Cheney, M. (2017). Needs of a silent minority: Mexican transgender asylum seekers. *Health Promotion Practice, 18*(3), 332–340. doi.org/10.1177/1524839917692750

Greytak, E. A., Kosciw, J. G., Villenas, C., & Giga, N. M. (2016). *From teasing to torment: School climate revisited: A survey of U.S. secondary school students and teachers.* GLSEN. www.glsen.org/research/teasing-torment-school-climate-revisited-survey-us-seconda

Horn, S., Kosciw, J. G., & Russell, S. (2009). Special issue introduction: New research on lesbian, gay, bisexual, and transgender youth: Studying lives in context. *Journal of Youth and Adolescence, 38*(7), 863–866. doi.org/10.1007/s10964-009-9420-1

Human Rights Campaign. (2012). *Growing up LGBT in America: HRC Youth Survey report key findings.* https://hrc.org/files/assets/resources/Growing-Up-LGBT-in-America_Report.pdf?_ga=2.47873575.1037792124.1593616704-1210519043.1593014079

Human Rights Campaign. (2018a). *Youth report.* www.hrc.org/resources/youth-report

Human Rights Campaign. (2018b, August 1). *Stances of faiths on LGBTQ issues: Roman Catholic Church.* www.hrc.org/resources/stances-of-faiths-on-lgbt-issues-roman-catholic-church

Human Rights Campaign. (2018c, August 1). *Stances of faiths on LGBTQ issues: Presbyterian Church (USA).* www.hrc.org/resources/stances-of-faiths-on-lgbt-issues-presbyterian-church-usa

Human Rights Campaign. (2018d, August 1). *Stances of faiths on LGBTQ issues: Reform Judaism.* www.hrc.org/resources/stances-of-faiths-on-lgbt-issues-reform-judaism

Human Rights Campaign. (2018e). *2018 LGBTQ youth report.* https://assets2.hrc.org/files/assets/resources/2018-YouthReport-NoVid.pdf?_ga=2.3915696.1217585561.1595800254-915330973.1595800254

Human Rights Campaign. (n.d.a) *Talking to grandparents and other adult family members.* www.hrc.org/resources/transgender-children-and-youth-talking-to-grandparents-and-other-adult-fami

Human Rights Campaign. (n.d.b). *Faith positions.* www.hrc.org/resources/faith-positions

Jenkins, W. (2020, June 22). *The Supreme Court reaffirmed LBGT protections against discrimination. How can we ensure those rights are realized?* Urban Wire. www.urban.org/urban-wire/supreme-court-reaffirmed-lbgt-protections-against-discrimination-how-can-we-ensure-those-rights-are-realized

Jones, S. W., Sood, A. B., Bearss, N., & Clauss-Ehlers, C. S. (2020). Lesbian, gay, bisexual, transgender, and queer youth and social justice. In C. S. Clauss-Ehlers, A. B. Sood, & M. D. Weist (Eds.), *Social justice for children and young people: International perspectives* (pp. 123–137). Cambridge, UK: Cambridge University Press.

Keith, E., & Gagliano, K. (2018). *Lack of trust in law enforcement hinders reporting of LBGTQ crimes.* The Center for Public Integrity. https://publicintegrity.org/politics/lack-of-trust-in-law-enforcement-hinders-reporting-of-lbgtq-crimes/

Kim, M., Wilson, L. M., Biery, N., & Frutos, B. (2019). The attitude of medical practices toward LGBTQ older adults before and after intervention. *Innovation in Aging, 3*(Suppl. 1), S491. doi.org/10.1093/geroni/igz038.1822

Mallory, C., Brown, T. N. T., & Conron, K. J. (2019, June). *Conversion therapy and LGBT youth.* Williams Institute. https://williamsinstitute.law.ucla.edu/publications/conversion-therapy-and-lgbt-youth/.

McCandless, S. (2018). LGBT homeless youth and policing. *Public Integrity, 20*(6), 558–570. doi.org/10.1080/10999922.2017.1402738

McConnell, E., Janulis, P., Phillips, G., Truong, R., & Birkett, M. (2018). Multiple minority stress and LGBT community resilience among sexual minority men. *Psychology of Sexual Orientation and Gender Diversity, 5*(1), 1–12. doi.org/10.1037/sgd0000265

Mereish, E., & Poteat, V. (2015). A relational model of sexual minority mental and physical health: The negative effects of shame on relationships, loneliness, and health. *Journal of Counseling Psychology, 62*(3), 425–437. doi.org/10.1037/cou0000088

Meyer, I. (1995). Minority stress and mental health in gay men. *Journal of Health and Social Behavior, 36*(1), 38–56. doi.org/10.2307/2137286

Meyer, I. H. (2003). Prejudice, social stress, and mental health in lesbian, gay, and bisexual populations: Conceptual issues and research evidence. *Psychological Bulletin, 129*(5), 674–697. doi.org/10.1037/0033-2909.129.5.674

Milan, T. (2017, July 16). *'Queen Sugar' actor Brian Michael Smith comes out as transgender.* NBC News. www.nbcnews.com/feature/nbc-out/queen-sugar-actor-brian-michael-smith-comes-out-transgender-n783451

Mills, K. (2015). APA's role in striking down prohibitions on same-sex marriage. *APA Monitor, 46*(8), 12.

Minero, E. (2018, April 19). *Schools struggle to support LGBTQ students.* Edutopia. www.edutopia.org/article/schools-struggle-support-lgbtq-students

Morandini, J., Blaszczynski, A., Dar-Nimrod, I., & Ross, M. (2015). Minority stress and community connectedness among gay, lesbian and bisexual Australians: A comparison of rural and metropolitan localities. *Australian and New Zealand Journal of Public Health, 39*(3), 260–266. doi.org/10.1111/1753-6405.12364

Morgan, E. M. (2013). Contemporary issues in sexual orientation and identity development in emerging adulthood. *Emerging Adulthood, 1*(1), 52–66. doi.org/10.1177/2167696812469187

Movement Advancement Project. (n.d.). *LGBTQ people in the workplace: Demographics, experiences and pathways to equity.* www.lgbtmap.org/lgbt-workers-brief

National Coalition for the Homeless. (n.d.). *LGBT homelessness.* https://nationalhomeless.org/issues/lgbt/

National LGBTQ Task Force. (2013, November 14). *LGBT workers of color are among the most disadvantaged in the American workforce.* www.thetaskforce.org/lgbt-workers-of-color-are-among-the-most-disadvantaged-in-the-american-workforce/

Newcomb, M. E., LaSala, M. C., Bouris, A., et al. (2019, March 7). The influence of families on LGBTQ youth health: A call to action for innovation in research and intervention development. *LGBT Health, 6*(4), 139–145. doi.org/10.1089/lgbt.2018.0157

Olson, K. R., Durwood, L., & McLaughlin, K. A. (2016). Mental health of transgender children who are supported in their identities. *Pediatrics, 137*, e2015323. doi.org/10.1542/peds.2018-1436

Paceley, M. S. (2015). *Social and community support among nonmetropolitan gender and sexual minority youth: A mixed methods study* [Doctoral dissertation, University of Illinois at Urbana-Champaign]. Ann Arbor, MI: ProQuest LLC.

Pachankis, J., Clark, K., Burton, C., et al. (2020). Sex, status, competition, and exclusion: Intraminority stress from within the gay community and gay and bisexual men's mental health. *Journal of Personality and Social Psychology, 119*(3), 713–740. doi.org/10.1037/pspp0000282

Parker, C., Hirsch, J., Philbin, M., & Parker, R. (2018). The urgent need for research and interventions to address family-based stigma and discrimination against lesbian, gay, bisexual, transgender, and queer youth. *Journal of Adolescent Health, 63*(4), 383–393. doi.org/10.1016/j.jadohealth.2018.05.018

Platt, L., Wolf, J., & Scheitle, C. (2018). Patterns of mental health care utilization among sexual orientation minority groups. *Journal of Homosexuality, 65*(2), 135–153. doi.org/10.1080/00918369.2017.1311552

Politico Staff. (2013, June 26). *26 gay-rights milestones.* Politico. www.politico.com/gallery/26-gay-rights-milestones?slide=25

Pride at Work. (2017, July 6). *Workplace discrimination.* www.prideatwork.org/issues/workplace-discrimination/

Ramgopal, K. (2018, June 22). *Only 0.1 percent of elected officials are LGBTQ, new report finds.* NBC News. www.nbcnews.com/feature/nbc-out/only-0-1-percent-elected-officials-are-lgbtq-new-report-n885871

Raynor, S. (2020, February 19). LGBT workplace issues: Why the majority of LGBT workers still hide their identity at work [Blog post]. *Everfi.* https://everfi.com/blog/workplace-training/lgbt-workplace-issues-hide-their-identity/

Reuters Staff. (2015, April 9). Obama calls for end to conversion therapy for LGBT youth. *Scientific American.* www.scientificamerican.com/article/obama-calls-for-end-to-conversion-therapy-for-lgbt-youth/

Rubinstein, G. (1995). The decision to remove homosexuality from the DSM: Twenty years later. *American Journal of Psychotherapy, 49*(3), 416–427. doi.org/10.1176/appi.psychotherapy.1995.49.3.416

Rutherford, K., McIntyre, J., Daley, A., & Ross, L. (2012). Development of expertise in mental health service provision for lesbian, gay, bisexual and transgender communities. *Medical Education, 46*(9), 903–913. doi.org/10.1111/j.1365-2923.2012.04272.x

Savage, R. (2020, February 26). *Nine countries seek to ban gay 'conversion therapy.'* Thomson Reuters Foundation. https://news.trust.org/item/20200225232358-ooujw/

Savin-Williams, R. C. (2005). *The new gay teenager.* Cambridge, MA: Harvard University Press.

Savin-Williams, R. C. (2016a). *Becoming who I am: Young men on being gay*. Cambridge, MA: Harvard University Press.

Savin-Williams, R. C. (2016b). Sexual orientation: Categories or continuum? Commentary on Bailey et al. *Psychology Science in the Public Interest: A Journal of the American Psychological Society*, *17*(2), 37–44. doi.org/10 .1177/1529100616637618

Savin-Williams, R. C. (2017). *Mostly straight: Sexual fluidity among men*. Cambridge, MA: Harvard University Press.

Shilo, G., Yossef, I., & Savaya, R. (2016). Religious coping strategies and mental health among religious Jewish gay and bisexual men. *Archives of Sexual Behavior*, *45*(6), 1551–1561. doi.org/10.1007/s10508-015-0567-4

Siegel, D. (2019). Transgender experiences and transphobia in higher education. *Sociology Compass*, *13*(10). doi.org/10.1111/soc4.12734

Smith, C., Cunningham, S., & Freyd, J. (2016). Sexual violence, institutional betrayal, and psychological outcomes for LGB college students. *Translational Issues in Psychological Science*, *2*(4), 351–360. doi.org/10.1037/tps0000094

Snapp, S., Watson, R., Russell, S., Diaz, R., & Ryan, C. (2015). Social support networks for LGBT young adults: Low cost strategies for positive adjustment. *Family Relations*, *64*(3), 420–430. doi.org/10.1111/fare.12124

Society for Community Research and Action. (n.d.). *What is community psychology?* www.scra27.org/what-we-do/what-community-psychology/

Soohinda, G., Singh, J. P., Sampath, H., & Dutta, S. (2019). Self-reported sexual orientation, relationships pattern, social connectedness, disclosure, and self-esteem in Indian men who use online gay dating websites. *Open Journal of Psychiatry and Allied Sciences*, *10*(1), 37–43. doi.org/10.5958/2394-2061.2019 .00010.7

Sopelsa, B. (2020, March 4). *Virginia becomes 20th state to ban conversion therapy for minors*. NBC News. www.nbcnews.com/feature/nbc-out/virginia-becomes-20th-state-ban-conversion-therapy-minors-n1148421

Spitzer, R. (2003). Can some gay men and lesbians change their sexual orientation? 200 participants reporting a change from homosexual to heterosexual orientation. *Archives of Sexual Behavior*, *32*(5), 403–417. doi.org/10.1023/ A:1025647527010

Spitzer, R. (2012). Spitzer reassesses his 2003 study of reparative therapy of homosexuality. *Archives of Sexual Behavior*, *41*(4), 757. doi.org/10.1007/s10508-012-9966-y

The Trevor Project. (2019, January 24). *Washington, D.C.'s ACT 22-573 becomes first U.S. law to include vulnerable LGBTQ adults in conversion therapy protections*. www.thetrevorproject.org/trvr_press/washington-d-c-s-act-22-573-becomes-first-u-s-law-to-include-vulnerable-lgbtq-adults-in-conversion-ther apy-protections/

Tomita, T. (2019). Gender-affirming medical interventions and mental health in transgender adults. *Psychology of Sexual Orientation and Gender Diversity*, *6*(2), 182–193. doi.org/10.1037/sgd0000316

Totenberg, N. (2020, June 15). *Supreme Court delivers major victory to LGBTQ employees*. NPR. www.npr.org/2020/06/15/863498848/supreme-court-delivers-major-victory-to-lgbtq-employees

Valentine, S., & Shipherd, J. (2018). A systematic review of social stress and mental health among transgender and gender non-conforming people in the United States. *Clinical Psychology Review*, *66*, 24–38. doi.org/10.1016/j.cpr.2018.03.003

Wang, T., Kelman, E., & Cahill, S. (2016, September). *What the new Affordable Care Act nondiscrimination rule means for providers and LGBT patients*. The Fenway Institute. https://fenwayhealth.org/wp-content/uploads/HHS-ACA-1557-LGBT-Non-Discimination-Brief.pdf

Wehse, M., Quinn, A., Legerski, E., & Reeves, B. (2018). *Online resources and the transgender community* [Doctoral dissertation, University of Wisconsin-Whitewater]. Ann Arbor, MI: ProQuest LLC.

White Hughto, J. M., Reisner, S. L., & Pachankis, J. E. (2015, November 11). Transgender stigma and health: A critical review of stigma determinants, mechanisms, and interventions. *Social Science & Medicine*, *147*, 222–231. doi.org/10.1016/j.socscimed.2015.11.010

Winderman, K., Martin, C., & Smith, N. (2018). Career indecision among LGB college students: The role of minority stress, perceived social support, and community affiliation. *Journal of Career Development*, *45*(6), 536–550. doi.org/10.1177/0894845317722860

Yep, I'm gay. (1997, April 14). *TIME Magazine* [Cover], *149*(15).

PART IV

Where Do We Go from Here?

Gaps and Opportunities for Community Psychology

29 Responding to Gaps in Research and Practice in Community Psychology

Tanya Graham

Community psychology is a globally diverse and continuously evolving field, in part due to the contested histories, meanings, and social dynamics that are intrinsic to the concept of "community" itself. This chapter identifies theories, topics, and methods that are underrepresented in empirical studies, and considers these trends from the perspective of locating research within a broader critical meta-analytic framework of understanding power relations. It begins with considering power as central to the conceptualization of community psychology research and practice. This discussion includes exploring how power dynamics permeate how we think about, write about, and work with communities. It is therefore necessary to further consider what is meant by the term "community" and how this connects to notions of privilege, dominance, marginalization, and power. The chapter then highlights the study of scholarly work as an important focus area in community psychology for students, practitioners, and scholars due to its value in promoting disciplinary reflexivity. It goes on to present selected findings from a retrospective study of published work in international community psychology journals. This study shows that continued reflexivity about the research gaps and future trajectory in community psychology is needed to shift dominant power relations and ensure greater theoretical and methodological openness, flexibility, and inclusivity in research and practice. The chapter concludes by presenting some thoughts about future imperatives for community psychologists.

29.1 Power as an Organizing Principle in Community Psychology

Several contemporary scholars in community psychology have voiced the need for considering the role of power in theory and practice, and bringing power into the forefront of activities in the field (Burton & Kagan, 2016; Fisher & Sonn, 2007; Smail, 1994, 2015). By definition, community psychology is concerned with the power differentials in society and the ways in which power relations affect the mental and physical state of individuals, groups, and communities (Fisher, Sonn, & Evans, 2007). Power also features as a prominent aspect of core values and principles guiding the field, such as social justice (Burton & Kagan, 2016). However, surprisingly, scholarly work in community psychology has neglected the centrality of power relations in both its content and methods. In much of the literature, power as a construct is virtually ignored or features only peripherally (Fisher & Sonn, 2007), even though much of the phenomena of interest to community psychologists are phenomena that the workings of power have given rise to (Smail, 1994). Smail (2015) maintains that psychological states of personal distress and unhappiness are intimately tied to experiences of social injustice and the effects of social inequality. Smail (2015) argues further that the social world, and the social institutions though which power operates, influence our thoughts, feelings, sensations, and relationships profoundly, and yet these have been separated from psychological understandings, including those dominant in community psychology (Smail, 1994).

The lack of attention to the workings of power in community psychology has, in part, been attributed to the scientist-practitioner model in which community psychologists are trained (Fisher et al., 2007). In contrast to a critical theory emphasis that foregrounds the workings of power relations, the scientist-practitioner model draws predominantly from a biomedical, positivist tradition. This tradition reifies the idea of scientific neutrality and the establishment of universal truths (Fisher et al., 2007). While the emphasis on value-free scientific understandings of communities has advanced the credibility of the field and consolidated its growth internationally, it has simultaneously detracted from the sociopolitical aspects of its stated ideals and their translation into theory and practice. Thus, the relevance of the knowledge generated in community psychology to the realities of those who are socially marginalized and living in adverse social conditions, is disputed.

This raises important questions for community psychologists about the relationship between epistemology and power (Fisher & Sonn, 2007). For Montero (2002), epistemological reflection is needed to consider questions about the producers of knowledge and the types of knowledge that are generated. This highlights a central epistemological paradox in the field. While striving for social transformation, published work consistently shows that scholars value individualized, objective rather than contextual and politicized models of theory and practice (Seedat, MacKenzie, & Stevens, 2004), that lack the critical social theoretical underpinnings evident in other forms of critical scholarship (Davidson et al., 2006). The lack of attention given to issues of power in scholarly work has therefore been implicated in perpetuating privilege and the domination of socially powerful groups (Angelique & Culley, 2007).

With an increasing global awareness of knowledge dynamics between countries in the Global South and North, community psychologists have become more aware of the need to develop a more power-centric community psychology that is cognizant of and sensitive to the power relations embedded within its theories, methods, and forms of practice. For some, this has prompted important debates about whether community psychology has ever been inherently critical at all (Evans et al., 2017). This is most notably evident in scholarship that refers to "critical community psychology" as a particular form of community psychology (see Kagan et al., 2011a). For others, it signals the need to reposition criticality within community psychology (Evans et al., 2017). Recentering criticality necessarily implies thinking about power.

Foucault (1982/1994) views power as a productive network that permeates throughout the entire social formation. Disciplinary power operates through "homogenous circuits capable of operating everywhere, in a continuous way" (Foucault, 1977, p. 80). Foucault's (1982/1994) coupling of power/knowledge illustrates that knowledge is part of the mechanism of power relations. Ideas can never be isolated from the institutions and the power relations that exist in a specific historical, geographical, and social context (Foucault, 1982/1994). However, in contrast to Marxist theory, Foucault (1982/1994) does not conceive of a binary between the powerful and powerless, but the constant reengagement of power relations. Any method of analysis is simply one reading of reality that is made possible by the relations of power it evokes, but an absence of any fixed forms of domination is desirable (Foucault, 1982/1994). Thus, community psychologists can focus on working in a range of areas where inequalities are entrenched, be they symbolic, discursive, related resource distribution, and processes of participation and decision-making or policy implementation, with a broader vision of establishing more equitable configurations of power.

Pierre Bourdieu (2004) provides insight into how power relations become entrenched in particular ways, and how this connects to knowledge practices. Bourdieu locates power relations both in the internal (unconscious) structures and practices and external structures. This includes the social actions arising from the interrelationship between the "*habitus*" and "*field*" (Bourdieu, 1980). Habitus and field constitute his reformulation of dichotomies such as agency and structural determinism, as being inseparable and dialectical (Wacquant, 2006). Thus, while Foucault sees power beyond agency or structure, Bourdieu views power as enacted and reenacted symbolically and culturally through the complex interplay of structure and agency (Bourdieu, 1980).

The habitus is the largely unconscious mental structures of social phenomena that exist internally in social agents within a particular social arena. They represent the shared generative dispositions of possibilities and constraints that exist within a social space (Bourdieu, 2004). The mental structures of the habitus are both conditioned by the social structures of the past and made malleable by exposure to changing social conditions (Wacquant, 2006). The field is comprised of a set of positions present in a social space (Bourdieu, 2004). The social structure of a particular field is reproduced in the convergence of the internalized possibilities and constraints of the habitus and the external possibilities and constraints in a field; and likewise contested when there are ruptures between the habitus and field (Wacquant, 2006). A circular, self-fulfilling logic is created through this interplay between the dispositions of the habitus and the positions of a field (Bourdieu, 1988).

Bourdieu further maintained that individuals within each field develop their own "*doxa*" – an unquestioned set of commonly held beliefs and opinions that would serve to unite them and would also direct their practices (Wacquant, 2006). The doxa of community psychology are the assumptions held by community psychologists about the field, its values and principles, and its views about the social world. These include accepted principles such as social justice, respect for diversity, and an emphasis on wellness. However, while these values may represent its ideals, they could overlook biases, support of the status quo through inaction or the neglect of social conditions, and thereby enact complex power relations. Thus, the commonly endorsed doxa of the field may direct the actions of community psychologists in specific ways that could lead us to be insufficiently critical of ourselves, the knowledge we produce, and our roles in society.

Bourdieu (2004) further advocates for reflexivity in academic research and argues that empirical work can reveal the logic of the social world. Reflexivity requires that we not only introspect about our own positionality but also critically reflect on the nature of our subdiscipline and the knowledge we produce – not to discredit this knowledge – but rather in order "to check and strengthen it" (Bourdieu, 2004, p. 4). Thus, the critique of research gaps in community psychology is vital for strengthening the field.

29.2 Power and Definitions of Community

Fundamental to any discussion of community psychology begins with consideration about the tensions inherent in the concept of "community" itself. In being such a central concept to the identity and doxa of community psychology, it is of vital importance to highlight that this is an intrinsically fraught and contentious term (Burton & Kagan, 2016). Although the concept of community is integral to community psychology and used in a widespread and manner, it has also garnered much critique, partly attributed to its ideological usage (Burton & Kagan, 2016). Thus, the term may be used in ways that mask or normalize deep-seated political agendas and serve to uphold the interests of the privileged.

Thus, it is important to consider the ways in which the term community is used. For instance, on what basis is a community defined, and for what purpose? Who decides who belongs together in a community and who is left out? What parameters are used to define communities and why? And what are the possible implications of these issues in terms of decision-making, participation, access to resources, inclusivity, representativity, historical, cultural, and symbolic significance? If we start to grasp the complexities of defining communities we can start to appreciate the multifaceted dimensions of community work itself – we can start to understand why community psychology can be so incredibly challenging. Yet, despite this inherent dilemma, the applied nature of community psychology requires that we nevertheless endeavor to define the parameters of communities, to impose the necessary focus and boundaries for engaging in community work.

In a pragmatic sense, then, communities can be seen as entities that serve as intermediaries between the individual and the social levels of society (Campbell & Murray, 2004). Thus, communities may include diverse and heterogeneous groups of people based in a common geographical area or locality, or they may be defined relationally as having a shared goal, purpose, social identity, or set of experiences (Campbell & Murray, 2004; Fox, Easpaig, & Watson, 2019; Kloos et al., 2012). In this way, communities may be self-defined, defined by others, or their membership may be incidental, with members otherwise sharing little in common (Fox et al., 2019). They may be comprised of cohesive groups of people that have long-standing connections and shared histories based on their mutual affiliations, or they may have weak social ties (Kloos et al., 2012). They may have finite or ever-shifting compositions. The concept of community suggests a single affiliation that is misleading, as people usually belong to multiple different and/or intersecting communities simultaneously, and therefore communities also exist in both a spatial dimension (be it social, functional, virtual, or geographical space) or temporal (historical, present, or imagined future space).

It may be useful to identify the characteristics of a particular community when engaged in community practice that involves service delivery or to engage in community research (Campbell & Murray, 2004), bearing in mind that there are objective, subjective, and temporal dimensions to who is considered a member. While communities may have positive connotations that suggest a sense of belonging and togetherness, this may not be the experience of all people within them. Thus, referring to communities may portray groups in a manner that conceals deeply painful social and political realities.

In reflecting on the ideological nature of defining communities, Burton and Kagan (2016) highlight that community is often used in the political sphere to garner support for a cause. In the Global North, for example, the promotion of notions of community inclusivity has been used to justify cuts in welfare spending to marginalized groups (such as the disabled or elderly), which may increase the burden of care for families and particularly women (Cool cited in Burton & Kagan, 2016).

Several scholars in the decolonial tradition have likewise pointed to the ideological aspects of the term community in the Global South. For example, defining groups of people as belonging to "communities" can also be the basis of grouping people in ways that may be othering, divisive, and used to control or manipulate resources or used within dominant ideologies to justify hierarchical social relations, exclusion, and oppression (Dutta, 2018). For example, Butchart and Seedat (1990) highlight that the term community was

used in South Africa under apartheid to implicitly support the state's segrega-
tionist policies of separate development and legislated racial difference, which
was used to maintain social inequalities. This, in itself, was a manifestation of
a more deeply entrenched history and system of colonial thought and practice,
and foregrounds the inherent racialization of communities in this context
(Carolissen et al., 2010). Thus, in South Africa using the term community
has been used to imply working with poor, Black, and/or marginalized populations (Painter, Terre Blanche, & Henderson, 2006) and this has also become
the perceived focus of community psychology (Carolissen et al., 2010). For
example, White, privileged students may refer to going "into the community"
as working in informal settlements occupied largely by poor Black people.
This illustrates how the very concept of community invokes complex power
relations that are intricately related to sociohistorical and geographical contexts, as well as larger global configurations.

Dutta (2018) argues that the use of the concept of community in community
psychology itself needs to be decolonized. This means awareness that the use
of the term community psychology is rooted in the ideologies of establishment
psychology, which some say has been used to perpetuate privilege and justify
social marginalization. For example, the assumption of community as an
already constituted, coherent group rather than one that is constructed, sets
up a power relation between "expert" (colonial) knowledge and reifies "the
community" as a homogenous, depoliticized object of inquiry (Dutta, 2018).

The discursive construction of communities as sites of human suffering or
intervention undermines the multiple relational possibilities between community psychologists and communities thereby entrenching the traditional
hierarchy of power that renders people and contexts as subservient to our
disciplinary expertise. Disrupting these traditional notions of community
involves acknowledging the multiplicity of relationships, practices, and know-
ledges that may be cocreated though the process of mutual rather than one-
dimensional engagement (Dutta, 2018).

This requires that community psychologists need to be cognizant of discourses of dominance and marginalization that may underpin how they define
communities. Thus, it is important to remain aware that communities are
profoundly structured by the social relations of the broader societies they are
embedded within, and are therefore deeply implicated in how these realities
are experienced (Campbell & Murray, 2004). This brings additional but
necessary complexity to the establishing focus of community psychology that
is important for students, academics, practitioners, and professionals who
engage in this sphere. Thinking about histories and relations of power is
therefore an important consideration in community research and practice,
and underpin existing divisions of privilege and marginalization. Structural
inequalities related to race, gender, and class are deeply entrenched systems of
power embedded within social structures and institutions. Discourses of marginalization shift continuously and new forms of marginalization and

exclusion are emerging all the time. Community psychology should focus on a broad spectrum of the population, with particular concern for marginalized positions, groups and identities, decentring dominant identities, and/or understanding the dynamics between dominance and marginalization. In research, scholarship should represent the diversity of community life so that lessons can be drawn about community functioning and community building across the globe. Whilst maintaining diversity, we would also expect community psychologists to foreground the position and voices of the socially excluded, as these are the most likely to be silenced.

29.3 The Study of Published Work in Community Psychology

Journals are highly complex sites of knowledge production that reflect the nexus of intrinsic and extrinsic knowledge and power unique to each discipline. Martin, Lounsbury, and Davidson (2004, p. 163) note that journal articles denote the focus of research in the field, and thereby highlight "the people, places, events, and ideas that shape it." The analysis of published work in community psychology is situated within a framework of sociopolitical influences and psychological disciplinary power. Scholars may be quite familiar with the routine processes and procedures of academic knowledge production and the culmination of intellectual assertion, exchange, modification, and censure in the formulation of published work. However, authors of research and academic writing in community psychology may not always be fully cognizant of the broader state of the collective of knowledge that is produced, as well as the ideological forces beneath, within, and beyond our field that we enact and reinforce as a collective, as well as the influences from our unique social context and global positioning that come to be represented in our work. For this reason, the studies of the trends in community psychology publications have played a vital role in providing the field with feedback on the relevant gaps and shortcomings in research, and have particularly highlighted areas of mismatch between its empirical basis and stated ideology (Jason et al., 2007). Thus, they have attested to the assertion that knowledge has the potential to reinscribe, contest, or disrupt the dominant power relations that exist both within and outside of community psychology, through its choices of theory and methods. This is important because it has implications for how community psychologists represent, think about, and practice in communities.

29.3.1 Research Synopsis

This section of the chapter presents selected findings from a larger study of trends in community psychology research (see Graham, 2014). The data presented here is drawn from the *American Journal of Community Psychology* (AJCP), *Journal of Community Psychology* (JCP), *Journal of*

Prevention and Intervention in the Community (JPIC), and *Journal of Community and Applied Social Psychology* (JCASP) from January 2000 to December 2009. Each of these journals occupies an esteemed position within community psychology globally. The AJCP and JCP have frequently appeared in a spectrum of research on knowledge production trends in community psychology, including trends related to social group representation and related asymmetries, such as a focus on gender (Angelique & Culley, 2000, 2003), culture and ethnicity (Bernal & Enchautegui-de-Jesus, 1994; Loo, Fong, & Iwamasa, 1988), as well as intersections of gender, culture, and other forms of social exclusion (Graham, 2017; Gutierez, 2010), interdisciplinary linkages with organizational psychology (Boyd, 2014; Boyd & Angelique, 2002), health psychology (Duncan, 1991), critical scholarship (Davidson et al., 2006), and trends related to general topics, methods, and theories (Graham & Ismail, 2011; Lounsbury et al., 1979; Lounsbury et al., 1980; Martin et al., 2004; Novaco & Monahan, 1980; Speer et al., 1992). Other analyses have focused on specific theoretical constructs, such as social power (Angelique et al., 2013), or topics, such as HIV/AIDS (Graham & Shirley, 2014). Some have also investigated publishing trends related to institutional ranking (Jason et al., 2007) and citation networks (Watling Neal, Janulis, & Collins, 2013). With the exception of the JCASP in Schruijer and Stephenson (2010), the JCASP and JPIC have been largely overlooked in previous research on publications trends, but these journals were included as they are valuable sources of international community psychology knowledge. In this study, only community-relevant articles of the JCASP were included in the analysis.

The findings presented here were selected from the analysis of empirical studies involving human participants, and address three main questions: (1) What theories do community psychologists use? (2) What methods do community psychologists use? and, lastly, (3) What topics do community psychologists study? This provides a basis from which gaps in community psychology, and ways of responding to these, are further discussed.

29.3.2 What Theories Do Community Psychologists Use?

The debate between advocating for the centrality of a particular theoretical framework for community psychology versus embracing greater epistemological diversity is long-standing (Toro, 2005). Proponents of particular varieties of theory have argued why their theoretical positions are most relevant over the years, and the issue of establishing conceptual primacy has been a recurring theme. While Toro (2005) raises the desirability and complementarity of maintaining theoretical diversity, studies of knowledge production have provided evidence that certain approaches are more dominant than others (Graham & Ismail, 2011). The data presented here includes an analysis of the explicit theories or use of theoretical constructs that uses a multiple response format to allow for more than one theoretical preference in a single article. Theories and their associated constructs were drawn from the community psychology literature, as well as iteratively from the data, and grouped as follows:

- **Cultural Diversity:** Cultural values, cultural diversity, cultural competence, acculturation, or an emphasis on local or indigenous knowledge.
- **Ecological:** Theories about the interaction between ecological levels or systems, and fit between person and environment, including organizational settings and processes.
- **Empowerment:** Use of empowerment theory or principles associated with social action, social justice, or participation in social structures, such as problematization, citizen participation, and conscientization.
- **Postmodern:** Theories that are social constructionist, postmodern, or post-structuralist (e.g., that use theorists such as Michel Foucault and Jacques Derrida).
- **Prevention:** Use of a public health or community mental health perspective, including health or mental health promotion, and the prevention of mental disorders/illness, physical illness, and associated risk and resilience factors.
- **Sense of Community (SOC):** Aspects of sense of community or support for community structures, social capital, and communal relationships.
- **Social Psychology:** Classic social psychology theories related to identity, stereotypes, prejudice, intergroup relations (e.g., attribution theory, social comparison theory, contact hypothesis, social identity theory).
- **Structuralist:** Structuralist critical theory, including postcolonial theory, Marxist theory, feminist theory, critical race theory, and activity theory.
- **Traditional:** Classic psychological theory (e.g., psychoanalysis, cognitive behavioral theory, attachment theory), other theories centered on the individual (e.g., sense of coherence), and theories related to the physiology of stress or models of health beliefs and behavior (e.g., health belief model, theory of reasoned action).

Theoretical trends are presented in Table 29.1 (N cases = 895; N responses = 1,386).

Table 29.1 shows that theories linked to the concept of *prevention* were by far the most popular (33.7%), followed by *traditional* psychological theories (16.7%) and *ecological* approaches (14.1%). Contrary to community psychology's ideals, most authors show a clear preference for biomedical epistemologies related to public health, ecological theories, or individualist psychological perspectives. Epistemologies related to empowerment, sense of community, and social psychology were more characteristic of articles in specific journals than pervasive features of community psychology scholarship. Critical, structuralist, political, postmodern, and economic theories were rarely or never utilized to understand community phenomena. This shows the closer alliance between community psychology, mainstream psychology, and the allied health fields. Any endeavor to shift this dominance will require

Table 29.1 *Theories in community psychology publications (2000–2009)*

	AJCP n (%)	JCP n (%)	JCASP n (%)	JPIC n (%)	All n (%)
Prevention	109 (23.7)	210 (45.5)	42 (22.8)	106 (37.7)	467 (33.7)
Traditional	142 (30.9)	40 (8.7)	23 (12.5)	27 (9.6)	232 (16.7)
Ecological	69 (15.0)	56 (12.1)	15 (8.2)	55 (19.6)	195 (14.1)
Empowerment	58 (12.6)	44 (9.5)	25 (13.6)	23 (8.2)	150 (10.8)
SOC	22 (4.8)	54 (11.7)	16 (8.7)	21 (7.5)	113 (8.2)
Cultural diversity	21 (4.6)	46 (10.0)	8 (4.3)	27 (9.6)	102 (7.4)
Structuralist	35 (7.6)	6 (1.3)	31 (16.8)	12 (4.3)	84 (6.1)
Social	1 (0.2)	2 (0.4)	10 (5.4)	6 (2.1)	19 (1.4)
Postmodern	0 (0.0)	0 (0.0)	0 (0.0)	0 (0.0)	0 (0.0)
Total (n responses)	459 (100.0)	462 (100.0)	184 (100.0)	281 (100.0)	1,386 (100.0)

strengthening other forms of interdisciplinarity, especially with regards to critical social sciences in order shift the doxa of the field. Queer theory, critical race theory, liberation theory, postcolonial/decolonization theory, and post-structuralist theory all have the potential to enhance the critical theoretical underpinnings of community psychology (Evans et al., 2017), but are fairly absent in published work.

29.3.3 What Methods Do Community Psychologists Use?

While previous trend analyses have revealed an overreliance on the traditional scientific approach, this was far more prominent in the earliest publications (see, e.g., Lounsbury et al., 1980; Novaco & Monahan, 1980). Speer et al. (1992) later identified the increased use of qualitative research methods in the 1980s. Studies of articles published in the 1990s continued to identify the dominance of quantitative research methods, but noted an increase in the use of qualitative methods and multimethod designs (Martin et al., 2004).

In the study reported here, the *research approach* was regarded as (1) *positivist* if the methodology involved numerical or scientific measurement, the use of correlational, experimental, or quasi-experimental research designs, quantitative data collection, and statistical analyses; (2) *interpretive* if the study involved the understanding of participants' subjective experiences and perceived meaning of phenomena, using qualitative data collection methods (e.g., unstructured interviews and participant observation); (3) *critical* if a study aimed to uncover and rectify power asymmetries; (4) *mixed method* if it used both quantitative and qualitative data collection, interpretation, and/or analyses; and an (5) *applied community method* if the research involved (a) a needs analysis, (b) policy research, (c) participatory action research, or (d) a program evaluation.

The results in Table 29.2 show the utilization of a range of research approaches, but most research articles were positivist in methodological orientation (69.1%). This was a consistent trend, though the proportion of positivist research was lower in some journals. *Interpretive* research (14.6%) and *applied* research (9.2%) followed by a substantial margin. *Critical* research was the least represented research paradigm (2.5%). While the inclusion of a variety of approaches, including applied and participatory community approaches, is encouraging, the results still suggest relatively entrenched dominance in terms of methodological preferences. The low level of research conducted with a critical paradigm is notable and suggests the marginalization of this approach in community psychology scholarship (Kagan et al., 2011b).

A further investigation into methods of data collection highlights further gaps (see Table 29.3). The first six methods categories discussed here were

Table 29.2 *Primary research approach in community psychology publications (2000–2009)*

	AJCP n (%)	JCP n (%)	JCASP n (%)	JPIC n (%)	All n (%)
Positivist	194 (82.6)	300 (80.0)	64 (44.4)	60 (42.6)	618 (69.1)
Interpretive	3 (1.3)	41 (10.9)	58 (40.3)	29 (20.6)	131 (14.6)
Applied	11 (4.7)	16 (4.3)	10 (6.9)	45 (31.9)	82 (9.2)
Mixed	7 (3.0)	18 (4.8)	10 (6.9)	7 (5.0)	42 (4.7)
Critical	20 (8.5)	0 (0.0)	2 (1.4)	0 (0.0)	22 (2.5)
Total	235 (100.0)	375 (100.0)	144 (100.0)	141 (100.0)	895 (100.0)

Table 29.3 *Method of data collection in community psychology publications (2000–2009)*

	AJCP n (%)	JCP n (%)	JCASP n (%)	JPIC n (%)	All n (%)
Survey	134 (57.0)	156 (46.1)	41 (28.5)	53 (37.6)	384 (42.9)
Multimethod	27 (11.5)	89 (23.7)	28 (19.4)	26 (18.4)	170 (19.0)
Test	16 (6.8)	55 (14.7)	2 (1.4)	1 (0.7)	74 (8.3)
Qualitative	25 (10.6)	36 (9.6)	55 (38.2)	18 (12.8)	134 (15.0)
Quasi-experimental	10 (4.3)	19 (5.1)	3 (2.1)	14 (9.9)	46 (5.1)
Experimental	12 (5.1)	11 (2.9)	7 (4.9)	7 (5.0)	37 (4.1)
Archival	3 (1.3)	9 (2.4)	0 (0.0)	8 (5.7)	20 (2.2)
Autobiography	0 (0.0)	0 (0.0)	0 (0.0)	14 (9.9)	16 (1.8)
Other	8 (2.4)	0 (0.0)	8 (5.6)	0 (0.0)	14 (1.6)
Total	235 (100.0)	375 (100.0)	144 (100.0)	141 (100.0)	895 (100.0)

developed by Zebian et al. (2007). These methods involved using (1) a self-report *survey* or structured questionnaire; (2) a standardized *test or scale*; (3) *experimental* methods; (4) *quasi-experimental* methods; (5) *qualitative* methods (e.g., semi-structured interviews and focus group discussions); and (6) *archival* studies that drew on preexisting records or data (e.g., hospital records, police statistics, reports). Additional categories emerged from the data that reflected new developments in data collection or methods specific to community psychology. These were (7) *multimethod* studies (more than one primary method) and (8) *autobiographies* in which the data was the life history or personal experiences of the author. Data that did not fall into these categories was coded as (9) *other*. This included the use of novel technological methods of data collection such as telephone recordings, video footage, and Geographic Information Systems (GIS) coordinates.

Interestingly, despite its strong positivist slant, there has been a staggering decline in the use of what Macleod (2004) terms "hard science" quantitative research designs, such as experimental and quasi-experimental research. For instance, only 4.1% of studies used experimental designs (5.1% in the AJCP and 2.9% in the JCP) and 5.1% used quasi-experimental designs (4.3% in the AJCP and 5.9% in the JCP) from 2000 to 2009. By comparison, Novaco and Monahan (1980) reported 51.8% of studies in the AJCP had experimental designs from 1973 to1978. Lounsbury et al. (1980) found that 39% used experimental designs in the AJCP and JCP, which then dropped to 22.0% in the 1984–1988 period (Speer et al., 1992), and then 9.3% in the AJCP from 1993 to 1998 (Martin et al., 2004). The reported use of quasi-experimental designs has showed a similar pattern of decline. Lounsbury et al. (1980) found that 58.0% used quasi-experimental designs from 1973 to 1978 in the AJCP and JCP, compared to a peak of 73.0% in 1984–1988 (Speer et al., 1992). A substantial decrease in the use of quasi-experimental designs was later reported in the AJCP to 19.8% in the years from 1993 to 1998 (Martin et al., 2004).

The low proportion of studies using this design reported here confirms the gains noted by Martin et al. (2004) in the use of more naturalistic research approaches. However, the current study suggests that survey research is now the most common form of research design, which is consistent with Orford's (2008) observation about a growing emphasis in community psychology on social epidemiology. The appropriateness of survey designs as a dominant data collection method for community psychology is questionable for those advocating for a more critical orientation. Though some shifts have been noted with respect to the greater inclusion of qualitative and mixed method research in community psychology, published research reflects the choice of less critical paradigms and methods. Qualitative analyses were largely restricted to content analysis or interpretive analytic methods, with critical thematic analysis or discourse analysis being extremely rare.

Burton and Kagan (2016) identify the tendency of community psychologists to settle for a restricted methodological repertoire, particularly noting the

prominence of statistical techniques such as multiple regression for understanding community phenomena. They are equally critical of authors that
show an exclusive "retreat to text" in preference to methods linked to community action and engagement. It is worthwhile thinking about the reasons for
such methodological enclaves or retreats, as they may be important social,
economic, or ideological factors underpinning them that we need to be more
cognizant of.

The representation of social groups in the samples of these published studies
has been explored in more detail elsewhere (see Graham, 2017). However, it is
important to note that power imbalances are similarly evident, which show the
historical dominance of privileged or mixed groups, and the continued exclusion of marginalized groups, in the methodological choices of researchers. For
example, Graham (2017) highlights that most empirical studies in community
psychology publications used data collected in North America (72.7%),
followed by Europe (14.3%) and then Australia (6.1%), showing the dominance of minority world countries in community psychology publications. The
overall patterns suggest that there is a paucity of research from Latin America,
Africa, and Asia (Graham, 2017). Most research in community psychology
journals from 2000 to 2009 involved participants comprised of US groups of
mixed ethnic composition, with limited focus on US *minority populations*
(African American, Hispanic and Native American, Asian American) that
was consistent with previous research on publication trends related to minority groups (Bernal & Enchautegui-de-Jesus, 1994; Loo et al., 1988). In the
studies that focused on marginalized groups, structural forms of social exclusion such as race/ethnicity, gender, and socioeconomic status featured most
strongly. A focus on these forms of structural inequality is important; however, there are several marginalized groups that remain neglected in community psychology, including the elderly, the unemployed, people with
disabilities, people with alternative gender identities and sexualities, migrants,
people in rural areas, and people living with HIV/AIDS, as well as intersections between these forms of social exclusion with structural inequalities
(Graham, 2017).

29.3.4 What Topics Do Community Psychologists Study?

Loo et al. (1988) argue that particular types of content are suggestive of a
field's level of commitment to a knowledge domain. From this perspective,
subject choice reflects the prioritization of particular content areas over
others. Examining trends in content thus has the potential to highlight shifts
in priorities over time. Previous studies of trends in knowledge production
have noted that the topics of research have changed over the past fifty years.
For example, Lounsbury et al. (1979) found that research in the 1970s
focused on the impact of social systems on individual functioning, particularly examining the effects of programs, policies, and interventions on

psychological variables among mentally ill populations. The salient topics were related to establishing the boundaries of community psychology, the training imperatives for community psychologists, a broader conceptual understanding of mental illness and a set of interventions to improve the situation of the mentally ill, and there was a limited focus on social issues (Lounsbury et al., 1979). In the 1980s, one of the notable shifts was a profound increase of 22% in studies on the topic of social support (Speer et al., 1992). In the 1990s, Martin et al. (2004) reported an increase in articles on *specific problem areas or issues* to 82%, with certain topics, like *HIV AIDS*, *violence/victimization*, and *prevention*, being sufficiently prominent to be independently coded for the first time (Martin et al., 2004).

Table 29.4 describes each of the topics evident from the publications that were studied from 2000 to 2009, and captures the complexity and range of topics in contemporary community psychology. Table 29.4 shows how each topic was categorized by providing a detailed description of the emerging themes, with illustrative examples of the types of concepts that were included within each topic area. This provides the researcher with a sense of the dominant ways of conceptualizing and writing about research foci in community psychology.

Table 29.5 presents the frequencies for topics in community psychology journals. The top five most frequent topics in descending order were (1) *child, youth, and family* (17.8%; $n = 365$); (2) *social networks and social support* (14.6%; $n = 299$); (3) *difference and exclusion* (11.6%; $n = 238$); (4) *mental health and mental illness* (11.2%; $n = 230$); and 5) *violence and abuse* (7.4%; $n = 152$). By and large, these trends were consistent across the journals.

The results reflect some interesting shifts that are worth pointing out. The focus on child, youth, and family development appears as the most popular and differentiated topic but did not appear as prominently in previous historical periods. This may reflect a broader contemporary trend toward a focus on children and the family, arguably part of the shift toward neoliberalism in society (Woolhouse, Day, & Rickett, 2019). Social networks and support and mental health and mental illness have been relatively consistent and popular topics in community psychology over the past two decades, but difference and exclusion has become more prominent, and, as in the 1990s, violence and abuse has remained an established feature of community psychology in the 2000s.

While these topics show diversity and consideration of individual, family and social issues, they were most often paired with the use of traditional psychological and preventionist approaches rather than critical or structuralist or poststructuralist theoretical frameworks, or critically oriented or participatory methodological choices. This suggests that while there have been gains in the prominence of social issues in community psychology, there remains a largely reductive, individualistic, and hierarchical understanding of well-being and community that may not place sufficient emphasis on the role of broader

Topic Name	Detailed Topic Description	Coding Examples
Mental health & mental illness	Indicators of wellness, adjustment, and psychopathology, including understanding, preventing, or treating a specific psychological condition or mental disorder; promoting mental health, well-being, adjustment, or quality of life; traditional forms of treatment and caregiving for the mentally ill; attitudes toward mental illness.	Psychiatric disability; serious mental illness; depressive symptoms; psychological well-being; burnout; suicide rates; mental health treatment; co-occurring mental disorders; general psychological distress; stressful life events; anxiety; aggression; psychological adjustment; help-seeking behavior; treatment choice; crisis intervention.
Social networks & social support	Understanding or measuring the role or effects of social networks; social cohesion; social capital; social support; components of sense of community.	Community connectedness; social support; social cohesion; social integration; promoting social capital; sense of community; quality of social support network; community integration; social disorganization; collective socialization; belongingness; structural and affiliative social support; social network analysis.
Difference & exclusion	The situation of socially marginalized groups; interaction between socially marginalized and powerful groups; social dynamics related to dimensions of diversity (e.g., age, gender, race, religion, culture, ethnicity, sexual orientation).	Bicultural stress, race, racism, cultural marginalization, cultural competence, patriarchal ideology, gender consciousness, addressing homophobia; negative attitudes to persons with physical disabilities; gender discrimination; prejudice and social values; acculturation; old-fashioned racism; ethnic and migrant differences.
Child, youth, & family	Children, adolescents, and families in all spheres of life, including development, influences, and outcomes.	Youth development; youth mentoring; behavioral problems; school participation; family detachment; parenthood transition; parental monitoring; academic success; parent–child relationship; developmental parenting; family milieu of children; children's school adjustment.
Neighborhood & residential	The description or effects of geographical and neighborhood characteristics or features related to the built environment and residential housing.	Environmental resources; residential stability; neighborhood effects; housing satisfaction; perception of neighborhood environment; perceptions of place; quality of physical environment; neighborhood planning.
Civic participation	The active participation and involvement of citizens in decisions affecting them and in effecting community transformation or change through community organizations, activities, and groups.	Community advocacy; community organizing; community action; activism; civic engagement; political participation; community leadership; resident participation; opportunities for increasing participation in community coalitions; community building using residents to drive change processes; political self-efficacy; citizen influence; control of resources; barriers to participation.

Table 29.4 (cont.)

Topic Name	Detailed Topic Description	Coding Examples
Violence & abuse	The predictors or effects of self-directed, interpersonal, and community violence or abuse, including violence and abuse of a physical, emotional, economic, or sexual nature, as well as all forms of exploitation and neglect.	Violence exposure; effects of victimization; bullying; disclosure of sexual assault; intimate partner violence; domestic violence; reporting physical assault; impact of community violence; adolescent violence; street violence; sexual coercion and consent.
Sexual outcomes & HIV/AIDS	Sexual practices and their effects, including sexual risk behavior, teenage pregnancy, knowledge of and risk for contracting STIs; the treatment and management of HIV/AIDS; as well as coping with associated stigma.	Perceptions about condom use; HIV/AIDS treatment; condom use self-efficacy; coping with HIV infection; HIV disclosure; HIV risk management; HIV-related stigma; risk of HIV exposure; knowledge of HIV; HIV prevention services.
Poverty, welfare, & homelessness	The experiences, risks for, or effects of homelessness, poverty, or being economically disadvantaged or a recipient of the welfare system.	Needs and experiences of homeless people; individuals with histories of homelessness; poverty; psychological sense of economic hardship; economic survival strategies; cross-national comparisons of homelessness; welfare recipients; street homelessness; reducing homelessness; rough sleeping; homeless achieving economic stability; life experiences of homeless adults; poor families receiving public assistance; homeless/housed families; risk and resilience related to homelessness; transition from welfare to work.
Substance use & abuse	The use or abuse of substances such as alcohol, drugs, and cigarettes, including substance risk identification and prevention, and the treatment of addiction and substance abuse.	Substance abuse recovery homes; substance abuse treatment; access to tobacco; determinants of dropout from a substance abuse case management program; substance abuse behaviors, norms, and attitudes; smokers' self-confidence to stop smoking; untreated heavy drinkers; drug misuse; levels of ecstasy use; heroin addiction; drug addiction and becoming drug-free; stable and escalating patterns of substance abuse.
Crime & criminal justice	The occurrence, incidence, or consequences of crime, attitudes about crime and safety in communities, and issues related to the criminal justice system.	Fear of crime; criminal legal system; concern about crime as a social problem; criminal victimization; crime prevention advice; knowledge of police activities; community policing; recidivism rates for offenders; exposure to neighborhood crime; incarceration; realities of the criminal justice system.

	issues related to HIV and sexual outcomes).	perception of health; injury events; risk for diabetes; accident frequency; disease risk; physical health; health disparities.
Disasters & war	The effects of widespread devastation due to natural disaster (e.g., flood or earthquake), man-made incidents, or national and international emergency or war.	Terrorism exposure; flood impact; disaster impact; natural disaster; September 11 terrorist attacks; Gulf war veterans; mass destruction and disaster, hurricane Katrina; exposure to the World Trade Center disaster; national community war effort.
Technology & media	The use or impact of the use of technology or forms of media (e.g., the Internet, newspapers, or television).	TV viewing; media stereotypes; mass media; media preference, interactive CD-ROM; internet technology; public communication campaigns; internet-based communication; technology divides.
Scale development & testing	The review, development, or novel use of any psychological or community-based scale.	Psychometric properties and scale development; psychometric properties of the multidimensional scale of perceived social support; reliability and validity of the sociopolitical control scale; psychometric properties of the volunteer functions inventory; psychometric scale properties; measurement; construct validity.
Intervention execution & evaluation	The description, assessment, or outcome of considerations related to intervention design, implementation, or evaluation.	Frameworks of program development; program evaluation; implementation problems; program efficacy; outcomes demonstration and evaluation; program adherence in real-world settings; target recipient responsivity; material quality; implementer prioritization.
Occupational issues	The description of factors related to the occupational status or challenges of individuals, or factors related to the work environment or organizational setting.	Involvement in organizational planning; organizational setting; shift of economic risk from employers to employees; staff reductions; organizational change; industrial conflict and dispute; perception of organizational fairness; effects of job demands; organizational processes.
Social policy & funding climate	The use, effects, or development of social and funding policies, including factors related to the political order and funding climate.	Social policy on future education; welfare to work policy; impact of welfare reform; policies on child welfare; federal and state policy; state loan programs; policy implementation gaps.
Human resources & training	The experiences of training and working in community psychology and other health and service professions and workers, including human resource considerations relating to paraprofessionals and community volunteers.	Volunteer training; professional development as a community psychologist; motivations of community psychologists in applied settings; training for social services; training of health professionals; mandatory community service; attracting students to community psychology programs; volunteering in community organizations.

Table 29.5 *Topic frequencies in community psychology publications (2000–2009)*

	AJCP n (%)	JCP n (%)	JCASP n (%)	JPIC n (%)	All n (%)
Child, youth, & family	107 (18.7)	162 (18.7)	43 (13.2)	53 (18.3)	365 (17.8)
Social networks & support	90 (15.7)	141 (16.3)	53 (16.3)	15 (5.2)	299 (14.6)
Difference & exclusion	69 (12.1)	88 (10.2)	52 (16.0)	29 (10.0)	238 (11.6)
Mental health & mental illness	64 (11.2)	97 (11.2)	36 (11.1)	33 (11.4)	230 (11.2)
Violence & abuse	44 (7.7)	66 (7.6)	19 (5.8)	23 (8.0)	152 (7.4)
Civic participation	22 (3.8)	57 (6.6)	24 (7.4)	12 (4.2)	115 (5.6)
Substance use & abuse	26 (4.5)	43 (5.0)	13 (4.0)	20 (6.9)	102 (5.0)
Welfare, poverty, & homelessness	36 (6.3)	28 (3.2)	11 (3.4)	15 (5.2)	90 (4.4)
Neighborhood & residential	24 (4.2)	40 (4.6)	9 (2.8)	6 (2.1)	79 (3.9)
Sexual outcomes & HIV/AIDS	20 (3.5)	16 (1.8)	11 (3.4)	17 (5.9)	64 (3.1)
Physical illness & injury	14 (2.4)	24 (2.8)	12 (3.7)	13 (4.5)	63 (3.1)
Intervention execution & evaluation	6 (1.0)	22 (2.5)	6 (1.8)	15 (5.2)	49 (2.4)
Work-related & organizational	12 (2.1)	17 (2.0)	10 (3.1)	6 (2.1)	45 (2.2)
Human resources & training	3 (0.5)	13 (1.5)	8 (2.5)	15 (8.7)	39 (1.9)
Crime & criminal justice	11 (1.9)	19 (2.2)	4 (1.2)	2 (0.7)	36 (1.8)
Media use & effects	3 (0.5)	9 (1.0)	8 (2.5)	6 (2.1)	26 (1.3)
Scale development & testing	6 (1.0)	16 (1.8)	1 (0.3)	3 (1.0)	26 (1.3)
Social policy & funding climate	10 (1.7)	0 (0.0)	3 (0.9)	4 (1.4)	17 (0.8)
Disasters & war	5 (0.9)	7 (0.8)	2 (0.6)	2 (0.7)	16 (0.8)
Total	572 (100.0)	865 (100.0)	325 (100.0)	289 (100.0)	2,051 (100.0)

social structures, access to power, and processes of inequality in understanding psychological and community phenomena. This can contribute to the perpetuation of victim-blaming ideologies that are prevalent in society (Ryan, 1971). This is similarly evident in the dominant disease-based models of mental health in mainstream psychology (Ahmed & Suffla, 2007). Ultimately, this points to the injustice of holding individuals responsible for their own health and distress, which may be influenced by social conditions beyond their control, such as race and class. It signals the importance of looking at broader social structures when thinking about psychological experiences, and making connections between these spheres. Ideologies that promote victim-blaming can be located as part of a broader neoliberal agenda that characterizes many postindustrialized countries.

The least frequent topics, in ascending order, were (1) disasters and war (0.8%; *n* = 16), (2) social policy and funding climate (0.8%; *n* = 17), (3) scale development and testing (1.3%; $n = 26$), (4) media use and effects (1.3%; $n = 26$), and (5) crime and criminal justice (1.8%; $n = 36$). Some topics appear to be fairly new areas for community psychologists in the journals that were investigated, such as media use and effects. Though the topic of disasters and war was proportionately very small, it is also significant to note that this is the first time this topic has emerged in community psychology, which may also highlight a shift in community psychology in response to national crises and significant global events.

Scale development and testing seemed low in comparison to previous studies, signaling that the use and development of scales and their psychometric properties may be decreasing in popularity, as has been similarly evident in mainstream psychology. It is suggested that we need to see greater engagement from community psychologists around topics related to the effects of neoliberalism on communities, issues of inequality between the Global North and Global South, and decolonization. Other issues that may become more evident in community psychology over the coming decades are topics related to environmental activism, sustainable development, and the food and water crisis (Burton & Kagan, 2016).

29.4 How Can Community Psychologists Respond to These Gaps?

Responding to the gaps in community psychology theory and practice requires adopting a stance of reflexivity, critical consciousness, and action in relation to several key areas that have been identified in this chapter. These are foregrounding aspects of our work that we may overlook or take for granted. The rationale for each is discussed in the following sections.

29.4.1 Nurturing Reflexivity, Critical Consciousness, and Critical Action

Reflexivity is a strategy through which community psychologists can understand the complex power relations and positionality dilemmas inherent in more critically oriented forms of community psychology (Suffla, Seedat, & Bawa, 2014). This involves thinking about reflexivity in terms of our own identity and positionality and as community psychologists, and how we can engage more meaningfully with people we work with. This includes gaining greater insights into our own positionality within dynamics of power, which can be thought about as a nuanced and multidimensional form of reflexivity that includes intellectual, relational, and emotional components (Burton & Kagan, 2016).

Reflexivity also extends to gaining greater understanding of those with whom community psychologists collaborate with in practice, be they community members, professionals from other disciplines, or students. It is important that we remain cognizant of the discourses and ideologies that shape our positions and choices and those of whom we engage with. Reflexivity is also needed about the nature of the research we conduct, the deeper motivations and possible effects of the choices we make, and the relational possibilities we create and foreclose on with others via the process of inquiry. Finally, reflexivity is needed with regard to power dynamics articulated by the dominant voices, ideas, and methods espoused within community psychology itself. This involves extending the frontiers of our awareness about the varied permutations of community psychology that exist around the world, as well as the broader global and social forces that shape knowledge generation. Relatedly, this also includes thinking about community psychology's positionality and ideological stance within the broader discipline of psychology.

Community psychology has established a global reach and footing. It has continued to pursue multiple trajectories and can be reinvigorated by changes in the social context and within psychology (Stevens, 2007). However, the current global neoliberal socioeconomic order and financial crisis have important implications for community psychologists, as these are associated with reduced funding for social interventions and welfare spending (Kagan et al., 2011b). However, the need for these interventions remains as pressing as ever, and community psychology can still position itself in terms of its unique contribution and its own agendas of social justice in research and action, both within and beyond psychology. This begins with reflexivity, which is linked to developing a *critical consciousness* about the social and structural basis of community phenomena that challenge power imbalances and generate alternate forms of knowledge through participatory methods (Suffla et al., 2014). Through developing critical consciousness, a community praxis of collective participation and *critical action* can be fostered. Critical action is created through deliberate efforts at social change, including social analysis, civic participation, and the creation of transformative social spaces. Critical action requires the clarification of theory and intention of social change, as well as leveraging positionality within change efforts (Kornbluh, Collins, & Kohfeldt, 2019).

29.4.2 Interdisciplinary and Extradisciplinary Collaboration

Community psychology can respond to gaps in its approach to knowledge and practice through dialogue and collaboration with partners and role players in diverse contexts. This involves commitment to a process of engaging with others about community work, both inside and outside the discipline. If we pay adequate attention to the diverse ways and contexts in which community psychology principles have been actualized in different parts of the world, we can promote fertile conceptual, contextual, and experiential grounds to strengthen the discipline.

Critical engagement can be offered related to community psychology through dialogue between academics and practitioners in varied global contexts. Dialogue needs to be fostered between community psychologists and community stakeholders. A renewed and increased commitment to interdisciplinary approaches is needed in community psychology, particularly with regard to understanding how community psychology research and intervention can be enriched and strengthened by the theories and methods of other disciplines.

An interdisciplinary community psychology approach is also necessary to address the complexity of social issues within which community psychologists engage (Kagan et al., 2011b). Here partnerships could fill gaps in community psychology's particular neglect of disciplines in the critical social sciences, such as sociology, political science, development studies, anthropology, and others. These theories are particularly relevant in the contemporary social world that is characterized by migration, globalization, and structural inequalities.

While the similitude between critical scholarship in the critical social sciences remains largely unexplored, this is fertile ground to enrich community psychology due to the confluence of values and aspirations (Davidson et al., 2006). This may require deliberate strategies on the part of community psychologists to forge and sustain interdisciplinary collaboration to compensate for the intrinsic bias of community psychologists toward the psychologization of community phenomena. This will address the insularity of community psychology in knowledge generation networks (Watling Neal et al., 2013).

Community psychology has much to gain from increased knowledge of the social, cultural, historical, and material aspects of communities. A key gap in knowledge requires a response that should translate into both theory and practice. Community psychologists can work at the boundaries of many disciplines and areas of professional practice. Community psychologists can also become more aware of the limits of their own knowledge (Kagan et al., 2011b) and seek appropriate collaboration, participation, and input from knowledgeable others to address these limitations and enhance the transformative potential of this knowledge.

29.4.3 Fostering Historicity

Fostering a sense of historicity is about developing an understanding that social and community phenomena occur within a particular time and place, and therefore have deeply embedded histories that shape their meanings (Hall, 2007). The histories of how ideas and events come to exist at a particular moment and the meanings they have in that historical context, as well as the possibilities they generate, and foreclose, are important. Understanding histories extends to understanding the multiple histories that exist of community psychology globally, and how these ideas surfaced and gained traction in different contexts in response to local contextual factors and disciplinary conditions within psychology (Stevens, 2007).

Understanding the connections between the past, present, and future involves developing a sensitivity to the importance of the role of context and the intricacies of power relations. We need to be aware of the histories of the contexts in which we engage as community psychologists, and how the power related to where we are today has been shaped by experiences of where we have been. When we start to observe and understand phenomena within their historical context, we also become more sensitive to interpreting what is needed for the future, and therefore open up possibilities for critical thinking and action. Within a decolonial mindset (a position that challenges the colonial origins of Western Scientific thought), our methodologies may be viewed as stemming from particular scientific traditions focused on the "other" that could be used to legitimize exclusion, marginalization, and oppression (Dutta, 2018). Meaningful critique that promotes shifts in power relations and a move away from such scientific traditions can only be generated from a position of understanding others, gaining insight into histories and different ways of knowing.

29.4.4 Promoting Methodological Pluralism and Innovation

Community psychologists are encouraged to develop competence in a range of research methodologies, especially those that promote participation and challenge the hierarchy of the traditional research relationship. They are encouraged to be open to alternative community-based strategies for both formal and informal means of information gathering. When we make certain research choices, we need to be aware that we are simultaneously excluding other possibilities, and can reflect upon our reasons for this (e.g., personal, social, institutional, and ideological), and the possible implications of these decisions –both intended and unintended.

Community psychologists are urged to critically evaluate the strengths and limitations of different methodologies. While some may argue that there are irreconcilable philosophical underpinnings to different methodological approaches, critical community psychologists emphasize the possibilities and advantages of using different methodologies (Burton & Kagan, 2016). Critical research paradigms support methodological flexibility, the use of a range of research methods, and the participation of communities in research. In the complex social world we find ourselves in today, one of the most valuable skills we can offer as community psychologists is our capacity for methodological reflexivity, versatility, innovation, and collective action. Community research methods can embrace creativity, inclusiveness, and explore opportunities for methodological advances and technological development.

One of the recent developments in community psychology has been the integration of technology into community research methods, including the use of data collection sources such as GIS coordinates, and the use of Photovoice. For example, Chirowodza et al. (2009) illustrate the value of combining the visualization capacity of GIS with participatory methods to capture the broader spatial and social contexts of communities and to map healthcare data. The Photovoice methodology uses photography as a tool for identifying and representing community strengths and concerns, in order to facilitate critical reflection, dialogue, and policy change (Wang & Burris, 1997). It has been particularly valuable in giving voice to the perspectives of historically marginalized populations in diverse contexts, such as the homeless, children and adolescents, women living in rural communities, people with disabilities, and survivors of gender-based violence (Lichty et al., 2019). More recent adaptions of the method within community psychology include pushing the boundaries of traditional photography to a larger scale through developing empowering online Photovoice platforms (see Lichty et al., 2019).

Researchers across the globe can now also access several large databases that harness technologies for getting community-level data fast. They have exposure to tools for community mapping, community profiling, census data, and other forms of collating population and neighborhood data. For example, Google Street View (freely available via Google's web page: http://maps.google.com) generates a synthesis of high-definition panoramic street views taken by camera-equipped cars that have driven down a particular street. This video footage provides a comprehensive 360° model of the streets that can be viewed as a virtual tour from any device (Odgers et al., 2012). Odgers et al. (2012) found Google Street View to be an innovative data collection methodology that is unobtrusive, cost-effective, and reliable in assessing children's neighborhood conditions. Several databases also exist that can be used to source population-level data. For example, UNdata (http//:data.un.org) provides free single-point internet access to global statistics on a range of areas such as agriculture, crime, gender, and population features, which can be used in education, policy development, and data dissemination (UNdata, 2020). The Gapminder database, an online tool produced by the Gapminder Foundation (www.gapminder.org), synthesizes data from global population, wealth, health, and development indicators (e.g., from the United Nations) and has an integrated data analysis program for exploring associations, as well as temporal and spatial patterns, in the data (LeBlanc, 2012).

The novel use of technology in community psychology extends not only to the evolution of research methods, but also opens up exciting prospects for enhancing research participation and community intervention (Milburn, 2016). These include the potential use of smartphones to enhance access and networking, information dissemination, and monitoring and evaluation efforts. Community psychologists in future generations will need to keep abreast of new developments in technology, and explore how these can be adapted for research and in efforts to contribute to methodological advancement in the field (Milburn, 2016).

Greater diversity of theory and methodology should be cultivated, along with flexibility, creativity, and the use of innovative methodological approaches

(Feis, 1990). The continued development of innovative methodologies for article analysis is also needed to support the generation of alternative forms of knowledge and practice. Here it would be useful to explore prospects for innovation for inquiry into the nature of community psychology scholarship. The enormity of the proliferation of publications that characterizes the current knowledge economy will make it increasingly more challenging to engage in research on trends in published work. However, publications are a multifarious and generative data source, and archival studies of published work can promote further reflexivity about shifting boundaries and power relations in the subdiscipline, as well as provide insights into its methodological, content, and theoretical concerns. Researching published work further provides vast opportunities for exploring new methodologies for data representation, reduction, and conversion and contributing to the advancement of mixed methods research, as well as potential for examining the longevity, interconnectedness, and influence of knowledge. Thus, the study of knowledge production in community psychology remains an area in which methodological aspects of data selection, representation, and analysis require future development.

29.4.5 Thinking about Who Benefits

In community psychology the role of research is integral to intervention. Research is conducted in many spaces both formally and informally, including industry, education, social development, health, and many other sectors. Much research in community psychology is conducted for funders, nongovernmental organizations (NGOs), community stakeholders, and government, and may be written up in technical reports, policy briefs, or other short reports that are never be published in academic fora. Likewise, academic research may never reach community partners. In some ways, the university has a unique intellectual role in actively devoting space, resources, and attention to the generation of ideas and thoughts about the world in a range of disciplines, but intellectuals need to become more socially engaged. One of its functions is to promote ideas, conversations, and shifts in thinking about complex topics and issues in society, but these should benefit a range of recipients, including students, academics, professionals, community leaders, and citizens of the broader public. The scrutiny of published work may signal which groups and ideas are privileged above others, and as such, where entrenched unequal power relations are evident. Reflexivity is needed to ensure that maximum benefit of community research is produced for a wide range of purposes, and actions should be geared to facilitate knowledge exchange between the public and academic spheres. Likewise, those community psychologists with "on the ground" community knowledge and experience need to influence spheres of knowledge production. In terms of knowledge generation across community psychology, particular attention is needed as to who benefits from the knowledge (and how) and who loses out (Fisher et al., 2007).

29.4.6 Shifting the Dominant Epistemological Frameworks in Community Psychology

This chapter has endeavored to respond to the decolonial imperative articulated by Dutta (2018) to "craft pathways that disrupt dominant modes of knowledge production and imagine non-hierarchical epistemic possibilities" in community psychology. Community psychologists often engage in critiques about psychology and broader social systems without sufficient self-critique about the more contentious aspects of this subdiscipline that may perpetuate privilege. While well-intentioned, community psychologists may be complicit in reinforcing existing hierarchies that support ideologies of social injustice. Community psychologists are encouraged to resist the commodification of knowledge into forms that reproduce acontextual, apolitical understandings of people – as these have widespread repercussions that uphold privilege and perpetuate social injustice against marginalized groups in the educational, health, economic, and social development spheres.

For community psychologists, the role of scholar and activist in the academy can be challenging, as this space reproduces social inequalities, especially for members of historically marginalized groups (Kornbluh et al., 2019). However, we should be mindful all the while of how we, even unwittingly, may recapitulate the status quo in this process, and foreclose on possibilities for alternative understandings about communities to exist. We therefore do need to take seriously the task of how we are positioned and position ourselves within communities, and how to create shifts in dominant power relations that allow for alternative positions and voices to emerge. In navigating this difficult terrain, we will need to try to resist the "grandiose rhetoric" that might at times characterize community psychology (Smail, 1994), as well as the paternalizing discourses of psychology and the helping professions more broadly (Dutta, 2018), which means being realistic and socially responsible in our roles as community psychologists.

It is also important to make space for ways of being, speaking, writing, and acting that are more nuanced, more polemical, and that promote greater epistemic reflexivity. In this regard it may be helpful to hold in mind the notion of the community psychologist as "boundary spanner" – meaning having the role of traversing social divides by occupying different positions (Rappaport, 2004). The efforts made to push the boundaries of the status quo, of our own levels of awareness, of the theories and methods we use, of the identities we assume, of how we relate to others, of knowledge, of discourse, may be among the ways to achieve this.

The gaps identified in theory, research, and practice suggest that we need to create narratives for community psychology that are reflexive, multifarious, nonhierarchical, authentic, socially, historically, and globally accountable, and challenging not only of others, but of ourselves, and our subdiscipline. These narratives need to question our "taken for granted" assumptions and may mean disrupting, unsettling, and even unlearning what we know to generate alternative ways of knowing. This chapter advocates working toward greater epistemic reflexivity and epistemic justice that foreground enactments of power, including those in knowledge-making practices. We need to expand our social theoretical base so that we can better account for how sociopolitical structures and histories in different societies shape our understandings of community life, promote the inclusion of critical social theories and critically oriented methodologies for community praxis, and find ways of engaging in interdisciplinary spaces. This can create innovative possibilities for alternative social analyses and prospects for action.

References

Ahmed, R., & Suffla, S. (2007). The mental health model: Preventing 'illness' or social inequality. In N. Duncan, B. Bowman, A. Naidoo, J. Pillay, & V. Roos (Eds.), *Community psychology: Analysis, context and action* (pp. 84–101). Cape Town, South Africa: University of Cape Town Press.

Angelique, H. L., & Culley, M. R. (2000). Searching for feminism: An analysis of CP literature relevant to women's concerns. *American Journal of Community Psychology*, *28*(6), 793–815. doi.org/10.1023/A:1005111800169

Angelique, H. L., & Culley, M. R. (2003). Feminism found: An examination of gender consciousness in community psychology. *Journal of Community Psychology*, *31*(3), 189–209. doi.org/10.1002/jcop.10050

Angelique, H. L., & Culley, M. R. (2007). History and theory of community psychology: An international perspective of community psychology in the United States – Returning to political, critical and ecological roots. In S. M. Reich, M. Reimer, I. Prilleltensky, & M. Montero (Eds.), *International community psychology: History and theories* (pp. 37–62). Irvine, CA: Springer.

Angelique, H. L., Rodriguez, R., Culley, M. R., Brown, R., & Binerre, A. J. (2013). (Em-)powering community psychology through an examination of social power. *Journal of Community Psychology*, *41*(6), 725–742. doi.org/10.1002/jcop.21567

Bernal, G., & Enchautegui-de-Jesus, N. (1994). Latinos and Latinas in community psychology: A review of the literature. *American Journal of Community Psychology*, *22*(4), 531–557. doi.org/10.1007/BF02506892

Bourdieu, P. (1980). *The logic of practice*. Stanford, CA: Stanford University Press.

Bourdieu, P. (1988). *Homo academicus*. Cambridge, UK: Polity Press.

Bourdieu, P. (2004). *Science of science and reflexivity*. Cambridge, UK: Polity Press.

Boyd, N. M. (2014). A 10-year retrospective of organisation studies in community psychology: Content, theory, and impact. *Journal of Community Psychology*, *42*(2), 237–254. doi.org/10.1002/jcop.21607

Boyd, N. M., & Angelique, H. (2002). Rekindling the discourse: Organisation studies in community psychology. *Journal of Community Psychology*, *30*(4), 325–348. doi.org/10.1002/jcop.10011

Burton, M., & Kagan, K. (2016). Theory and practice for a critical community psychology in the UK. *Psicología, Conocimiento y Sociedad*, *5*(2), 182–205.

Butchart A., & Seedat, M. A. (1990). Within and without: Images of community and implications for South African psychology. *Social Science & Medicine, 31*(10), 1093–1102. doi.org/10.1016/0277-9536(90)90231-G

Campbell, C., & Murray, M. (2004). Community health psychology: Promoting analysis and action for social change. *Journal of Health Psychology, 9*(2), 187–195. doi.org/10.1177/1359105304040886

Carolissen, R., Rohleder, P., Bozalek, V., & Leibowitz, B. (2010). "Community psychology is for poor, black people": Pedagogy and teaching of community psychology in South Africa. *Equity and Excellence in Education, 43*(4), 495–510. doi.org/10.1080/10665684.2010.516695

Chirowodza, A., van Rooyen, H., Joseph, P., et al. (2009). Using participatory methods and geographic information systems (GIS) to prepare for an HIV community-based trial in Vulindlela, South Africa. *Journal of Community Psychology, 37*(1), 41–57. doi.org/10.1002/jcop.20294

Davidson, H., Evans, S., Ganote, C., et al. (2006). Power and action in critical theory across disciplines: Implications for critical community psychology. *American Journal of Community Psychology, 38,* 35–49. doi.org/10.1007/s10464-006-9061-4

Duncan, D. F. (1991). Health psychology and community psychology: A comparison through content analysis of representative journals. *Psychological Reports, 69* (3), 1225–1226. doi.org/10.2466/pr0.1991.69.3f.1225

Dutta, U. (2018). Decolonizing "community" in community psychology. *American Journal of Community Psychology, 62*(3–4), 272–282. doi.org/10.1002/ajcp.12281

Evans, S. D., Duckett, P., Lawthom, R., & Kivell, N. (2017). Positioning the critical in community psychology. In M. A. Bond, I. Serrano-García, & C. B. Keys (Eds.), *APA handbook of community psychology: Vol. 1 – Theoretical foundations, core concepts, and emerging challenges* (pp. 107–127). Washington, DC: American Psychological Association.

Feis, C. L. (1990). Reflections on a conference: Daring to be different – A graduate student's perspective. In P. Tolan, F. Chertok, C. Keys, & L. Jason (Eds.), *Researching community psychology: Issues of theory and methods* (pp. 201–205). Washington, DC: American Psychological Association.

Fisher, A. T., & Sonn, C. C. (2007). Power in community psychology theory and practice. *Journal of Community & Applied Social Psychology, 17*(4), 255–257. doi.org/10.1002/casp.930

Fisher, A. T., Sonn, C. C., & Evans, S. D. (2007). The place and function of power in community psychology: Philosophical and practical issues. *Journal of Community & Applied Social Psychology, 17*(4), 258–267. doi.org/10.1002/casp.934

Foucault, M. (1977). *Discipline and punish: The birth of the prison.* London: Allen Lane.

Foucault, M. (1982/1994). The subject and power. In J. D. Faubion (Ed.), *Michel Foucault: Power – Essential works of Foucault 1954–1984* (pp. 326–348). London, UK: Penguin Books.

Fox, R., Easpaig, B. N. G., & Watson, L. (2016). Making space for community critical methodology: Stories from the Australian context. *American Journal of Community Psychology, 63*(1–2), 227–238. doi.org/10.1002/ajcp.12302

Graham, T. M. (2014). *Patterns of dominance and marginality in community psychology knowledge production: A critical analysis of published work* [Unpublished doctoral thesis]. University of the Witwatersrand.

Graham, T. M. (2017). Who's left out and who's still on the margins? Social exclusion in community psychology journals. *Journal of Community Psychology, 45*(2), 193–209. doi.org/10.1002/jcop.21842

Graham, T. M., & Ismail, T. (2011). Content and method trends in the *Journal of Community Psychology* between 2003 and 2007. *Journal of Community Psychology, 39*(2), 121–135. doi.org/10.1002/jcop.20420

Graham, T. M., & Shirley, A. (2014). Theoretical and methodological characteristics of scholarly work on HIV in community psychology. In S. Cooper & K. Ratele (Eds.), *Psychology serving humanity: Proceedings of the 30th International Congress of Psychology: Vol. 1. Majority world psychology* (pp. 253–272). New York: Psychology Press.

Gutierrez, R. E. (2010). Whom do we study: An analysis of diversity in the community psychology literature from 1973 to 2007. *College of Liberal Arts & Social Sciences Theses and Dissertations*, Paper 38. http://via.library.depaul.edu/etd/38

Hall, J. R. (2007). Historicity and sociohistorical research. In W. Outhwaite & S. P. Turner (Eds.), *The SAGE handbook of social science methodology* (pp. 82–101). Los Angeles: SAGE Publications.

Jason, L. A., Pokorny, S. B., Patka, M., Adams, M., & Morello, T. (2007). Ranking institutional settings based on publications in community psychology journals. *Journal of Community Psychology, 35*(8), 967–979. doi.org/10.1002/jcop.20206

Kagan, C., Burton, M., Duckett, P., Lawthom, R., & Siddiquee, A. (2011a). *Critical community psychology*. Chichester, UK: BPS Blackwell.

Kagan, C., Duggan, K., Richards, M., & Siddiiquee, A. (2011b). Community psychology. In P. R. Martin, F. M. Cheung, M. C. Knowles, et al. (Eds.), *IAAP handbook of applied psychology* (pp. 471–499). Oxford, UK: Blackwell.

Kloos, B., Hill, J., Thomas, E., et al. (2012). *Community psychology: Linking individuals and communities* (3rd ed.). Belmont, CA: Wadsworth Cengage Learning.

Kornbluh, M., Collins, C., & Kohfeldt, D. (2019). Navigating activism within the academy: Consciousness building and social justice identity formation. *Journal of Community & Applied Social Psychology, 30*(2), 1–13. doi.org/10.1002/casp.2434

Le Blanc, D. (2012). Gapminder: Using a world of human ecology data to teach students critical thinking skills. *Bulletin of the Ecological Society of America, 93*(4), 358–372. doi.org/10.1890/0012-9623-93.4.358

Lichty, L. F., Kornbluh, M., Mortensen, J., & Foster-Fishman, P. (2019). Claiming online space for empowering methods: Taking Photovoice to scale online. *Global Journal of Community Psychology Practice, 10*(3), 1–26. http://gjcpp.org/

Loo, C., Fong, K. T., & Iwamasa, G. (1988). Ethnicity and cultural diversity: An analysis of work published in community psychology journals, 1965–1985. *Journal of Community Psychology, 16*(3), 332–349. doi.org/10.1002/1520-6629(198807)16:3<332::AID-JCOP2290160308>3.0.CO;2-8

Lounsbury, J. W., Cook, M. P., Leader, D. S., Rubeiz, G., & Meares, E. P. (1979). Community psychology: Boundary problems, psychological perspectives, and an empirical overview of the field. *American Psychologist, 34*(6), 554–557. doi.org/10.1037/0003-066X.34.6.554

Lounsbury, J. W., Leader, D. S., & Meares, E. P. (1980). An analytic review of research in community psychology. *American Journal of Community Psychology, 8*(4), 415–441. doi.org/10.1007/BF00912

Macleod, C. (2004). South African psychology and 'relevance': Continuing challenges. *South African Journal of Psychology, 34*(4), 613–629. doi.org/10.1177/008124630403400407

Martin, P. P., Lounsbury, D. W., & Davidson, W. S. (2004). AJCP as a vehicle for improving community life: An historic-analytic review of the journal's contents. *American Journal of Community Psychology, 34*(3–4), 163–173. doi.org/10.1007/s10464-004-7412-6

Milburn, N. G. (2016). Commentary on the future of community psychology: Perspective of a research community psychologist. *American Journal of Community Psychology, 58*(3–4), 245–250. doi.org/10.1002/ajcp.1206

Montero, M. (2002). On the construction of reality and truth: Towards an epistemology of community social psychology. *American Journal of Community Psychology, 30*(4), 571–584. doi.org/10.1023/A:1015864103005

Novaco, R. W., & Monahan, J. (1980). Research in community psychology: An analysis of work published in the first six years of the *American Journal of Community Psychology*. *American Journal of Community Psychology, 8*(2), 131–145. doi.org/10.1007/BF00912656

Odgers, C. L., Caspi, A., Bates, C. J., Sampson, R. J., & Moffitt, T. E. (2012). Systematic social observation of children's neighborhoods using Google Street View: A reliable and cost-effective method. *Journal of Child Psychology and Psychiatry, 53*(10), 1009–1017. doi.org/10.1111/j.1469-7610.2012.02565.x

Orford, J. (2008). *Community psychology: Challenges, controversies and emerging consensus*. Chichester, UK: John Wiley & Sons.

Painter, D., Terre Blanche, M., & Henderson, J. (2006). Critical psychology in South Africa: Histories, themes and prospects. *Annual Review of Critical Psychology, 5*, 212–235. www.discourseunit.com/arcp/5

Rappaport, J. (2004). On becoming a community psychologist: The intersection of autobiography and history. *Journal of Prevention and Intervention in the Community, 28*(1–2), 15–39. doi.org/10.1300/J005v28n01_02

Ryan, W. (1971). *Blaming the victim*. New York: Pantheon Books.

Schruijer, S. G. L., & Stephenson, G. M. (2010). Trends and developments in community and applied social psychology: JCASP 1991–2010. *Journal of Community & Applied Social Psychology, 20*(6), 437–444. doi.org/10.1002/casp.1069

Seedat, M., MacKenzie, S., & Stevens, G. (2004). Trends and redress in community psychology during 10 years of democracy (1994–2003): A journal-based perspective. *South African Journal of Psychology, 34*(4), 595–612. doi.org/10.1177/008124630403400406

Smail, D. (1994). Community psychology and politics. *Journal of Community & Applied Social Psychology, 4*(1), 3–10. doi.org/10.1002/casp.2450040103

Smail, D. (2015). *The origins of unhappiness: A new understanding of personal distress*. London, UK: Karnac Books.

Speer, P., Dey, A., Griggs, P., et al. (1992). In search of community: An analysis of community psychology research from 1984–1988. *American Journal of Community Psychology*, *20*(2), 195–209. doi.org/10.1007/BF00940836

Stevens, G. (2007). Histories and possibilities: The international emergence and development of community psychology. In N. Duncan, B. Bowman, A. Naidoo, J. Pillay, & V. Roos (Eds.), *Community psychology: Analysis, context and action* (pp. 27–50). Cape Town, South Africa: University of Cape Town Press.

Suffla, S., Seedat, M., & Bawa, U. (2014). Reflexivity as enactment of critical community psychologies: Dilemmas of voice and positionality in a multi-country Photovoice study. *Journal of Community Psychology*, *43*(1), 9–21. doi.org/10.1002/jcop.21691

Toro, P. A. (2005). Community psychology: Where do we go from here? *American Journal of Community Psychology*, *35*(1–2), 9–16. doi.org/10.1007/s10464-005-1883-y

UNdata. (2020). *About UNdata*. https:// data.un.org/Host.aspx?Content=About

Wacquant, L. (2006). Pierre Bourdieu. In R. Stones (Ed.), *Key contemporary thinkers* (pp. 215–230). London, UK: Macmillan.

Wang, C., & Burris, M. A. (1997). Photovoice: Concept, methodology, and use for participatory needs assessment. *Health Education & Behaviour*, *24*(3), 369–387. doi.org/10.1177/109019819702400309

Watling Neal, J., Janulis, P., & Collins, C. (2013). Is community psychology too insular? A network analysis of journal citations. *Journal of Community Psychology*, *41*(5), 549–564. doi.org/10.1002/jcop.21556

Woolhouse, S., Day, K., & Rickett, B. (2019). "Growing your own herbs" and "cooking from scratch": Contemporary discourses around good mothering, food, and class-related identities. *Journal of Community and Applied Social Psychology*, *29*(4), 285–296. doi.org/10.1002/casp.2400

Zebian, S., Alamuddin, R., Maalouf, M., & Chatila, Y. (2007). Developing an appropriate psychology through culturally sensitive research practices in the Arabic speaking world: A content analysis of psychological research published between 1950 and 2004. *Journal of Cross-Cultural Psychology*, *38*(2), 91–122. doi.org/10.1177/0022022106295442

30 Rewriting the Community Psychology Narrative

A Contextual, Interdisciplinary, Inclusive, Empowerment Approach

Caroline S. Clauss-Ehlers

Throughout this volume, we have explored the impact and application of community psychology from interdisciplinary and contextual perspectives. Our journey started with an introductory chapter that calls communities and community psychologists to social action amid systemic oppression including differential health access related to the COVID-19 global pandemic and transnational outrage at police brutality and racial violence. This first chapter asked the question: *Doesn't all psychology incorporate community psychology?* We return to this question in this concluding chapter.

Subsequent to Chapter 1, with its identification of the gap between community psychology's original focus on a social action vision and the current status of the literature, the chapters that followed addressed this aperture by representing a new narrative for community psychology. This new narrative includes theoretical, empirical, practical, and professional considerations that incorporate the following: addressing systemic oppression, a community-informed research and practice approach, empowerment across diverse communities, and transnational perspectives of wellness. The overarching lens that framed these contributions was contextual and interdisciplinary. This approach demonstrated the importance of community psychology locating community considerations within a contextual framework. To do so, it presents a model that underscores the importance of collaborating across disciplines to avoid an insular understanding of complex community issues. Case illustrations highlighted the significance of understanding power dynamics in community psychology endeavors, including the importance of community identification, empowerment, and collaboration in research, policy, and practice. Foundational themes in the first part of this book address what we mean by a psychological sense of community (PSOC), an understanding of power relations and how communities can navigate power to promote change, ethical considerations in community psychology, and understanding definitions of wellness across "geo-cultural dimensions" (Chapter 5). The presentation of foundational themes in the first part of the book, like other chapters, shifts the community psychology narrative with regard to our theoretical framework for the discipline. It challenges community psychology's overwhelming usage of traditional theoretical approaches, and instead incorporates transnational, empowerment, and community engagement understandings.

In the second part of the book, we turned to look at contextual and interdisciplinary considerations in community-based research and evaluation. These chapters present a new narrative approach for community psychology through illustrations of a research framework that moves away from positivist approaches (e.g., scientific measurement using numerical values) and instead, reflects diverse research methodologies. For instance, this part of the book highlights the importance of conducting culturally responsive community needs assessments; multitiered approaches to community-based program evaluation; and the important roles that participatory action research and community-centered research can play in generating knowledge from a qualitative, ethnographic perspective where community members are not only included in research, they are informing it. Further, these chapters demonstrate how knowledge generated by community-focused research could, and should, be shared with the community in alignment with community goals and vision.

We then moved to the third part of the book that emphasized community psychology in action. Here critical themes and case illustrations emerged that highlighted contemporary topics relevant to the practice of community psychology in the twenty-first century. Such topics included: women and leadership, community resilience, disaster risk reduction, consumer recovery, violence prevention, developmental neuropsychology for adolescents, public policy, family support services for seriously ill children, faith healing camps, social media, educational access, climate change, local governments and service provision, a public health approach to juvenile delinquency, public service organizations and community empowerment, women and immigration, adolescents and young adults with neurodevelopmental disabilities, mental health on college campuses, and supporting LGBTQ+ communities. Each chapter's action-oriented approach furthers the proposed new community psychology narrative with a focus on context, social action, ecological understanding, and awareness of power relations. We can see the new narrative emerging through chapter case studies, many of which address topic areas currently underrepresented in the community psychology literature (e.g., see Chapters 14, 16, and 23).

The concluding part of this book focuses on responding to gaps in research and practice in community psychology. Part IV examines various "theories, topics, and methods that are underrepresented" (Chapter 29, p. 623). The paragraphs that follow expand upon this discussion and advocate for all psychologists to engage in efforts to fill these significant gaps and work toward changing the community psychology narrative.

I have enormous gratitude toward the authors who have contributed to this book. They represent a range of experiences and countries including Peru, Ghana, Australia, the United States, Japan, South Africa, and Canada. This reflects a transnational approach to community psychology, although more transnational participation and collaboration is needed. It has been a wonderful opportunity to work with a committed Cambridge University Press editorial team. I greatly appreciate the collaboration with Janka Romero, who first talked about a book project of this nature when we met at the 15th European Congress of Psychology in Amsterdam during Summer 2017. Emily Watton has been a wonderful ongoing presence and support who helped see this work through to fruition. Ilaria Tassistro was an enormous support in helping us organize content. Penny Harper was an amazing copy editor, Vinithan Sethumadhaven was a wonderful project manager, and Grace Morris kept us moving forward to production. Many thanks to Erica Garagiola whose work as a student and research assistant made invaluable contributions to this project.

Through work on this project the past four years and learning about the status of the community psychology literature as a result, I am left with the conclusion that *the field has moved away from its original drive of social action and community empowerment. There is a disconnection between community psychology's initial aspirations (e.g., social justice, empowerment, community support) and the reality of the field in terms of theoretical, research, and practice output.*

I am struck by Tanya Graham's finding of a mismatch between empirical and stated ideology with research output that is often less likely to take a critical approach and less likely to focus on understanding community within the context of power relations. Graham (Chapter 29) encourages us to incorporate reflexivity in our work as community psychologists.

Working on this project over the past several years has left me with this thought: *We need to shift the community psychology narrative, as operationalized in the previous chapters, so that community psychologists engage in reflexivity about power dynamics and privilege, consider sociopolitical aspects of communities, and collaborate outside of the community psychology discipline with interdisciplinary domestic and transnational partners. This means examining structural issues and the ecological context that has an impact on both community experience and one's experience of the community. As the broader literature reads, community psychology is at risk of maintaining the status quo, and staying siloed by not shifting the narrative in ways that, ironically, return the field to its initial vision, and are beneficial and contributive across a global context.*

The following paragraphs highlight critical areas to address to change the community psychology narrative. These areas include more inclusive theoretical approaches, more inclusive research methodologies, more inclusive practice approaches, and changing how we think about teaching, training, tenure, and promotion within academia. Figure 30.1 presents a visual depiction of rewriting the community psychology narrative with regard to theoretical perspectives, research approaches, practice, and teaching. The current status of each area is presented followed by proposed steps to shift the narrative.

30.1 Critical Areas to Change the Community Psychology Narrative

30.1.1 Diverse Theoretical Perspectives: Status of the Literature

A starting point to change the community psychology narrative is for the field to incorporate and develop diverse theoretical perspectives. Such diversification is

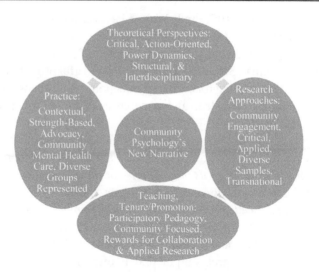

Figure 30.1 *Changing the community psychology narrative: a contextual, interdisciplinary, inclusive, empowerment approach*

necessary to address contemporary situations such as the COVID-19 global pandemic and systemic racism. The current status of the literature shows a preponderance of a couple theoretical approaches being overrepresented, with more ecological/contextual approaches underrepresented. According to Graham's analysis (Chapter 29), for instance, more than 50% of community psychology journals incorporate prevention (33.7%) or traditional psychological theoretical (16.7%) approaches in their work. In contrast, only 14.1% of community psychology journal articles take an ecological approach, 10.8% take an empowerment approach, 7.4% take a cultural diversity approach, and a mere 6.1% incorporate a structuralist perspective. The preponderance of prevention and traditional psychological theoretical approaches as compared to the dearth of more contextual, structural approaches suggests that community psychology's current theoretical foundation risks not conceptualizing the experiences of communities from a sociocultural perspective that explores structural issues and power dynamics that may lead to oppression, empowerment, or a complex combination of both. This is a departure from a prior community psychology narrative that incorporated this perspective more fully.

30.1.2 Diverse Theoretical Perspectives: Steps to Change the Narrative

Building on Graham's important analysis of the theoretical approaches used in community psychology, incorporating an interdisciplinary approach is one strategy to rewrite the community psychology narrative. As demonstrated in *Handbook* chapters, by collaborating with disciplines such as philosophy, public health, psychiatry, counseling, anthropology, education, health sciences, philosophy, medical ethics, political science, and history, it is hoped that community psychology theoretical approaches can adopt a more comprehensive, synergistic framework. Through interdisciplinary collaboration, community psychology can apply critical action and structuralist frameworks that address the complexity of social issues such as contextual considerations and an analysis of power dynamics.

30.1.3 Diverse Ways of Generating Knowledge through Research: Status of the Literature

We see a narrow approach reflected in community psychology research when we consider Graham's finding (Chapter 29) that an overwhelming 69.1% of community psychology research takes a positivist approach to the generation of new knowledge (e.g., research that uses numerical data). This percentage is in stark contrast to the 9.2% of publications that incorporate an applied community approach, with strategies including needs analysis (see Chapter 6); evaluation (see Chapter 7); policy research (see Chapter 11); or participatory action research (see Chapter 18); the 4.7% of publications that take a mixed method approach (e.g., a combination of qualitative and quantitative data); and the 2.5% of community psychology publications that incorporate a critical research approach that addresses power dynamics.

The reality of the status of research in community psychology journals is further amplified when we consider Graham's finding (Chapter 29) that 42.9% of journal articles use a survey method for data collection. This means that a questionnaire method is the research methodology most often published in community psychology journals. The overriding use of the survey method is in contrast with other methods such as the 15% of qualitative studies, the 2.2% of archival methods, and the 1.8% of autobiographical methods that are employed (Chapter 29). These findings underscore the lack of diverse approaches to generating new knowledge through the research enterprise (Kidd et al., 2018). By not incorporating a diversification of research approaches, we lose our understanding of specific community aspects. We lose the ability to understand how evidence-based interventions can be tailored to specific community needs (Clauss-Ehlers, 2017).

30.1.4 Diverse Ways of Generating Knowledge through Research: Steps to Change the Narrative

The new narrative for community psychology research can consider ways to design empirical investigation. Research perspectives can be informed by communities, not just researchers. One strategy is to reenvision how we understand the research enterprise. A way to do this is to think about research not only as science, but also as storytelling. Research can tell a story about a community's experience.

Autobiographical research, for instance, allows research participants to share their stories about an experience through writing or oral presentation (Clauss-Ehlers, 2020; Piana et al., 2010). Not only does the autobiographical narrative approach provide data that addresses the complexities of situations, it also gives back to the community. For instance, in Piana and colleagues' (2010) autobiographical narrative study about adolescents diagnosed with diabetes, adolescents engaged in daily self-writing activities where they shared what it was like for them to discover they had diabetes. This study found that the adolescent participants reported that this self-writing activity, while challenging, also had "a strong liberating effect" (p. 56). This is but one example of how diverse research methodologies can be implemented in ways that not only contribute to new knowledge, but also give back to the community. Participatory research approaches can lead to new research designs that are inclusive of communities and community members (Clauss-Ehlers, 2020; Clauss-Ehlers et al., 2019; Chapter 8).

Research approach and design can be further diversified to produce a more critical, contextual literature, through engagement in interdisciplinary work. States Graham (Chapter 29, p. 643): "This may require deliberate strategies on the part of community psychologists to forge and sustain interdisciplinary collaboration to compensate for the intrinsic bias of community psychologists toward the psychologization of community phenomena. This will address the insularity of community psychology in knowledge generation networks." By building community and interdisciplinary partnerships, community psychology becomes more relevant and responsive to communities and their members.

30.1.5 A Diverse Community Psychology Practice: Status of Practice

We return now to the question of: *Doesn't all psychology incorporate community psychology?* If we are taking a contextual approach that understands individuals, couples, families, and organizations within their ecological frameworks, we could say that it does. Understanding human behavior in the context of the surrounding environment, in and of itself, involves understanding community.

And yet, despite this rationale, we know from research that, across the globe, most people with a mental illness do not receive treatment (Thornicroft, Deb, & Henderson, 2016). What has come to be known as a significant "treatment gap" refers to those in need of mental health treatment who never receive it (Thornicroft et al., 2016). Adding to the treatment gap is psychotherapy discontinuation where client(s) engage in treatment but end therapy before it is clinically recommended. Research indicates that most clients attend two therapy sessions and then stop treatment (Swift & Greenberg, 2012). This reality only adds to the treatment gap.

While an explanation of hypotheses about why clients drop out of treatment is beyond the scope of this chapter, environmental factors that contribute to attrition are relevant to community psychology. A client unable to access care due to a lack of insurance coverage, for instance, is a key environmental factor in psychotherapy discontinuation (Barrett et al., 2008). In addition, a medical model focused on disease risks taking a deficit approach to clinical work, making clients responsible for their "health and distress" (Chapter 29).

Community psychology also lacks research on various groups and thus provides limited insight about how such research might inform practice. These include "the elderly, the unemployed, people with disabilities, people with alternative gender identities and sexualities, migrants, people in rural areas, and people living with HIV/AIDS, as well as intersections between these forms of social exclusion with structural inequalities" (Chapter 29, p. 635). In addition to Graham's (Chapter 29) thoughtful analysis, other underrepresented groups and topics in the community psychology field include: religion and faith-based communities, the impact of climate change on communities, the role of social media and sense of community, the impact of forced migration on communities, the effect of human trafficking on families and communities, and intergenerational trauma, none of which are listed in topic frequencies in community psychology journals from 2000 to 2009 (Chapter 29). If the literature does not reflect experiences of underrepresented groups, we risk not developing relevant evidence-based interventions that are responsive to the needs of diverse communities. This trickles down to not having a literature in place that can be integrated into training a future mental health workforce that is responsive to these varied community requirements.

30.1.6 A Diverse Community Psychology Practice: Steps to Change the Narrative

Community psychologists can contribute to rewriting the practice narrative in several ways. Efforts are being made globally to address the treatment gap through the provision of community mental health care. The policy aspect here is that governments invest in building mental health capacity in their countries so that those with mental health issues can receive treatment (Clauss-Ehlers, Sood, & Weist, 2020). That such national investments have remained low is "a level of disregard that has been described as structural or systemic discrimination" (Thornicroft et al., 2016, p. 276). Community psychologists can participate in measures to increase mental health capacity beyond specialist care services to provide supports "in primary, community health care services, and in population-level and community-level platforms" (Thornicroft et al., 2016, p. 282).

Community psychologists can address the treatment gap through advocacy efforts that seek to make treatment accessible across diverse community groups. Advocacy can occur at local, state, and national levels and include efforts to promote policy change. We saw one such change occur in the face of the COVID-19 crisis when school systems approved teletherapy platforms so that students could receive counseling remotely. In taking a strength-based approach to working with communities, community psychologists can build partnerships, collaborate with community stakeholders, and engage in a bidirectional relationship that includes reflexivity about one's role (Clauss-Ehlers et al., 2019).

Finally, community psychology and clinical community psychology practice can rewrite the narrative through research and practice that incorporates the experiences of groups who have been underrepresented in the literature. Research informs practice. Research creates an evidence-base for clinical intervention. We need research on the process of culturally adaptive approaches to clinical interventions (Clauss-Ehlers, 2017). We need research to provide insight and clinical implications among those affected by climate change, COVID-19, social media, human trafficking, generational trauma, forced migration, detention, incarceration, aging, disability status, gender inequity, mental health and health disparity, the digital divide, complicated grief related to separation from parting loved ones due to COVID-19 safety measures, chronic illness, HIV/AIDS, child and adolescent mental health, and religion- and faith-based communities. We need practice-oriented efforts to build global mental health capacity through transnational partnerships and shared resources (Clauss-Ehlers et al., 2020).

30.1.7 A System That Perpetuates Itself: Teaching, Tenure, and Promotion

Changing any narrative involves self-reflection, awareness, and intentionality. It also involves systemic change to address structural issues that promote current outcomes. Shifting the community psychology narrative involves thinking about structural issues in teaching, training, tenure, and promotion that support an a-contextual, siloed approach to the field. Each is addressed in the following paragraphs.

30.1.7.1 Teaching

A challenge for community psychology and clinical community psychology training programs is to find a balance between learning about core competencies and being able to incorporate a diverse, contextual perspective. While students may didactically learn about key concepts such as empowerment, sense of community, and liberation, the skill aspect of the community psychologist's role is much more complex. It involves interpersonal skills and an ability to collaborate with communities, understand communities, and demonstrate cultural humility in doing so (Hook et al., 2017).

One strategy to support the development of community psychology skills involves active engagement on the part of students in the classroom. A pedagogical model of student engagement and participation to cocreate classroom knowledge contrasts with more traditional lecture approaches where students hear and digest content. Participatory pedagogy "redefines the student's role from a passive listener and optional discussant to an active participant in the teaching and learning process. It encourages thinking deeply and critically, reflecting on and sharing experiences and prior knowledge, solving problems and actively applying new knowledge gained through course content" (Collins et al., 2016, p. 5). Community-based practicum and fieldwork experiences allow students to learn via active engagement in the community. Through such engagement, students can share what they have learned with classmates while also hearing about the experiences of their peers.

Engaged pedagogy has several benefits for training future generations of community psychologists. In their description of the community psychology course they took as a graduate training requirement, Collins and colleagues (2016) discuss how the instructor's engaged, interactive approach encouraged their creativity and critical thinking. Through participatory pedagogy, the students shared that they learned to "[think] ecologically when applying [community psychology] concepts to community programs," "[simulate the start of community program development," and "[experience] systemic inequity and build sociocultural and cross-cultural competence" (Collins et al., 2016, pp. 7, 9, 11, respectively).

These participatory learning experiences prompted community psychology students to learn about how to apply diverse theoretical perspectives to understand the ecological context of community issues, learn skills related to partnering with community stakeholders, and engage in reflexivity about one's own privilege while learning about systemic oppression. These learning themes directly correspond with rewriting the community psychology narrative in theory, research, and practice. It is hoped that students who engage in this type of learning environment can be future leaders who approach the field from an inclusive framework.

30.1.7.2 Tenure and Promotion

Just as *Handbook* chapters identify structural issues leading to systemic inequity, so too the academic aspect of the field has its own structural framework that imposes limitations. One such limitation includes a devaluing of professional research collaboration. Among many higher education research institutions collaboration is not rewarded. For instance, it is often the case that the tenure process values single-authored publications, that can be viewed as a requirement for tenure and promotion. This reward structure interferes with the collaborative work that the field needs to be engaged in to move forward.

Higher education structures also interfere with rewriting the community psychology narrative so that it can move beyond survey research (e.g., research participants complete questionnaires) to incorporate diverse research approaches and methodologies that capture community experiences. This recommendation can also be in contrast to the reward system for tenure and promotion. Tenure and promotion processes often examine the quantity of research output with committees and outside reviewers counting the number of the candidate's peer-reviewed publications. The number of publications and the impact of the journals in which they are published are often key contributors to success with tenure and promotion.

The overvaluing of numerical output is in contrast with a community psychology narrative that values nonsurvey approaches. For instance, community-focused data collection processes are likely to be more time-consuming than relying on a convenience sample (e.g., college undergraduates) for data. Further, qualitative and mixed methods approaches often take more time to implement than a quantitative approach. Qualitative data, for instance, may involve the researcher's time in conducting interviews.

Collaborating with communities and building effective partnerships takes time, often years (Clauss-Ehlers, 2020). When conducting community research, given that communities are dynamic, and most likely not engaging in research for college credit for their research course, the sample size may naturally be smaller. This work risks being devalued by the norms of a positivist research approach that views sample size as indicative of statistical significance (Clauss-Ehlers, 2020). Hence, the structure of what is valued for tenure and promotion is in direct contrast to diverse research approaches and methods that may produce fewer publications.

In addition to interdisciplinary approaches to theory and research, another way in which community psychology can be rewritten is through an emphasis on transnational collaboration. This focus is important so that community psychology reflects our global society, and not merely a North American perspective. Again, however, transnational research is time-consuming. It involves developing partnerships with colleagues from other countries, travel time, and even a more extensive Institutional Review Board (IRB) process that accounts for transnational research participants. A combination of these factors is likely to lead to a decrease in research output and, hence, a structural devaluation of a transnational approach to research.

It is understandable that faculty might rely upon research approaches and methods valued by some institutions of higher education. Some higher education research institutions and faculty are moving away from a more traditional focus on research to value a more holistic research and advancement process. Institutions of higher education are encouraged to engage in their own reflexivity regarding reward systems in efforts to promote systemic change. It would be very easy, and cost-effective, for instance, to change tenure and promotion processes so that more weight is given to research that partners with communities outside of one's own university, includes transnational samples, and goes beyond a survey approach. Higher education institutions can take the lead in making these changes, thus supporting the shift in the community psychology narrative, as well as the narratives in many other fields.

30.2 Conclusion

To conclude, rewriting the community psychology narrative involves looking at our own in-house structural issues. Through an honest appraisal, we can extend this important field of psychology to close the gap between community needs and the status of the field. Rewriting the community psychology narrative involves addressing systemic issues in theory, research, practice, teaching, and tenure and promotion practices.

Theory and research will benefit from interdisciplinary approaches that consider community context. The diversification of theoretical approaches is encouraged – with an invitation for community psychology theorists to explore other theories in their work such as ecological, empowerment, culturally diverse, structural, and sense of community approaches. Similarly, community psychology research will benefit from contributions that move beyond a positivist, quantitative survey approach. Community psychology researchers are encouraged to advance the field through applied, critical, and mixed methods research approaches. The field and the academy are encouraged to value other methods of data collection more highly including qualitative research, autobiographical, and archival research methods.

For practice, rewriting the community psychology narrative involves addressing the modal number of two therapy sessions before client attrition. Community psychologists can contribute greatly by exploring this as a practice issue, and applying the science of community psychology to address it. Also of great need are innovations to deliver community mental health care in low-, middle-, and high-income countries (Thornicroft et al., 2016). Several groups have been underrepresented in community psychology research, which has implications for practice. Graham (Chapter 29) provides a thoughtful review of topic frequencies and omissions (see Table 29.5). Overall, there is agreement with Graham's analysis (Chapter 29) that while the community psychology literature has moved forward with addressing social justice issues, there is a need for practitioners and community psychology scientists to examine them from a structural perspective that integrates power dynamics, systemic inequity, and the larger sociocultural context (Clauss-Ehlers et al., 2019).

Finally, the field and higher education perpetuate inequities through a valuing of some contributions over others. Institutions of higher education have an opportunity to address such inequity by valuing diverse types of research, research collaborations, and the time-intensive process of community-focused research and related initiatives. Using participatory pedagogy in teaching practice can provide students with the complex skills needed to collaborate with communities and further contribute to a pipeline of next-generation community psychologists. *It is imperative to shift the narrative so that voices that are muffled can be heard, and communities who are invisible become palpable.*

References

Barrett, M. S., Chua, W., Crits-Christoph, P., Gibbons, M., & Thompson, D. (2008). Early withdrawal from mental health treatment: Implications for psychotherapy practice. *Psychotherapy: Theory, Research, Practice, Training, 45*(2), 247–267. doi.org/10.1037/0033-3204.45.2.247

Clauss-Ehlers, C. S. (2017). In search of an evidence-based approach to understand and promote effective parenting practices. *Couple and Family Psychology: Research and Practice, 6*(3), 135–153. doi.org/10.1037/cfp0000082

Clauss-Ehlers, C. S. (2020). Exploration of psychological well-being, resilience, ethnic identity, and meaningful events among a group of youth in Northern England: An autobiographical narrative intervention pilot study. *Adolescent Psychiatry, 10*(2), 92–109. doi.org/10.2174/2210676610666200226090427

Clauss-Ehlers, C. S., Chiriboga, D., Hunter, S. J., Roysircar, G., & Tummala-Narra, P. (2019). APA Multicultural Guidelines executive summary: Ecological approach to context, identity, and intersectionality. *American Psychologist, 74*(2), 232–244. doi.org/10.1037/amp0000382

Clauss-Ehlers, C. S., Sood, A. B., & Weist, M. D. (2020). *Social justice for children and young people: International perspectives.* Cambridge, UK: Cambridge University Press.

Collins, K., Keys, C., Mihelicova, M., et al. (2016). Addressing the community psychology competency dialectic through participatory pedagogy. *Global Journal of Community Psychology Practice, 7*(4), 1–71.

Hook, J. N., Davis, D., Owen, J., & DeBlaere, C. (2017). *Cultural humility: Engaging diverse identities in therapy.* Washington, DC: American Psychological Association.

Kidd, S., Davidson, L., Frederick T., & Kral, M. J. (2018). Reflecting on participatory, action-oriented research methods in community psychology: Progress, problems, and paths forward. *American Journal of Community Psychology, 61*(1–2), 76–87. doi.org/10.1002/ajcp.12214

Piana, N., Maldonato, A., Bloise, D., et al. (2010). The narrative-autobiographical approach in the group education of adolescents with diabetes: A qualitative research on its effects. *Patient Education and Counseling, 80*(1), 56–63. doi.org/10.1016/j.pec.2009.10.020

Swift, J. K., & Greenberg, R. P. (2012). Premature discontinuation in adult psychotherapy: A meta-analysis. *Journal of Consulting and Clinical Psychology, 80*(4), 547–559. doi.org/10.1037/a0028226

Thornicroft, G., Deb, T., & Henderson, C. (2016). Community mental health care worldwide: Current status and further developments. *World Psychiatry, 15*(3), 276–286. doi.org/10.1002/wps.20349

Index